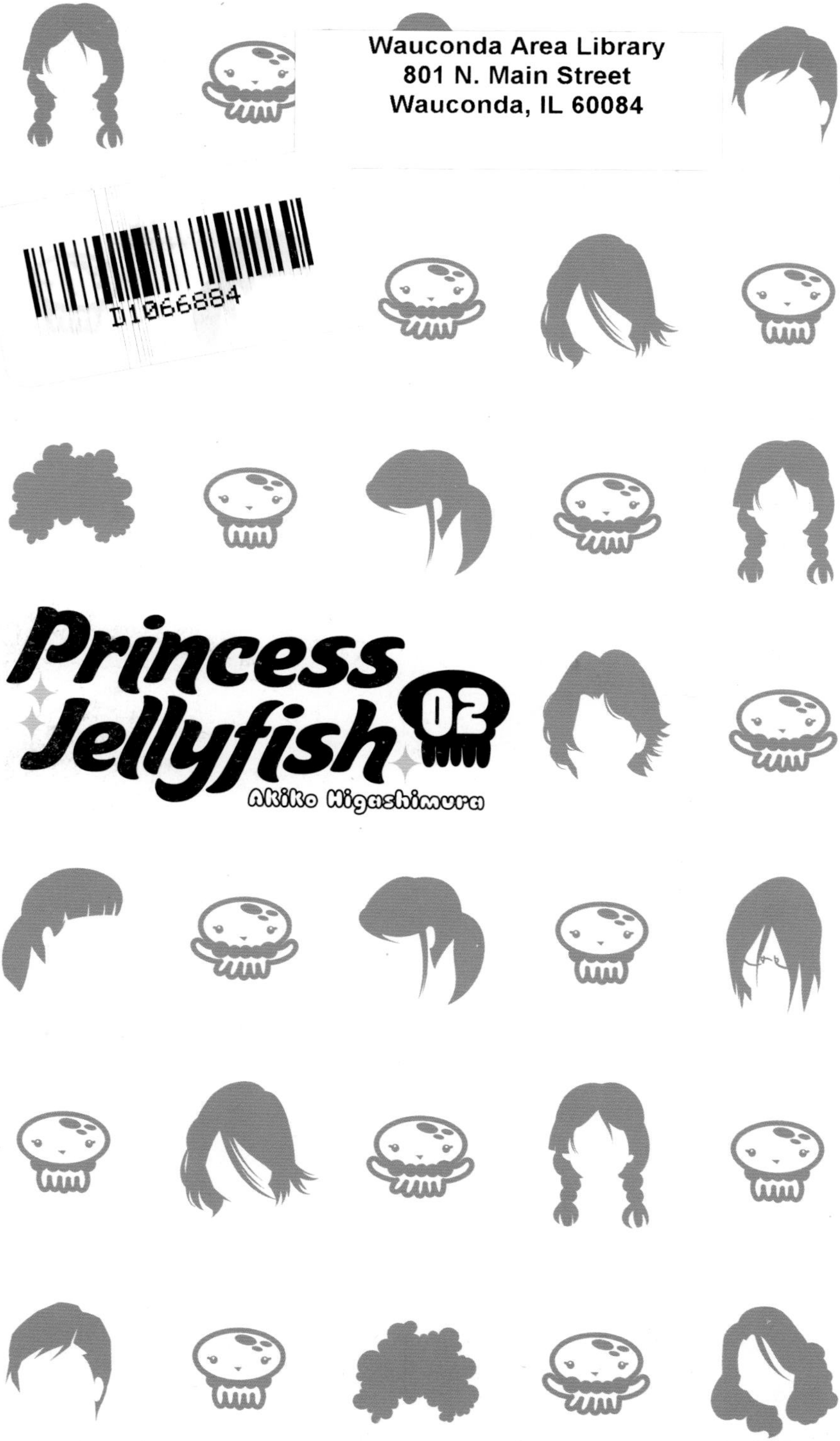

Princess Jellyfish 02

Akiko Higashimura

DEAREST READERS!

I GUESS GIRLS REALLY DO
ASPIRE TO BE PRINCESSES,
NO MATTER THEIR AGE, HUH?!
BUT IT'S SO HARD TO FIND
THE RIGHT OCCASION TO
DON A DRESS!
NOWADAYS, YOU CAN BUY
COSPLAY-TYPE DRESSES FOR
PRETTY CHEAP ONLINE!
DEAREST READERS,
JUST LIKE KURANOSUKE,
GO AHEAD AND DO WHATEVER
YOU REALLY WANT TO DO!

-AKIKO HIGASHIMURA

Episode 13

WE'LL BUY IT...
...THIS AMAMIZU-KAN!

So we're Amars... the ones who just said we'd buy the place...
...we're also all unemployed NEETs...

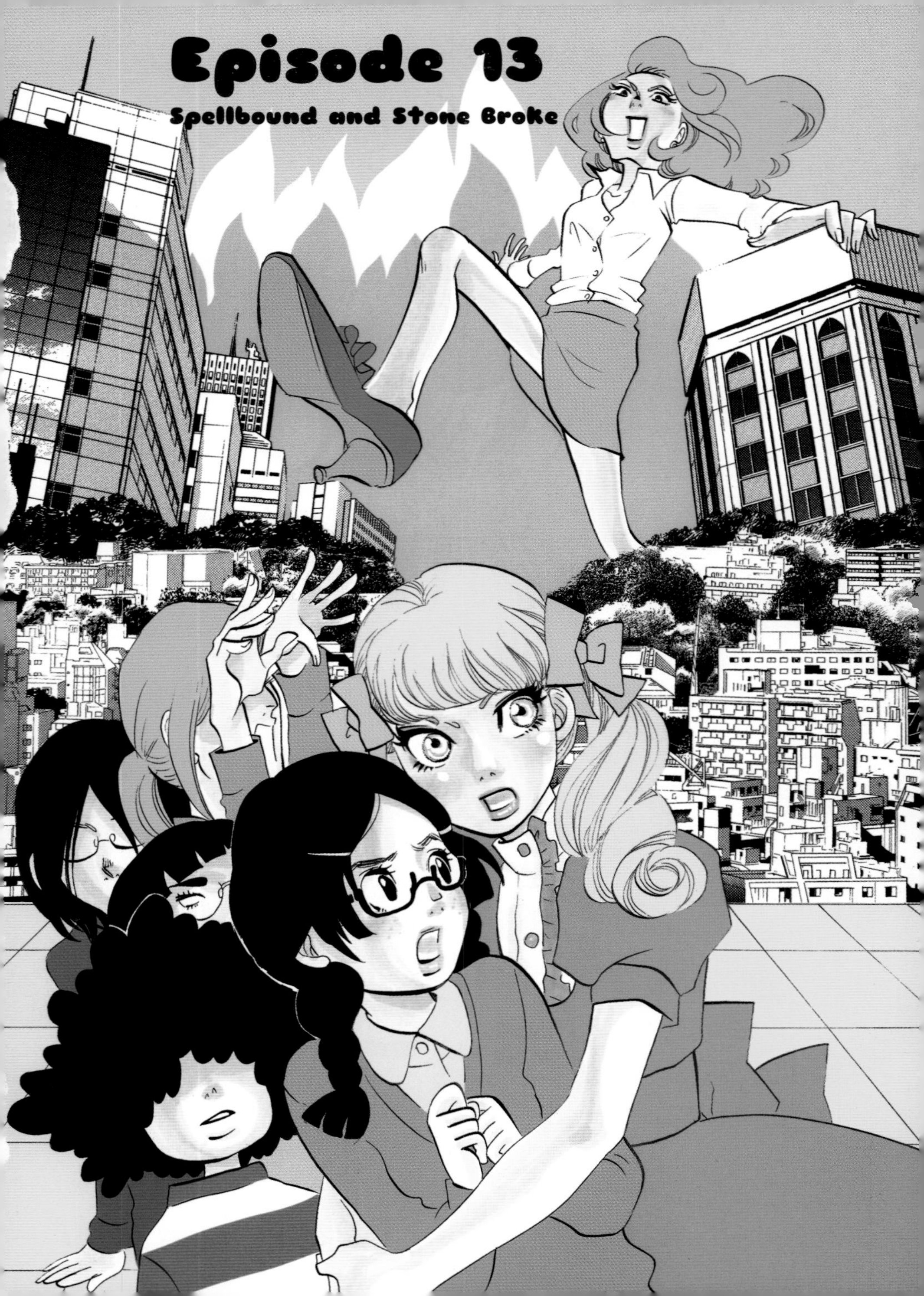
Episode 13
Spellbound and Stone Broke

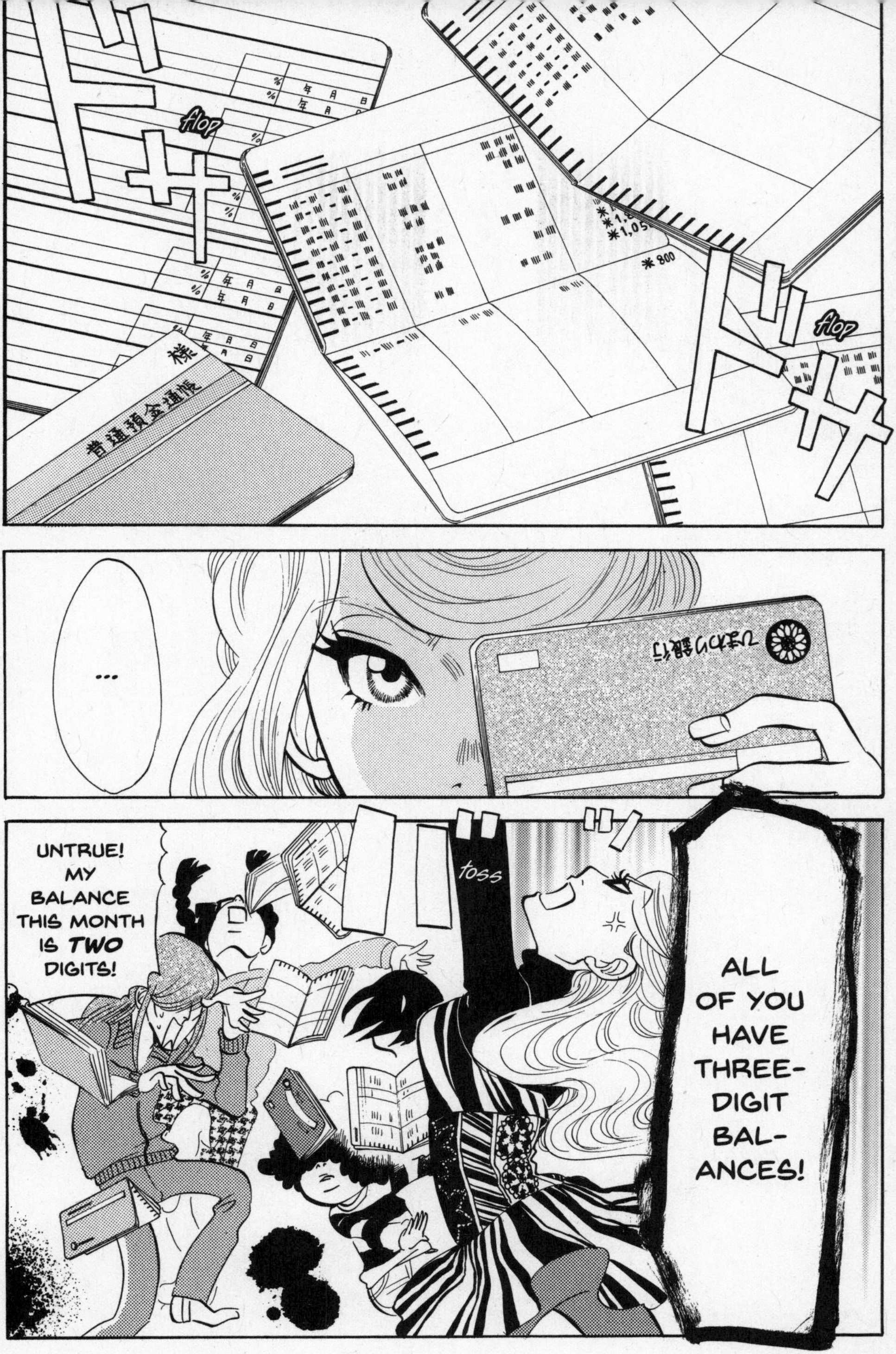
ドサッ
flop
ドサッ
flop
普通預金通帳
様
...
バッ
toss
ALL OF YOU HAVE THREE-DIGIT BALANCES!
UNTRUE! MY BALANCE THIS MONTH IS *TWO* DIGITS!

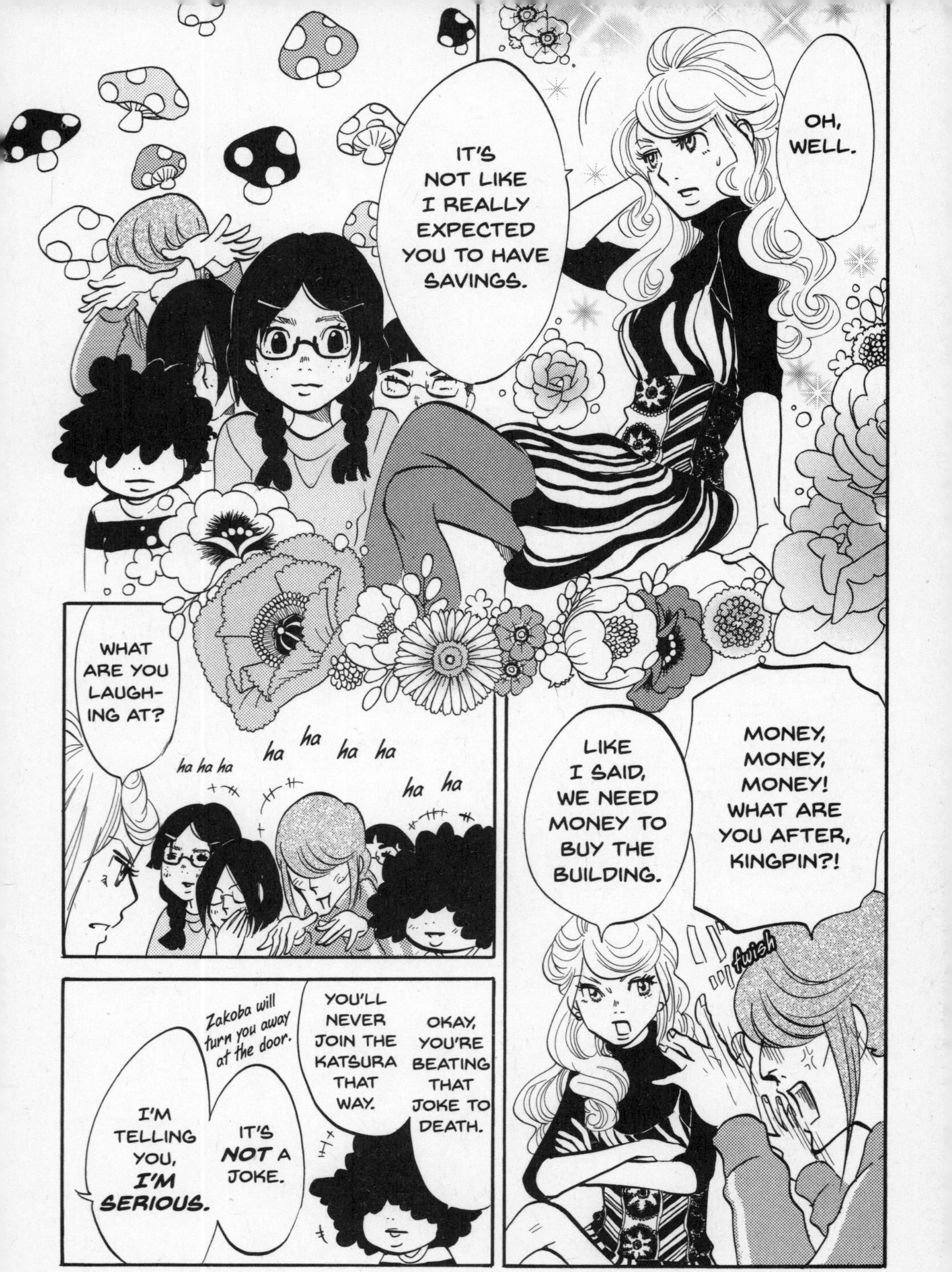
OH, WELL.
IT'S NOT LIKE I REALLY EXPECTED YOU TO HAVE SAVINGS.
MONEY, MONEY, MONEY! WHAT ARE YOU AFTER, KINGPIN?!
LIKE I SAID, WE NEED MONEY TO BUY THE BUILDING.
fwish
WHAT ARE YOU LAUGHING AT?
ha ha ha ha
ha ha
ha ha ha
OKAY, YOU'RE BEATING THAT JOKE TO DEATH.
YOU'LL NEVER JOIN THE KATSURA THAT WAY.
Zakoba will turn you away at the door.
IT'S **NOT** A JOKE.
I'M TELLING YOU, **I'M SERIOUS.**

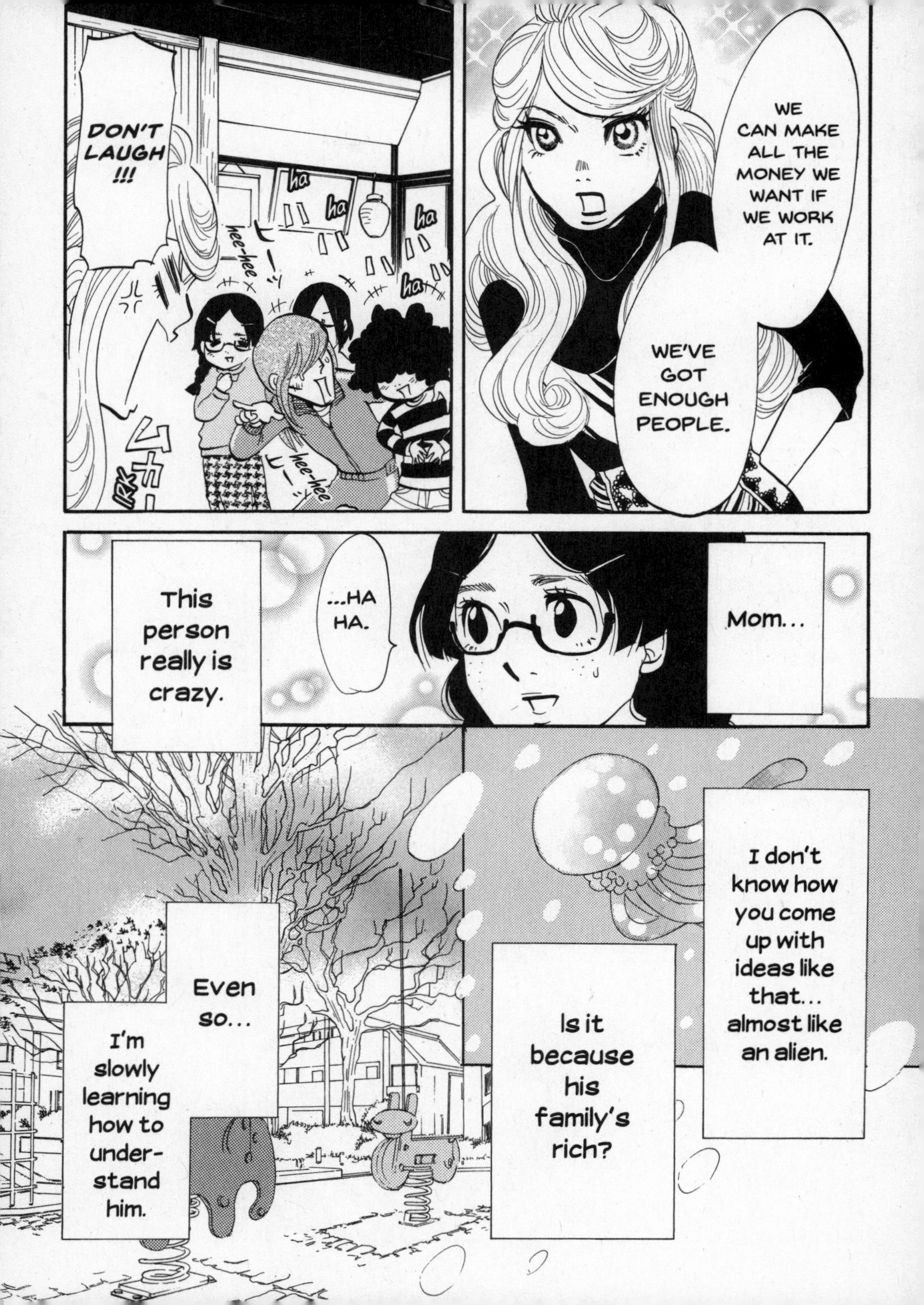
WE CAN MAKE ALL THE MONEY WE WANT IF WE WORK AT IT.
WE'VE GOT ENOUGH PEOPLE.
DON'T LAUGH!!!
ha
ha
ha
ha
hee-hee
hee-hee
IRK
Mom...
...HA HA.
This person really is crazy.
I don't know how you come up with ideas like that... almost like an alien.
Is it because his family's rich?
Even so...
I'm slowly learning how to under-stand him.

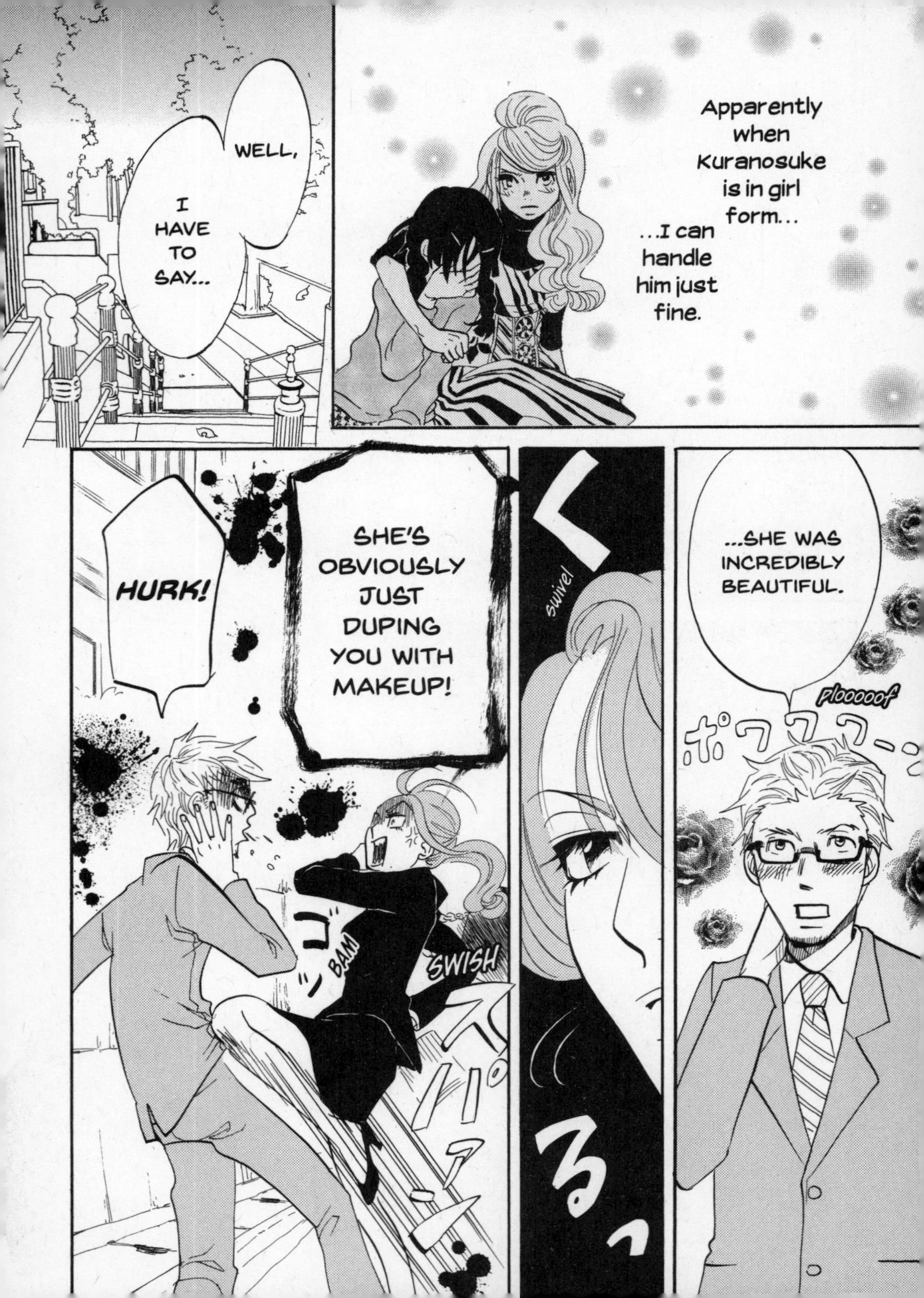
Apparently when Kuranosuke is in girl form...
...I can handle him just fine.
WELL, I HAVE TO SAY...
...SHE WAS INCREDIBLY BEAUTIFUL.
Plooooof
swivel
SHE'S OBVIOUSLY JUST DUPING YOU WITH MAKEUP!
HURK!
SWISH
BAM

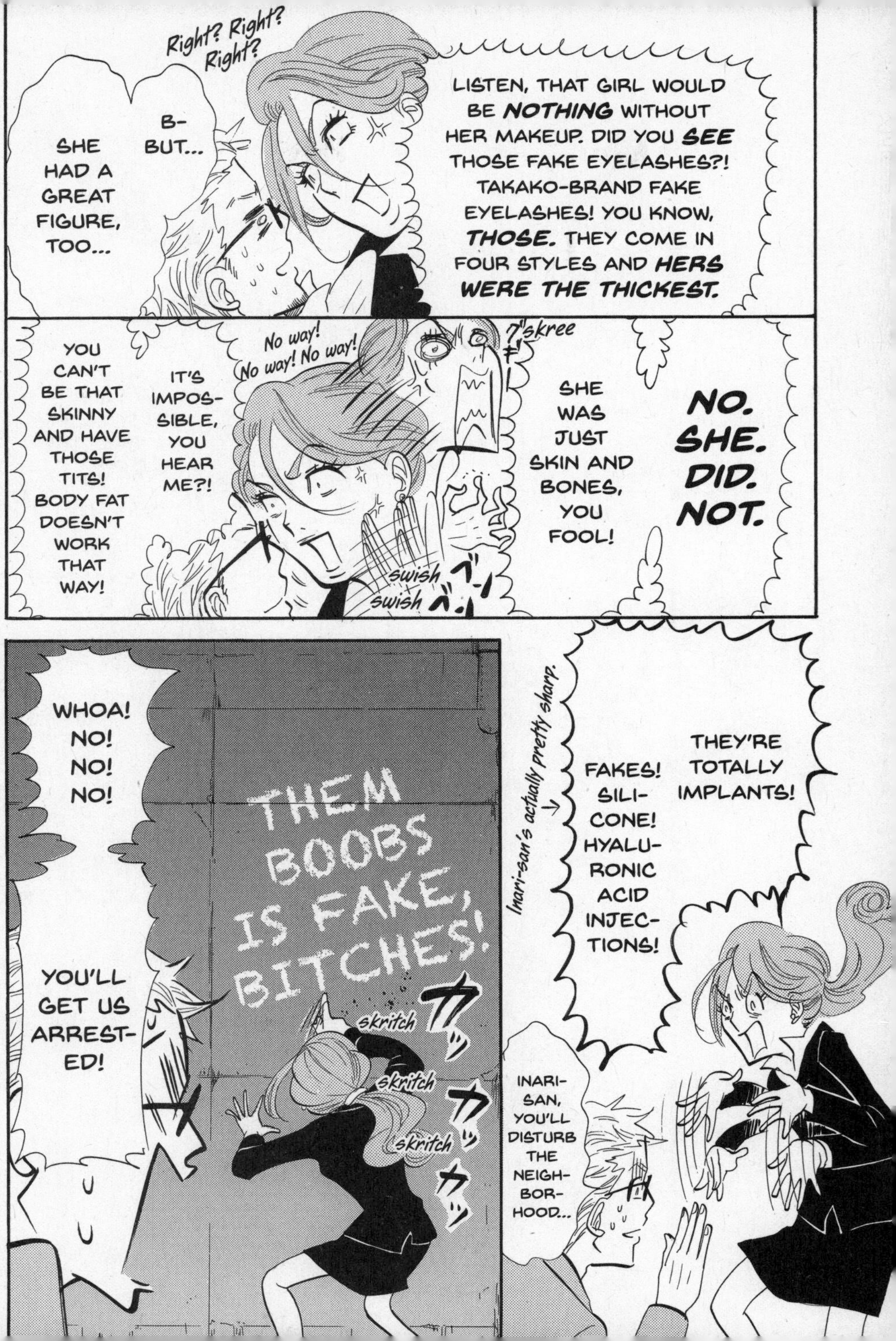
Right? Right? Right?
LISTEN, THAT GIRL WOULD BE NOTHING WITHOUT HER MAKEUP. DID YOU SEE THOSE FAKE EYELASHES?! TAKAKO-BRAND FAKE EYELASHES! YOU KNOW, THOSE. THEY COME IN FOUR STYLES AND HERS WERE THE THICKEST.
B- BUT...
SHE HAD A GREAT FIGURE, TOO...
NO. SHE. DID. NOT.
SHE WAS JUST SKIN AND BONES, YOU FOOL!
skree
No way! No way! No way!
IT'S IMPOSSIBLE, YOU HEAR ME?!
YOU CAN'T BE THAT SKINNY AND HAVE THOSE TITS! BODY FAT DOESN'T WORK THAT WAY!
swish
swish
THEY'RE TOTALLY IMPLANTS!
FAKES! SILICONE! HYALURONIC ACID INJECTIONS!
Inari-san's actually pretty sharp.
INARI-SAN, YOU'LL DISTURB THE NEIGHBORHOOD...
THEM BOOBS IS FAKE, BITCHES!
WHOA! NO! NO! NO!
skritch
skritch
skritch
YOU'LL GET US ARRESTED!

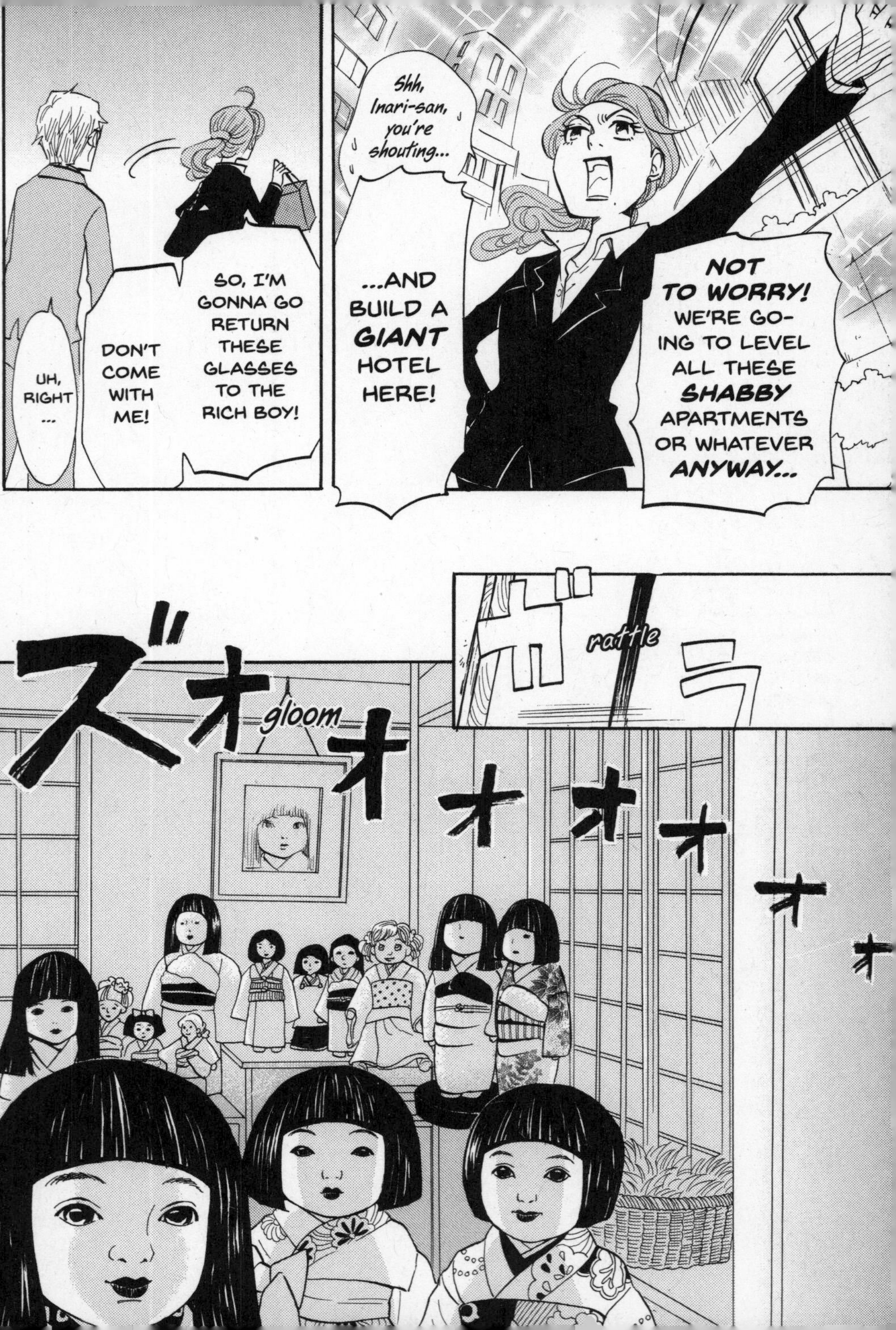
NOT TO WORRY! WE'RE GOING TO LEVEL ALL THESE SHABBY APARTMENTS OR WHATEVER ANYWAY...
...AND BUILD A GIANT HOTEL HERE!
Shh, Inari-san, you're shouting...
SO, I'M GONNA GO RETURN THESE GLASSES TO THE RICH BOY!
DON'T COME WITH ME!
UH, RIGHT ...
ガラ
rattle
ズオオオオオオ
gloom

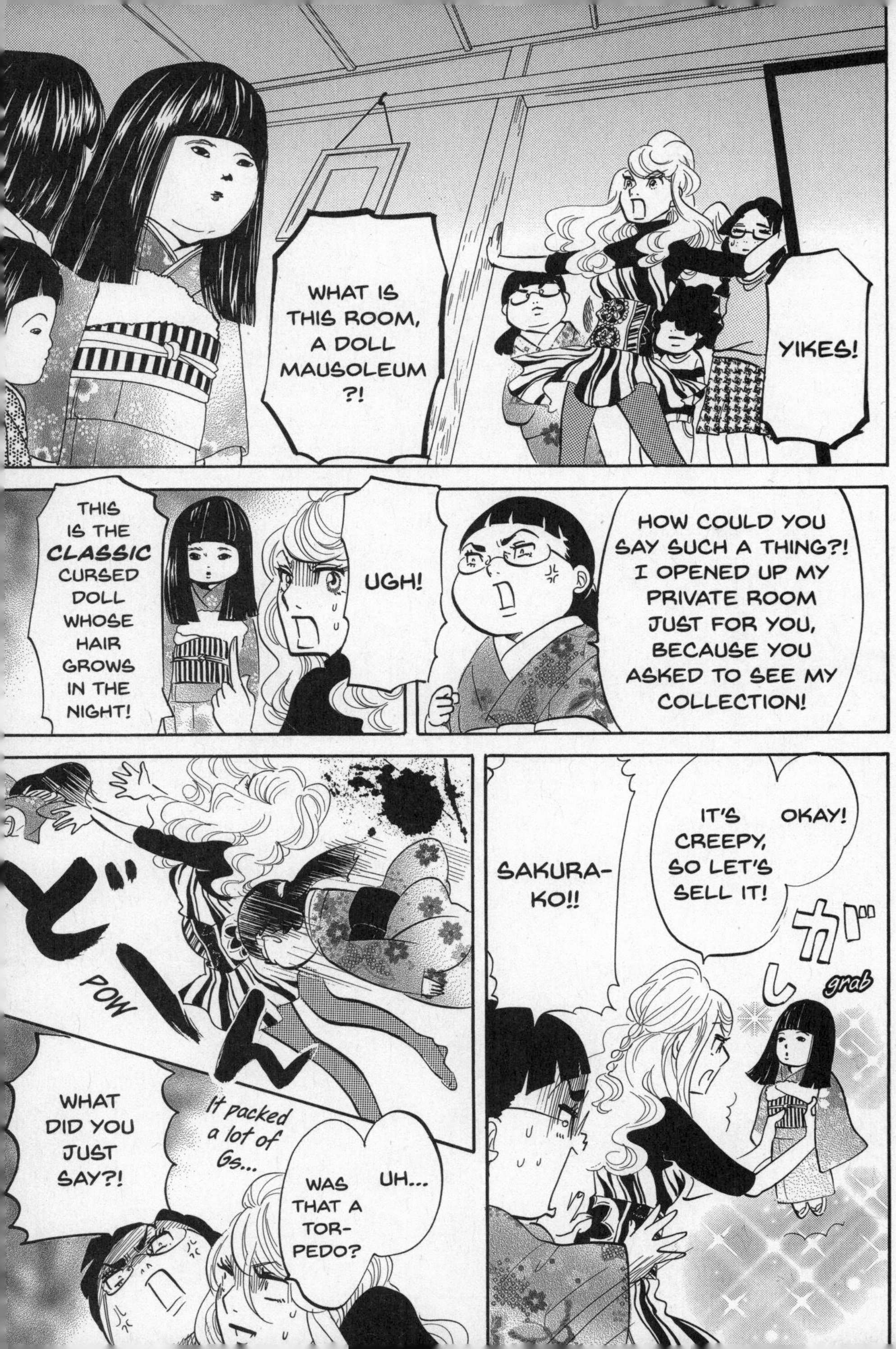
YIKES!
WHAT IS THIS ROOM, A DOLL MAUSOLEUM?!
HOW COULD YOU SAY SUCH A THING?! I OPENED UP MY PRIVATE ROOM JUST FOR YOU, BECAUSE YOU ASKED TO SEE MY COLLECTION!
UGH!
THIS IS THE **CLASSIC** CURSED DOLL WHOSE HAIR GROWS IN THE NIGHT!
OKAY!
IT'S CREEPY, SO LET'S SELL IT!
SAKURA-KO!!
grab
POW
It packed a lot of Gs...
UH...
WAS THAT A TORPEDO?
WHAT DID YOU JUST SAY?!

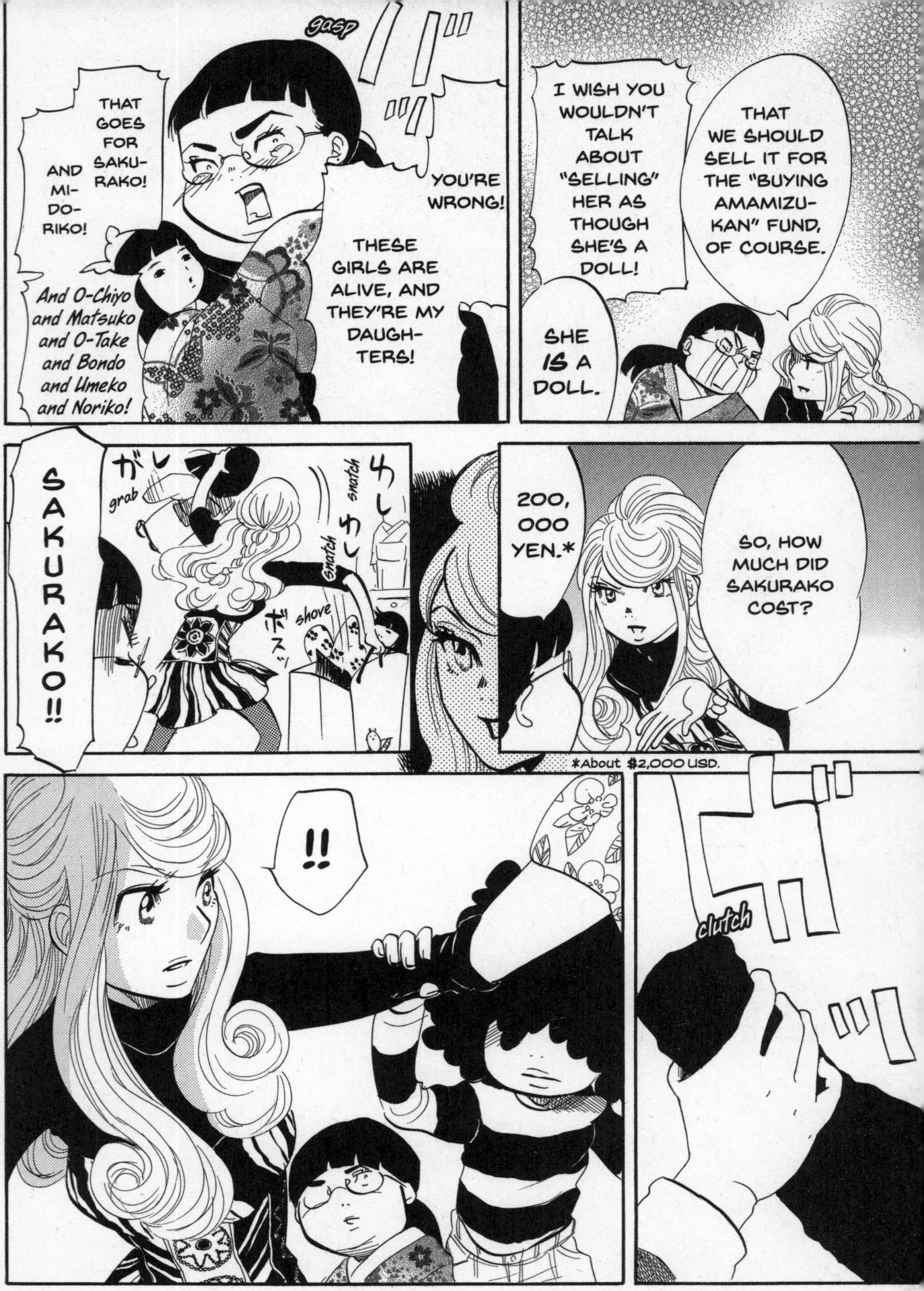
THAT WE SHOULD SELL IT FOR THE "BUYING AMAMIZUKAN" FUND, OF COURSE.
I WISH YOU WOULDN'T TALK ABOUT "SELLING" HER AS THOUGH SHE'S A DOLL!
SHE IS A DOLL.
gasp
YOU'RE WRONG!
THESE GIRLS ARE ALIVE, AND THEY'RE MY DAUGHTERS!
THAT GOES FOR SAKURAKO!
AND MIDORIKO!
And O-Chiyo and Matsuko and O-Take and Bondo and Umeko and Noriko!
SO, HOW MUCH DID SAKURAKO COST?
200,000 YEN.*
snatch
snatch
grab
snatch
shove
SAKURAKO!!
*About $2,000 USD.
clutch
!!

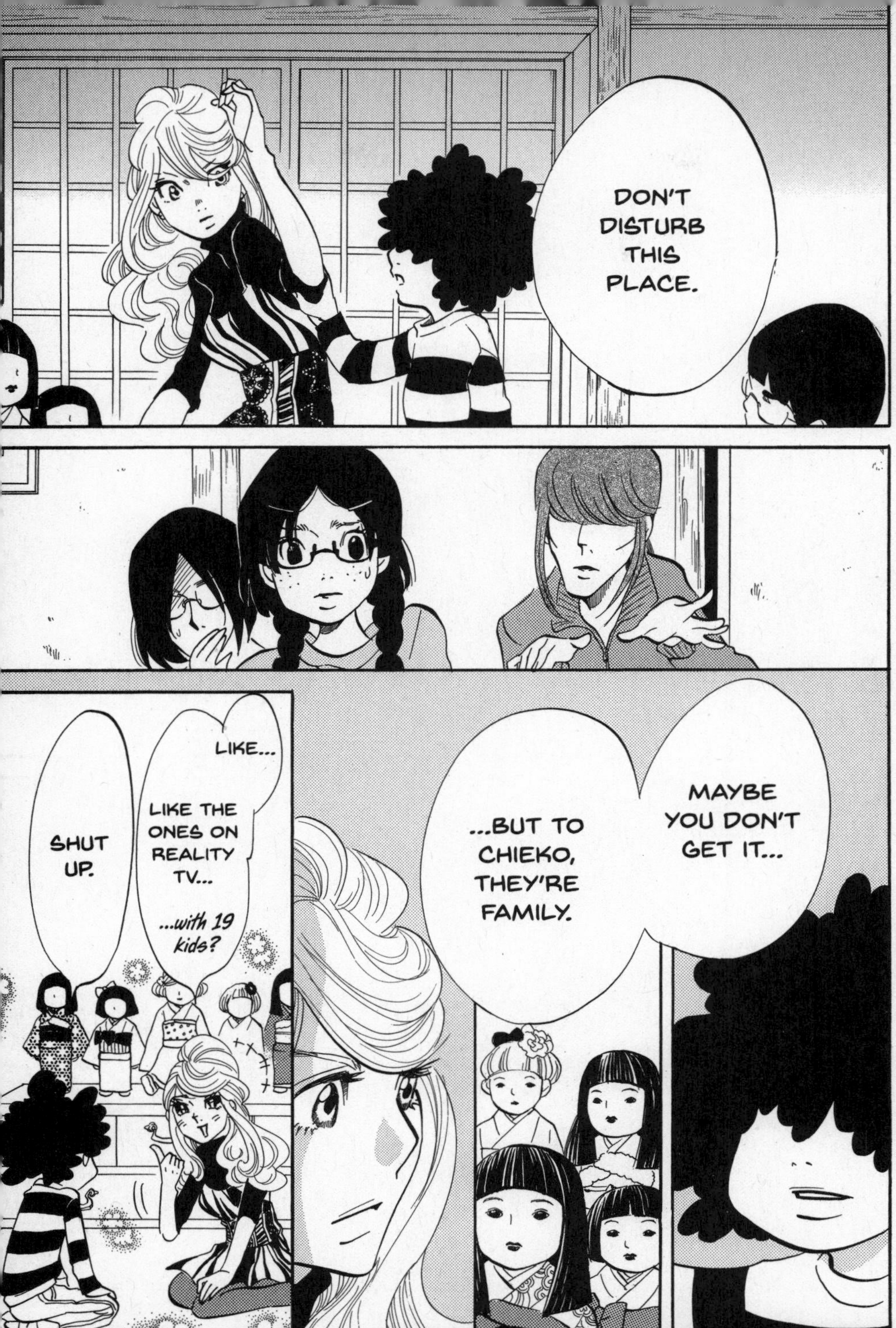
DON'T DISTURB THIS PLACE.
MAYBE YOU DON'T GET IT...
...BUT TO CHIEKO, THEY'RE FAMILY.
LIKE...
LIKE THE ONES ON REALITY TV...
...with 19 kids?
SHUT UP.

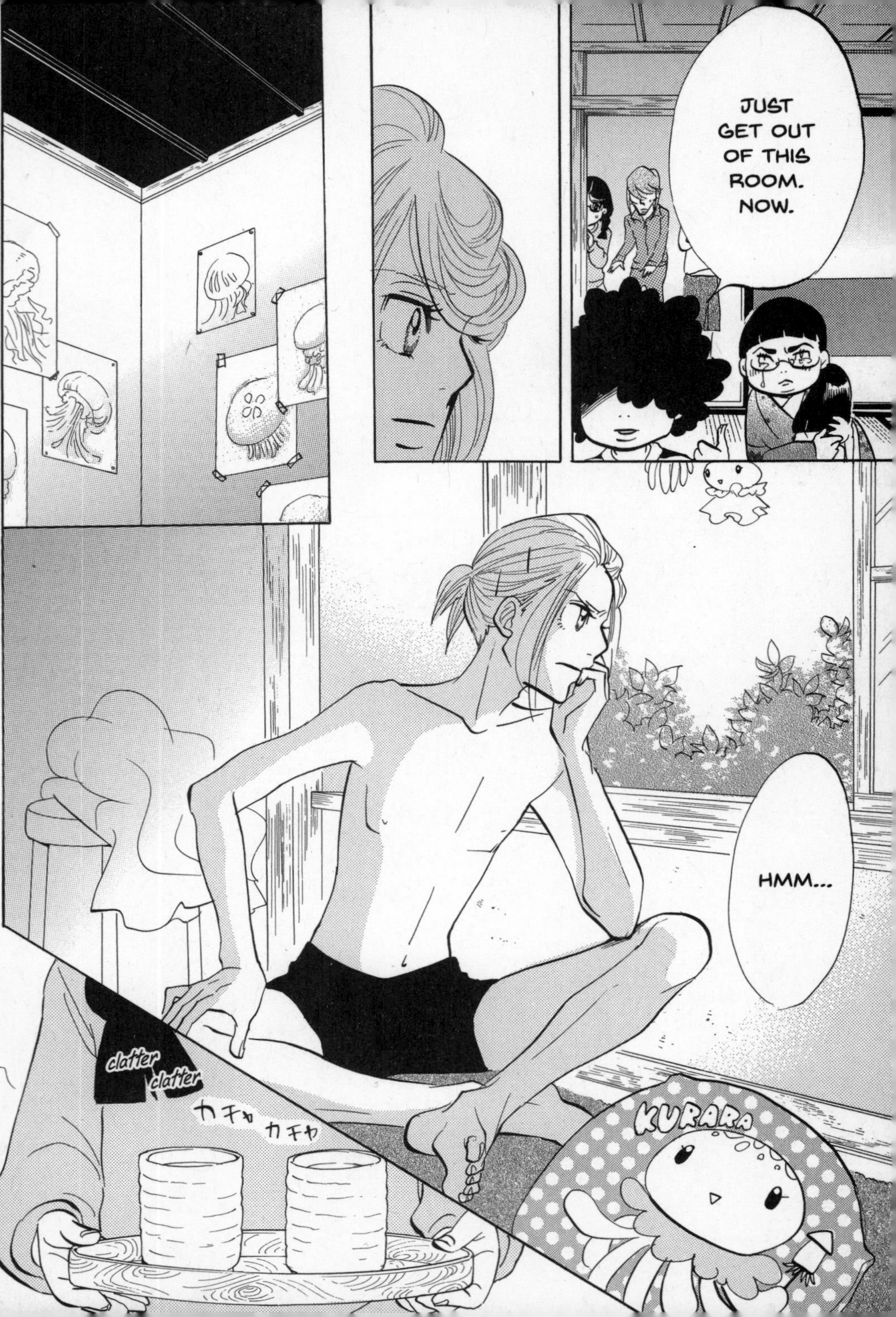
JUST GET OUT OF THIS ROOM. NOW.
HMM...
clatter clatter
カチャ カチャ
KURARA

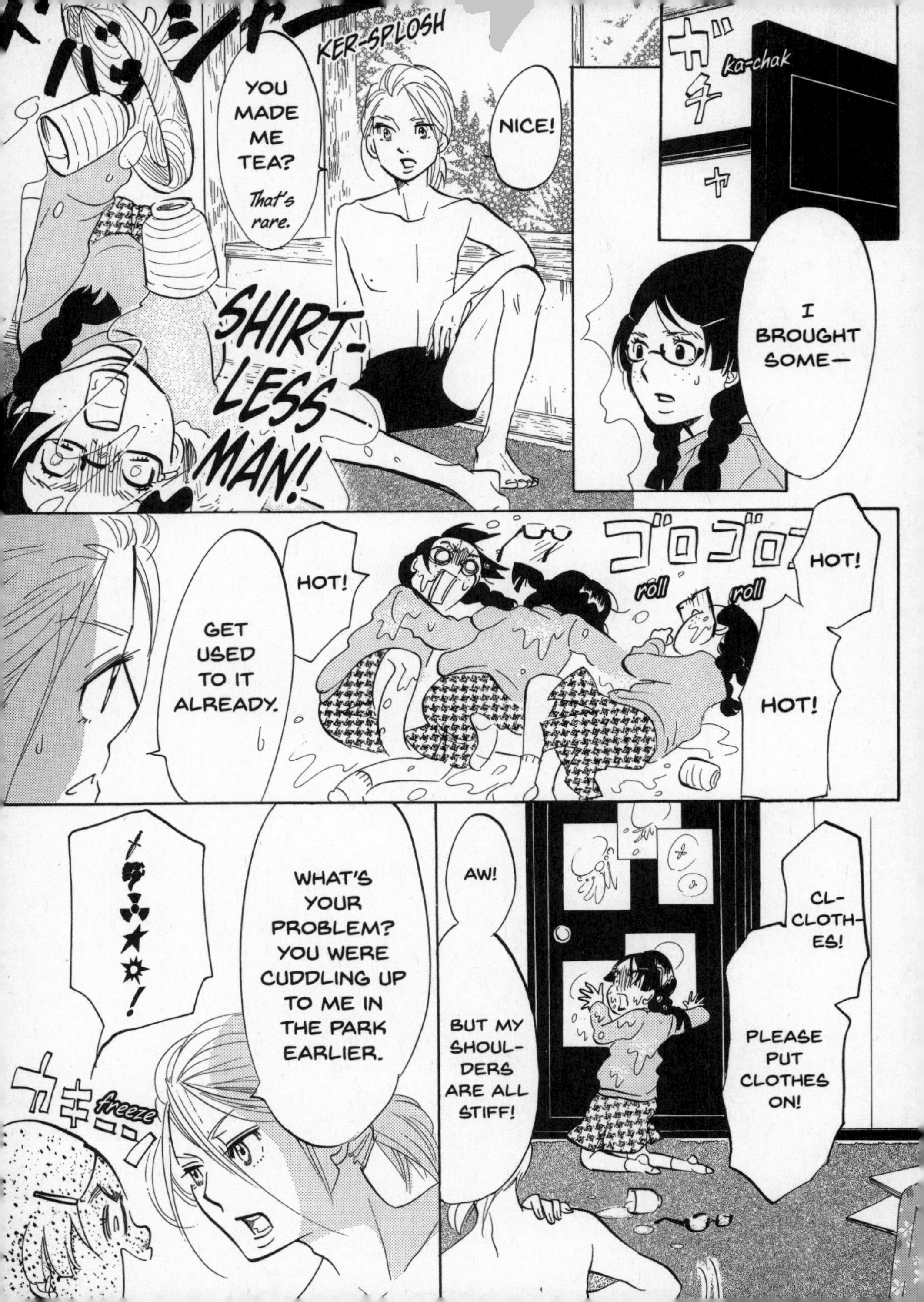
ガチャ
ka-chak
I BROUGHT SOME—
ズバシャー
KER-SPLOSH
NICE!
YOU MADE ME TEA? That's rare.
SHIRT-LESS MAN!
HOT!
ゴロゴロ
roll roll
HOT!
HOT!
GET USED TO IT ALREADY.
CL-CLOTHES!
PLEASE PUT CLOTHES ON!
AW!
BUT MY SHOULDERS ARE ALL STIFF!
WHAT'S YOUR PROBLEM? YOU WERE CUDDLING UP TO ME IN THE PARK EARLIER.
カキーン
freeze

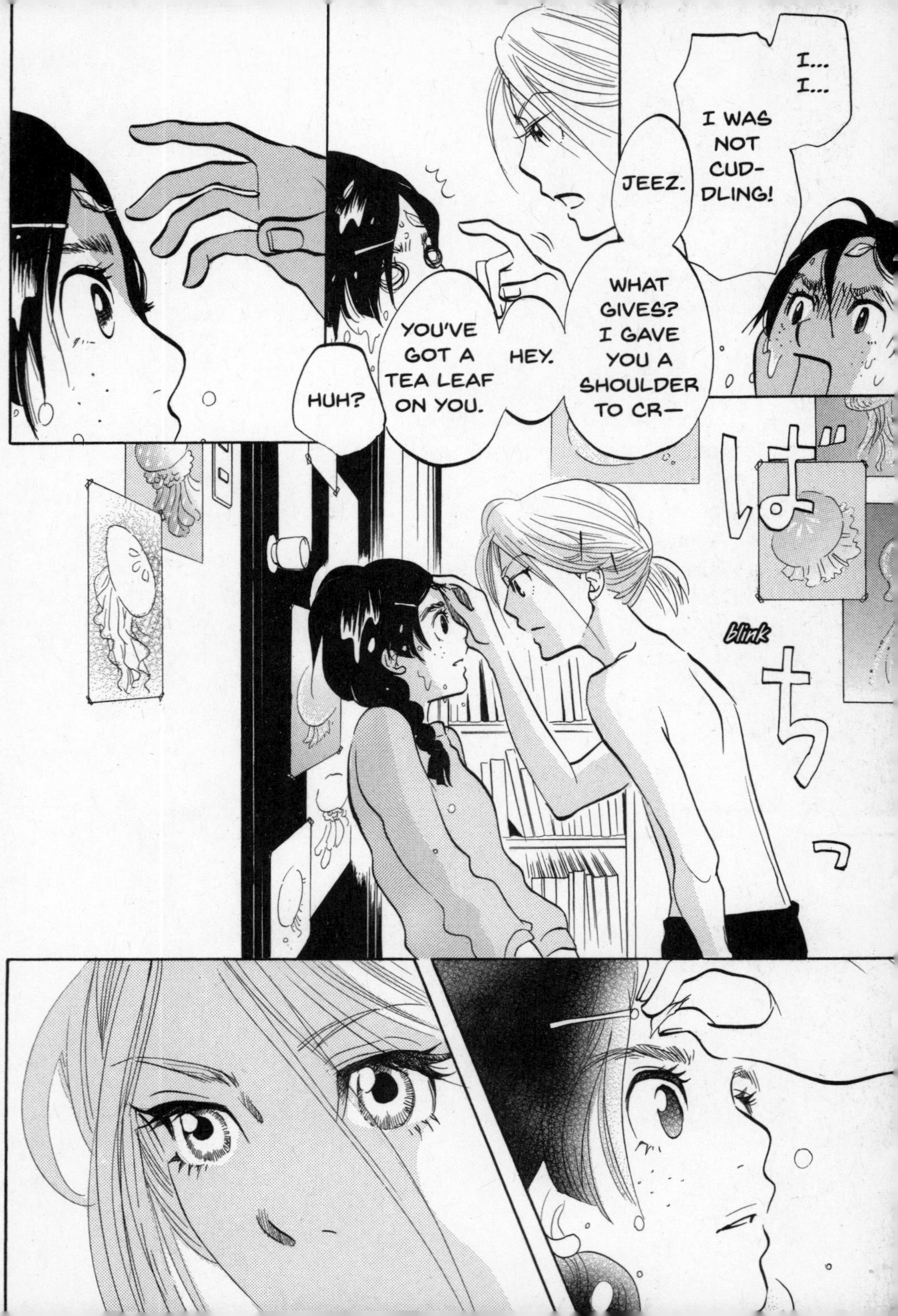
I...
I...
I WAS NOT CUD-DLING!
JEEZ.
WHAT GIVES? I GAVE YOU A SHOULDER TO CR—
HEY.
YOU'VE GOT A TEA LEAF ON YOU.
HUH?
ばちっ
blink

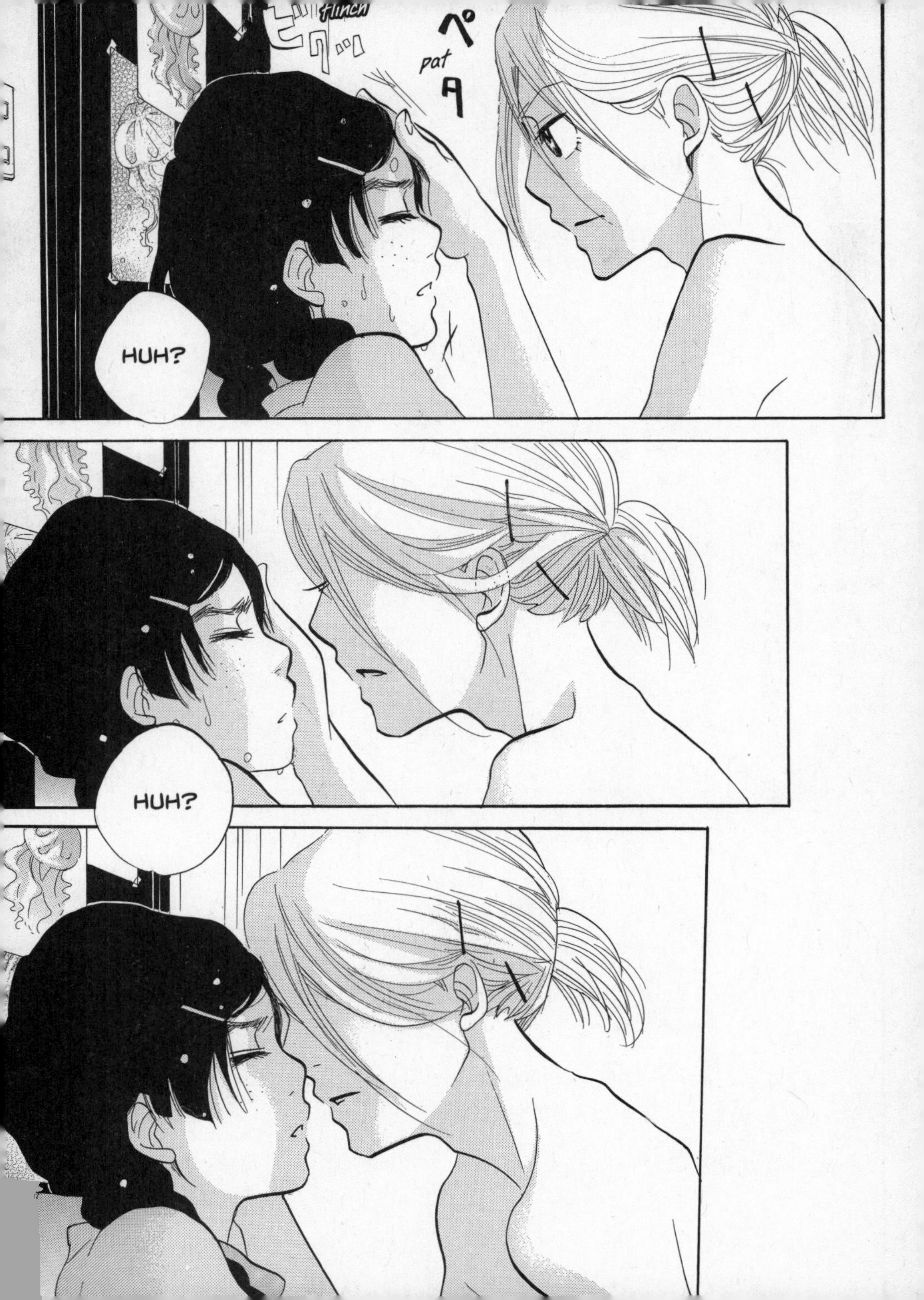
ビクッ
flinch
ペタ
pat
HUH?
HUH?

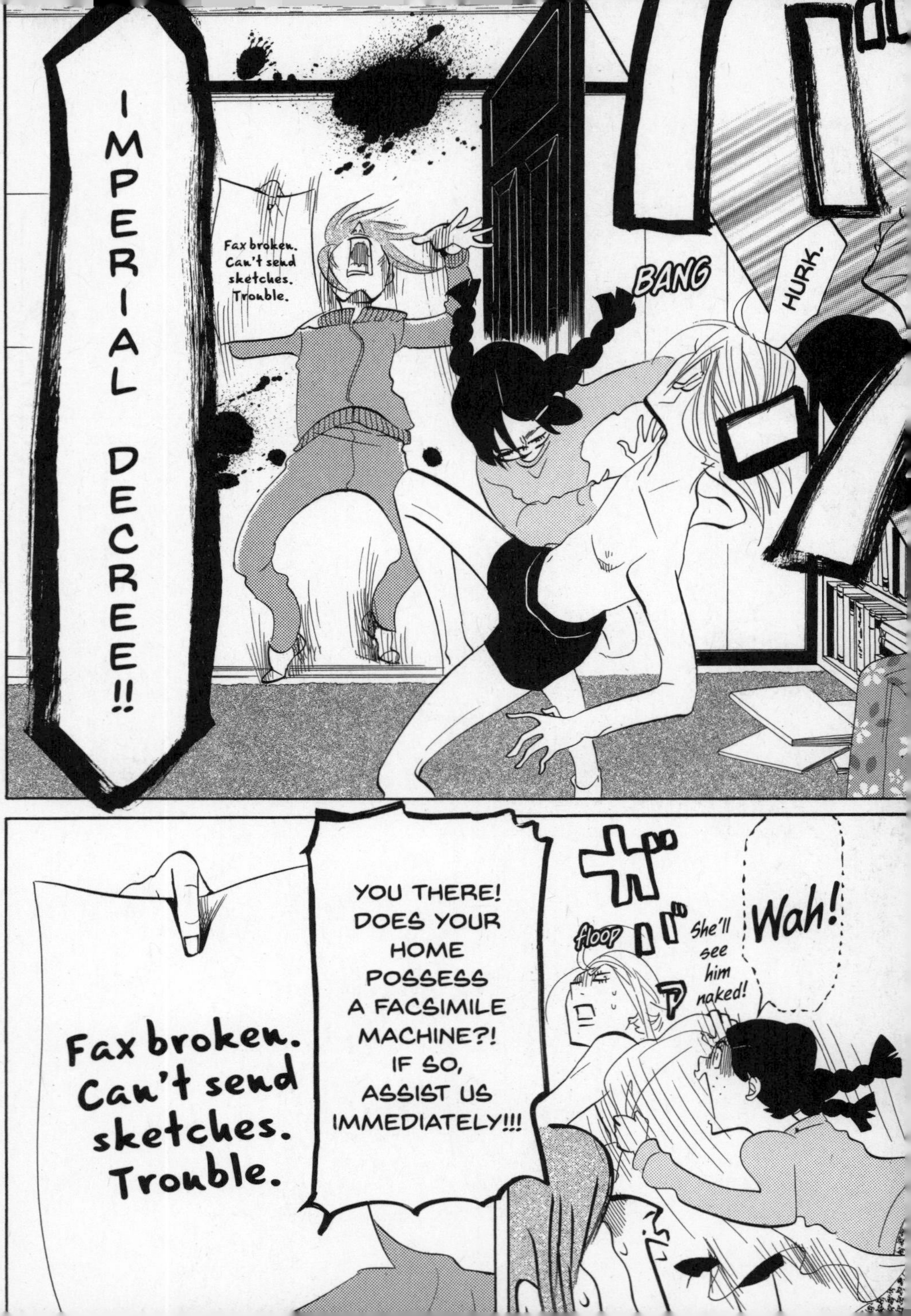
HURK.
BANG
Fax broken. Can't send sketches. Trouble.
IMPERIAL DECREE!!
Wah!
She'll see him naked!
floop
YOU THERE! DOES YOUR HOME POSSESS A FACSIMILE MACHINE?! IF SO, ASSIST US IMMEDIATELY!!!
Fax broken. Can't send sketches. Trouble.

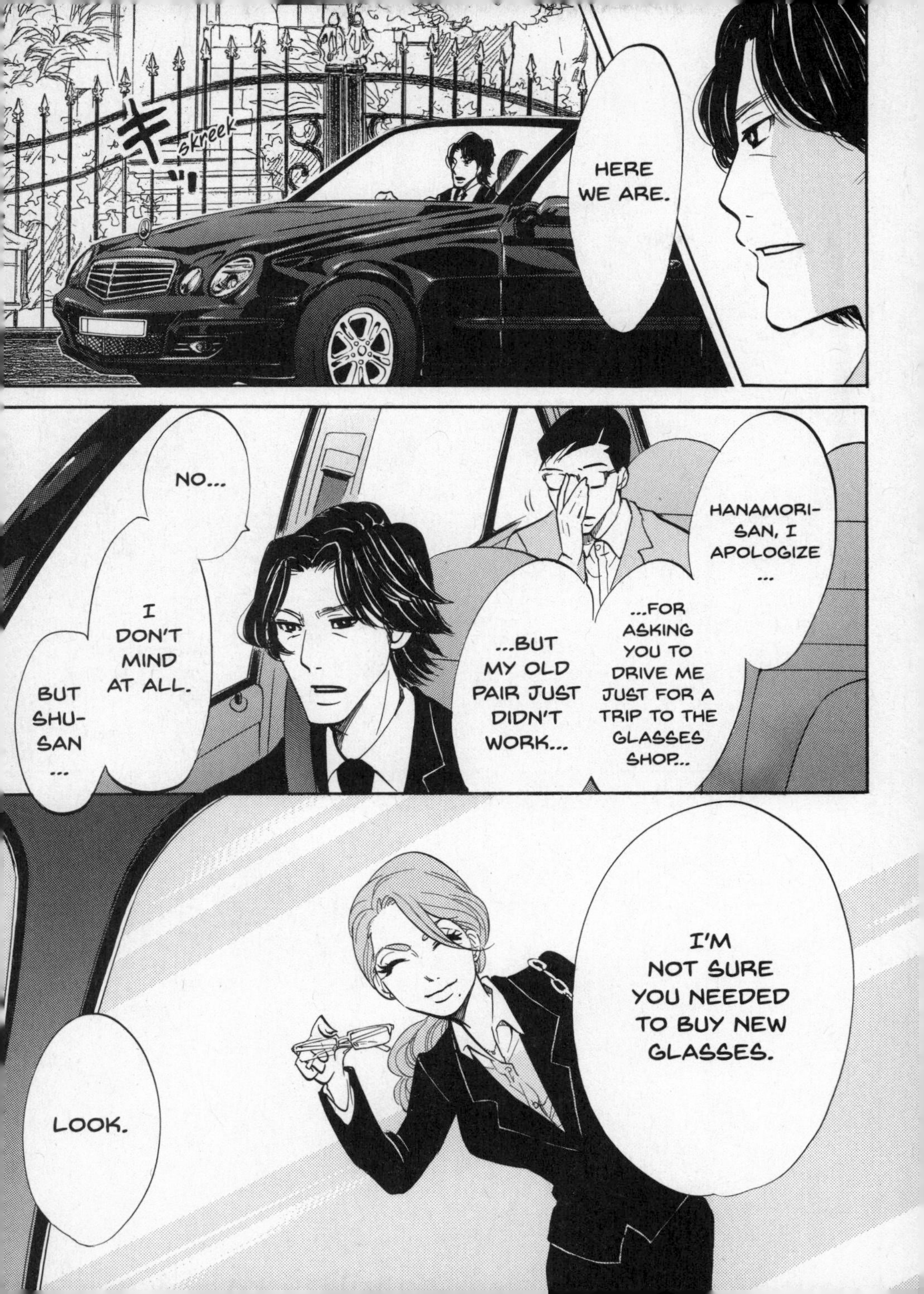
HERE WE ARE.
キッ skreek
HANAMORI-SAN, I APOLOGIZE...
...FOR ASKING YOU TO DRIVE ME JUST FOR A TRIP TO THE GLASSES SHOP...
...BUT MY OLD PAIR JUST DIDN'T WORK...
NO...
I DON'T MIND AT ALL.
BUT SHU-SAN...
I'M NOT SURE YOU NEEDED TO BUY NEW GLASSES.
LOOK.

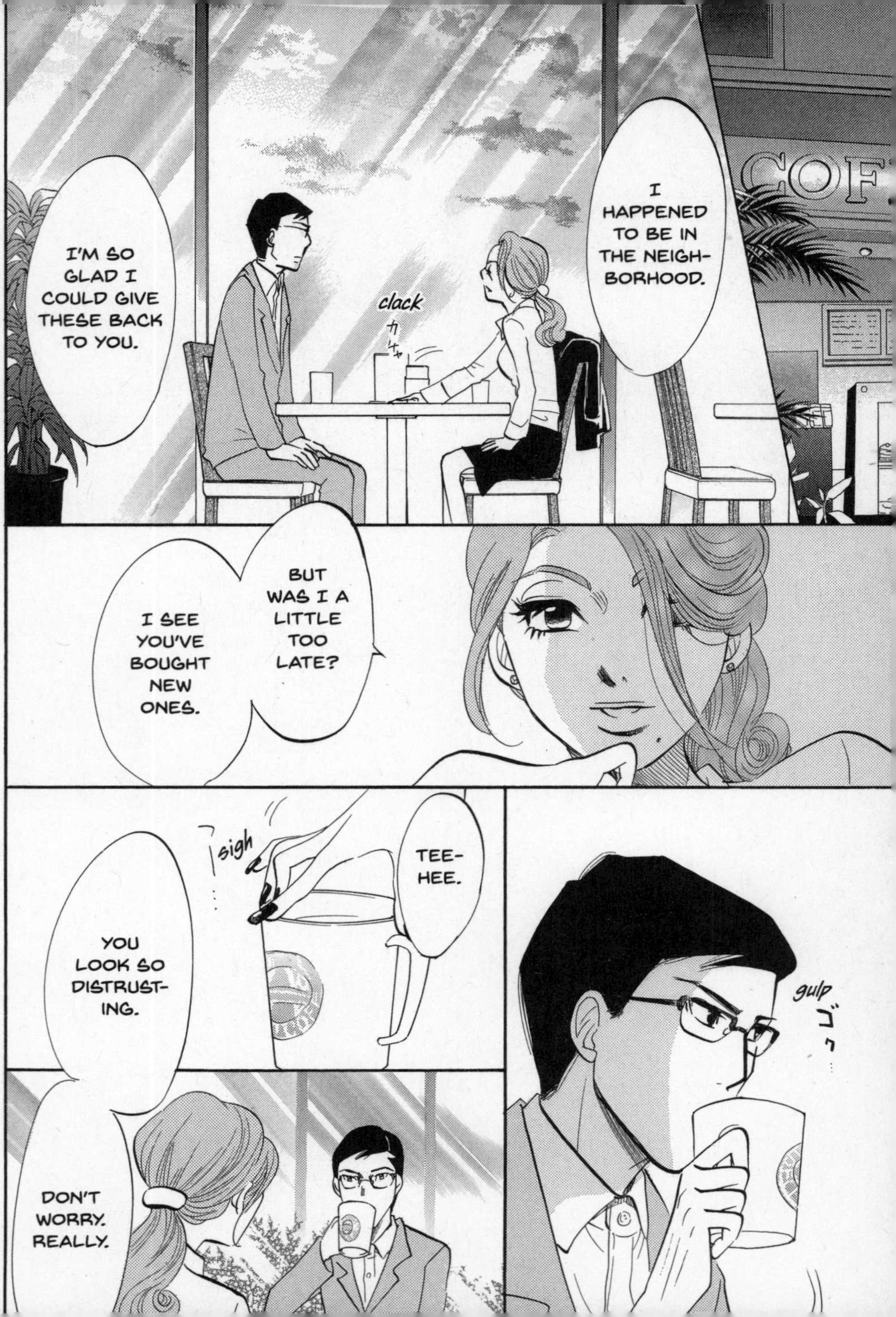
COF
I HAPPENED TO BE IN THE NEIGHBORHOOD.
clack
カチャ
I'M SO GLAD I COULD GIVE THESE BACK TO YOU.
BUT WAS I A LITTLE TOO LATE?
I SEE YOU'VE BOUGHT NEW ONES.
gulp
ゴク
TEE-HEE.
sigh
YOU LOOK SO DISTRUSTING.
DON'T WORRY. REALLY.

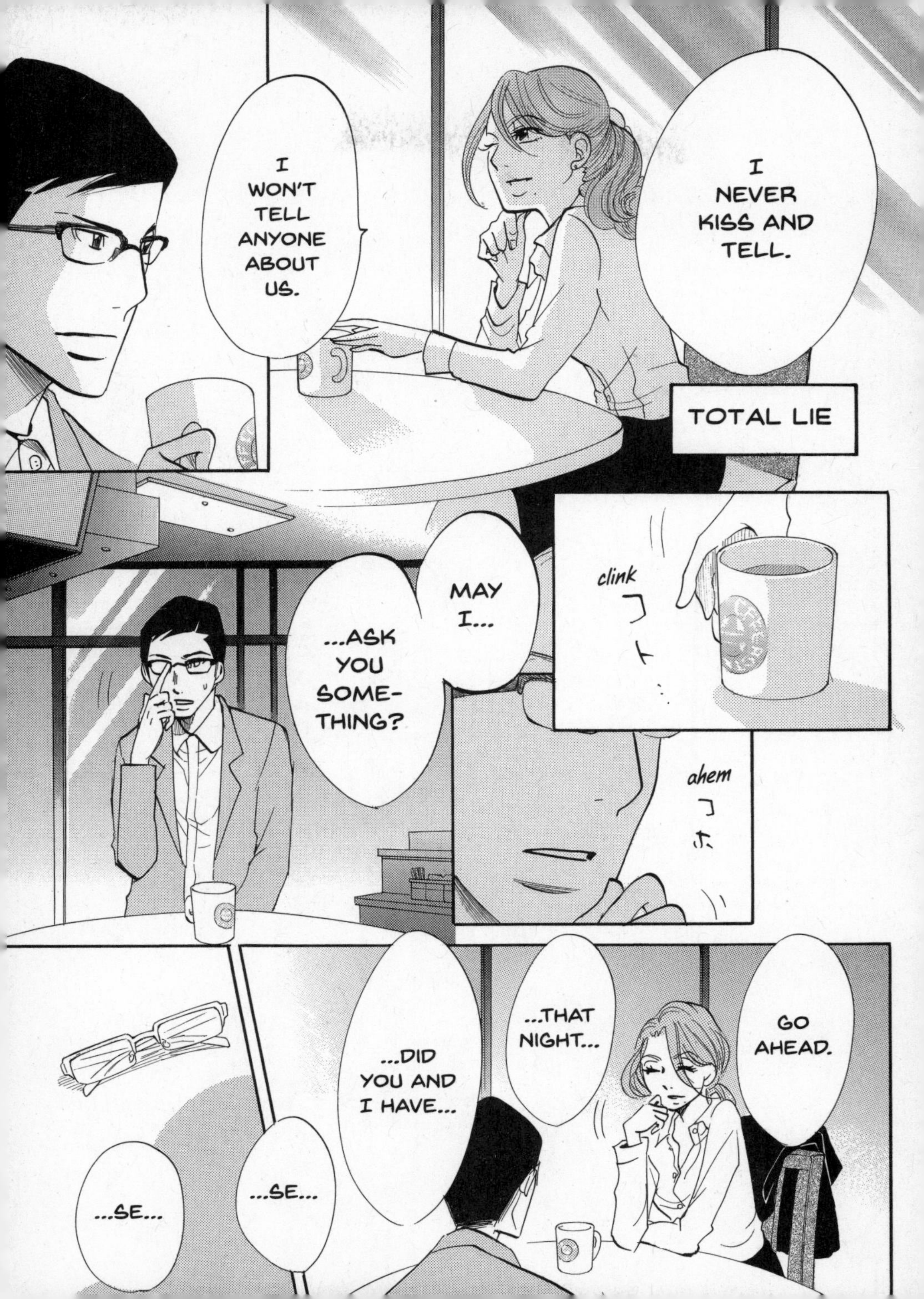
I NEVER KISS AND TELL.
TOTAL LIE
I WON'T TELL ANYONE ABOUT US.
clink
コト
ahem
コホ
MAY I...
...ASK YOU SOME-THING?
GO AHEAD.
...THAT NIGHT...
...DID YOU AND I HAVE...
...SE...
...SE...

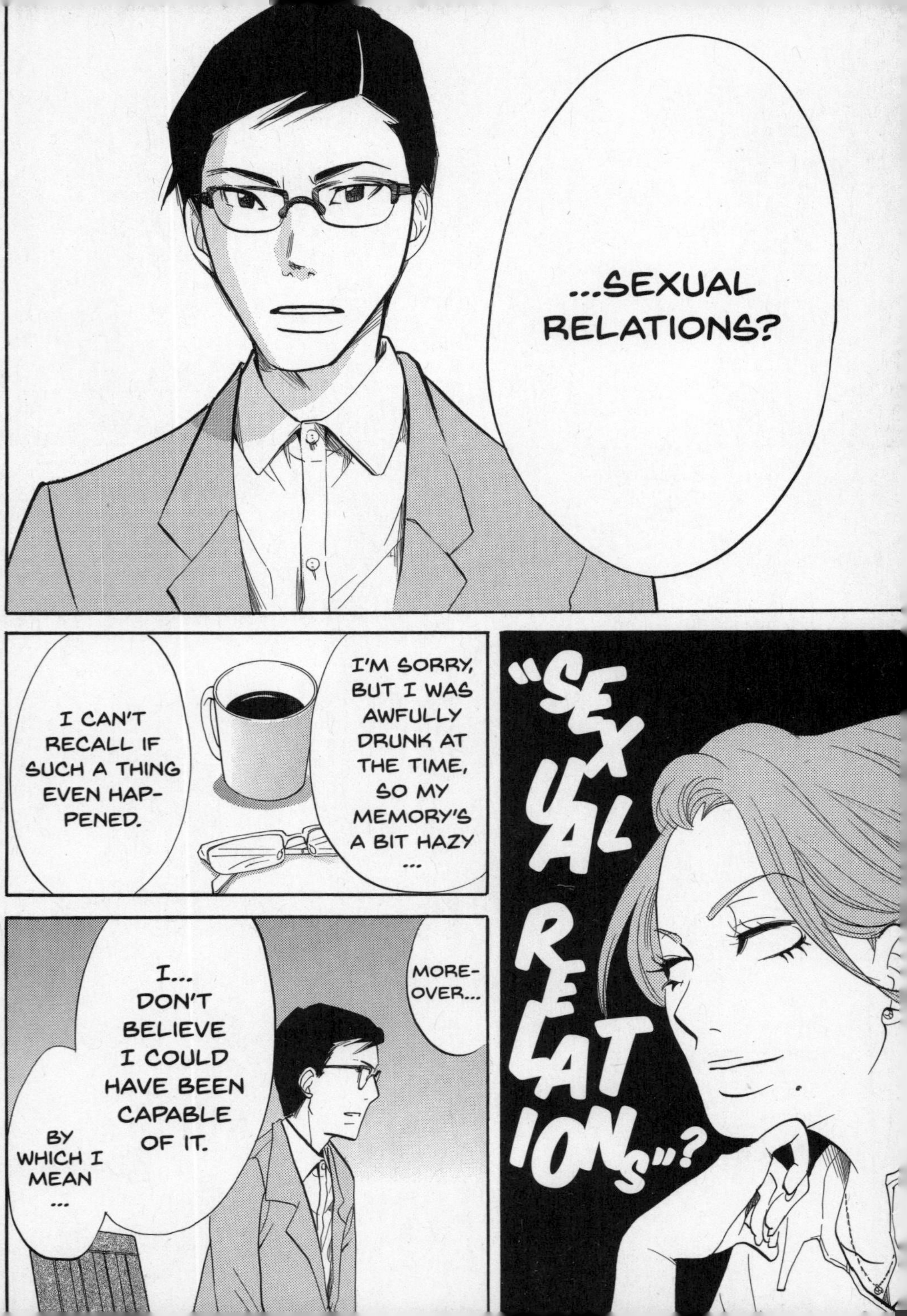
...SEXUAL RELATIONS?
"SEXUAL RELATIONS"?
I'M SORRY, BUT I WAS AWFULLY DRUNK AT THE TIME, SO MY MEMORY'S A BIT HAZY ...
I CAN'T RECALL IF SUCH A THING EVEN HAP-PENED.
MORE-OVER...
I... DON'T BELIEVE I COULD HAVE BEEN CAPABLE OF IT.
BY WHICH I MEAN ...

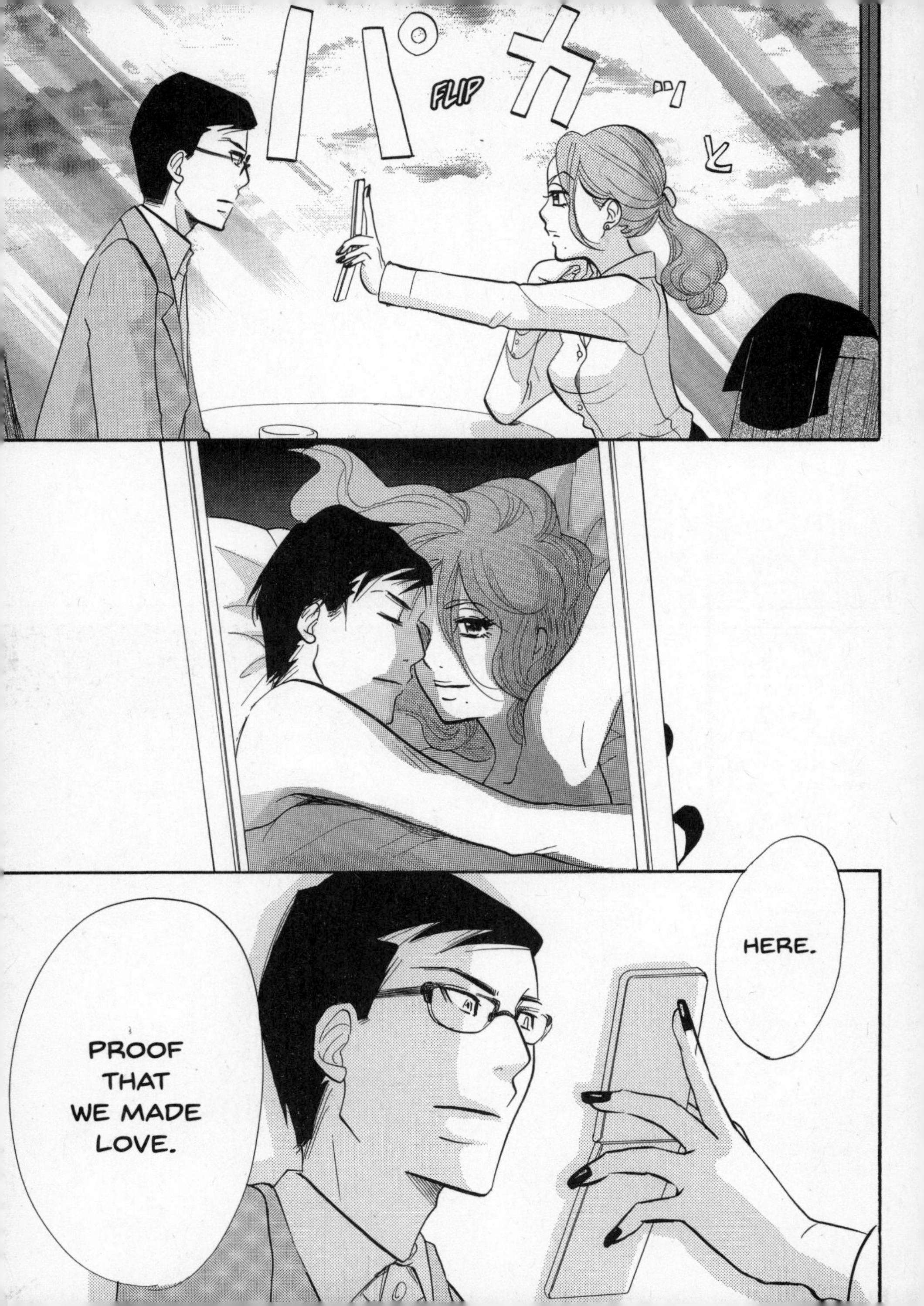
パ
FLIP
カッ
と
HERE.
PROOF THAT WE MADE LOVE.

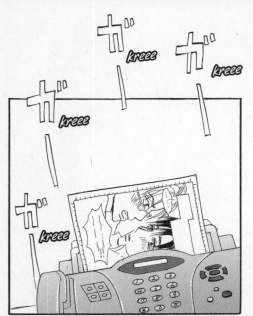

ガ"
kreee

ガ"
kreee

ガ"
kreee

ガ"
kreee

ガ"
kreee

...

ガ"
kreee

...

phoo
phoo

ガ"
kreee

ガ"
kreee

...

kreee
ガ"
ガ"
kreee

slurp
ズズズ・・・
slurp

BOB DYLA

-26-

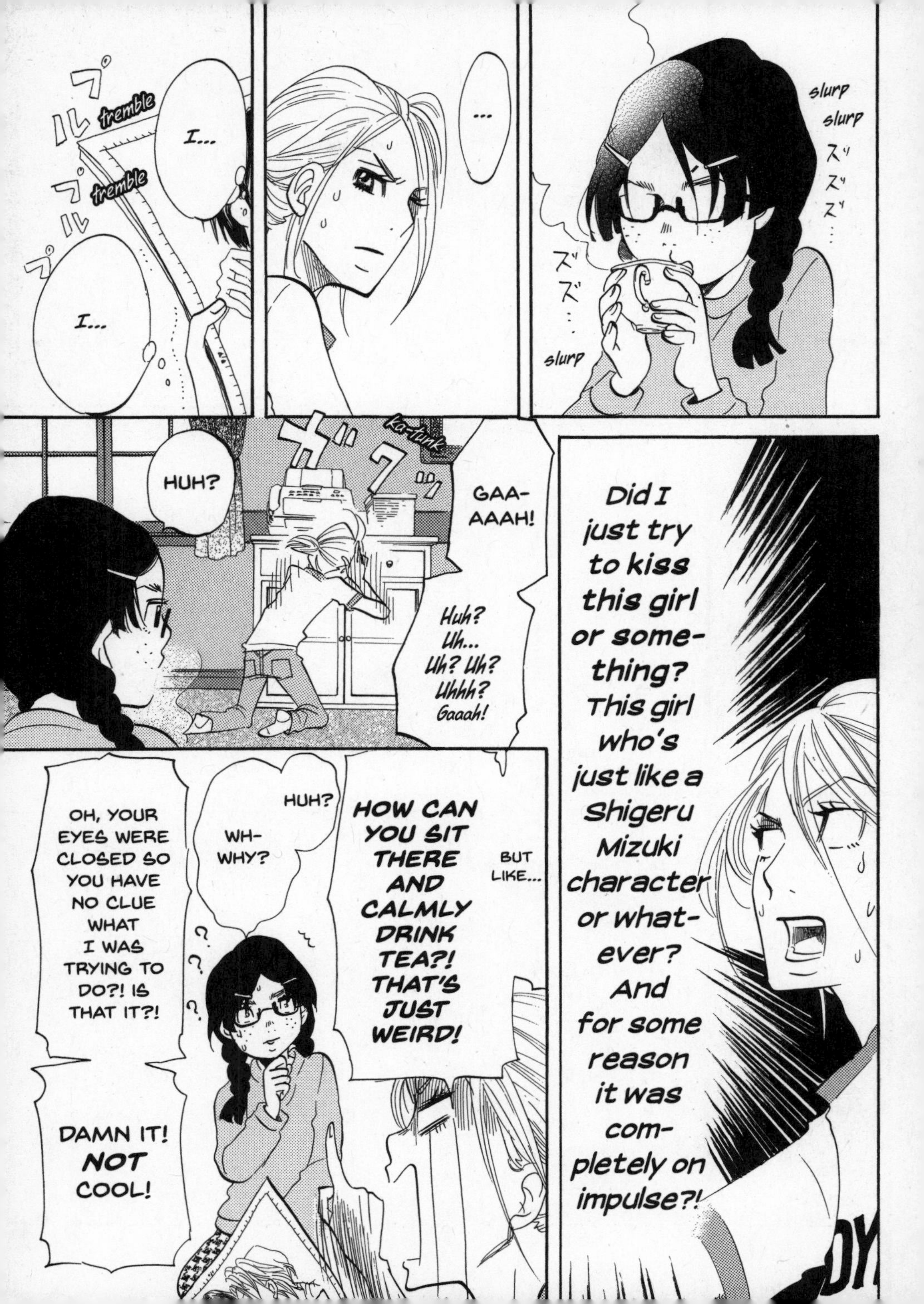

slurp
slurp
ズズズ…
ズズ…
slurp
...
I...
プルプル
tremble
tremble
I...
Did I just try to kiss this girl or some-thing? This girl who's just like a Shigeru Mizuki character or what-ever? And for some reason it was com-pletely on impulse?!
GAA-AAAH!
ka-tunk
Huh? Uh... Uh? Uh? Uhhh? Gaaah!
HUH?
BUT LIKE...
HOW CAN YOU SIT THERE AND CALMLY DRINK TEA?! THAT'S JUST WEIRD!
HUH?
WH-WHY?
OH, YOUR EYES WERE CLOSED SO YOU HAVE NO CLUE WHAT I WAS TRYING TO DO?! IS THAT IT?!
DAMN IT! NOT COOL!

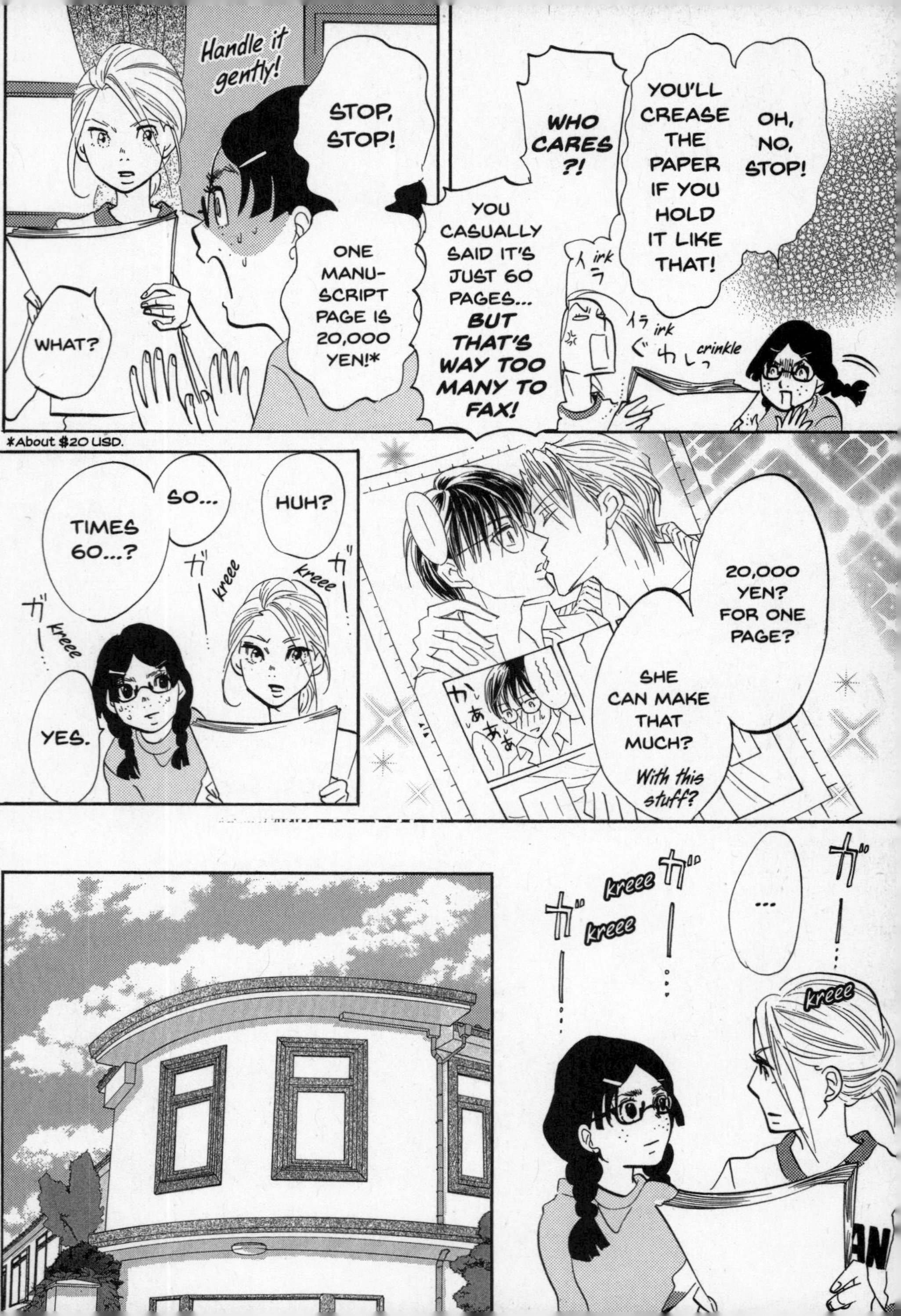
OH, NO, STOP!
YOU'LL CREASE THE PAPER IF YOU HOLD IT LIKE THAT!
irk
irk
crinkle
WHO CARES?!
YOU CASUALLY SAID IT'S JUST 60 PAGES... BUT THAT'S WAY TOO MANY TO FAX!
STOP, STOP!
Handle it gently!
ONE MANU-SCRIPT PAGE IS 20,000 YEN!*
WHAT?
20,000 YEN? FOR ONE PAGE?
SHE CAN MAKE THAT MUCH?
With this stuff?
HUH?
SO...
TIMES 60...?
kreee
kreee
kreee
YES.
kreee
...
kreee
kreee

*About $20 USD.

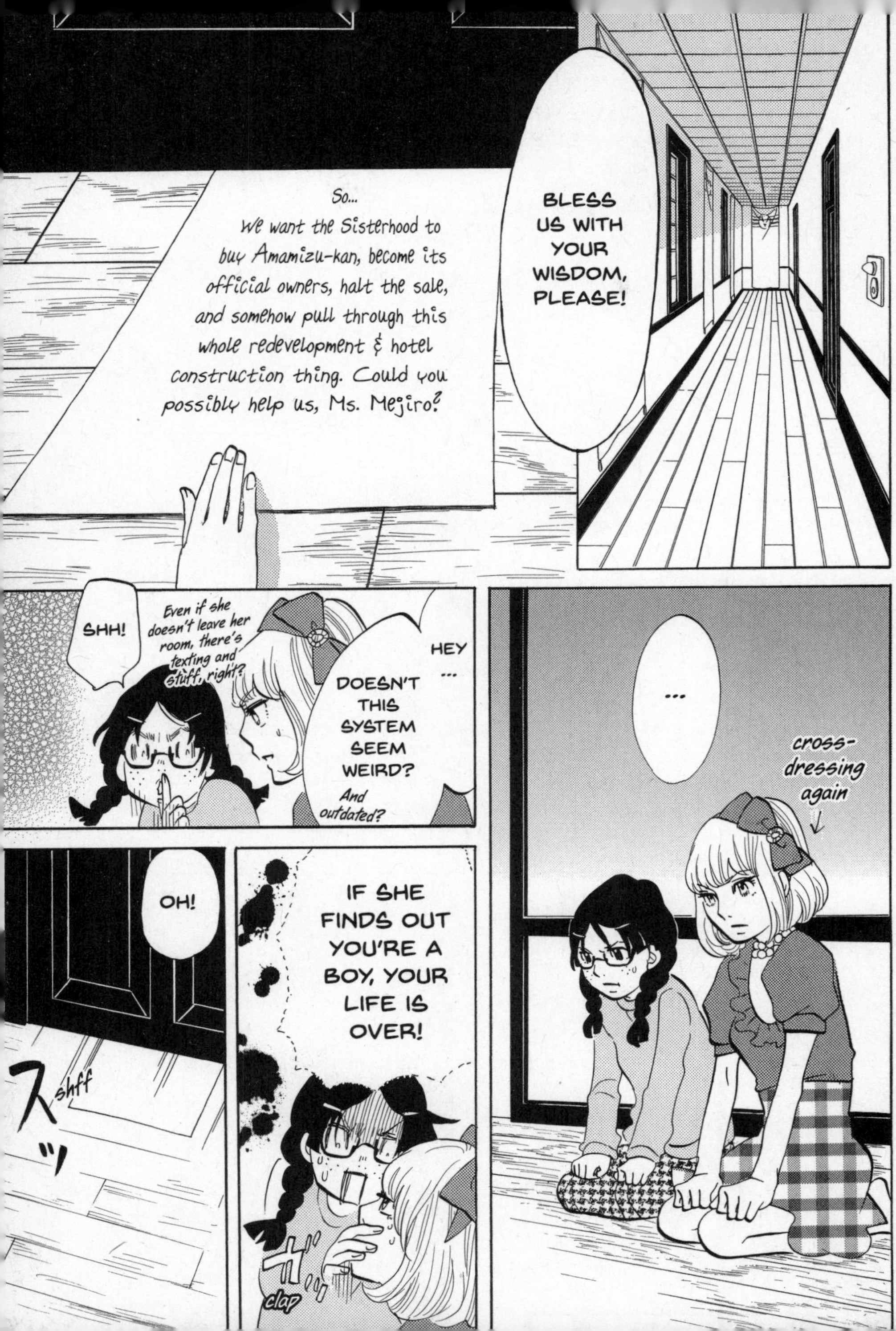
BLESS US WITH YOUR WISDOM, PLEASE!
So... We want the Sisterhood to buy Amamizu-kan, become its official owners, halt the sale, and somehow pull through this whole redevelopment & hotel construction thing. Could you possibly help us, Ms. Mejiro?
...
cross-dressing again
HEY ...
DOESN'T THIS SYSTEM SEEM WEIRD?
And outdated?
Even if she doesn't leave her room, there's texting and stuff, right?
SHH!
IF SHE FINDS OUT YOU'RE A BOY, YOUR LIFE IS OVER!
clap
OH!
shff

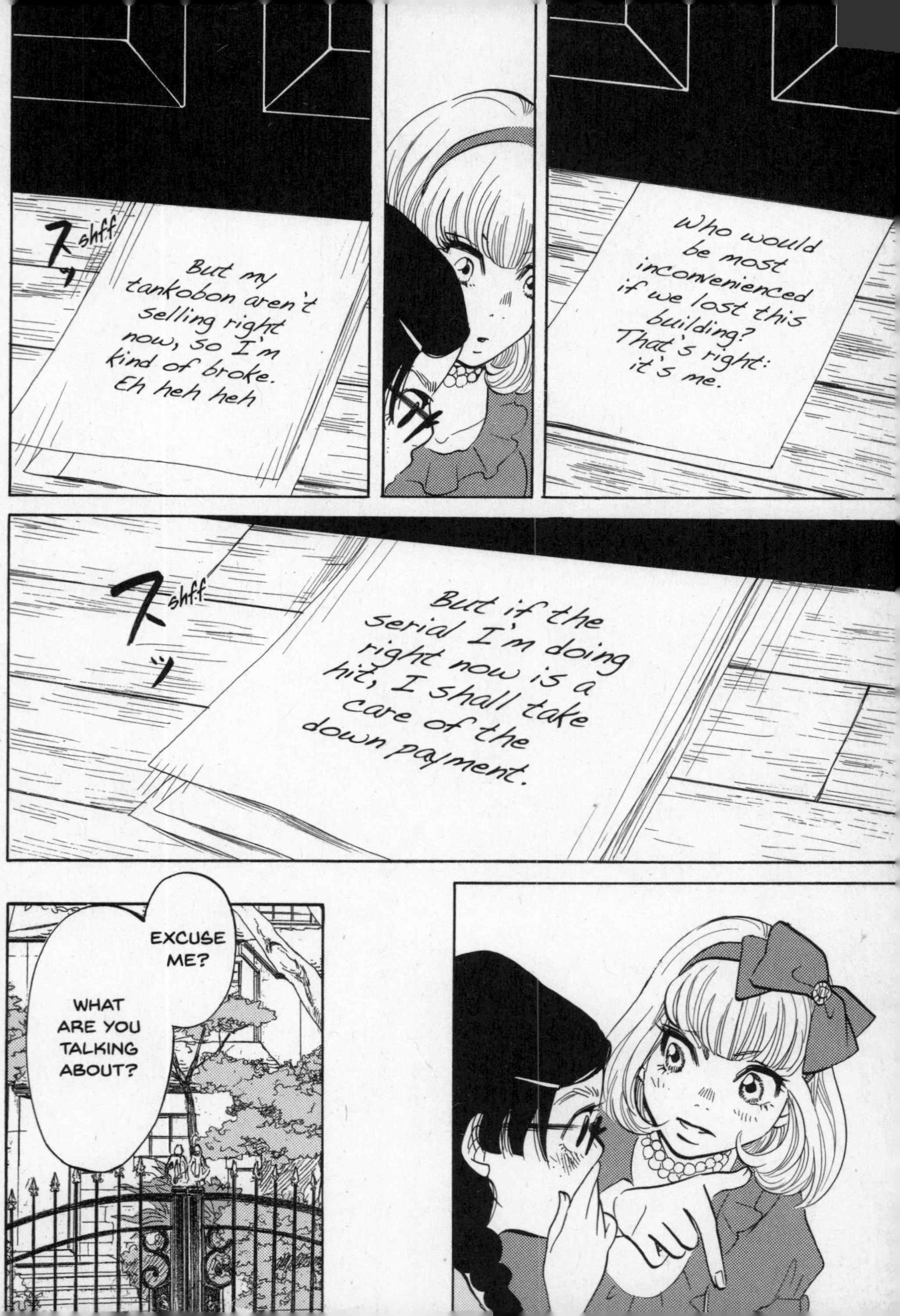
Who would be most inconvenienced if we lost this building? That's right: it's me.
スッ shff
But my tankobon aren't selling right now, so I'm kind of broke. Eh heh heh
スッ shff
But if the serial I'm doing right now is a hit, I shall take care of the down payment.
EXCUSE ME?
WHAT ARE YOU TALKING ABOUT?

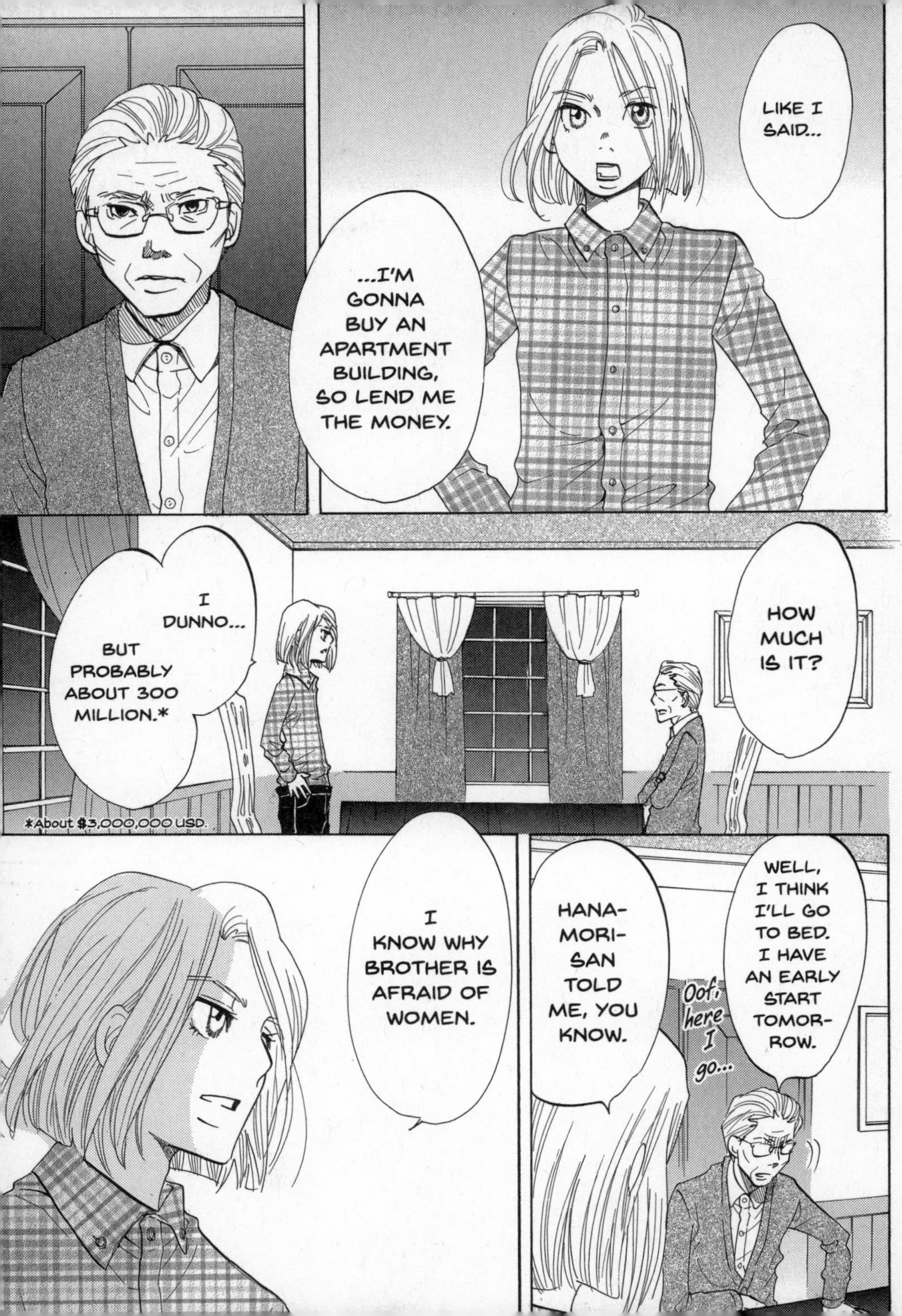
LIKE I SAID...
...I'M GONNA BUY AN APARTMENT BUILDING, SO LEND ME THE MONEY.
HOW MUCH IS IT?
I DUNNO... BUT PROBABLY ABOUT 300 MILLION.*
*About $3,000,000 USD.
WELL, I THINK I'LL GO TO BED. I HAVE AN EARLY START TOMORROW.
Oof, here I go...
HANAMORI-SAN TOLD ME, YOU KNOW.
I KNOW WHY BROTHER IS AFRAID OF WOMEN.

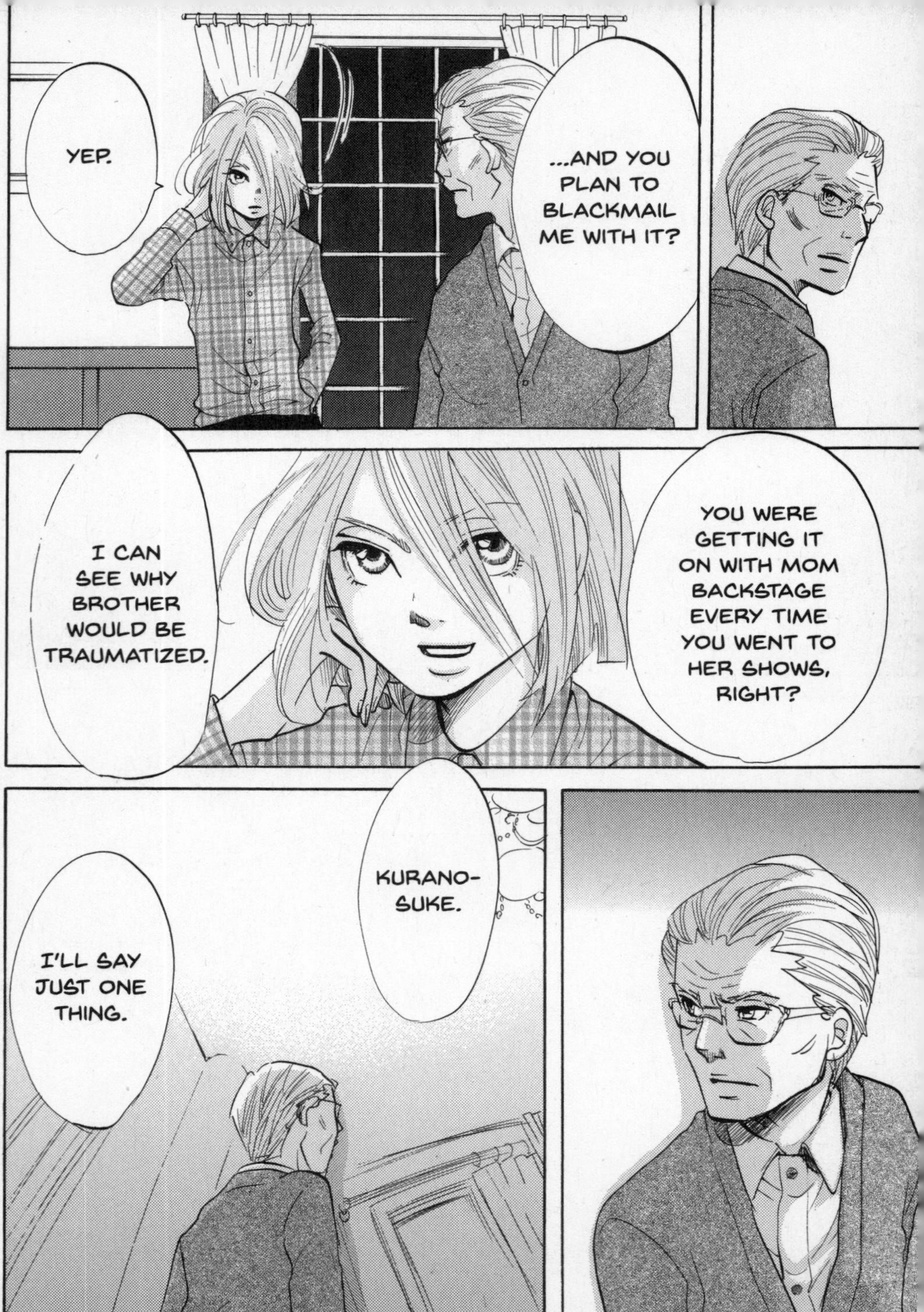
...AND YOU PLAN TO BLACKMAIL ME WITH IT?
YEP.
YOU WERE GETTING IT ON WITH MOM BACKSTAGE EVERY TIME YOU WENT TO HER SHOWS, RIGHT?
I CAN SEE WHY BROTHER WOULD BE TRAUMATIZED.
KURANO-SUKE.
I'LL SAY JUST ONE THING.

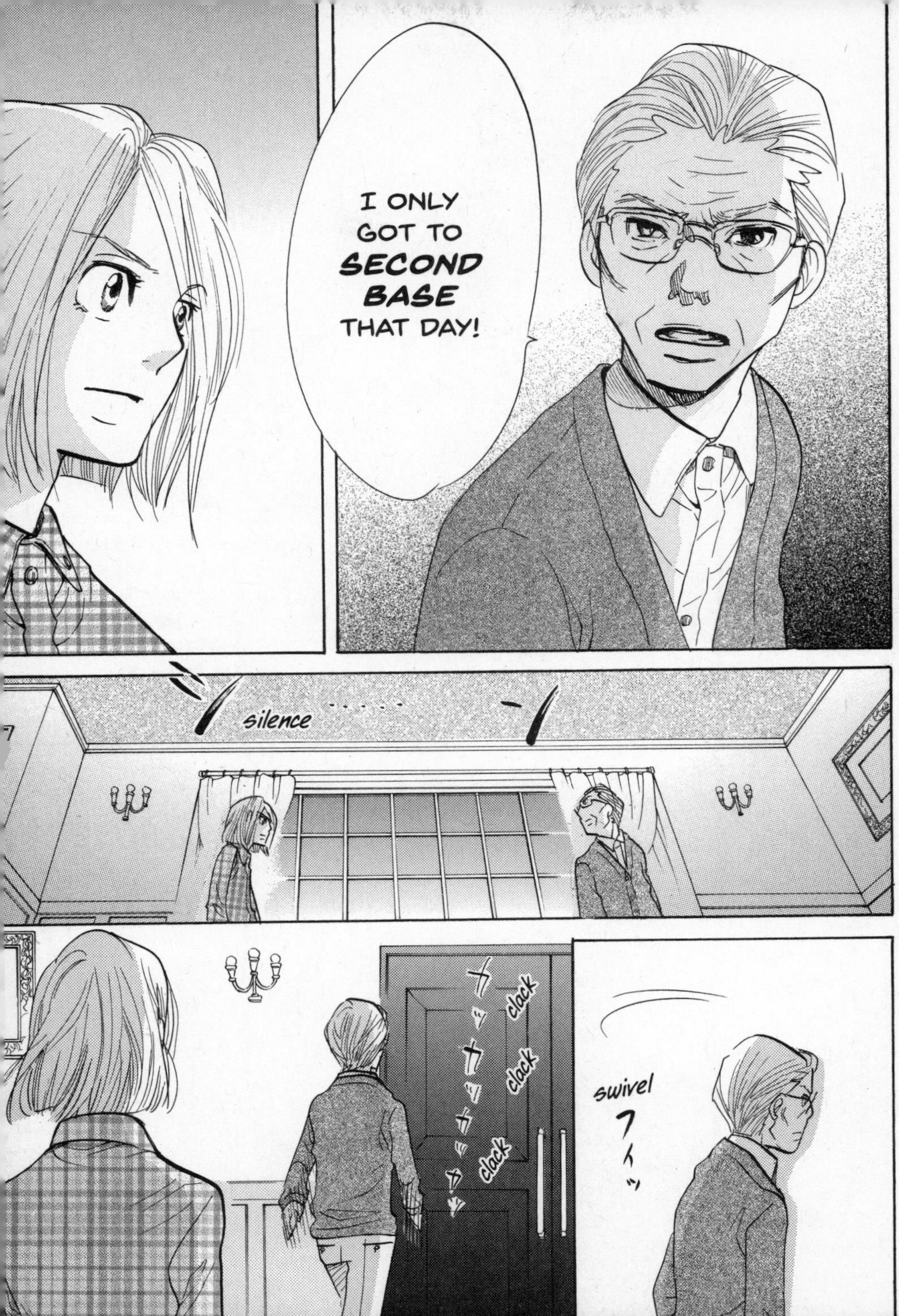
I ONLY GOT TO SECOND BASE THAT DAY!
silence
.....
swivel
フィッ
clack clack clack
カッカッカッ

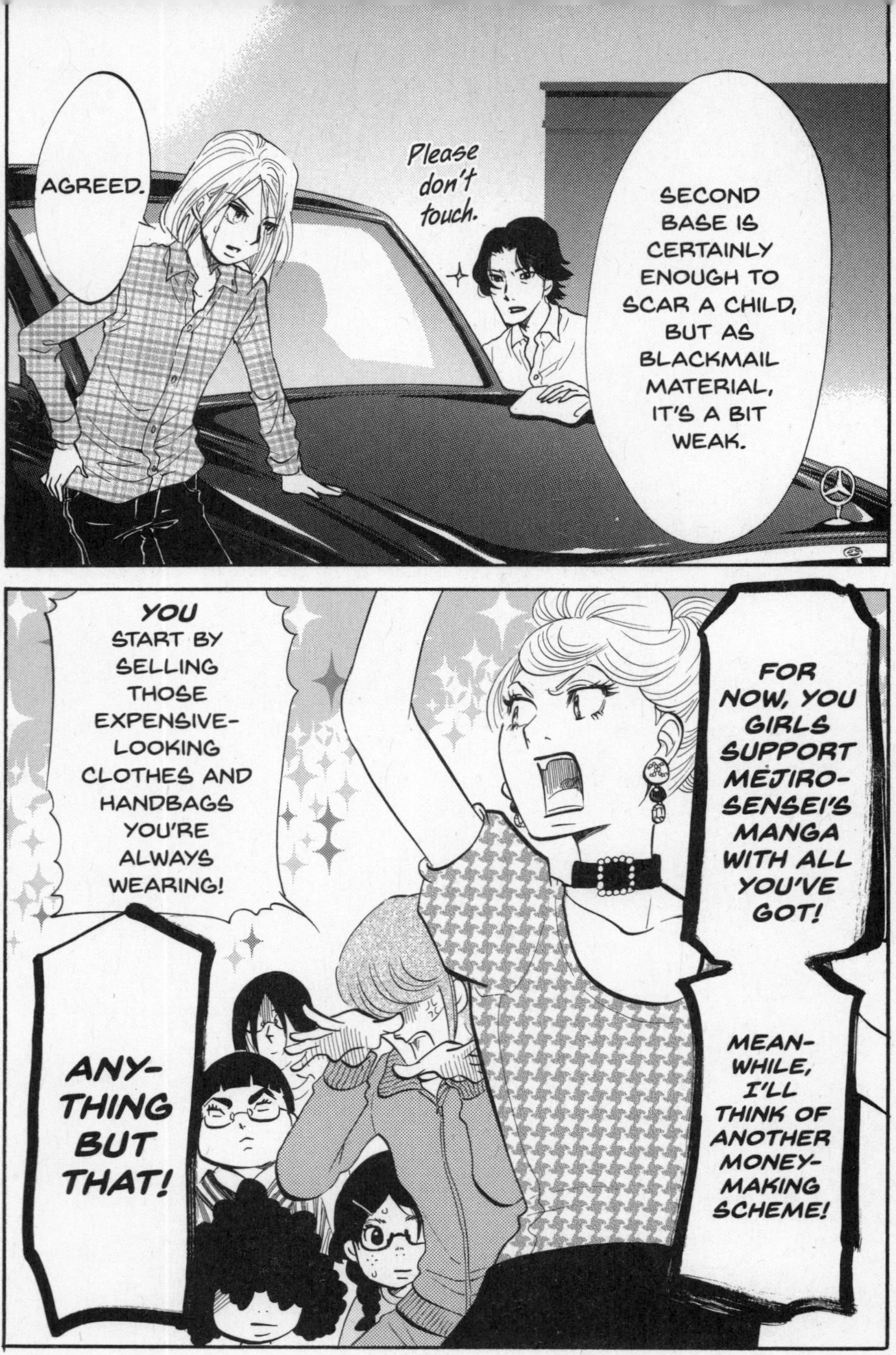
SECOND BASE IS CERTAINLY ENOUGH TO SCAR A CHILD, BUT AS BLACKMAIL MATERIAL, IT'S A BIT WEAK.
Please don't touch.
AGREED.
FOR NOW, YOU GIRLS SUPPORT MEJIRO-SENSEI'S MANGA WITH ALL YOU'VE GOT!
YOU START BY SELLING THOSE EXPENSIVE-LOOKING CLOTHES AND HANDBAGS YOU'RE ALWAYS WEARING!
MEAN-WHILE, I'LL THINK OF ANOTHER MONEY-MAKING SCHEME!
ANY-THING BUT THAT!

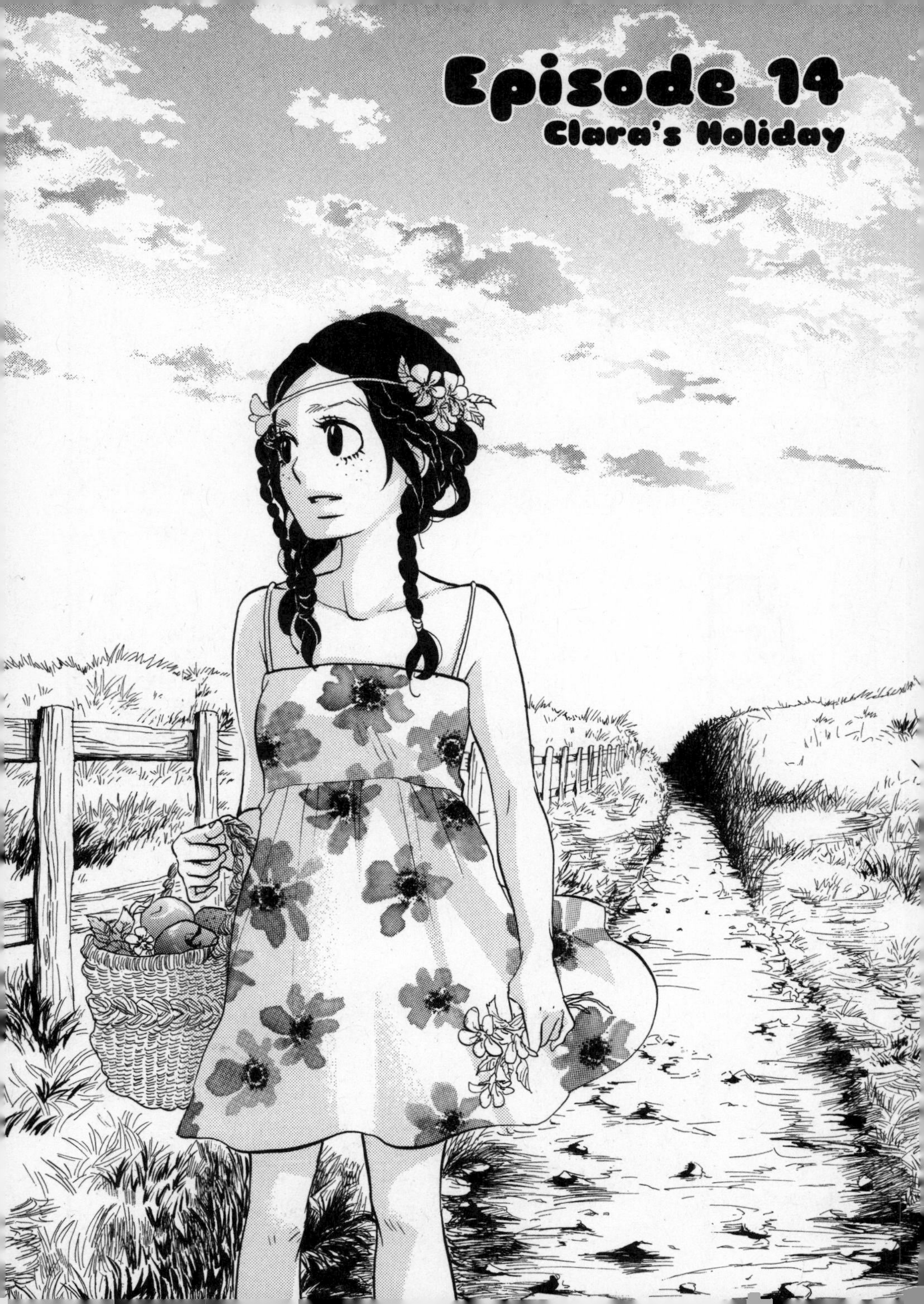
Episode 14
Clara's Holiday

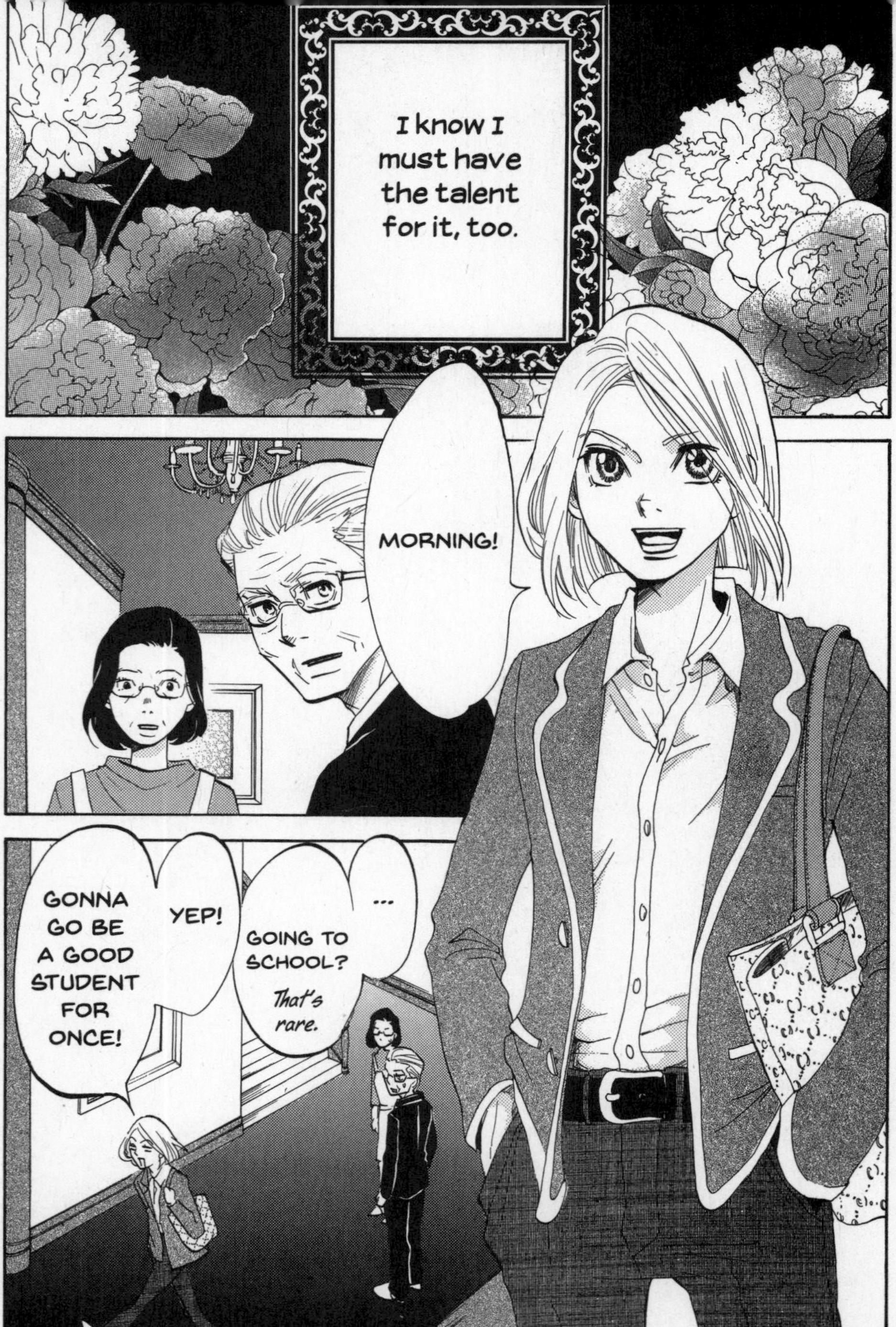
I know I must have the talent for it, too.
MORNING!
...
GOING TO SCHOOL?
That's rare.
YEP!
GONNA GO BE A GOOD STUDENT FOR ONCE!

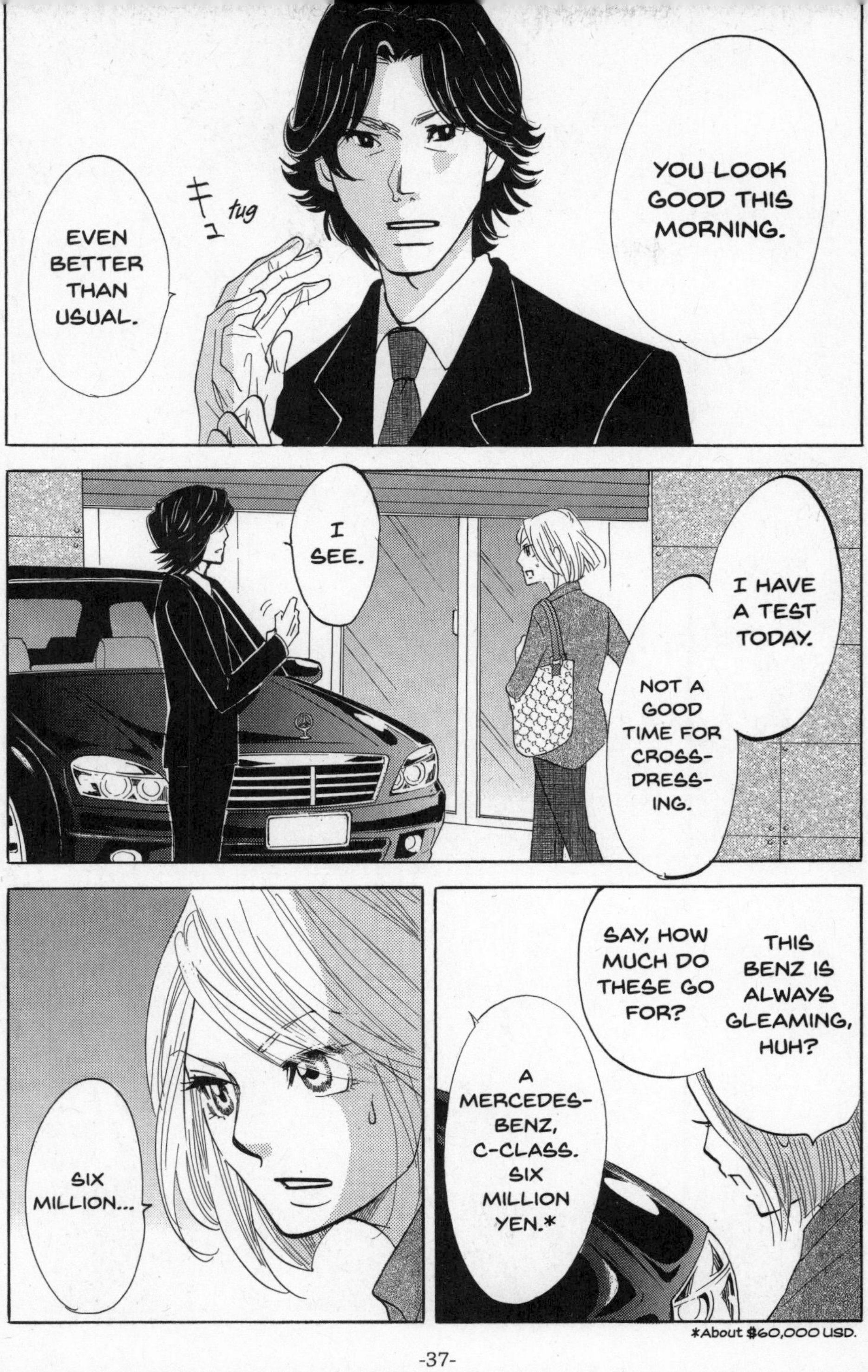
YOU LOOK GOOD THIS MORNING.
キュ tug
EVEN BETTER THAN USUAL.
I HAVE A TEST TODAY.
NOT A GOOD TIME FOR CROSS-DRESSING.
I SEE.
THIS BENZ IS ALWAYS GLEAMING, HUH?
SAY, HOW MUCH DO THESE GO FOR?
A MERCEDES-BENZ, C-CLASS. SIX MILLION YEN.*
SIX MILLION...

*About $60,000 USD.

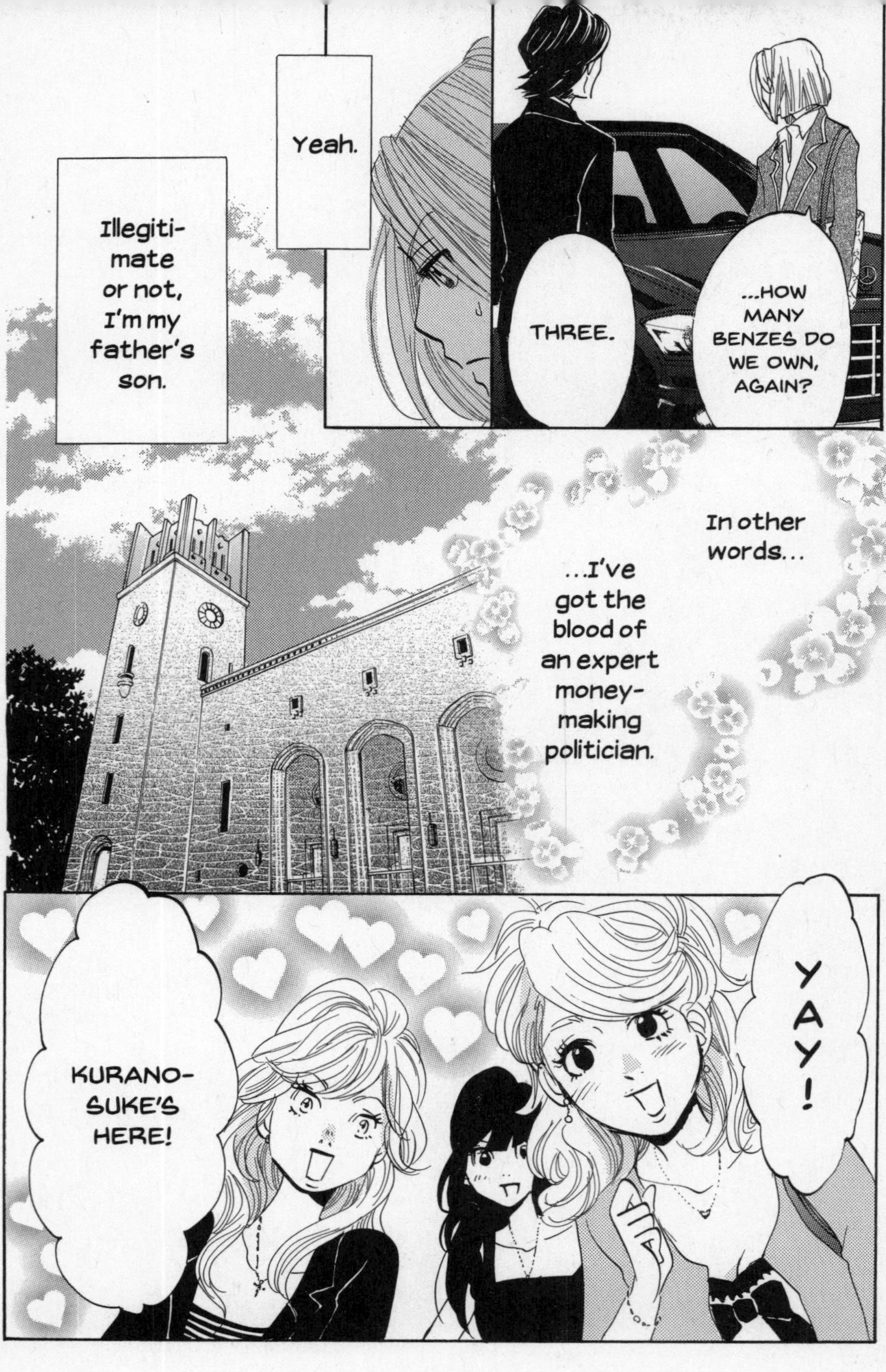
...HOW MANY BENZES DO WE OWN, AGAIN?
THREE.
Yeah.
Illegitimate or not, I'm my father's son.
In other words...
...I've got the blood of an expert money-making politician.
YAY!
KURANOSUKE'S HERE!

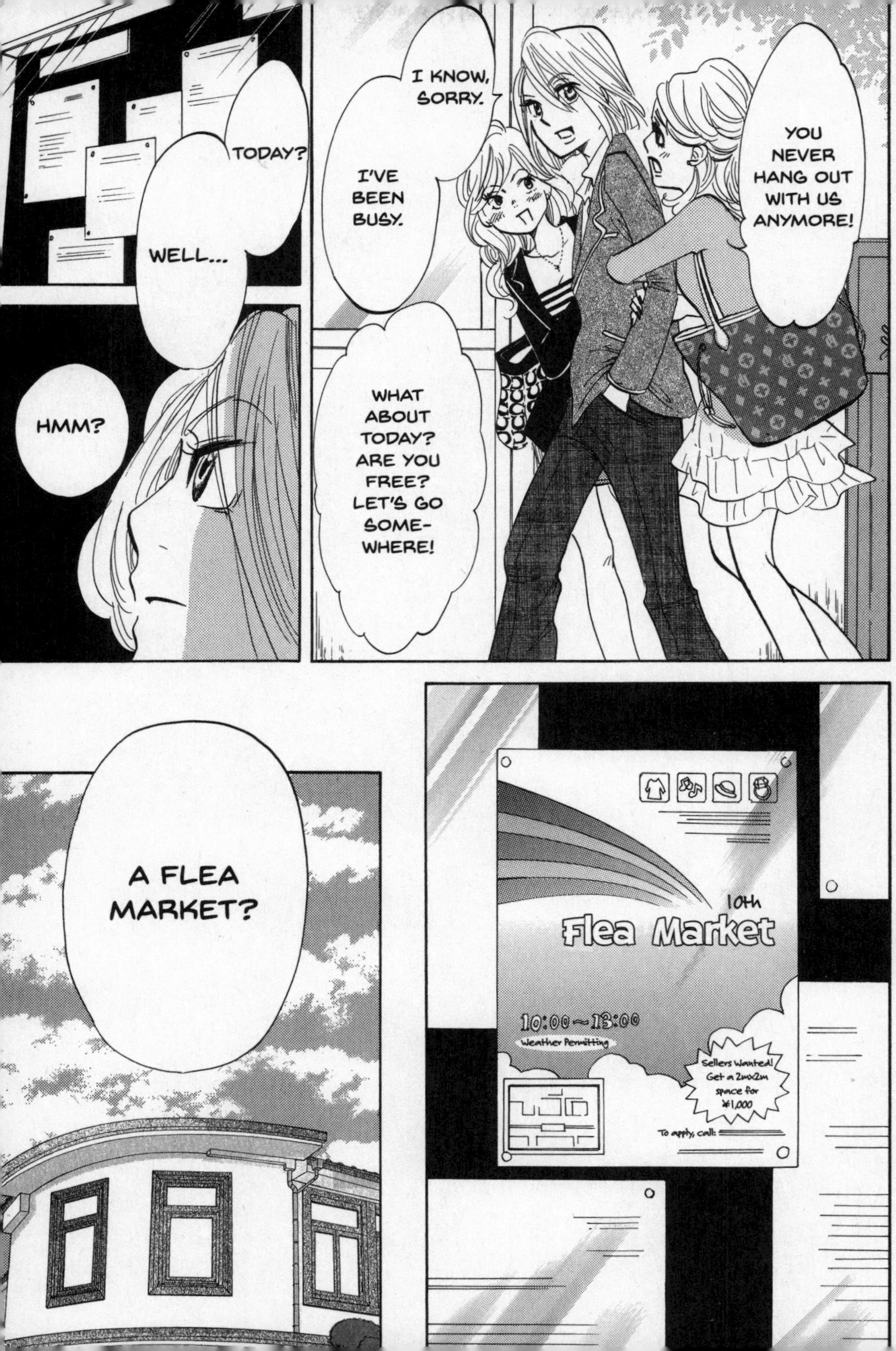
YOU NEVER HANG OUT WITH US ANYMORE!
I KNOW, SORRY.
I'VE BEEN BUSY.
WHAT ABOUT TODAY? ARE YOU FREE? LET'S GO SOME-WHERE!
TODAY?
WELL...
HMM?
10th
Flea Market
10:00~13:00
Weather Permitting
Sellers Wanted! Get a 2mx2m space for ¥1,000
To apply, call:
A FLEA MARKET?

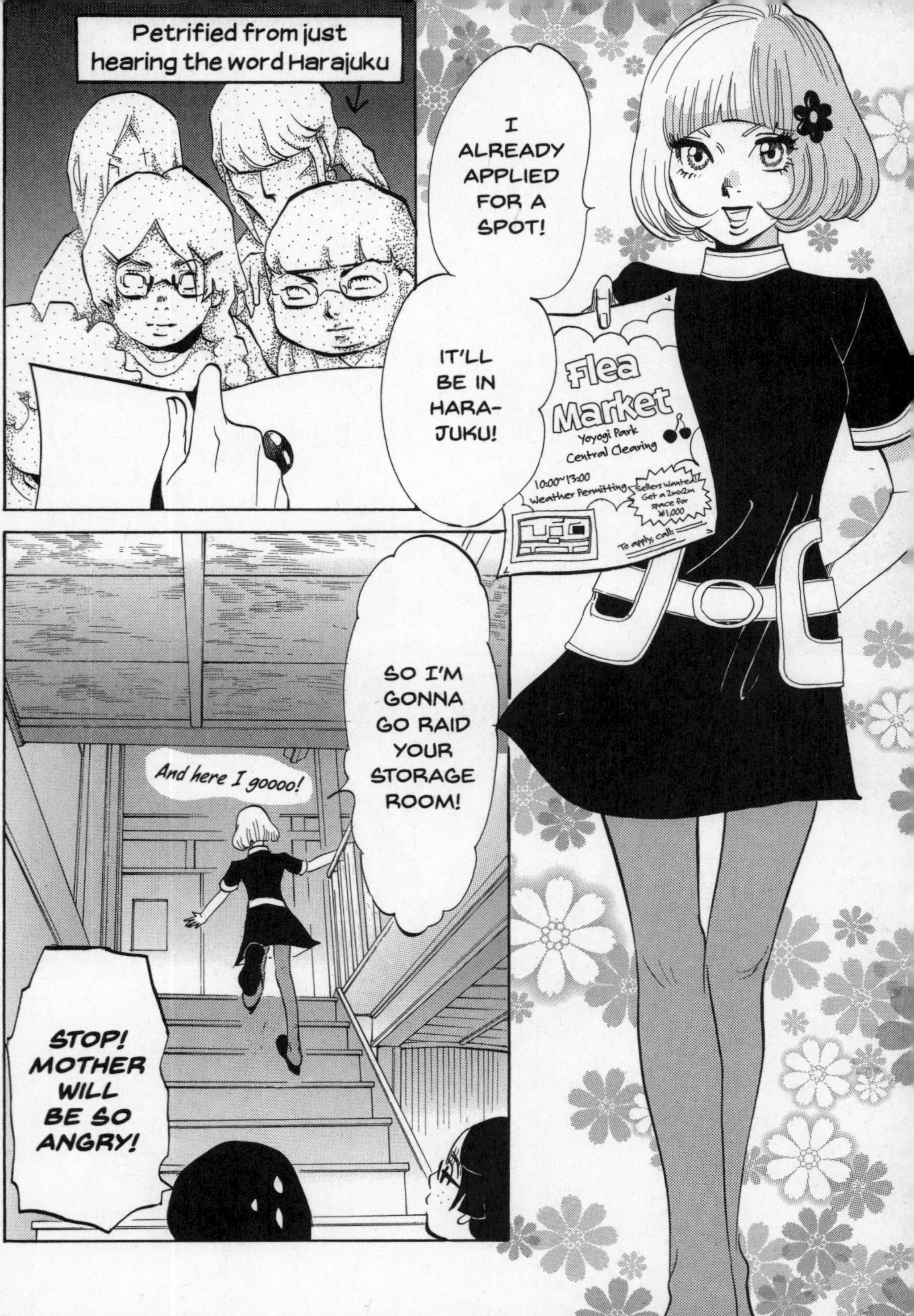
I ALREADY APPLIED FOR A SPOT!
IT'LL BE IN HARA-JUKU!
Flea Market
Yoyogi Park Central Clearing
10:00~13:00 Weather Permitting
Sellers Wanted! Get a 2mx2m space for ¥1,000
To apply, call:
SO I'M GONNA GO RAID YOUR STORAGE ROOM!
Petrified from just hearing the word Harajuku
And here I goooo!
STOP! MOTHER WILL BE SO ANGRY!

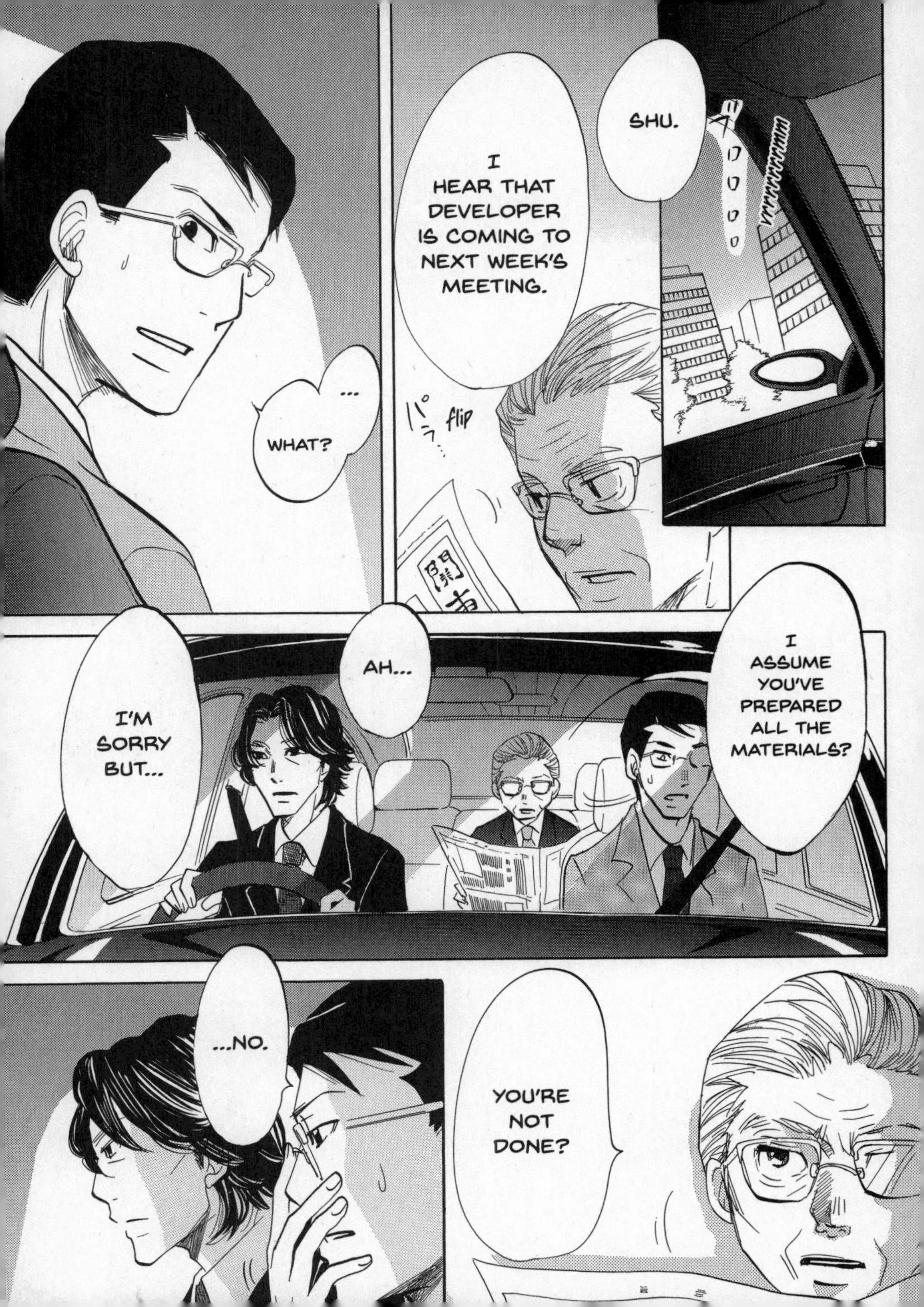
vrrrrrrmmm
ブロロロロ
SHU.
I HEAR THAT DEVELOPER IS COMING TO NEXT WEEK'S MEETING.
パラ…
flip
... WHAT?
I ASSUME YOU'VE PREPARED ALL THE MATERIALS?
AH...
I'M SORRY BUT...
YOU'RE NOT DONE?
...NO.

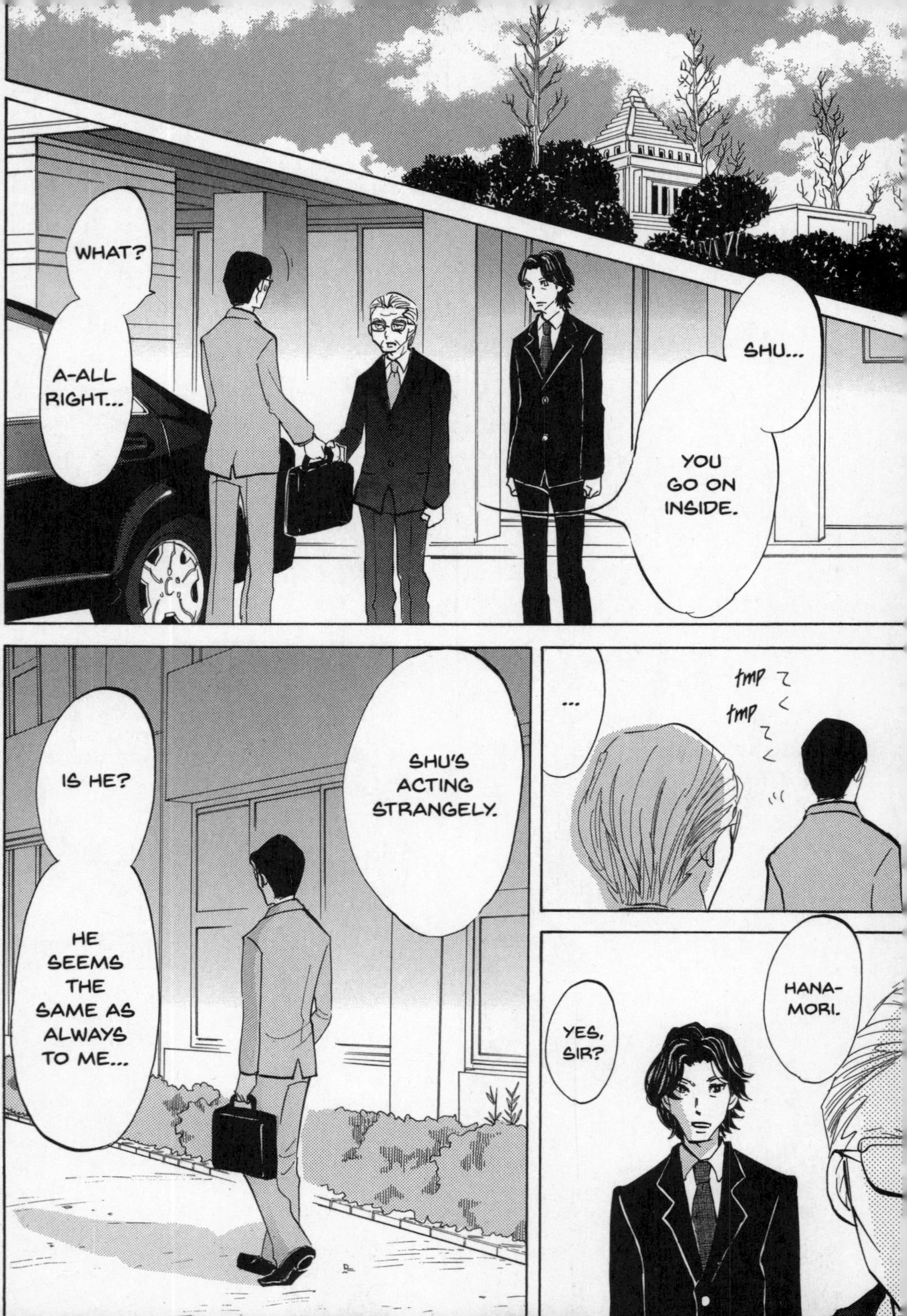
SHU...
YOU GO ON INSIDE.
WHAT?
A-ALL RIGHT...
...
tmp
tmp
HANA-MORI.
YES, SIR?
SHU'S ACTING STRANGELY.
IS HE?
HE SEEMS THE SAME AS ALWAYS TO ME...

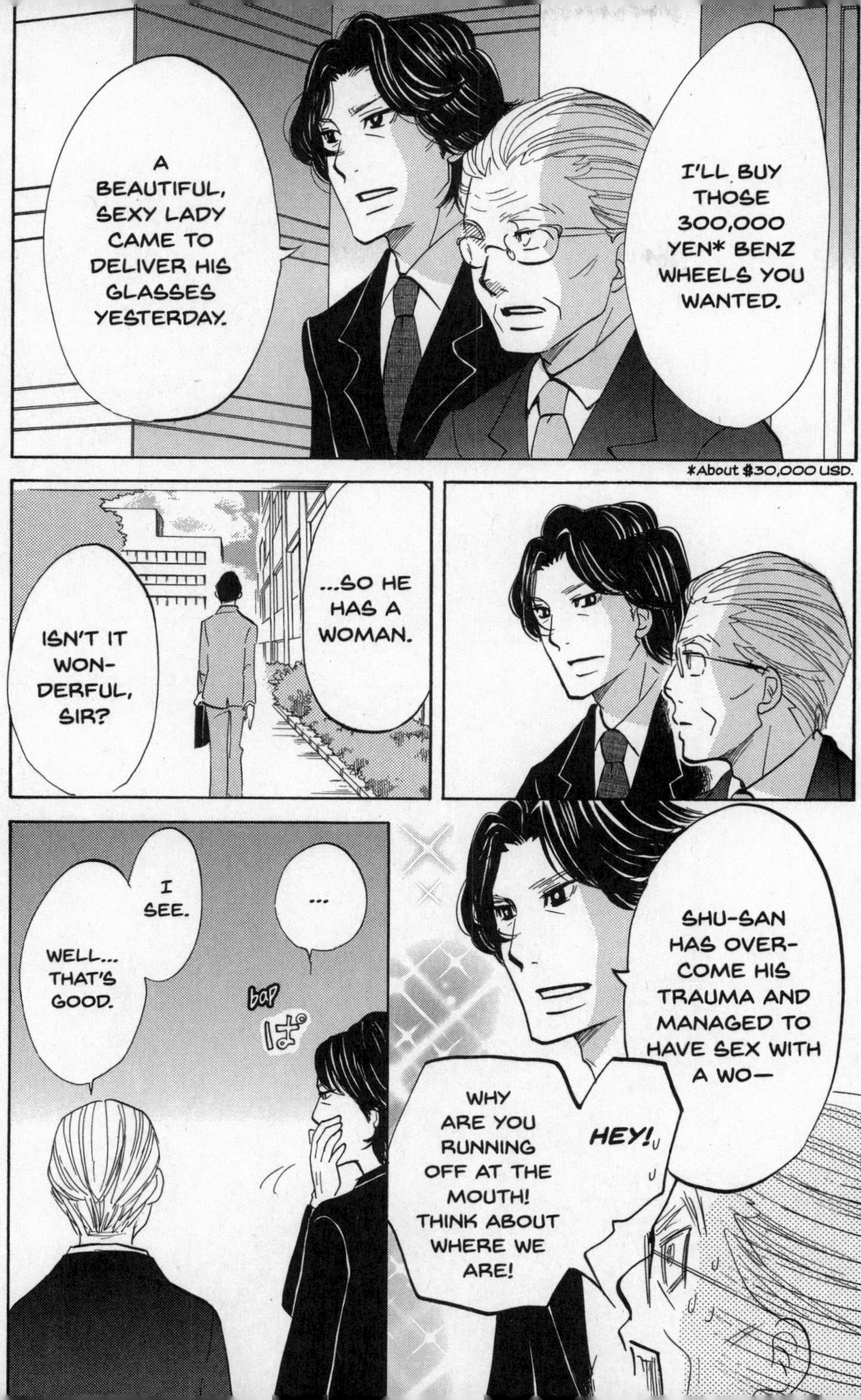
I'LL BUY THOSE 300,000 YEN* BENZ WHEELS YOU WANTED.
A BEAUTIFUL, SEXY LADY CAME TO DELIVER HIS GLASSES YESTERDAY.
*About $30,000 USD.
...SO HE HAS A WOMAN.
ISN'T IT WON-DERFUL, SIR?
SHU-SAN HAS OVER-COME HIS TRAUMA AND MANAGED TO HAVE SEX WITH A WO—
HEY!
WHY ARE YOU RUNNING OFF AT THE MOUTH! THINK ABOUT WHERE WE ARE!
...
I SEE.
WELL... THAT'S GOOD.
bap
ぱ

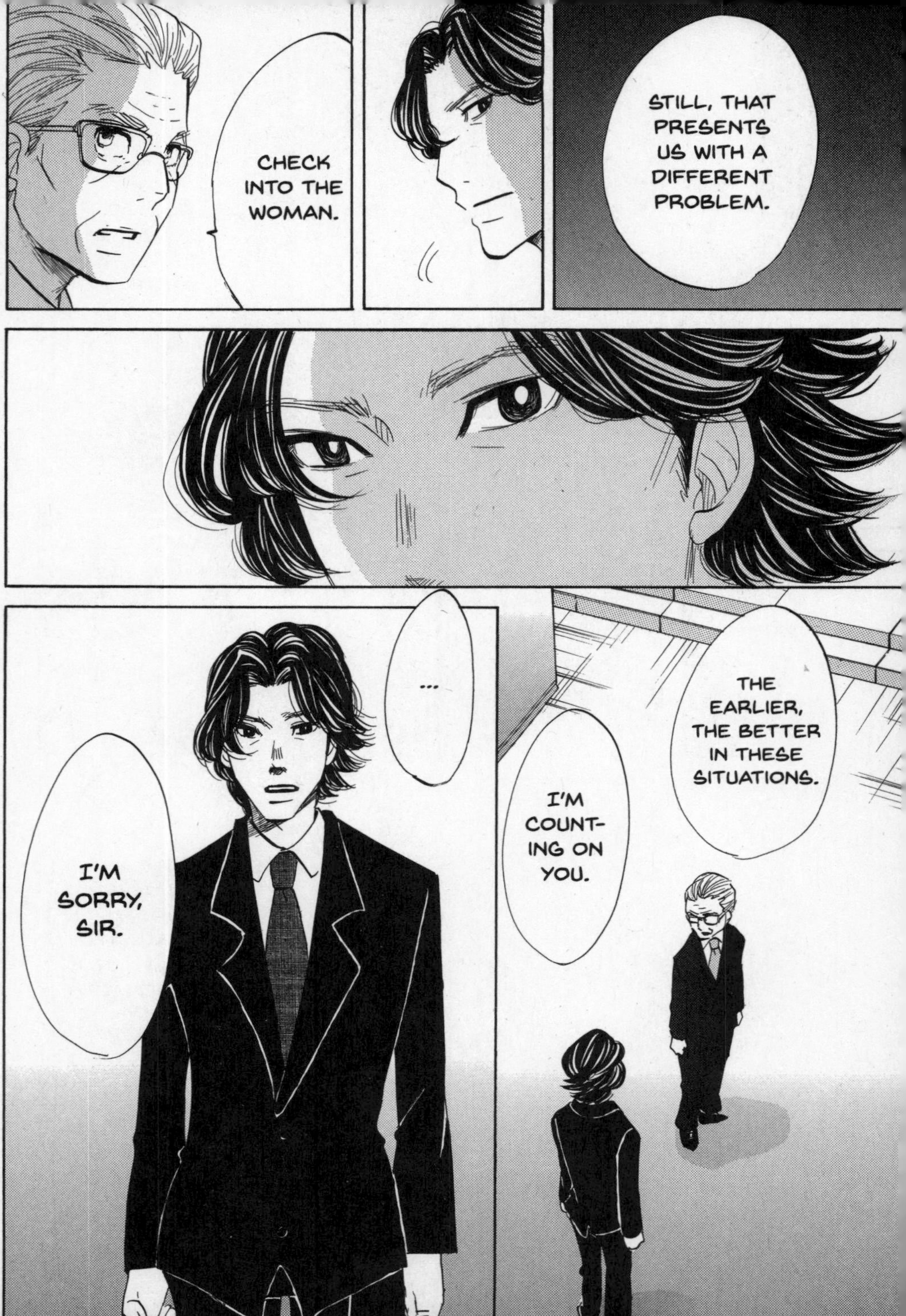
STILL, THAT PRESENTS US WITH A DIFFERENT PROBLEM.
CHECK INTO THE WOMAN.
THE EARLIER, THE BETTER IN THESE SITUATIONS.
I'M COUNT-ING ON YOU.
...
I'M SORRY, SIR.

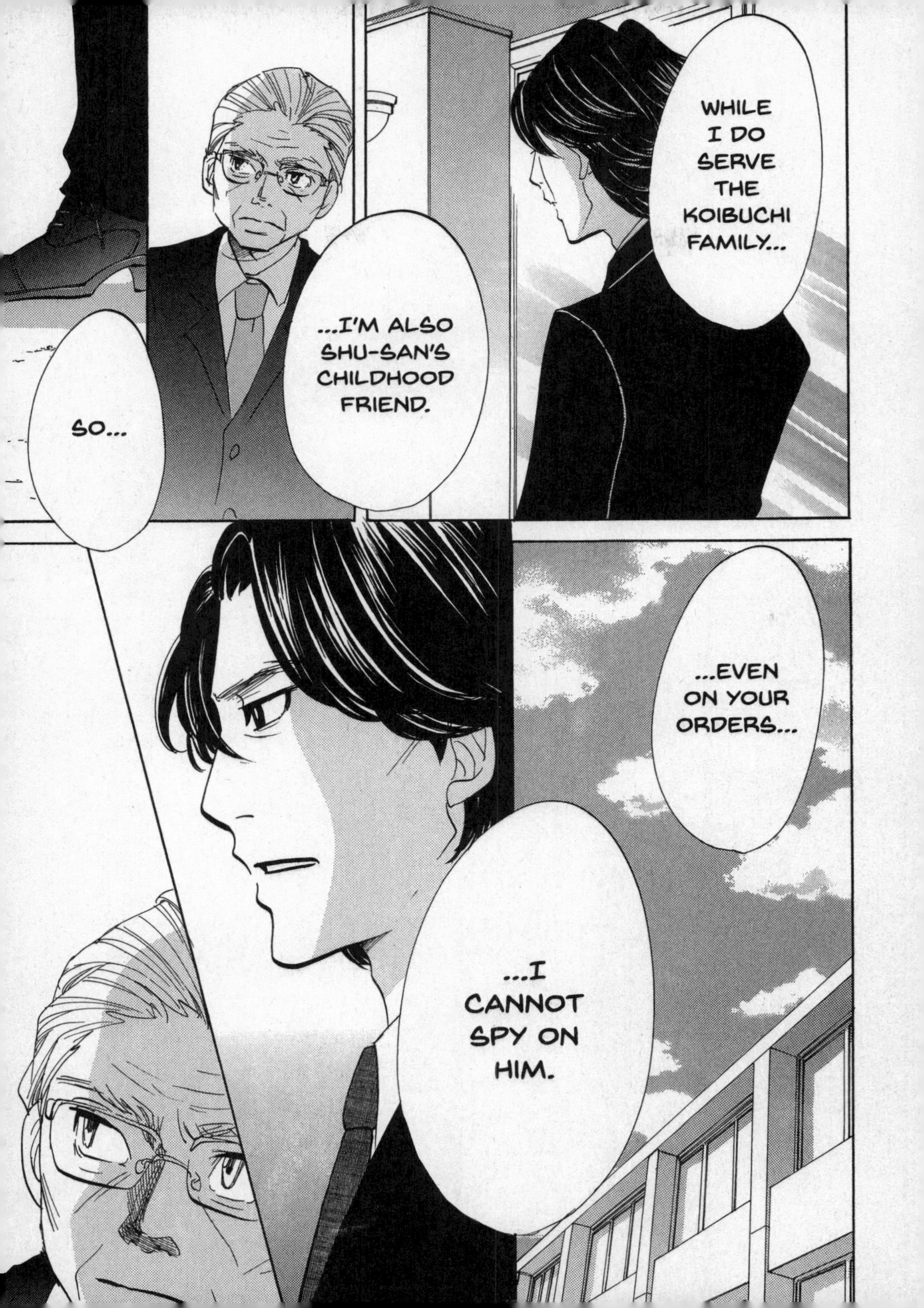
WHILE I DO SERVE THE KOIBUCHI FAMILY...
...I'M ALSO SHU-SAN'S CHILDHOOD FRIEND.
SO...
...EVEN ON YOUR ORDERS...
...I CANNOT SPY ON HIM.

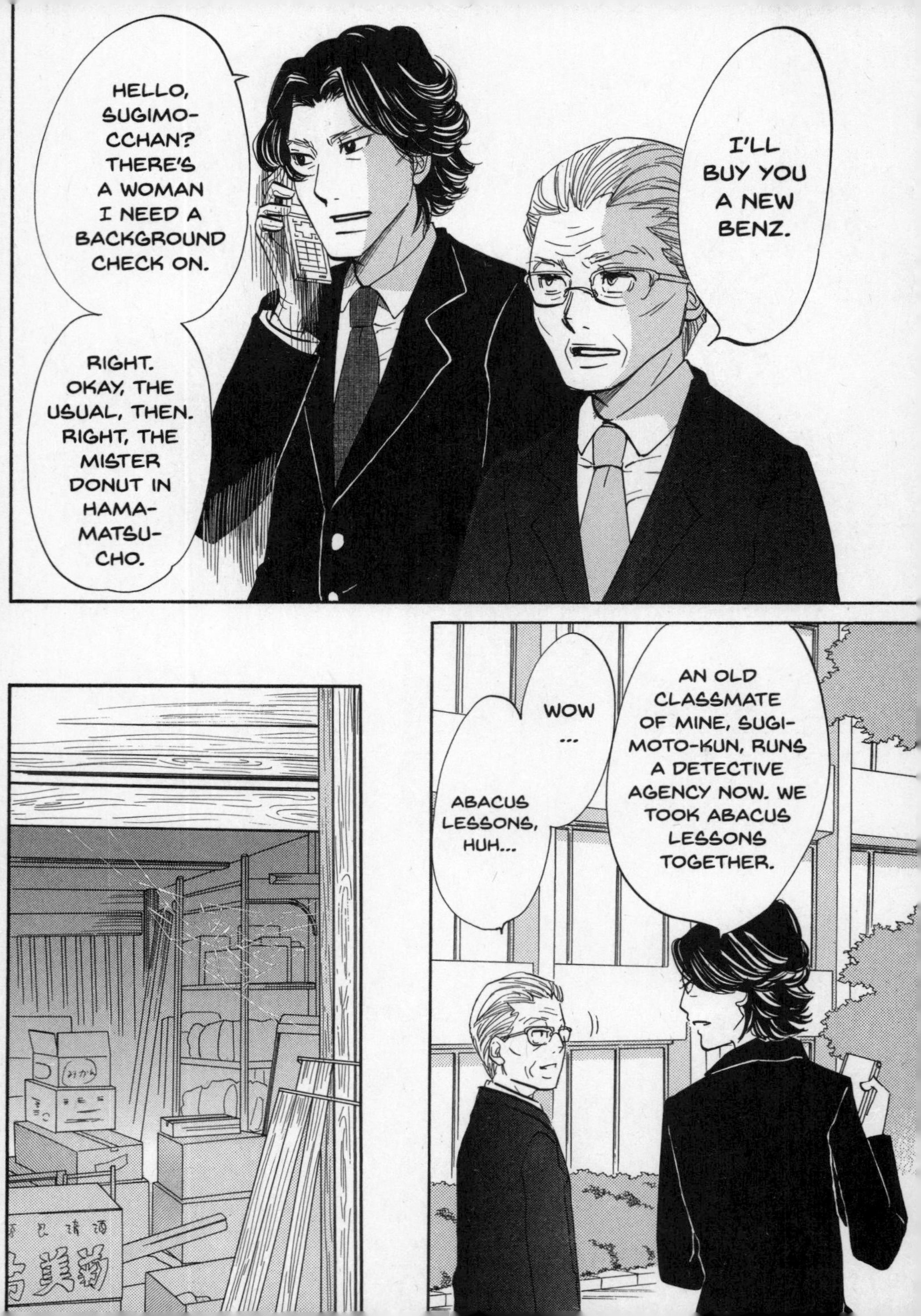
I'LL BUY YOU A NEW BENZ.
HELLO, SUGIMOCCHAN? THERE'S A WOMAN I NEED A BACKGROUND CHECK ON.
RIGHT. OKAY, THE USUAL, THEN. RIGHT, THE MISTER DONUT IN HAMAMATSUCHO.
AN OLD CLASSMATE OF MINE, SUGIMOTO-KUN, RUNS A DETECTIVE AGENCY NOW. WE TOOK ABACUS LESSONS TOGETHER.
WOW ...
ABACUS LESSONS, HUH...

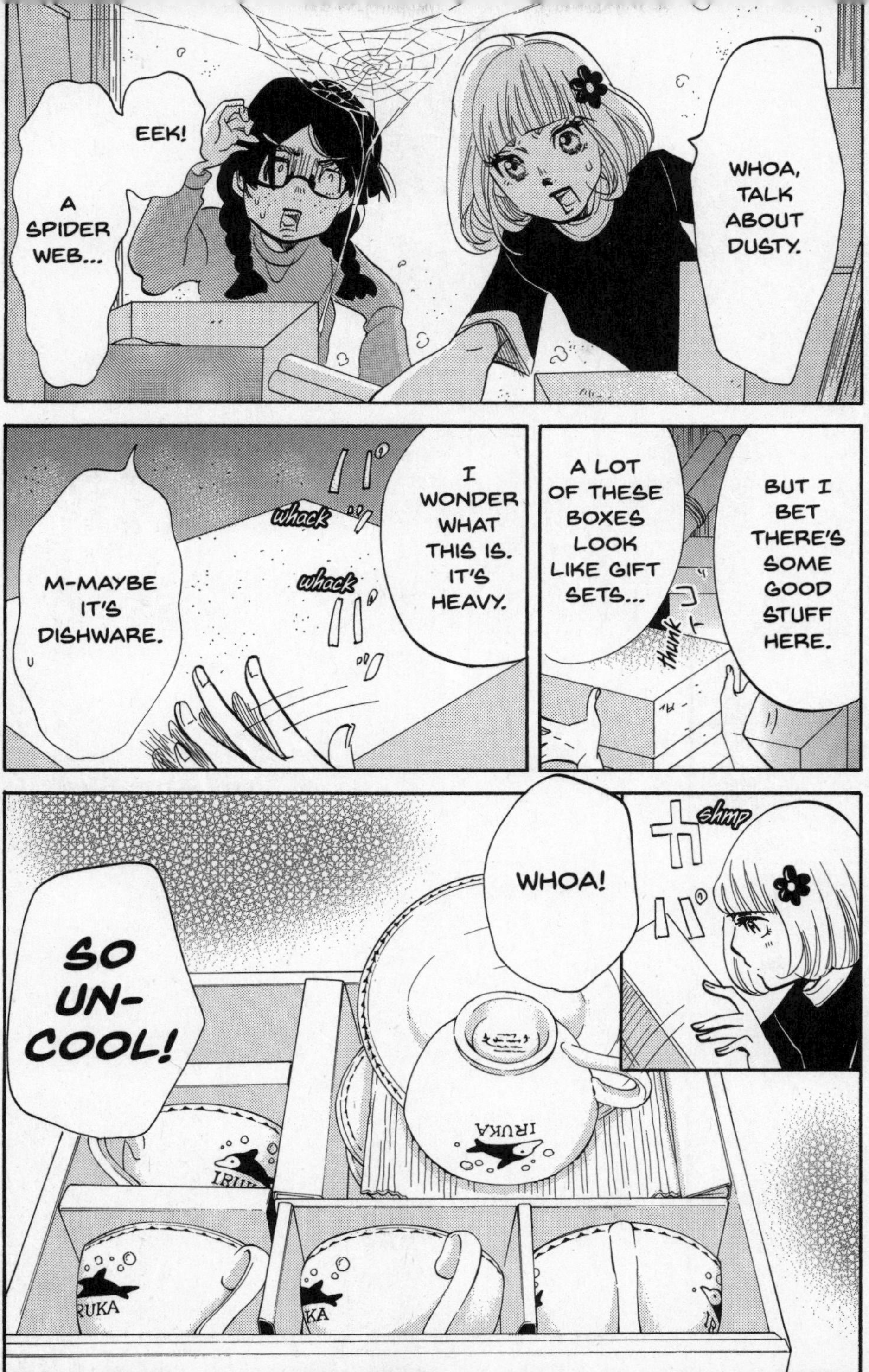
WHOA, TALK ABOUT DUSTY.
EEK!
A SPIDER WEB...
BUT I BET THERE'S SOME GOOD STUFF HERE.
A LOT OF THESE BOXES LOOK LIKE GIFT SETS...
thunk
I WONDER WHAT THIS IS. IT'S HEAVY.
whack
whack
M-MAYBE IT'S DISHWARE.
shmp
WHOA!
SO UN-COOL!
IRUKA

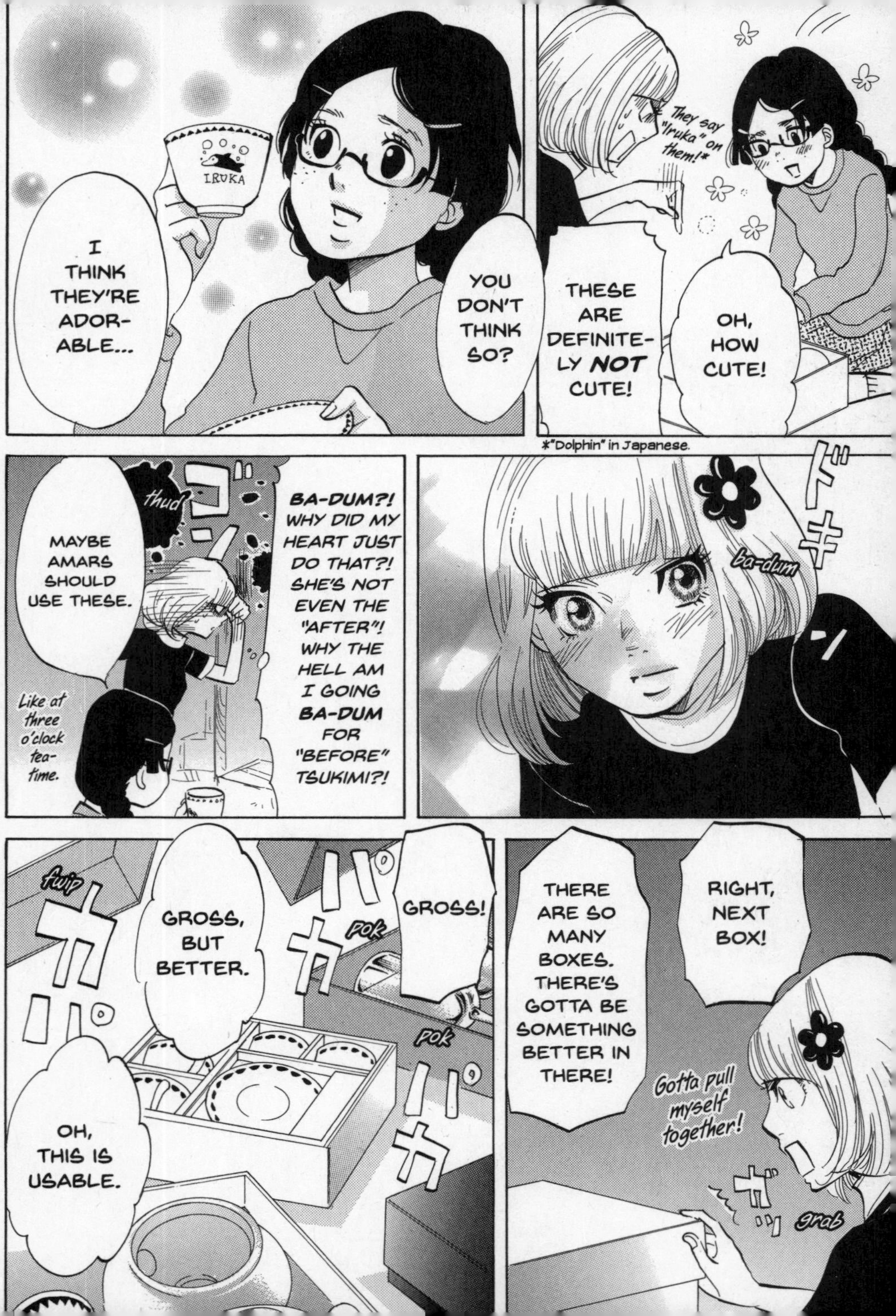
OH, HOW CUTE!
They say "Iruka" on them!*
THESE ARE DEFINITE-LY **NOT** CUTE!
YOU DON'T THINK SO?
I THINK THEY'RE ADOR-ABLE...
*"Dolphin" in Japanese.
ba-dum
BA-DUM?! WHY DID MY HEART JUST DO THAT?! SHE'S NOT EVEN THE "AFTER"! WHY THE HELL AM I GOING **BA-DUM** FOR "BEFORE" TSUKIMI?!
thud
MAYBE AMARS SHOULD USE THESE.
Like at three o'clock tea-time.
RIGHT, NEXT BOX!
THERE ARE SO MANY BOXES. THERE'S GOTTA BE SOMETHING BETTER IN THERE!
Gotta pull myself together!
grab
GROSS!
pok
GROSS, BUT BETTER.
fwip
pok
OH, THIS IS USABLE.

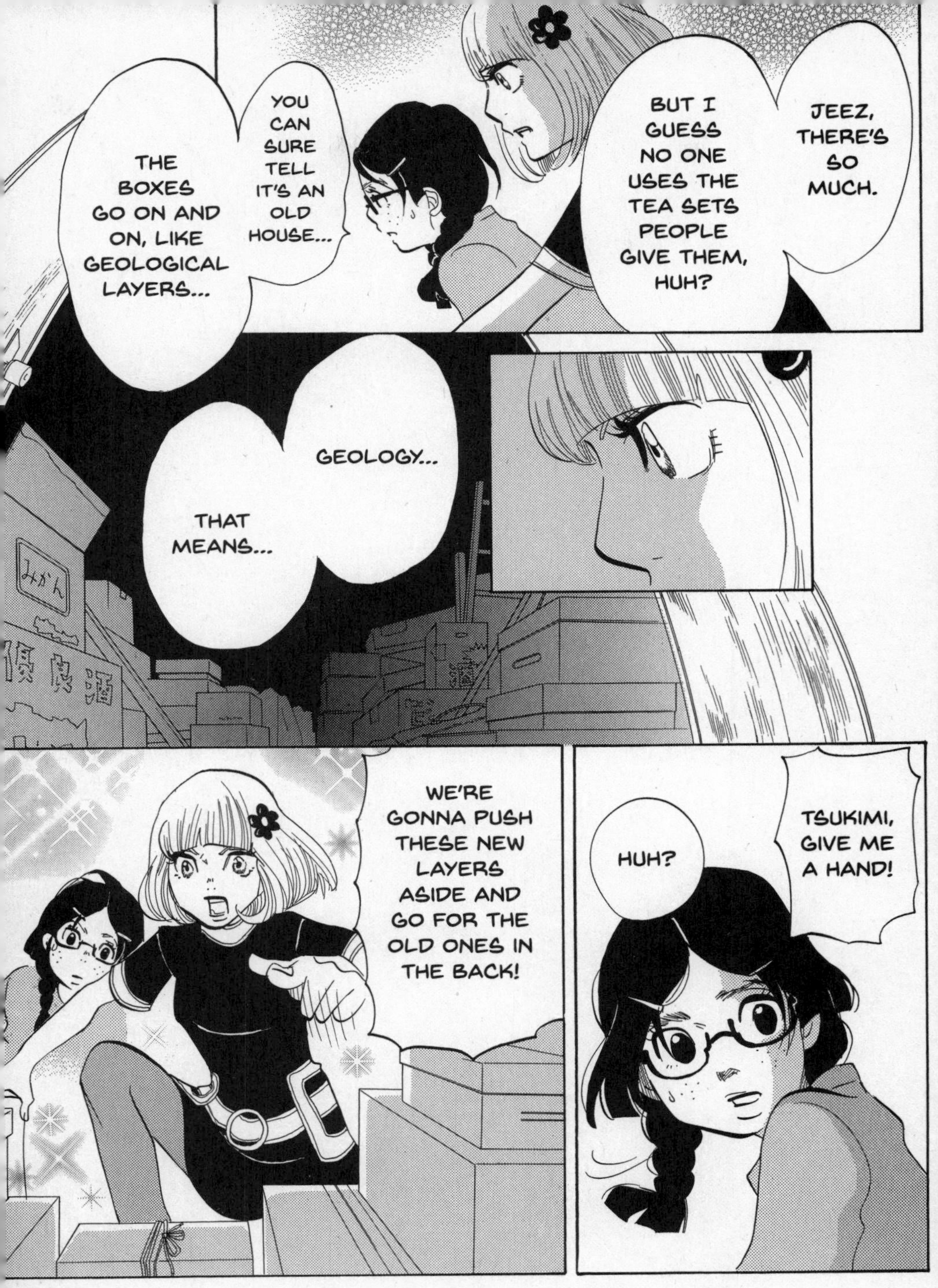
JEEZ, THERE'S SO MUCH.
BUT I GUESS NO ONE USES THE TEA SETS PEOPLE GIVE THEM, HUH?
YOU CAN SURE TELL IT'S AN OLD HOUSE...
THE BOXES GO ON AND ON, LIKE GEOLOGICAL LAYERS...
GEOLOGY...
THAT MEANS...
みかん
TSUKIMI, GIVE ME A HAND!
HUH?
WE'RE GONNA PUSH THESE NEW LAYERS ASIDE AND GO FOR THE OLD ONES IN THE BACK!

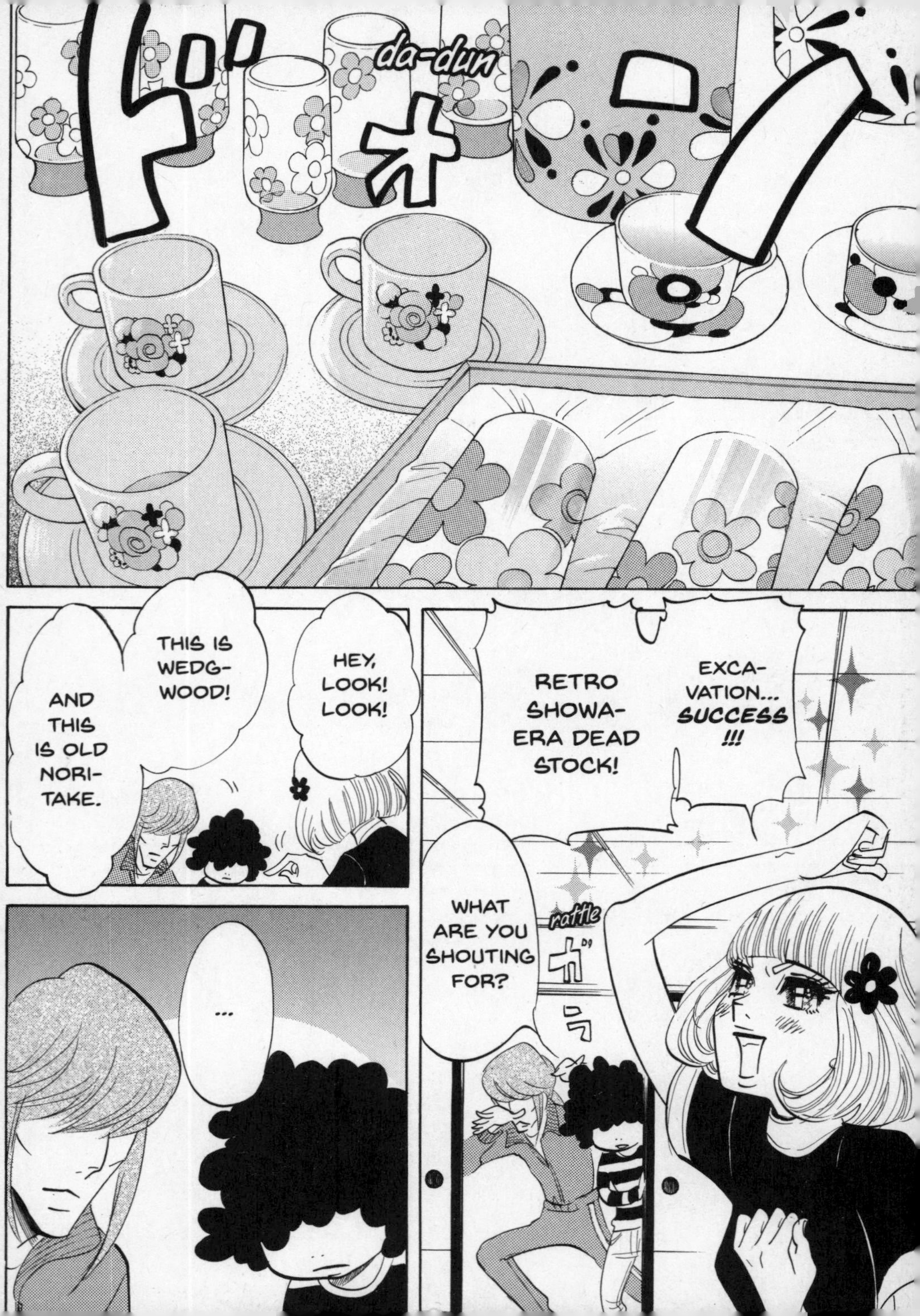
da-dun
RETRO SHOWA-ERA DEAD STOCK! EXCAVATION... SUCCESS!!!
rattle
WHAT ARE YOU SHOUTING FOR?
HEY, LOOK! LOOK!
THIS IS WEDGWOOD!
AND THIS IS OLD NORITAKE.
...

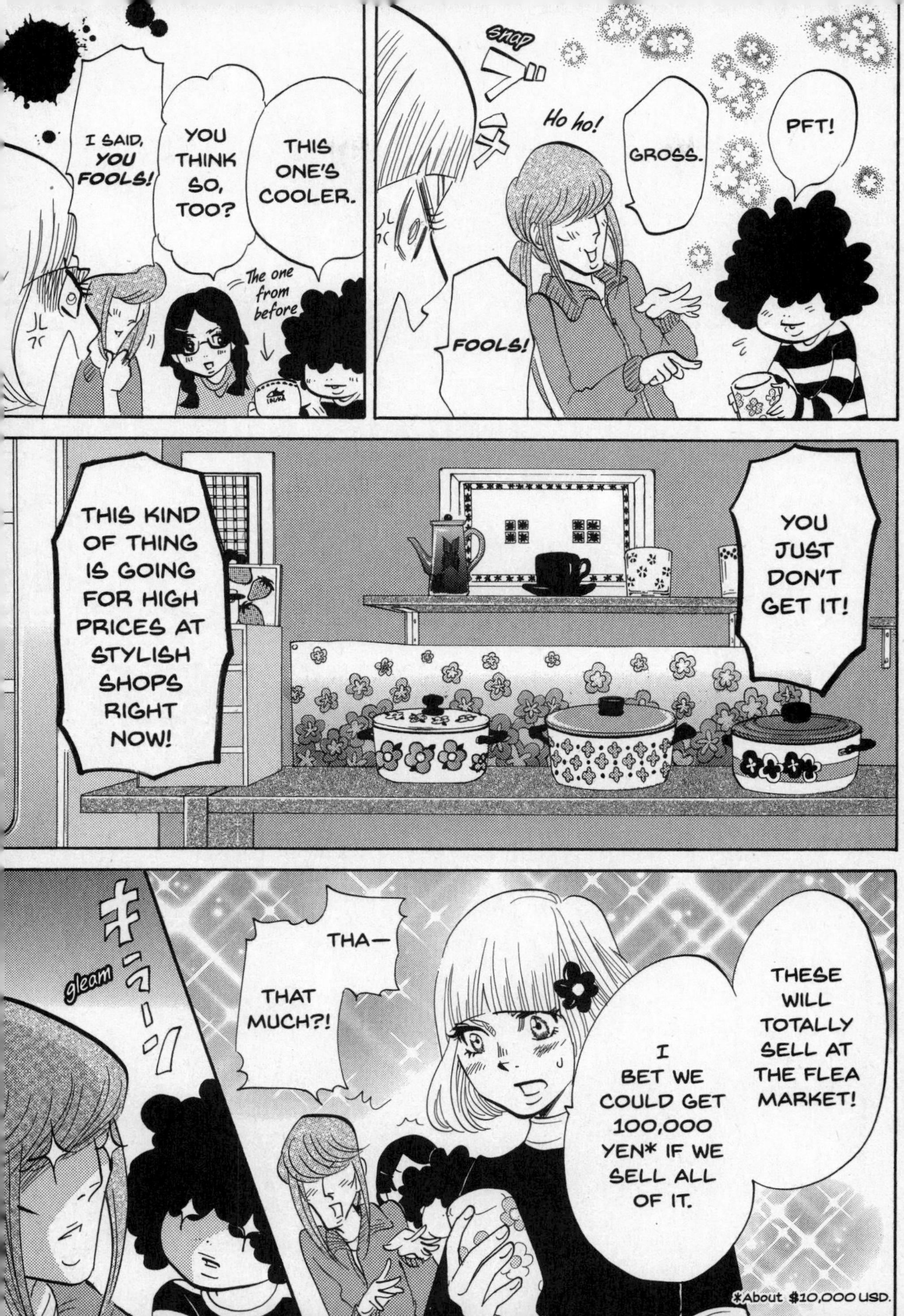
PFT!
GROSS.
Ho ho!
Snap
FOOLS!
THIS ONE'S COOLER.
YOU THINK SO, TOO?
I SAID, YOU FOOLS!
The one from before
YOU JUST DON'T GET IT!
THIS KIND OF THING IS GOING FOR HIGH PRICES AT STYLISH SHOPS RIGHT NOW!
THESE WILL TOTALLY SELL AT THE FLEA MARKET!
I BET WE COULD GET 100,000 YEN* IF WE SELL ALL OF IT.
THA—
THAT MUCH?!
gleam
*About $10,000 USD.

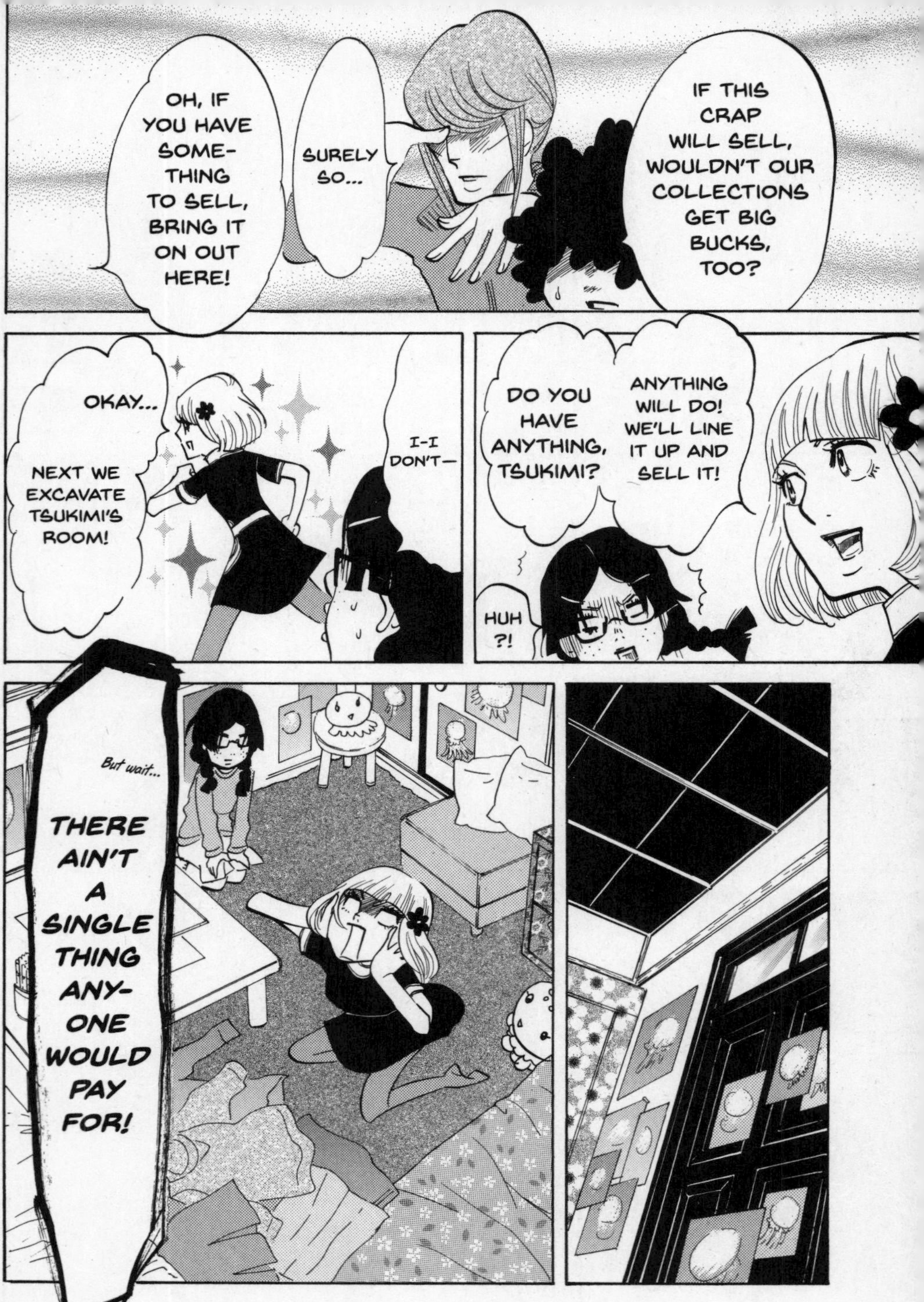
IF THIS CRAP WILL SELL, WOULDN'T OUR COLLECTIONS GET BIG BUCKS, TOO?
SURELY SO...
OH, IF YOU HAVE SOME-THING TO SELL, BRING IT ON OUT HERE!
ANYTHING WILL DO! WE'LL LINE IT UP AND SELL IT!
DO YOU HAVE ANYTHING, TSUKIMI?
HUH ?!
I-I DON'T—
OKAY...
NEXT WE EXCAVATE TSUKIMI'S ROOM!
But wait...
THERE AIN'T A SINGLE THING ANY-ONE WOULD PAY FOR!

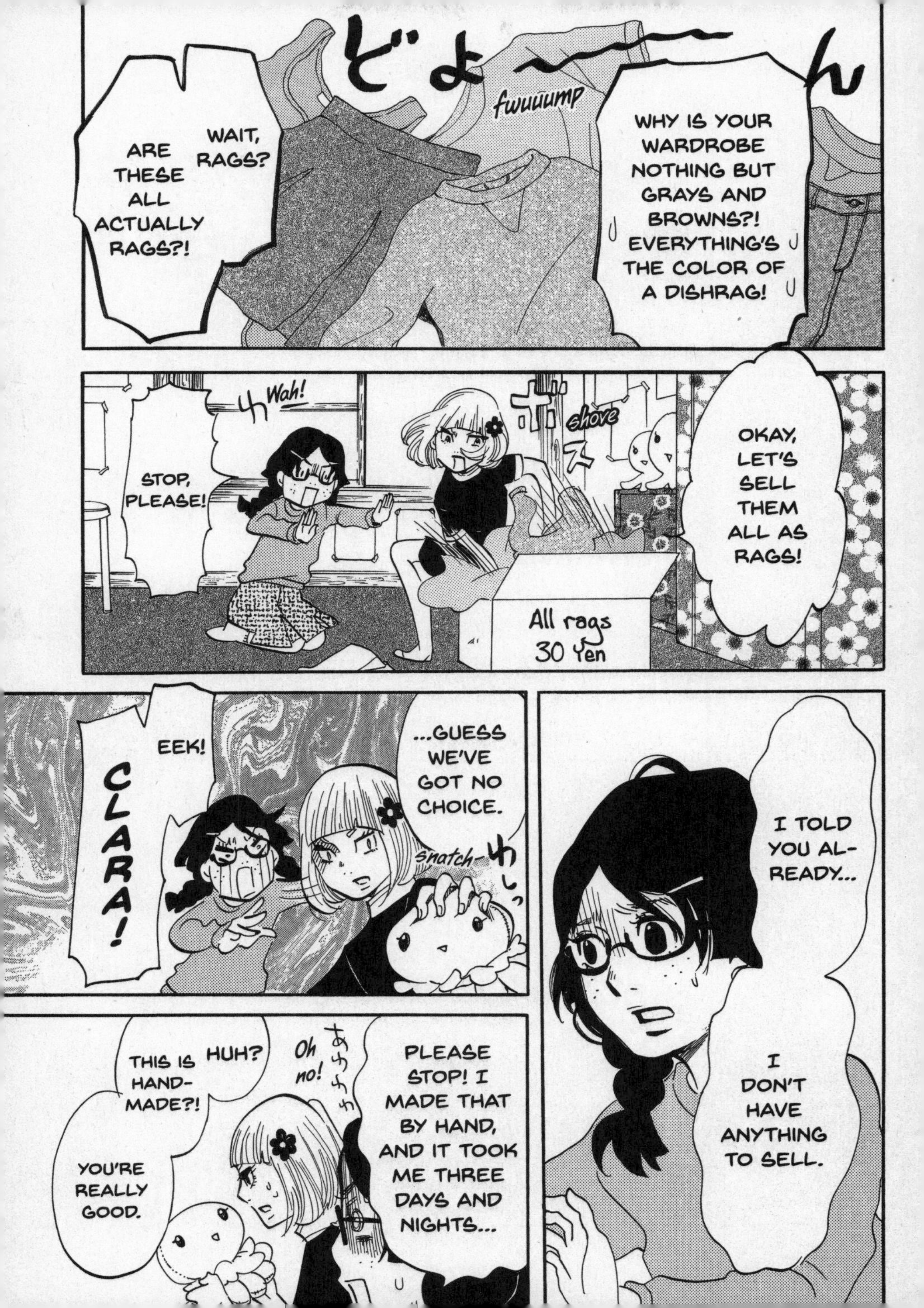
どよ〜〜ん
fwuuuump
WHY IS YOUR WARDROBE NOTHING BUT GRAYS AND BROWNS?! EVERYTHING'S THE COLOR OF A DISHRAG!
WAIT, RAGS?
ARE THESE ALL ACTUALLY RAGS?!
OKAY, LET'S SELL THEM ALL AS RAGS!
shove
Wah!
STOP, PLEASE!
All rags 30 Yen
I TOLD YOU AL-READY...
I DON'T HAVE ANYTHING TO SELL.
...GUESS WE'VE GOT NO CHOICE.
snatch
わしっ
EEK!
CLARA!
PLEASE STOP! I MADE THAT BY HAND, AND IT TOOK ME THREE DAYS AND NIGHTS...
Oh no!
HUH?
THIS IS HAND-MADE?!
YOU'RE REALLY GOOD.

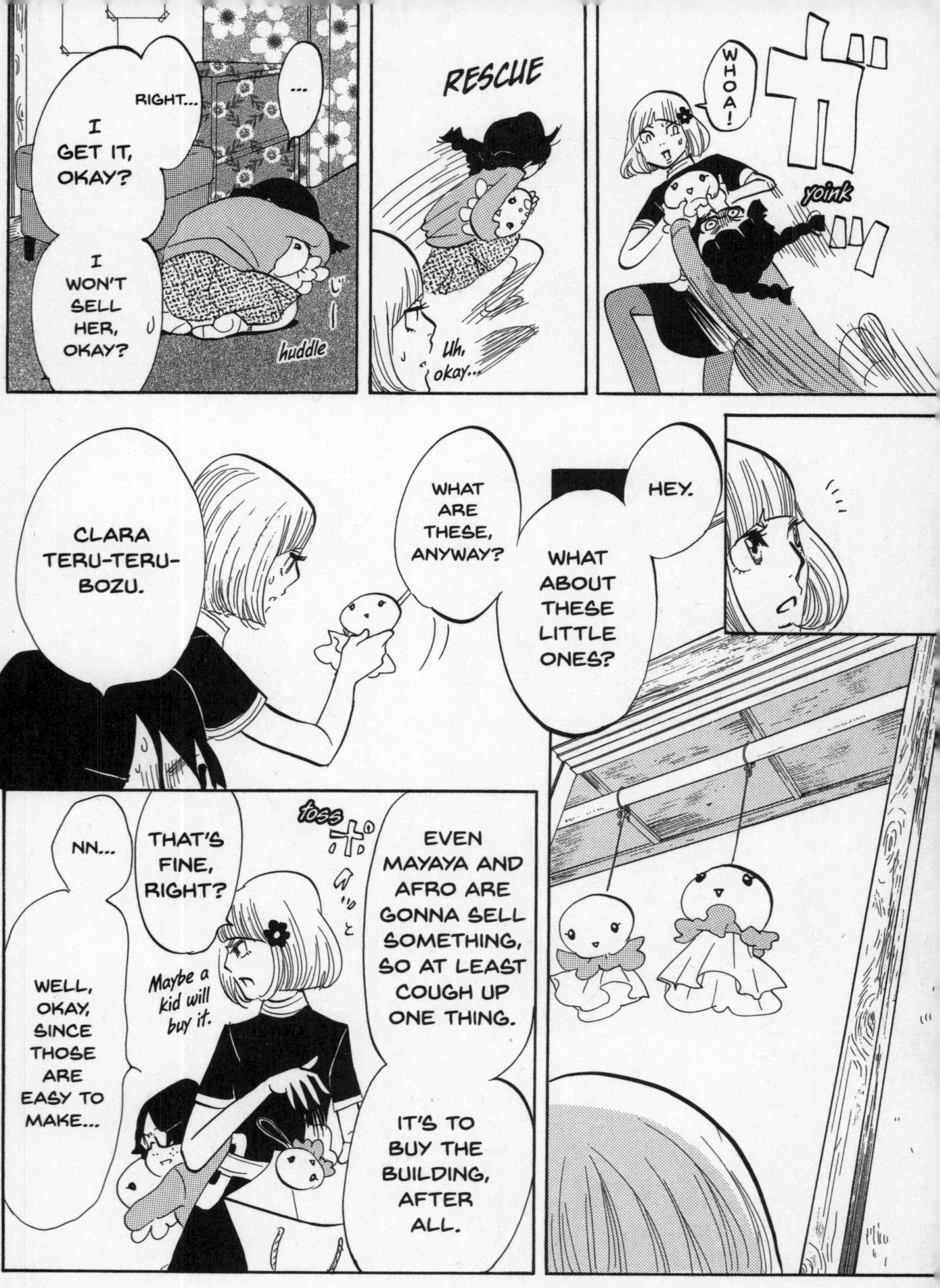
WHOA!
yoink
RESCUE
Uh, okay...
...
RIGHT...
I GET IT, OKAY?
I WON'T SELL HER, OKAY?
huddle
HEY.
WHAT ABOUT THESE LITTLE ONES?
WHAT ARE THESE, ANYWAY?
CLARA TERU-TERU-BOZU.
EVEN MAYAYA AND AFRO ARE GONNA SELL SOMETHING, SO AT LEAST COUGH UP ONE THING.
IT'S TO BUY THE BUILDING, AFTER ALL.
toss
THAT'S FINE, RIGHT?
NN...
Maybe a kid will buy it.
WELL, OKAY, SINCE THOSE ARE EASY TO MAKE...

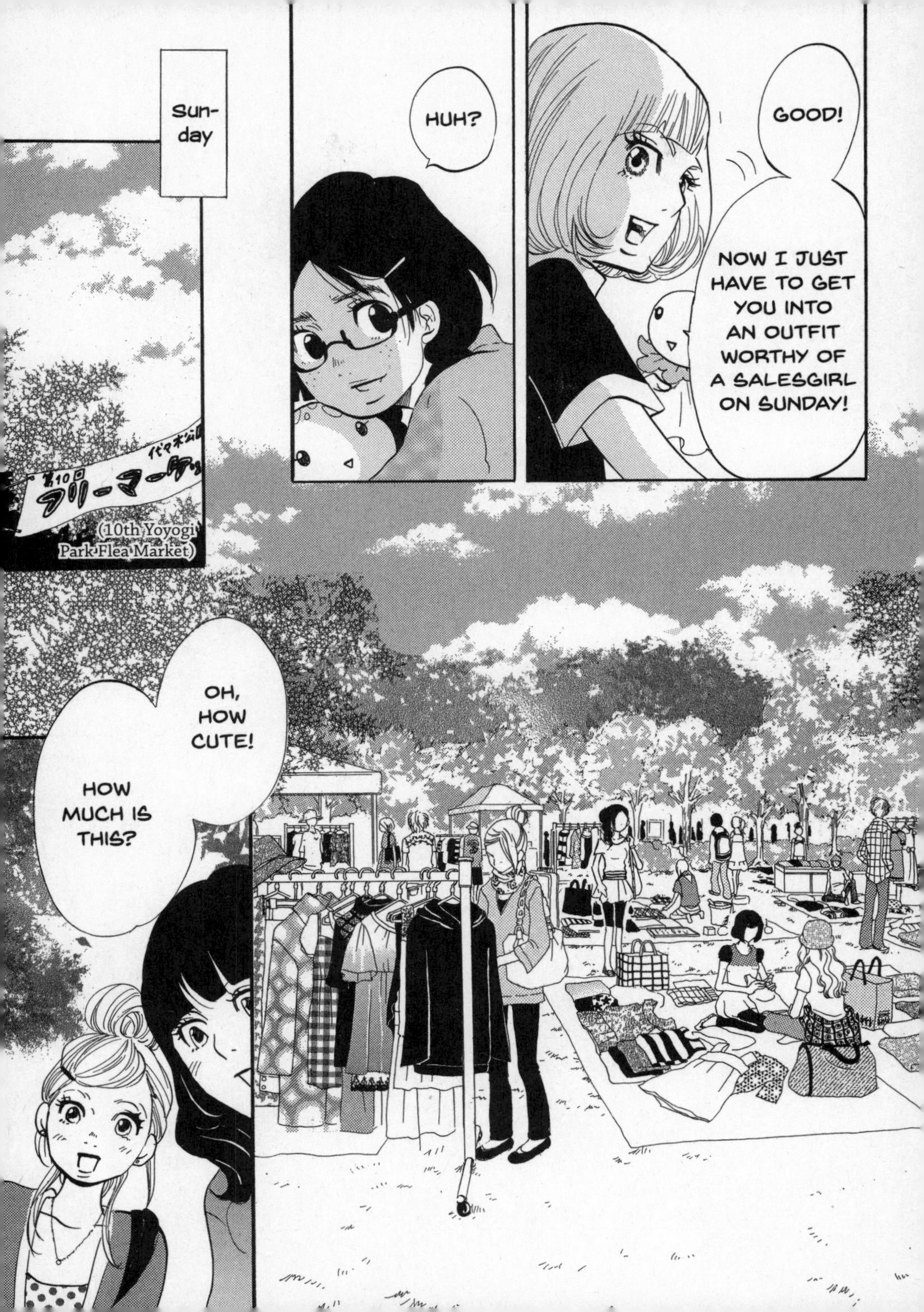
GOOD!
NOW I JUST HAVE TO GET YOU INTO AN OUTFIT WORTHY OF A SALESGIRL ON SUNDAY!
HUH?
Sun-day
(10th Yoyogi Park Flea Market)
OH, HOW CUTE!
HOW MUCH IS THIS?

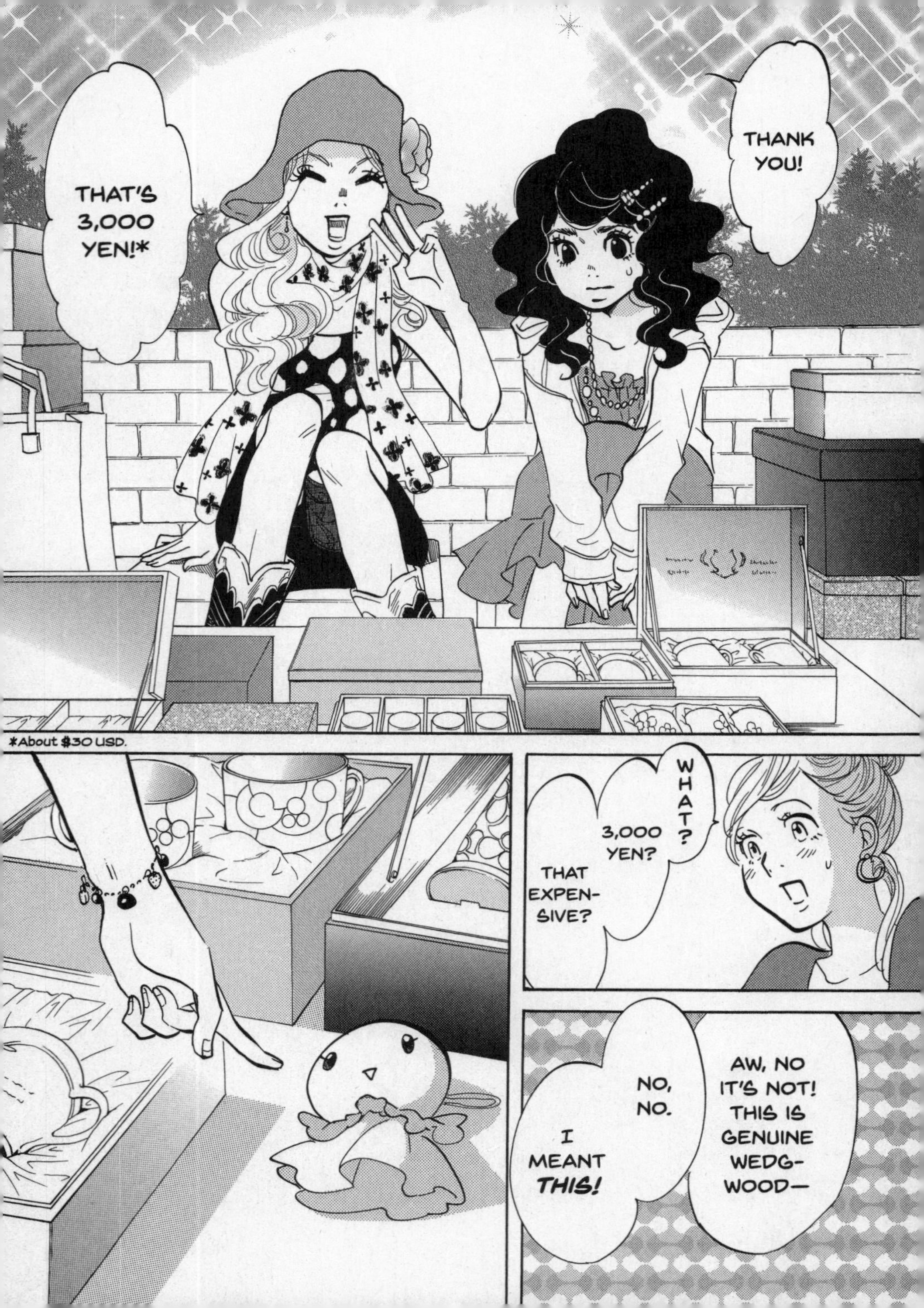
THANK YOU!
THAT'S 3,000 YEN!*
WHAT?
3,000 YEN?
THAT EXPEN-SIVE?
AW, NO IT'S NOT! THIS IS GENUINE WEDG-WOOD—
NO, NO.
I MEANT *THIS!*

*About $30 USD.

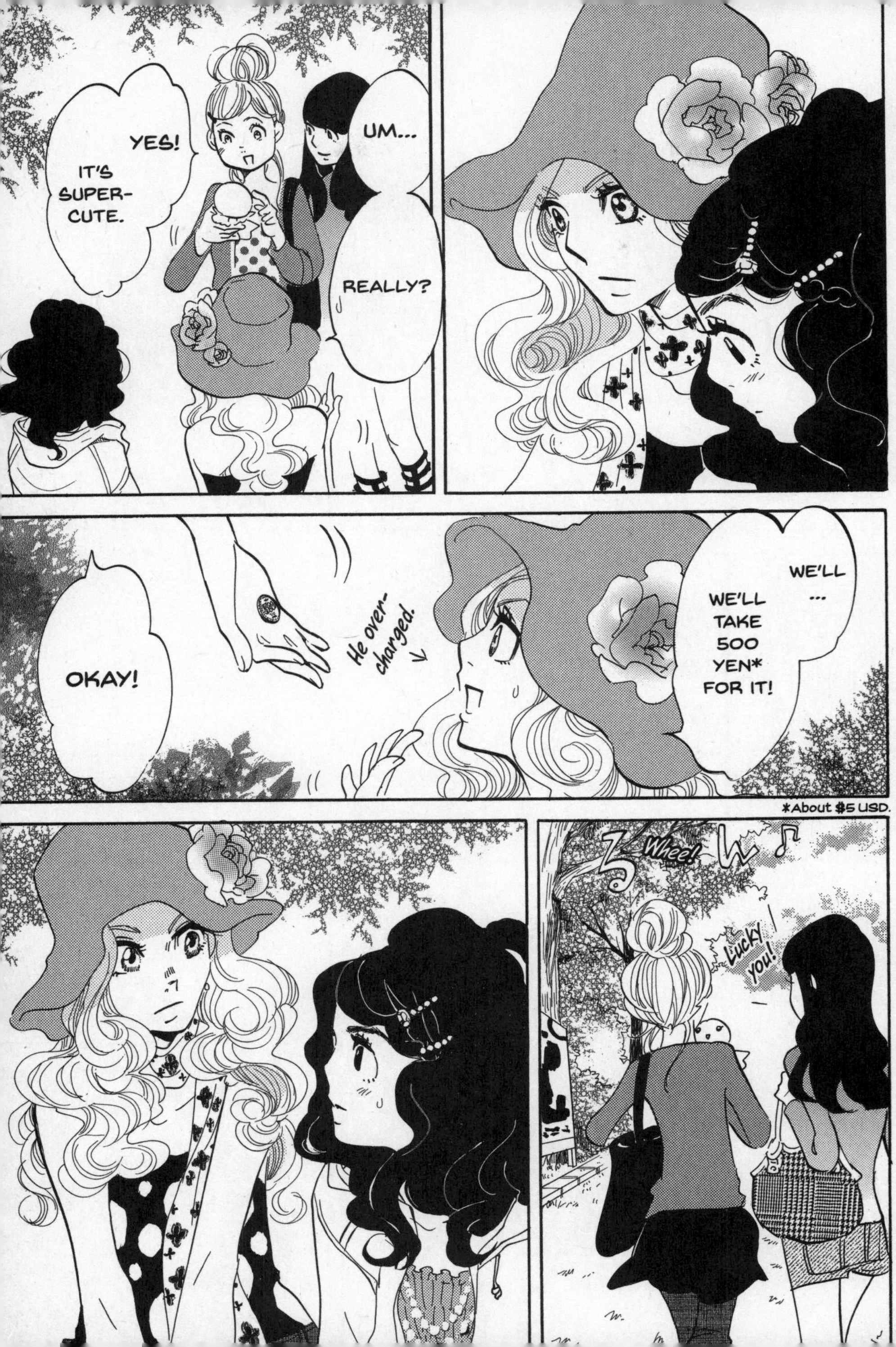
UM... REALLY?
YES! IT'S SUPER-CUTE.
WE'LL ... WE'LL TAKE 500 YEN* FOR IT!
He over-charged.
OKAY!
Whee!
Lucky you!

*About $5 USD.

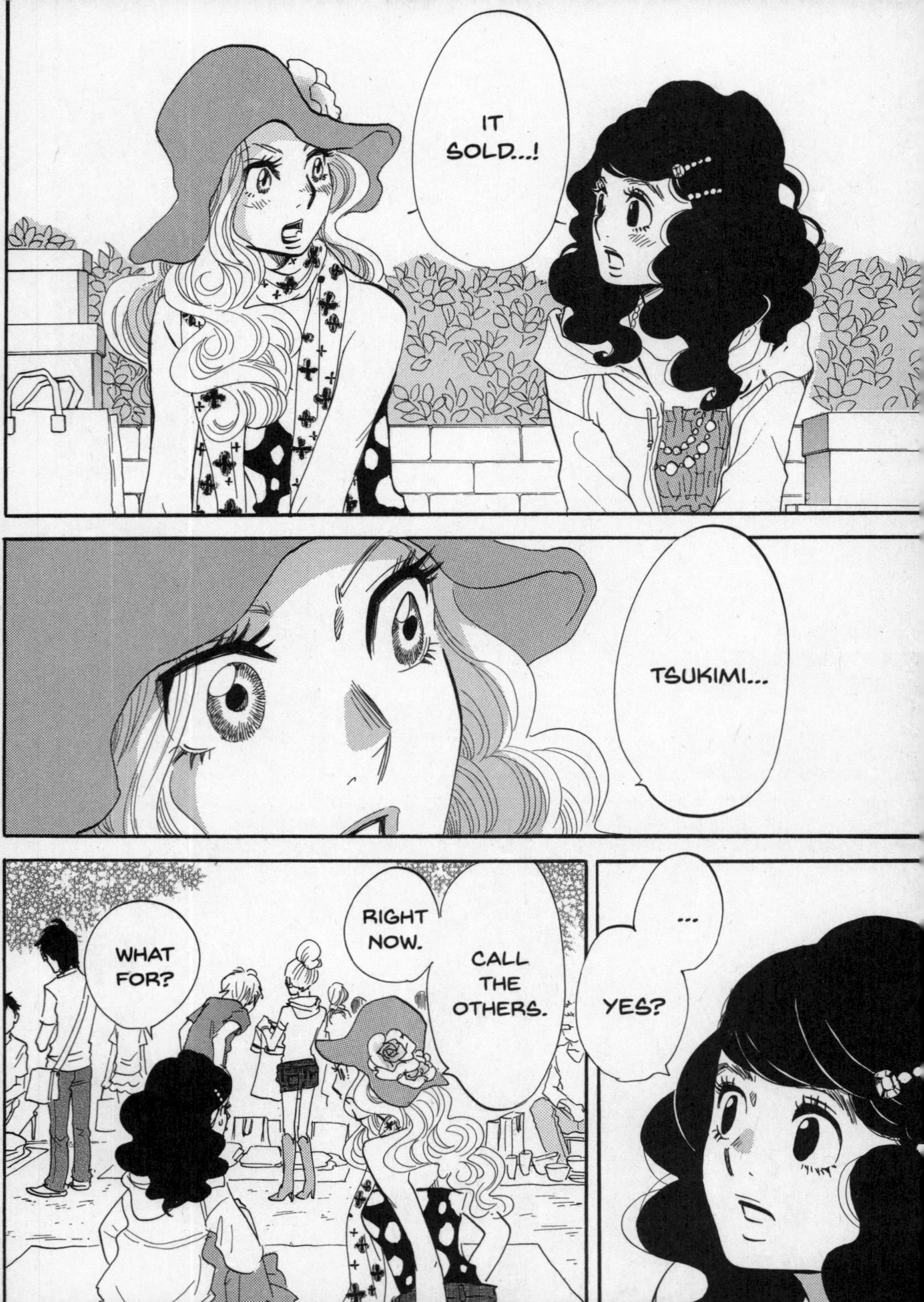
IT SOLD...!
TSUKIMI...
...
YES?
CALL THE OTHERS.
RIGHT NOW.
WHAT FOR?

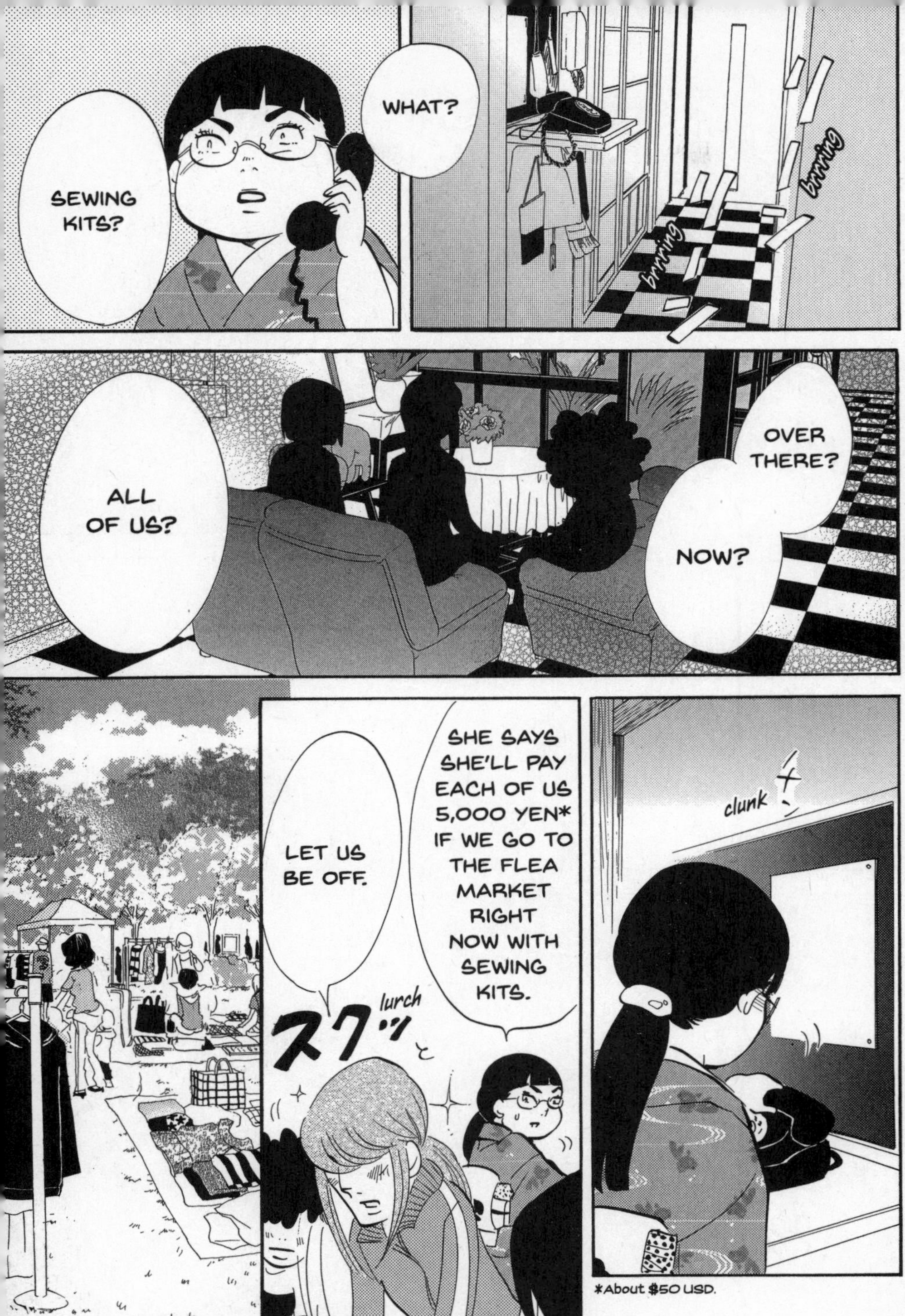
brrring
brrring
WHAT?
SEWING KITS?
OVER THERE?
NOW?
ALL OF US?
clunk
SHE SAYS SHE'LL PAY EACH OF US 5,000 YEN* IF WE GO TO THE FLEA MARKET RIGHT NOW WITH SEWING KITS.
LET US BE OFF.
lurch
スクッと

*About $50 USD.

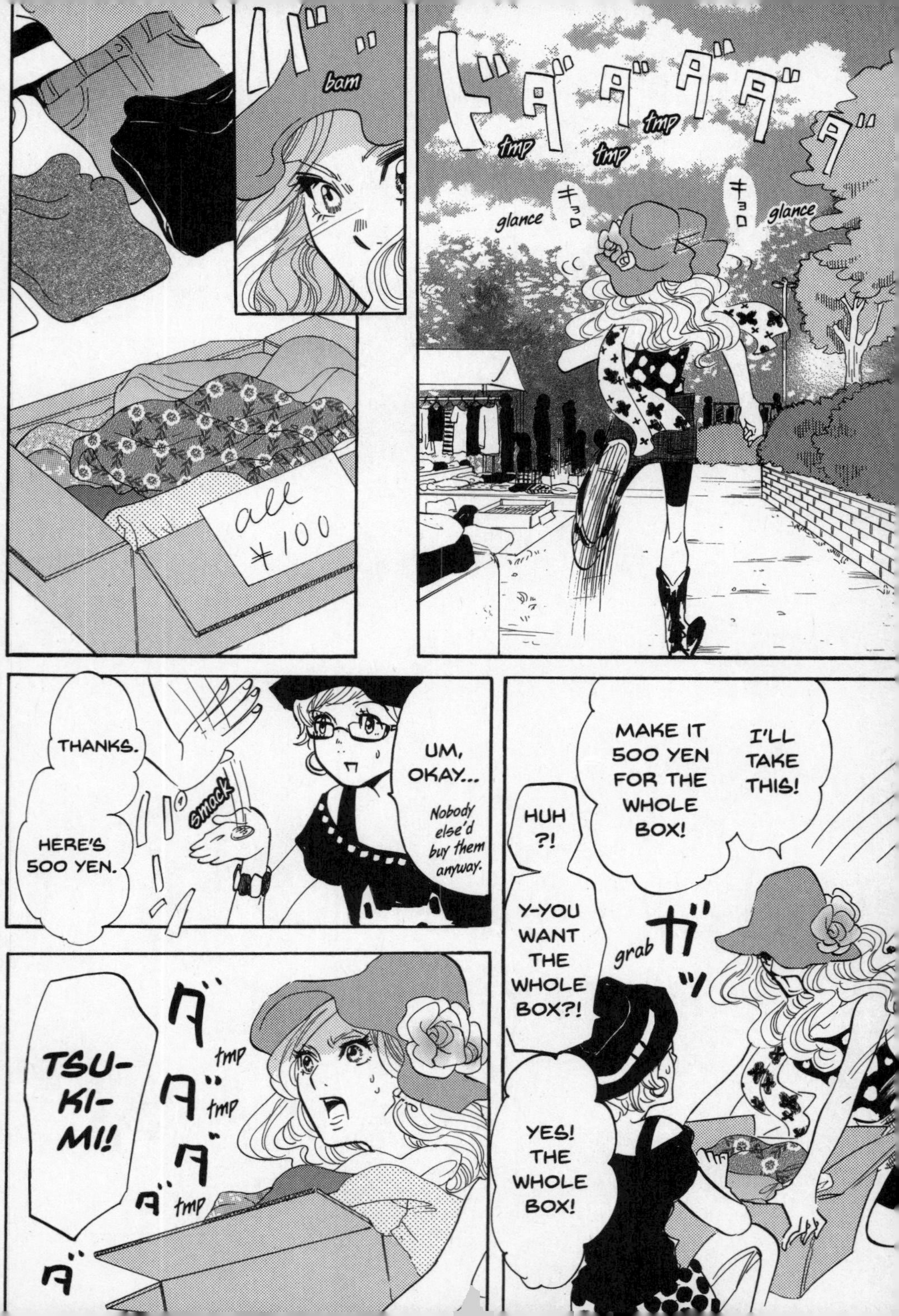

ドダダダダダ
tmp
tmp
tmp
キョロ
glance
キョロ
glance
バ
bam
all ¥100
I'LL TAKE THIS!
MAKE IT 500 YEN FOR THE WHOLE BOX!
HUH?!
Y-YOU WANT THE WHOLE BOX?!
ガッ
grab
YES! THE WHOLE BOX!
UM, OKAY...
Nobody else'd buy them anyway.
HERE'S 500 YEN.
smack
THANKS.
ダダダダダ
tmp
tmp
tmp
TSU-KI-MI!

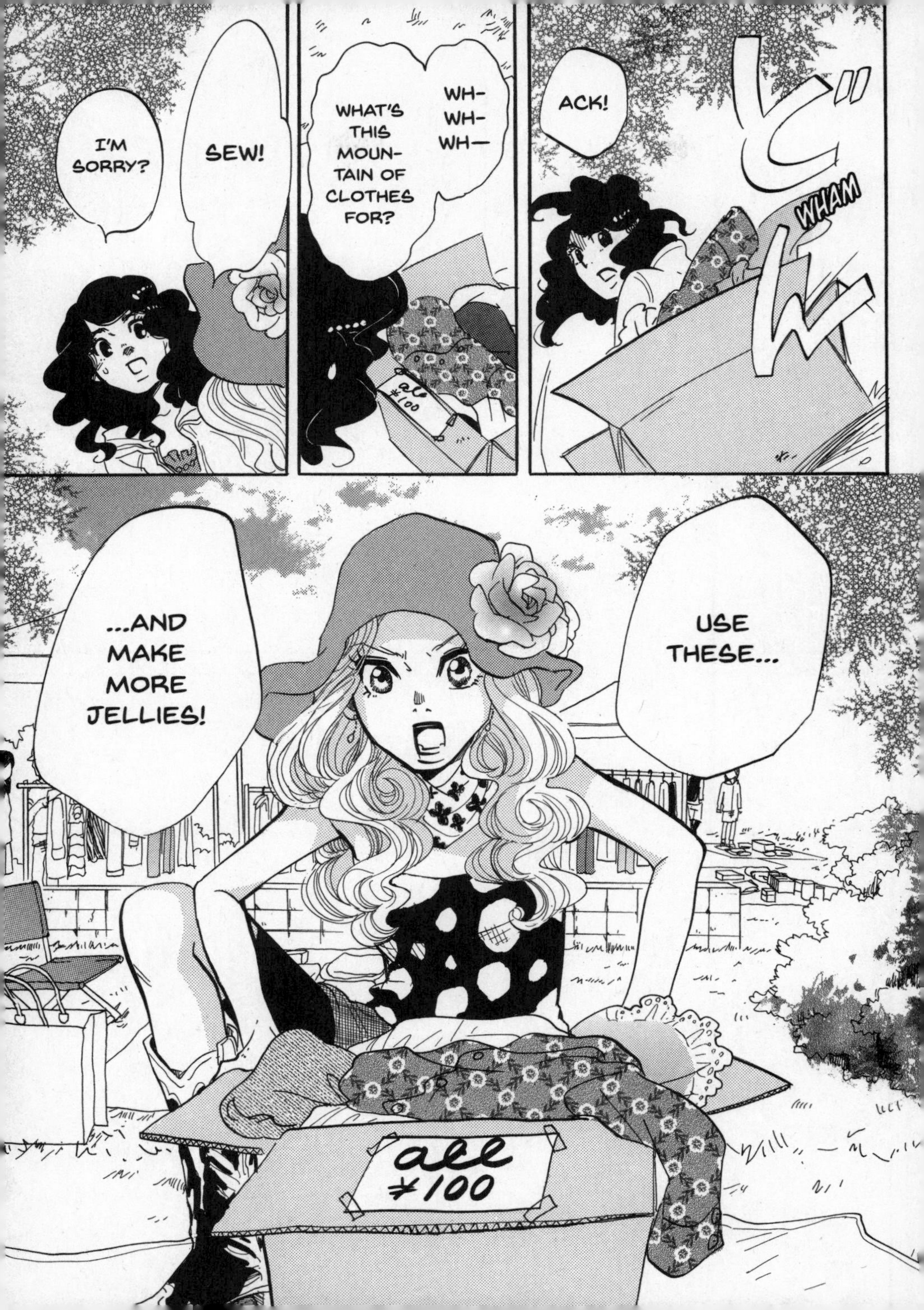
ACK!
WHAM
WH- WH- WH—
WHAT'S THIS MOUNTAIN OF CLOTHES FOR?
SEW!
I'M SORRY?
all ¥100
USE THESE...
...AND MAKE MORE JELLIES!
all ¥100

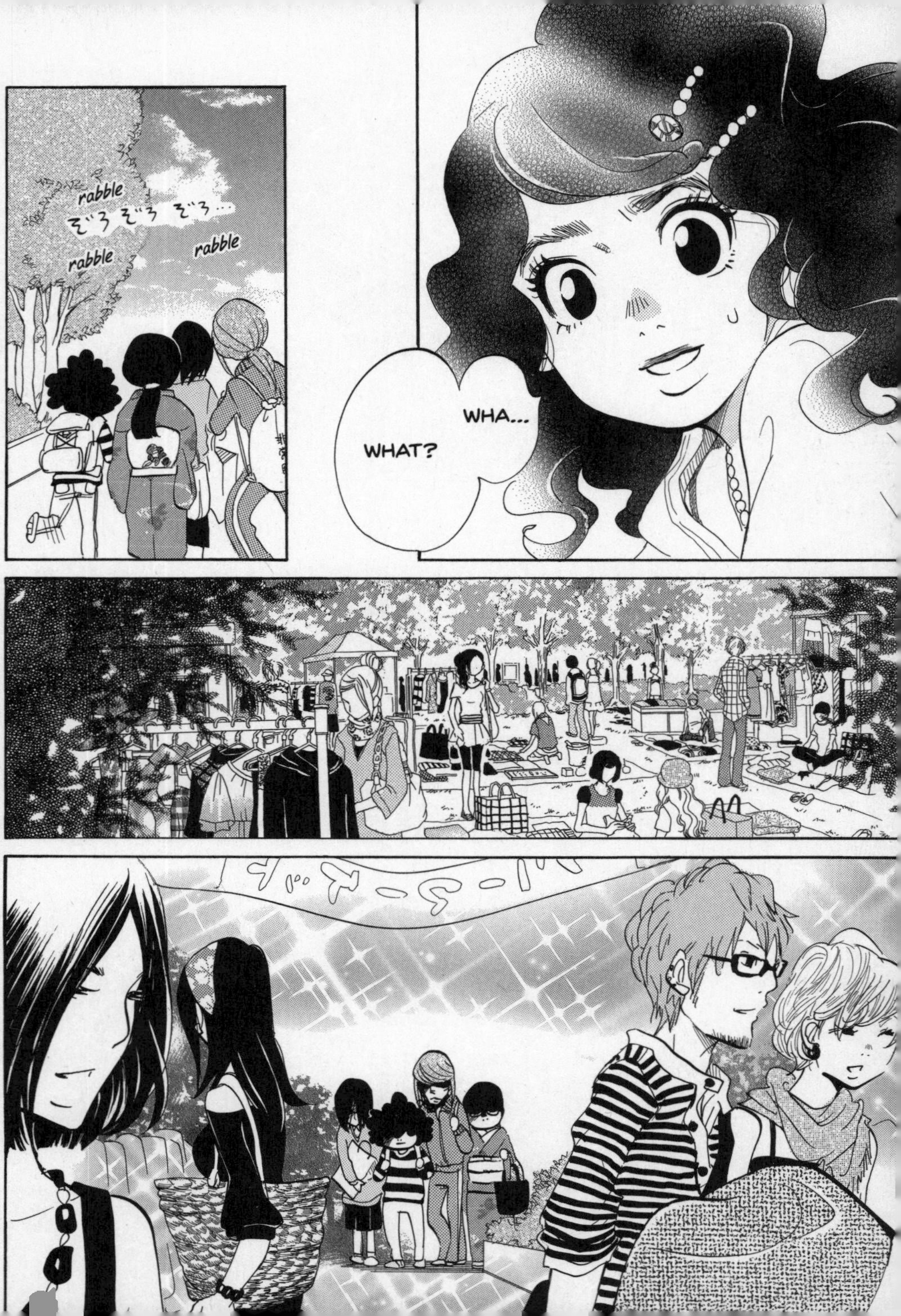
WHA...
WHAT?
rabble
ぞろぞろぞろ…
rabble
rabble

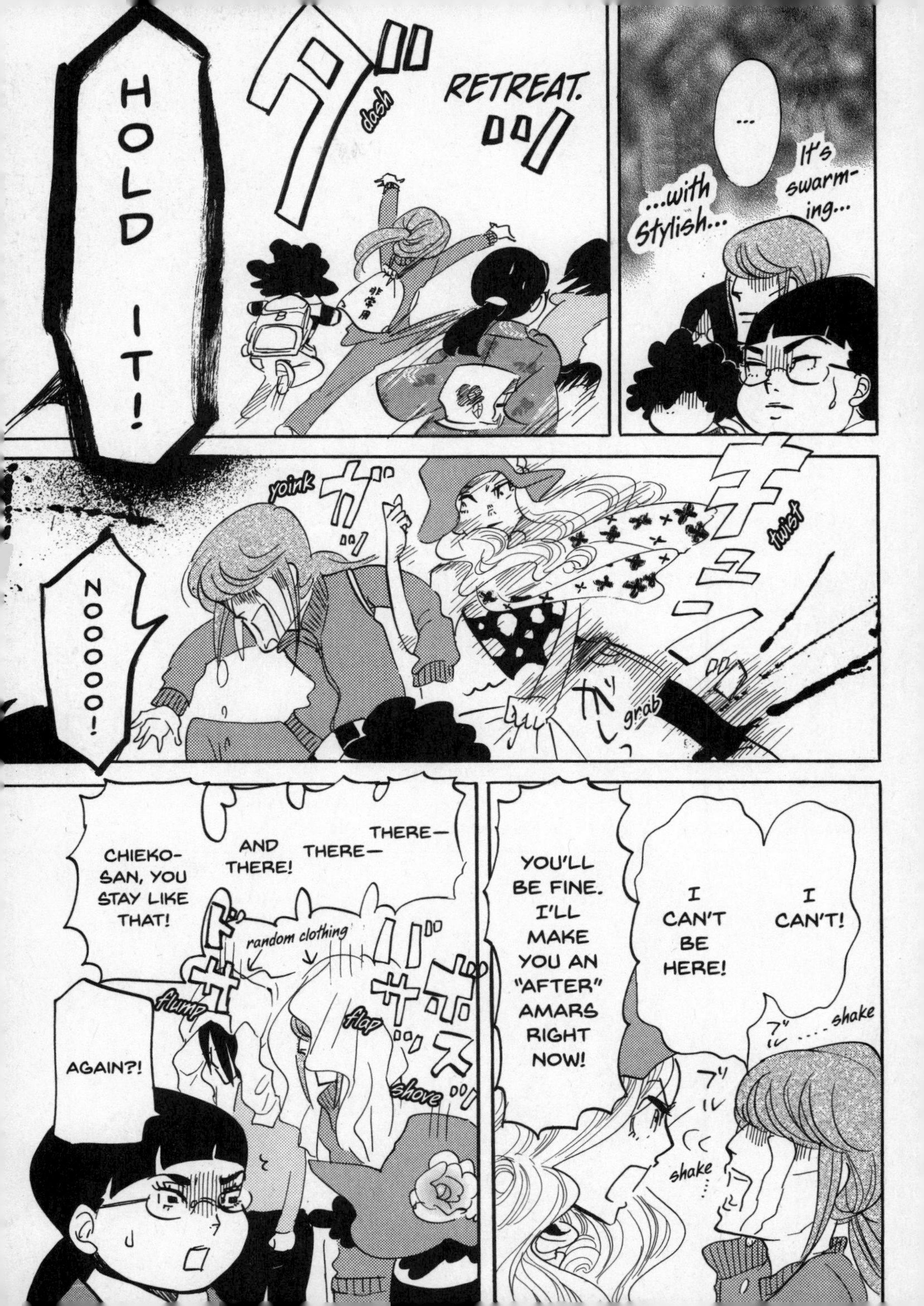
...
It's swarming...
...with Stylish...
RETREAT.
dash
HOLD IT!
twist
yoink
grab
NOOOOOO!
I CAN'T!
I CAN'T BE HERE!
YOU'LL BE FINE. I'LL MAKE YOU AN "AFTER" AMARS RIGHT NOW!
shake
shake
THERE—
THERE—
AND THERE!
CHIEKO-SAN, YOU STAY LIKE THAT!
random clothing
flap
shove
flump
AGAIN?!

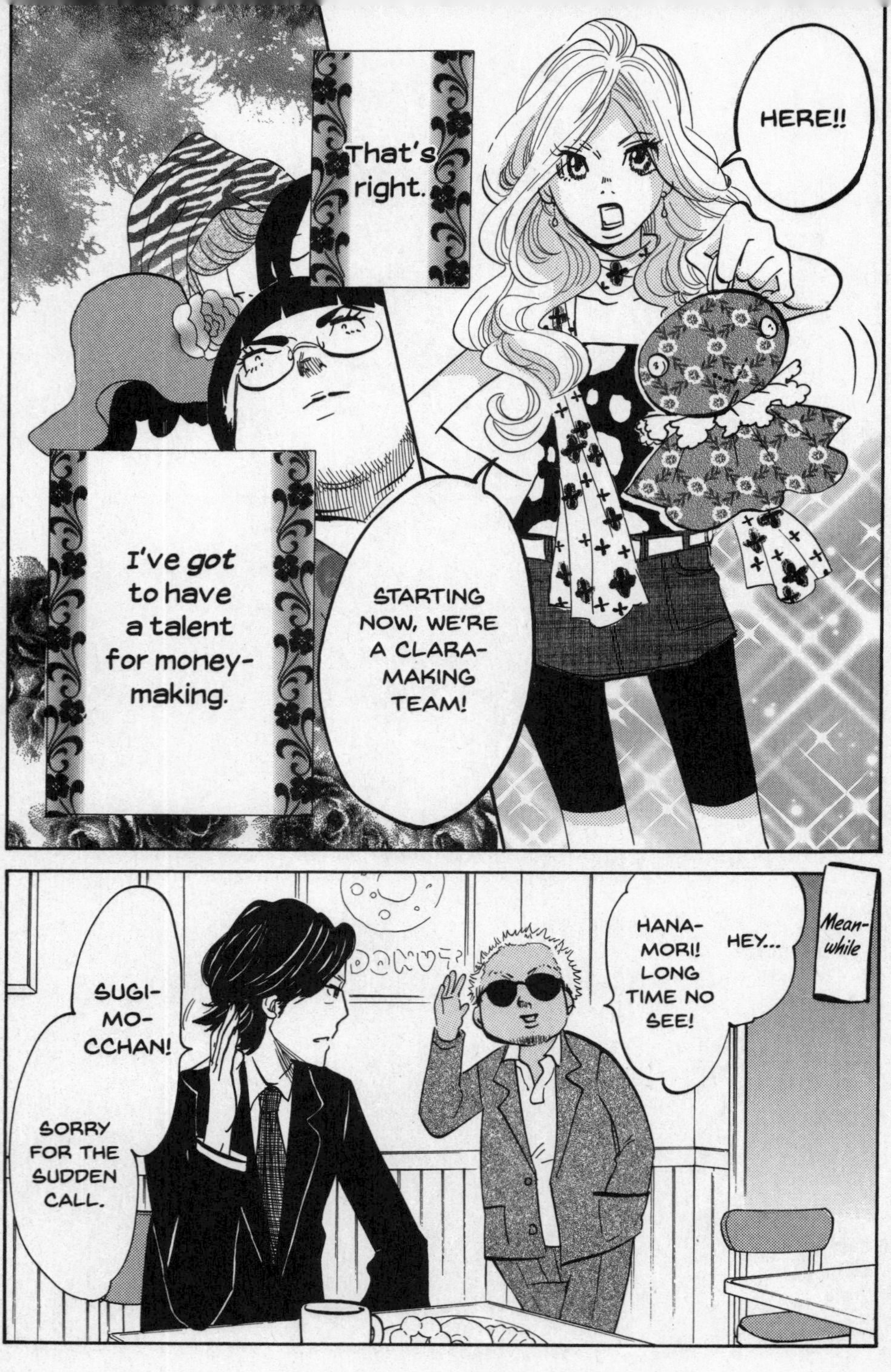
HERE!!
That's right.
STARTING NOW, WE'RE A CLARA-MAKING TEAM!
I've *got* to have a talent for money-making.
Mean-while
HEY... HANA-MORI! LONG TIME NO SEE!
SUGI-MO-CCHAN!
SORRY FOR THE SUDDEN CALL.

Episode 15

Million Dollar Baby

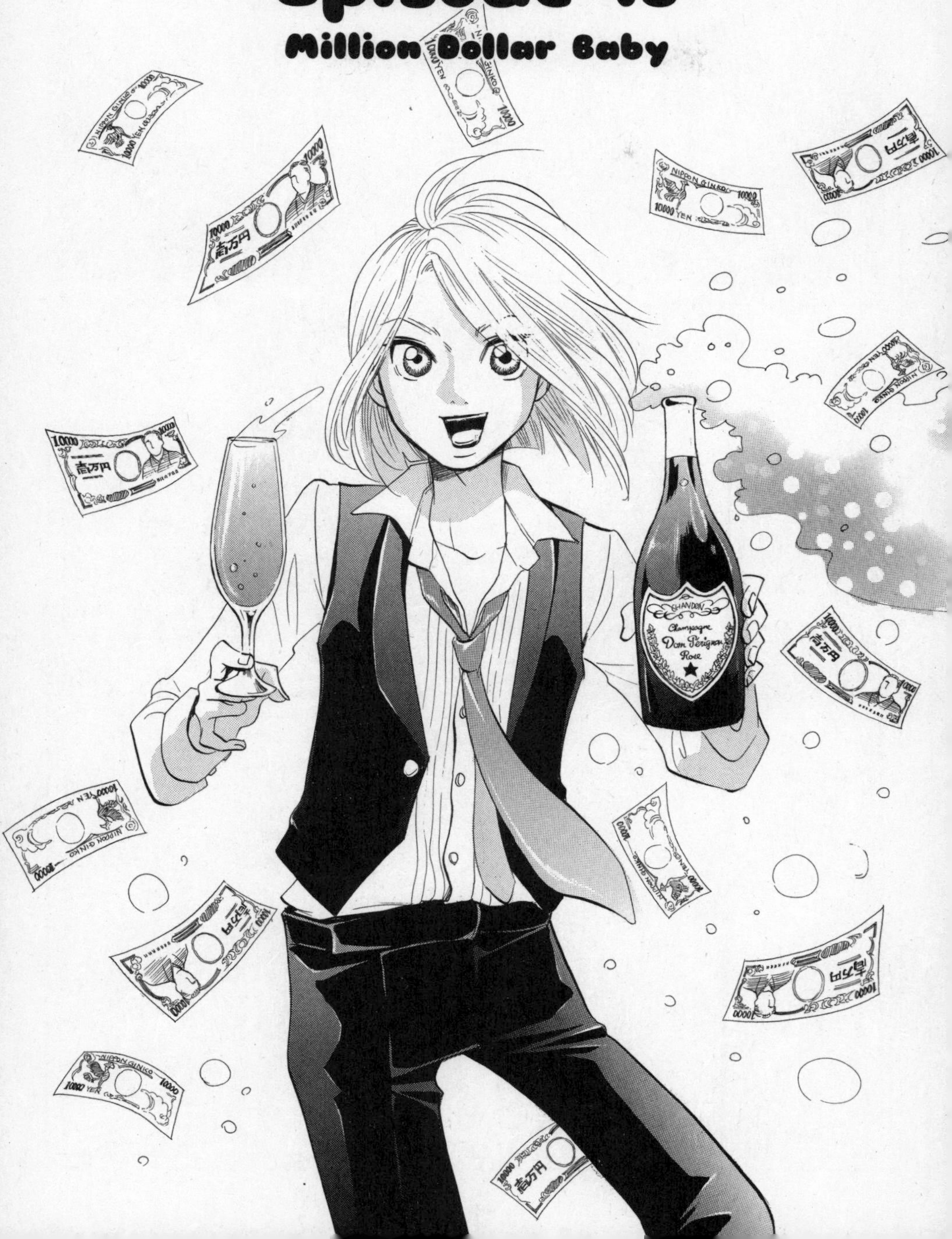
CHANDON
Champagne
Dom Pérignon
Rose

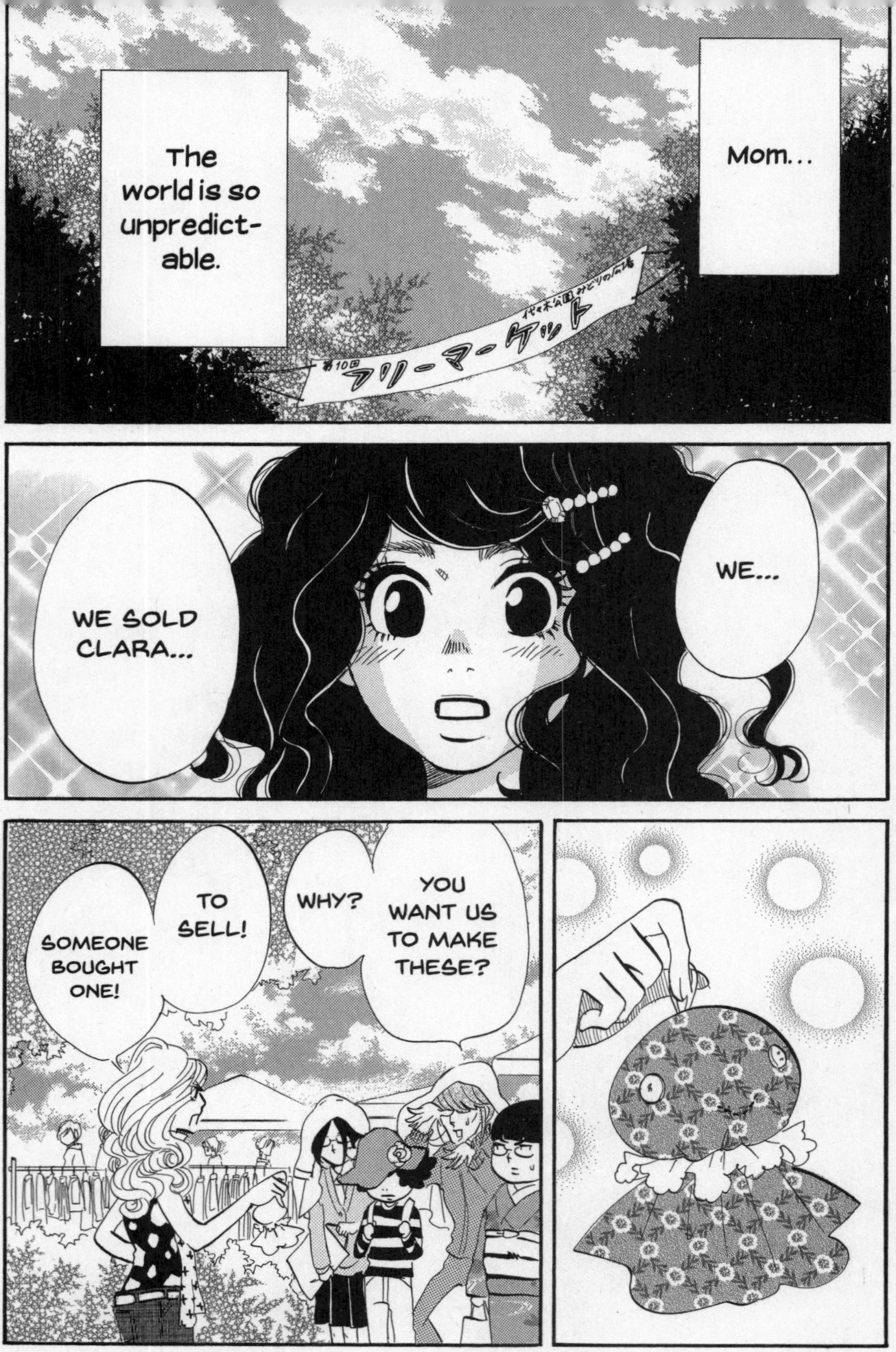
Mom...
The world is so unpredict-able.
第10回 フリーマーケット
代々木公園 みどりの広場
WE...
WE SOLD CLARA...
YOU WANT US TO MAKE THESE?
WHY?
TO SELL!
SOMEONE BOUGHT ONE!

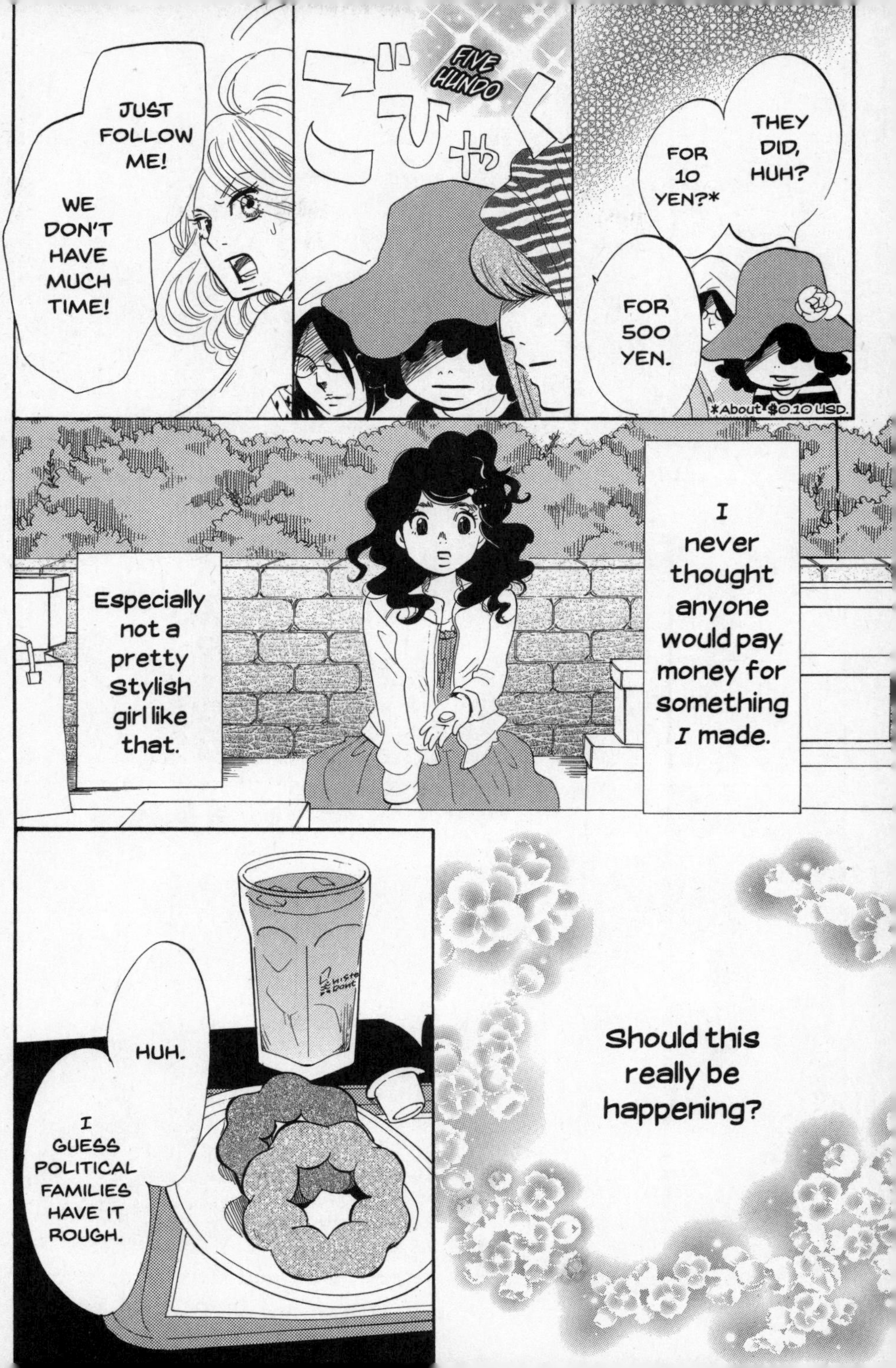
THEY DID, HUH?
FOR 10 YEN?*
FOR 500 YEN.
*About $0.10 USD.
ごひゃく
FIVE HUNDO
JUST FOLLOW ME!
WE DON'T HAVE MUCH TIME!
I never thought anyone would pay money for something I made.
Especially not a pretty Stylish girl like that.
Should this really be happening?
HUH.
I GUESS POLITICAL FAMILIES HAVE IT ROUGH.

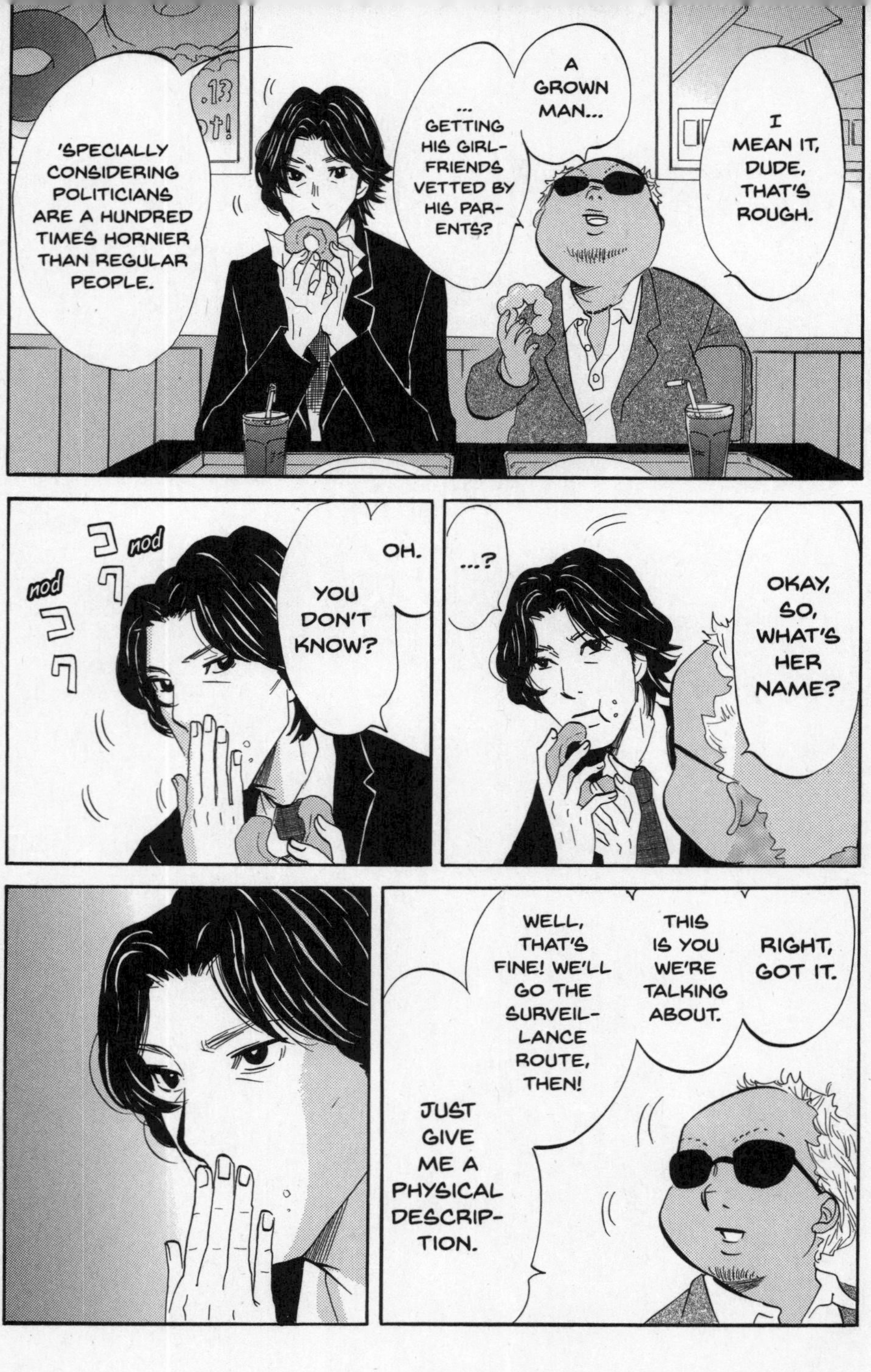
I MEAN IT, DUDE, THAT'S ROUGH.
A GROWN MAN...
...GETTING HIS GIRL-FRIENDS VETTED BY HIS PAR-ENTS?
'SPECIALLY CONSIDERING POLITICIANS ARE A HUNDRED TIMES HORNIER THAN REGULAR PEOPLE.
OKAY, SO, WHAT'S HER NAME?
...?
OH.
YOU DON'T KNOW?
コク nod
コク nod
RIGHT, GOT IT.
THIS IS YOU WE'RE TALKING ABOUT.
WELL, THAT'S FINE! WE'LL GO THE SURVEIL-LANCE ROUTE, THEN!
JUST GIVE ME A PHYSICAL DESCRIP-TION.

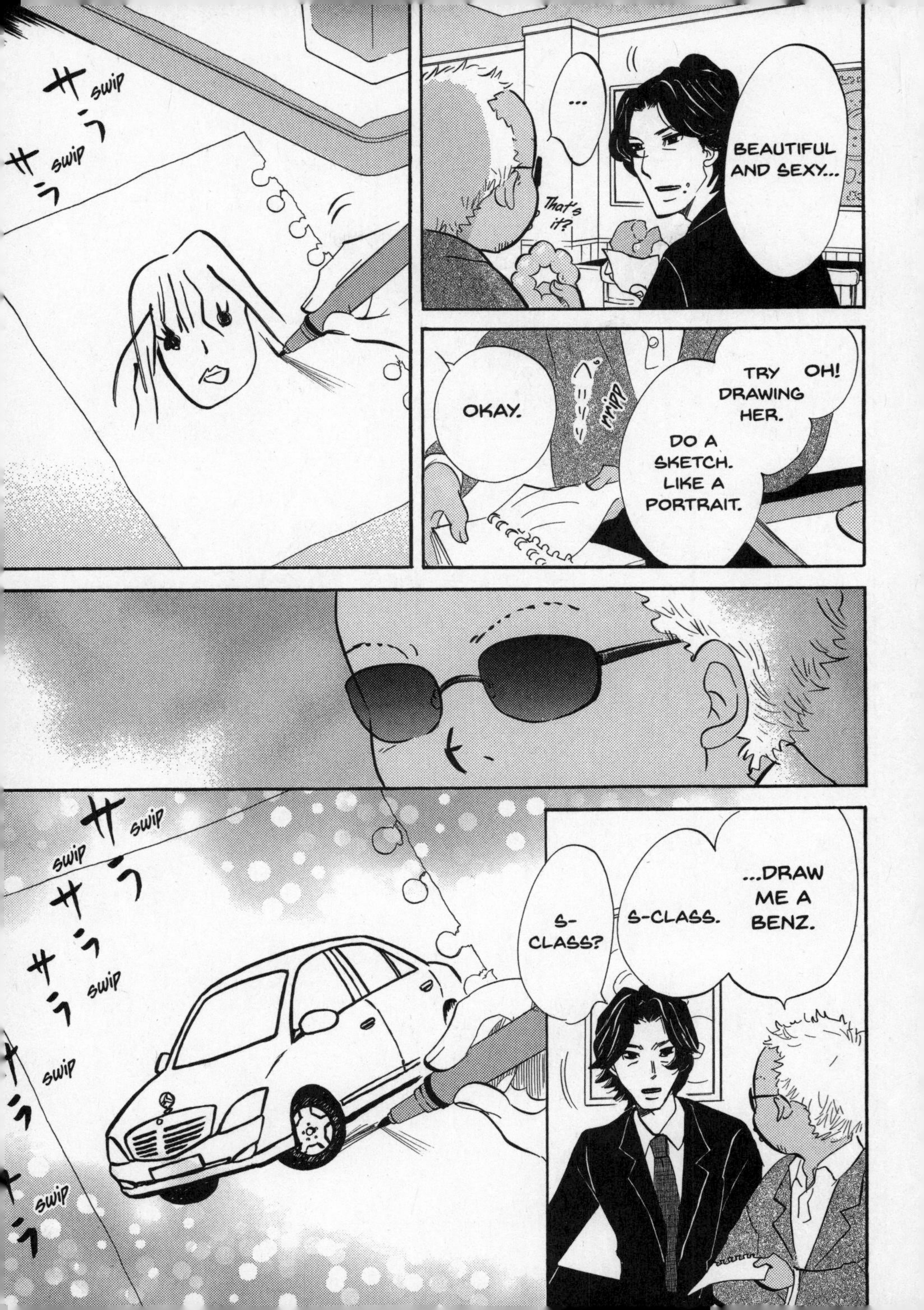
...
BEAUTIFUL AND SEXY...
That's it?
OH!
TRY DRAWING HER.
DO A SKETCH. LIKE A PORTRAIT.
rrrip
OKAY.
サ swip
ラ
サ swip
ラ
...DRAW ME A BENZ.
S-CLASS.
S-CLASS?
サ swip
ラ
サ swip
ラ
サ swip
ラ
swip
ラ
swip
ラ

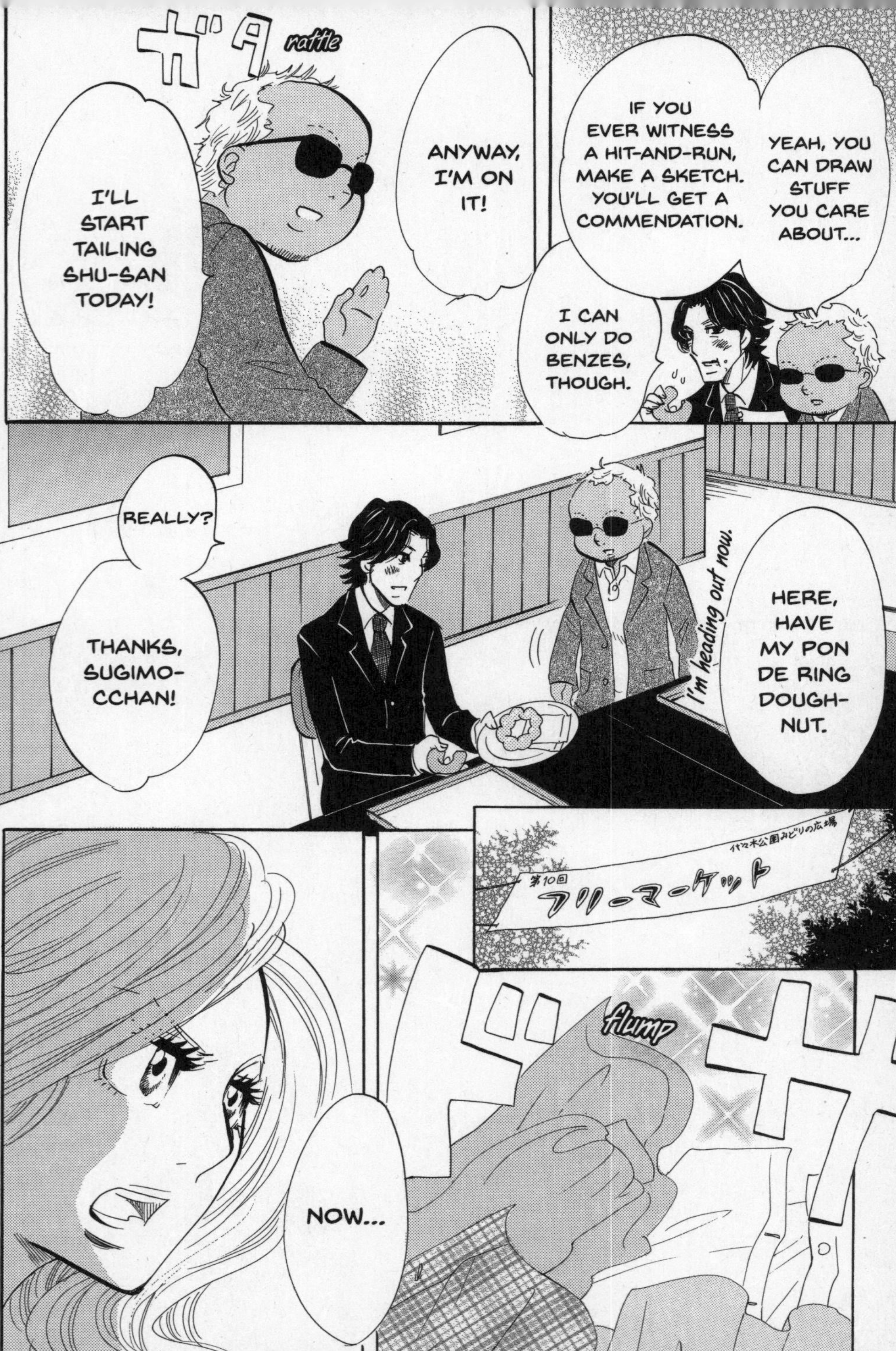
YEAH, YOU CAN DRAW STUFF YOU CARE ABOUT...
IF YOU EVER WITNESS A HIT-AND-RUN, MAKE A SKETCH. YOU'LL GET A COMMENDATION.
I CAN ONLY DO BENZES, THOUGH.
ガタ
rattle
ANYWAY, I'M ON IT!
I'LL START TAILING SHU-SAN TODAY!
I'm heading out now.
HERE, HAVE MY PON DE RING DOUGHNUT.
REALLY?
THANKS, SUGIMO-CCHAN!
代々木公園みどりの広場
第10回
フリーマーケット
ドサ
flump
NOW...

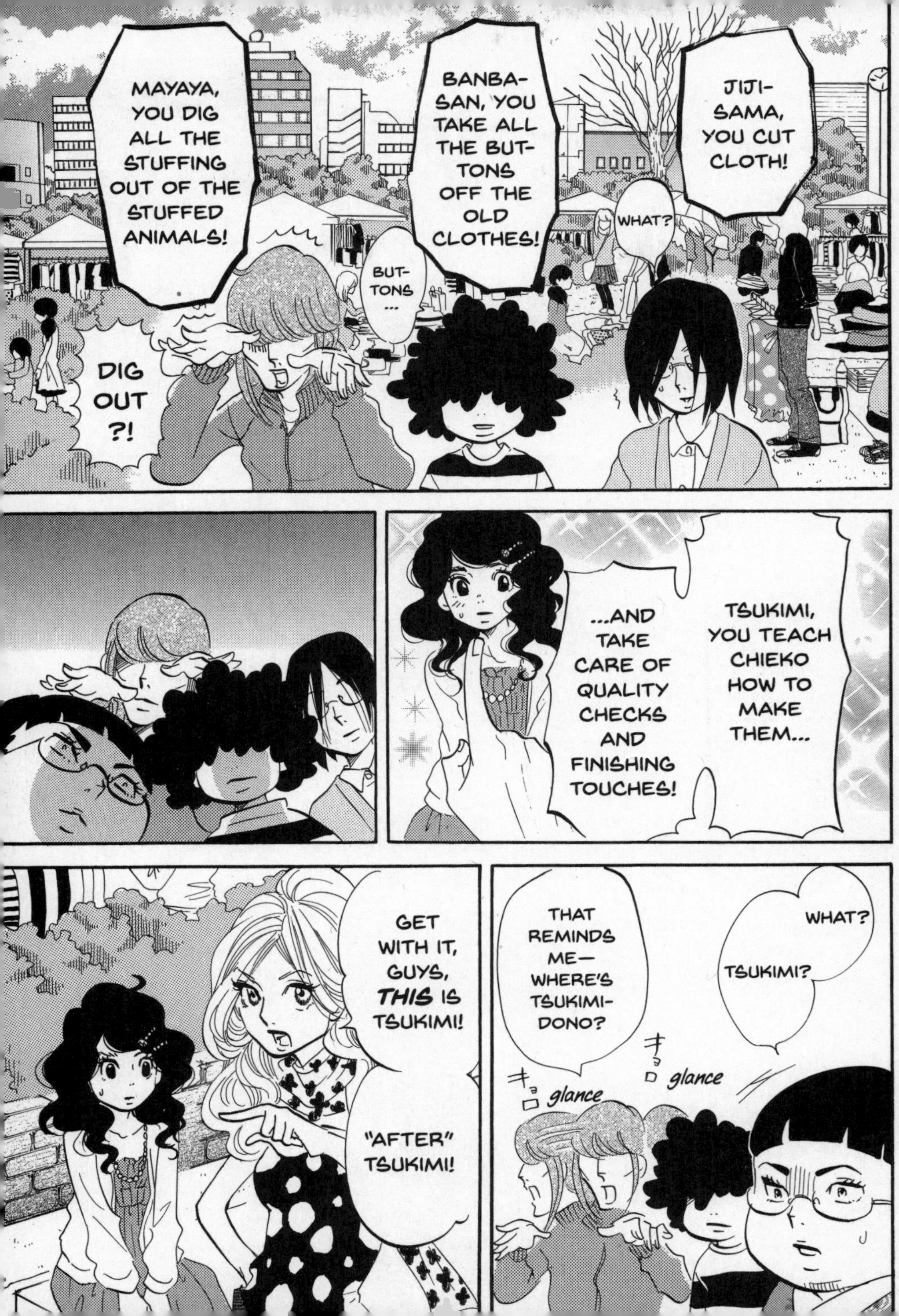
JIJI-SAMA, YOU CUT CLOTH!
WHAT?
BANBA-SAN, YOU TAKE ALL THE BUTTONS OFF THE OLD CLOTHES!
BUTTONS...
MAYAYA, YOU DIG ALL THE STUFFING OUT OF THE STUFFED ANIMALS!
DIG OUT?!
TSUKIMI, YOU TEACH CHIEKO HOW TO MAKE THEM...
...AND TAKE CARE OF QUALITY CHECKS AND FINISHING TOUCHES!
WHAT?
TSUKIMI?
THAT REMINDS ME—WHERE'S TSUKIMI-DONO?
glance
glance
GET WITH IT, GUYS, **THIS** IS TSUKIMI!
"AFTER" TSUKIMI!

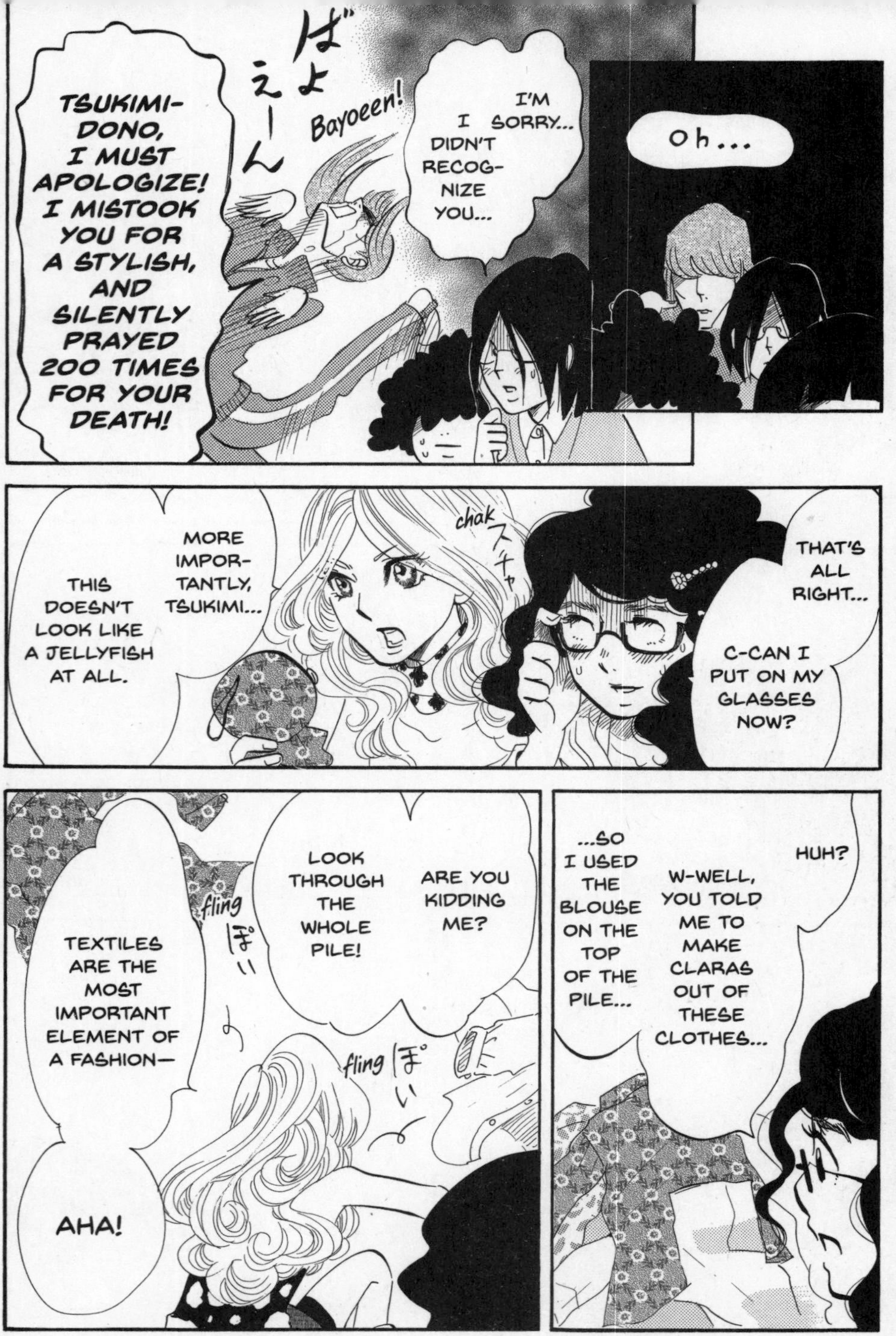

Oh...
I'M SORRY... I DIDN'T RECOGNIZE YOU...
ばよえーん
Bayoeen!
TSUKIMI-DONO, I MUST APOLOGIZE! I MISTOOK YOU FOR A STYLISH, AND SILENTLY PRAYED 200 TIMES FOR YOUR DEATH!
THAT'S ALL RIGHT...
C-CAN I PUT ON MY GLASSES NOW?
スチャ
chak
MORE IMPORTANTLY, TSUKIMI...
THIS DOESN'T LOOK LIKE A JELLYFISH AT ALL.
HUH?
W-WELL, YOU TOLD ME TO MAKE CLARAS OUT OF THESE CLOTHES...
...SO I USED THE BLOUSE ON THE TOP OF THE PILE...
ARE YOU KIDDING ME?
LOOK THROUGH THE WHOLE PILE!
ぽい
fling
ぽい
fling
TEXTILES ARE THE MOST IMPORTANT ELEMENT OF A FASHION—
AHA!

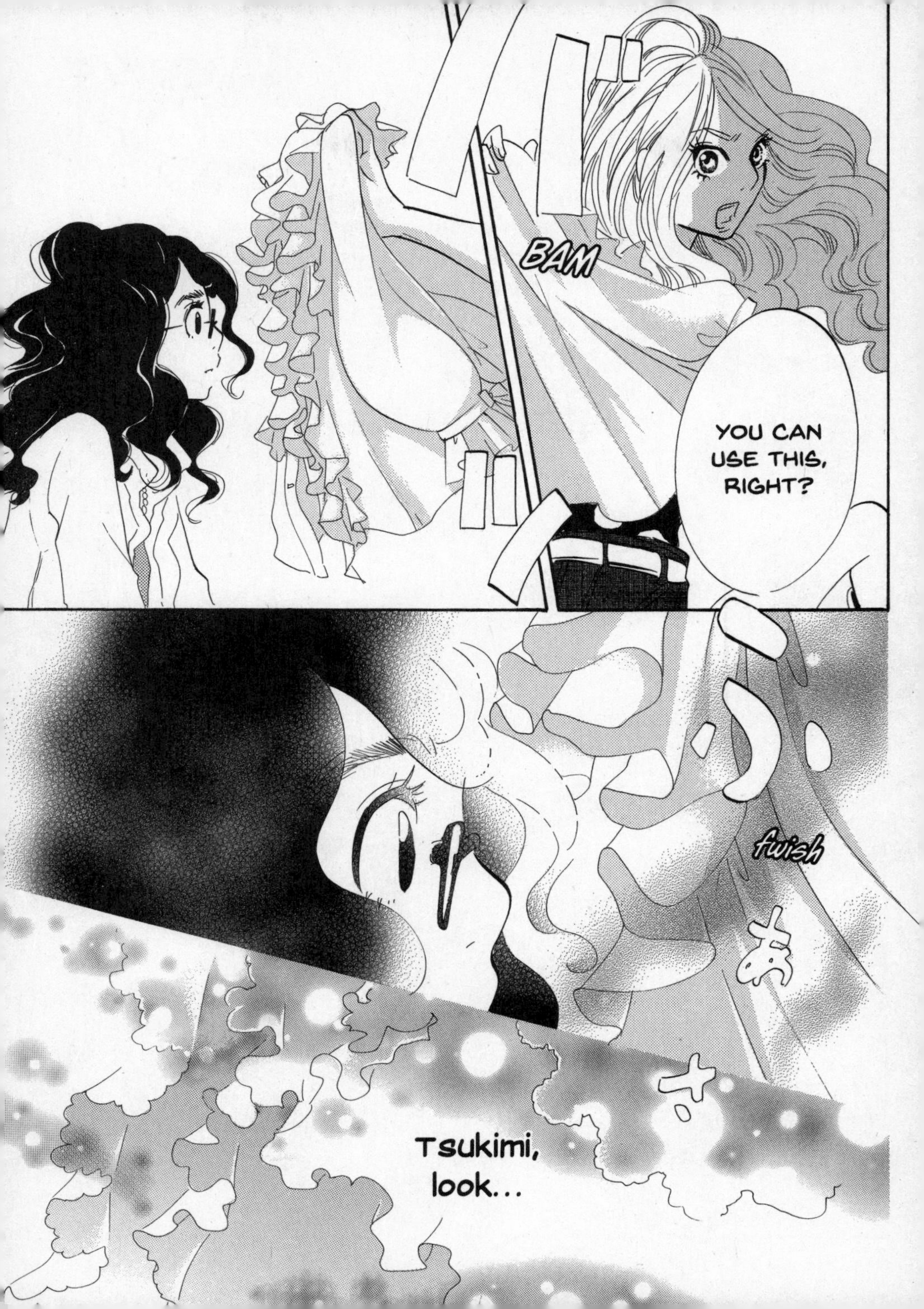
BAM
YOU CAN USE THIS, RIGHT?
fwish
Tsukimi, look...

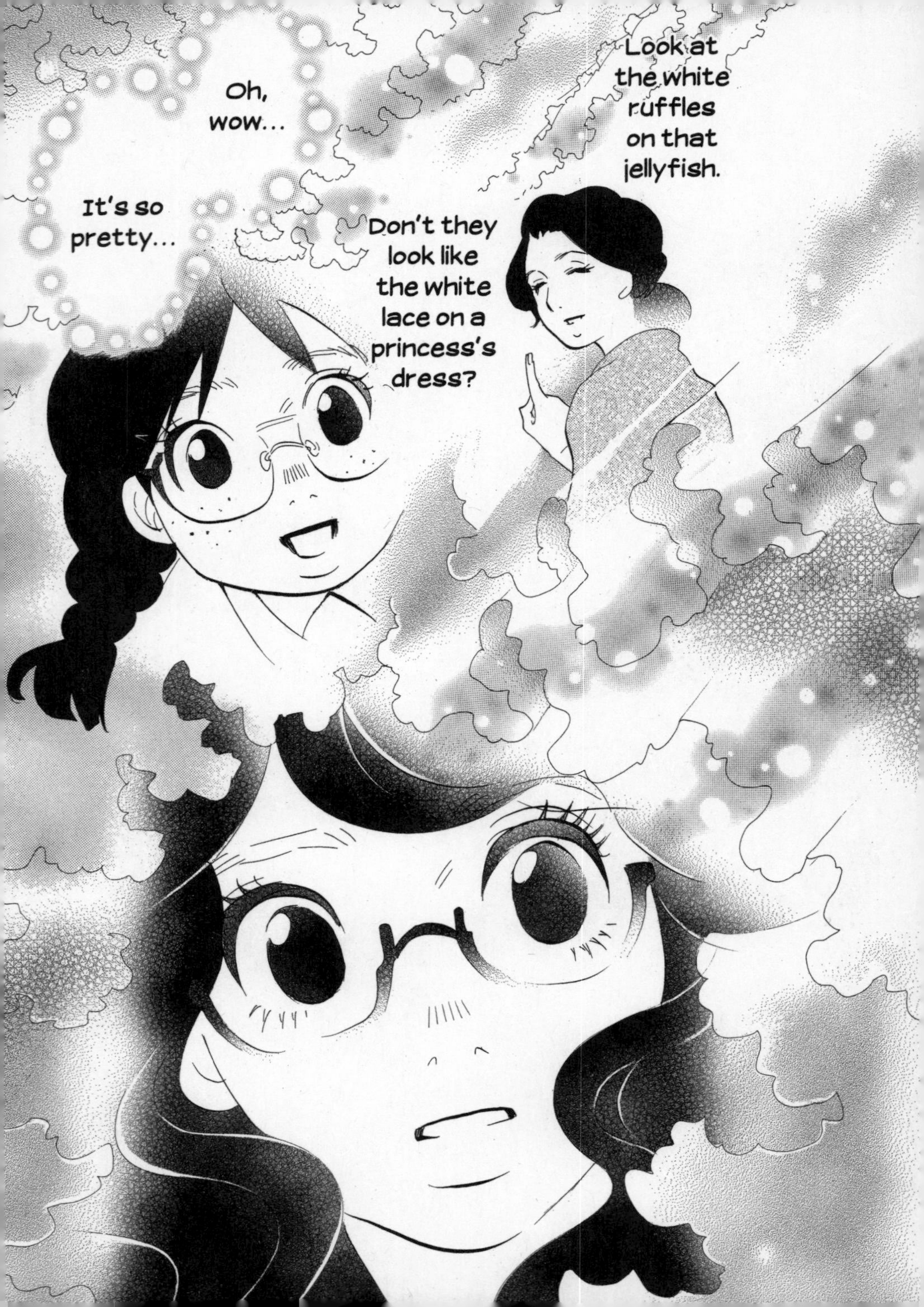
Look at the white ruffles on that jellyfish.
Don't they look like the white lace on a princess's dress?
Oh, wow...
It's so pretty...

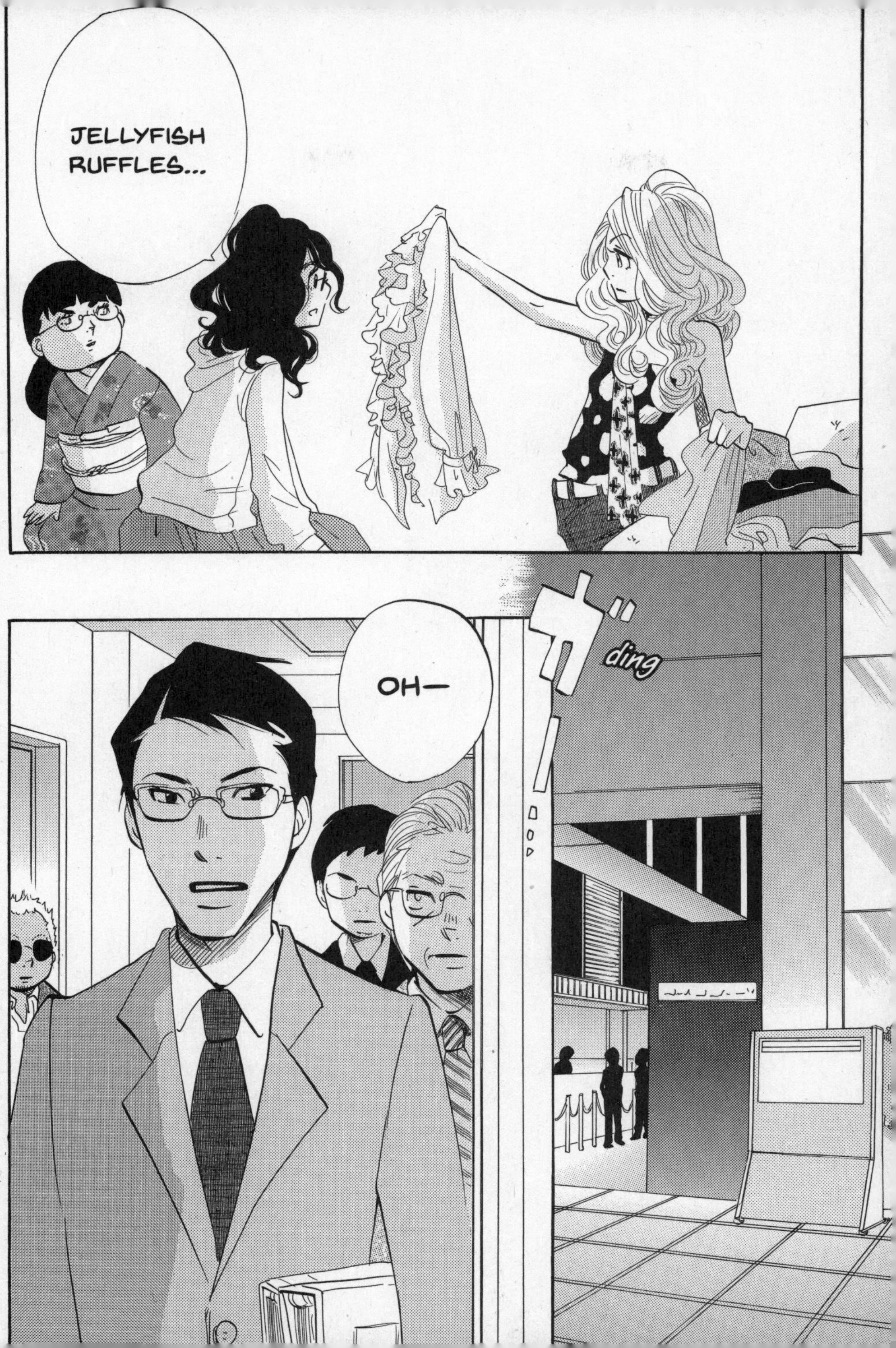
JELLYFISH RUFFLES...
ding
OH—

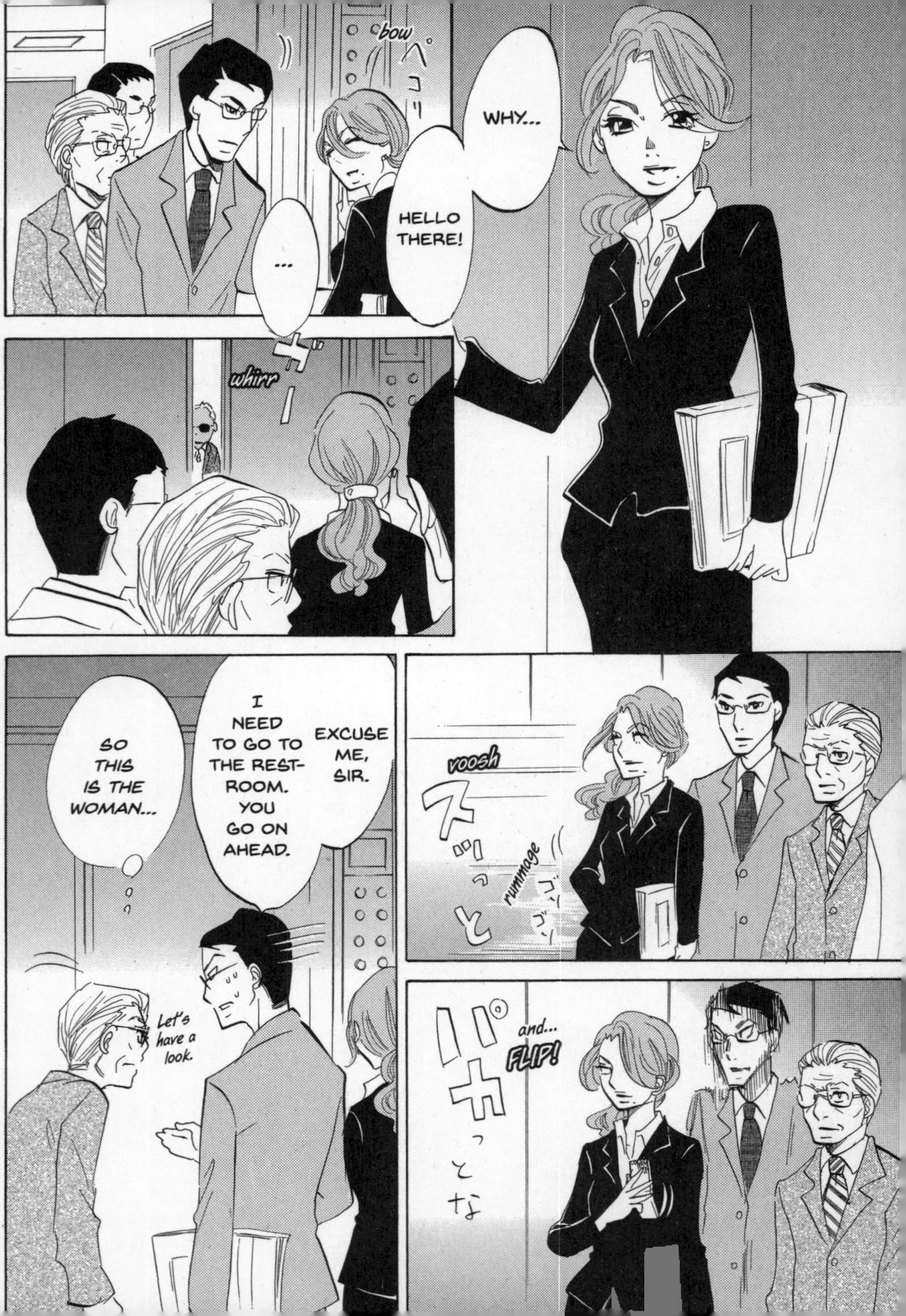
WHY...
HELLO THERE!
bow
...
whirr
voosh
rummage
and...
FLIP!
EXCUSE ME, SIR.
I NEED TO GO TO THE REST-ROOM. YOU GO ON AHEAD.
SO THIS IS THE WOMAN...
Let's have a look.

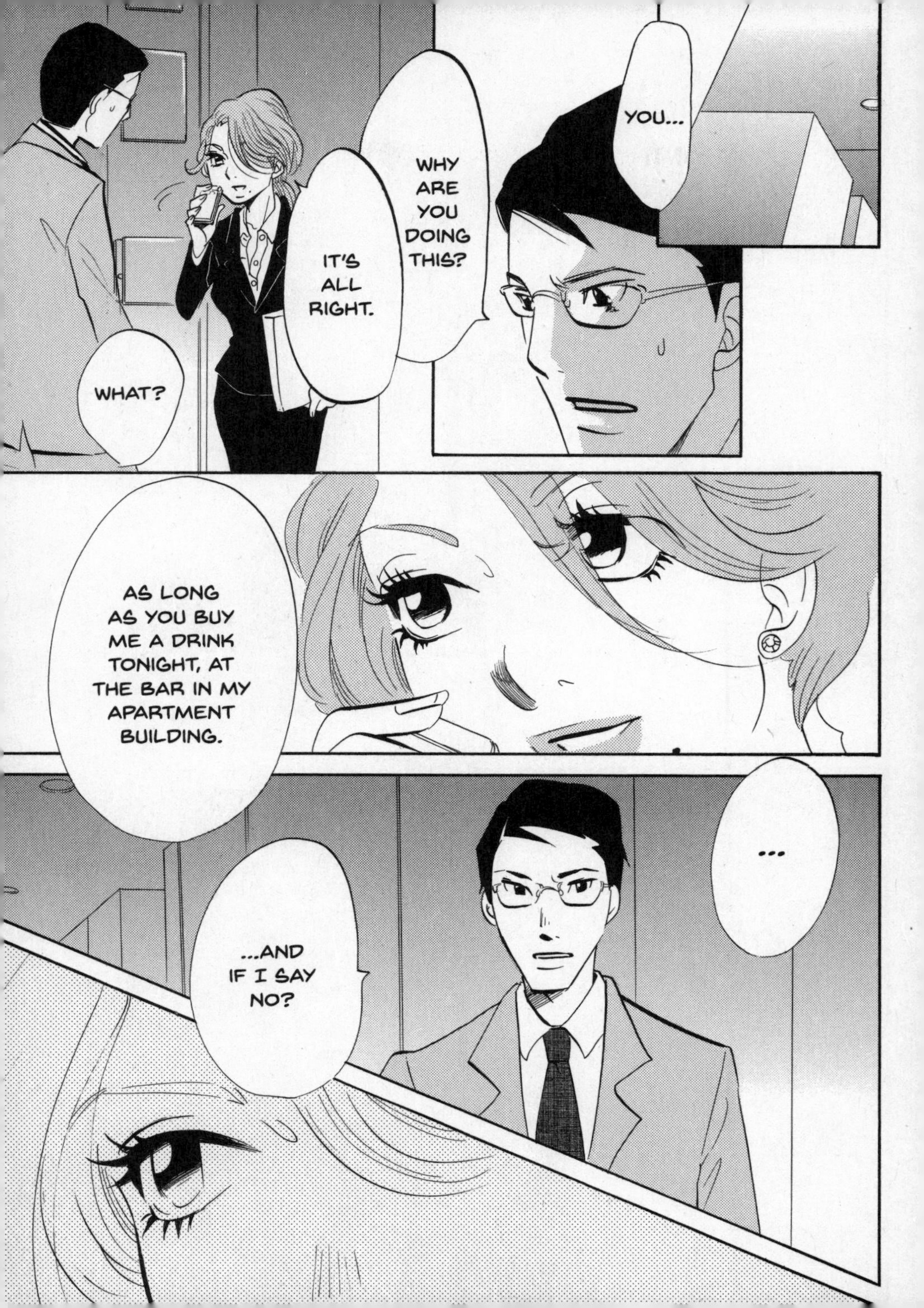
YOU...
WHY ARE YOU DOING THIS?
IT'S ALL RIGHT.
WHAT?
AS LONG AS YOU BUY ME A DRINK TONIGHT, AT THE BAR IN MY APARTMENT BUILDING.
...
...AND IF I SAY NO?

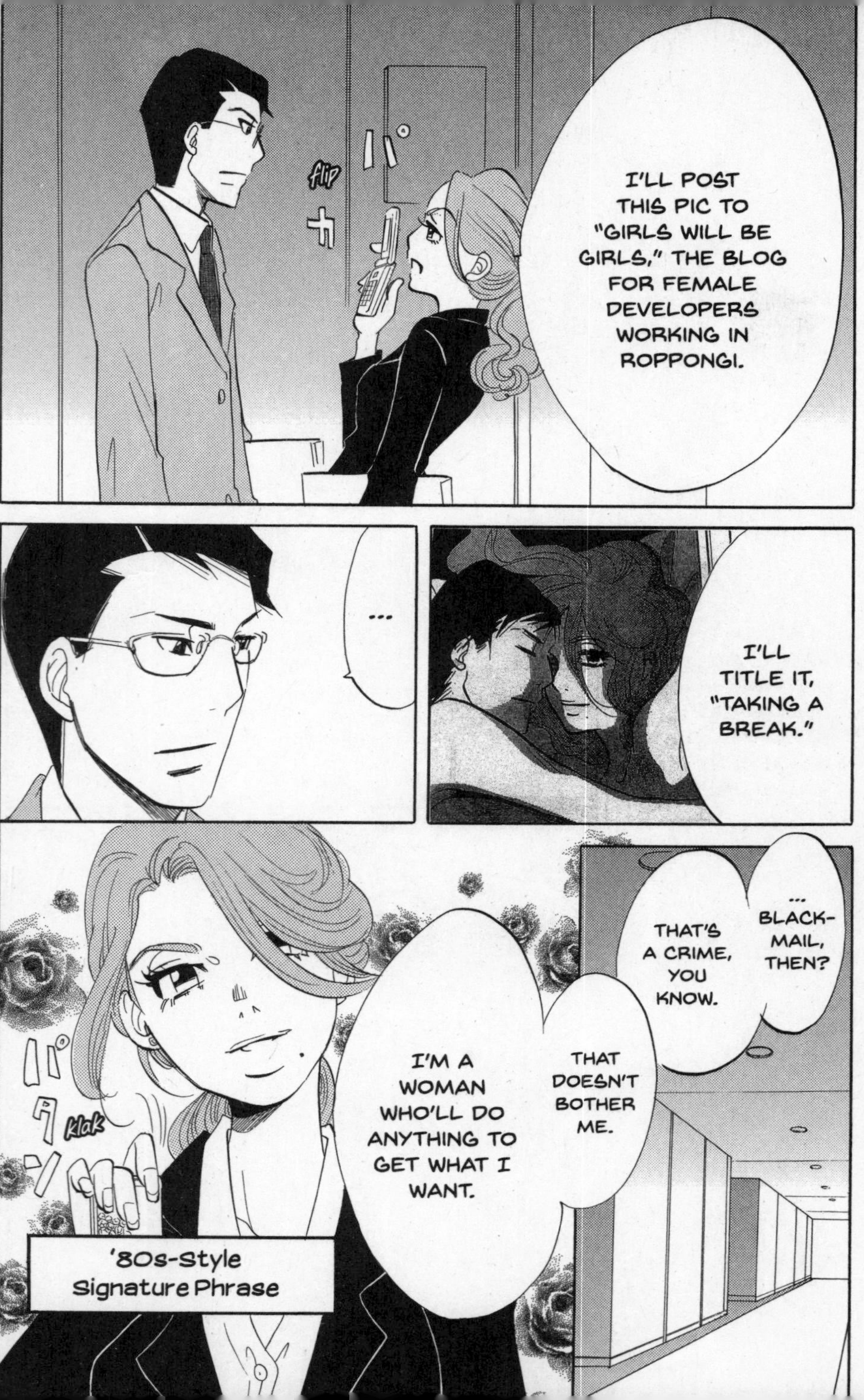
flip
I'LL POST THIS PIC TO "GIRLS WILL BE GIRLS," THE BLOG FOR FEMALE DEVELOPERS WORKING IN ROPPONGI.
I'LL TITLE IT, "TAKING A BREAK."
...
... BLACK-MAIL, THEN?
THAT'S A CRIME, YOU KNOW.
THAT DOESN'T BOTHER ME.
I'M A WOMAN WHO'LL DO ANYTHING TO GET WHAT I WANT.
klak
'80s-Style Signature Phrase

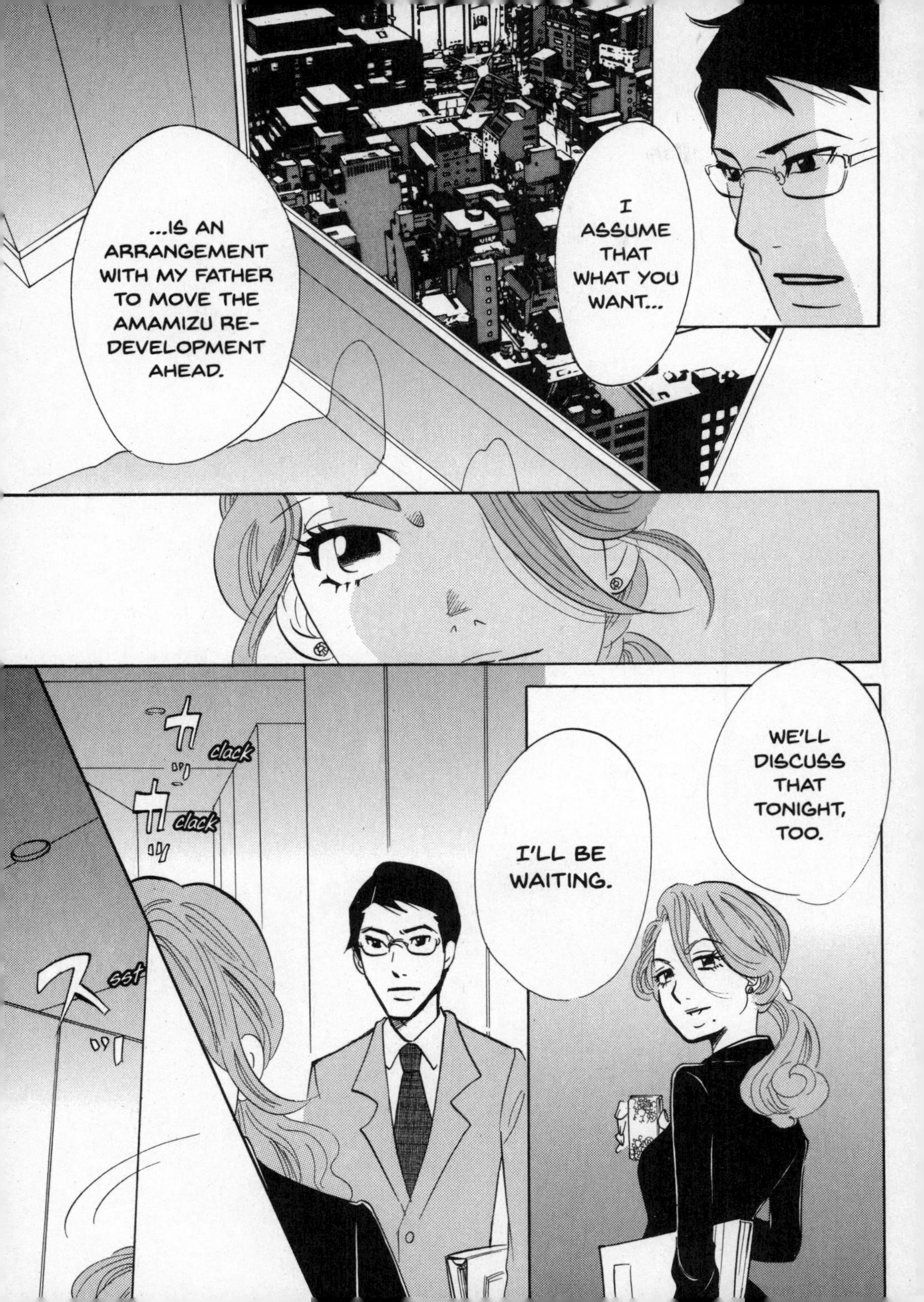
I ASSUME THAT WHAT YOU WANT...
...IS AN ARRANGEMENT WITH MY FATHER TO MOVE THE AMAMIZU RE-DEVELOPMENT AHEAD.
WE'LL DISCUSS THAT TONIGHT, TOO.
I'LL BE WAITING.
clack
clack
sst

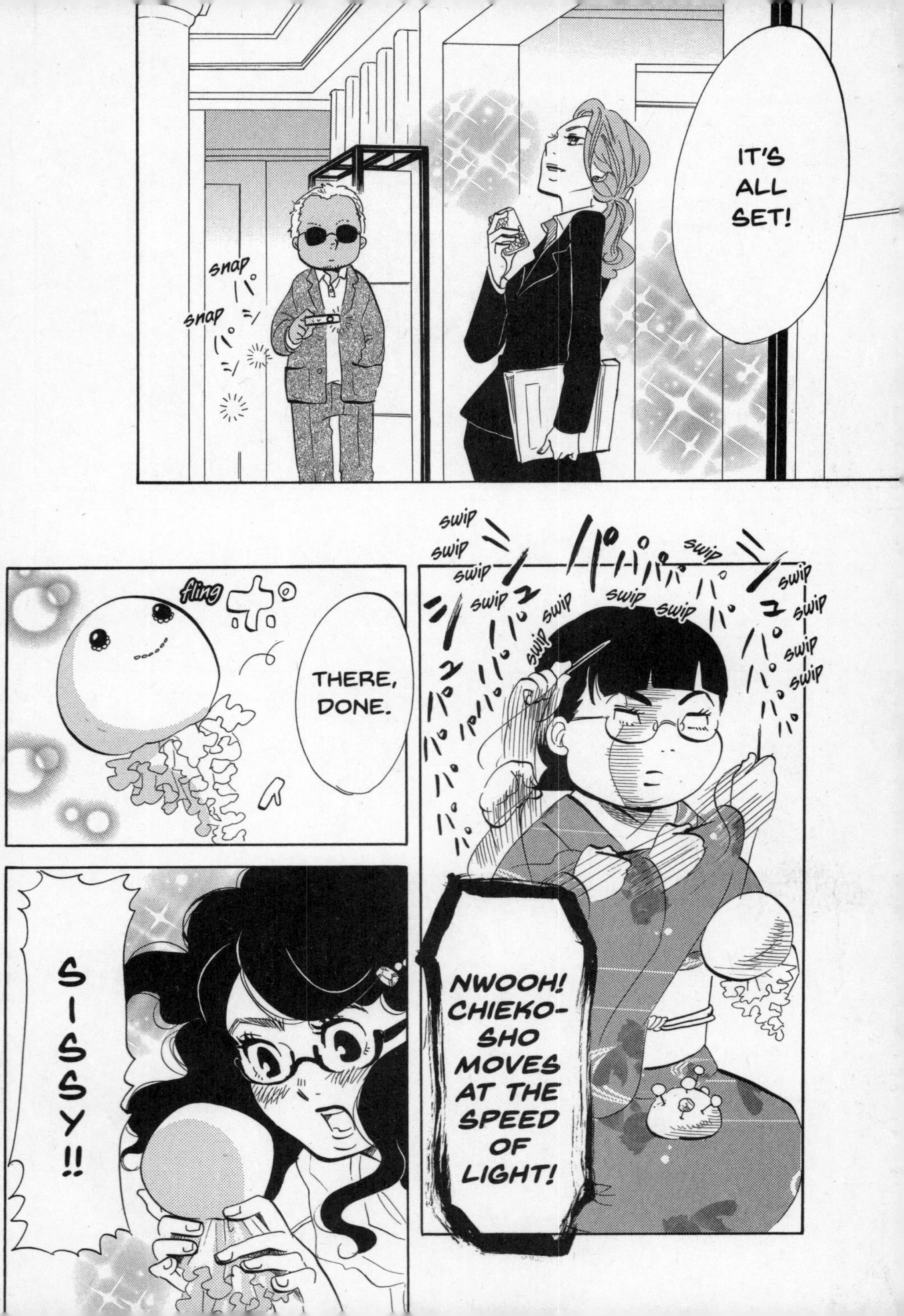
IT'S ALL SET!
snap
snap
swip swip swip swip swip swip swip swip swip swip swip swip swip
NWOOH! CHIEKO-SHO MOVES AT THE SPEED OF LIGHT!
fling
THERE, DONE.
SISSY!!

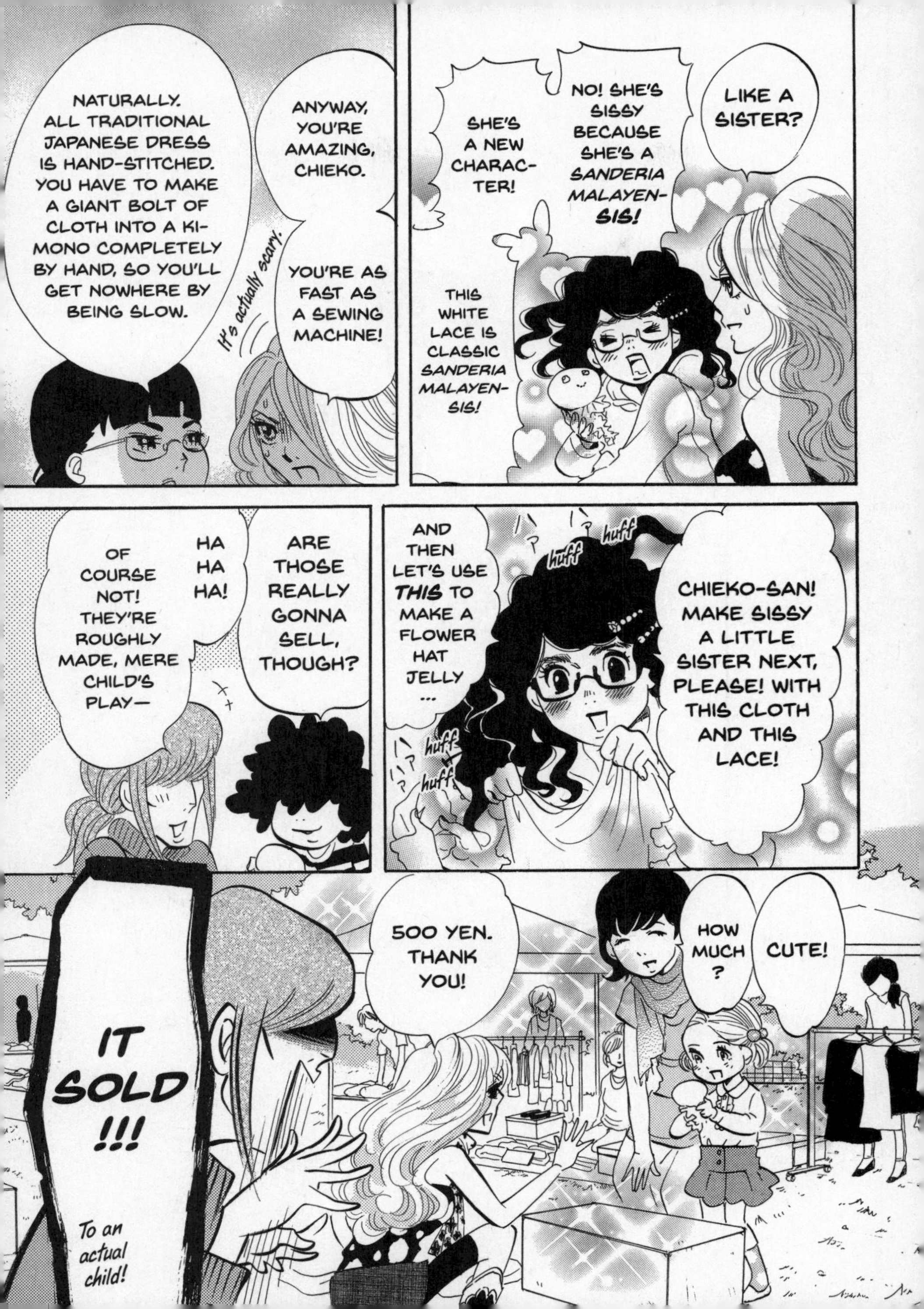
LIKE A SISTER?
NO! SHE'S SISSY BECAUSE SHE'S A SANDERIA MALAYENSIS!
SHE'S A NEW CHARACTER!
THIS WHITE LACE IS CLASSIC SANDERIA MALAYENSIS!
ANYWAY, YOU'RE AMAZING, CHIEKO.
YOU'RE AS FAST AS A SEWING MACHINE!
It's actually scary.
NATURALLY. ALL TRADITIONAL JAPANESE DRESS IS HAND-STITCHED. YOU HAVE TO MAKE A GIANT BOLT OF CLOTH INTO A KIMONO COMPLETELY BY HAND, SO YOU'LL GET NOWHERE BY BEING SLOW.
huff huff
CHIEKO-SAN! MAKE SISSY A LITTLE SISTER NEXT, PLEASE! WITH THIS CLOTH AND THIS LACE!
AND THEN LET'S USE THIS TO MAKE A FLOWER HAT JELLY ...
huff huff
ARE THOSE REALLY GONNA SELL, THOUGH?
HA HA HA!
OF COURSE NOT! THEY'RE ROUGHLY MADE, MERE CHILD'S PLAY—
CUTE!
HOW MUCH?
500 YEN. THANK YOU!
IT SOLD!!!
To an actual child!

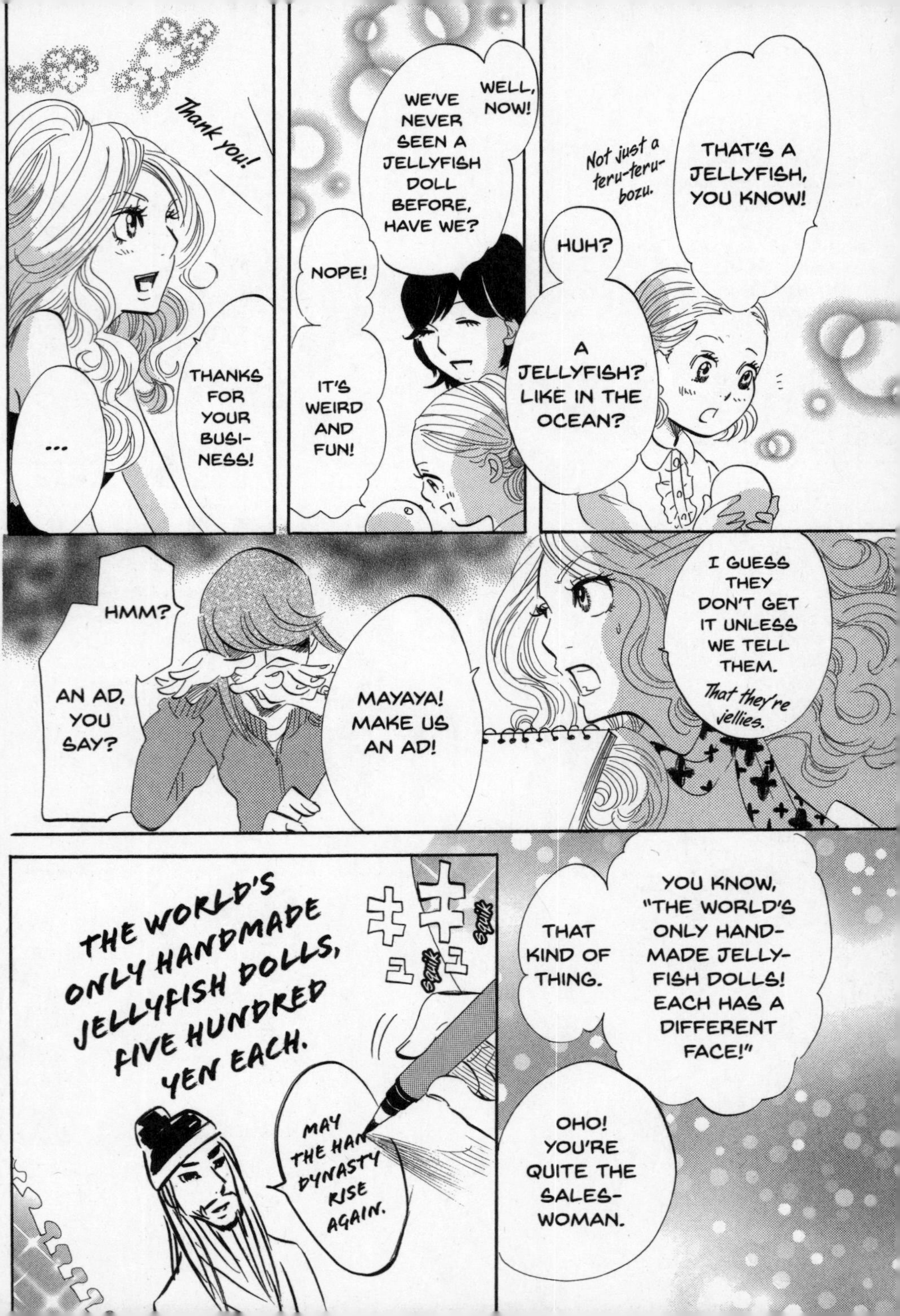
THAT'S A JELLYFISH, YOU KNOW!
Not just a teru-teru-bozu.
HUH?
A JELLYFISH? LIKE IN THE OCEAN?
WELL, NOW!
WE'VE NEVER SEEN A JELLYFISH DOLL BEFORE, HAVE WE?
NOPE!
IT'S WEIRD AND FUN!
Thank you!
THANKS FOR YOUR BUSINESS!
...
I GUESS THEY DON'T GET IT UNLESS WE TELL THEM.
That they're jellies.
MAYAYA! MAKE US AN AD!
HMM?
AN AD, YOU SAY?
YOU KNOW, "THE WORLD'S ONLY HANDMADE JELLYFISH DOLLS! EACH HAS A DIFFERENT FACE!"
THAT KIND OF THING.
OHO! YOU'RE QUITE THE SALESWOMAN.
squik
squik
THE WORLD'S ONLY HANDMADE JELLYFISH DOLLS, FIVE HUNDRED YEN EACH.
MAY THE HAN DYNASTY RISE AGAIN.

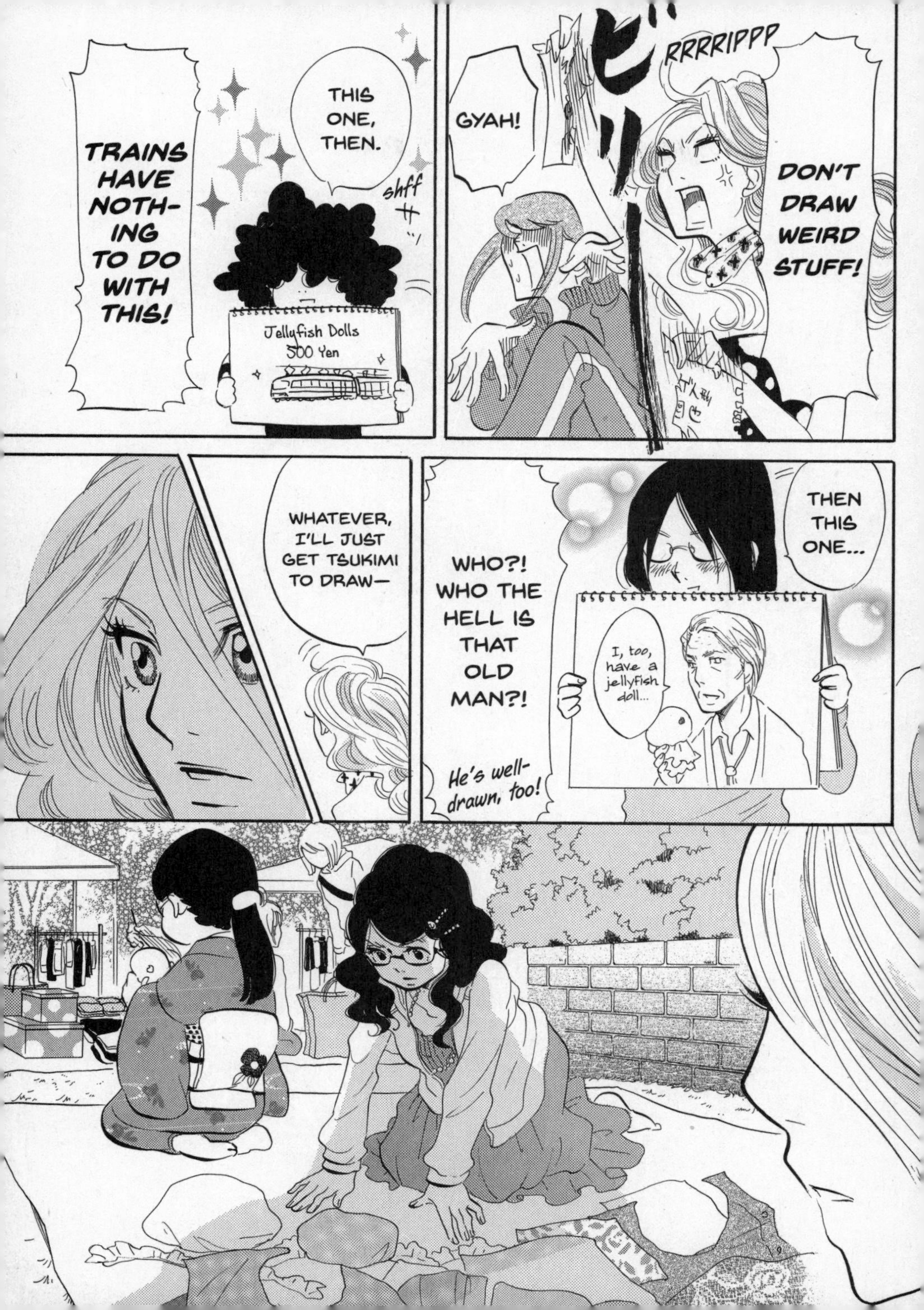
RRRRIPPP
DON'T DRAW WEIRD STUFF!
GYAH!
THIS ONE, THEN.
shff
Jellyfish Dolls
500 Yen
TRAINS HAVE NOTH-ING TO DO WITH THIS!
THEN THIS ONE...
I, too, have a jellyfish doll...
WHO?! WHO THE HELL IS THAT OLD MAN?!
He's well-drawn, too!
WHATEVER, I'LL JUST GET TSUKIMI TO DRAW—

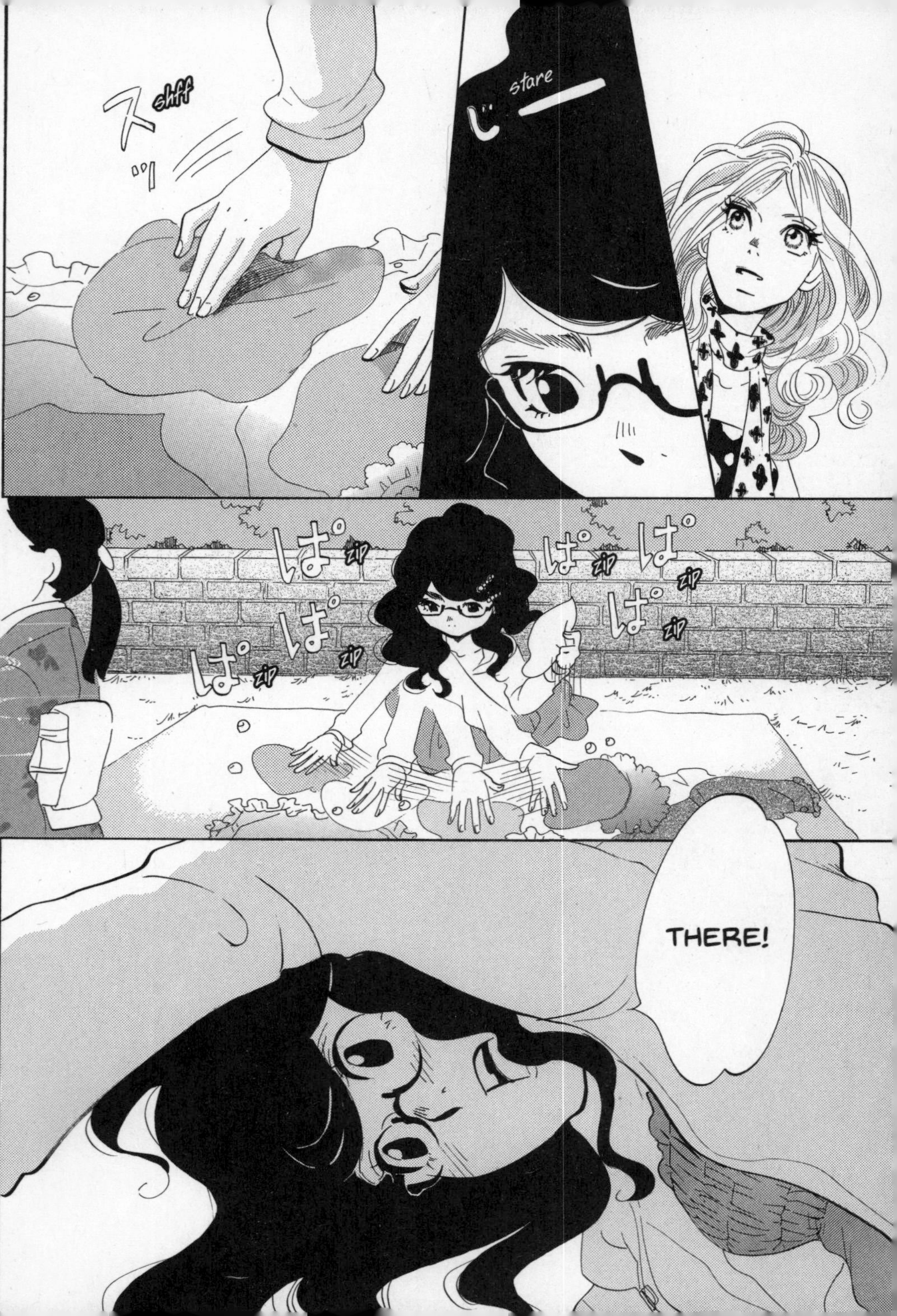

じー
stare
スッ
shff
ぱ
zip
ぱ
zip
ぱ
zip
ぱ
zip
ぱ
zip
ぱ
zip
THERE!

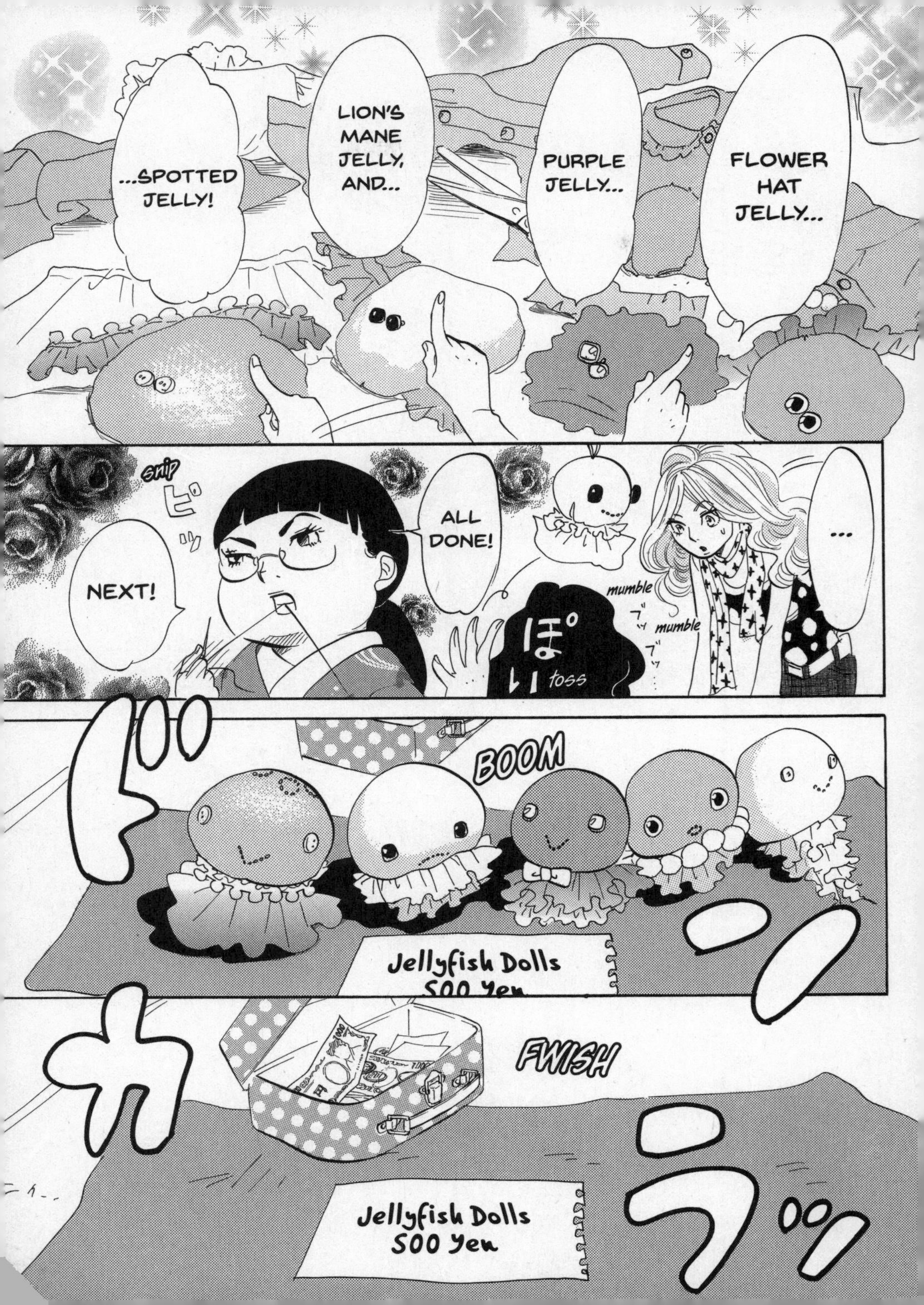

FLOWER HAT JELLY...
PURPLE JELLY...
LION'S MANE JELLY, AND...
...SPOTTED JELLY!
...
mumble
mumble
toss
ぽい
ALL DONE!
NEXT!
snip
BOOM
Jellyfish Dolls 500 Yen
FWISH
Jellyfish Dolls 500 Yen

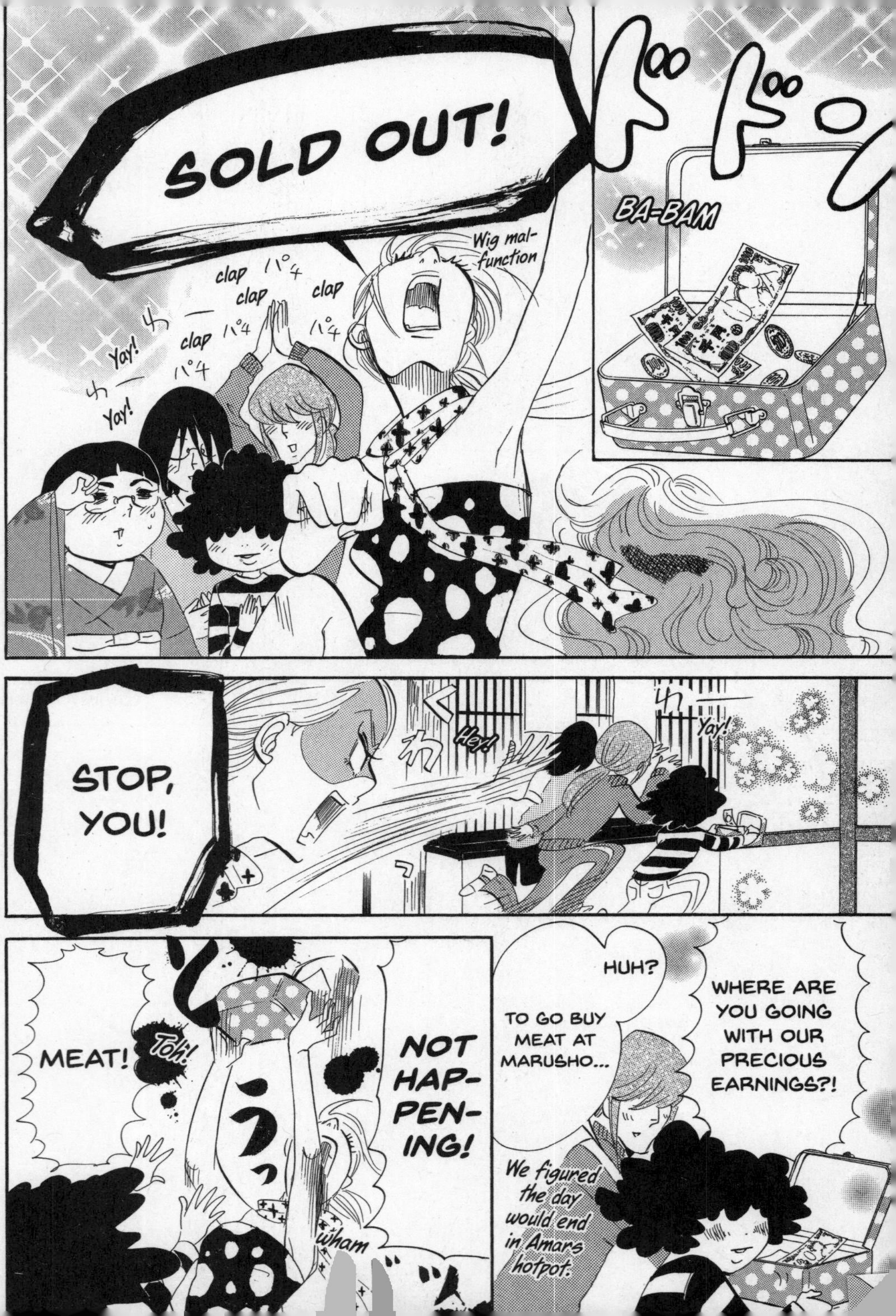
BA-BAM
SOLD OUT!
Wig mal-function
clap
clap
clap
clap
Yay!
Yay!
STOP, YOU!
Hey!
Yay!
WHERE ARE YOU GOING WITH OUR PRECIOUS EARNINGS?!
HUH?
TO GO BUY MEAT AT MARUSHO...
We figured the day would end in Amars hotpot.
NOT HAP-PEN-ING!
MEAT!
Toh!
wham

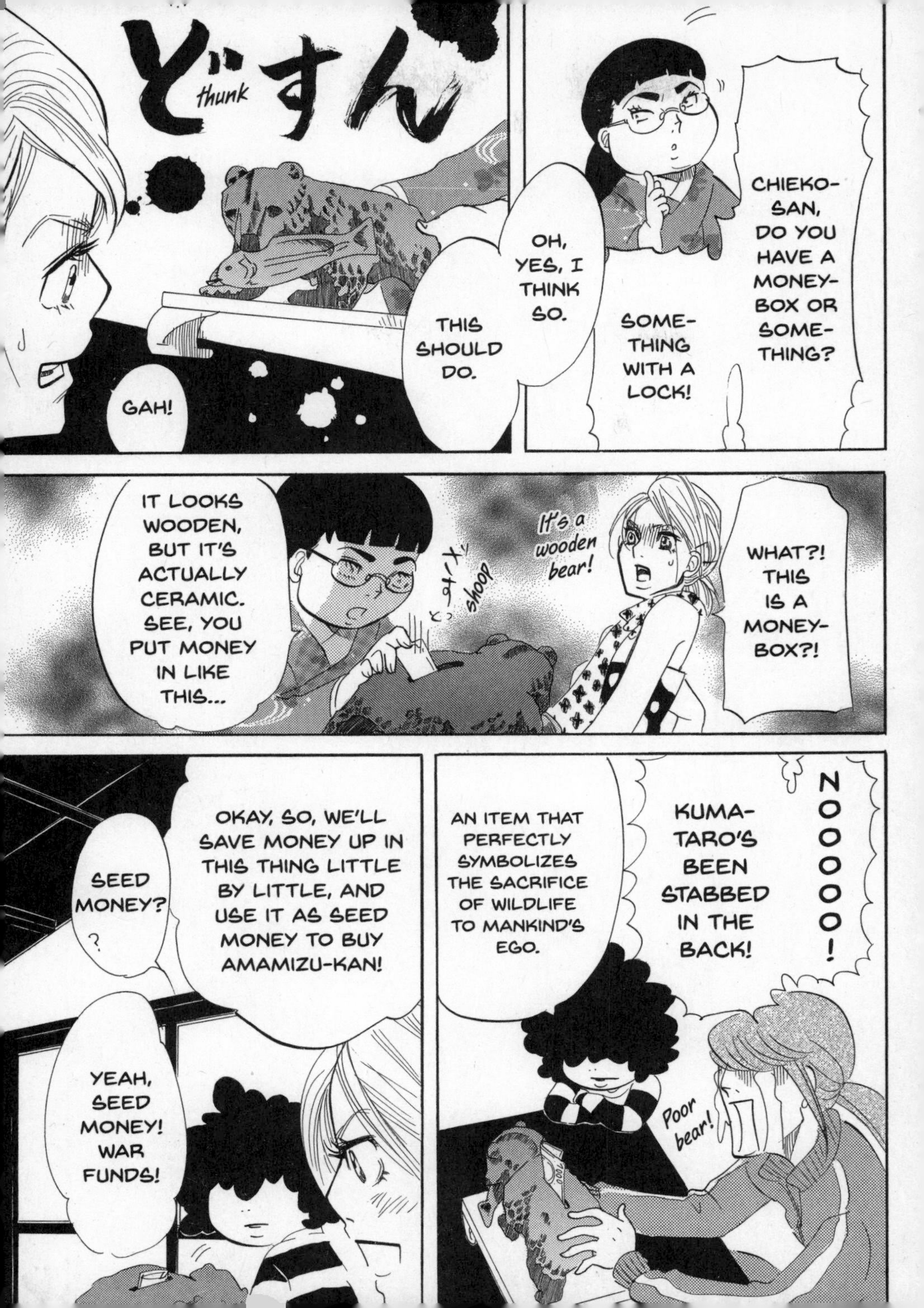
CHIEKO-SAN, DO YOU HAVE A MONEY-BOX OR SOME-THING?
SOME-THING WITH A LOCK!
OH, YES, I THINK SO.
どすん
thunk
THIS SHOULD DO.
GAH!
WHAT?! THIS IS A MONEY-BOX?!
It's a wooden bear!
shoop
IT LOOKS WOODEN, BUT IT'S ACTUALLY CERAMIC. SEE, YOU PUT MONEY IN LIKE THIS...
NOOOOOO!
KUMA-TARO'S BEEN STABBED IN THE BACK!
AN ITEM THAT PERFECTLY SYMBOLIZES THE SACRIFICE OF WILDLIFE TO MANKIND'S EGO.
Poor bear!
OKAY, SO, WE'LL SAVE MONEY UP IN THIS THING LITTLE BY LITTLE, AND USE IT AS SEED MONEY TO BUY AMAMIZU-KAN!
SEED MONEY?
?
YEAH, SEED MONEY! WAR FUNDS!

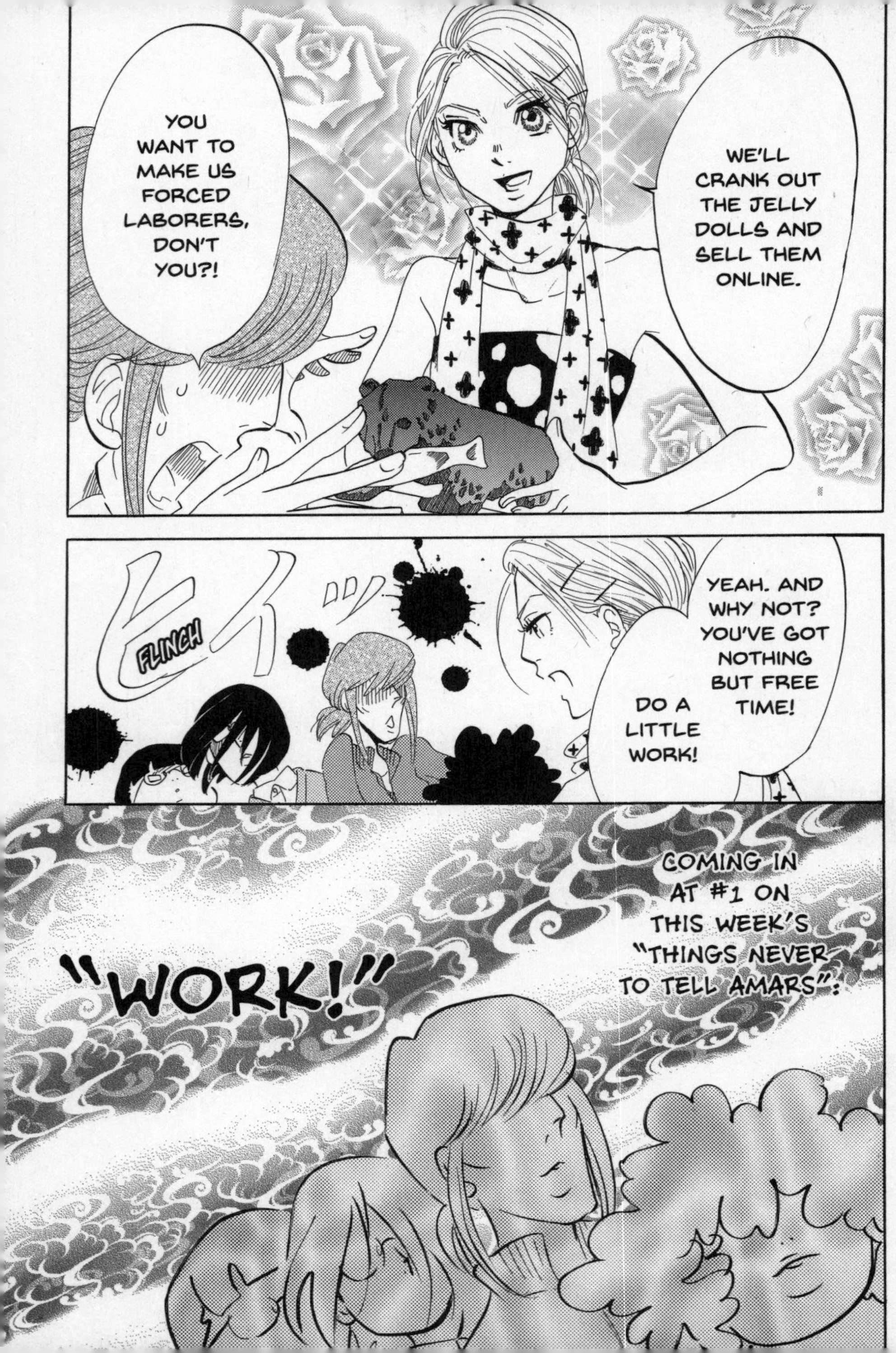
WE'LL CRANK OUT THE JELLY DOLLS AND SELL THEM ONLINE.
YOU WANT TO MAKE US FORCED LABORERS, DON'T YOU?!
YEAH. AND WHY NOT? YOU'VE GOT NOTHING BUT FREE TIME!
DO A LITTLE WORK!
FLINCH
COMING IN AT #1 ON THIS WEEK'S "THINGS NEVER TO TELL AMARS":
"WORK!"

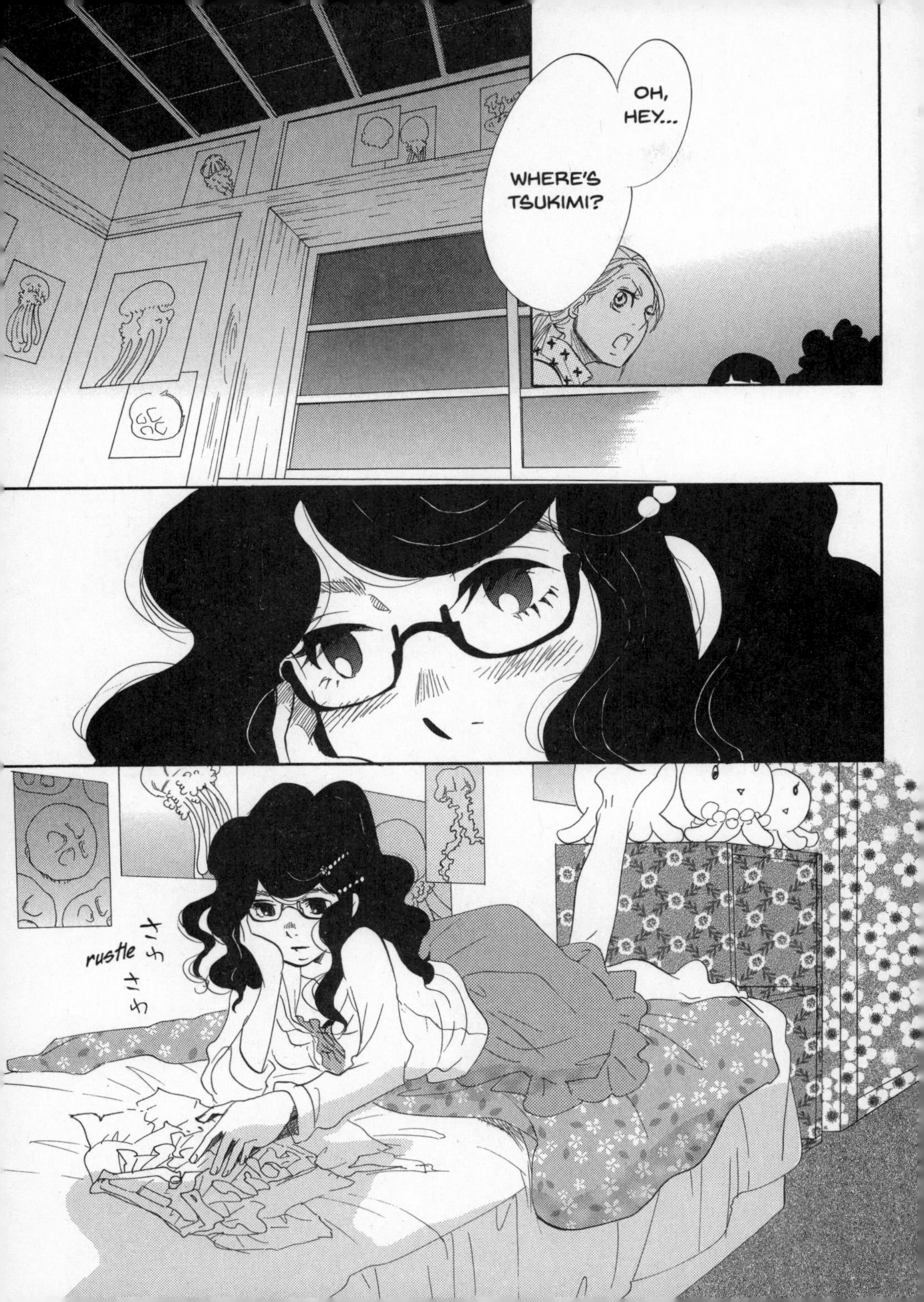
OH, HEY...
WHERE'S TSUKIMI?
さわ さわ
rustle

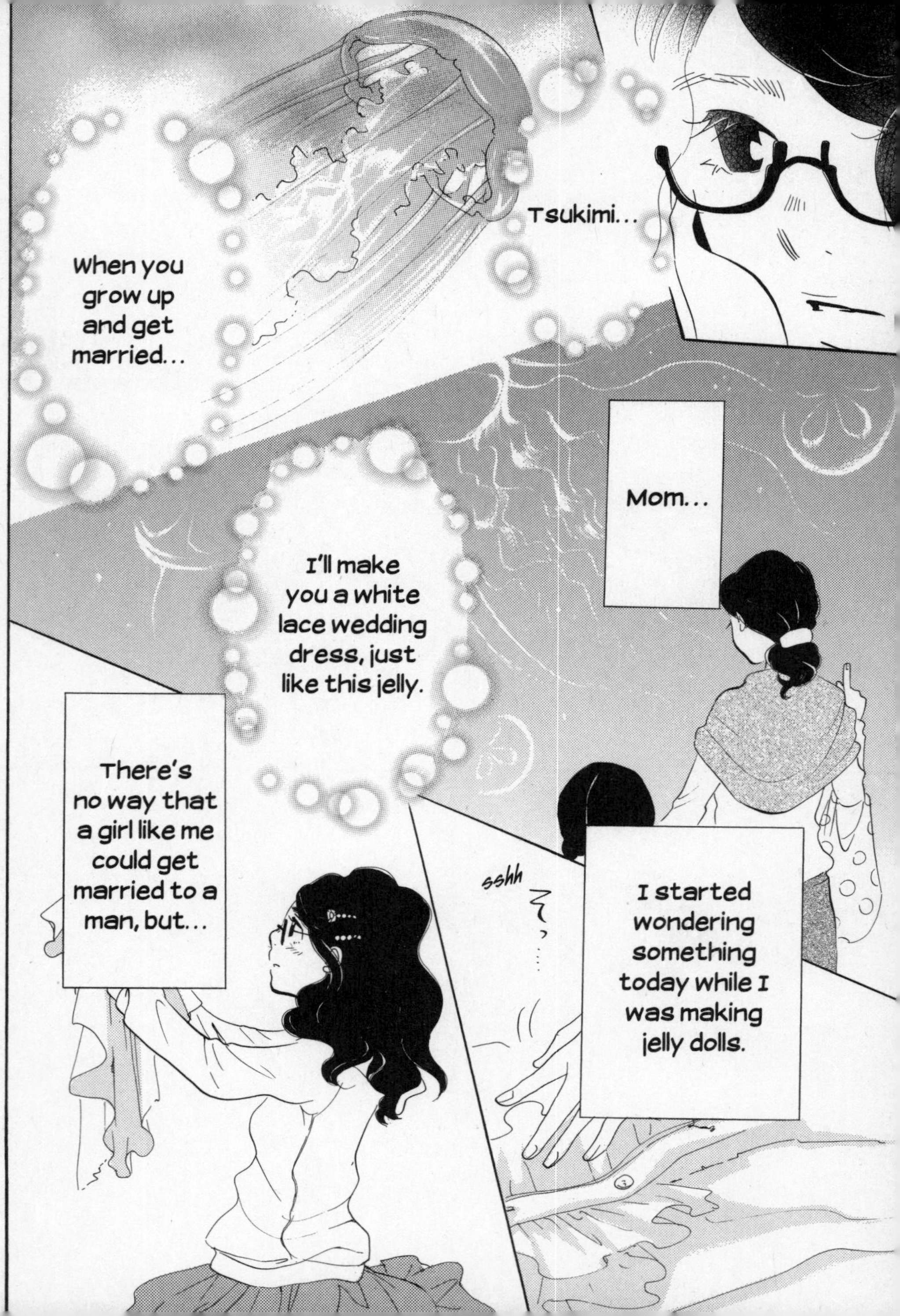
Tsukimi...
When you grow up and get married...
Mom...
I'll make you a white lace wedding dress, just like this jelly.
sshh
I started wondering something today while I was making jelly dolls.
There's no way that a girl like me could get married to a man, but...

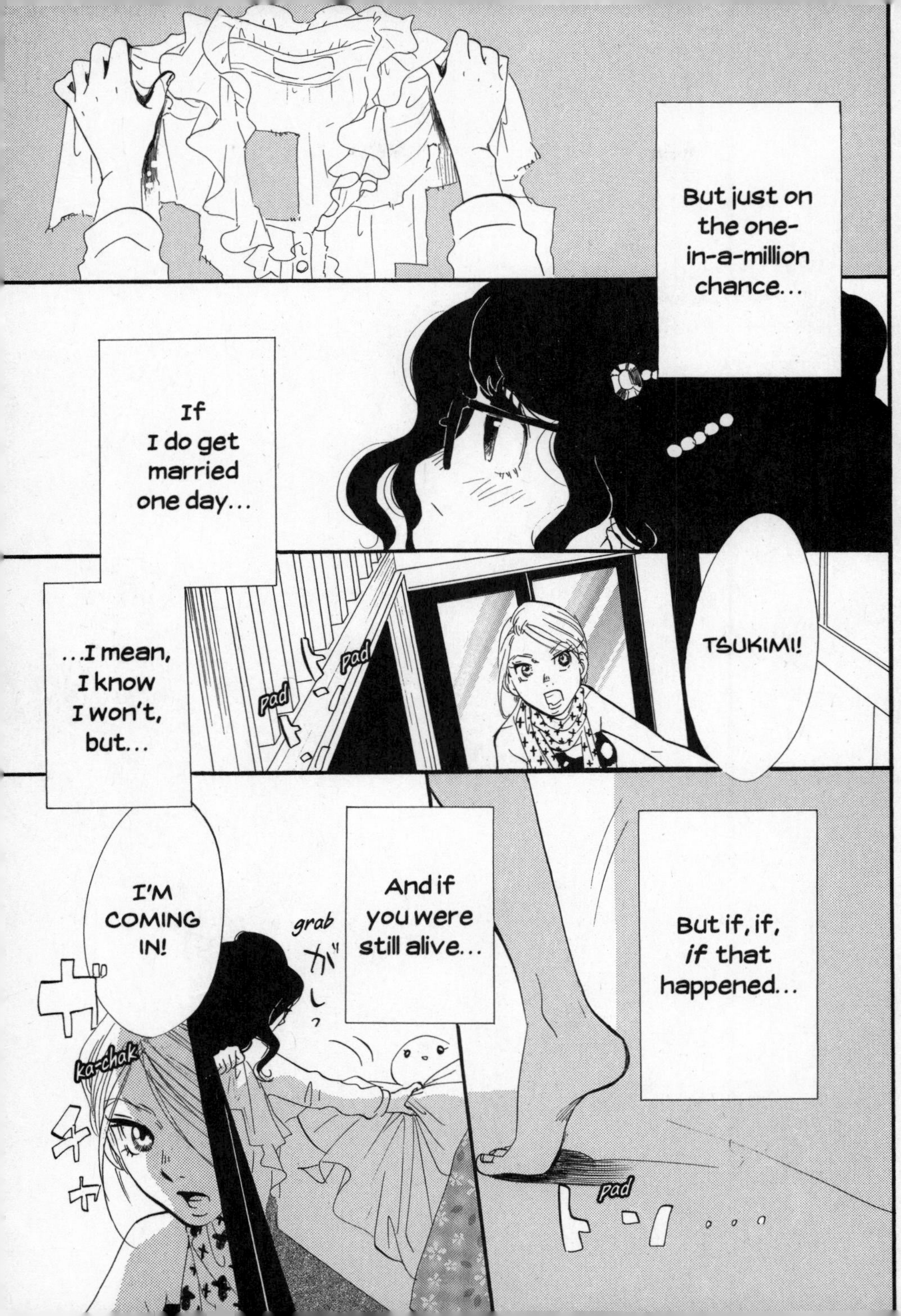
But just on the one-in-a-million chance...
If I do get married one day...
TSUKIMI!
pad
pad
...I mean, I know I won't, but...
But if, if, *if* that happened...
And if you were still alive...
pad
grab
I'M COMING IN!
ka-chak

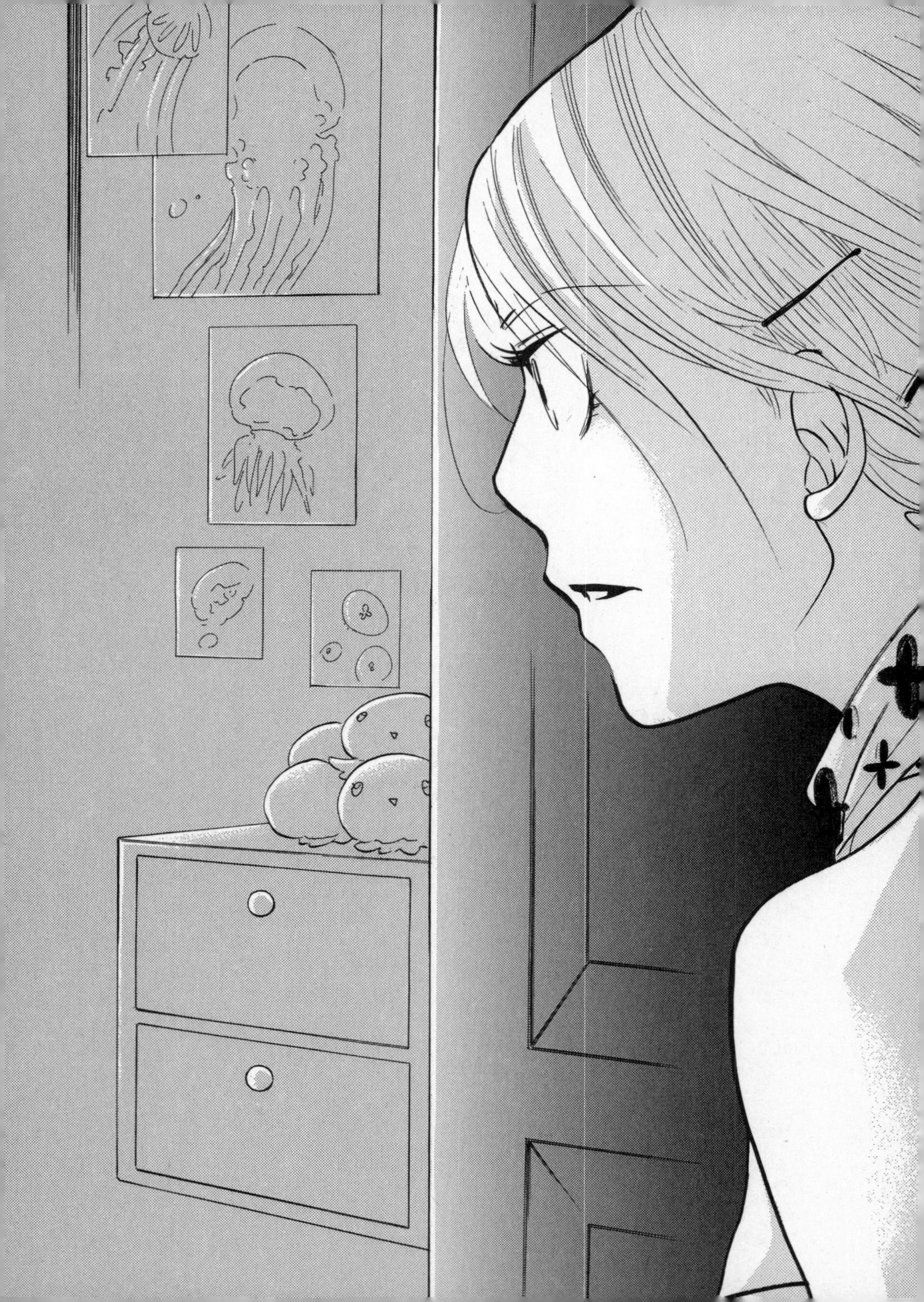

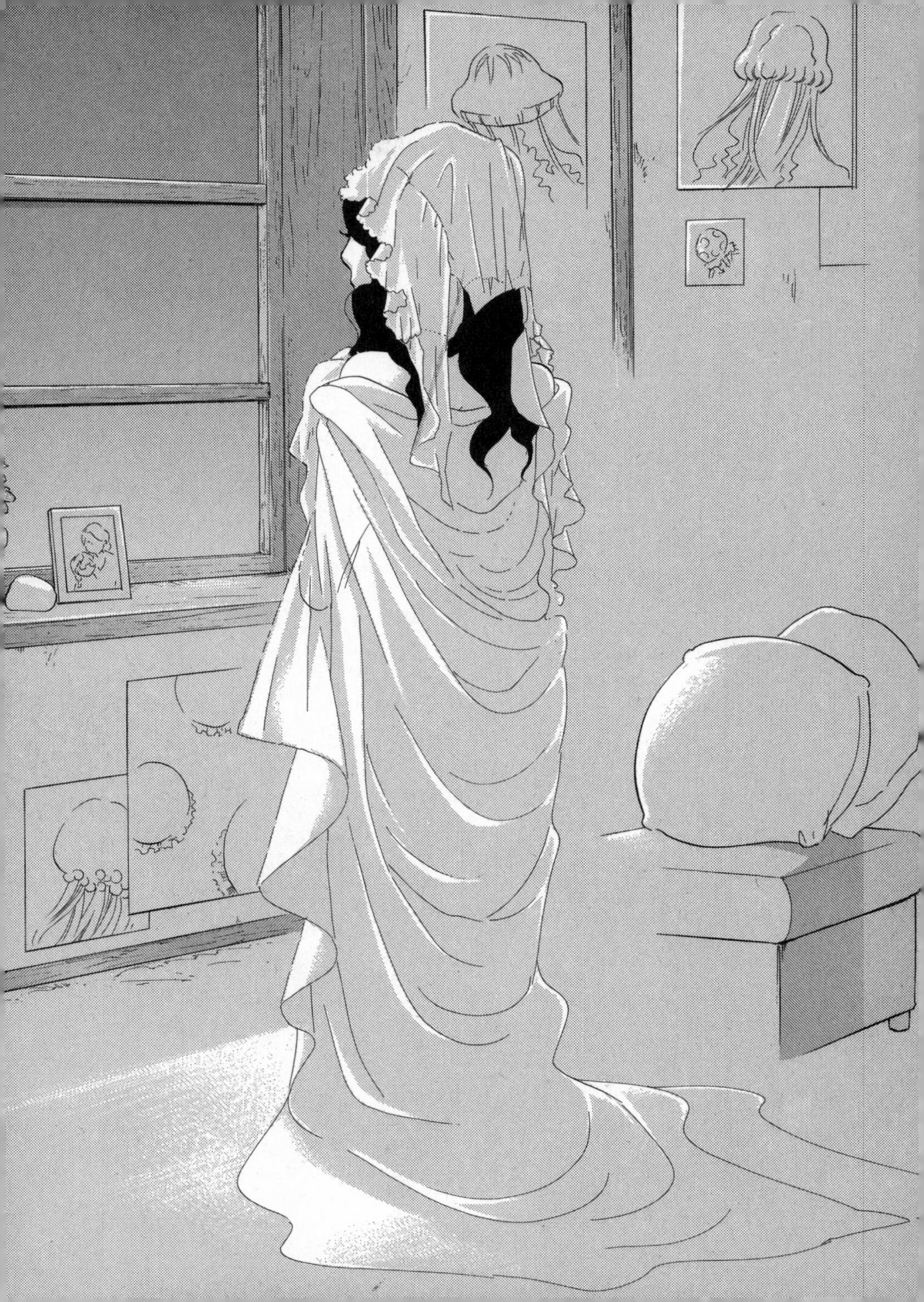

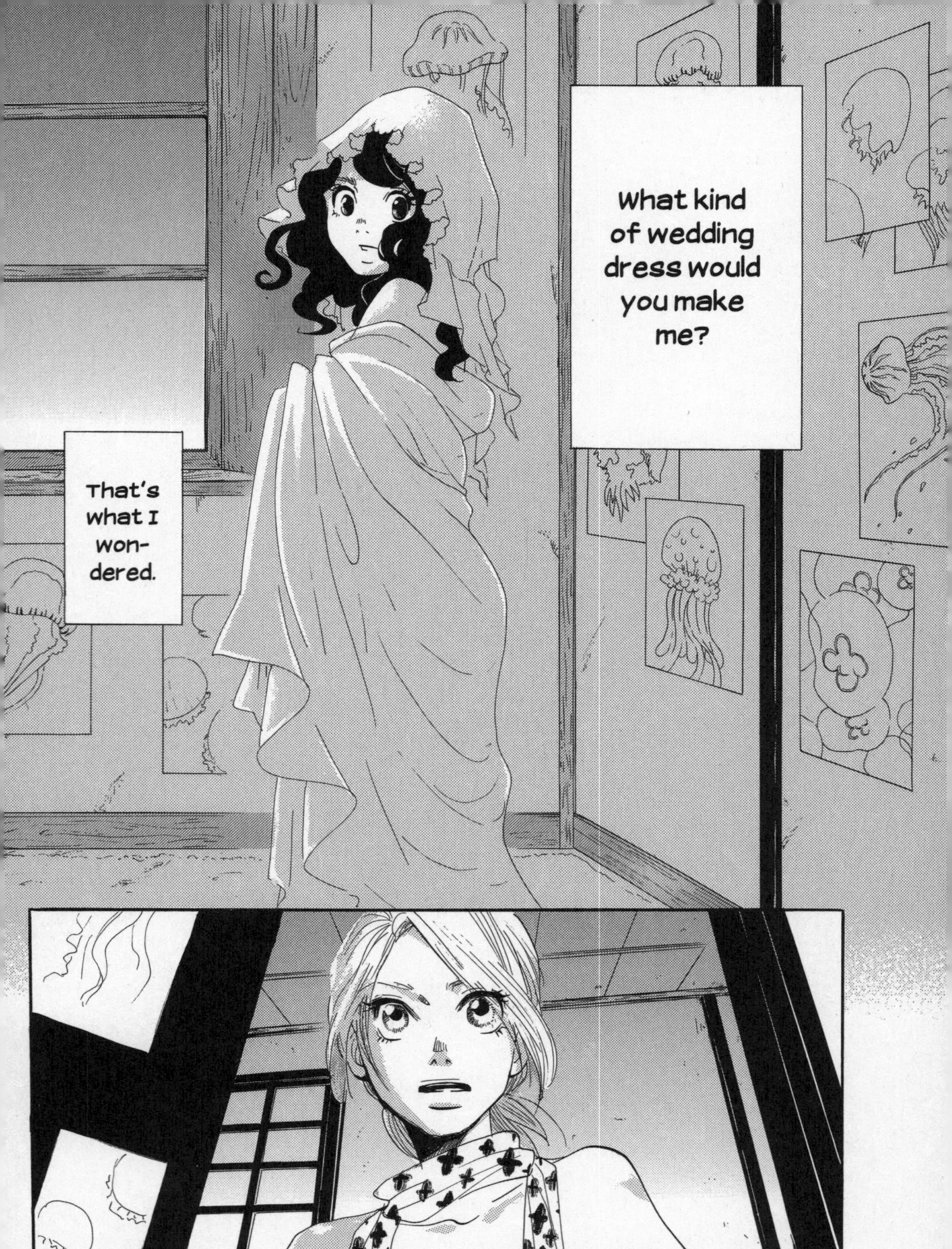
What kind of wedding dress would you make me?
That's what I wondered.

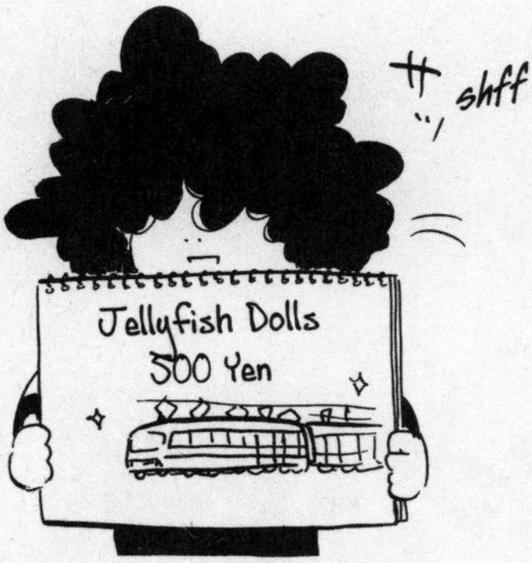
shff
Jellyfish Dolls
500 Yen

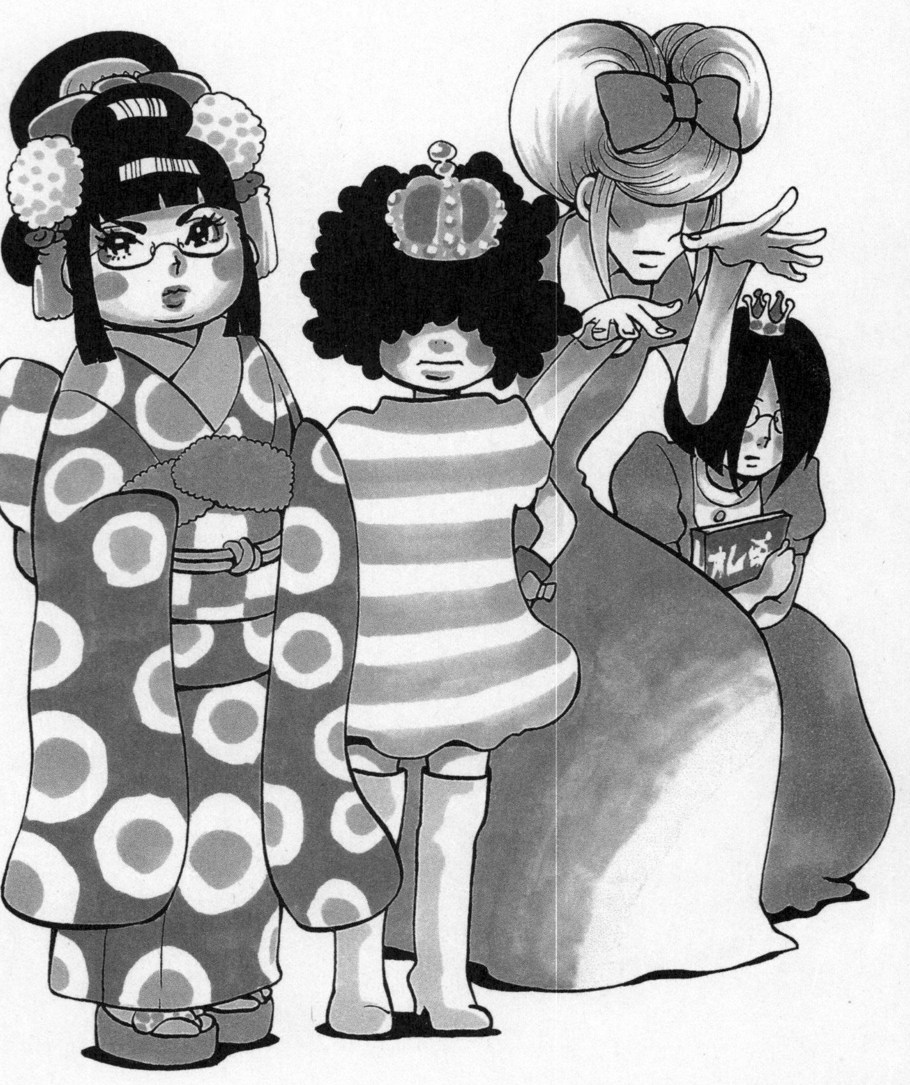

Episode 16
Romeo & Juliet?

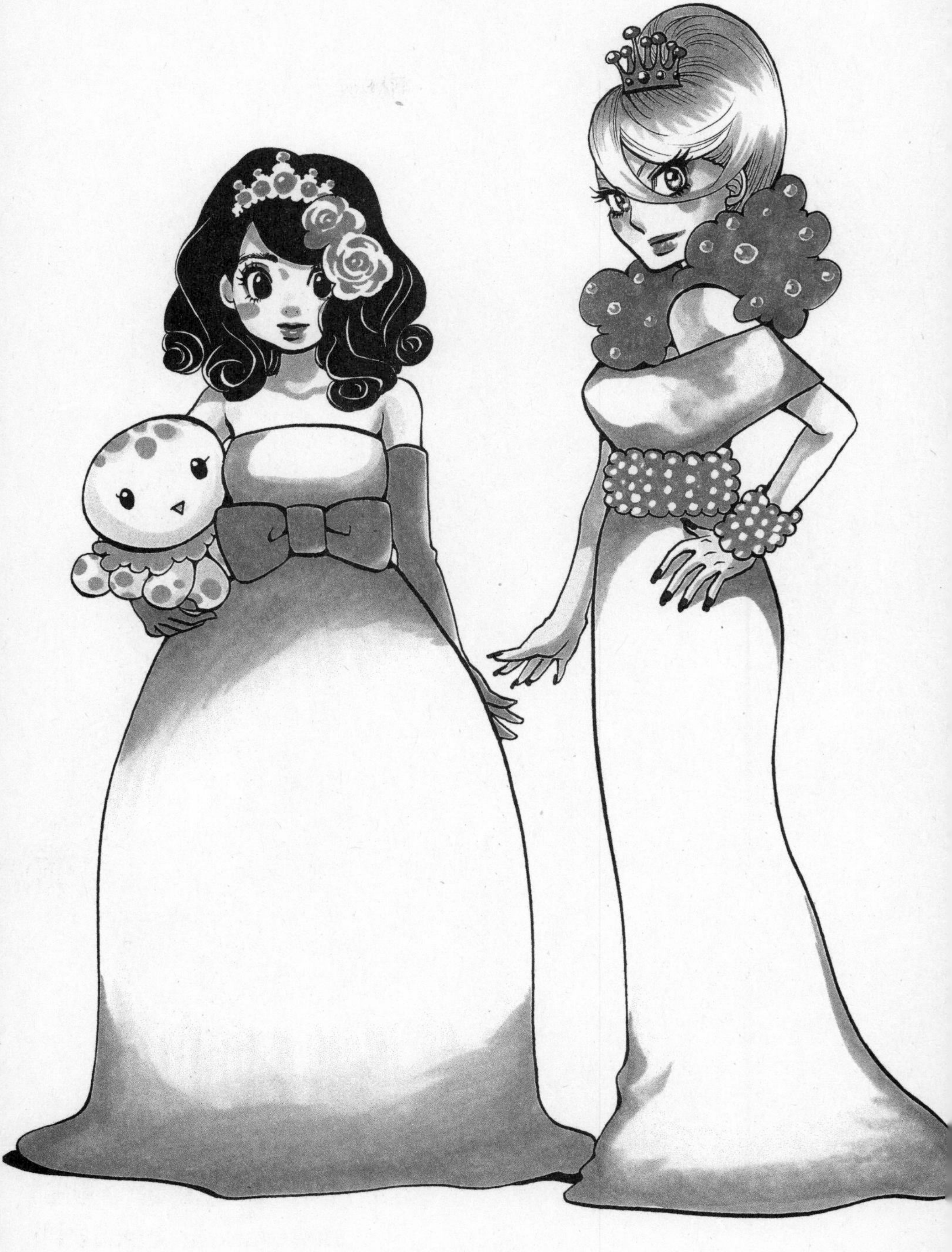

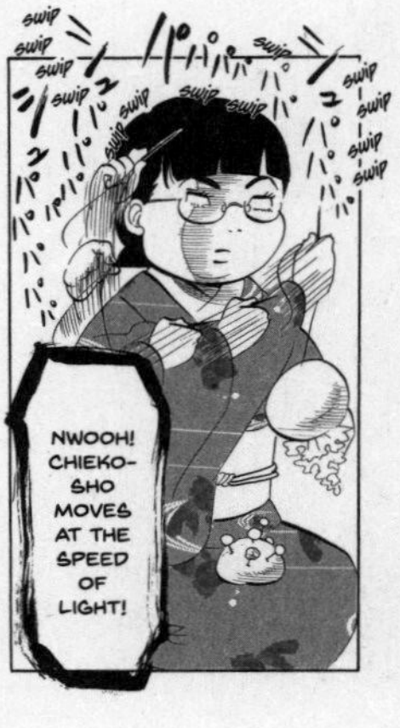
swip swip swip
swip
swip swip
swip swip swip
NWOOH! CHIEKO-SHO MOVES AT THE SPEED OF LIGHT!

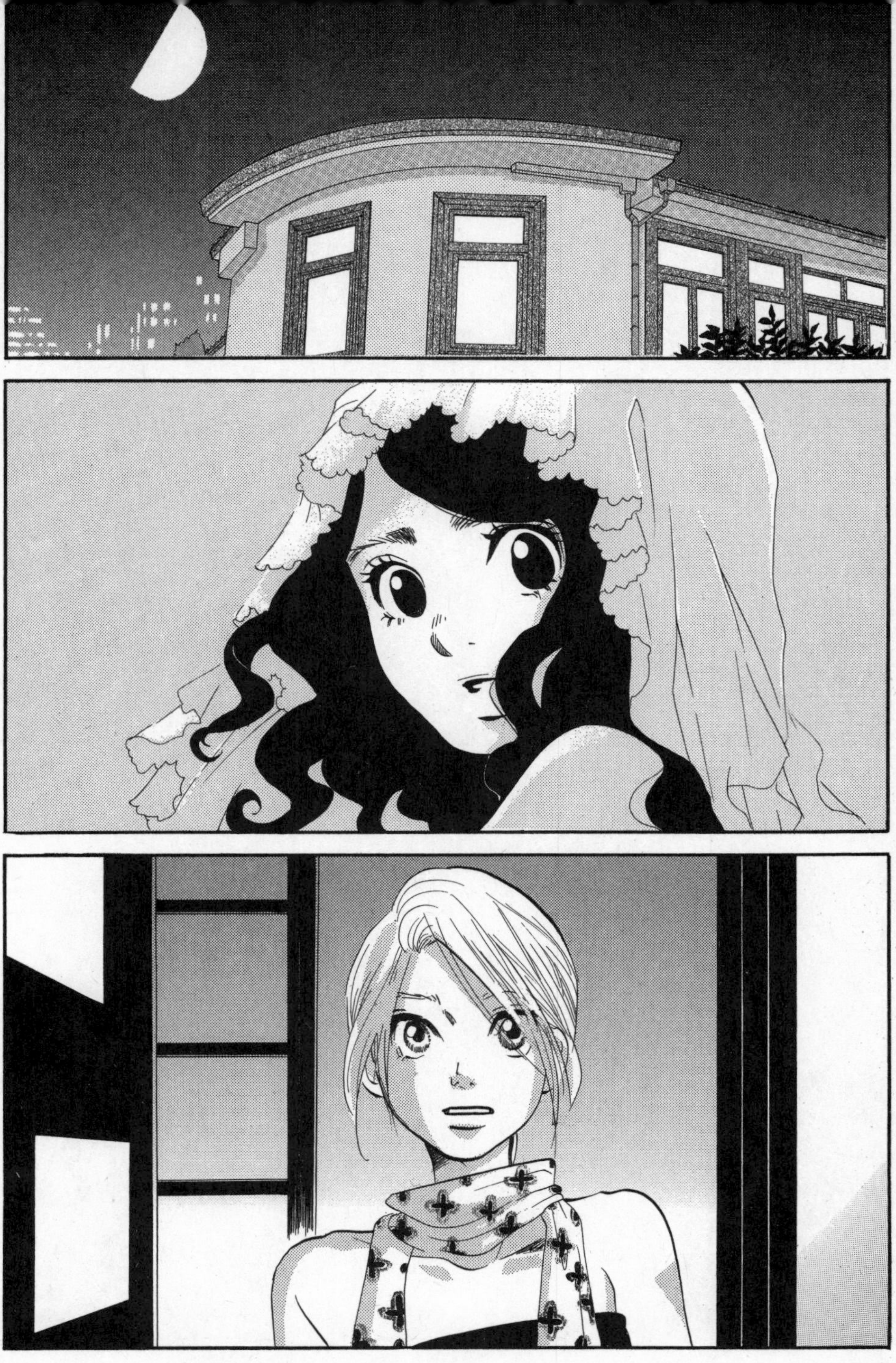

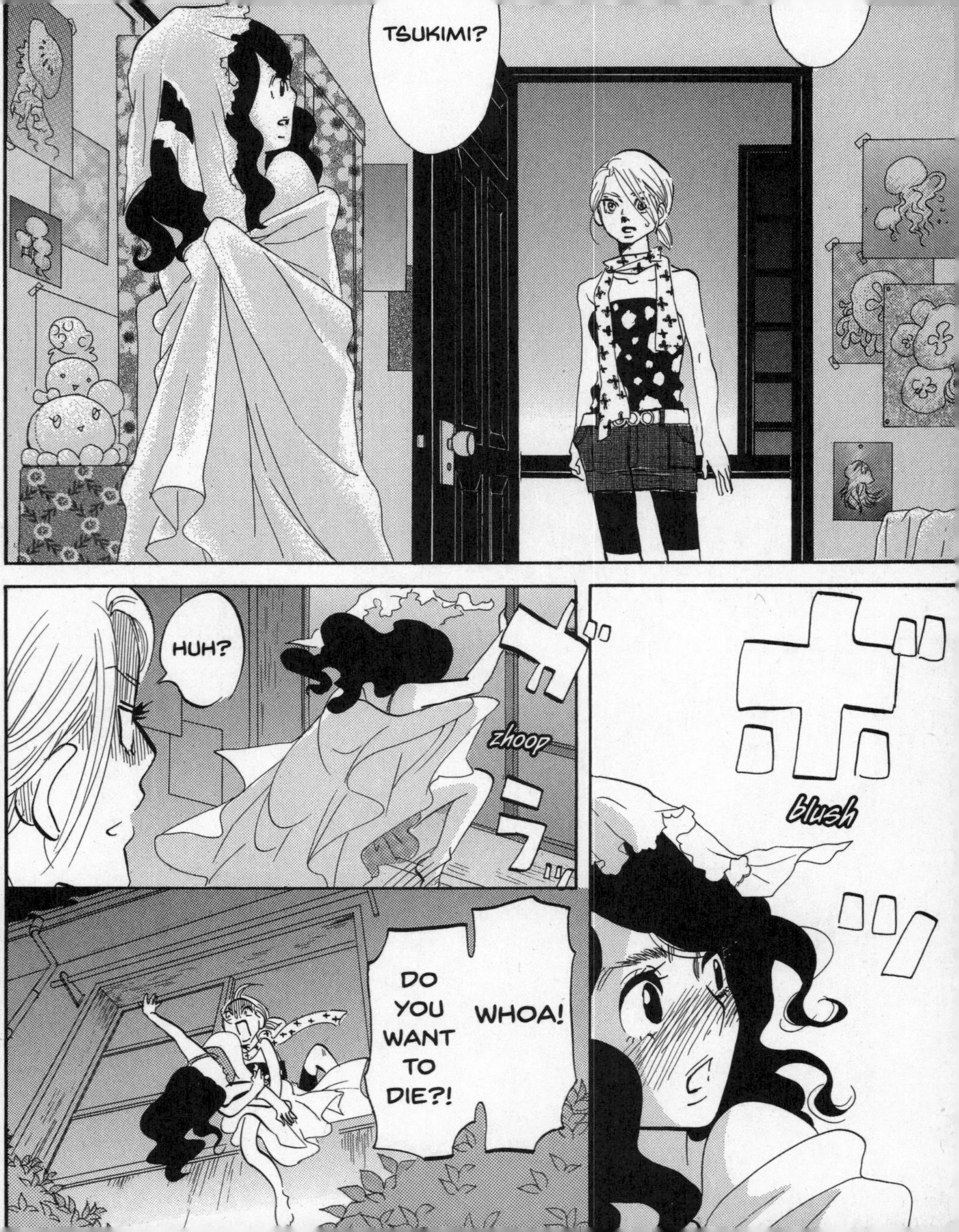
TSUKIMI?
blush
HUH?
zhoop
WHOA!
DO YOU WANT TO DIE?!

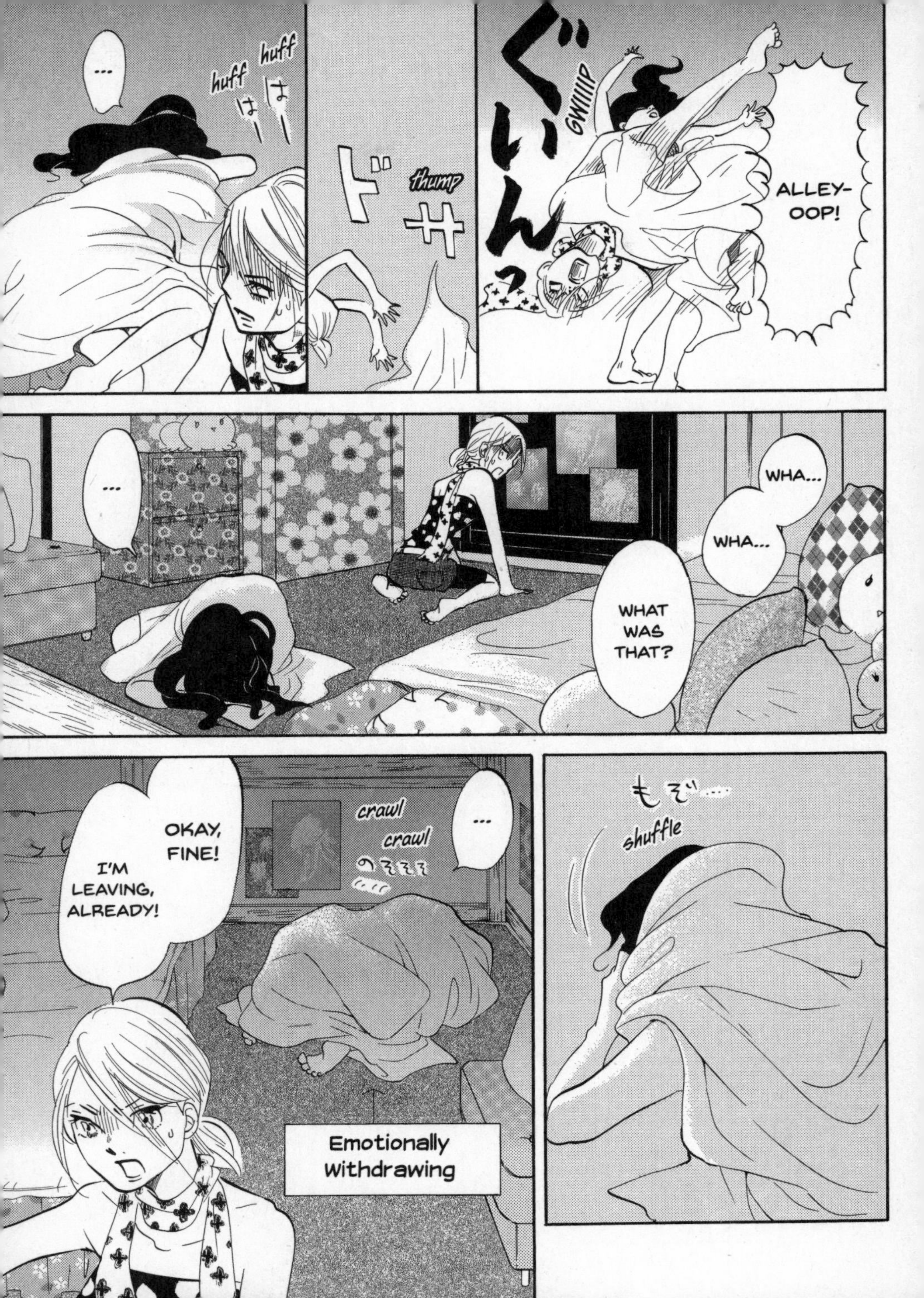
ぐいんっ
GWIIIIP
ALLEY-OOP!
ドサ
thump
...
huff huff huff
はーはー
WHA...
WHA...
WHAT WAS THAT?
...
もぞ...
shuffle
...
crawl crawl
のそそそ
OKAY, FINE!
I'M LEAVING, ALREADY!
Emotionally Withdrawing

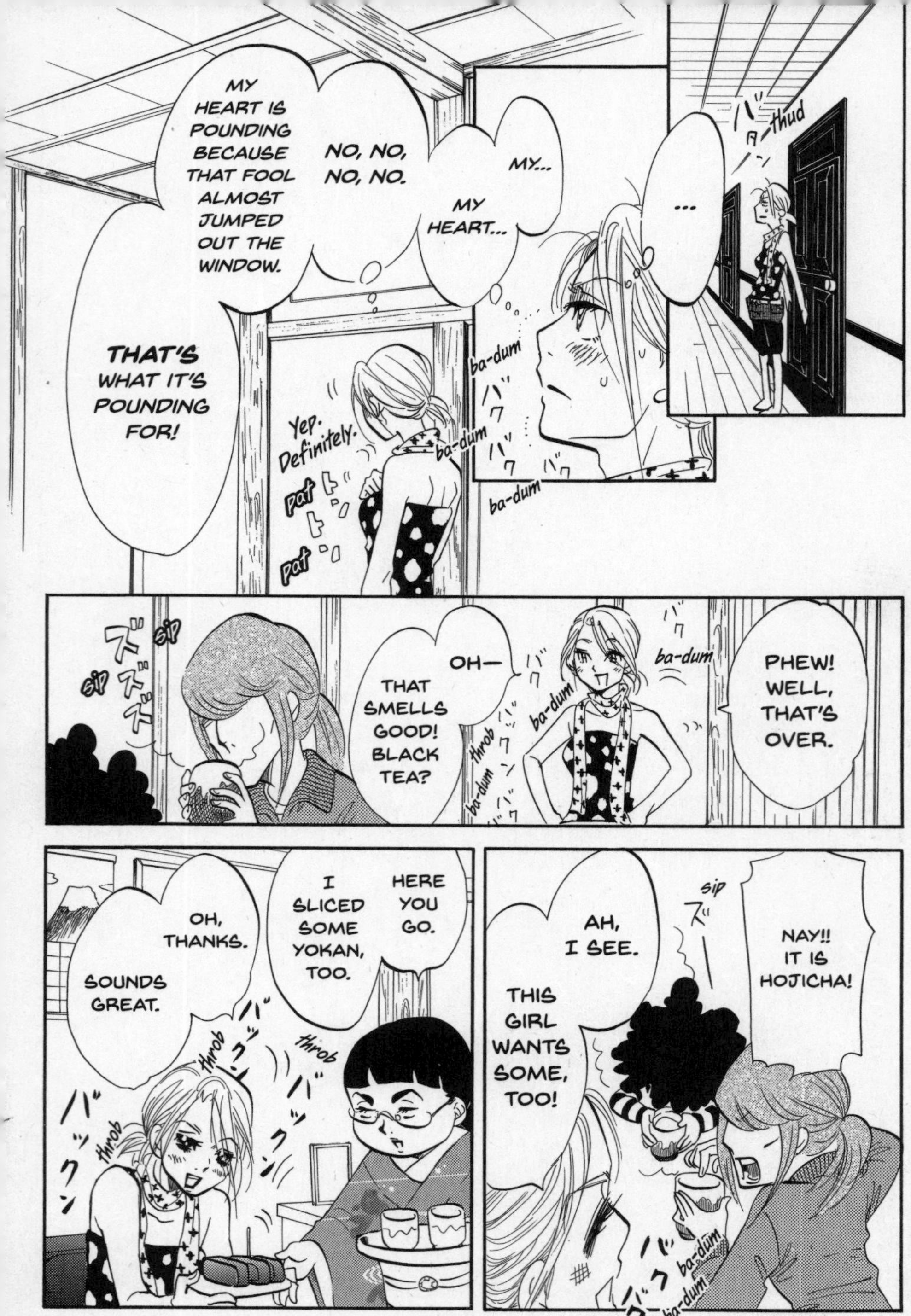
thud
...
MY...
MY HEART...
ba-dum
ba-dum
ba-dum
NO, NO, NO, NO.
MY HEART IS POUNDING BECAUSE THAT FOOL ALMOST JUMPED OUT THE WINDOW.
THAT'S WHAT IT'S POUNDING FOR!
Yep. Definitely.
pat
pat
PHEW! WELL, THAT'S OVER.
ba-dum
ba-dum
throb
ba-dum
OH—
THAT SMELLS GOOD! BLACK TEA?
sip
sip
sip
NAY!! IT IS HOJICHA!
AH, I SEE.
THIS GIRL WANTS SOME, TOO!
ba-dum
ba-dum
HERE YOU GO.
I SLICED SOME YOKAN, TOO.
OH, THANKS.
SOUNDS GREAT.
throb
throb
throb

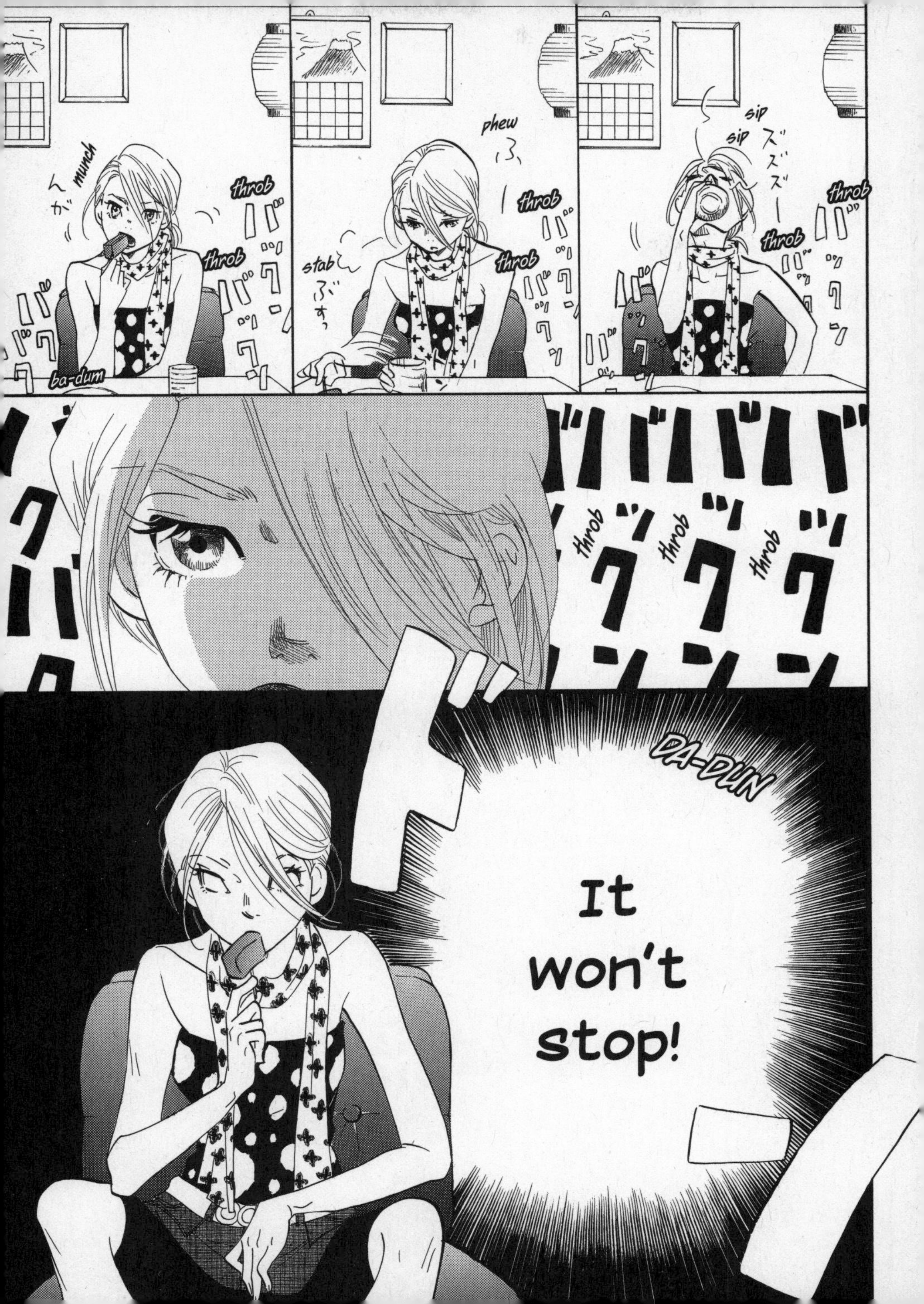

sip
sip
throb
throb
phew
throb
throb
stab
munch
throb
throb
ba-dum
throb
throb
throb
DA-DUN
It won't stop!

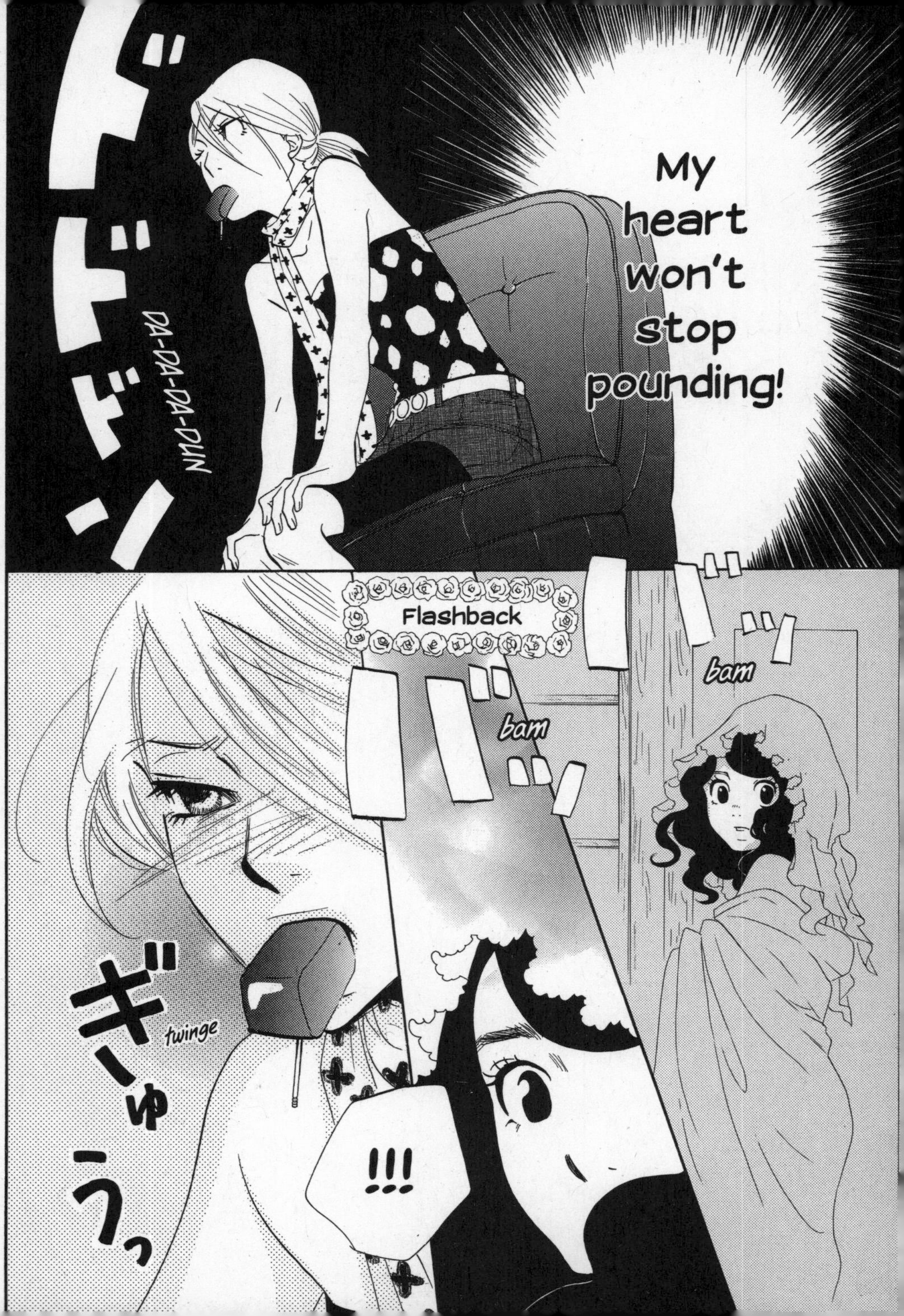

My heart won't stop pounding!
ドドドドン
DA-DA-DA-DUN
Flashback
bam
bam
!!!
ギューゅうっ
twinge

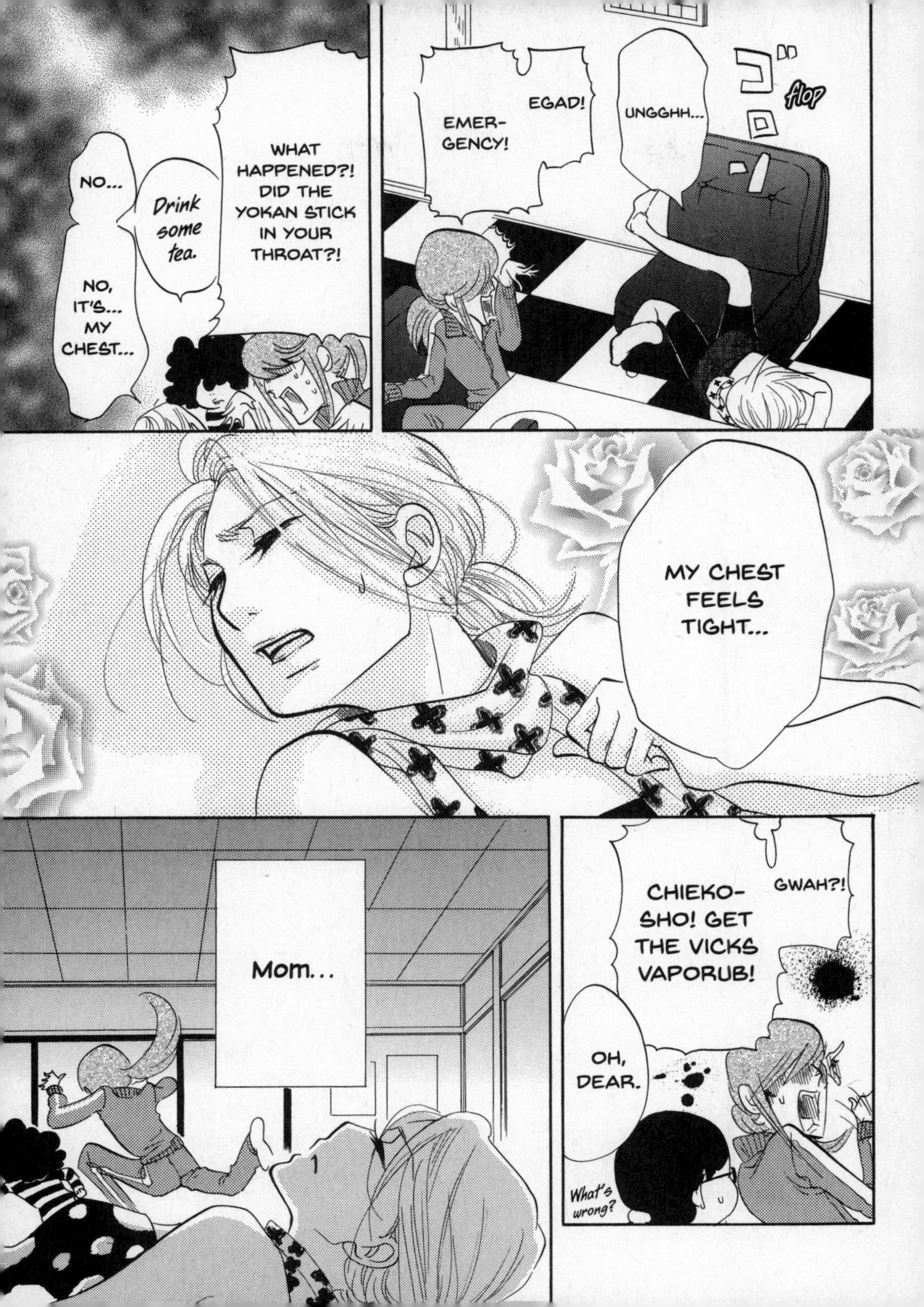
flop
UNGGHH...
EGAD!
EMER-GENCY!
WHAT HAPPENED?! DID THE YOKAN STICK IN YOUR THROAT?!
Drink some tea.
NO...
NO, IT'S... MY CHEST...
MY CHEST FEELS TIGHT...
GWAH?!
CHIEKO-SHO! GET THE VICKS VAPORUB!
OH, DEAR.
What's wrong?
Mom...

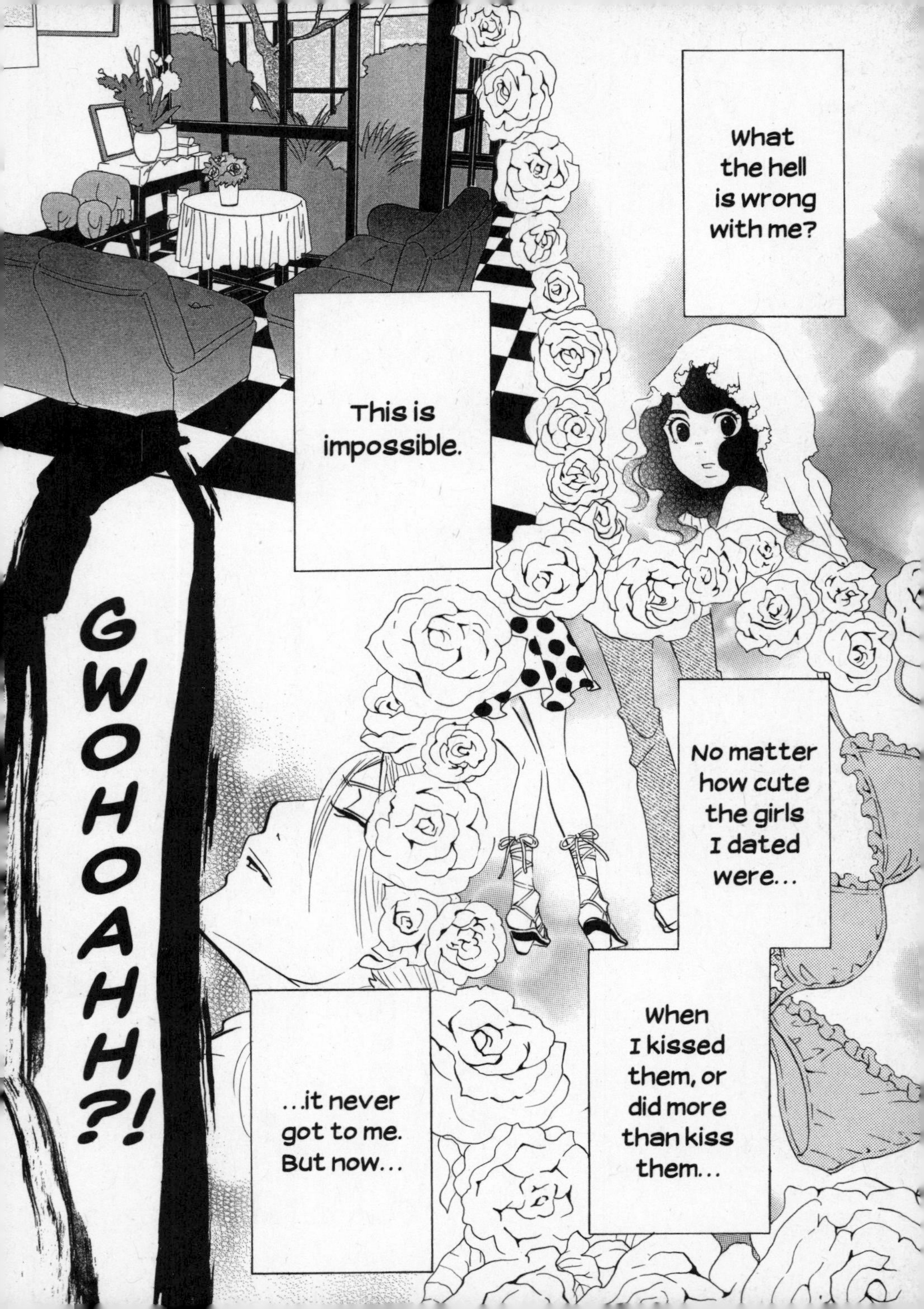
What the hell is wrong with me?
This is impossible.
No matter how cute the girls I dated were...
When I kissed them, or did more than kiss them...
...it never got to me. But now...
GWOHOAHH?!

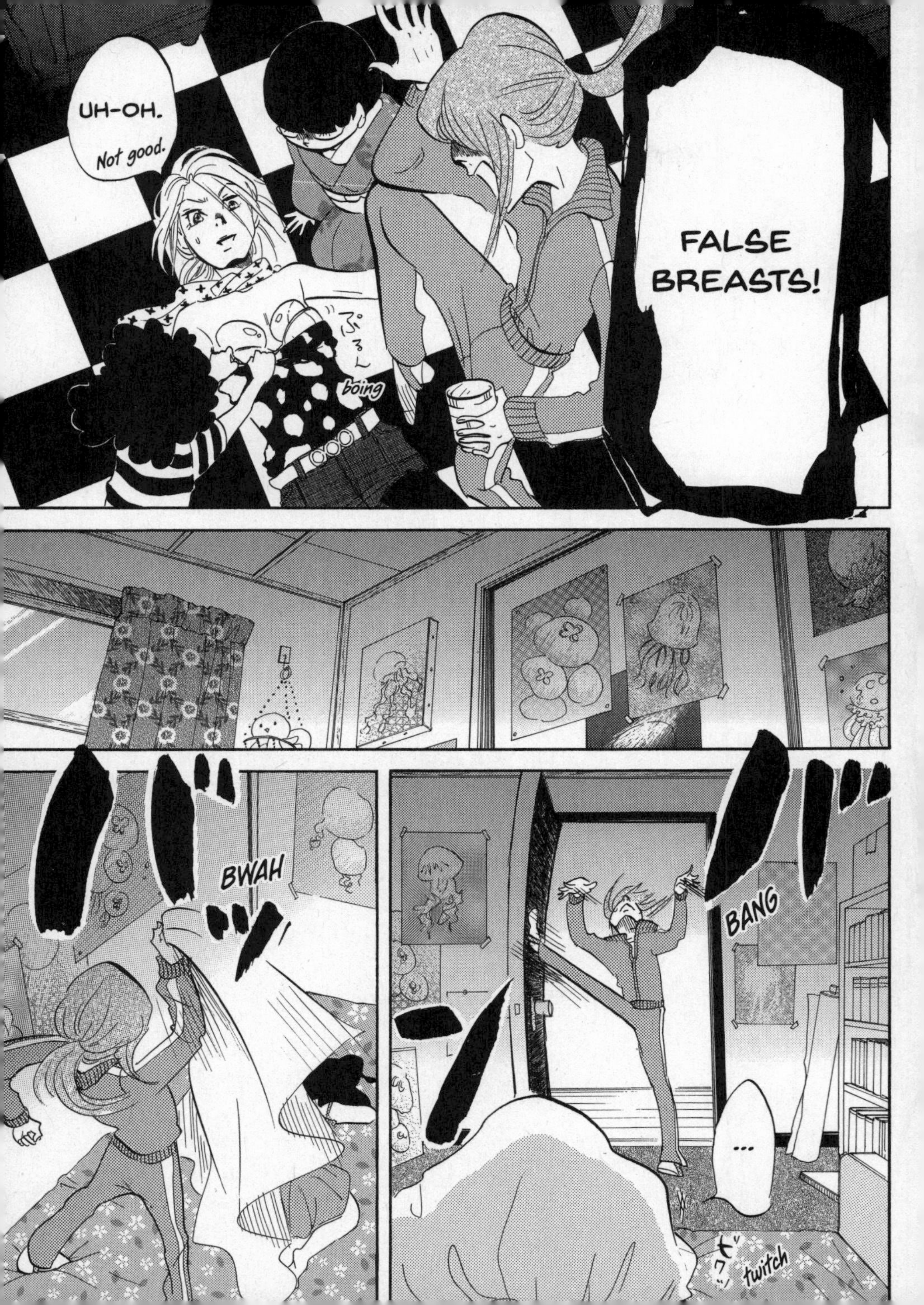
FALSE BREASTS!
UH-OH.
Not good.
ぷるん
boing
BANG
...
ビクッ
twitch
BWAH

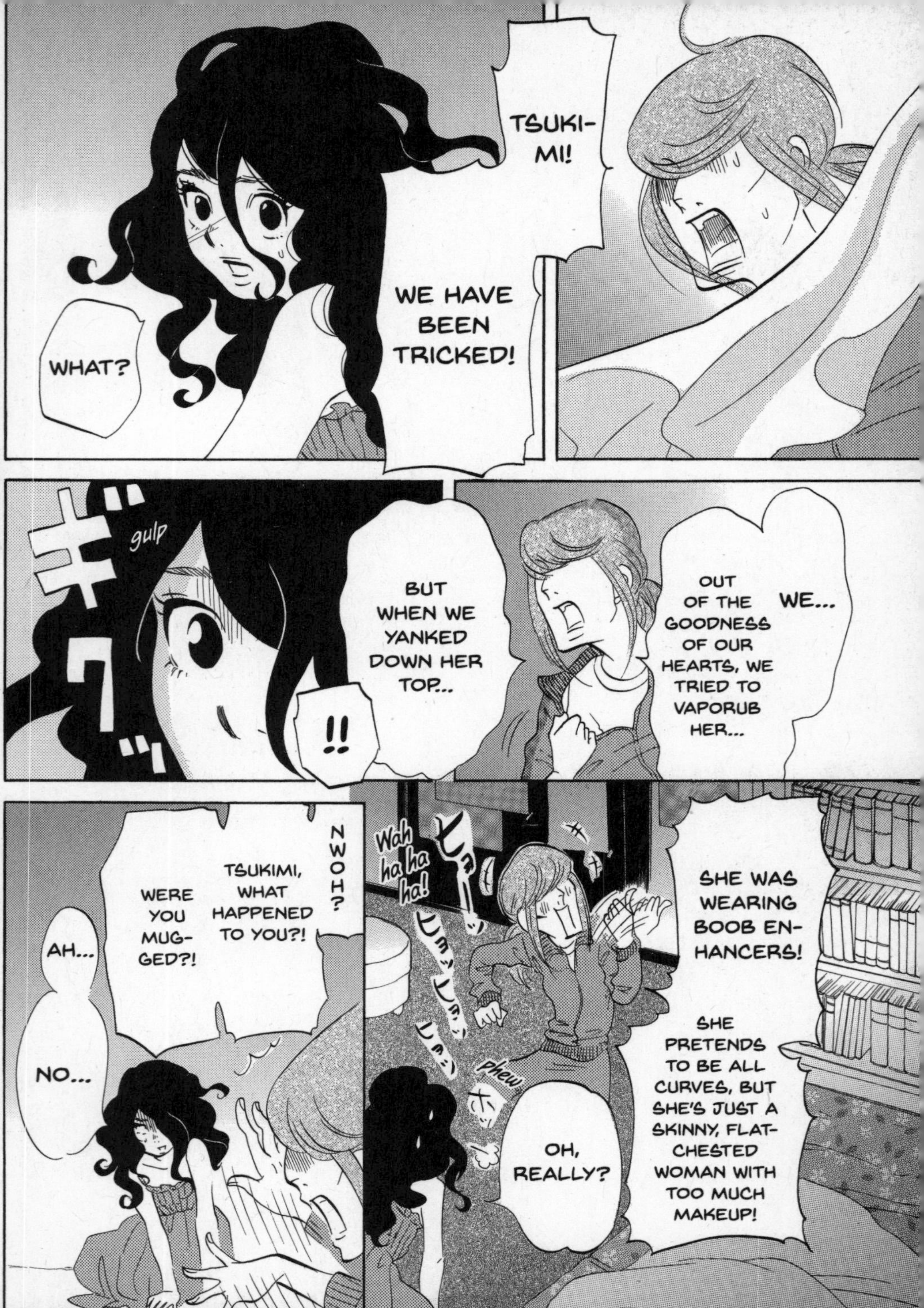

TSUKI-MI!
WE HAVE BEEN TRICKED!
WHAT?
WE...
OUT OF THE GOODNESS OF OUR HEARTS, WE TRIED TO VAPORUB HER...
BUT WHEN WE YANKED DOWN HER TOP...
!!
gulp
SHE WAS WEARING BOOB EN-HANCERS!
SHE PRETENDS TO BE ALL CURVES, BUT SHE'S JUST A SKINNY, FLAT-CHESTED WOMAN WITH TOO MUCH MAKEUP!
Wah ha ha ha!
phew
OH, REALLY?
NWOH?
TSUKIMI, WHAT HAPPENED TO YOU?!
WERE YOU MUG-GED?!
AH...
NO...

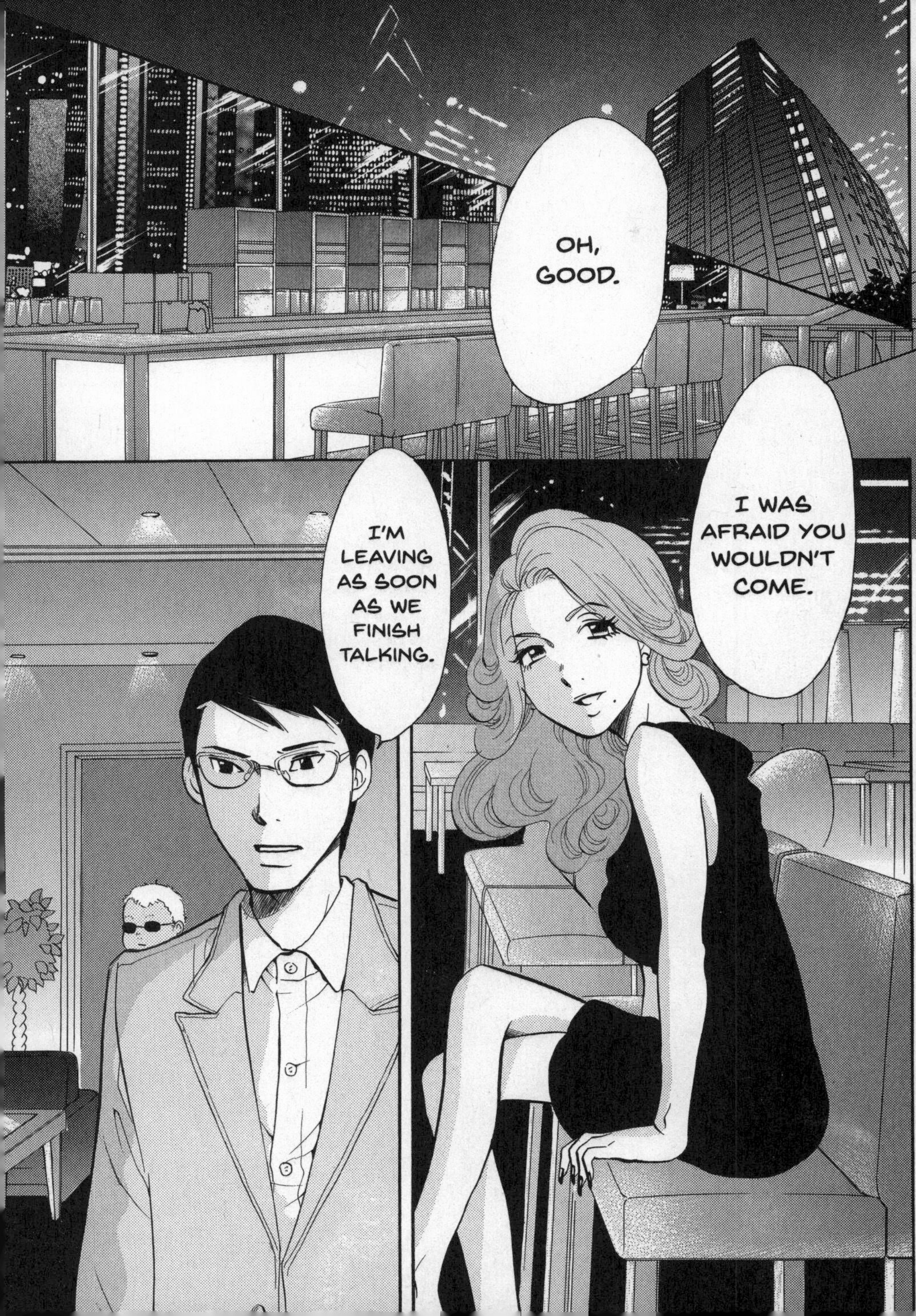
OH, GOOD.
I WAS AFRAID YOU WOULDN'T COME.
I'M LEAVING AS SOON AS WE FINISH TALKING.

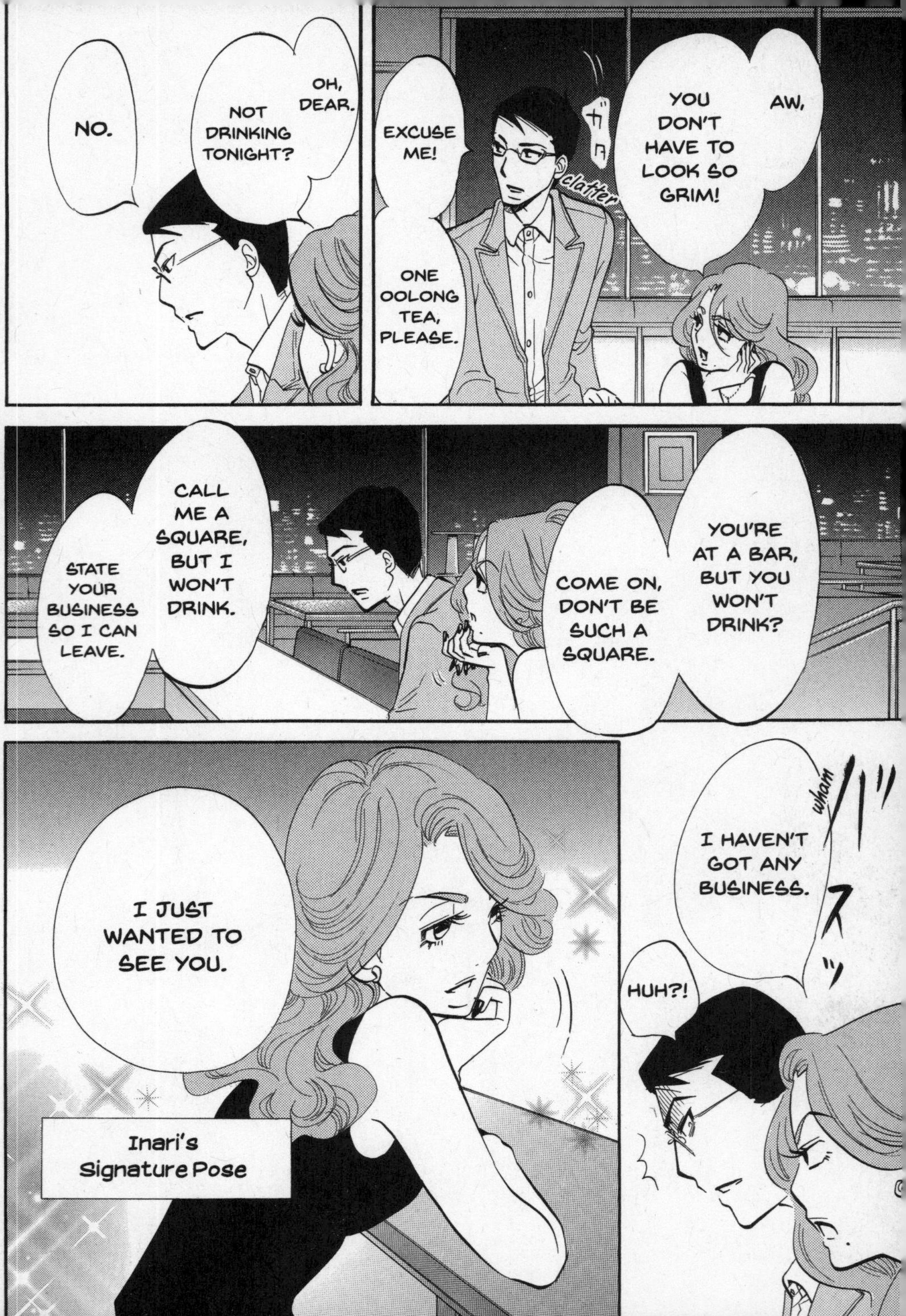
AW, YOU DON'T HAVE TO LOOK SO GRIM!
ガタ
clatter
EXCUSE ME!
ONE OOLONG TEA, PLEASE.
OH, DEAR. NOT DRINKING TONIGHT?
NO.
YOU'RE AT A BAR, BUT YOU WON'T DRINK?
COME ON, DON'T BE SUCH A SQUARE.
CALL ME A SQUARE, BUT I WON'T DRINK.
STATE YOUR BUSINESS SO I CAN LEAVE.
I HAVEN'T GOT ANY BUSINESS.
wham
HUH?!
I JUST WANTED TO SEE YOU.
Inari's Signature Pose

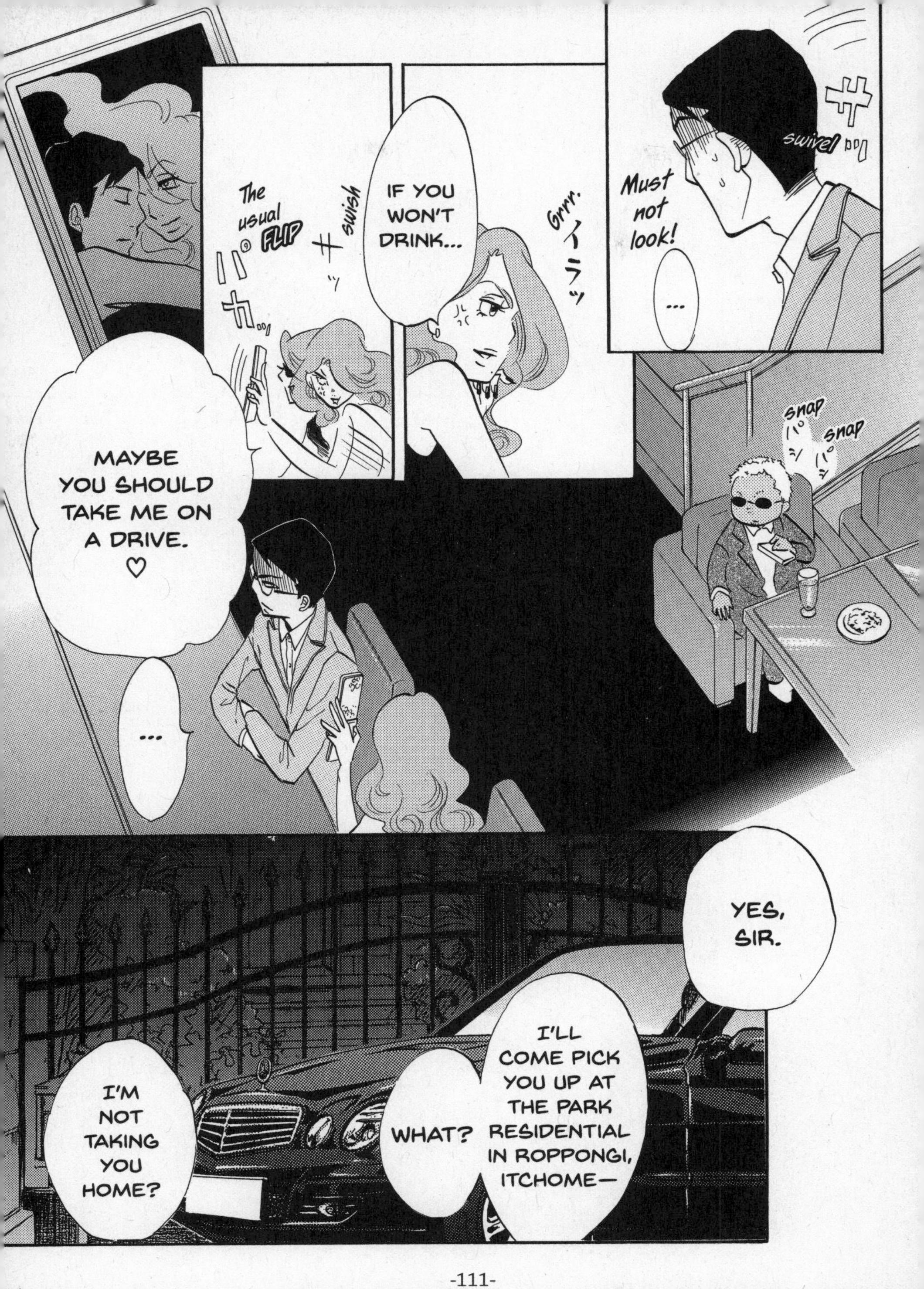
swivel
Must not look!
...
IF YOU WON'T DRINK...
Grrr.
The usual FLIP
swish
snap
snap
MAYBE YOU SHOULD TAKE ME ON A DRIVE. ♡
...
YES, SIR.
I'LL COME PICK YOU UP AT THE PARK RESIDENTIAL IN ROPPONGI, ITCHOME—
WHAT?
I'M NOT TAKING YOU HOME?

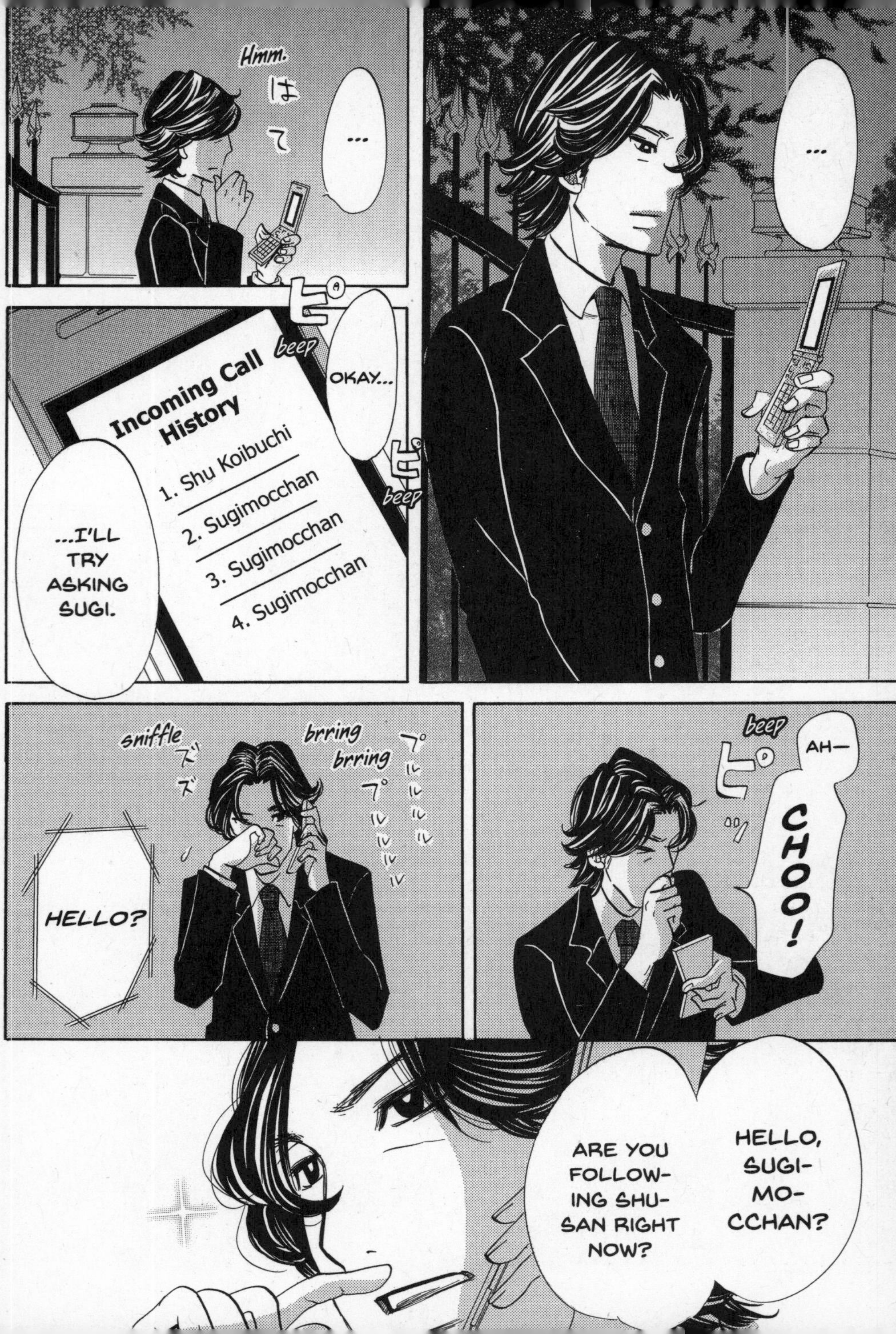
...
Hmm.
はて
...
beep
ピ
OKAY...
ピ
beep
Incoming Call History
1. Shu Koibuchi
2. Sugimocchan
3. Sugimocchan
4. Sugimocchan
...I'LL TRY ASKING SUGI.
beep
ピ
AH—CHOO!
sniffle
ズズ
brring brring
プルルルル
プルルルル
HELLO?
HELLO, SUGI-MO-CCHAN?
ARE YOU FOLLOW-ING SHU-SAN RIGHT NOW?

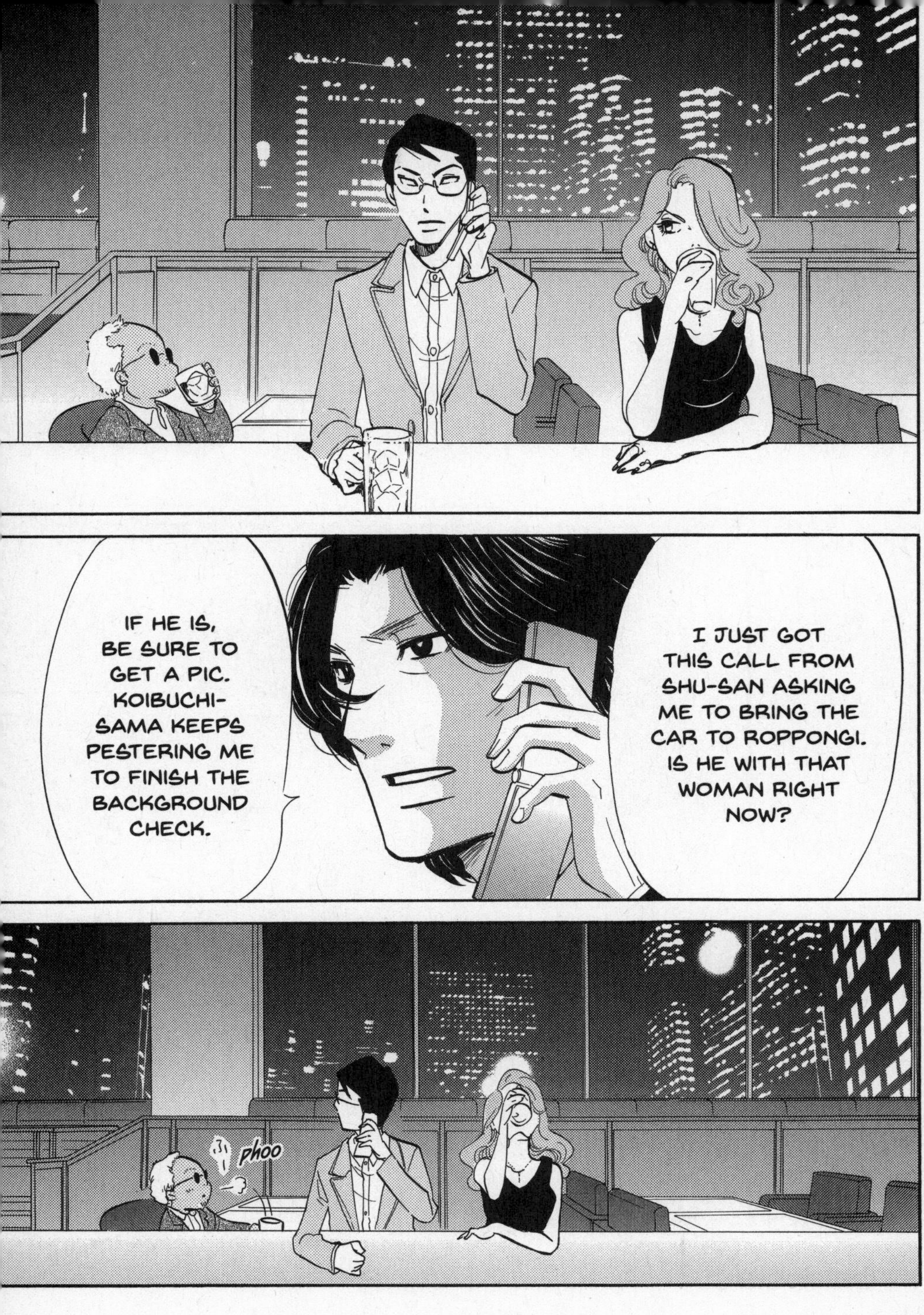
I JUST GOT THIS CALL FROM SHU-SAN ASKING ME TO BRING THE CAR TO ROPPONGI. IS HE WITH THAT WOMAN RIGHT NOW?
IF HE IS, BE SURE TO GET A PIC. KOIBUCHI-SAMA KEEPS PESTERING ME TO FINISH THE BACKGROUND CHECK.
phoo

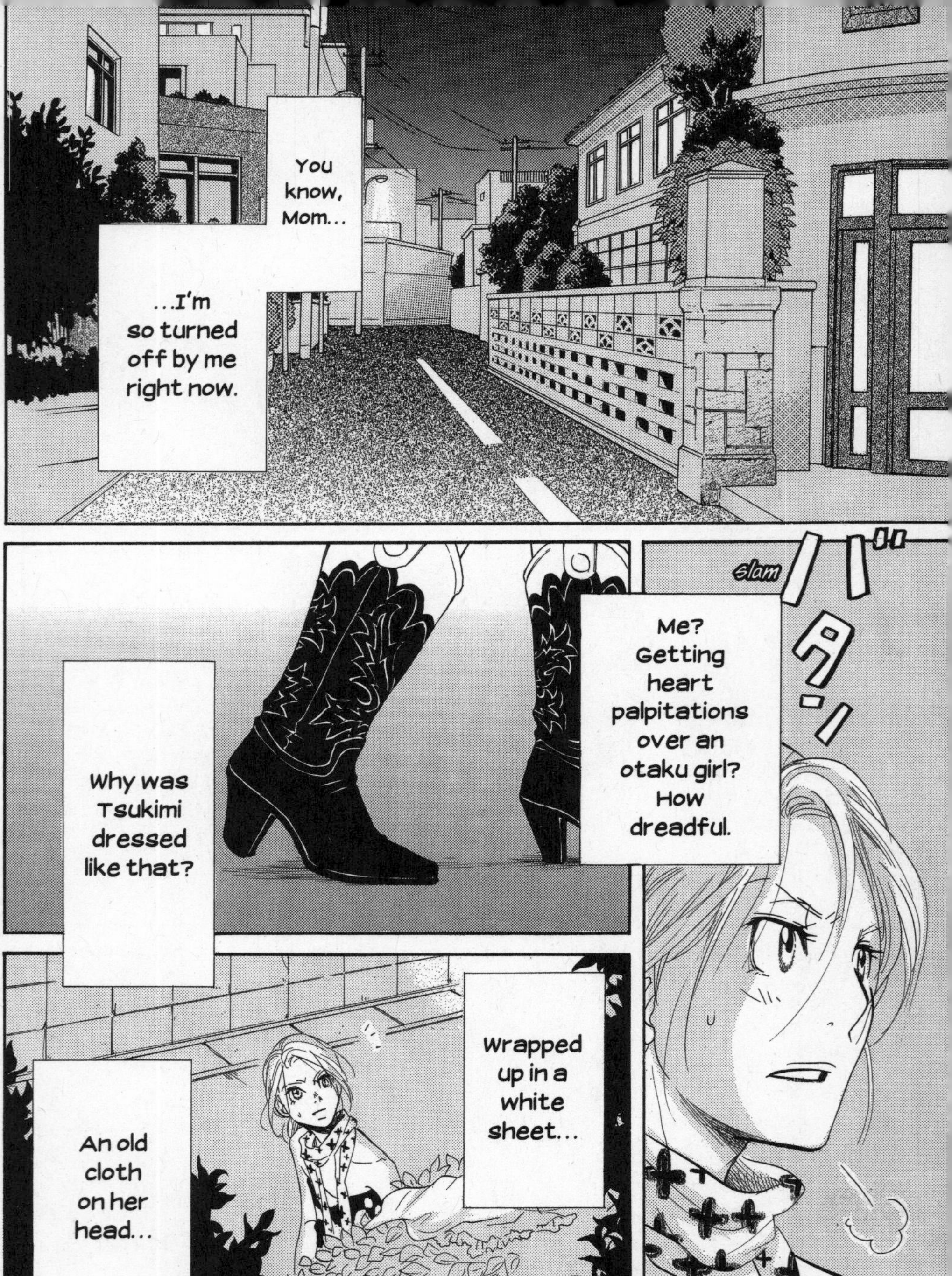
You know, Mom...
...I'm so turned off by me right now.
slam
Me? Getting heart palpitations over an otaku girl? How dreadful.
Why was Tsukimi dressed like that?
Wrapped up in a white sheet...
An old cloth on her head...

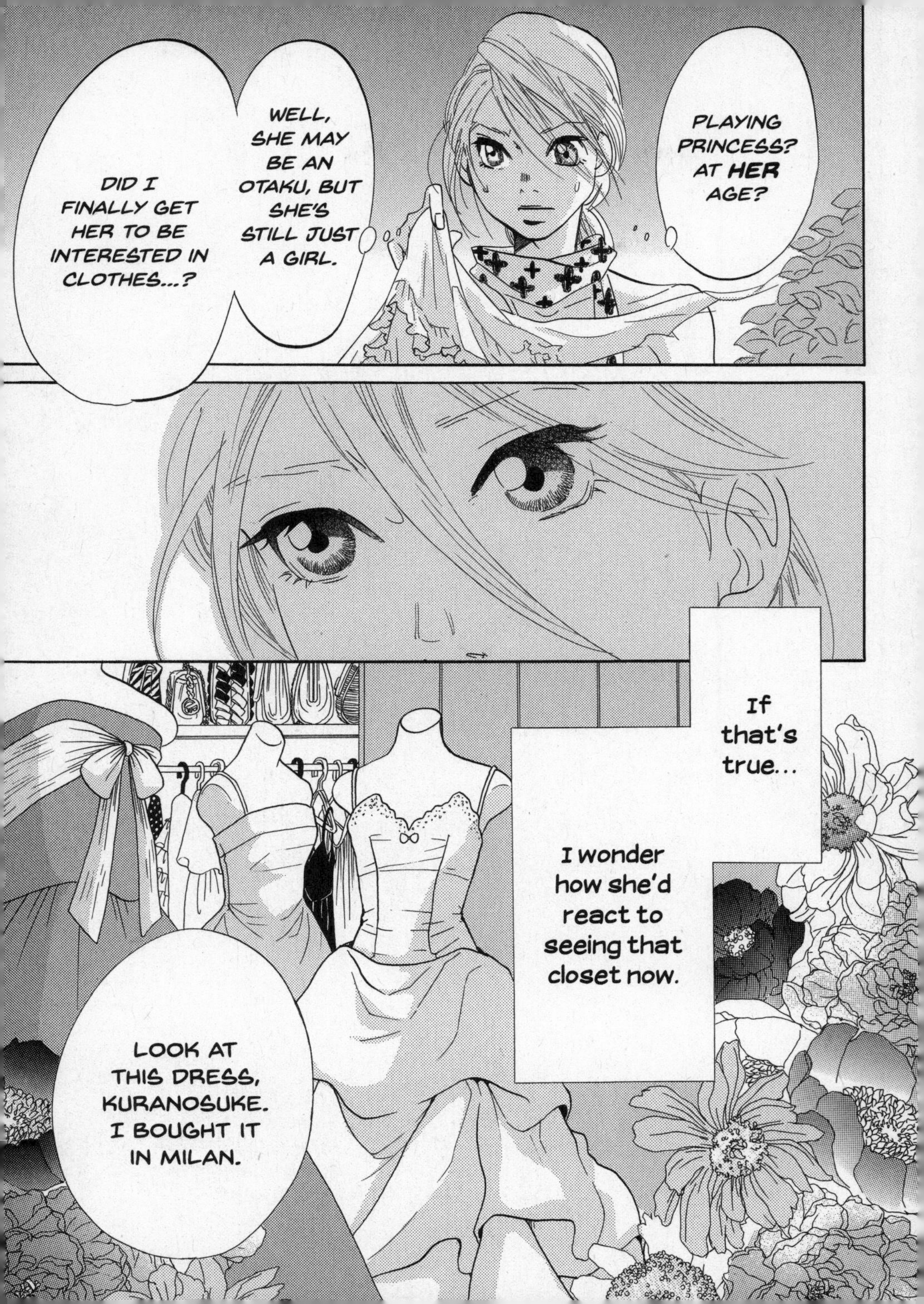
PLAYING PRINCESS? AT **HER** AGE?
WELL, SHE MAY BE AN OTAKU, BUT SHE'S STILL JUST A GIRL.
DID I FINALLY GET HER TO BE INTERESTED IN CLOTHES...?
If that's true...
I wonder how she'd react to seeing that closet now.
LOOK AT THIS DRESS, KURANOSUKE. I BOUGHT IT IN MILAN.

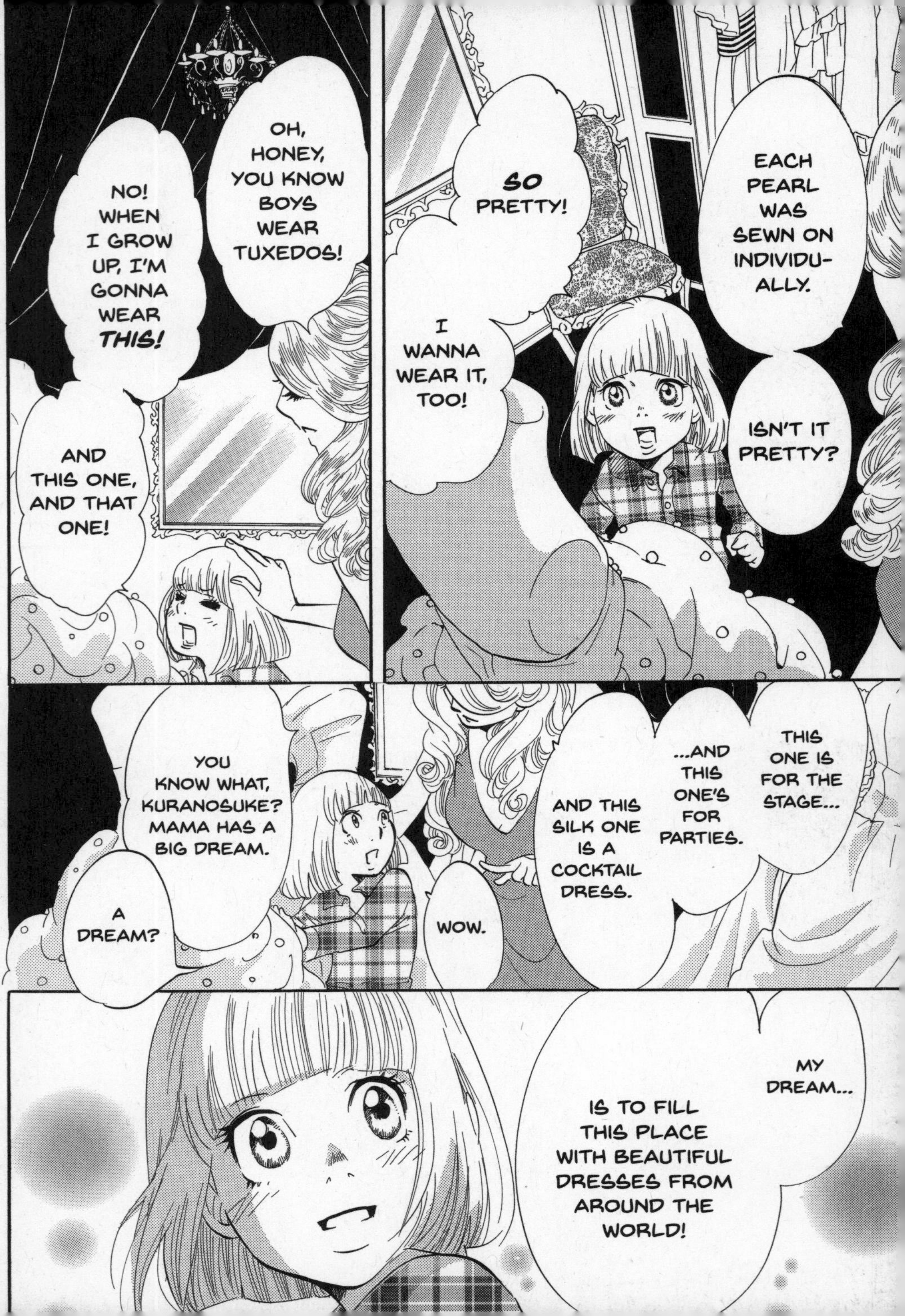
EACH PEARL WAS SEWN ON INDIVIDU-ALLY.
SO PRETTY!
I WANNA WEAR IT, TOO!
ISN'T IT PRETTY?
OH, HONEY, YOU KNOW BOYS WEAR TUXEDOS!
NO! WHEN I GROW UP, I'M GONNA WEAR *THIS!*
AND THIS ONE, AND THAT ONE!
THIS ONE IS FOR THE STAGE...
...AND THIS ONE'S FOR PARTIES.
AND THIS SILK ONE IS A COCKTAIL DRESS.
WOW.
YOU KNOW WHAT, KURANOSUKE? MAMA HAS A BIG DREAM.
A DREAM?
MY DREAM...
IS TO FILL THIS PLACE WITH BEAUTIFUL DRESSES FROM AROUND THE WORLD!

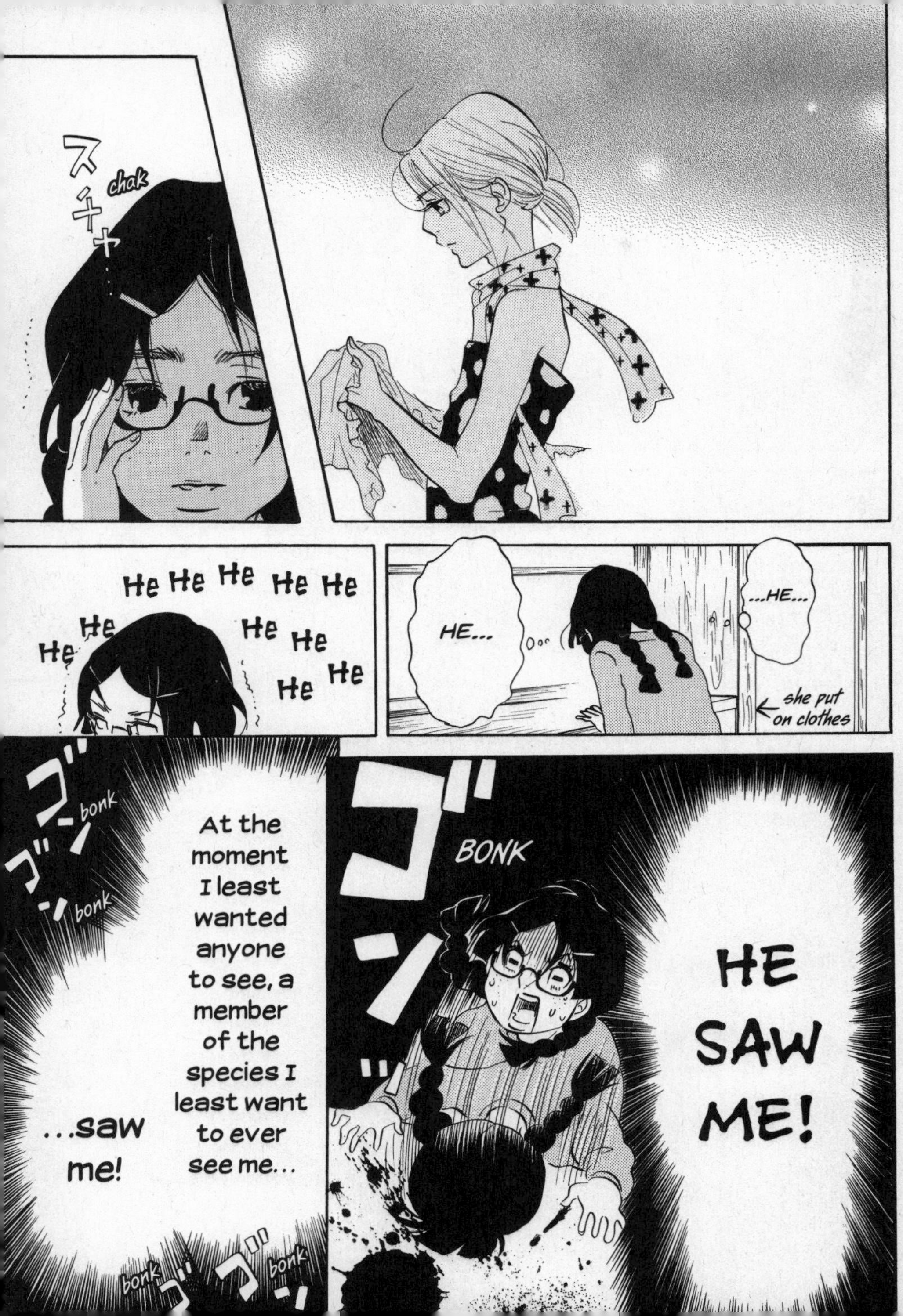
chak
...HE...
HE...
she put on clothes
He He He He He He He He He He He He
BONK
HE SAW ME!
bonk
bonk
At the moment I least wanted anyone to see, a member of the species I least want to ever see me...
...saw me!
bonk
bonk

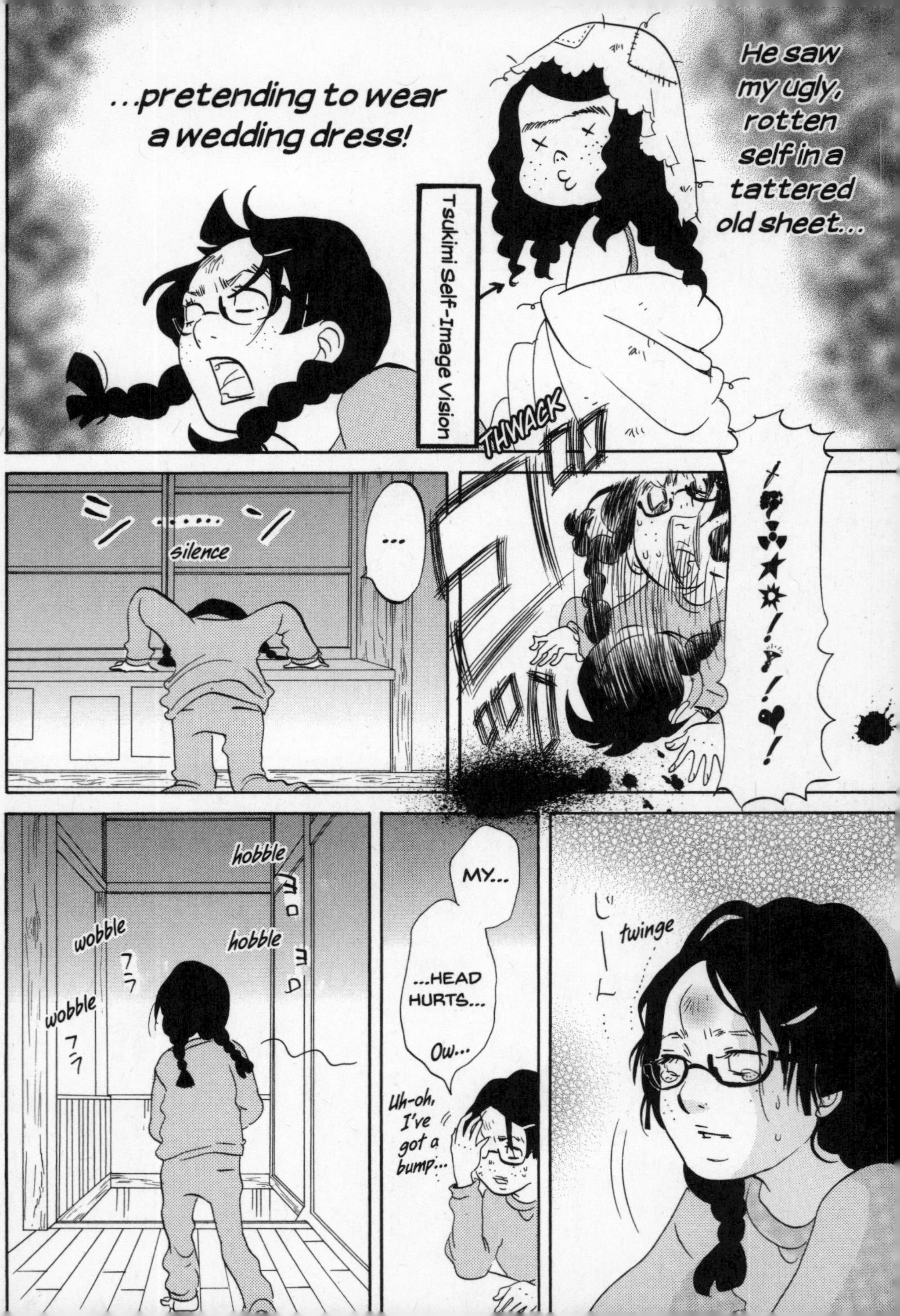

He saw my ugly, rotten self in a tattered old sheet...
...pretending to wear a wedding dress!
Tsukimi Self-Image Vision
THWACK
...
silence
twinge
MY...
...HEAD HURTS...
Ow...
Uh-oh, I've got a bump...
hobble
hobble
wobble
wobble

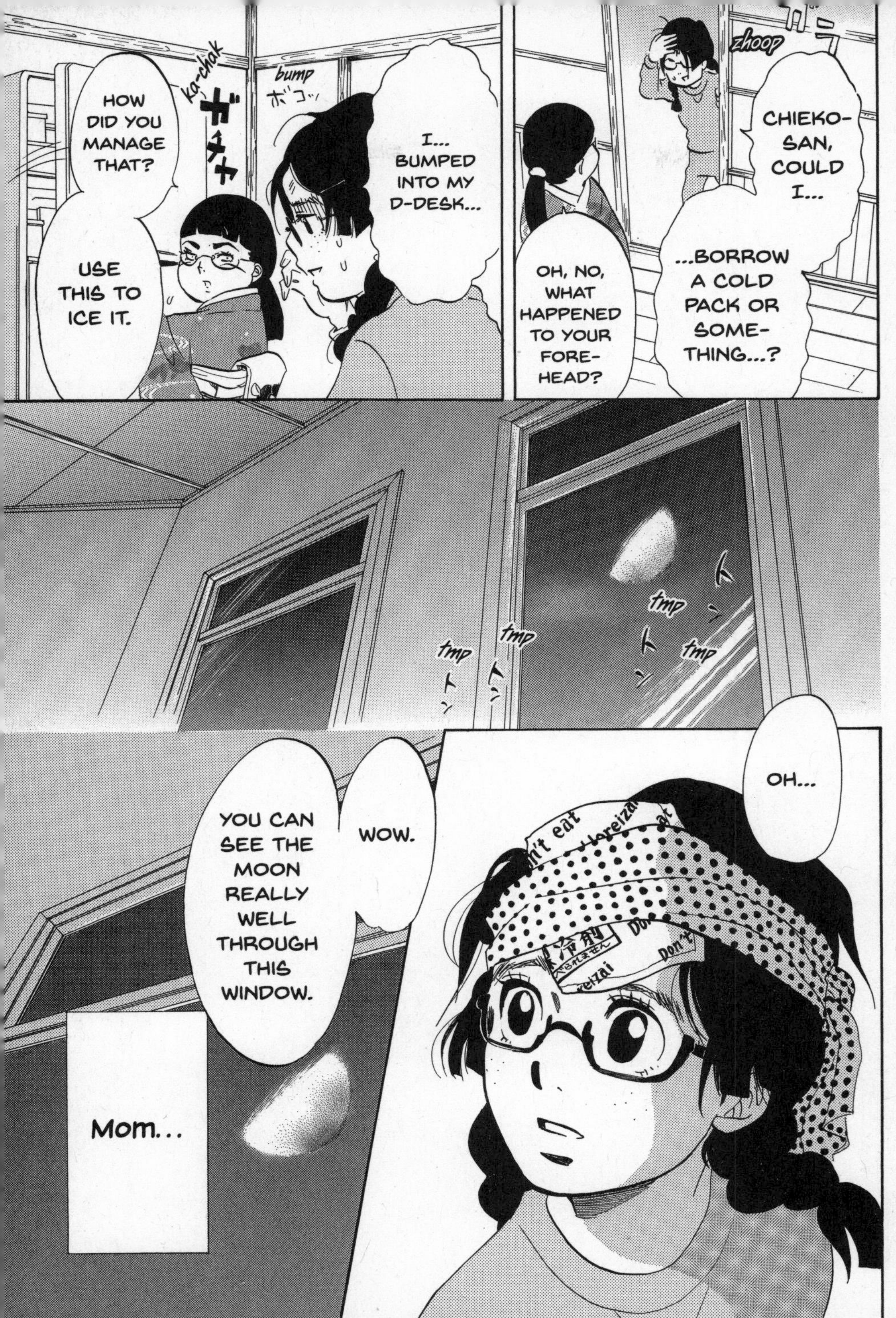
zhoop
CHIEKO-SAN, COULD I...
...BORROW A COLD PACK OR SOME-THING...?
OH, NO, WHAT HAPPENED TO YOUR FORE-HEAD?
bump
I... BUMPED INTO MY D-DESK...
ka-chak
HOW DID YOU MANAGE THAT?
USE THIS TO ICE IT.
tmp
tmp
tmp
tmp
OH...
WOW.
YOU CAN SEE THE MOON REALLY WELL THROUGH THIS WINDOW.
Mom...

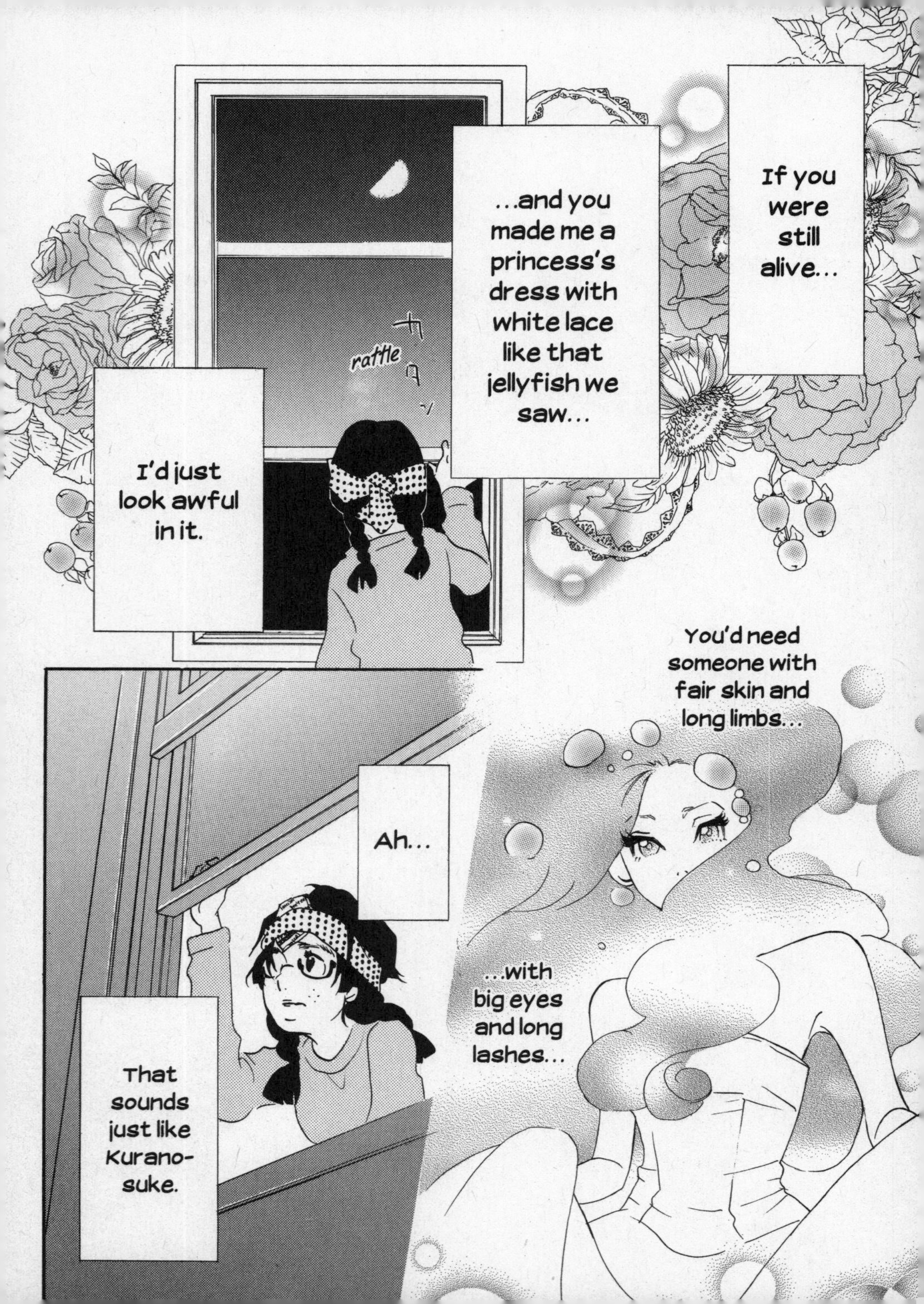

If you were still alive...
...and you made me a princess's dress with white lace like that jellyfish we saw...
rattle
I'd just look awful in it.
You'd need someone with fair skin and long limbs...
...with big eyes and long lashes...
Ah...
That sounds just like Kurano-suke.

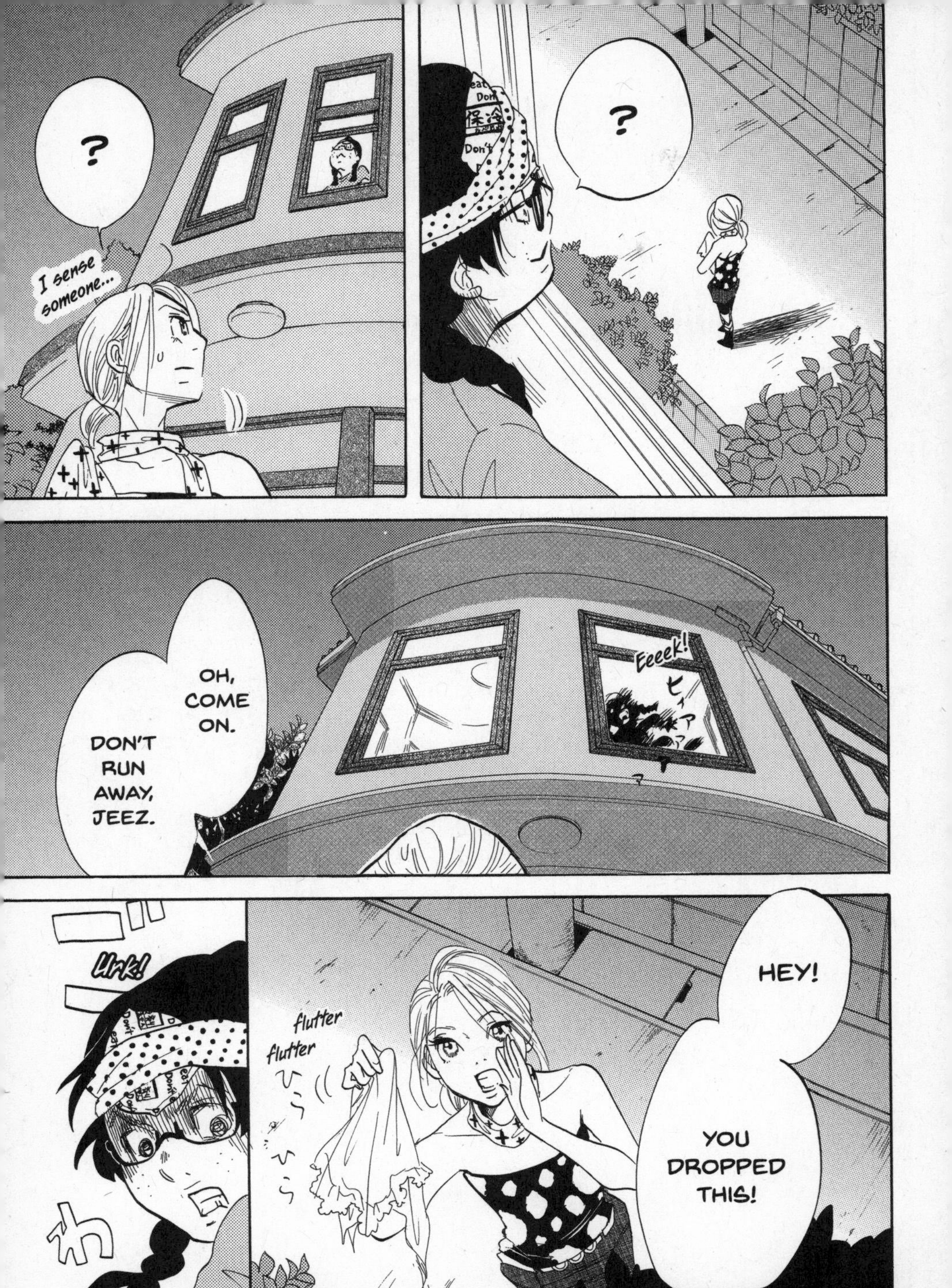
?
?
I sense someone...
Eeeek!
OH, COME ON. DON'T RUN AWAY, JEEZ.
HEY!
YOU DROPPED THIS!
flutter flutter
ひら ひら
Urk!
わ

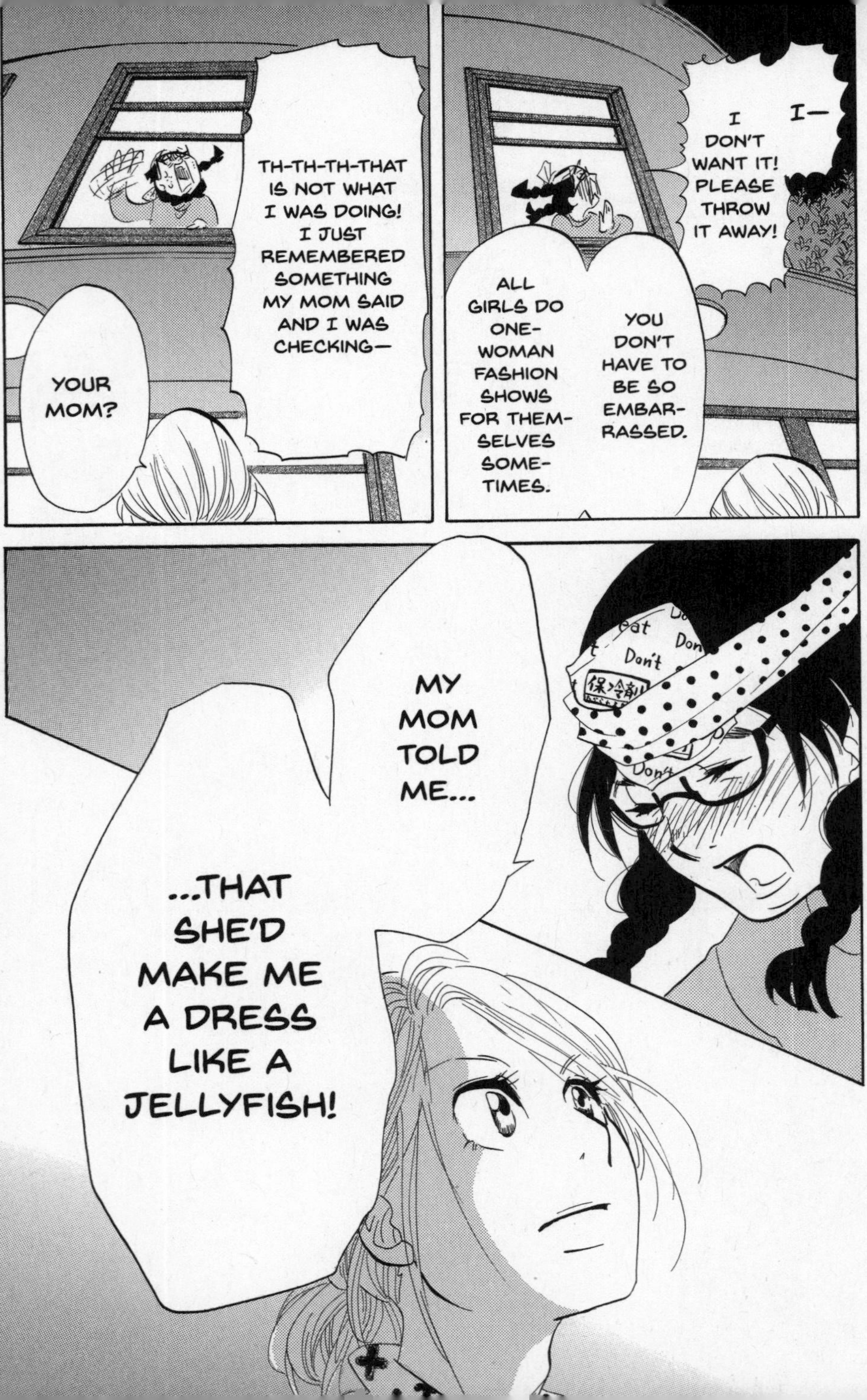
I— I DON'T WANT IT! PLEASE THROW IT AWAY!
YOU DON'T HAVE TO BE SO EMBARRASSED.
ALL GIRLS DO ONE-WOMAN FASHION SHOWS FOR THEMSELVES SOMETIMES.
TH-TH-TH-THAT IS NOT WHAT I WAS DOING! I JUST REMEMBERED SOMETHING MY MOM SAID AND I WAS CHECKING—
YOUR MOM?
MY MOM TOLD ME...
...THAT SHE'D MAKE ME A DRESS LIKE A JELLYFISH!

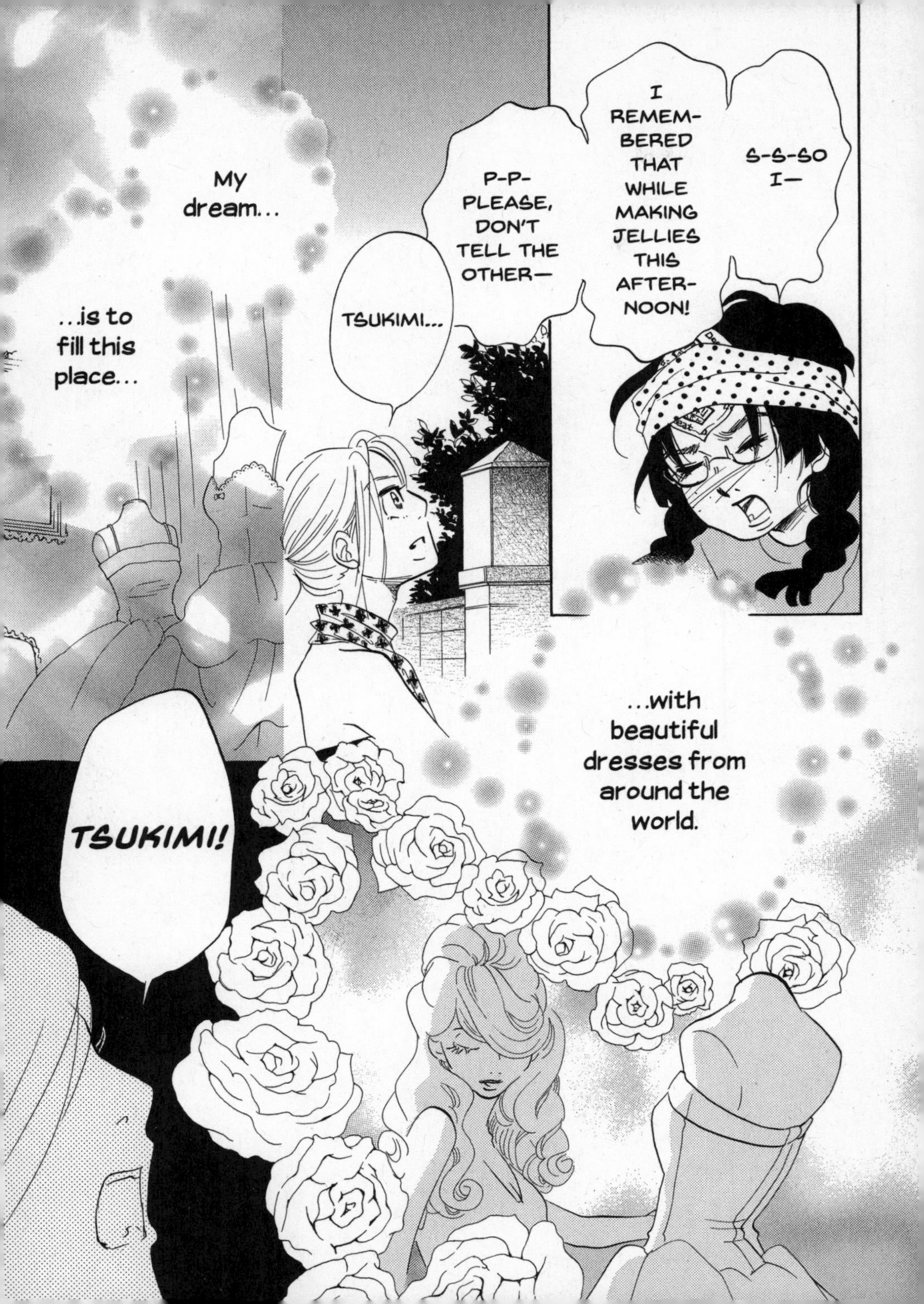
S-S-SO I—
I REMEMBERED THAT WHILE MAKING JELLIES THIS AFTERNOON!
P-P-PLEASE, DON'T TELL THE OTHER—
TSUKIMI...
My dream...
...is to fill this place...
...with beautiful dresses from around the world.
TSUKIMI!

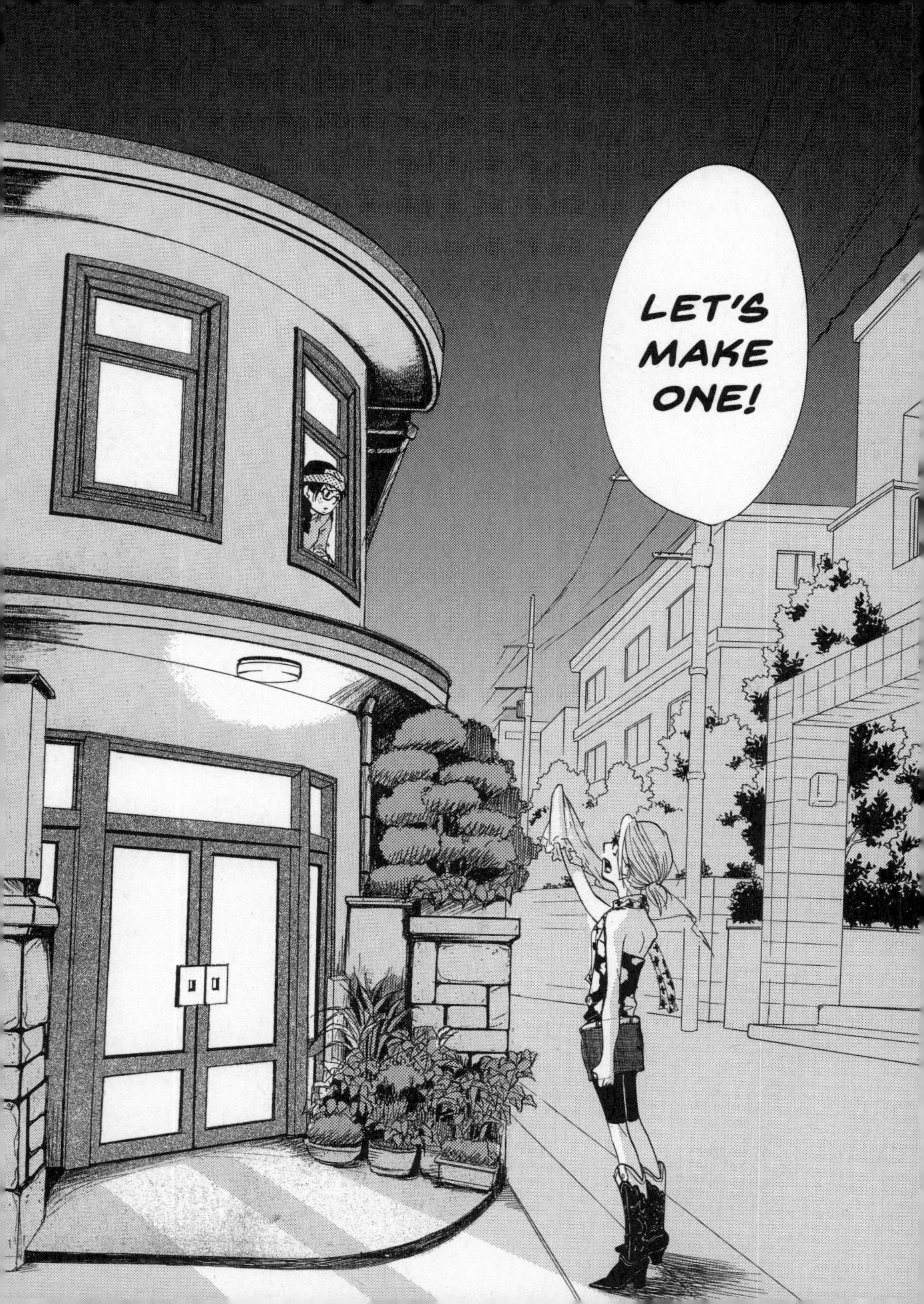
LET'S MAKE ONE!

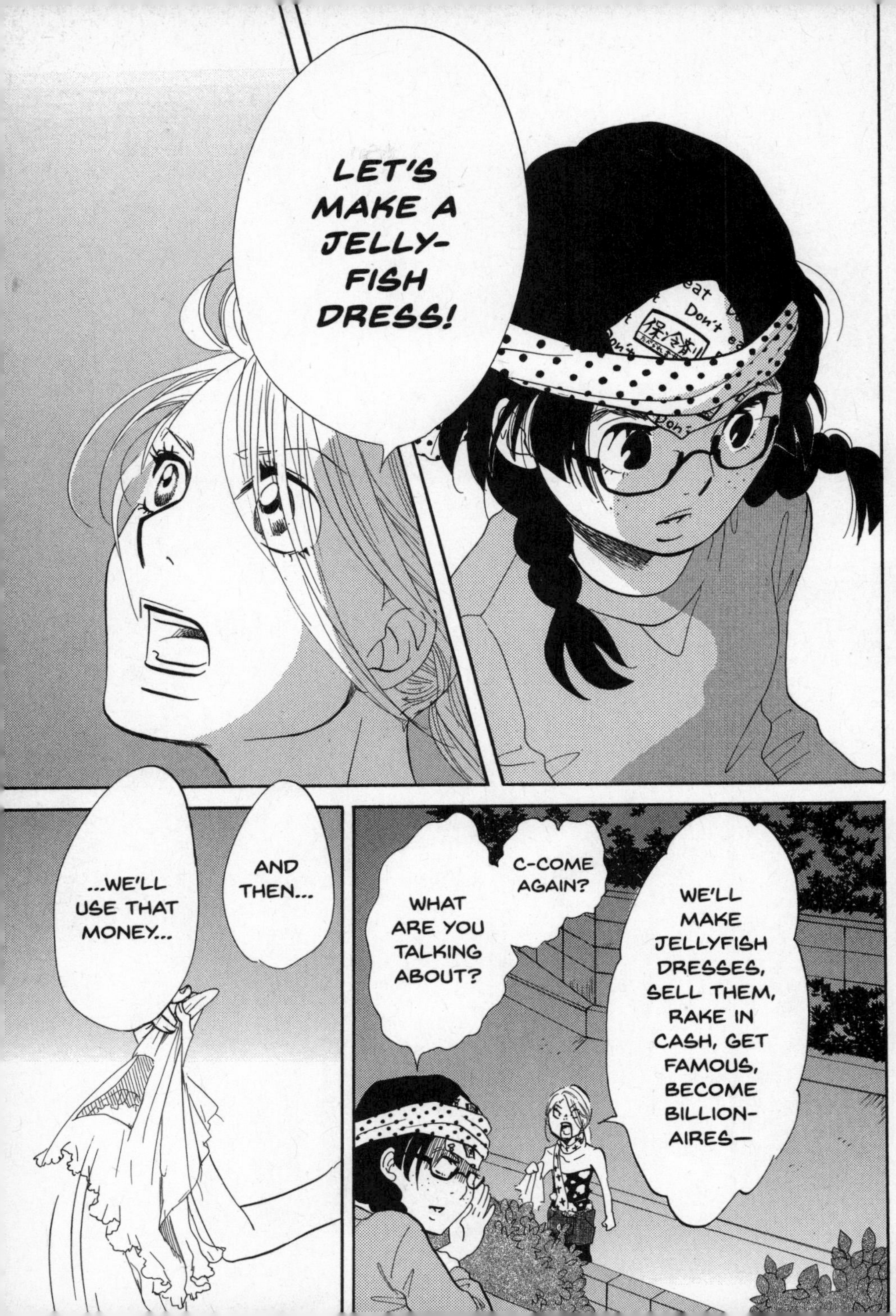
LET'S MAKE A JELLY-FISH DRESS!
WE'LL MAKE JELLYFISH DRESSES, SELL THEM, RAKE IN CASH, GET FAMOUS, BECOME BILLION-AIRES—
C-COME AGAIN?
WHAT ARE YOU TALKING ABOUT?
AND THEN...
...WE'LL USE THAT MONEY...

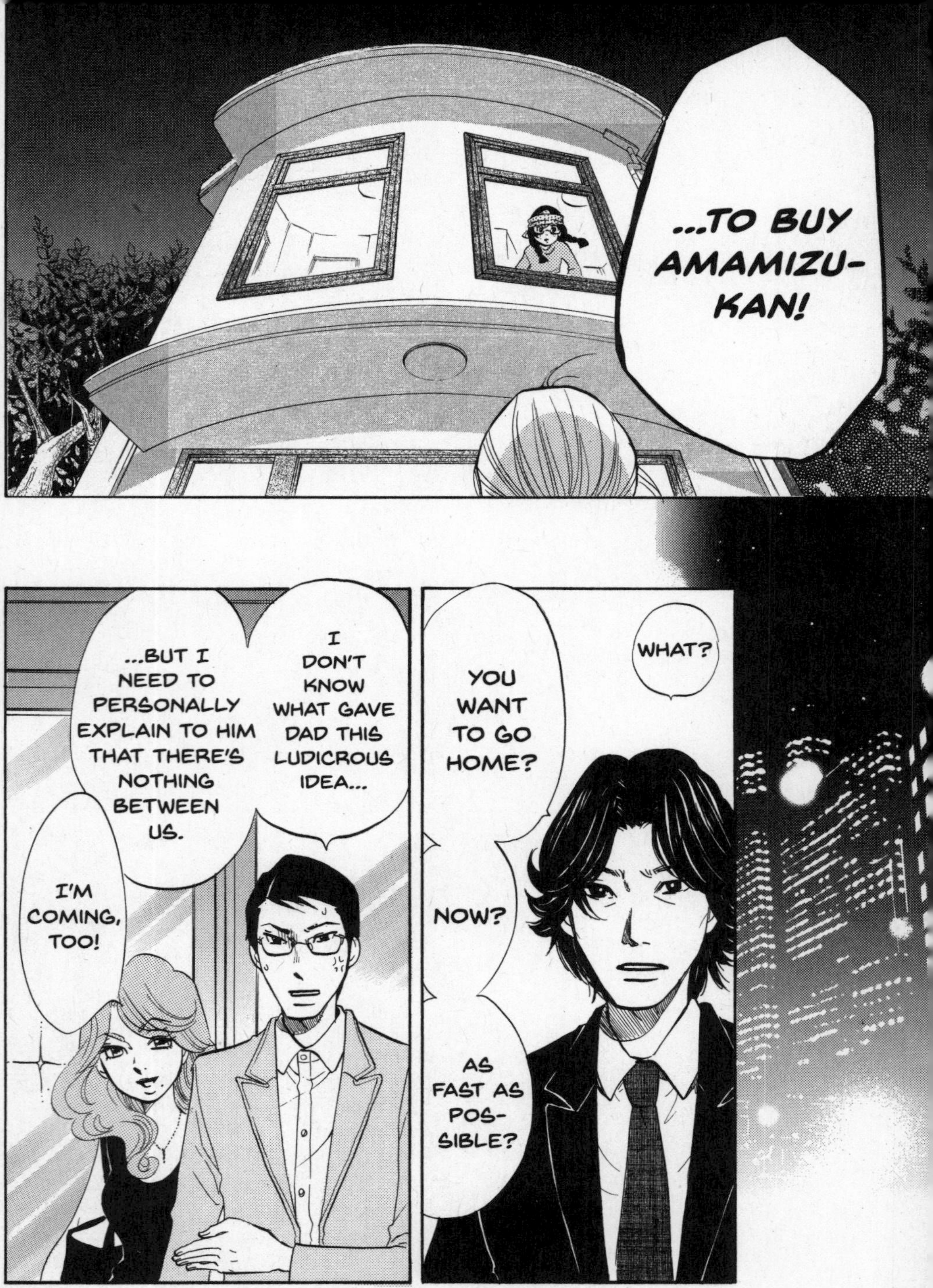
...TO BUY AMAMIZU-KAN!
WHAT?
YOU WANT TO GO HOME?
NOW?
AS FAST AS POS-SIBLE?
I DON'T KNOW WHAT GAVE DAD THIS LUDICROUS IDEA...
...BUT I NEED TO PERSONALLY EXPLAIN TO HIM THAT THERE'S NOTHING BETWEEN US.
I'M COMING, TOO!

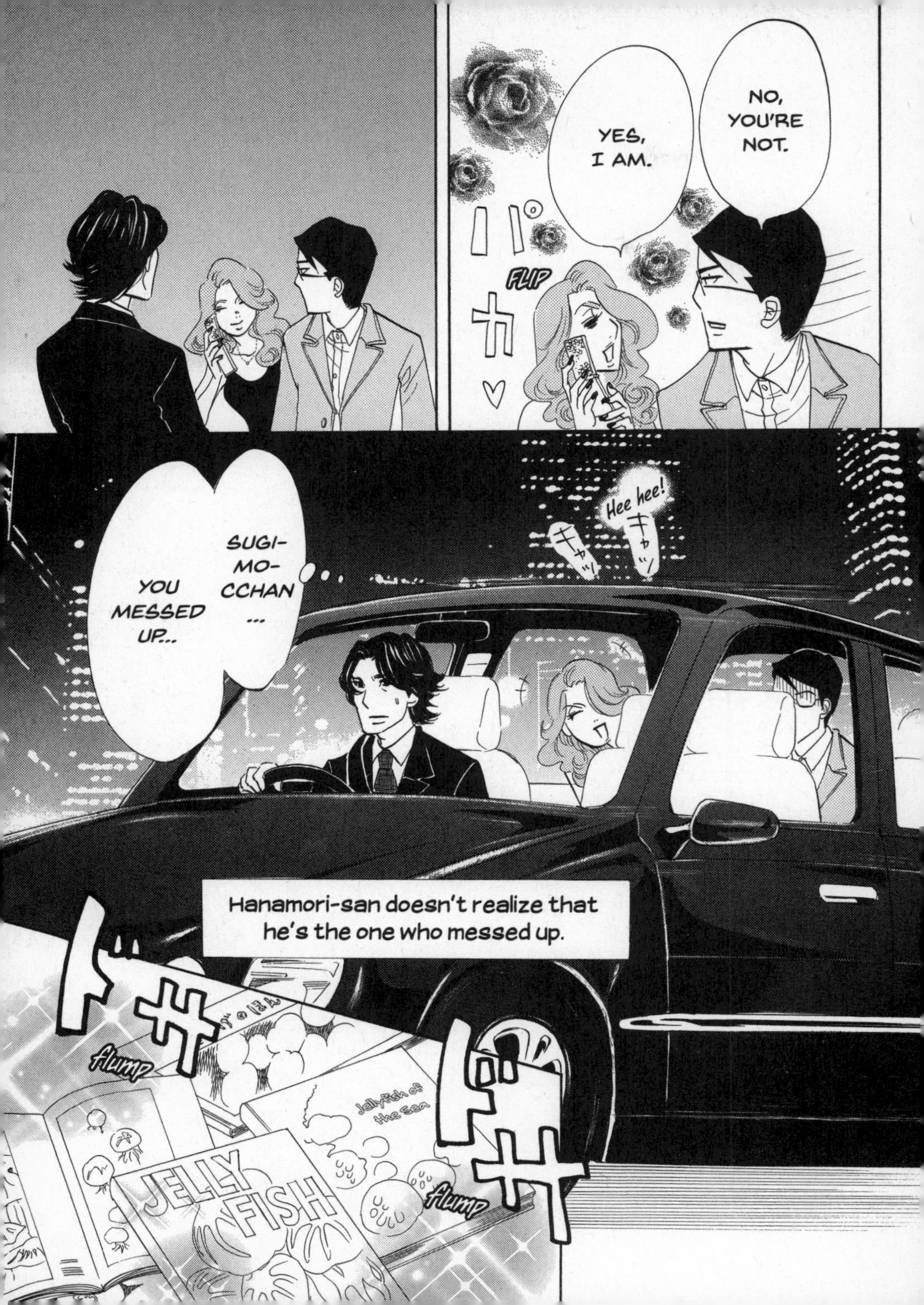
NO, YOU'RE NOT.
YES, I AM.
パカ
FLIP
♥
Hee hee!
キャッ キャッ
SUGI-MO-CCHAN...
YOU MESSED UP...
Hanamori-san doesn't realize that he's the one who messed up.
ドサッ
flump
Jellyfish of the Sea
JELLY FISH
ドサッ
flump

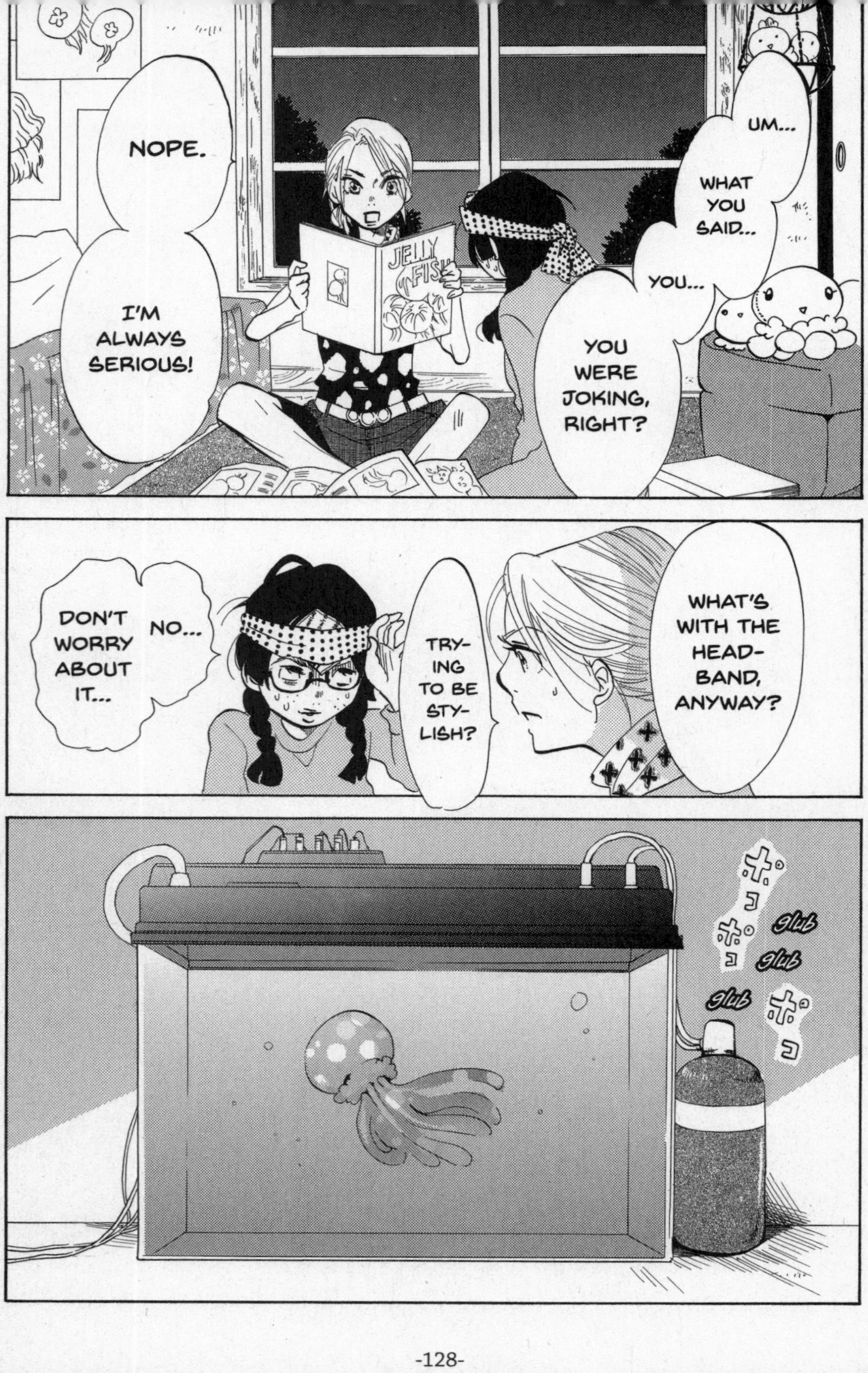
UM...
WHAT YOU SAID...
YOU...
YOU WERE JOKING, RIGHT?
NOPE.
I'M ALWAYS SERIOUS!
WHAT'S WITH THE HEAD-BAND, ANYWAY?
TRY-ING TO BE STY-LISH?
NO...
DON'T WORRY ABOUT IT...
ポコ
ポコ
ポコ
glub
glub
glub

Episode 17
A Moment to Remember

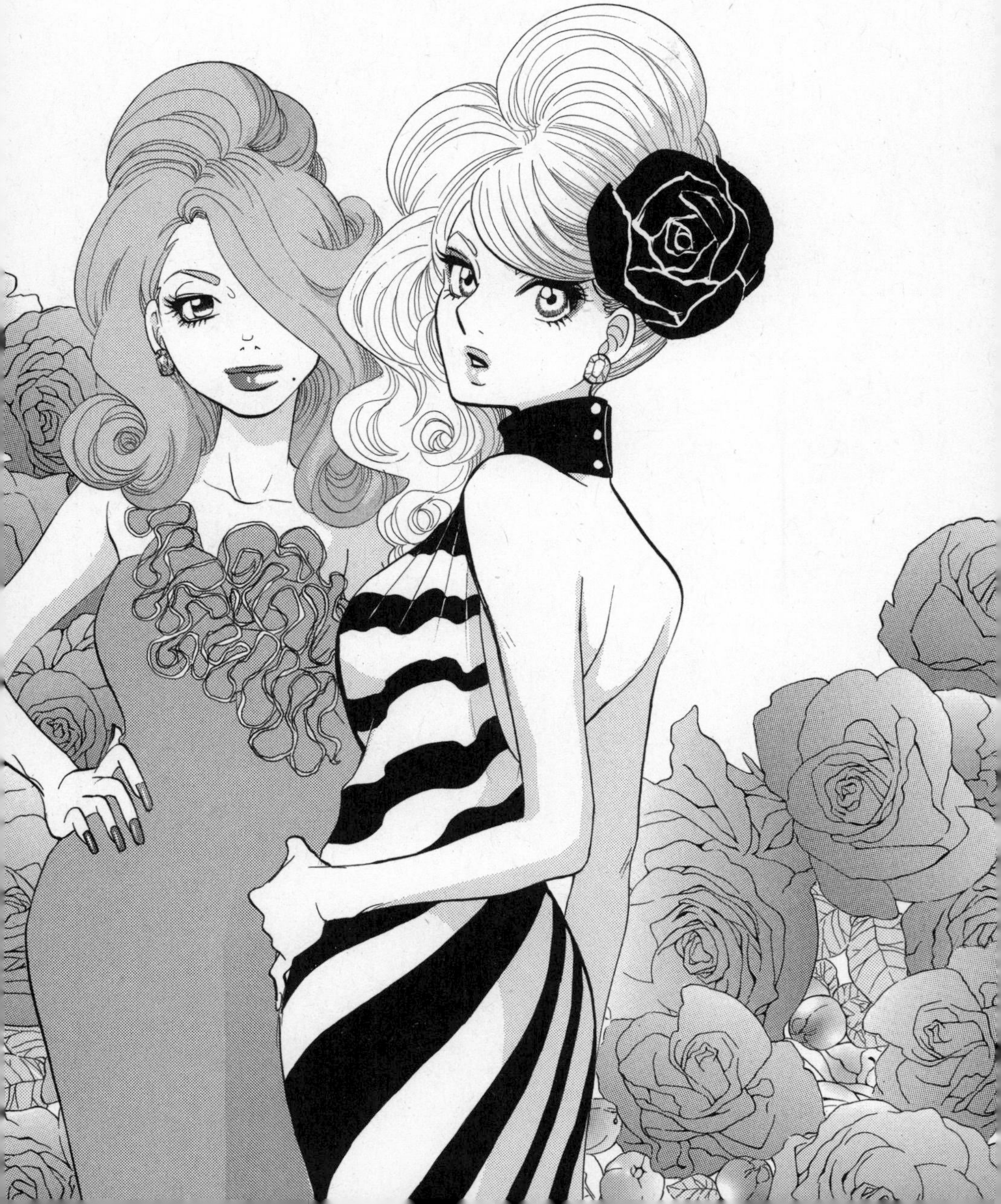

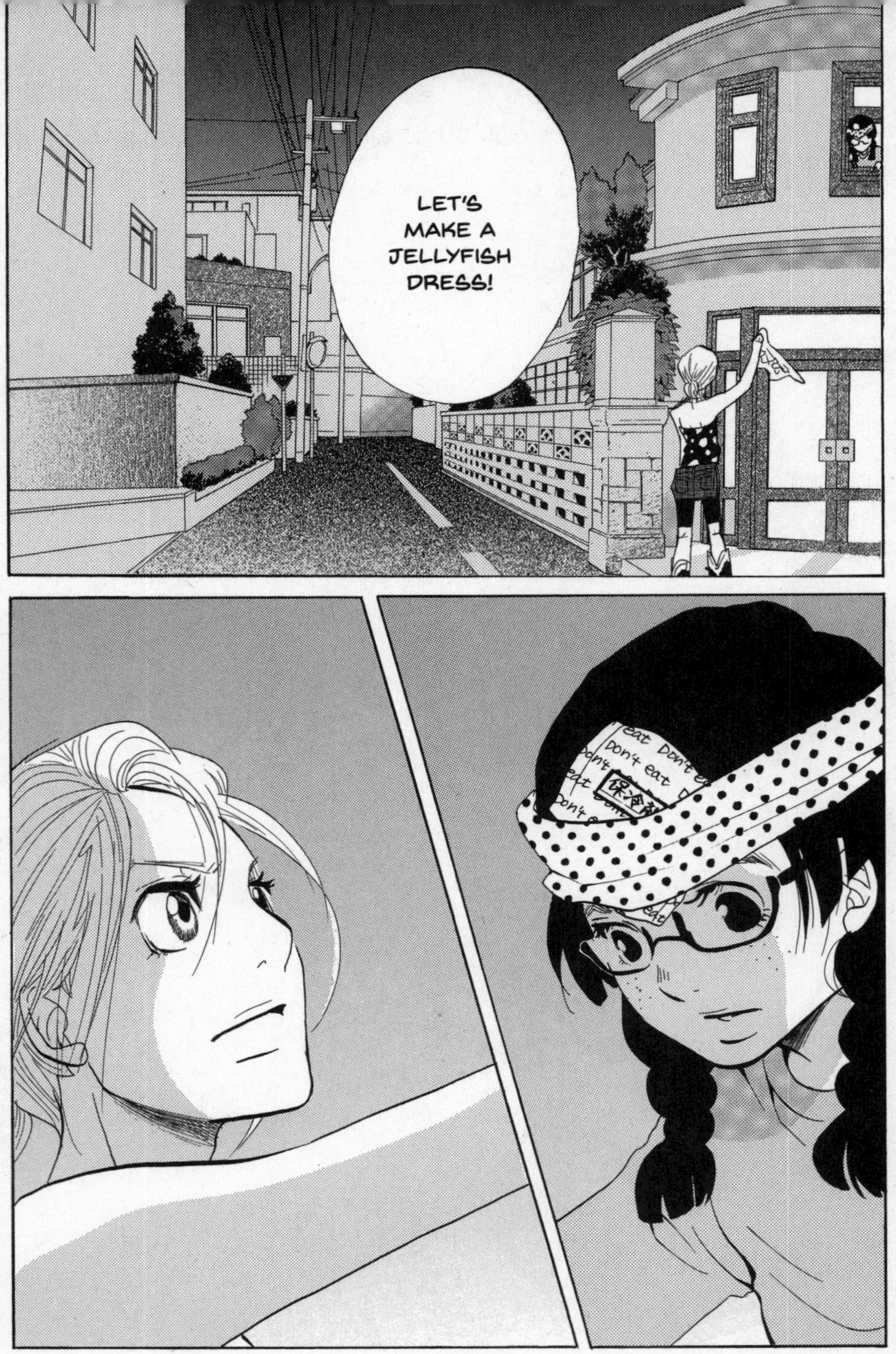
LET'S MAKE A JELLYFISH DRESS!

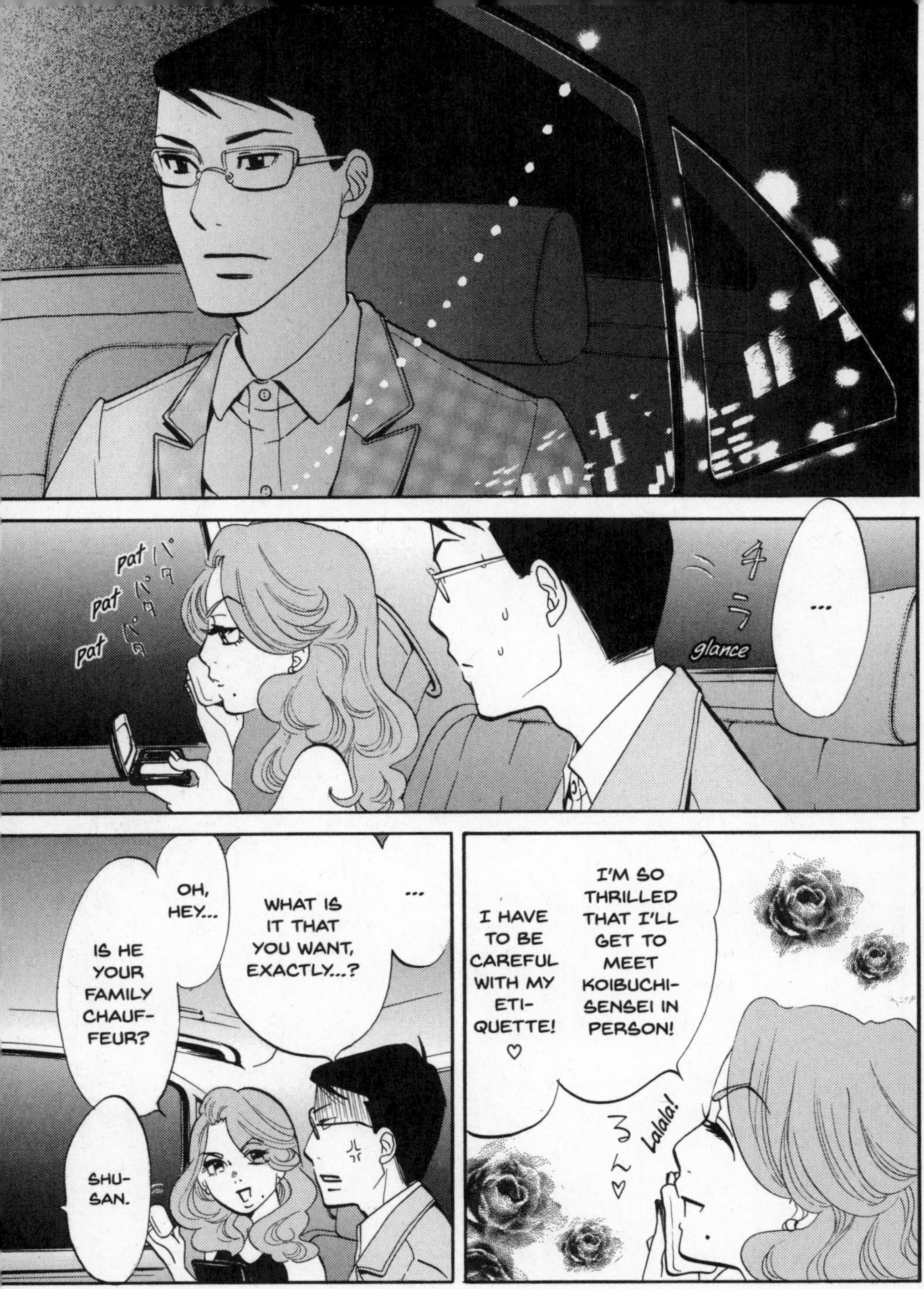
...
チラ
glance
pat パタ
pat パタ
pat パタ
I'M SO THRILLED THAT I'LL GET TO MEET KOIBUCHI-SENSEI IN PERSON!
I HAVE TO BE CAREFUL WITH MY ETI-QUETTE! ♡
Lalala!
るん♡
...
WHAT IS IT THAT YOU WANT, EXACTLY...?
OH, HEY...
IS HE YOUR FAMILY CHAUF-FEUR?
SHU-SAN.

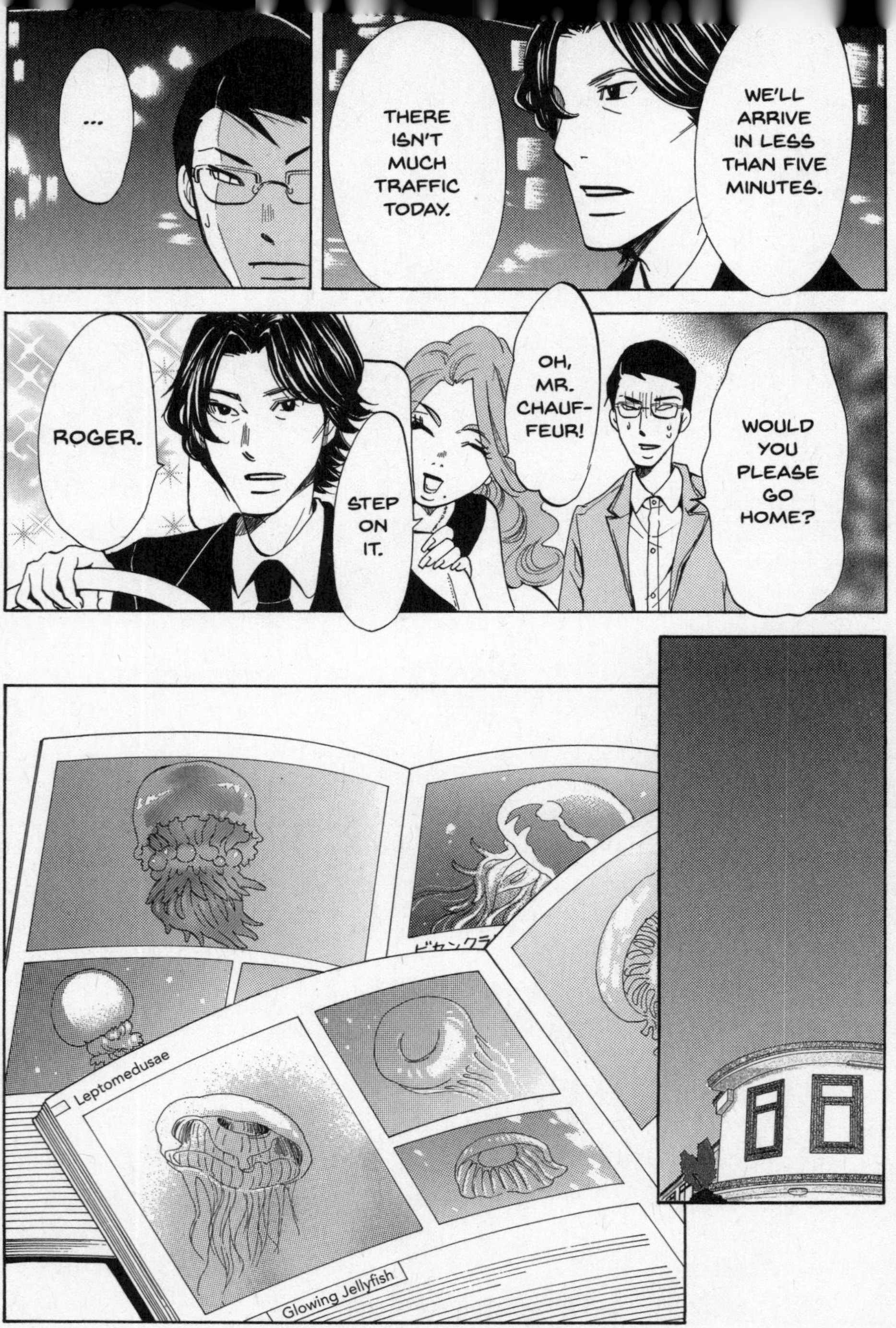
WE'LL ARRIVE IN LESS THAN FIVE MINUTES.
THERE ISN'T MUCH TRAFFIC TODAY.
...
WOULD YOU PLEASE GO HOME?
OH, MR. CHAUFFEUR!
STEP ON IT.
ROGER.
Leptomedusae
Glowing Jellyfish

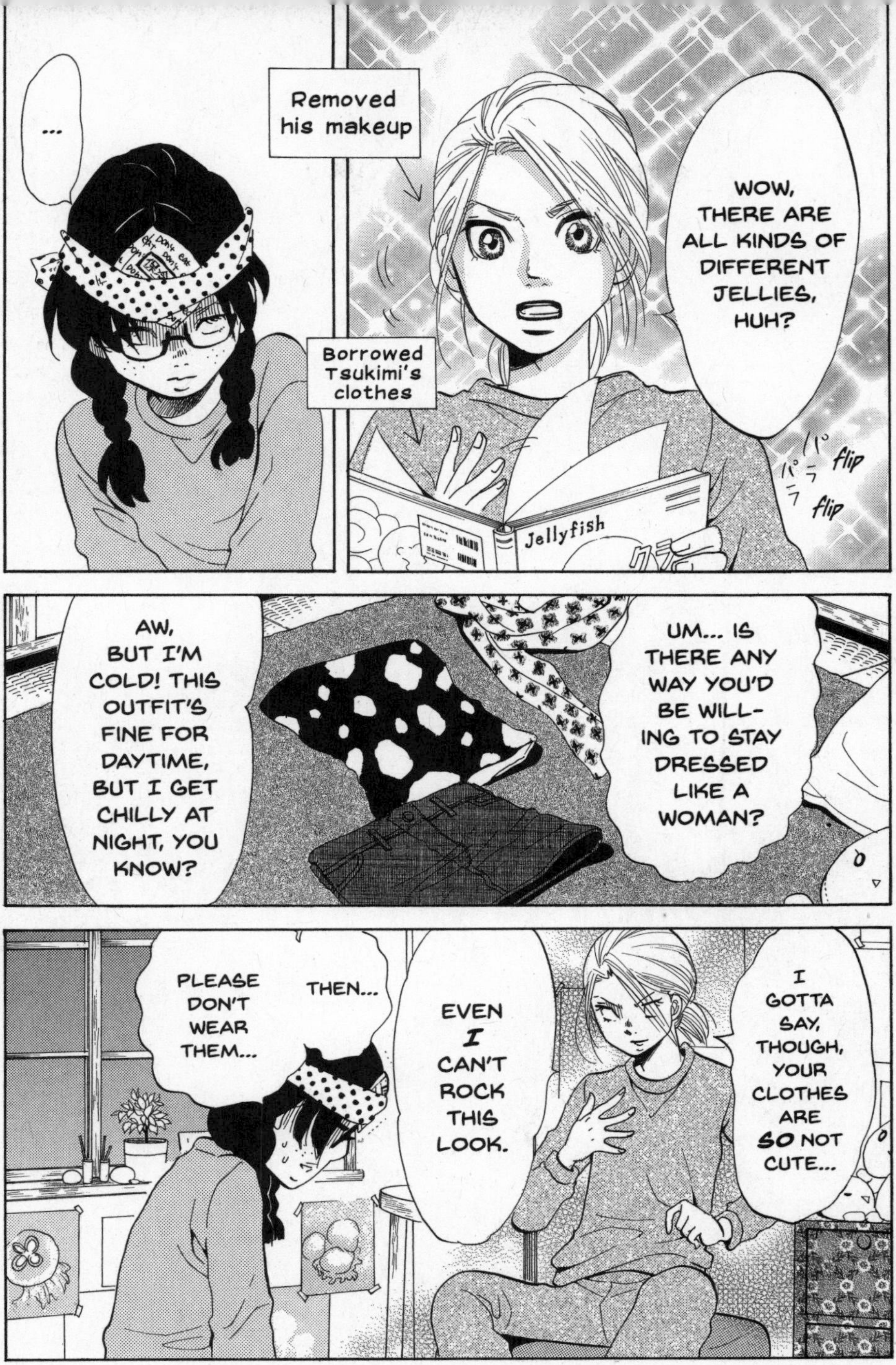
WOW, THERE ARE ALL KINDS OF DIFFERENT JELLIES, HUH?
Removed his makeup
flip
flip
Borrowed Tsukimi's clothes
Jellyfish
...
UM... IS THERE ANY WAY YOU'D BE WILL- ING TO STAY DRESSED LIKE A WOMAN?
AW, BUT I'M COLD! THIS OUTFIT'S FINE FOR DAYTIME, BUT I GET CHILLY AT NIGHT, YOU KNOW?
I GOTTA SAY, THOUGH, YOUR CLOTHES ARE **SO** NOT CUTE...
EVEN *I* CAN'T ROCK THIS LOOK.
THEN...
PLEASE DON'T WEAR THEM...

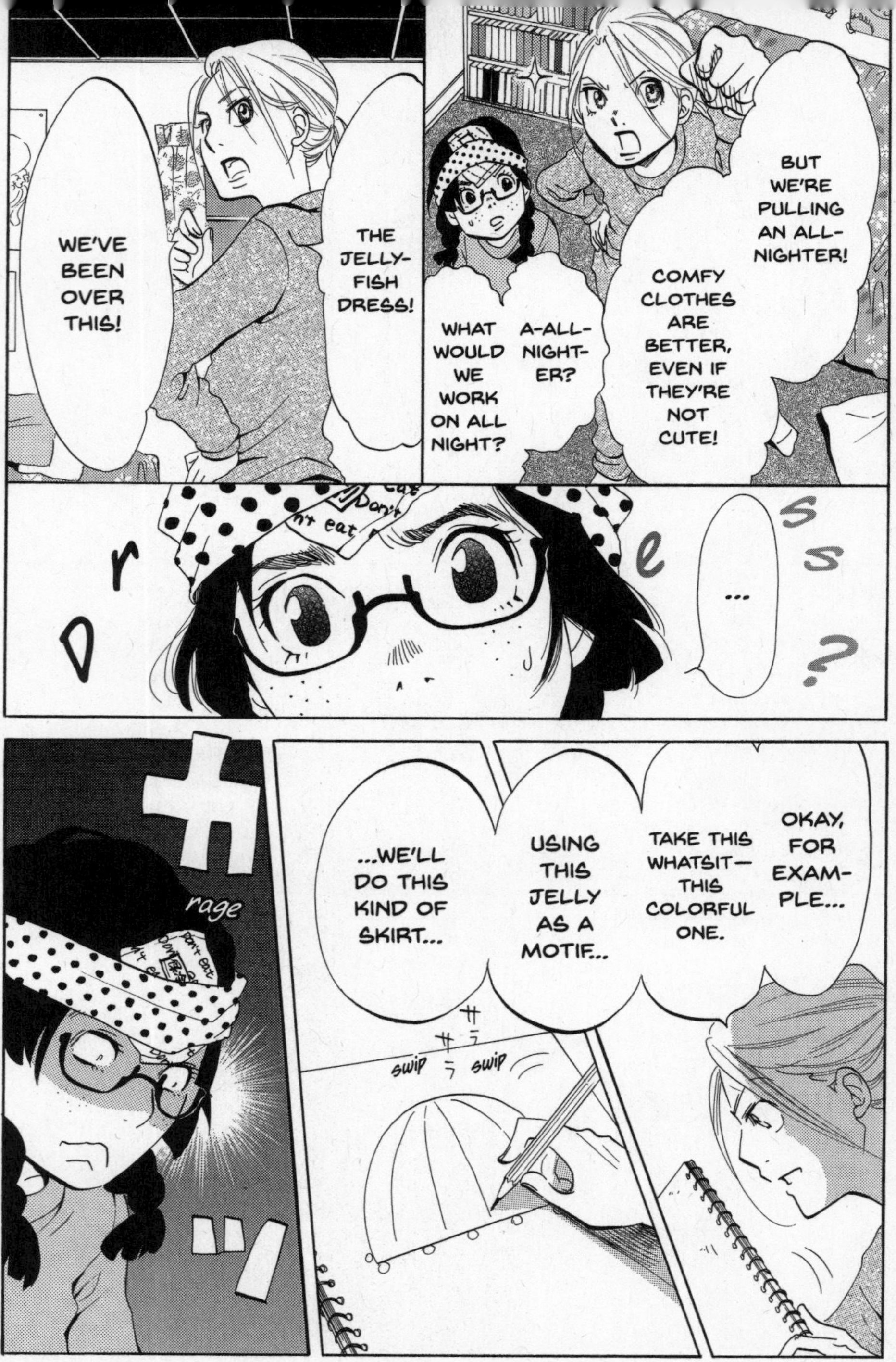

BUT WE'RE PULLING AN ALL-NIGHTER!
COMFY CLOTHES ARE BETTER, EVEN IF THEY'RE NOT CUTE!
A-ALL-NIGHT-ER?
WHAT WOULD WE WORK ON ALL NIGHT?
THE JELLY-FISH DRESS!
WE'VE BEEN OVER THIS!
D r e s s ?
...
OKAY, FOR EXAMPLE...
TAKE THIS WHATSIT—THIS COLORFUL ONE.
USING THIS JELLY AS A MOTIF...
...WE'LL DO THIS KIND OF SKIRT...
サラ サラ
swip swip
カッ
rage

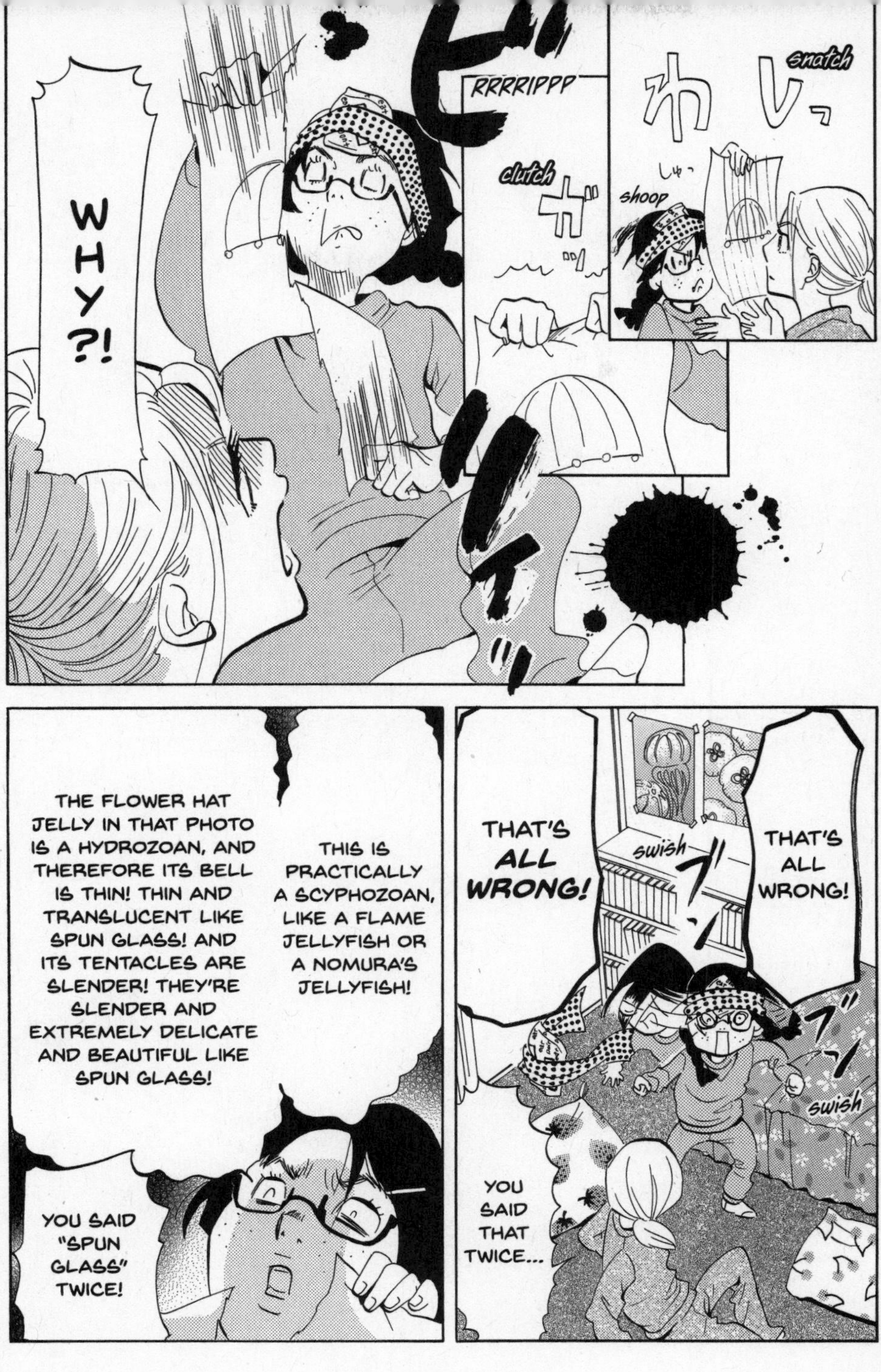
snatch
shoop
RRRRIPPP
clutch
WHY?!
THAT'S ALL WRONG!
THAT'S ALL WRONG!
swish
swish
YOU SAID THAT TWICE...
THE FLOWER HAT JELLY IN THAT PHOTO IS A HYDROZOAN, AND THEREFORE ITS BELL IS THIN! THIN AND TRANSLUCENT LIKE SPUN GLASS! AND ITS TENTACLES ARE SLENDER! THEY'RE SLENDER AND EXTREMELY DELICATE AND BEAUTIFUL LIKE SPUN GLASS!
THIS IS PRACTICALLY A SCYPHOZOAN, LIKE A FLAME JELLYFISH OR A NOMURA'S JELLYFISH!
YOU SAID "SPUN GLASS" TWICE!

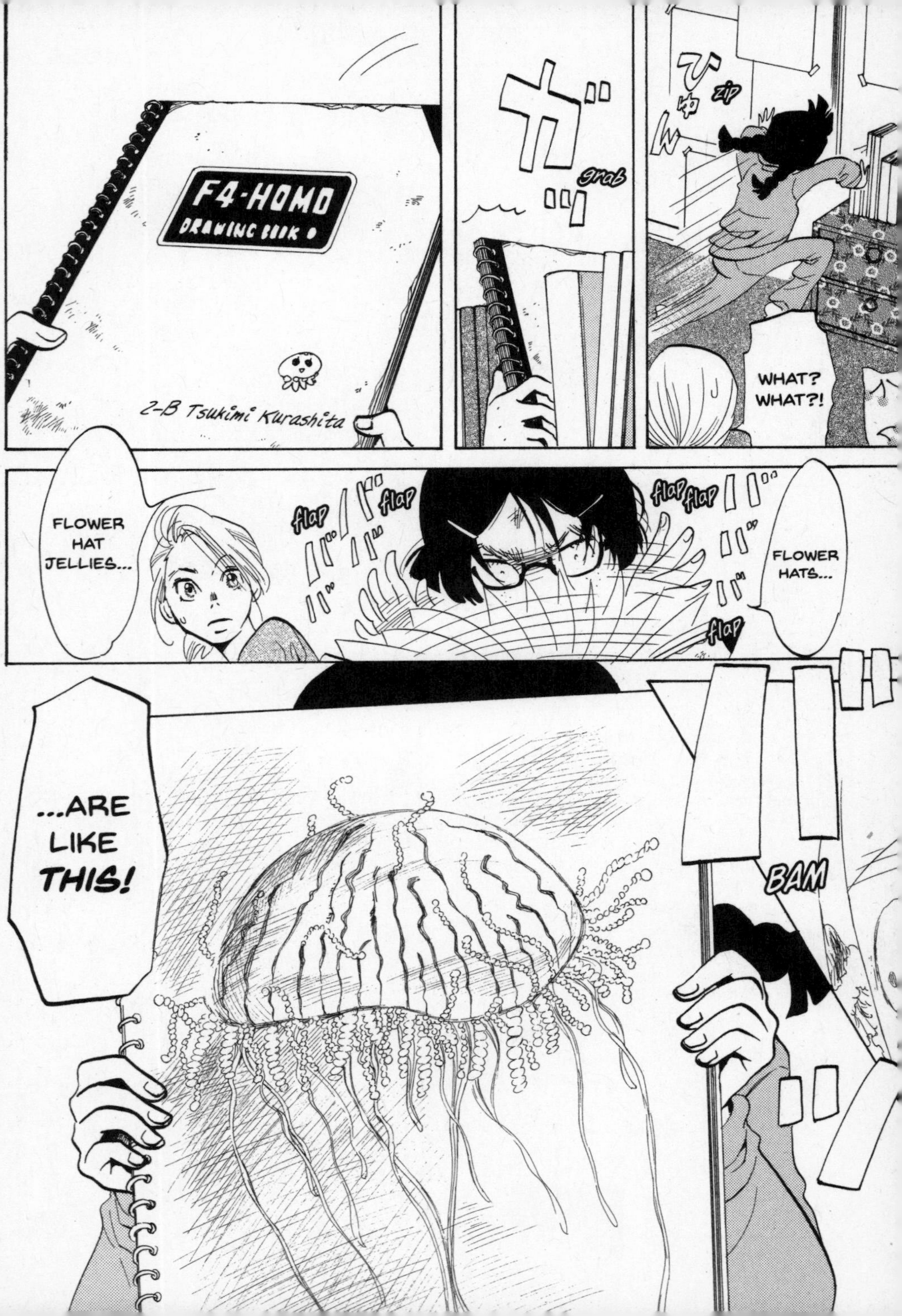
ひゅん
zip
WHAT? WHAT?!
ガッ
grab
F4-HOMO
DRAWING BOOK 0
2-B Tsukimi Kurashita
flap flap
FLOWER HATS...
flap
flap
flap
FLOWER HAT JELLIES...
BAM
...ARE LIKE THIS!

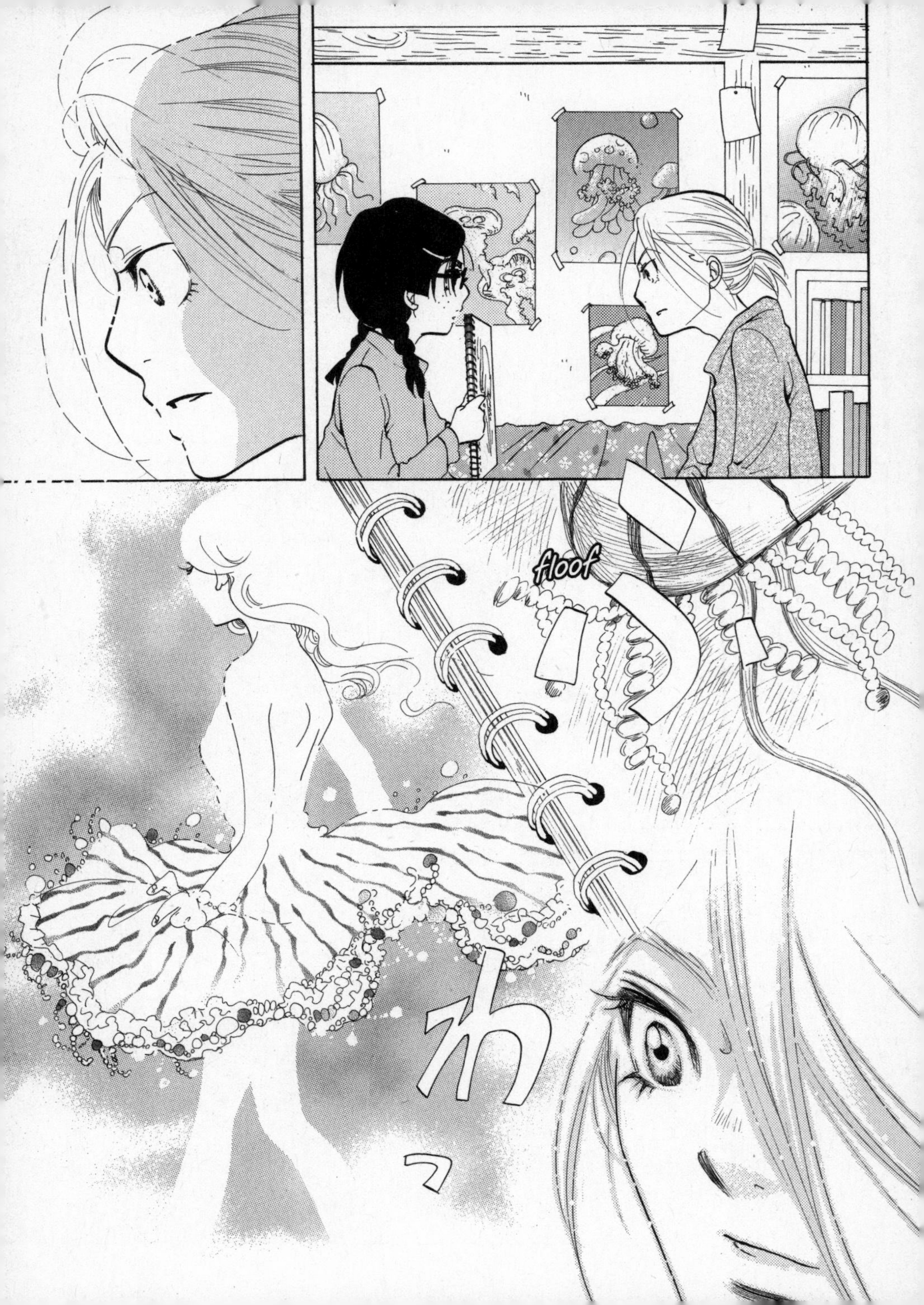
floof
わっ

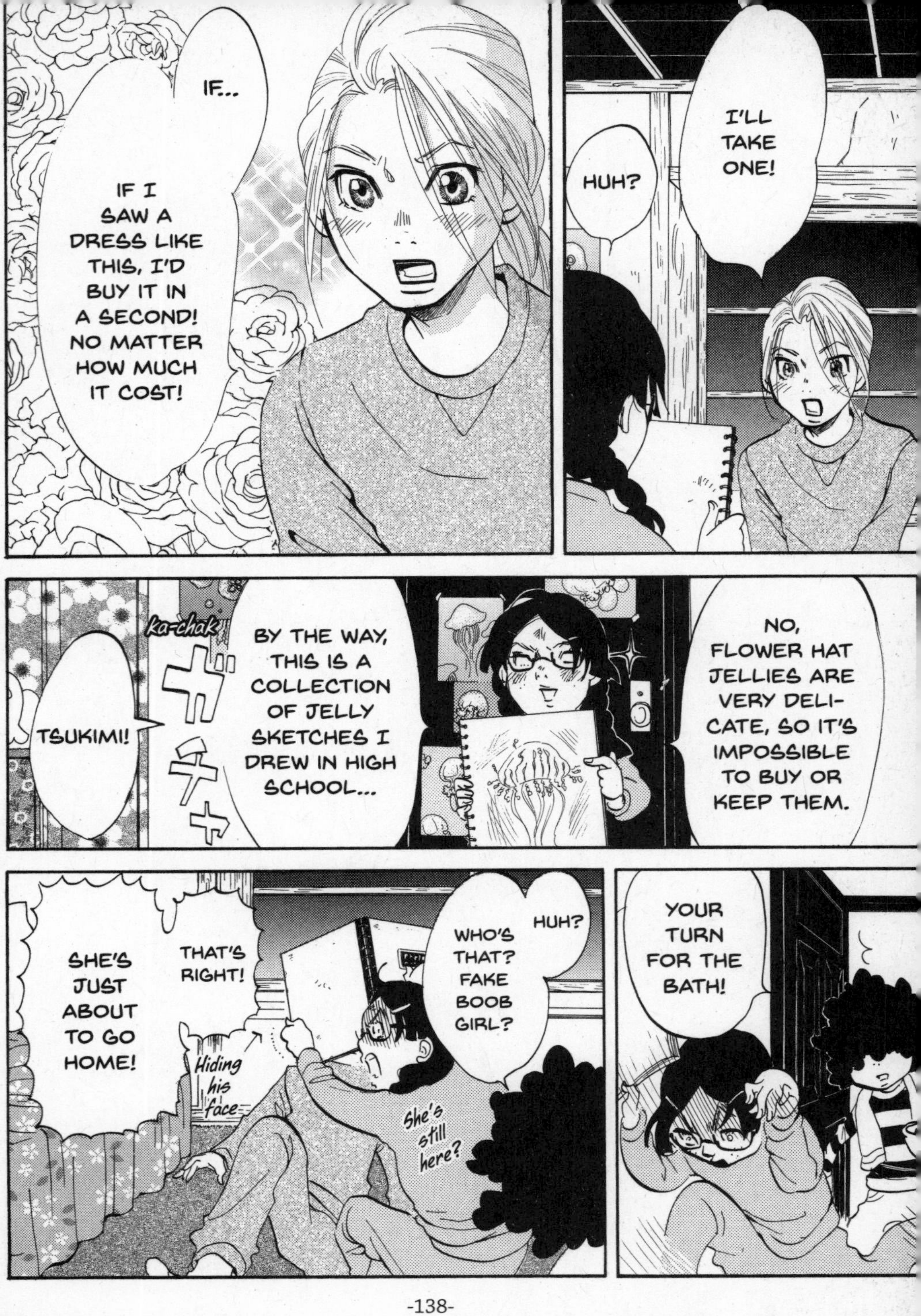

I'LL TAKE ONE!
HUH?
IF...
IF I SAW A DRESS LIKE THIS, I'D BUY IT IN A SECOND! NO MATTER HOW MUCH IT COST!
NO, FLOWER HAT JELLIES ARE VERY DELI-CATE, SO IT'S IMPOSSIBLE TO BUY OR KEEP THEM.
BY THE WAY, THIS IS A COLLECTION OF JELLY SKETCHES I DREW IN HIGH SCHOOL...
ka-chak
ガチャ
TSUKIMI!
YOUR TURN FOR THE BATH!
HUH?
WHO'S THAT? FAKE BOOB GIRL?
She's still here?
THAT'S RIGHT!
SHE'S JUST ABOUT TO GO HOME!
Hiding his face

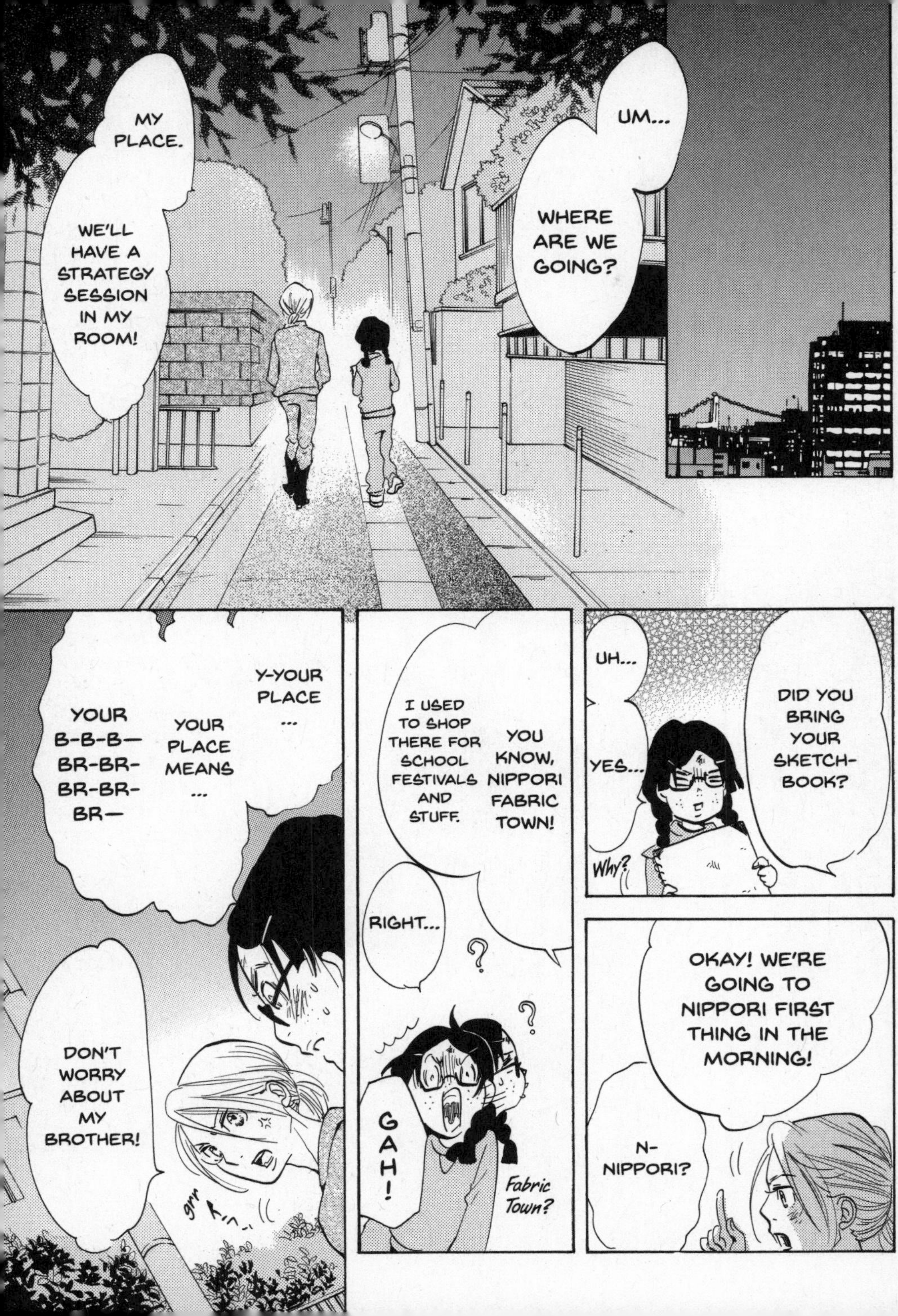
UM...
WHERE ARE WE GOING?
MY PLACE.
WE'LL HAVE A STRATEGY SESSION IN MY ROOM!
DID YOU BRING YOUR SKETCH-BOOK?
UH...
YES...
Why?
OKAY! WE'RE GOING TO NIPPORI FIRST THING IN THE MORNING!
N-NIPPORI?
YOU KNOW, NIPPORI FABRIC TOWN!
I USED TO SHOP THERE FOR SCHOOL FESTIVALS AND STUFF.
RIGHT...
GAH!
Fabric Town?
Y-YOUR PLACE ...
YOUR PLACE MEANS ...
YOUR B-B-B— BR-BR-BR-BR-BR—
DON'T WORRY ABOUT MY BROTHER!
grr

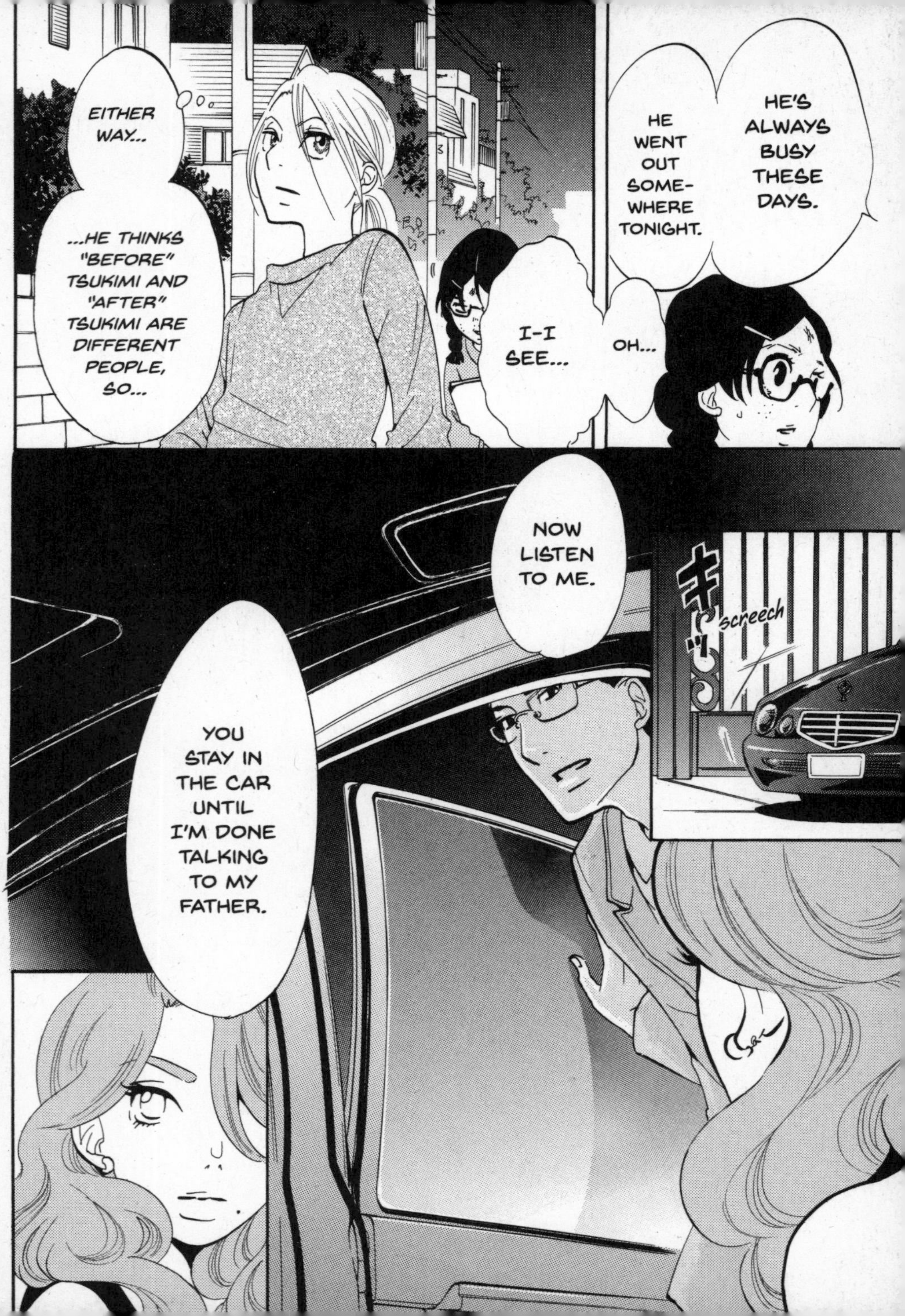
HE'S ALWAYS BUSY THESE DAYS.
HE WENT OUT SOME-WHERE TONIGHT.
OH...
I-I SEE...
EITHER WAY...
...HE THINKS "BEFORE" TSUKIMI AND "AFTER" TSUKIMI ARE DIFFERENT PEOPLE, SO...
screech
NOW LISTEN TO ME.
YOU STAY IN THE CAR UNTIL I'M DONE TALKING TO MY FATHER.

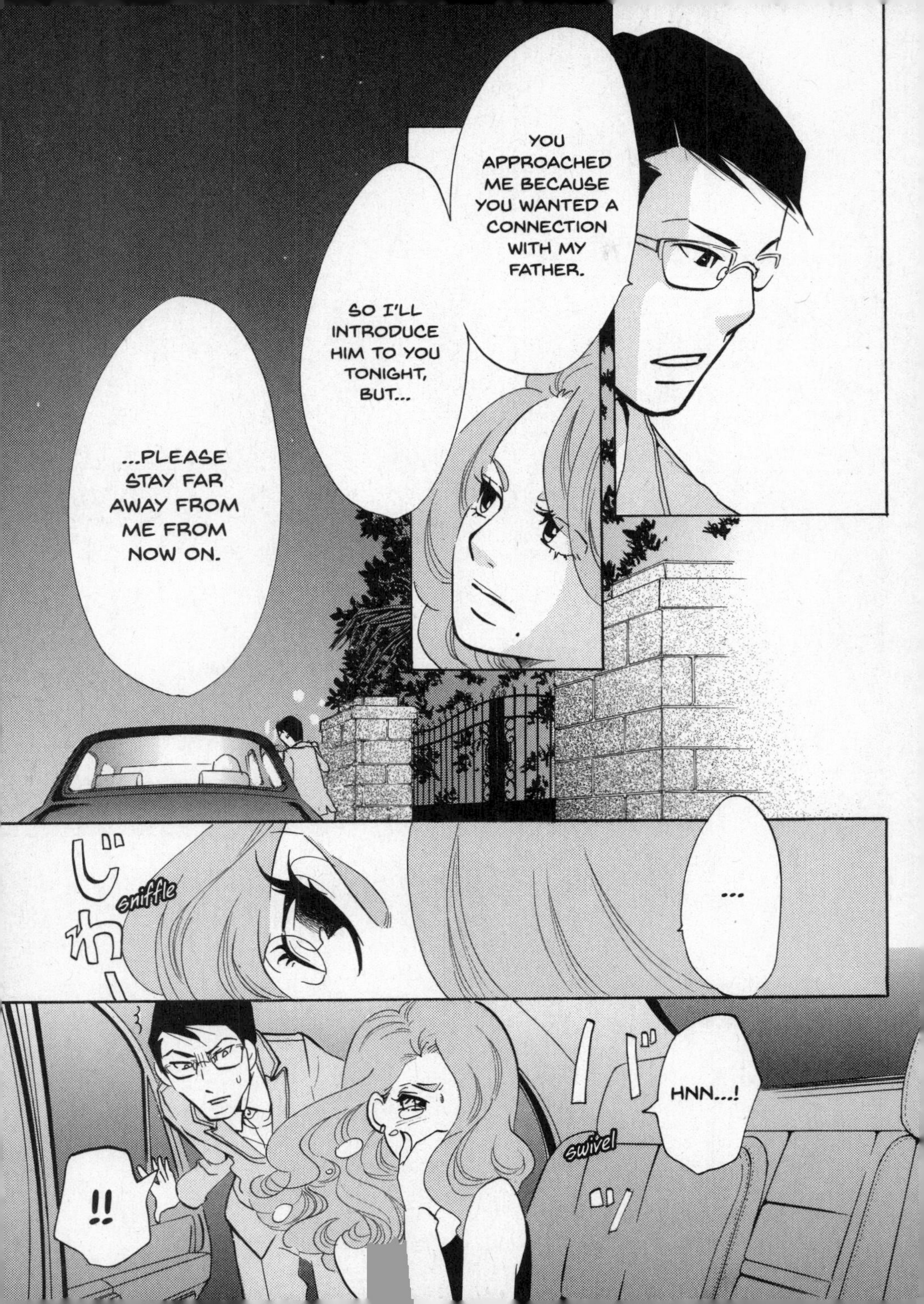
YOU APPROACHED ME BECAUSE YOU WANTED A CONNECTION WITH MY FATHER.
SO I'LL INTRODUCE HIM TO YOU TONIGHT, BUT...
...PLEASE STAY FAR AWAY FROM ME FROM NOW ON.
...
sniffle
HNN...!
swivel
!!

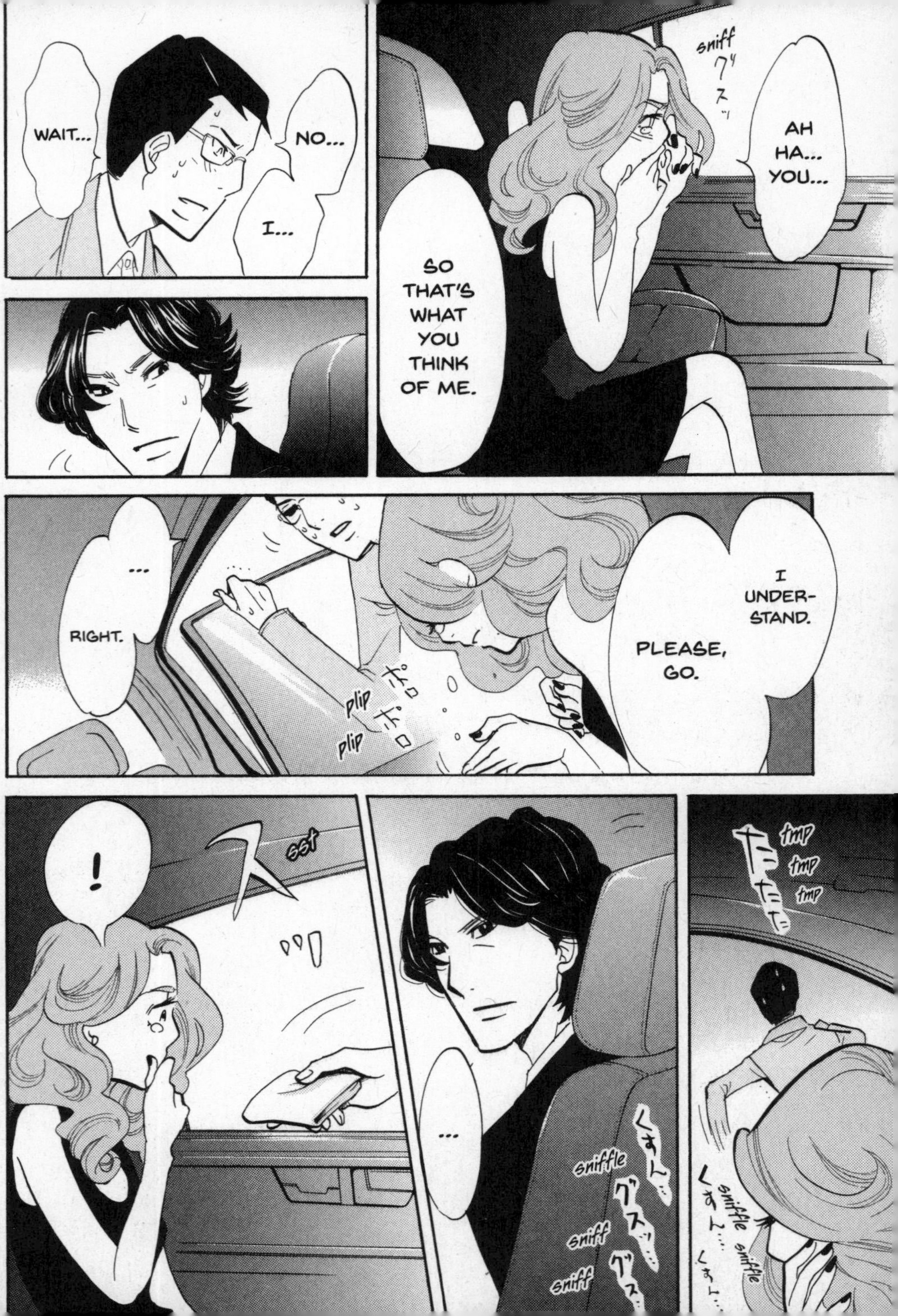
sniff
グズッ
AH HA... YOU...
SO THAT'S WHAT YOU THINK OF ME.
NO...
I...
WAIT...
I UNDERSTAND.
PLEASE, GO.
plip
plip
ポロ ポロ
... RIGHT.
tmp tmp tmp
たたた
sniffle
くすん...
sniffle
くすん...
sniffle
くすん...
グス...
sniff
グス...
sniff
...
sst
ス
!

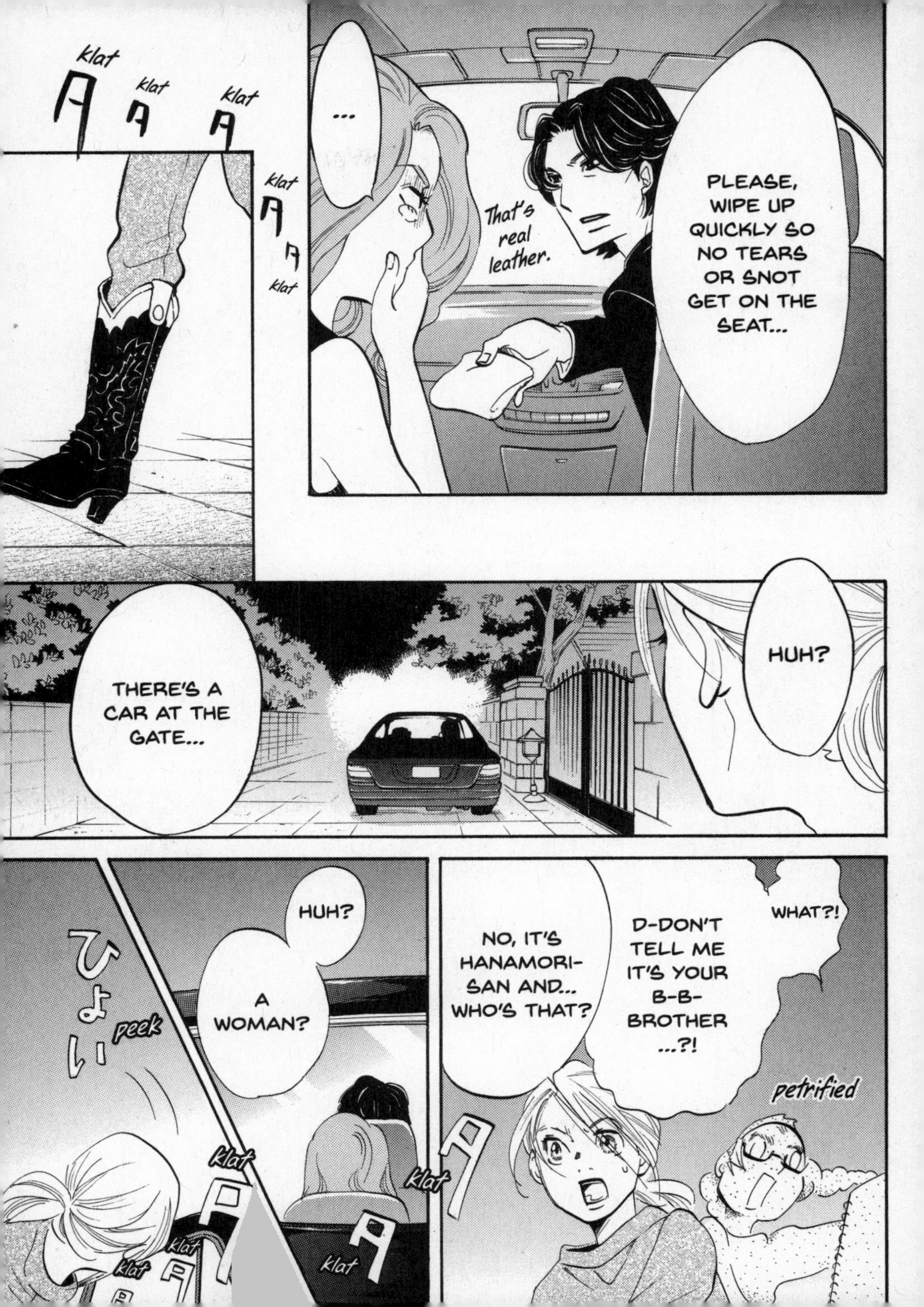
PLEASE, WIPE UP QUICKLY SO NO TEARS OR SNOT GET ON THE SEAT...
That's real leather.
...
klat
klat
klat
klat
klat
HUH?
THERE'S A CAR AT THE GATE...
WHAT?!
D-DON'T TELL ME IT'S YOUR B-B-BROTHER ...?!
NO, IT'S HANAMORI-SAN AND... WHO'S THAT?
petrified
klat
HUH?
A WOMAN?
ひょい
peek
klat
klat
klat
klat

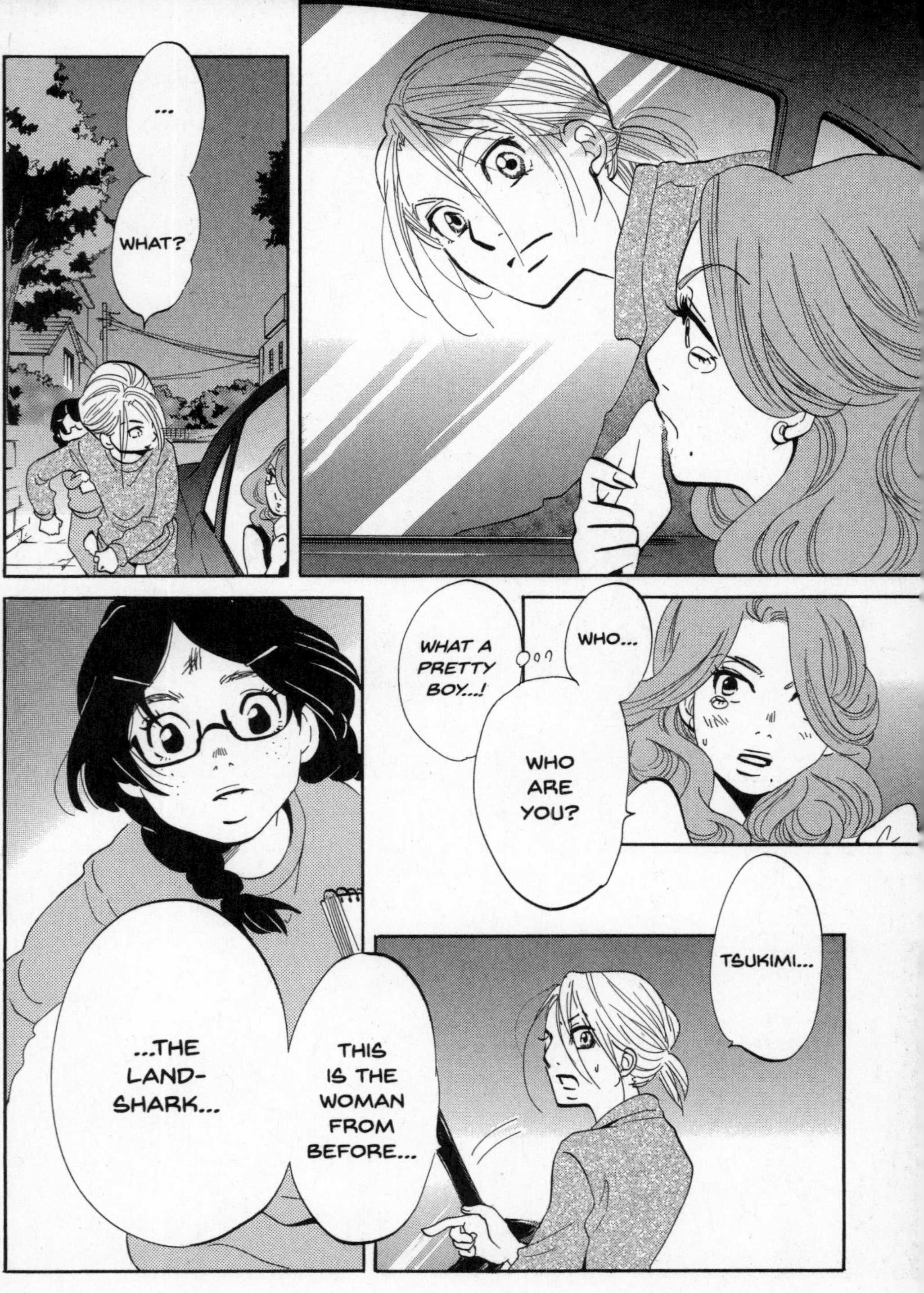
...
WHAT?
WHO...
WHO ARE YOU?
TSUKIMI...
THIS IS THE WOMAN FROM BEFORE...
WHAT A PRETTY BOY...!
...THE LAND-SHARK...

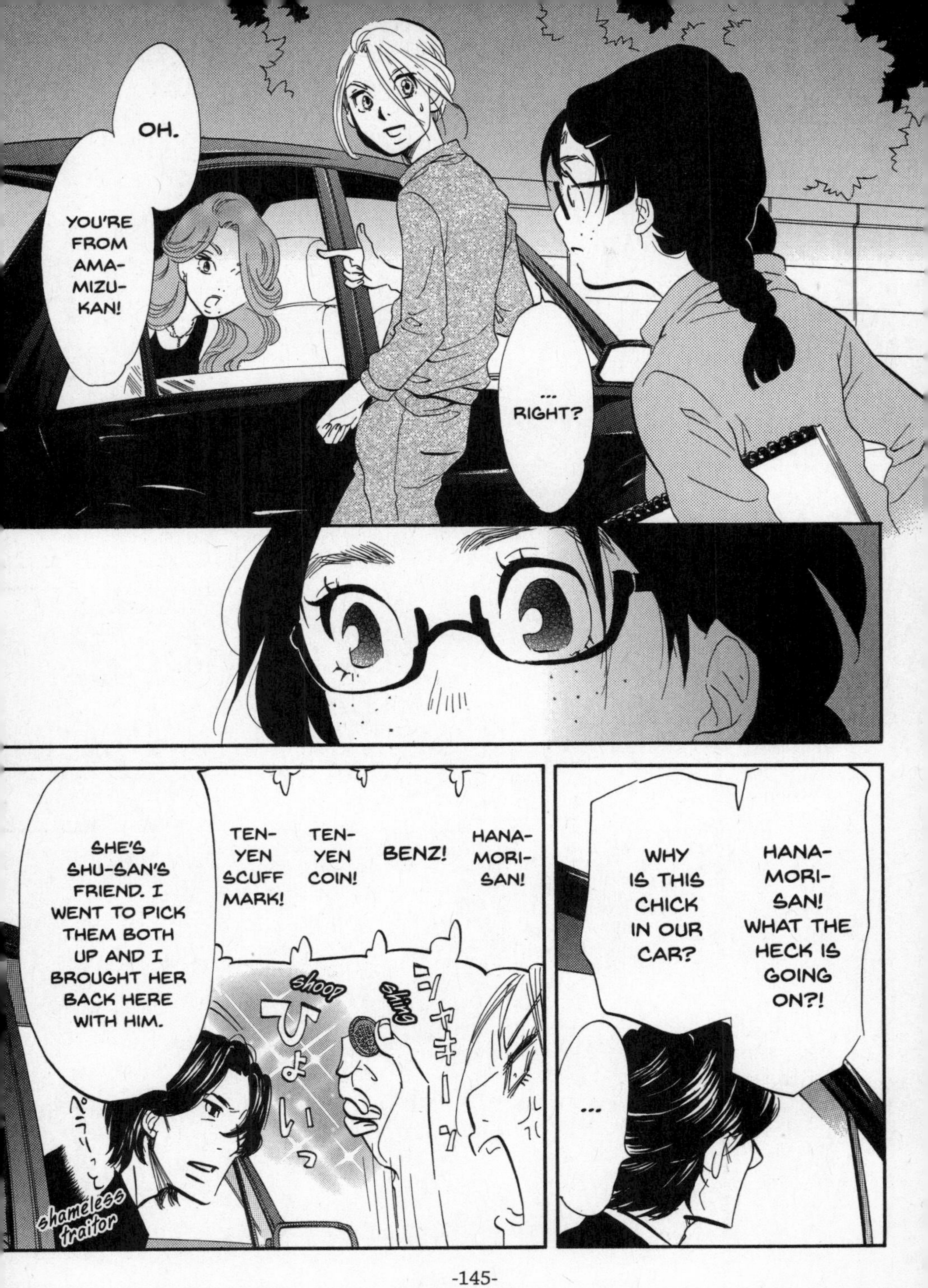
OH.
YOU'RE FROM AMA-MIZU-KAN!
...RIGHT?
HANA-MORI-SAN! WHAT THE HECK IS GOING ON?!
WHY IS THIS CHICK IN OUR CAR?
...
HANA-MORI-SAN!
BENZ!
TEN-YEN COIN!
TEN-YEN SCUFF MARK!
shing
shoop
SHE'S SHU-SAN'S FRIEND. I WENT TO PICK THEM BOTH UP AND I BROUGHT HER BACK HERE WITH HIM.
shameless traitor

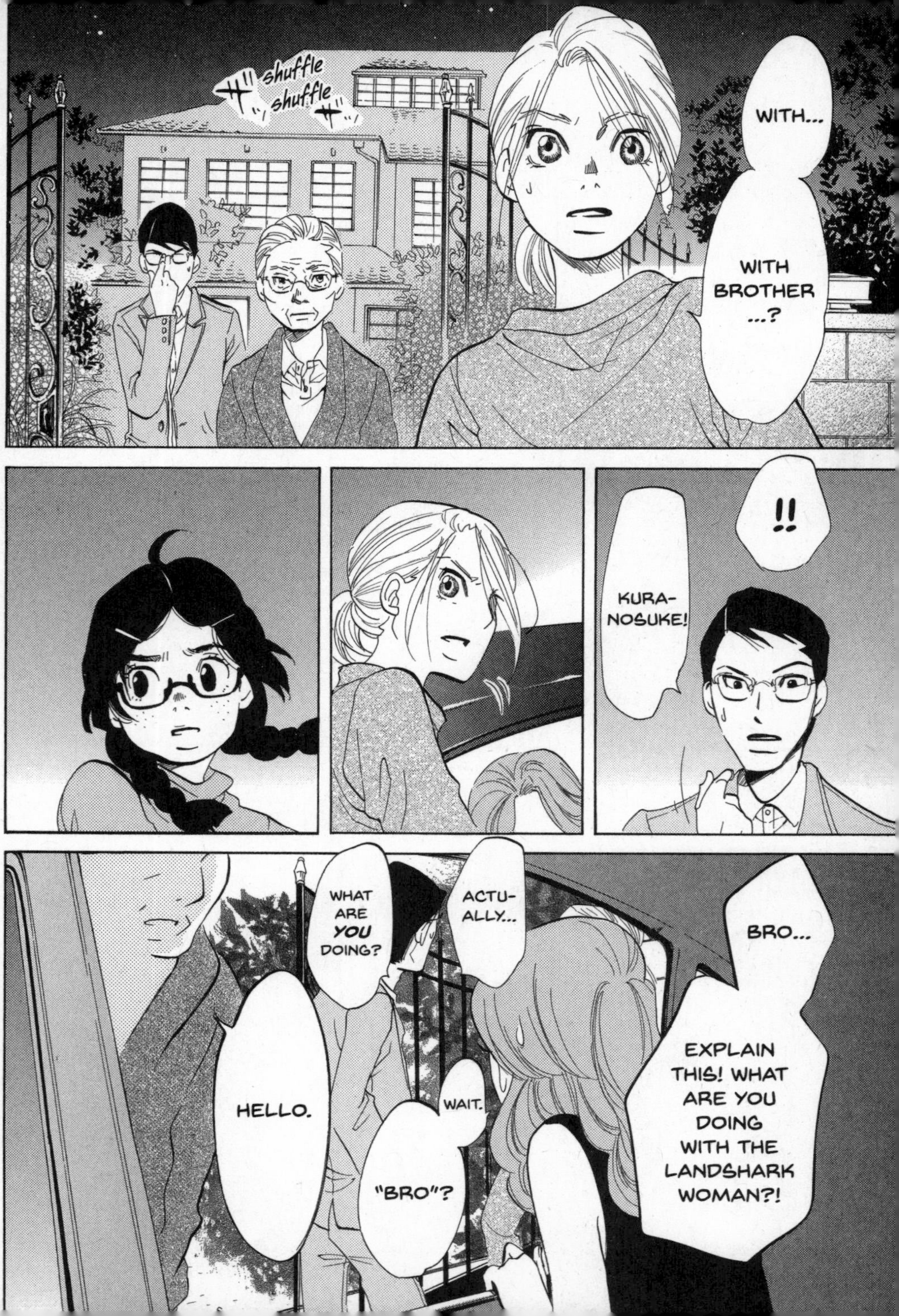
WITH...
WITH BROTHER ...?
shuffle shuffle
!!
KURA-NOSUKE!
BRO...
EXPLAIN THIS! WHAT ARE YOU DOING WITH THE LANDSHARK WOMAN?!
ACTU-ALLY...
WHAT ARE *YOU* DOING?
WAIT.
"BRO"?
HELLO.

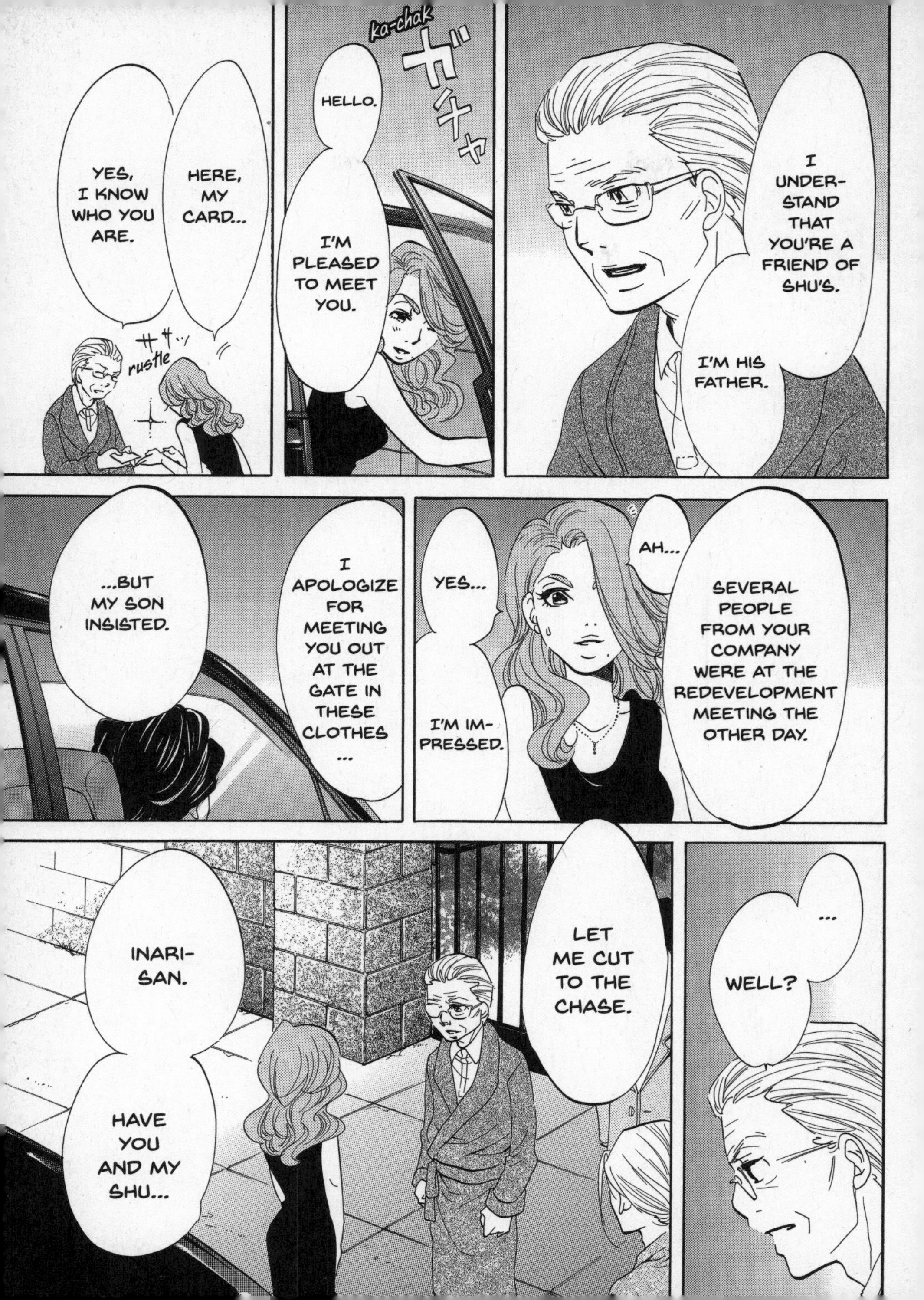
I UNDERSTAND THAT YOU'RE A FRIEND OF SHU'S.
I'M HIS FATHER.
ka-chak
HELLO.
I'M PLEASED TO MEET YOU.
HERE, MY CARD...
YES, I KNOW WHO YOU ARE.
rustle
SEVERAL PEOPLE FROM YOUR COMPANY WERE AT THE REDEVELOPMENT MEETING THE OTHER DAY.
AH...
YES...
I'M IMPRESSED.
I APOLOGIZE FOR MEETING YOU OUT AT THE GATE IN THESE CLOTHES...
...BUT MY SON INSISTED.
...
WELL?
LET ME CUT TO THE CHASE.
INARI-SAN.
HAVE YOU AND MY SHU...

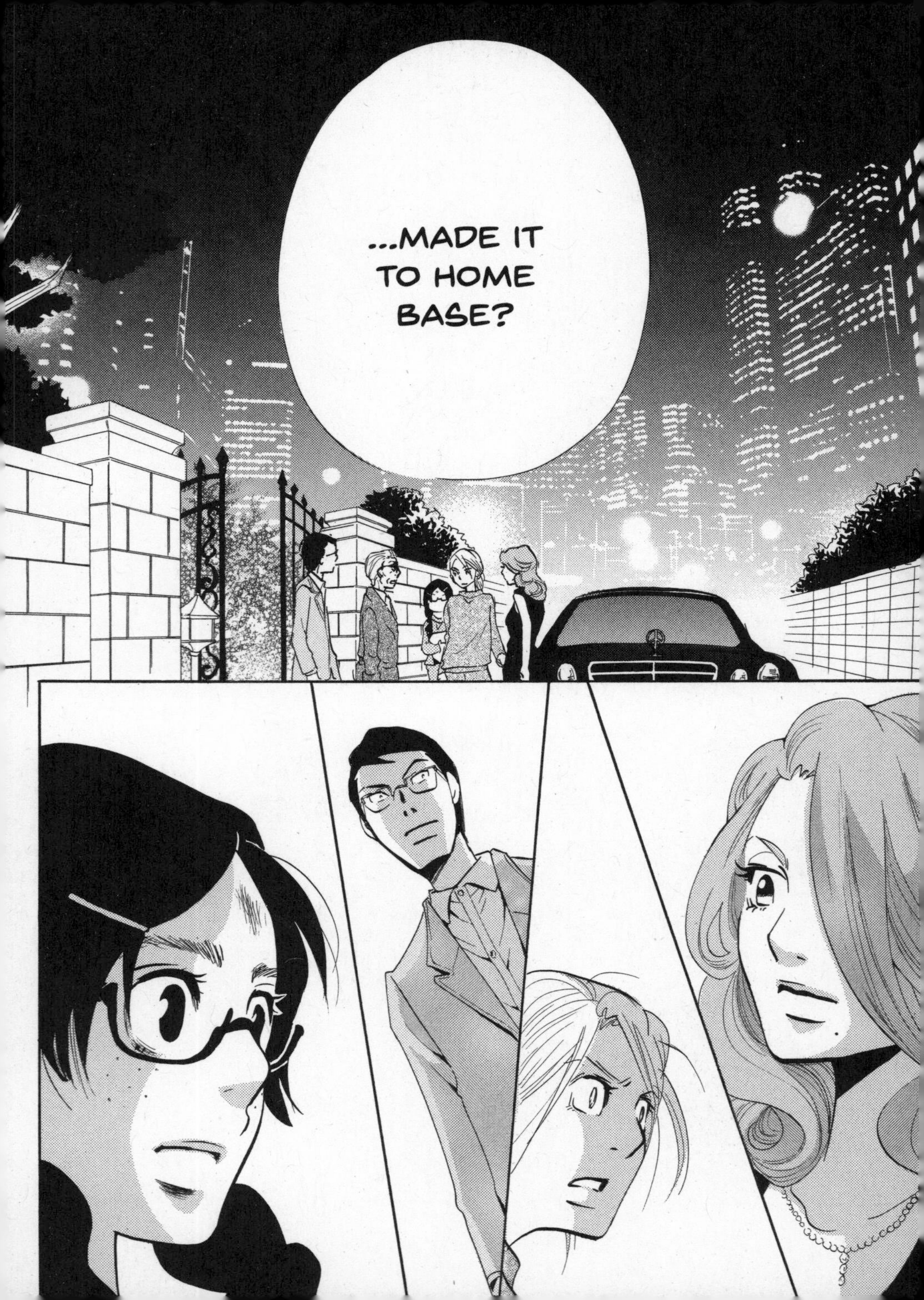
...MADE IT TO HOME BASE?

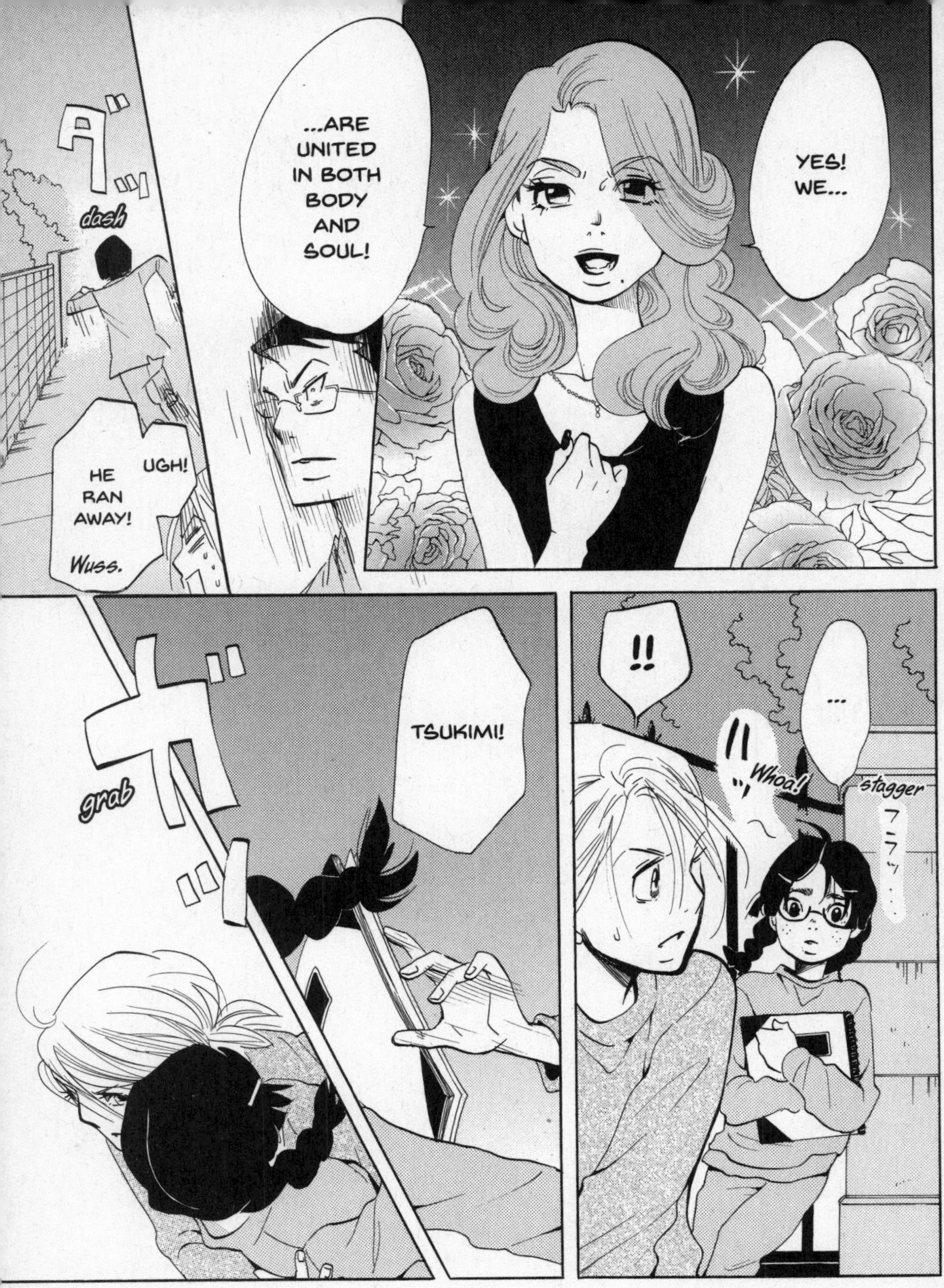
YES! WE...
...ARE UNITED IN BOTH BODY AND SOUL!
dash
UGH!
HE RAN AWAY!
Wuss.
!!
...
Whoa!
stagger
フラッ・・・
TSUKIMI!
grab

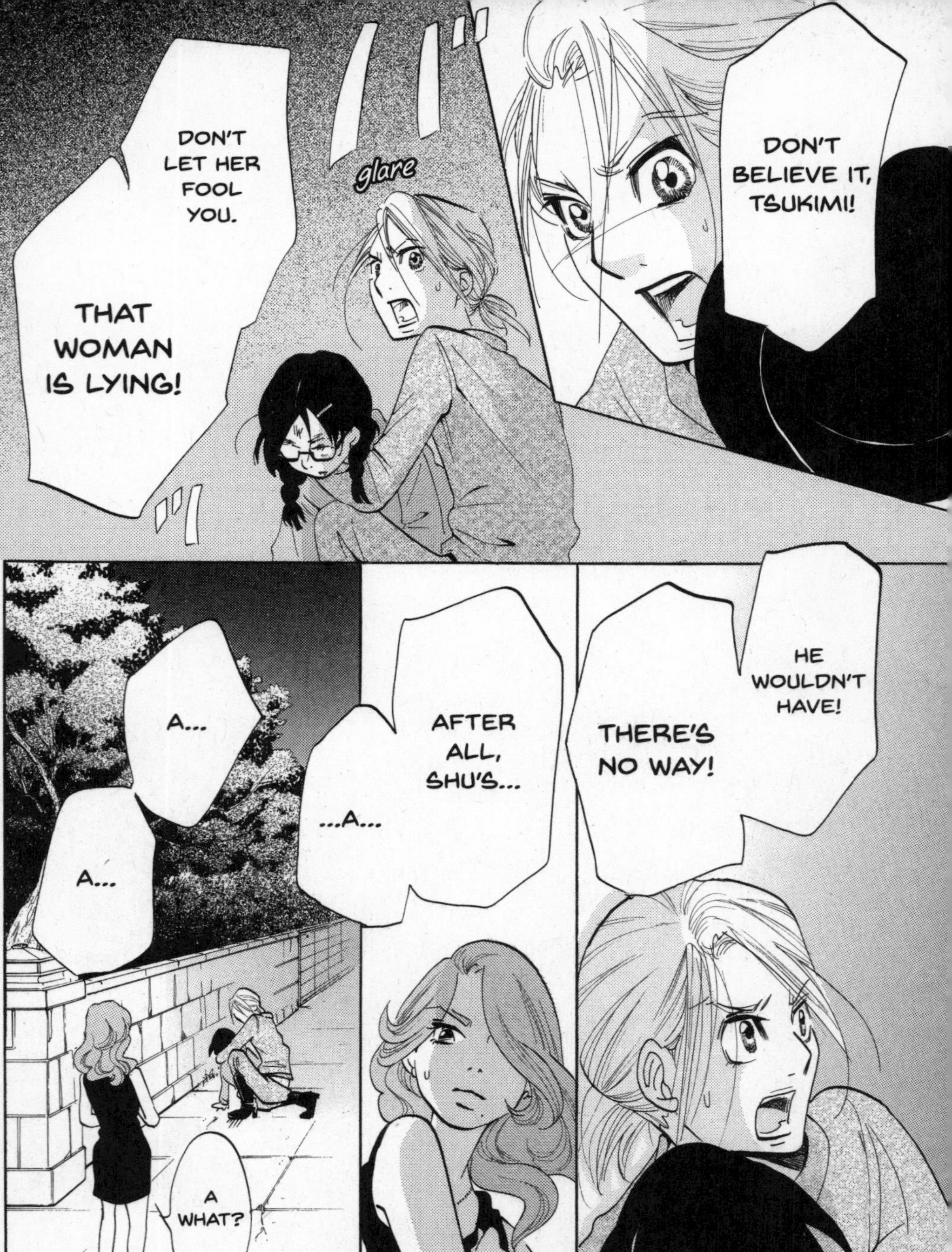
DON'T BELIEVE IT, TSUKIMI!
DON'T LET HER FOOL YOU.
glare
THAT WOMAN IS LYING!
HE WOULDN'T HAVE!
THERE'S NO WAY!
AFTER ALL, SHU'S...
...A...
A...
A...
A WHAT?

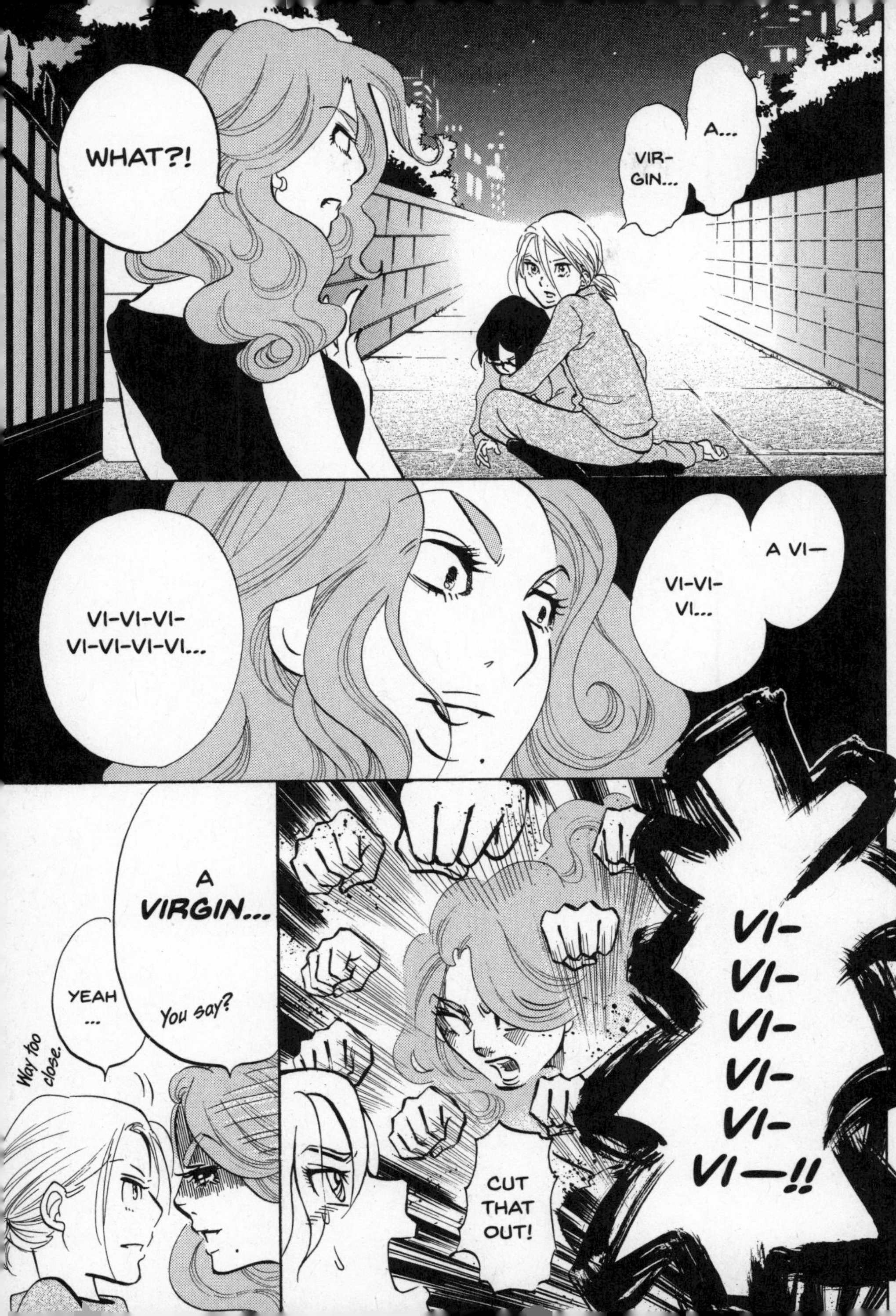
A... VIR-GIN...
WHAT?!
A VI— VI-VI-VI...
VI-VI-VI-VI-VI-VI-VI...
VI-VI-VI-VI-VI-VI—!!
CUT THAT OUT!
A VIRGIN... You say?
YEAH ...
Way too close.

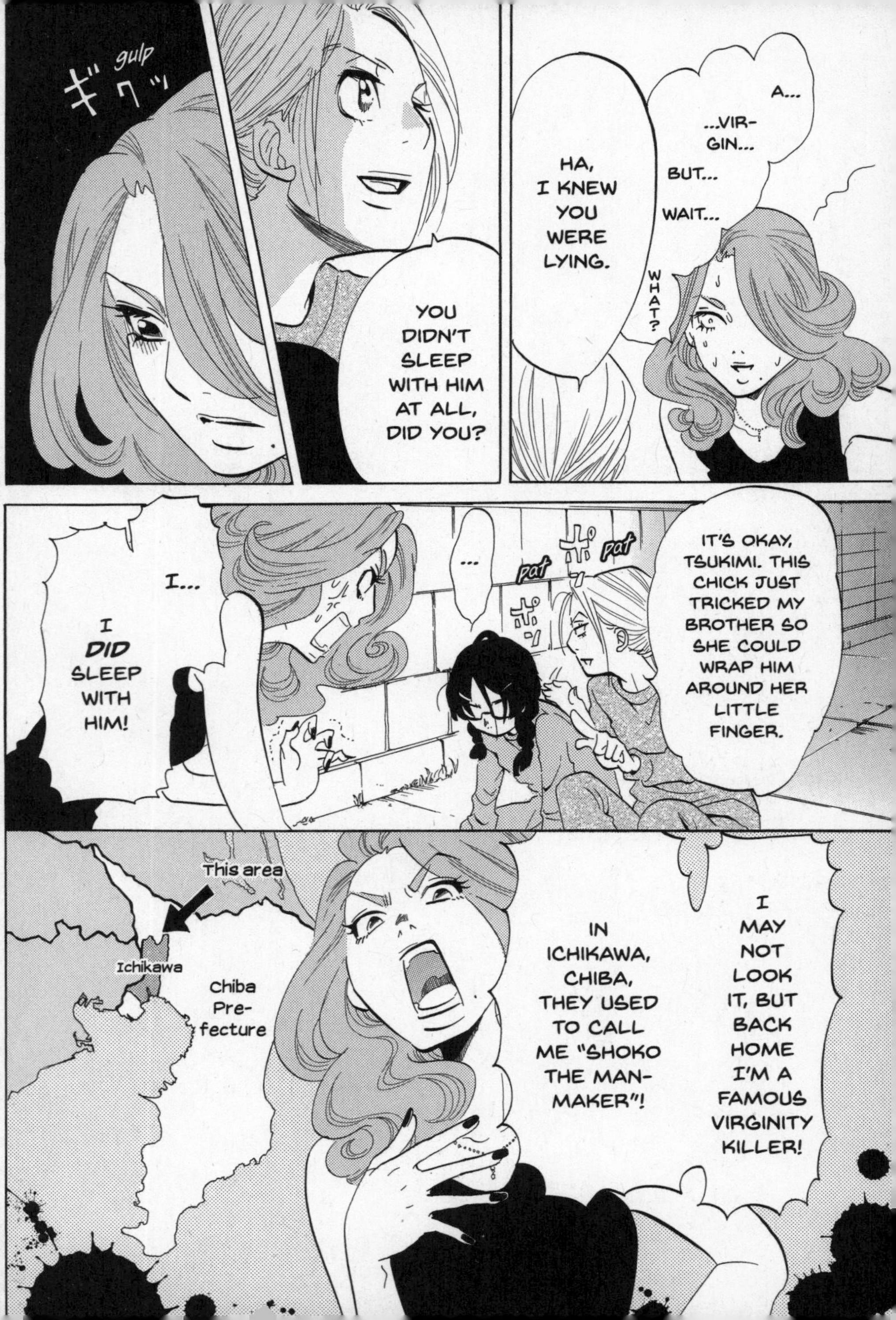
A... ...VIR-GIN... BUT... WAIT...
HA, I KNEW YOU WERE LYING.
WHAT?
YOU DIDN'T SLEEP WITH HIM AT ALL, DID YOU?
gulp
ギクッ
IT'S OKAY, TSUKIMI. THIS CHICK JUST TRICKED MY BROTHER SO SHE COULD WRAP HIM AROUND HER LITTLE FINGER.
pat
ポン
pat
ポン
...
I...
I DID SLEEP WITH HIM!
I MAY NOT LOOK IT, BUT BACK HOME I'M A FAMOUS VIRGINITY KILLER!
IN ICHIKAWA, CHIBA, THEY USED TO CALL ME "SHOKO THE MAN-MAKER"!
This area
Ichikawa
Chiba Prefecture

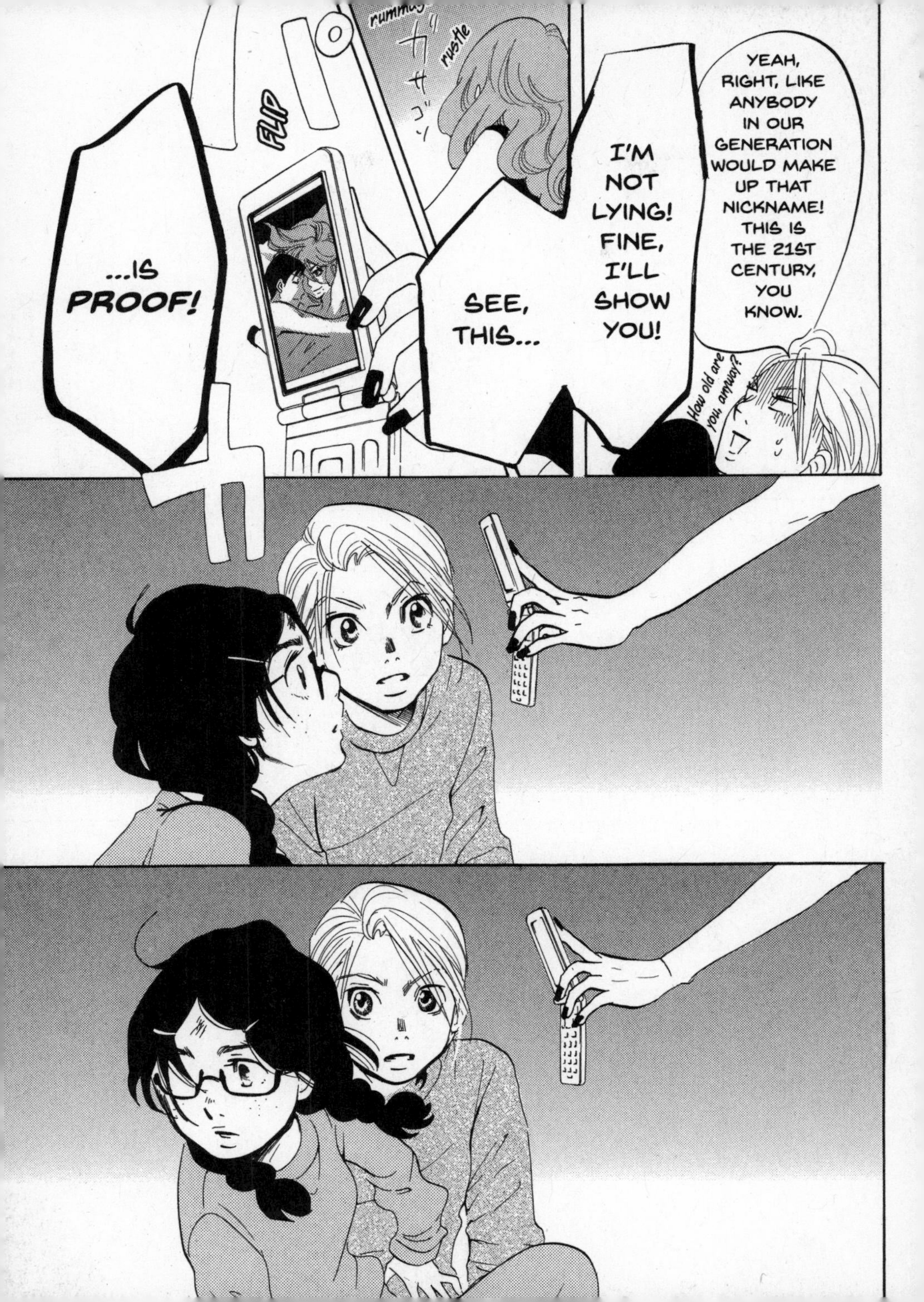
YEAH, RIGHT, LIKE ANYBODY IN OUR GENERATION WOULD MAKE UP THAT NICKNAME! THIS IS THE 21ST CENTURY, YOU KNOW.
How old are you, anyway?
rustle
rummage
I'M NOT LYING! FINE, I'LL SHOW YOU!
FLIP
SEE, THIS...
...IS PROOF!

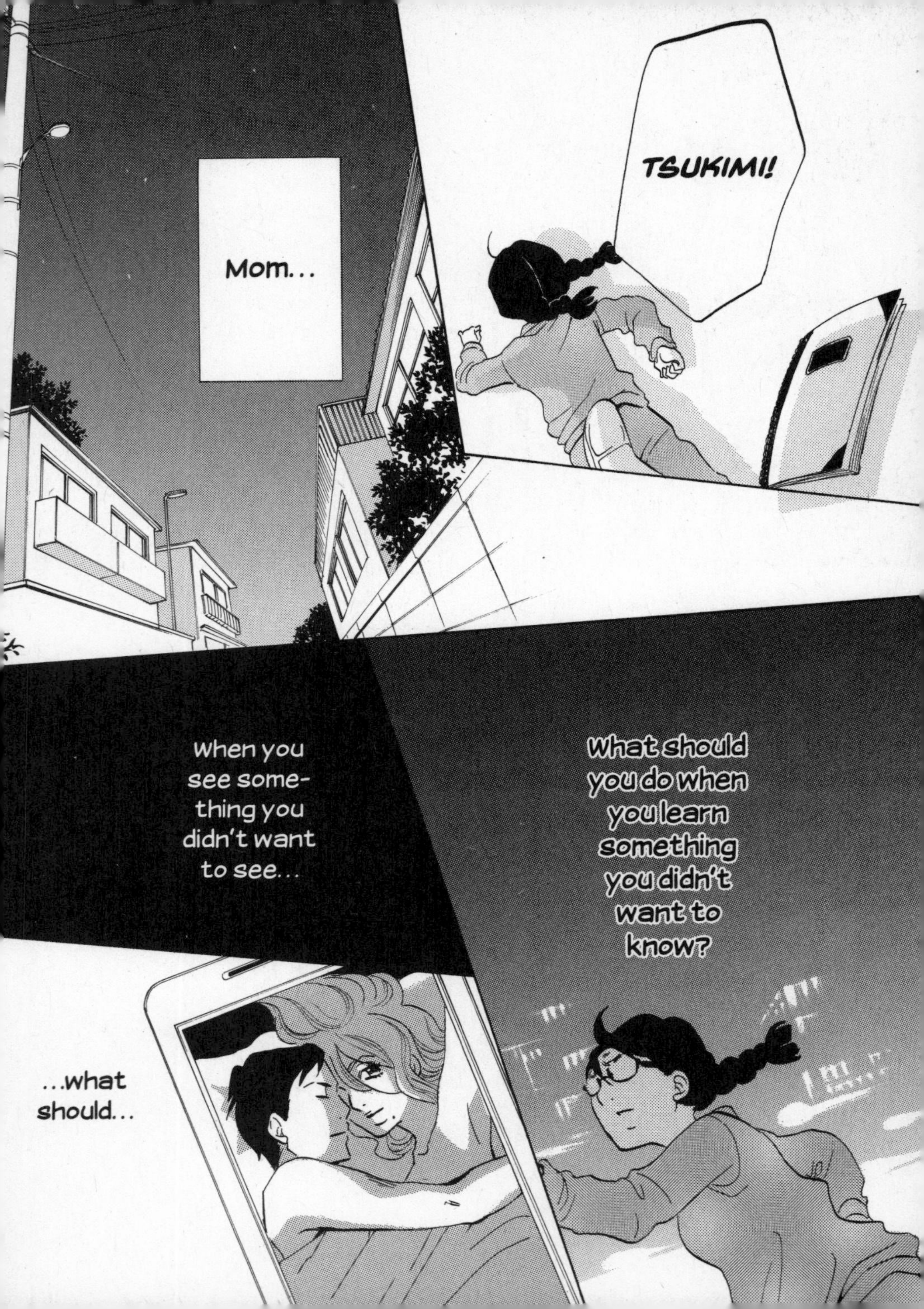
TSUKIMI!
Mom...
What should you do when you learn something you didn't want to know?
When you see some-thing you didn't want to see...
...what should...

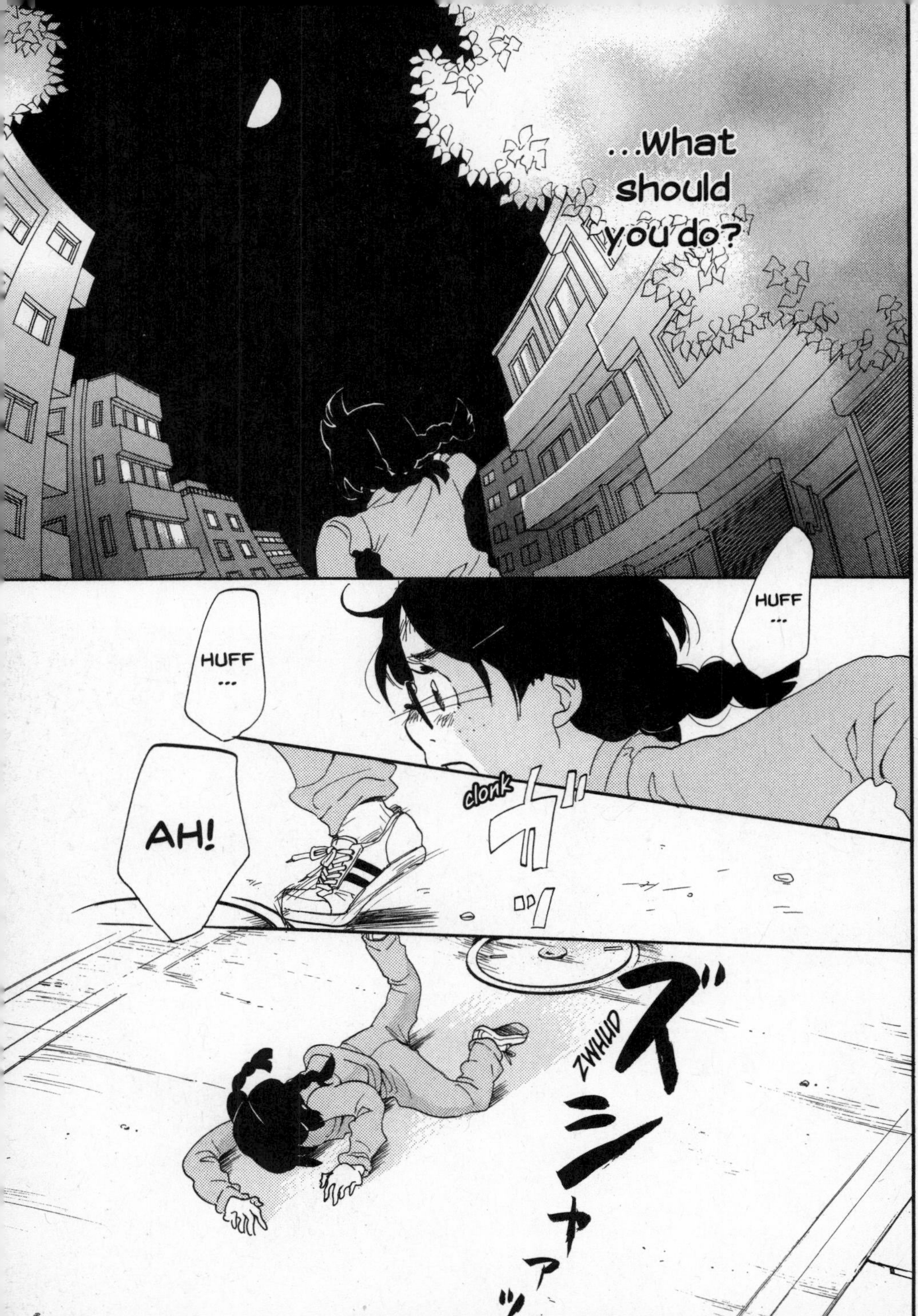
...What should you do?
HUFF ...
HUFF ...
clonk
AH!
ZWHUD
ズシャアッ

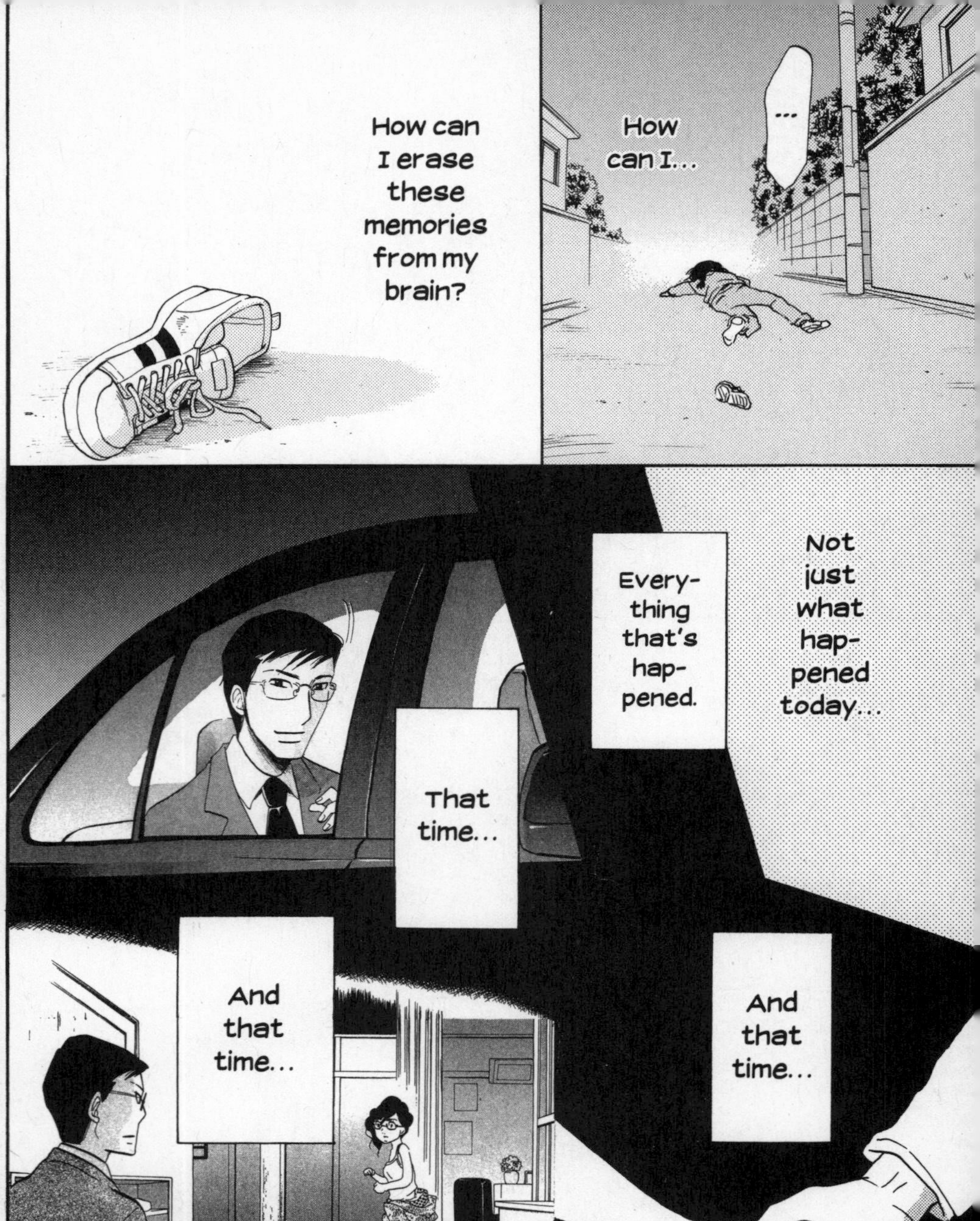
...
How can I...
How can I erase these memories from my brain?
Not just what happened today...
Everything that's happened.
That time...
And that time...
And that time...

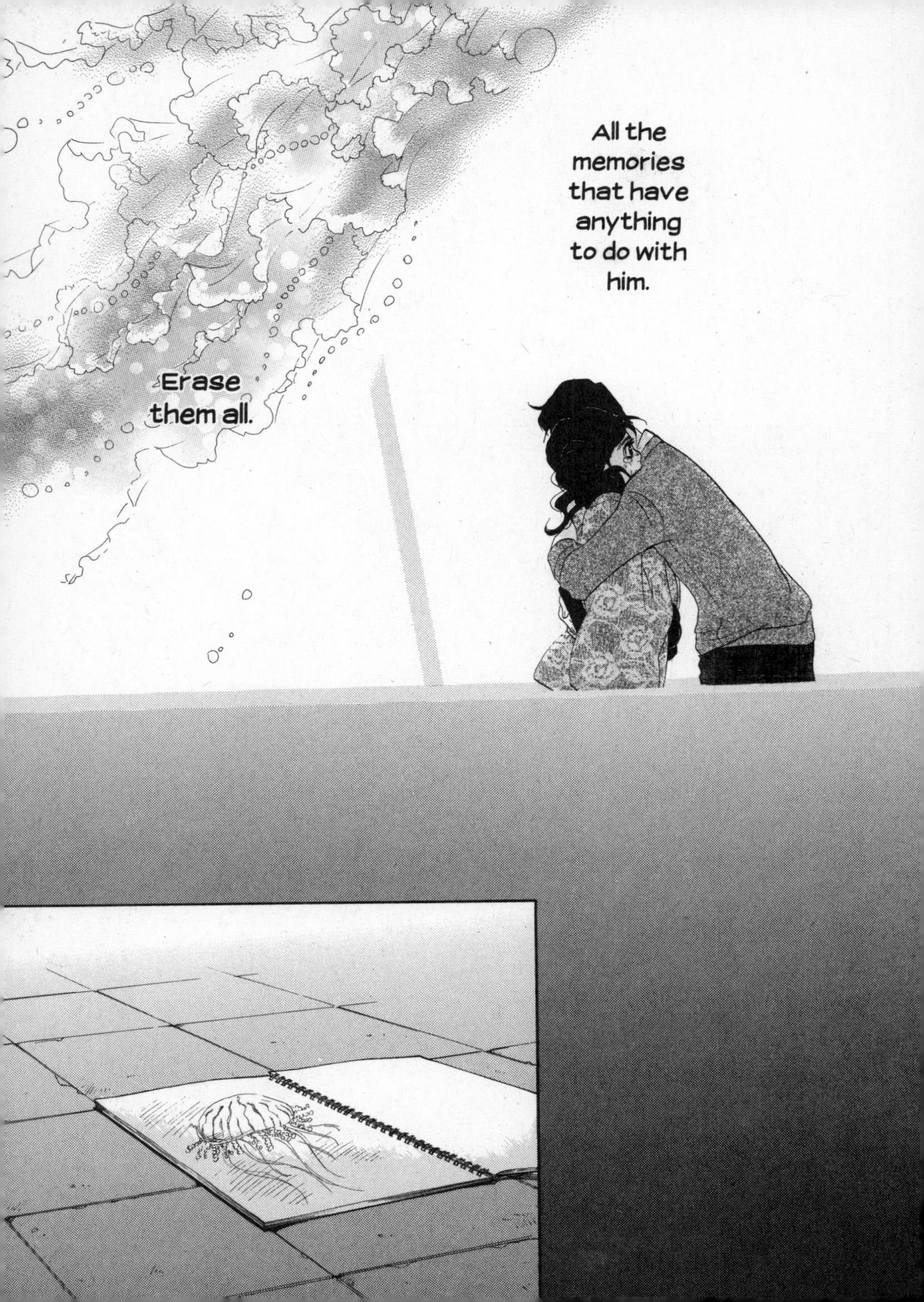
All the memories that have anything to do with him.
Erase them all.

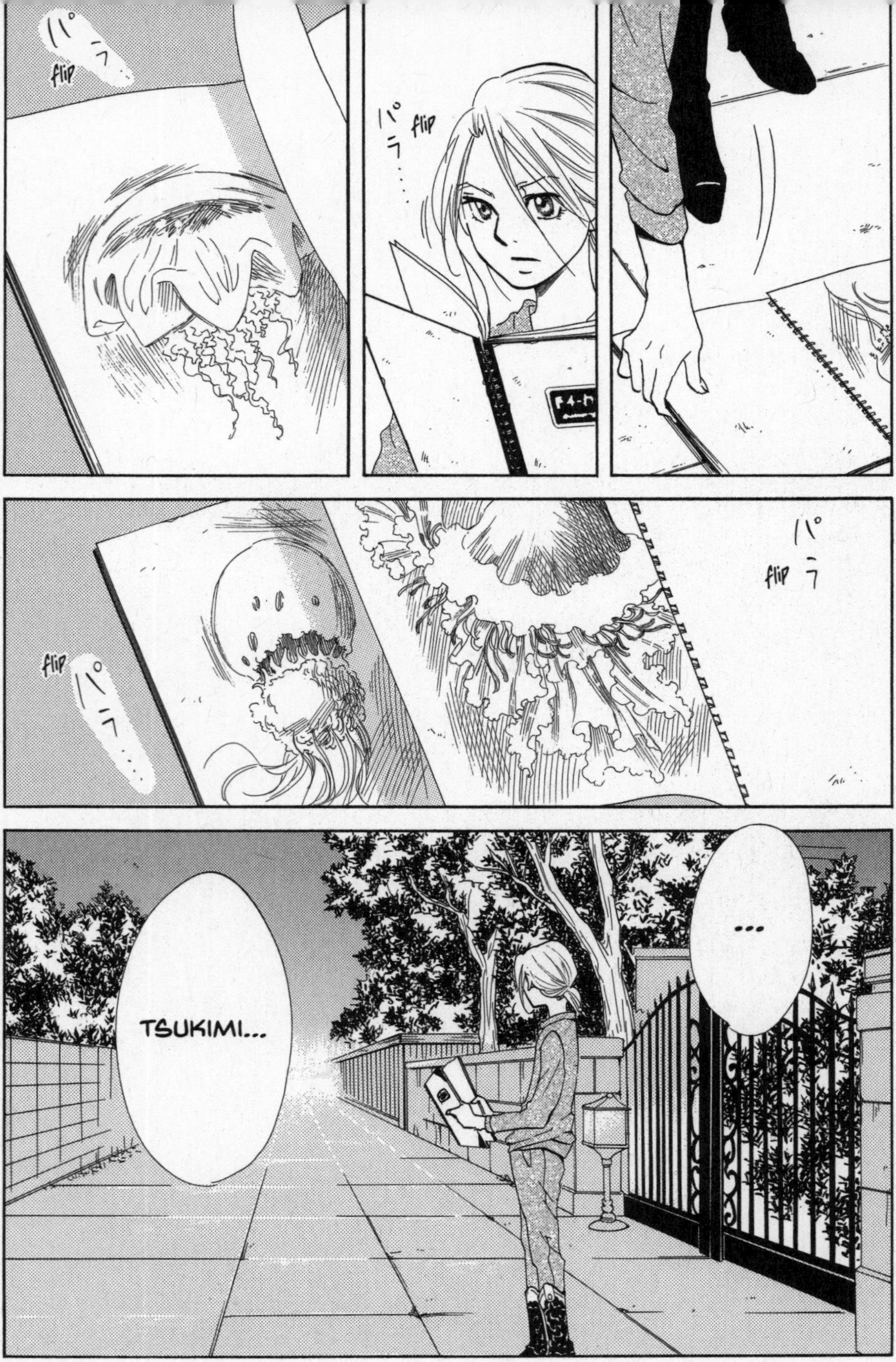
パラ…
flip
パラ…
flip
パラ
flip
flip
パラ…
…
TSUKIMI…

Episode 18
Deep Blue Sea

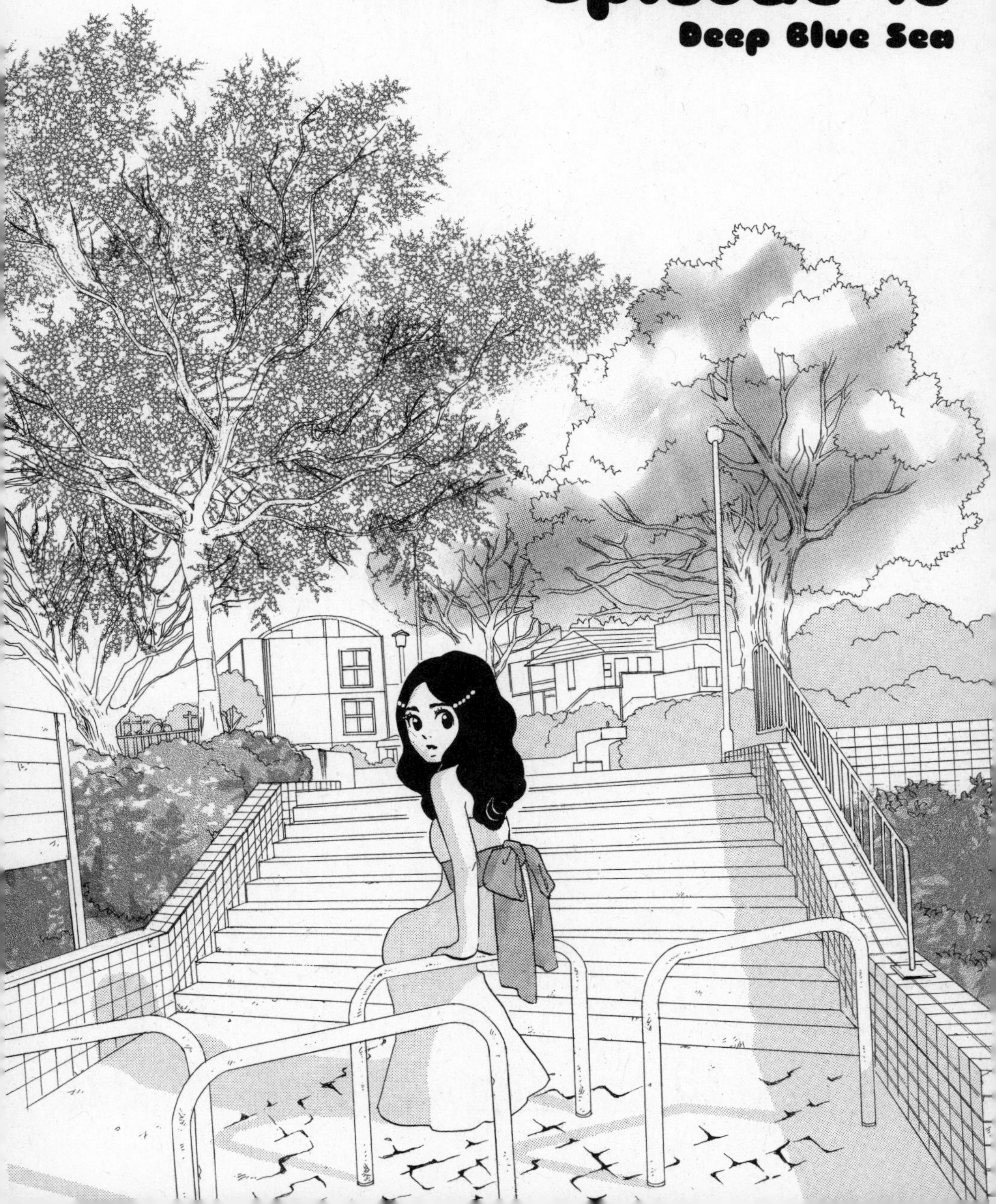

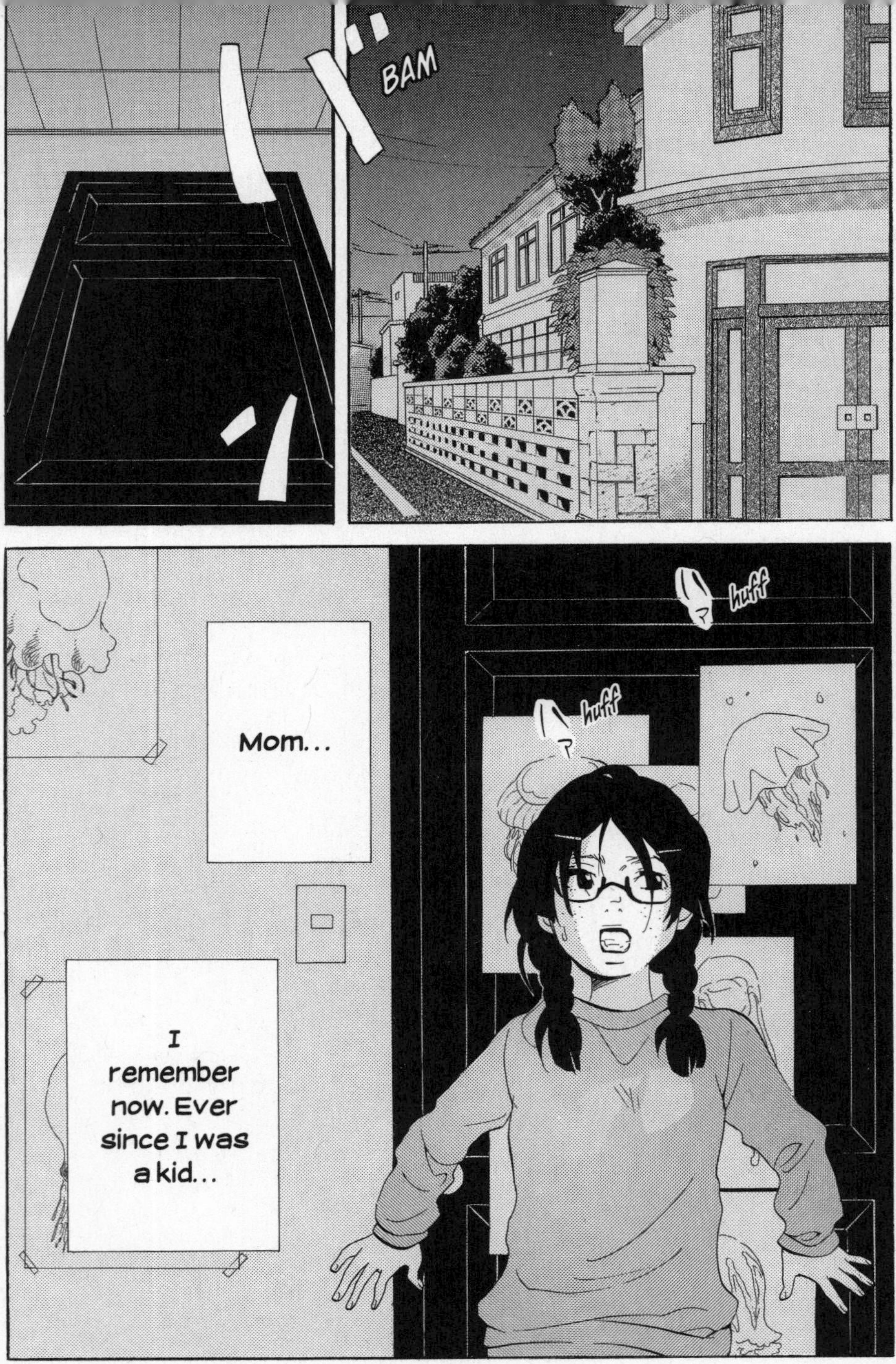
BAM
ハァ huff
ハァ huff
Mom...
I remember now. Ever since I was a kid...

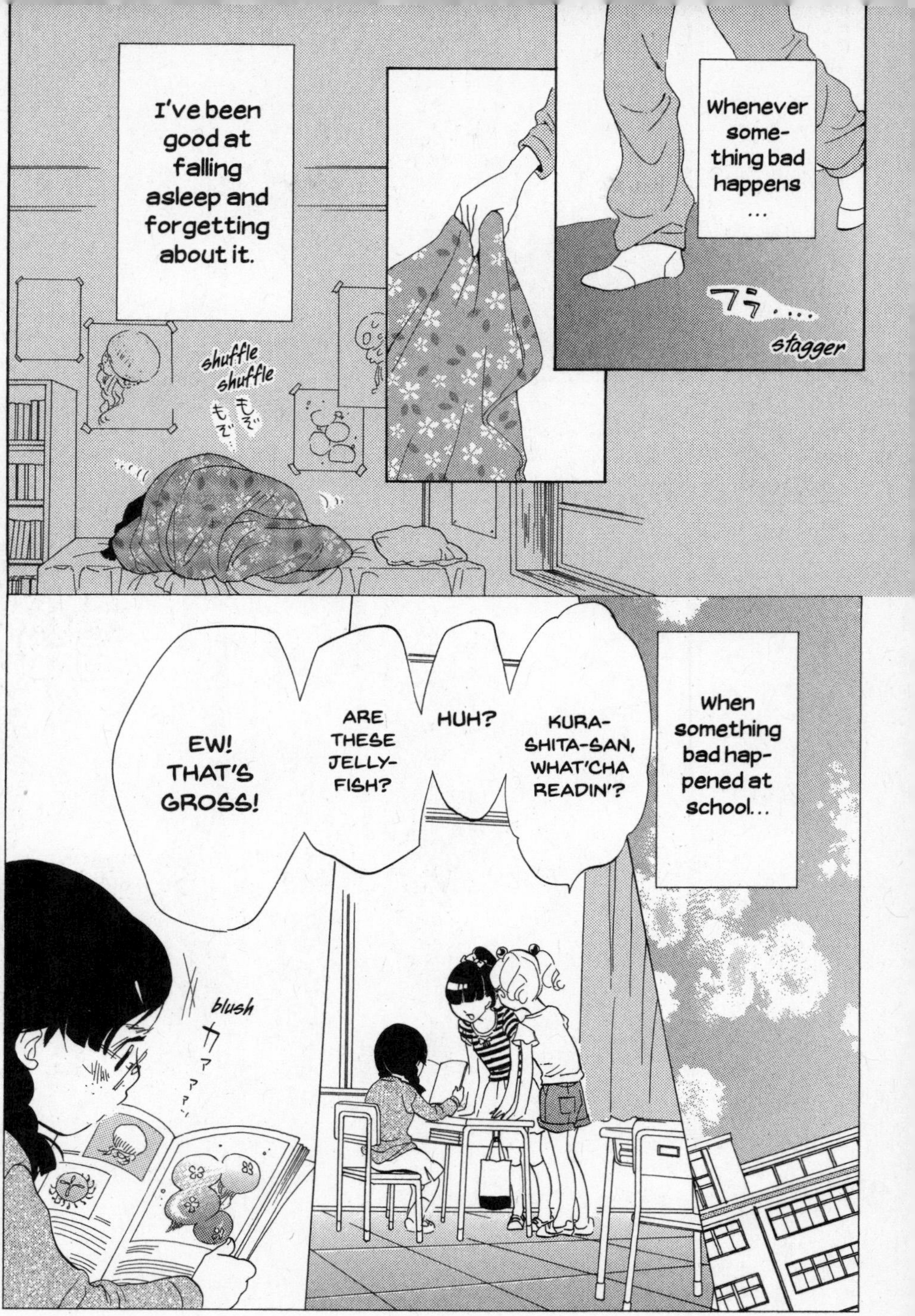
Whenever something bad happens ...
フラ…
stagger
I've been good at falling asleep and forgetting about it.
shuffle shuffle
もぞもぞ
When something bad happened at school...
KURA-SHITA-SAN, WHAT'CHA READIN'?
HUH?
ARE THESE JELLY-FISH?
EW! THAT'S GROSS!
blush
カァァ

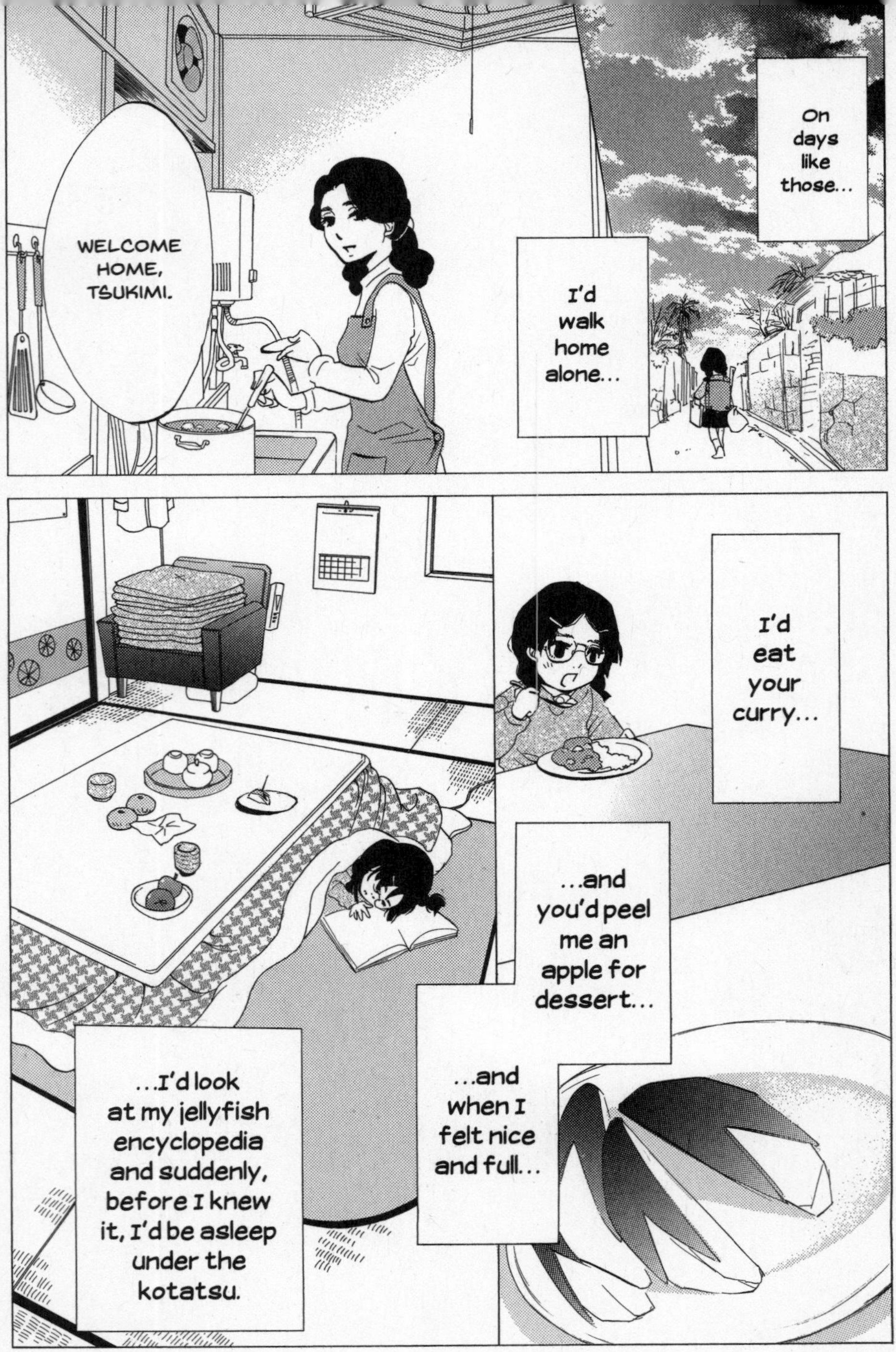
On days like those...
I'd walk home alone...
WELCOME HOME, TSUKIMI.
I'd eat your curry...
...and you'd peel me an apple for dessert...
...and when I felt nice and full...
...I'd look at my jellyfish encyclopedia and suddenly, before I knew it, I'd be asleep under the kotatsu.

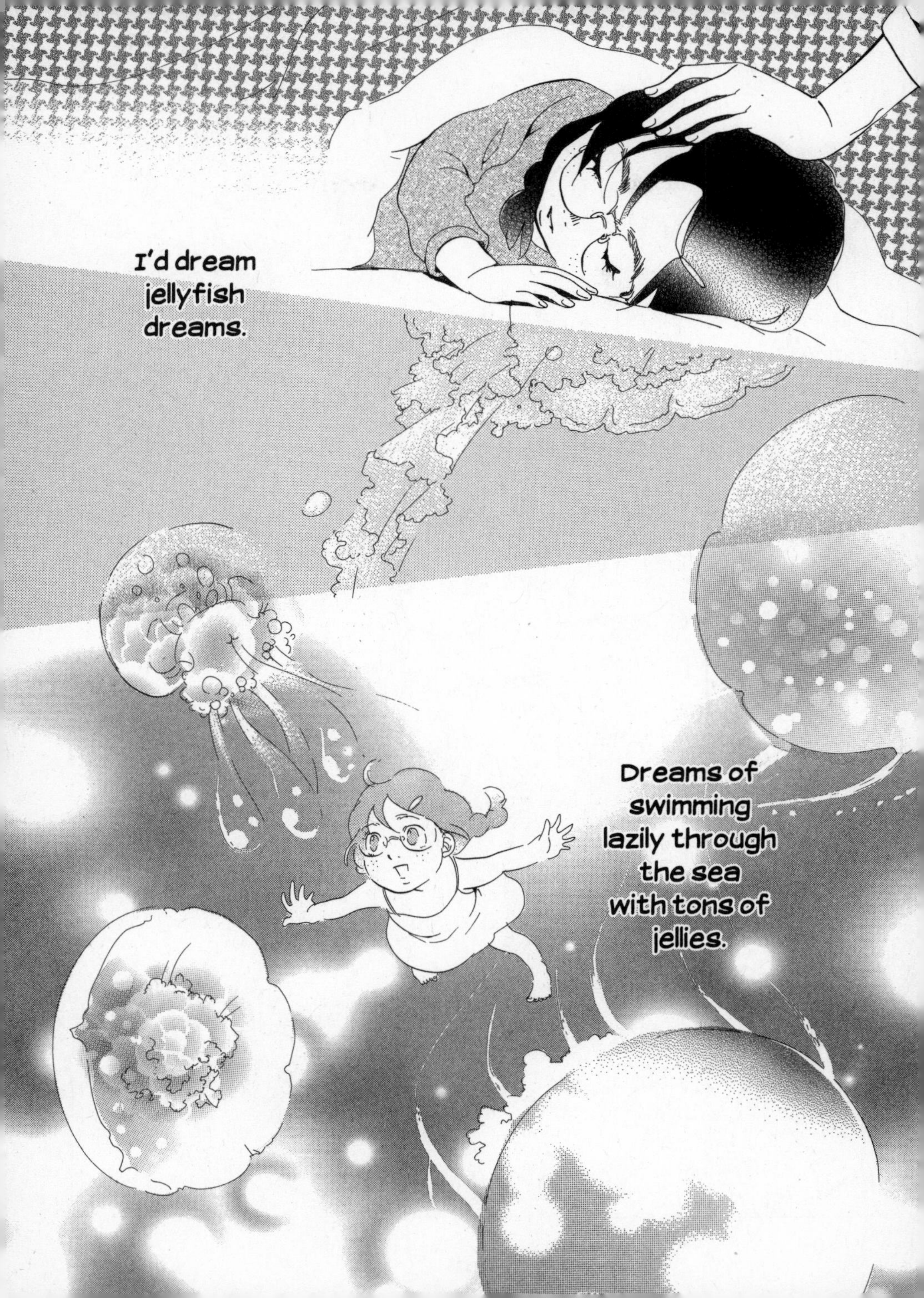
I'd dream jellyfish dreams.
Dreams of swimming lazily through the sea with tons of jellies.

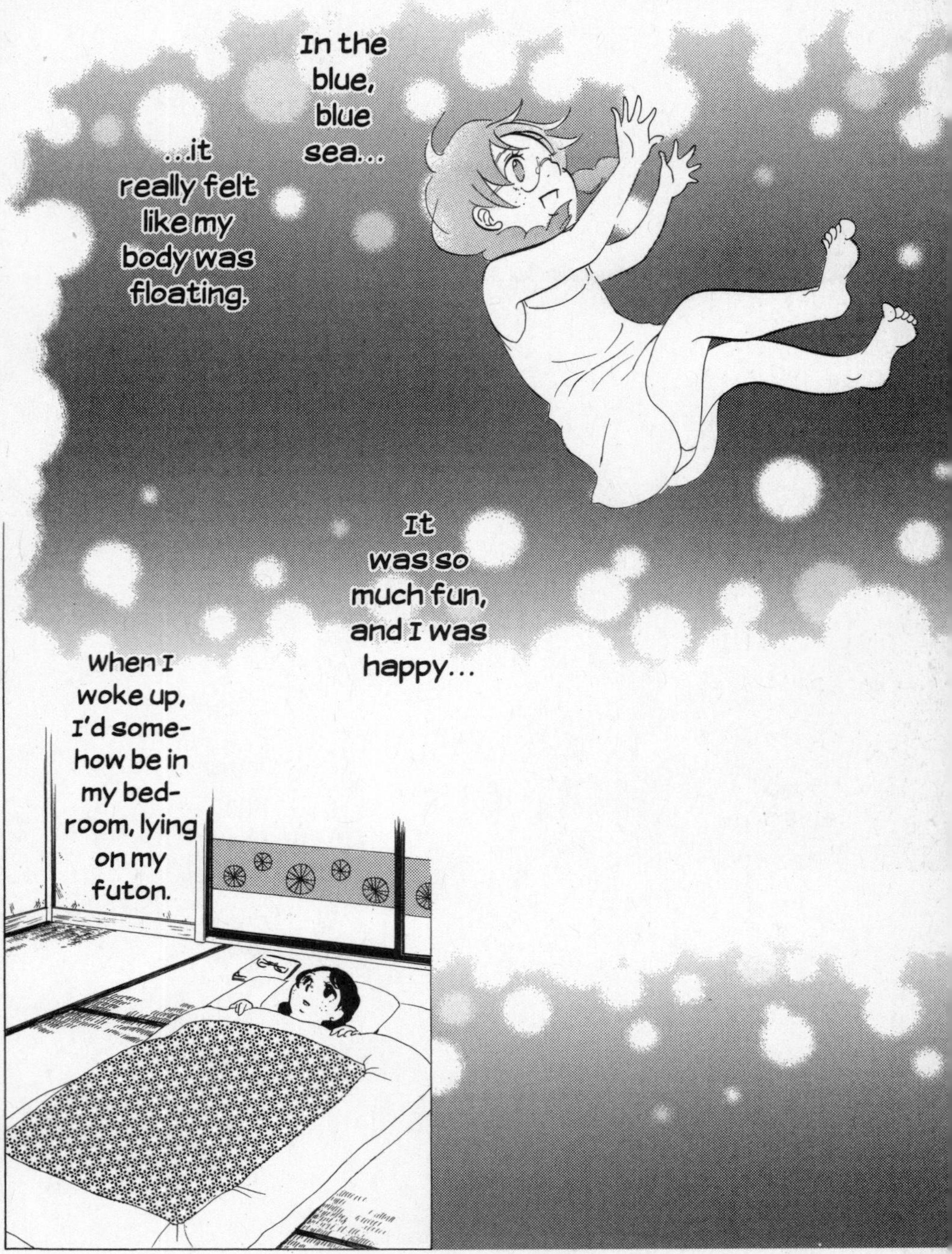
In the blue, blue sea...
...it really felt like my body was floating.
It was so much fun, and I was happy...
When I woke up, I'd some-how be in my bed-room, lying on my futon.

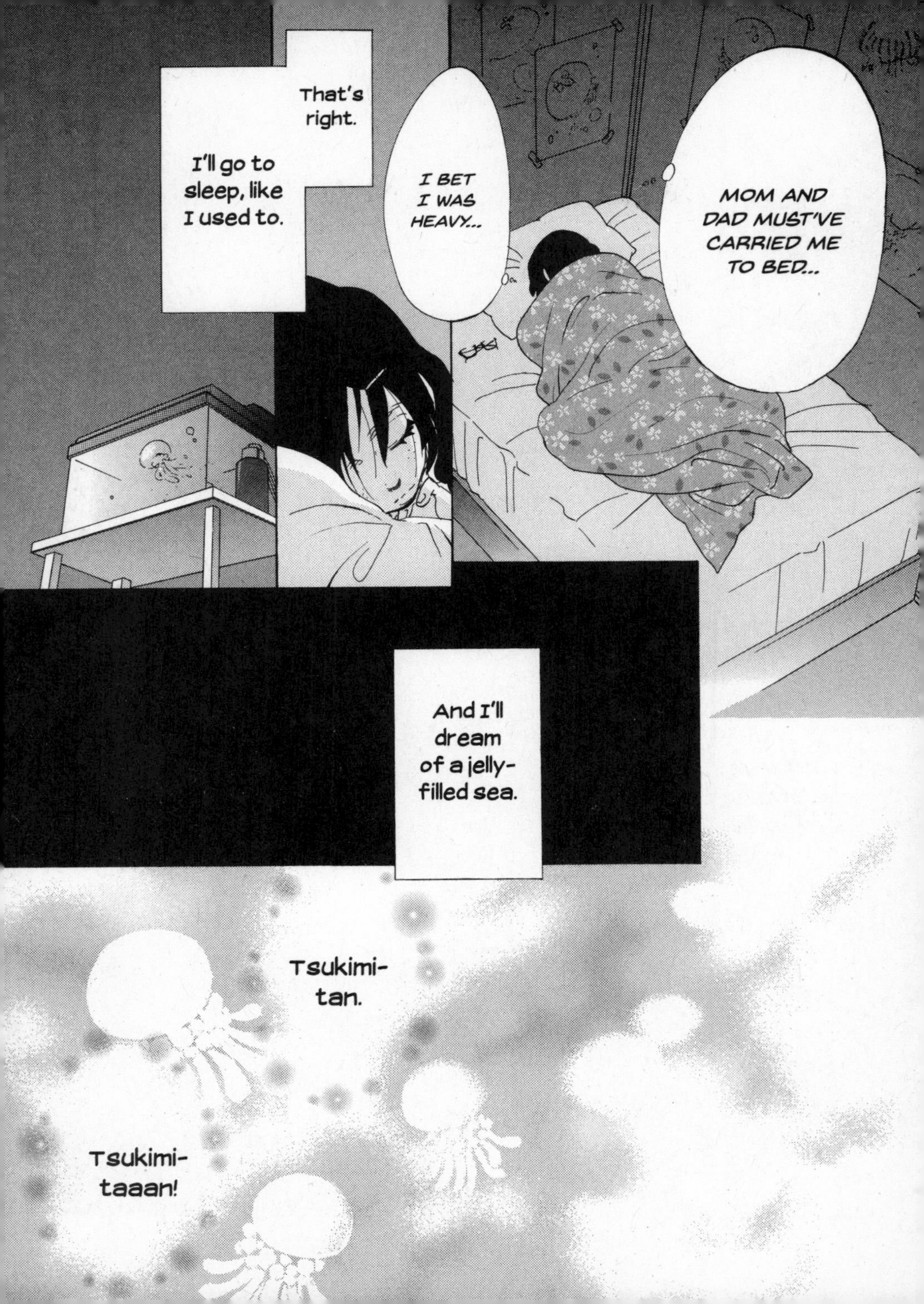
MOM AND DAD MUST'VE CARRIED ME TO BED...
I BET I WAS HEAVY...
That's right.
I'll go to sleep, like I used to.
And I'll dream of a jelly-filled sea.
Tsukimi-tan.
Tsukimi-taaan!

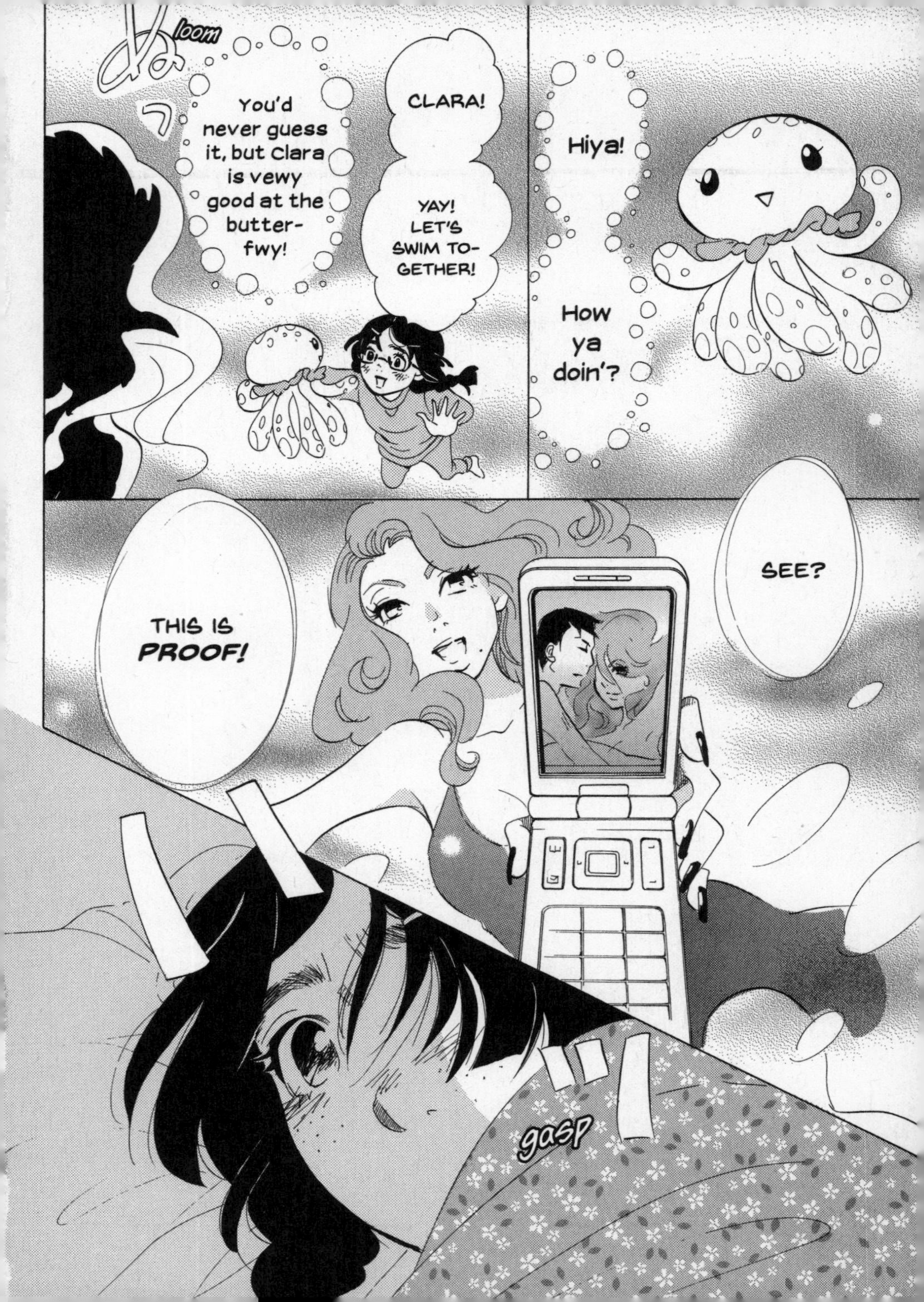

Hiya!
How ya doin'?
CLARA!
YAY! LET'S SWIM TO-GETHER!
You'd never guess it, but Clara is vewy good at the butter-fwy!
bloom
SEE?
THIS IS **PROOF!**
gasp

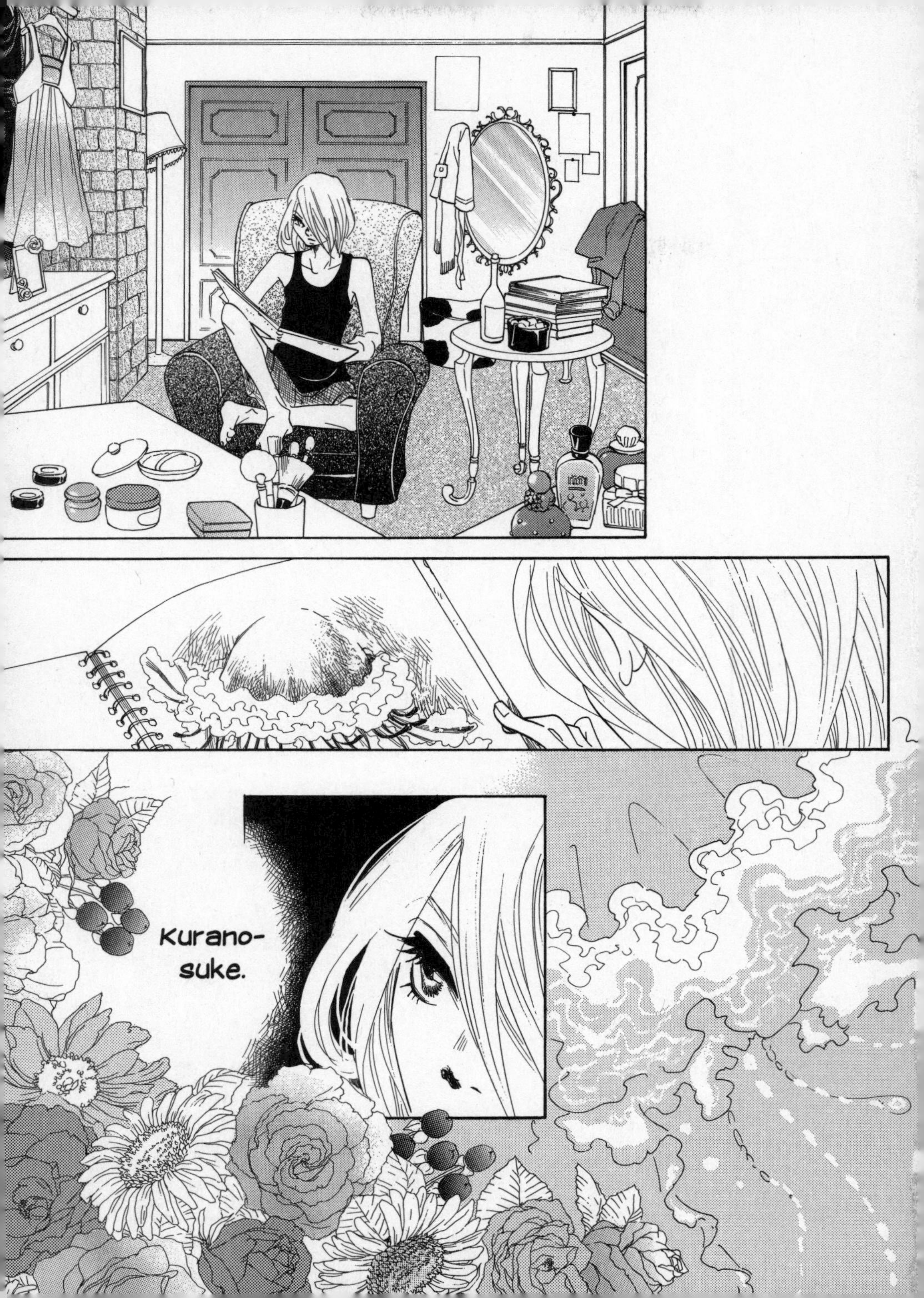
Kurano-suke.

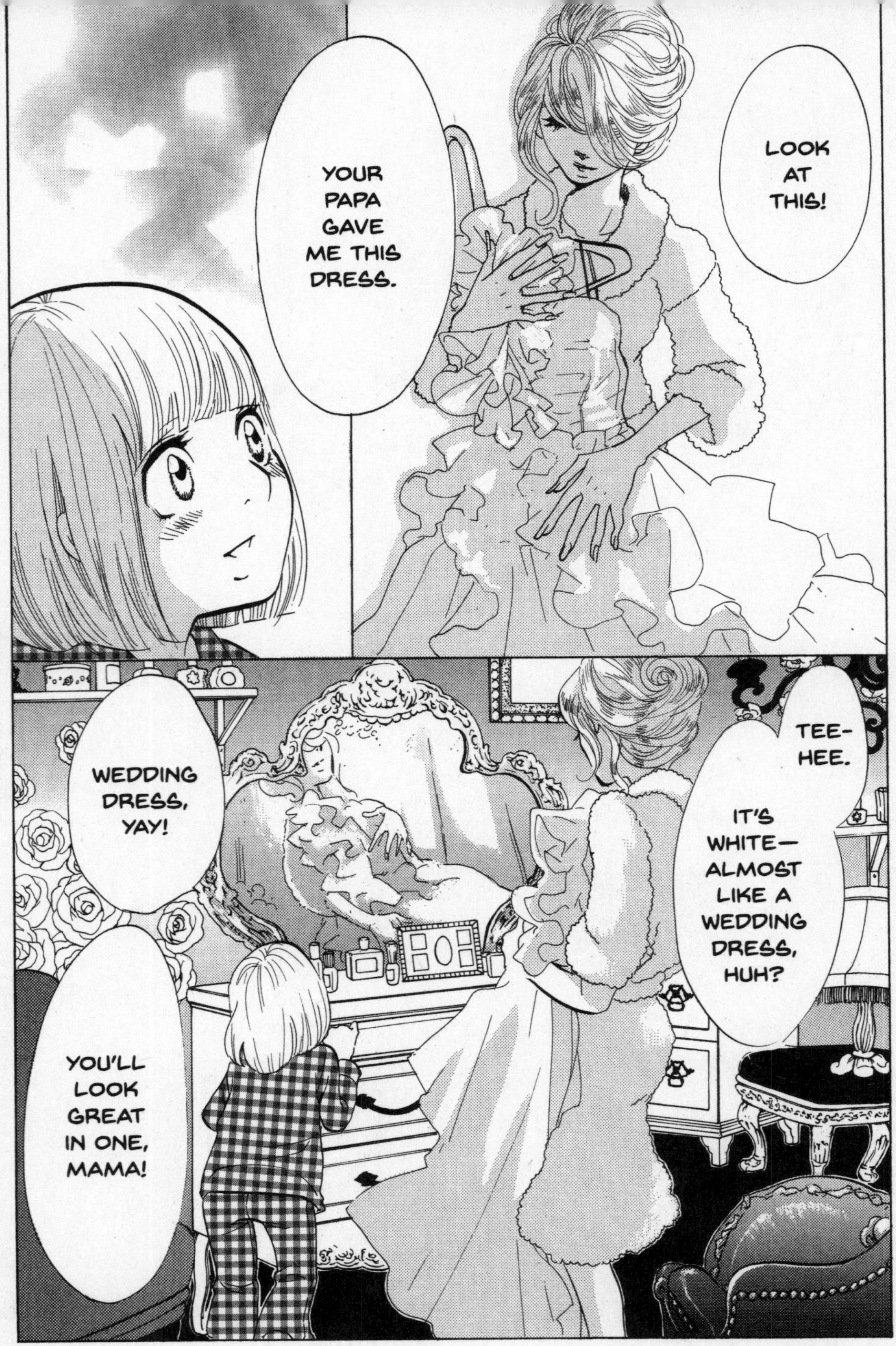
LOOK AT THIS!
YOUR PAPA GAVE ME THIS DRESS.
TEE-HEE.
IT'S WHITE—ALMOST LIKE A WEDDING DRESS, HUH?
WEDDING DRESS, YAY!
YOU'LL LOOK GREAT IN ONE, MAMA!

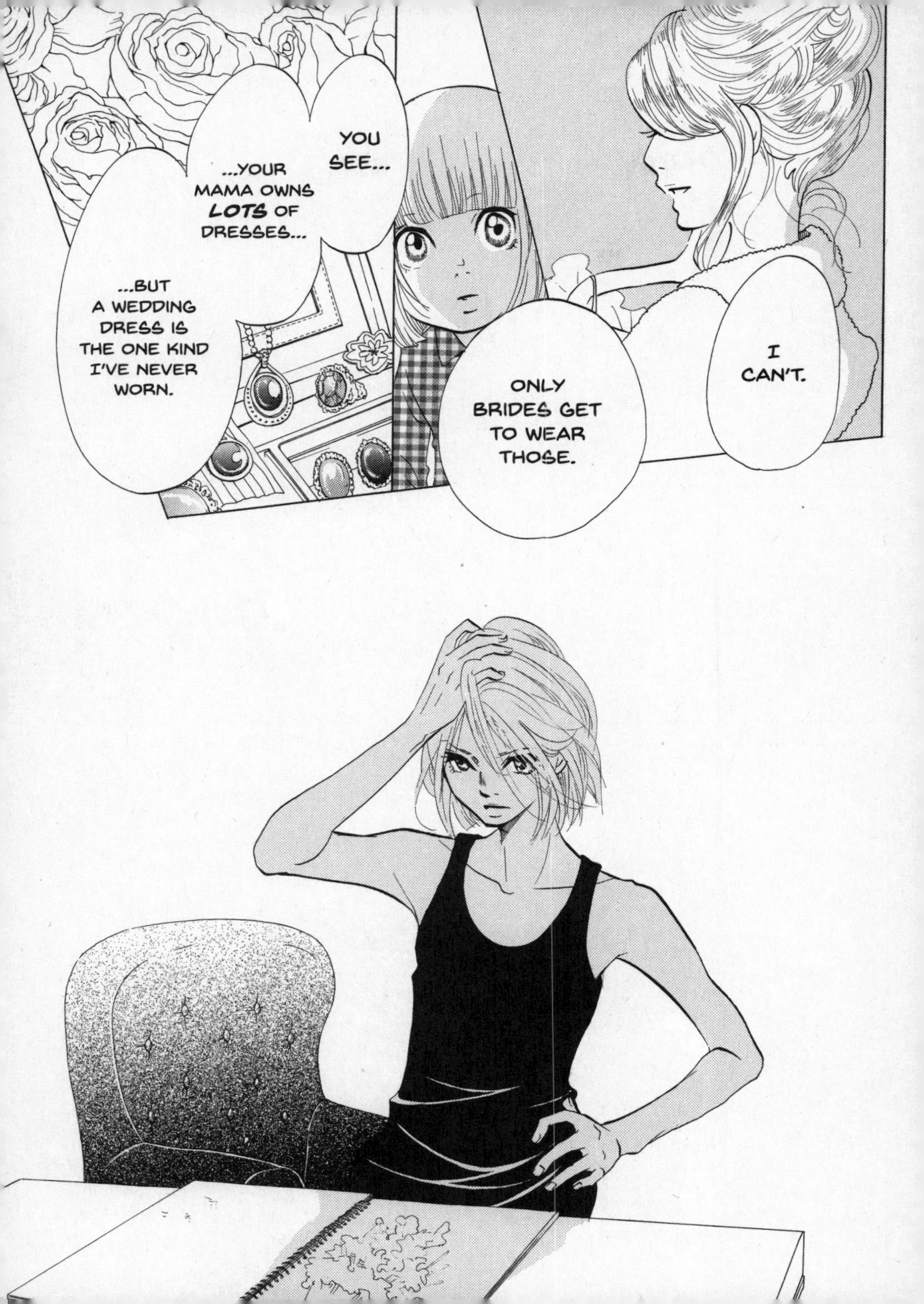
YOU SEE...
...YOUR MAMA OWNS LOTS OF DRESSES...
...BUT A WEDDING DRESS IS THE ONE KIND I'VE NEVER WORN.
ONLY BRIDES GET TO WEAR THOSE.
I CAN'T.

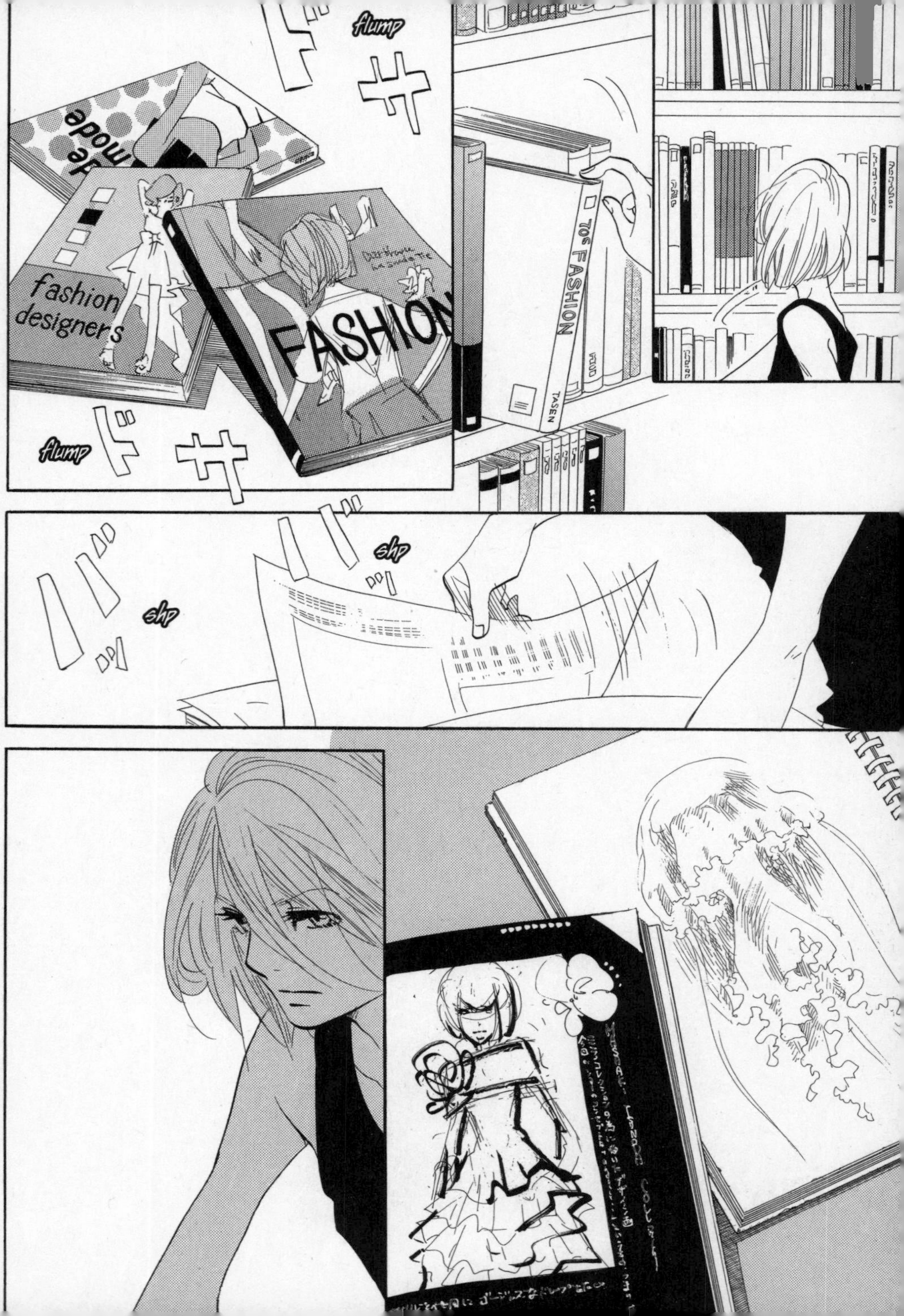
70s FASHION
TASEN
flump
mode
fashion designers
FASHION
flump
shp
shp

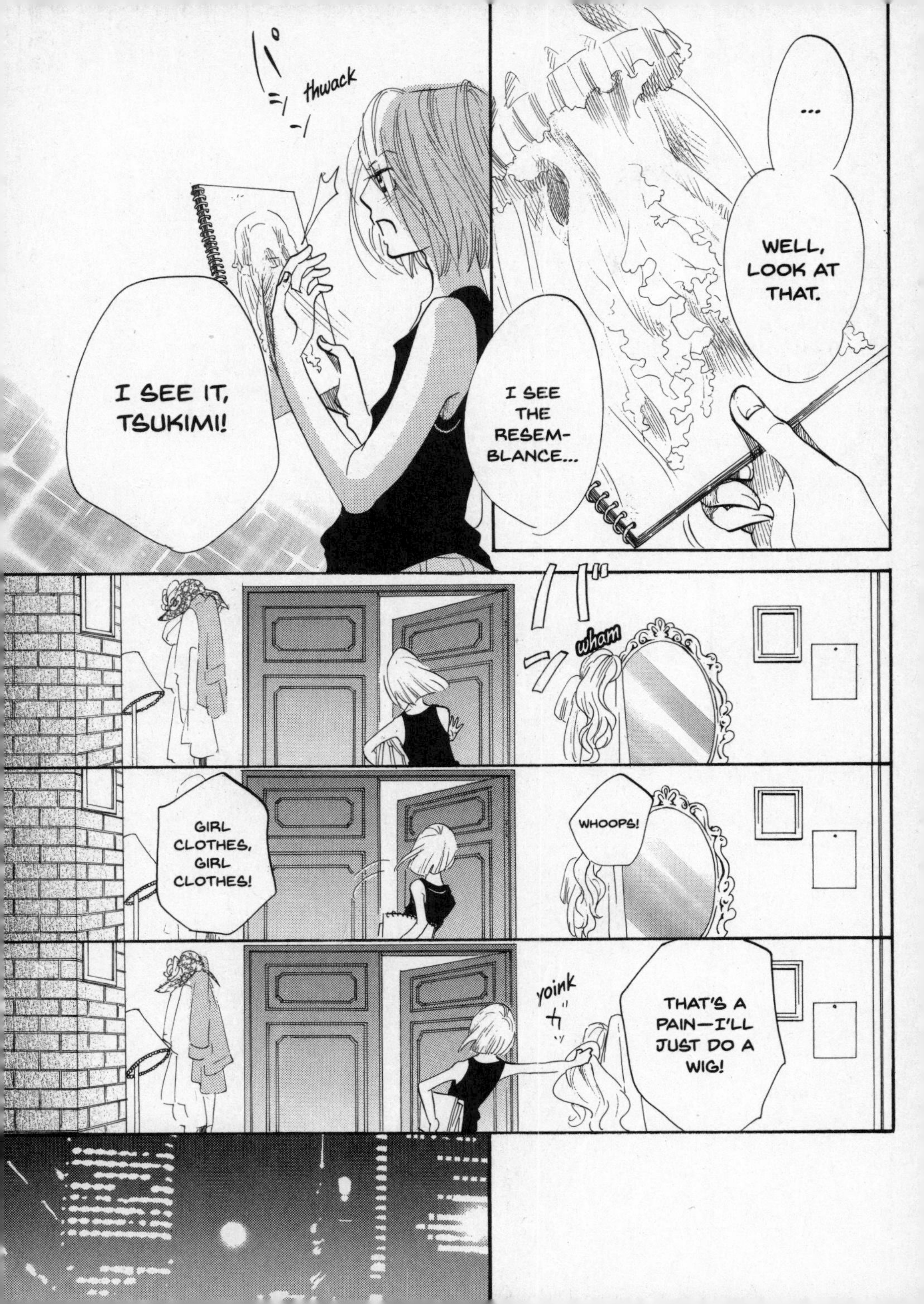
...
WELL, LOOK AT THAT.
I SEE THE RESEMBLANCE...
thwack
I SEE IT, TSUKIMI!
wham
WHOOPS!
GIRL CLOTHES, GIRL CLOTHES!
THAT'S A PAIN—I'LL JUST DO A WIG!
yoink

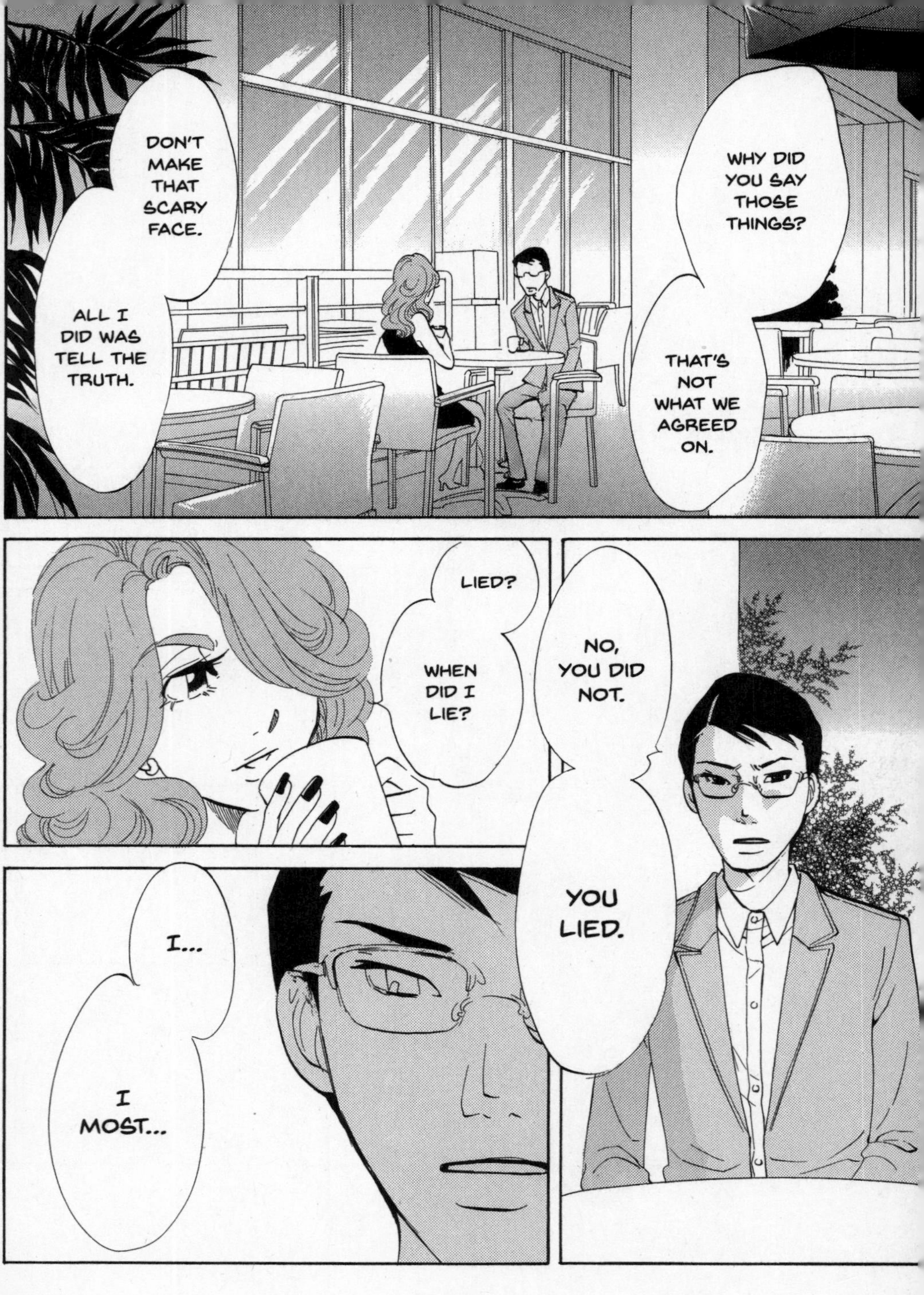
WHY DID YOU SAY THOSE THINGS?
THAT'S NOT WHAT WE AGREED ON.
DON'T MAKE THAT SCARY FACE.
ALL I DID WAS TELL THE TRUTH.
NO, YOU DID NOT.
YOU LIED.
LIED?
WHEN DID I LIE?
I...
I MOST...

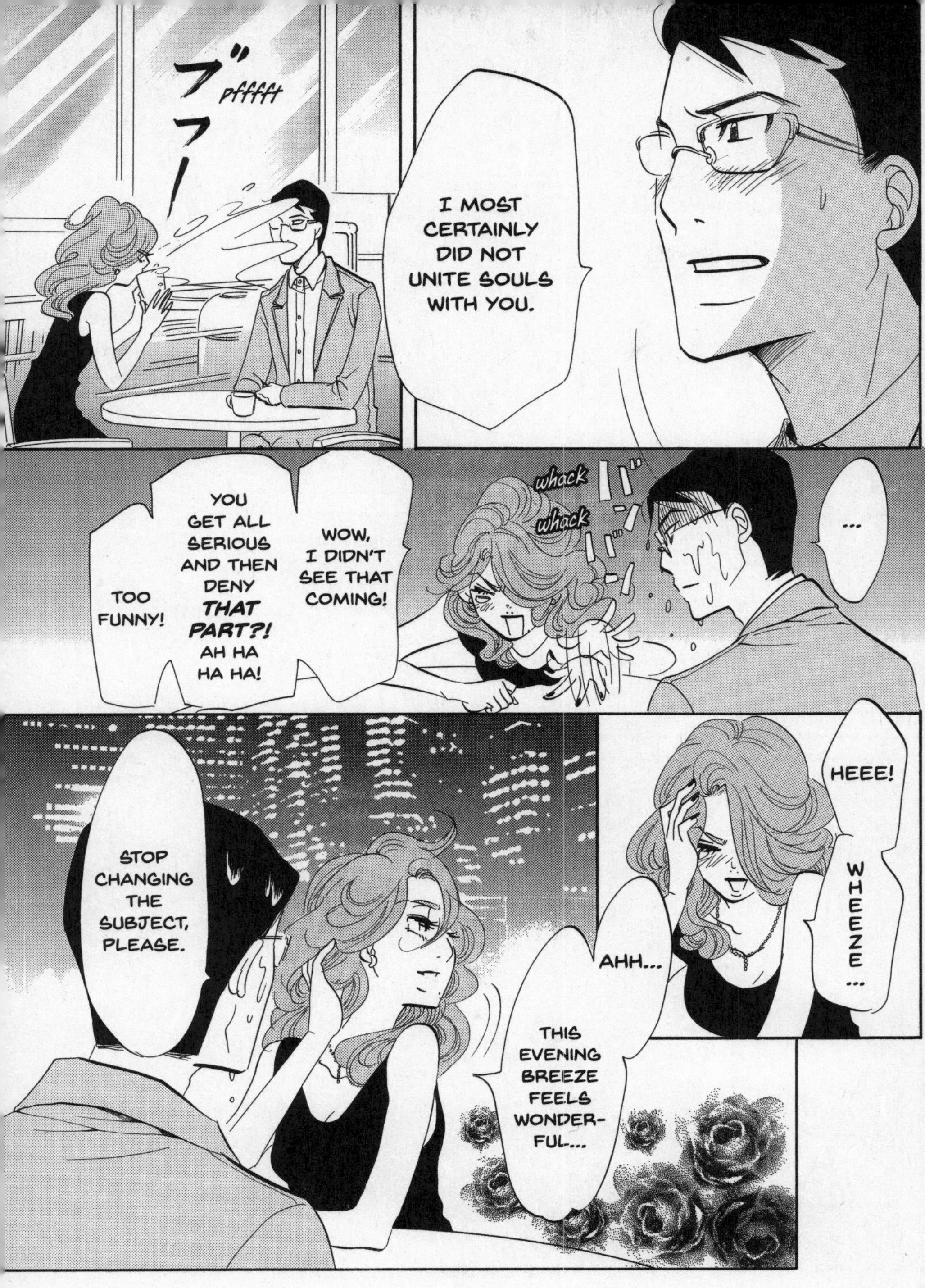
I MOST CERTAINLY DID NOT UNITE SOULS WITH YOU.
ブフー
pfffft
...
whack
whack
WOW, I DIDN'T SEE THAT COMING!
YOU GET ALL SERIOUS AND THEN DENY THAT PART?! AH HA HA HA!
TOO FUNNY!
HEEE!
WHEEZE...
AHH...
THIS EVENING BREEZE FEELS WONDER-FUL...
STOP CHANGING THE SUBJECT, PLEASE.

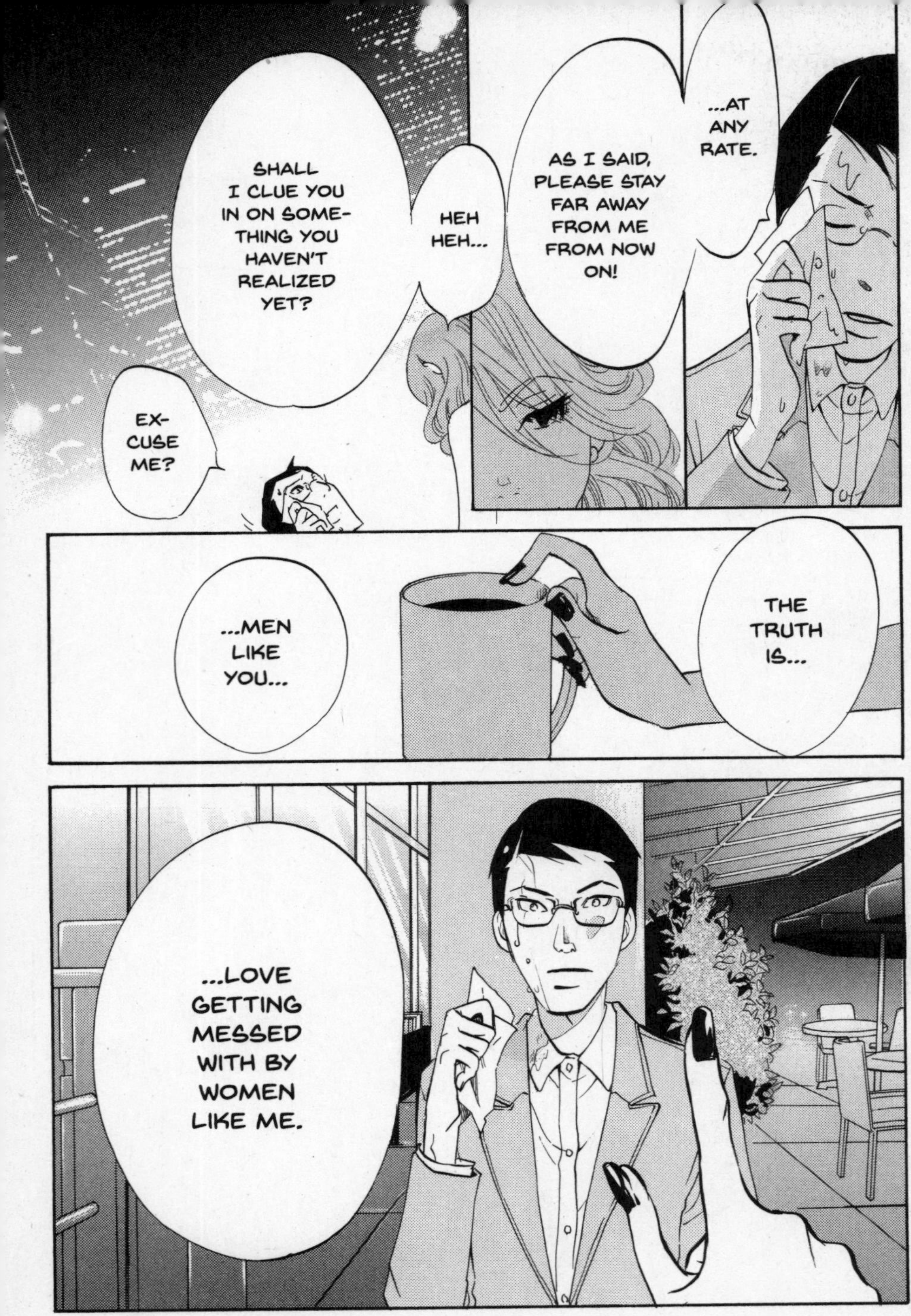
...AT ANY RATE.
AS I SAID, PLEASE STAY FAR AWAY FROM ME FROM NOW ON!
HEH HEH...
SHALL I CLUE YOU IN ON SOMETHING YOU HAVEN'T REALIZED YET?
EXCUSE ME?
THE TRUTH IS...
...MEN LIKE YOU...
...LOVE GETTING MESSED WITH BY WOMEN LIKE ME.

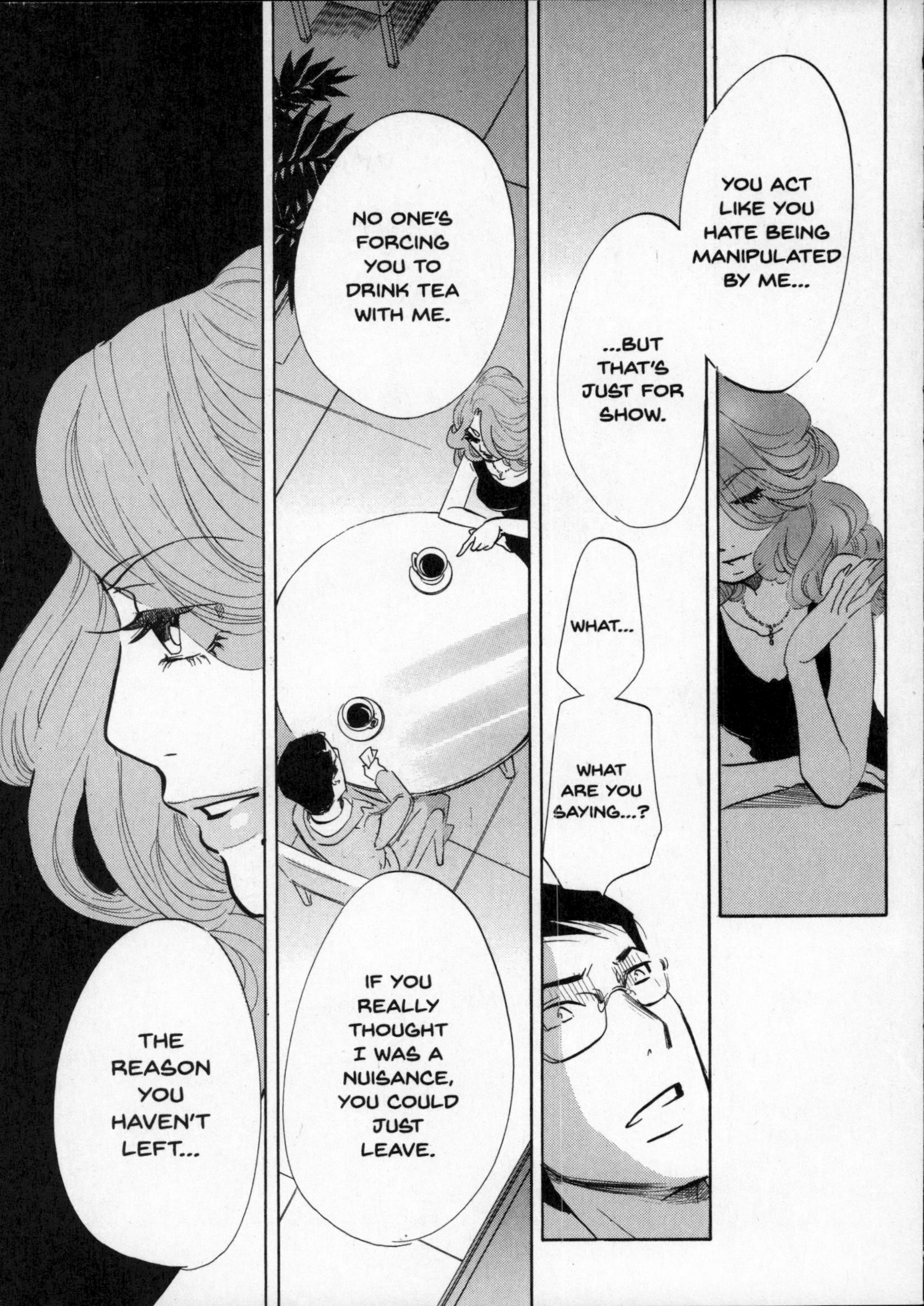
YOU ACT LIKE YOU HATE BEING MANIPULATED BY ME...
...BUT THAT'S JUST FOR SHOW.
WHAT...
WHAT ARE YOU SAYING...?
NO ONE'S FORCING YOU TO DRINK TEA WITH ME.
IF YOU REALLY THOUGHT I WAS A NUISANCE, YOU COULD JUST LEAVE.
THE REASON YOU HAVEN'T LEFT...

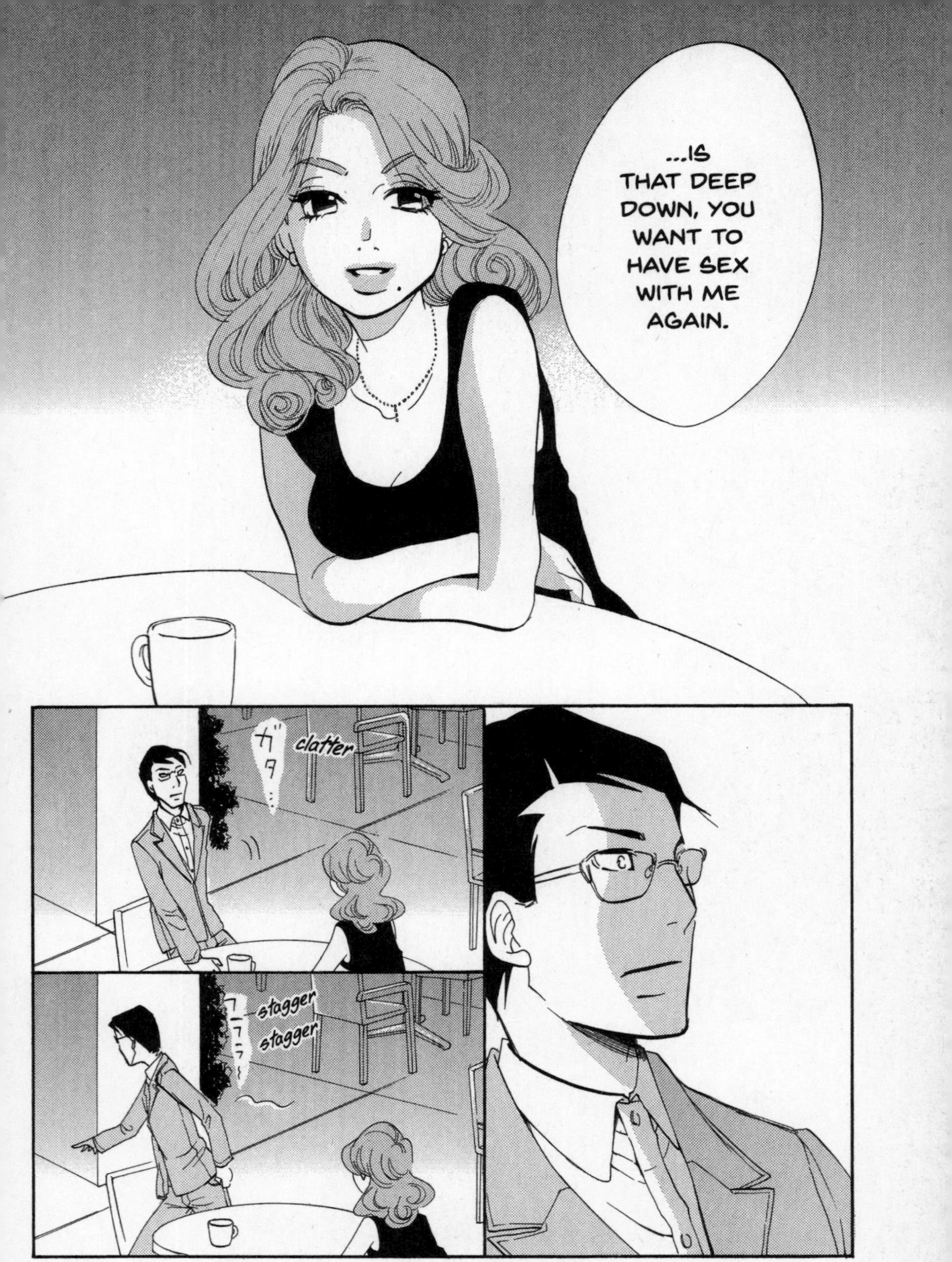
...IS THAT DEEP DOWN, YOU WANT TO HAVE SEX WITH ME AGAIN.
ガタ…
clatter
フラフラ～
stagger stagger

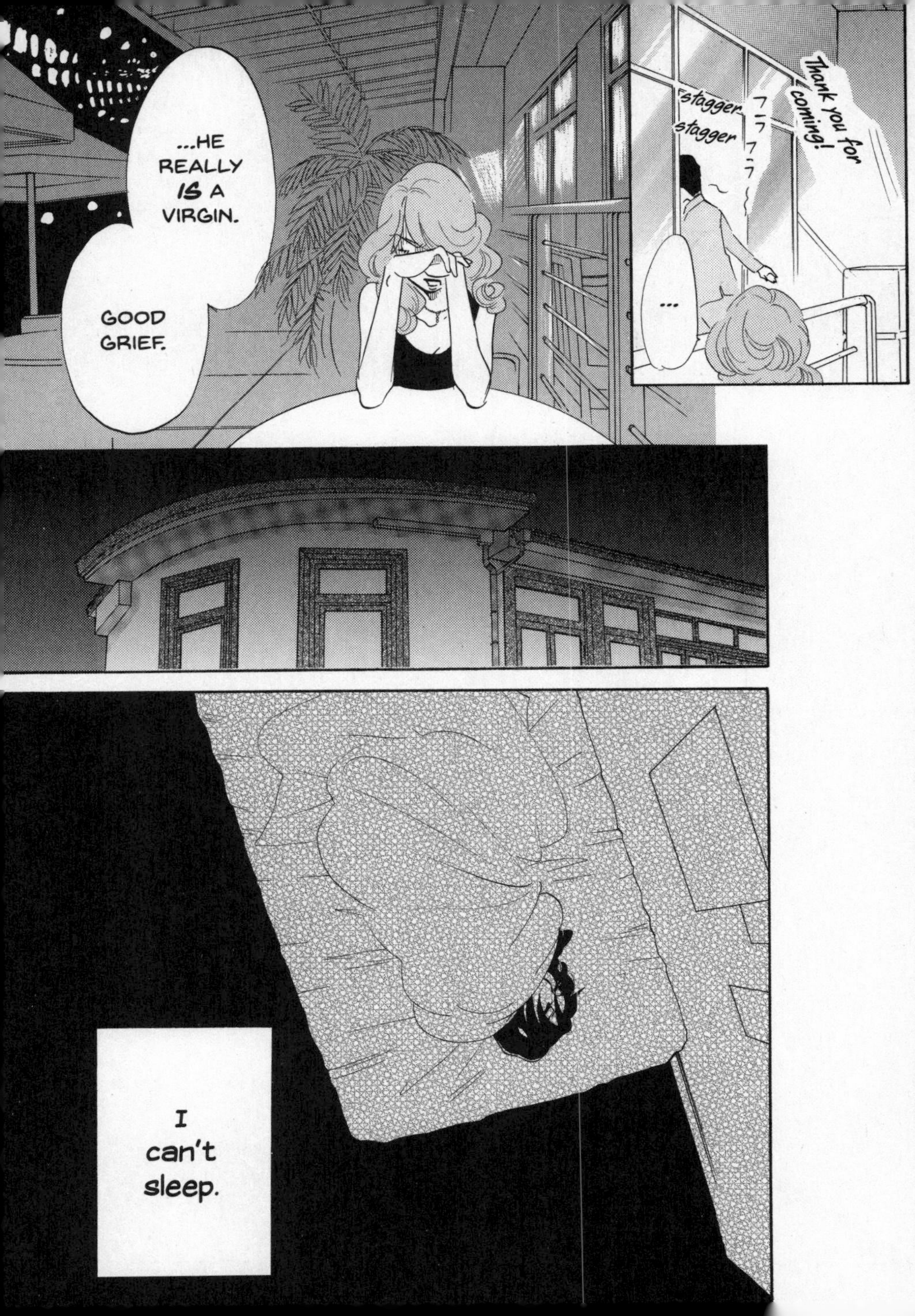
Thank you for coming!
stagger stagger
...
...HE REALLY IS A VIRGIN.
GOOD GRIEF.
I can't sleep.

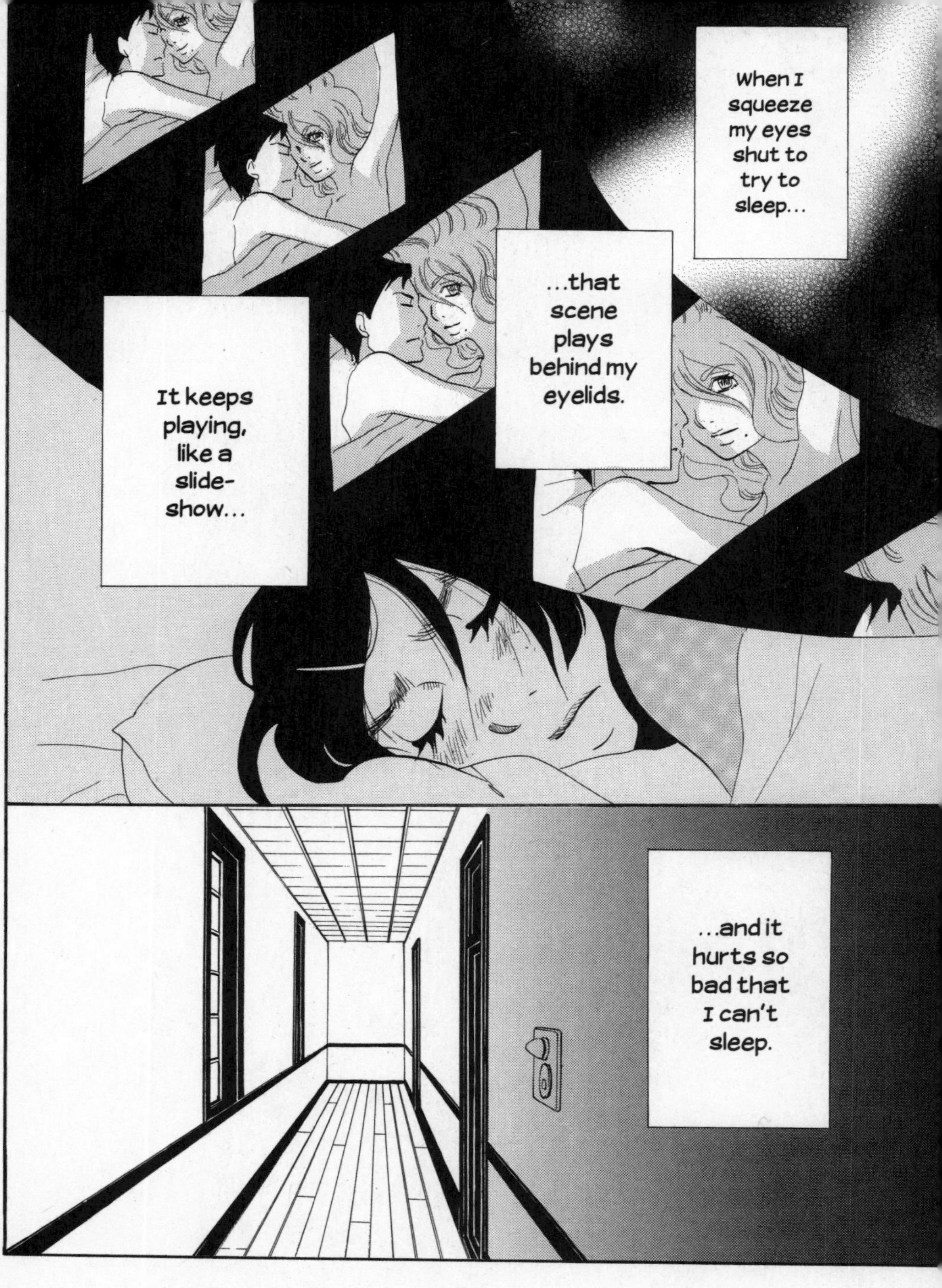
When I squeeze my eyes shut to try to sleep...
...that scene plays behind my eyelids.
It keeps playing, like a slide-show...
...and it hurts so bad that I can't sleep.

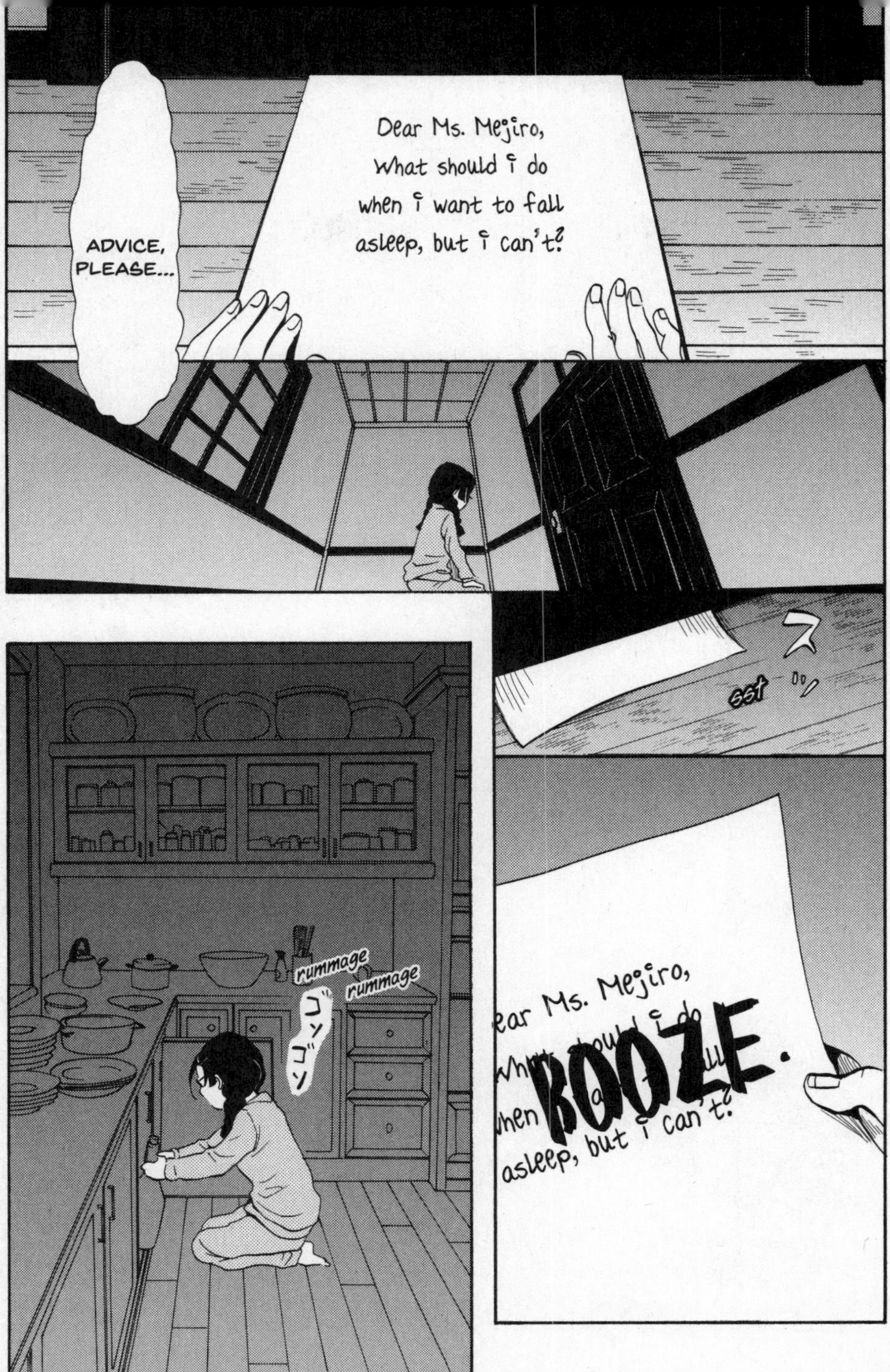
Dear Ms. Mejiro,
What should i do
when i want to fall
asleep, but i can't?
ADVICE, PLEASE...
スッ
sst
ear Ms. Mejiro,
when
asleep, but i can't?
BOOZE.
ゴソゴソ
rummage
rummage

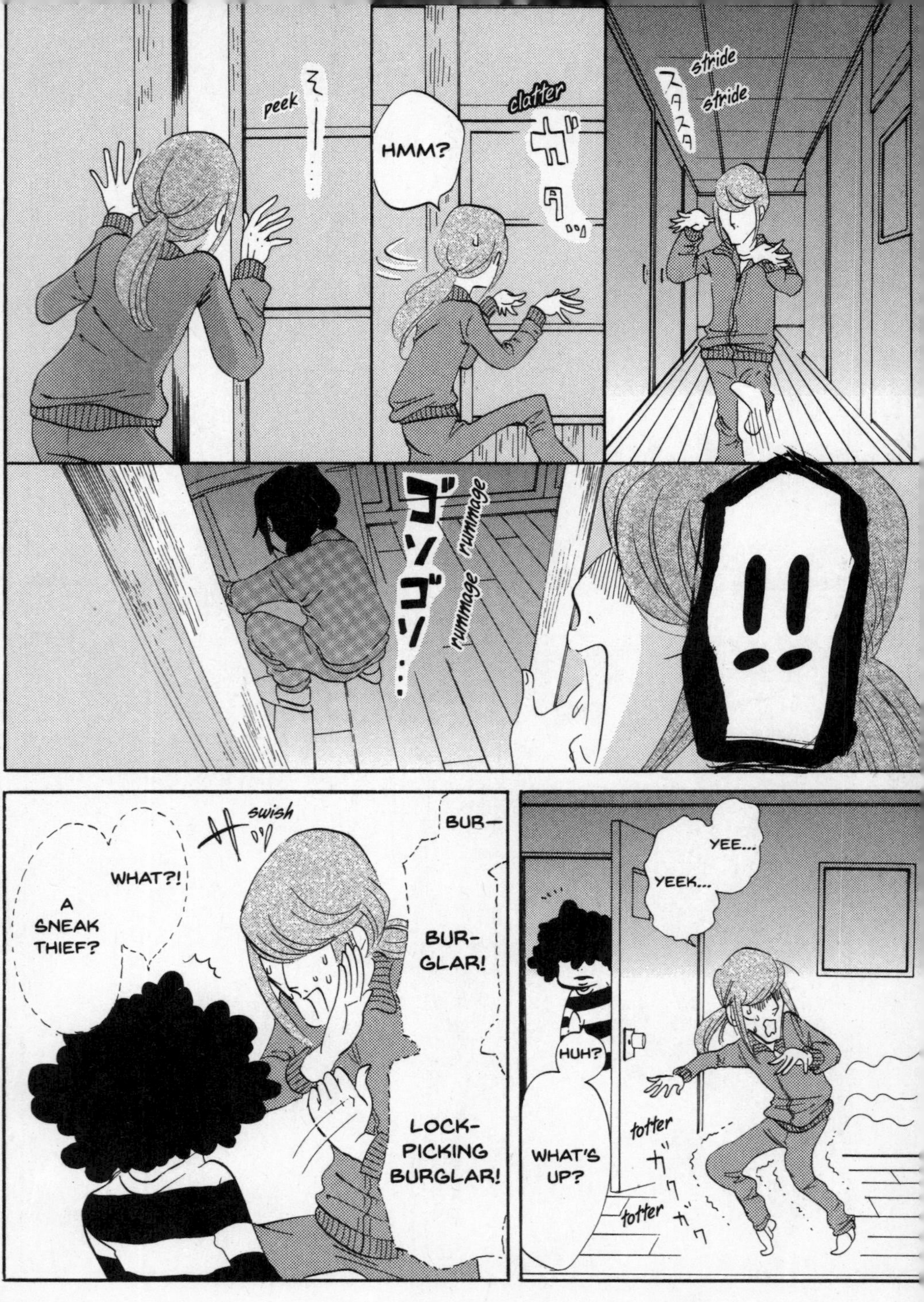
stride
スタスタ
stride
clatter
ガタ
HMM?
peek
!!
ゴソゴソ…
rummage
rummage
YEE...
YEEK...
HUH?
WHAT'S UP?
totter
ガクガク
totter
BUR—
BURGLAR!
LOCK-PICKING BURGLAR!
swish
WHAT?!
A SNEAK THIEF?

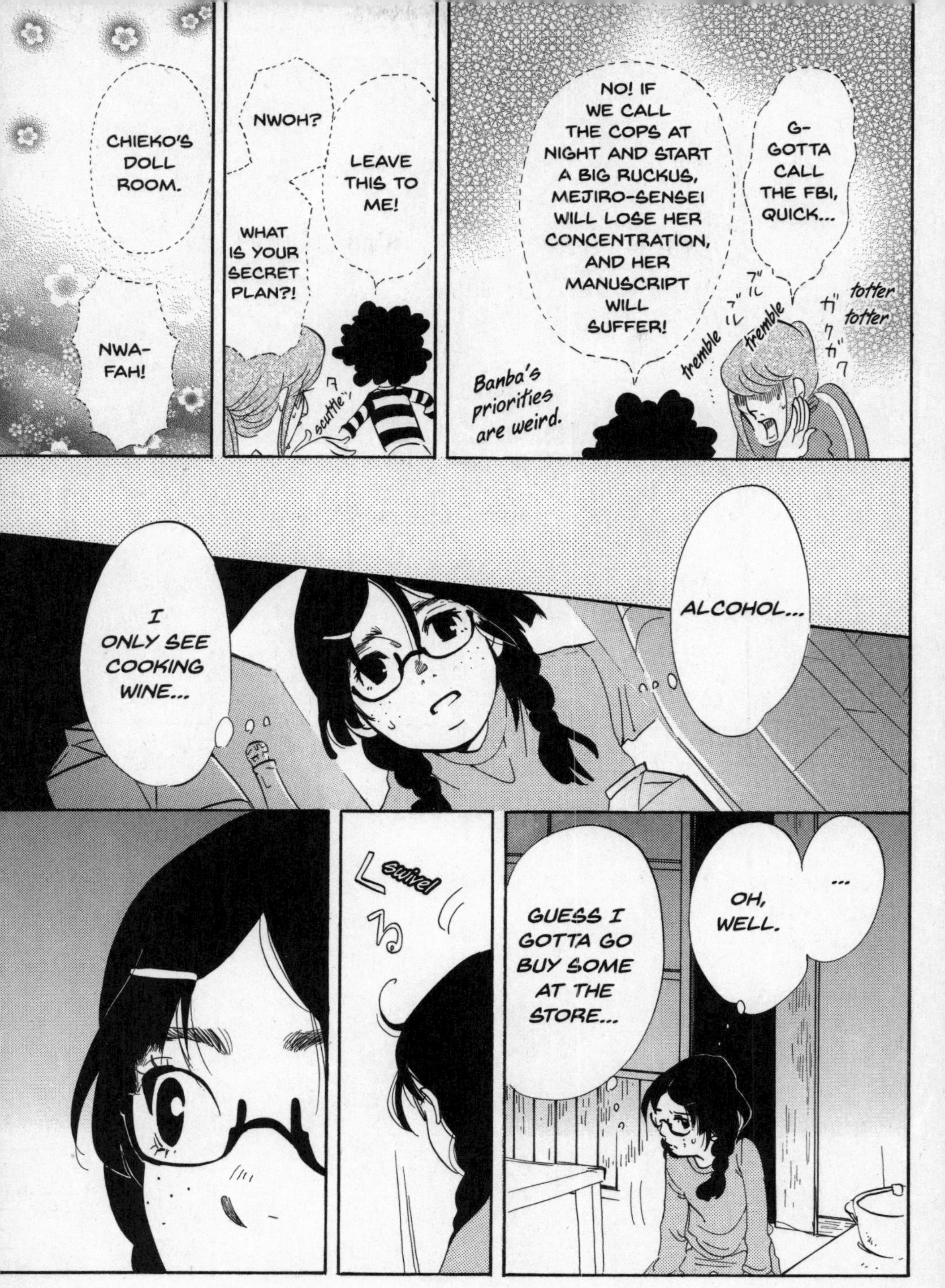
G-GOTTA CALL THE FBI, QUICK...
totter totter
tremble tremble
NO! IF WE CALL THE COPS AT NIGHT AND START A BIG RUCKUS, MEJIRO-SENSEI WILL LOSE HER CONCENTRATION, AND HER MANUSCRIPT WILL SUFFER!
Banba's priorities are weird.
LEAVE THIS TO ME!
NWOH?
WHAT IS YOUR SECRET PLAN?!
scuttle
CHIEKO'S DOLL ROOM.
NWA-FAH!
ALCOHOL...
I ONLY SEE COOKING WINE...
...
OH, WELL.
GUESS I GOTTA GO BUY SOME AT THE STORE...
swivel

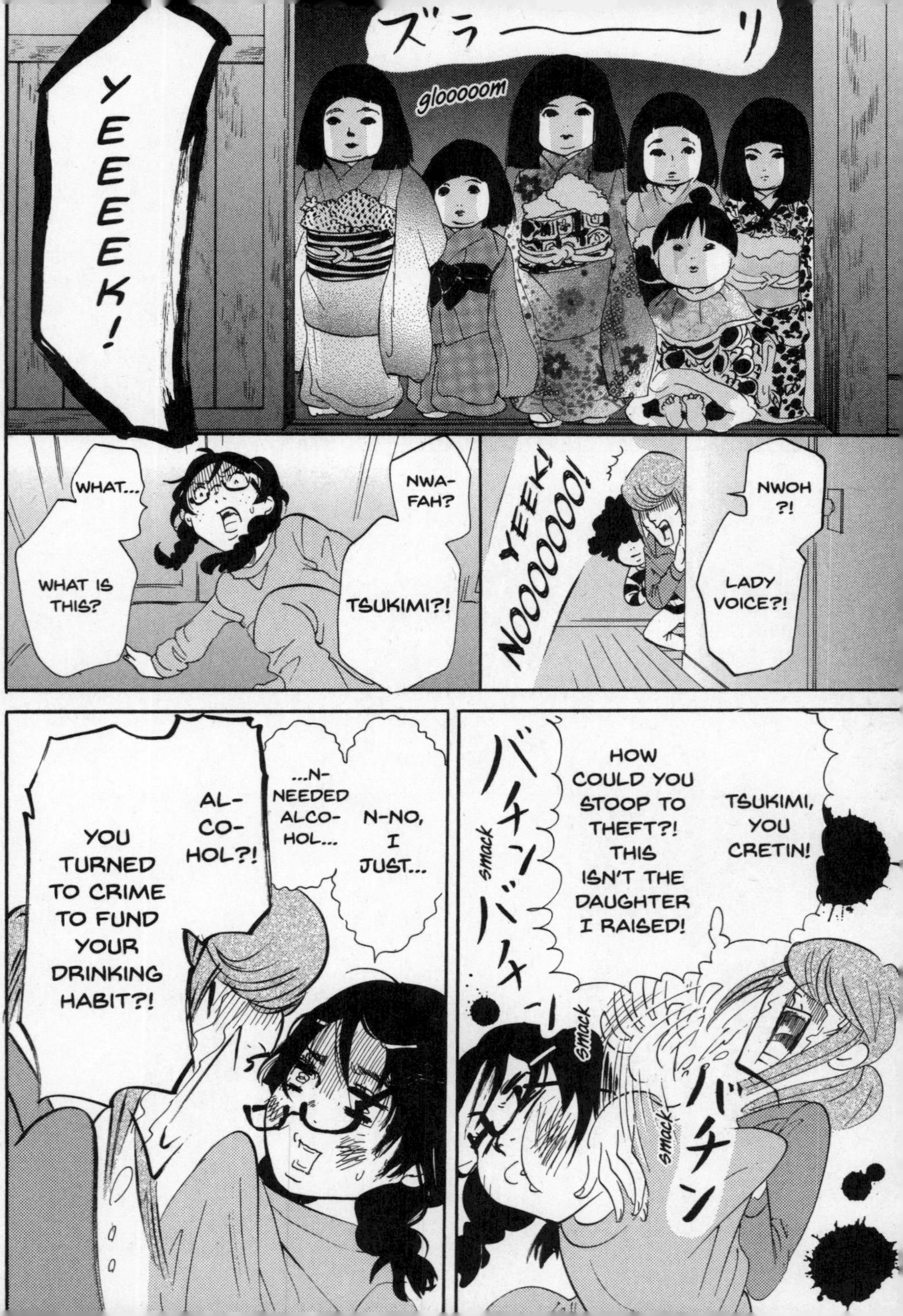
ズラーーーリ
gloooom
YEEEEEK!
NWOH ?!
LADY VOICE?!
YEEK! NOOOOOOO!
NWA-FAH?
TSUKIMI?!
WHAT...
WHAT IS THIS?
TSUKIMI, YOU CRETIN!
HOW COULD YOU STOOP TO THEFT?! THIS ISN'T THE DAUGHTER I RAISED!
バチンバチーン
smack
smack
バチン
smack
N-NO, I JUST...
...N-NEEDED ALCO-HOL...
AL-CO-HOL?!
YOU TURNED TO CRIME TO FUND YOUR DRINKING HABIT?!

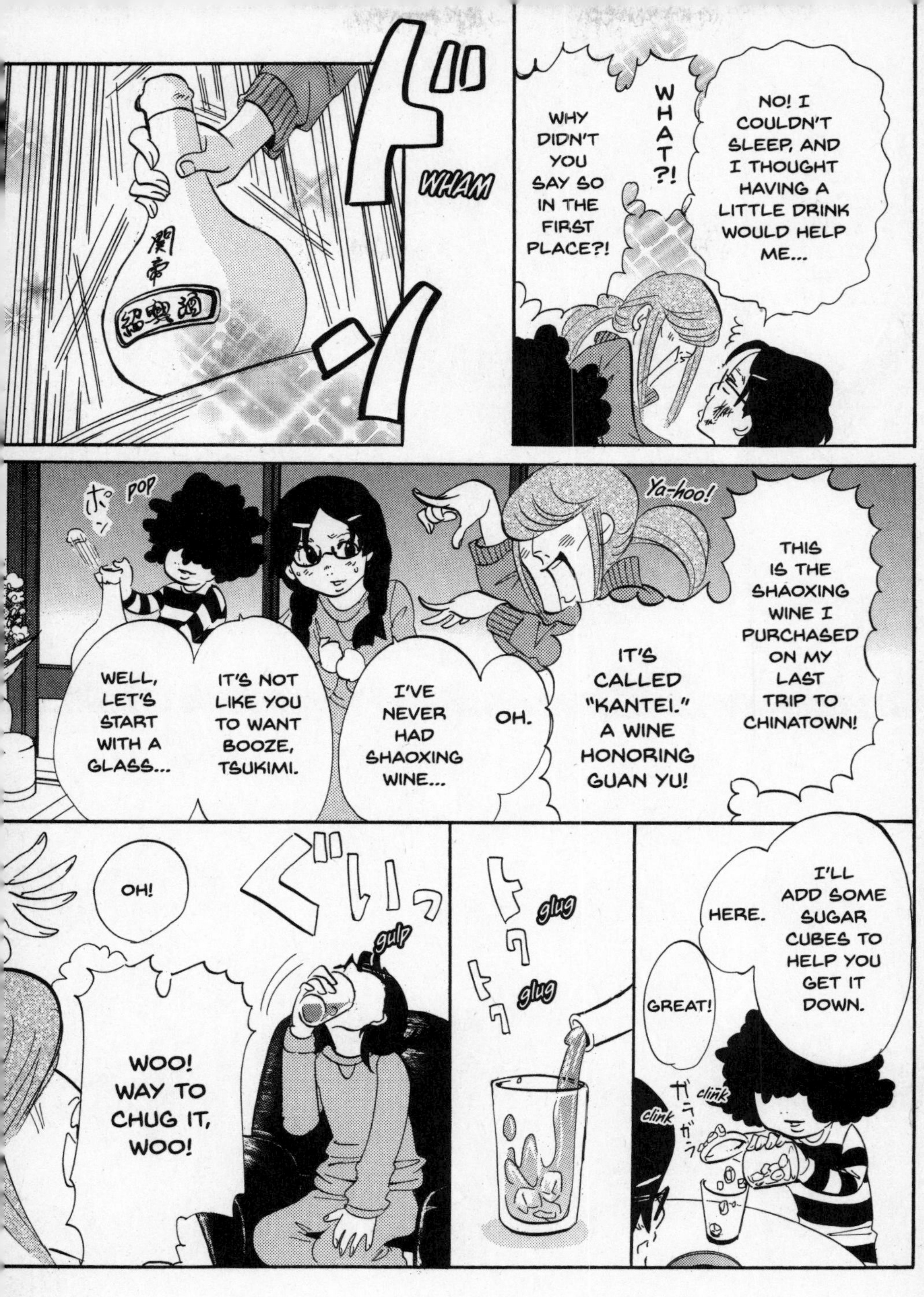
NO! I COULDN'T SLEEP, AND I THOUGHT HAVING A LITTLE DRINK WOULD HELP ME...
WHAT?!
WHY DIDN'T YOU SAY SO IN THE FIRST PLACE?!
WHAM
関帝
紹興酒
Ya-hoo!
THIS IS THE SHAOXING WINE I PURCHASED ON MY LAST TRIP TO CHINATOWN!
IT'S CALLED "KANTEI." A WINE HONORING GUAN YU!
OH.
I'VE NEVER HAD SHAOXING WINE...
IT'S NOT LIKE YOU TO WANT BOOZE, TSUKIMI.
WELL, LET'S START WITH A GLASS...
pop
I'LL ADD SOME SUGAR CUBES TO HELP YOU GET IT DOWN.
HERE.
GREAT!
clink
clink
glug
glug
OH!
gulp
WOO! WAY TO CHUG IT, WOO!

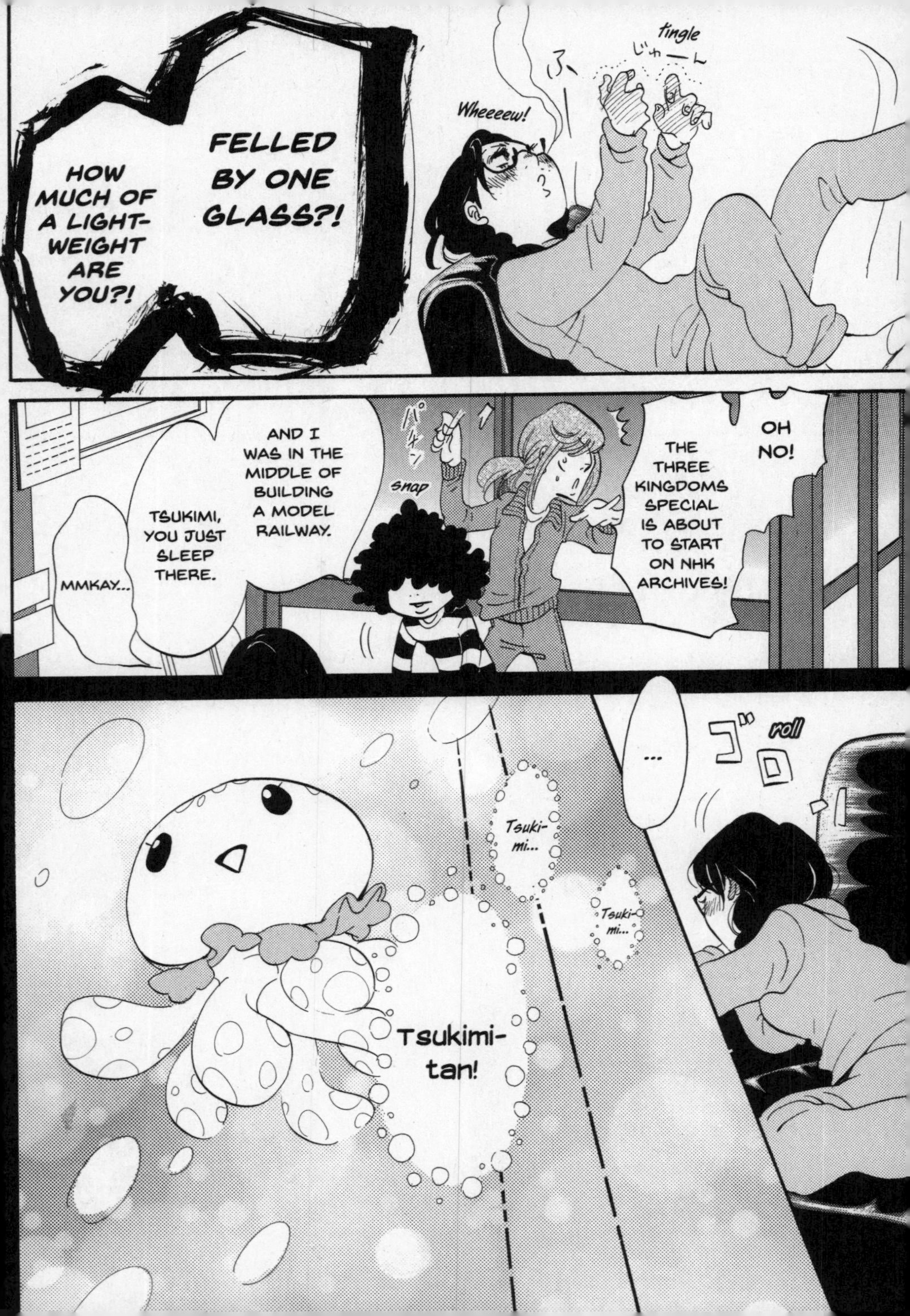
tingle
じゃーん
ふ
Wheeeew!
FELLED BY ONE GLASS?!
HOW MUCH OF A LIGHT-WEIGHT ARE YOU?!
OH NO!
THE THREE KINGDOMS SPECIAL IS ABOUT TO START ON NHK ARCHIVES!
パキン
snap
AND I WAS IN THE MIDDLE OF BUILDING A MODEL RAILWAY.
TSUKIMI, YOU JUST SLEEP THERE.
MMKAY...
ゴロ
roll
...
Tsuki-mi...
Tsuki-mi...
Tsukimi-tan!

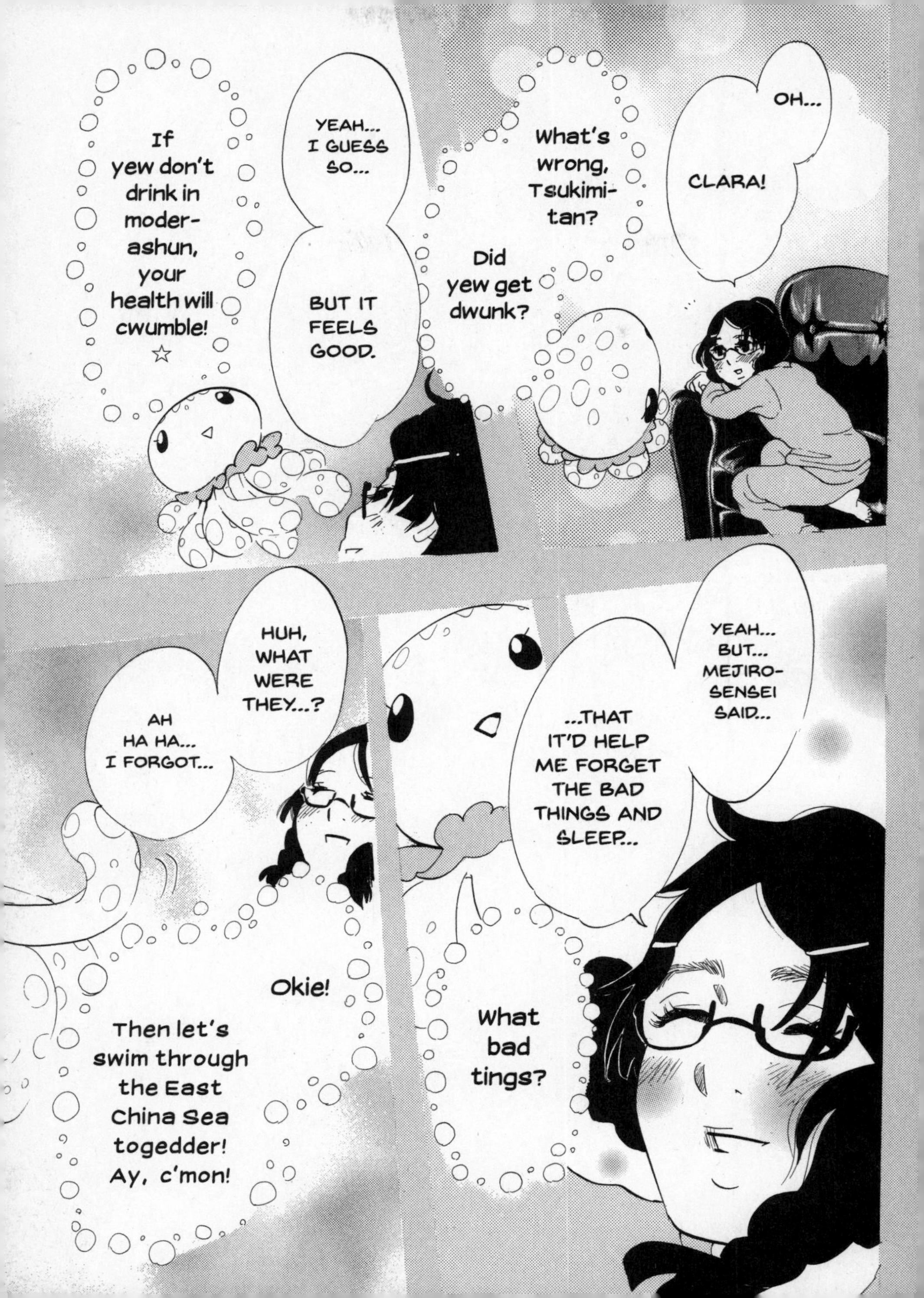
OH... CLARA!
What's wrong, Tsukimi-tan?
Did yew get dwunk?
YEAH... I GUESS SO...
BUT IT FEELS GOOD.
If yew don't drink in moder-ashun, your health will cwumble! ☆
YEAH... BUT... MEJIRO-SENSEI SAID...
...THAT IT'D HELP ME FORGET THE BAD THINGS AND SLEEP...
What bad tings?
HUH, WHAT WERE THEY...?
AH HA HA... I FORGOT...
Okie!
Then let's swim through the East China Sea togedder! Ay, c'mon!

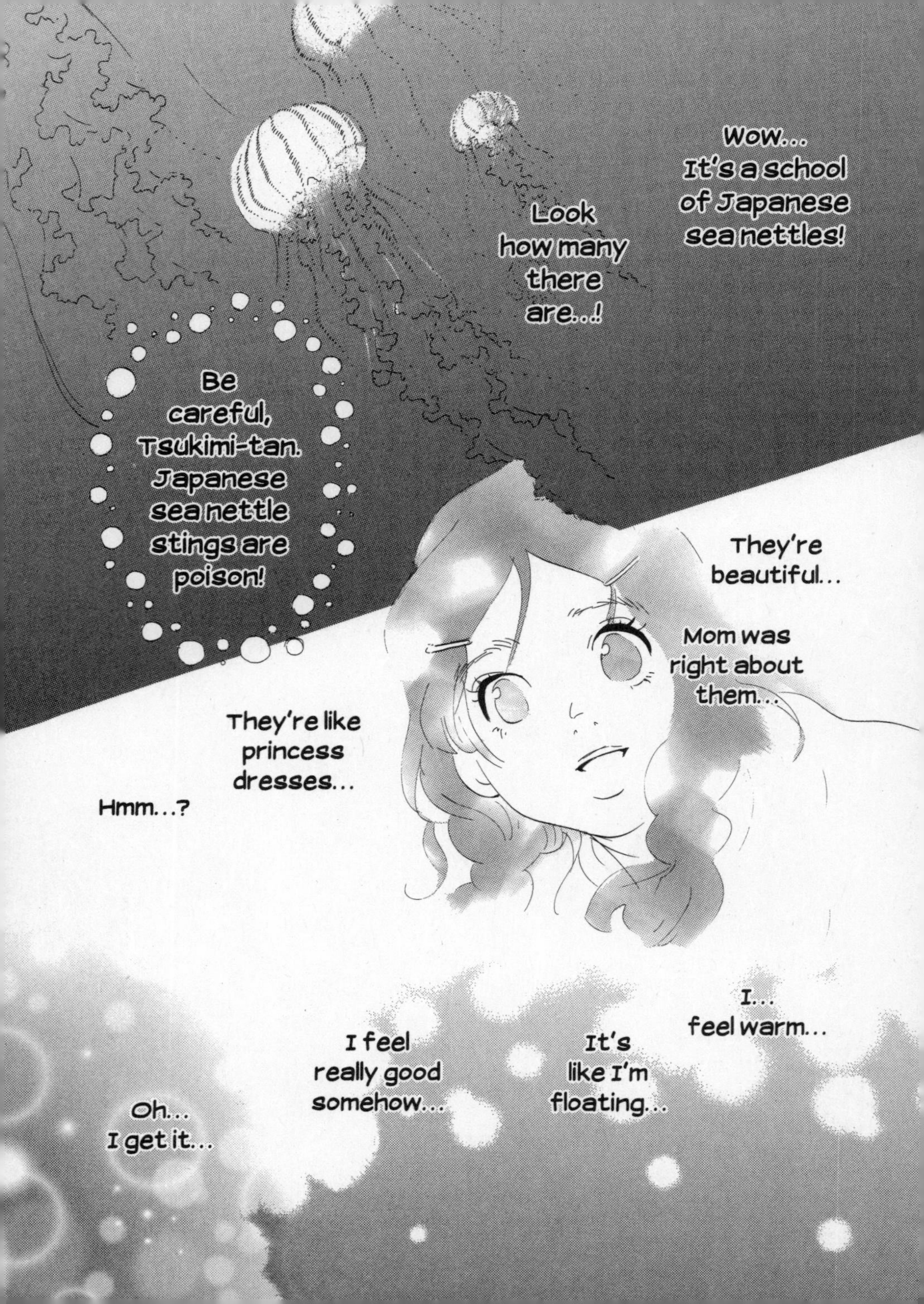
Wow... It's a school of Japanese sea nettles!
Look how many there are...!
Be careful, Tsukimi-tan. Japanese sea nettle stings are poison!
They're beautiful...
Mom was right about them...
They're like princess dresses...
Hmm...?
I... feel warm...
It's like I'm floating...
I feel really good somehow...
Oh... I get it...

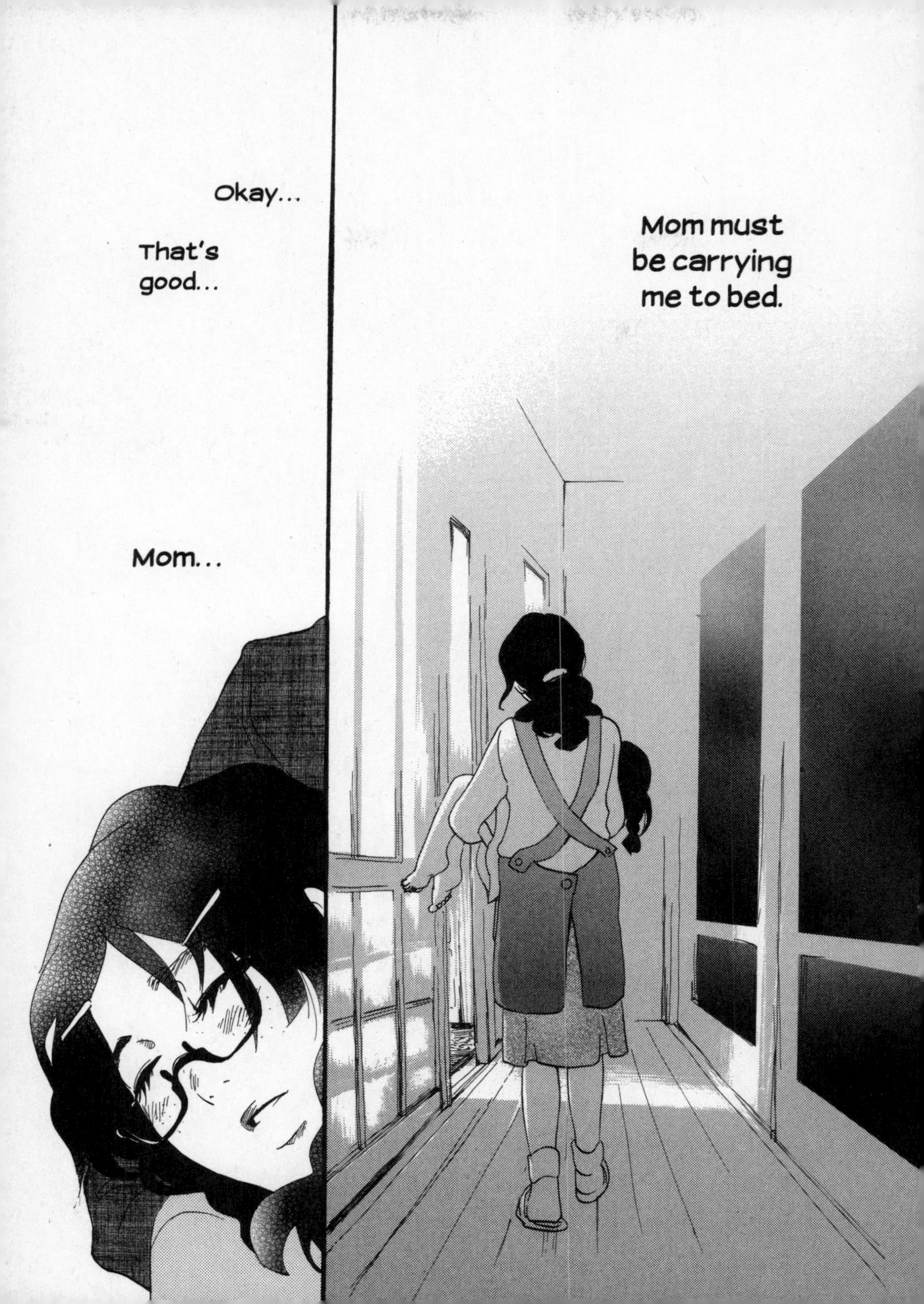
Mom must be carrying me to bed.
Okay...
That's good...
Mom...

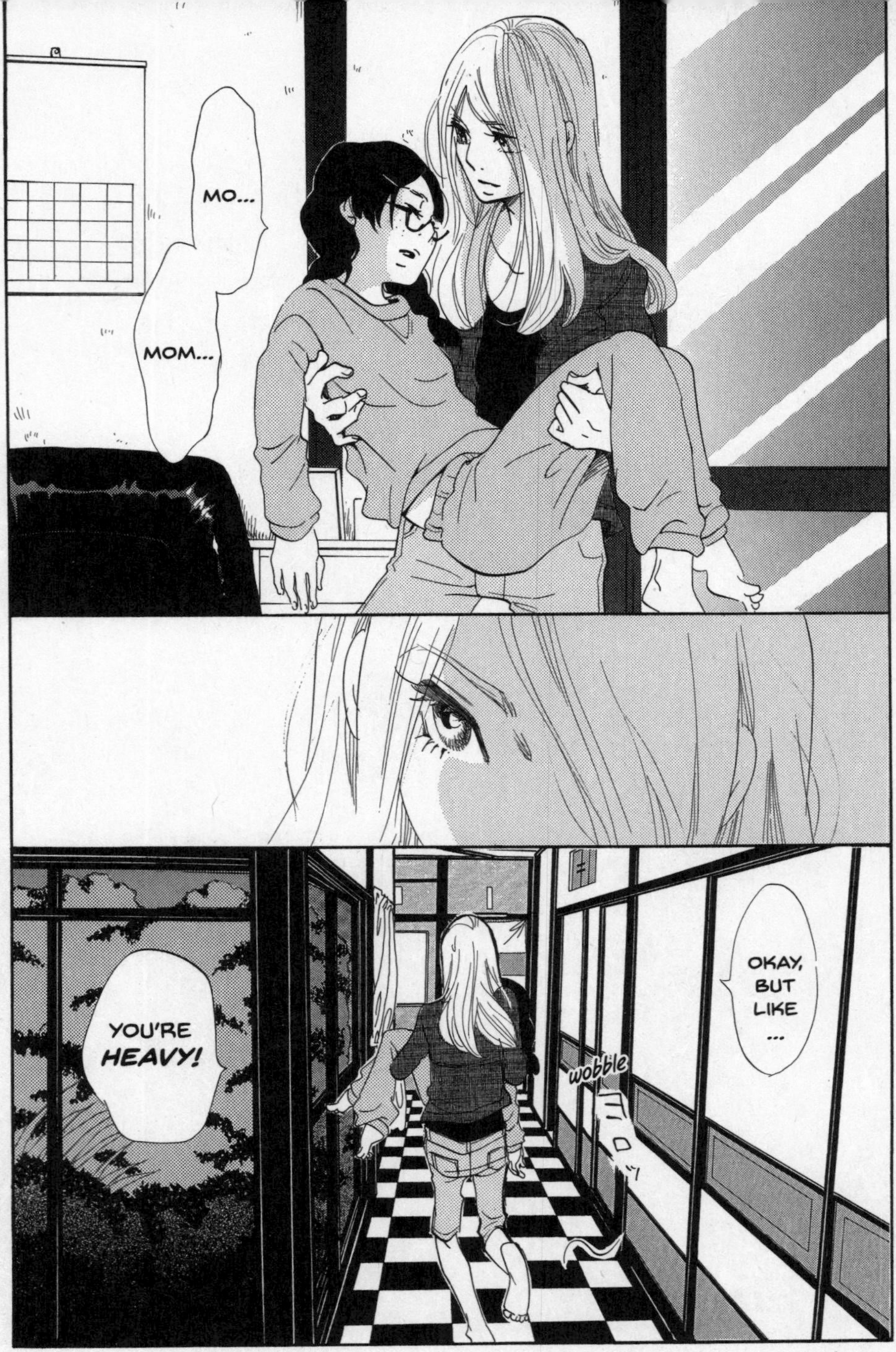
MO...
MOM...
OKAY, BUT LIKE ...
wobble
YOU'RE HEAVY!

Seen by an assistant!

When the Penélope Cruz movie "*Vicky Cristina Barcelona*" was announced a while after Higashimura-sensei drew the first chapter of "Jelly, Higashimura, Barcelona," she became genuinely angry. She yelled, "They ripped off my title!"

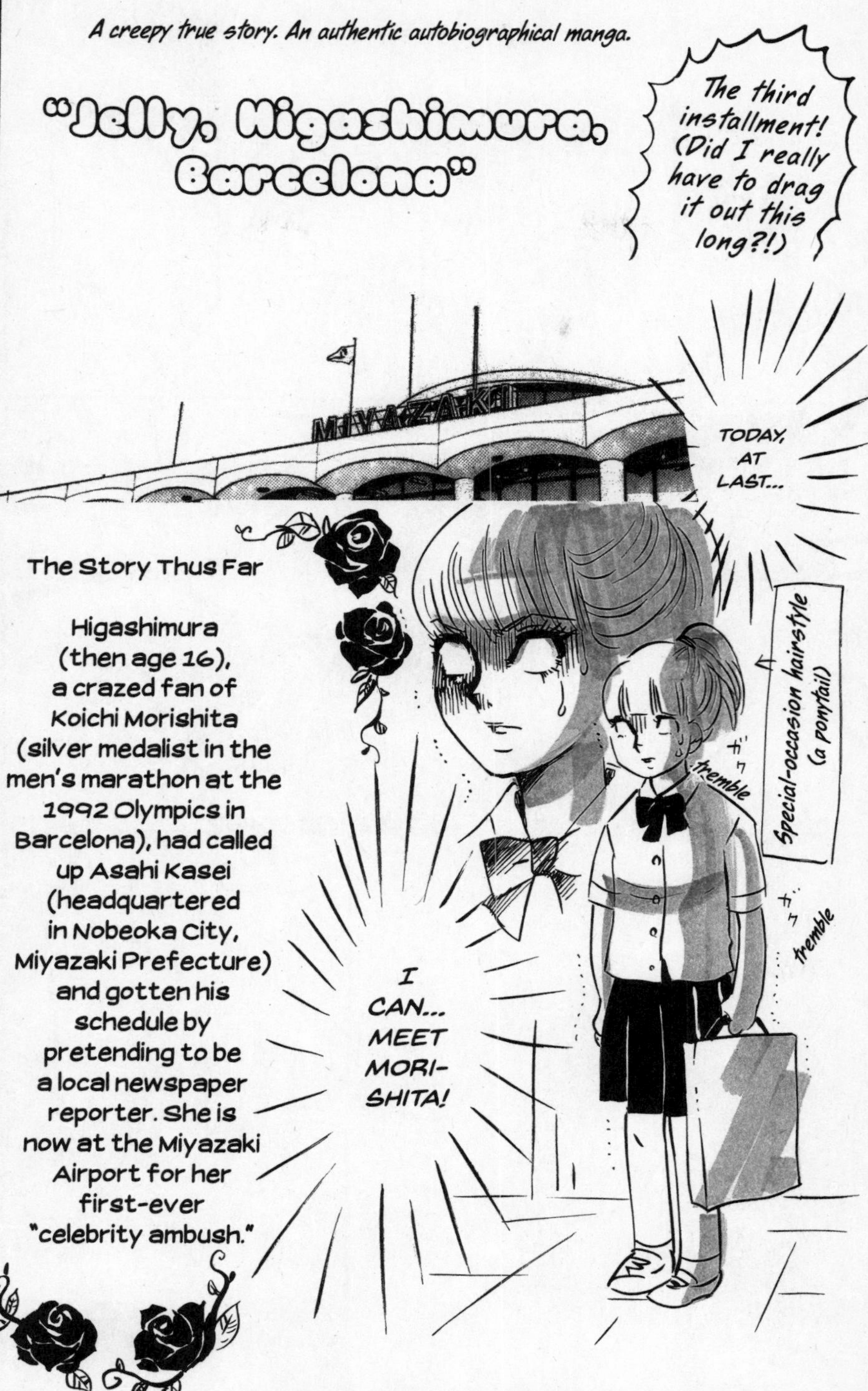
A creepy true story. An authentic autobiographical manga.
"Jelly, Higashimura, Barcelona"
The third installment! (Did I really have to drag it out this long?!)
MIYAZAKI
TODAY, AT LAST...
Special-occasion hairstyle (a ponytail)
tremble
tremble
I CAN... MEET MORI-SHITA!
The Story Thus Far
Higashimura (then age 16), a crazed fan of Koichi Morishita (silver medalist in the men's marathon at the 1992 Olympics in Barcelona), had called up Asahi Kasei (headquartered in Nobeoka City, Miyazaki Prefecture) and gotten his schedule by pretending to be a local newspaper reporter. She is now at the Miyazaki Airport for her first-ever "celebrity ambush."

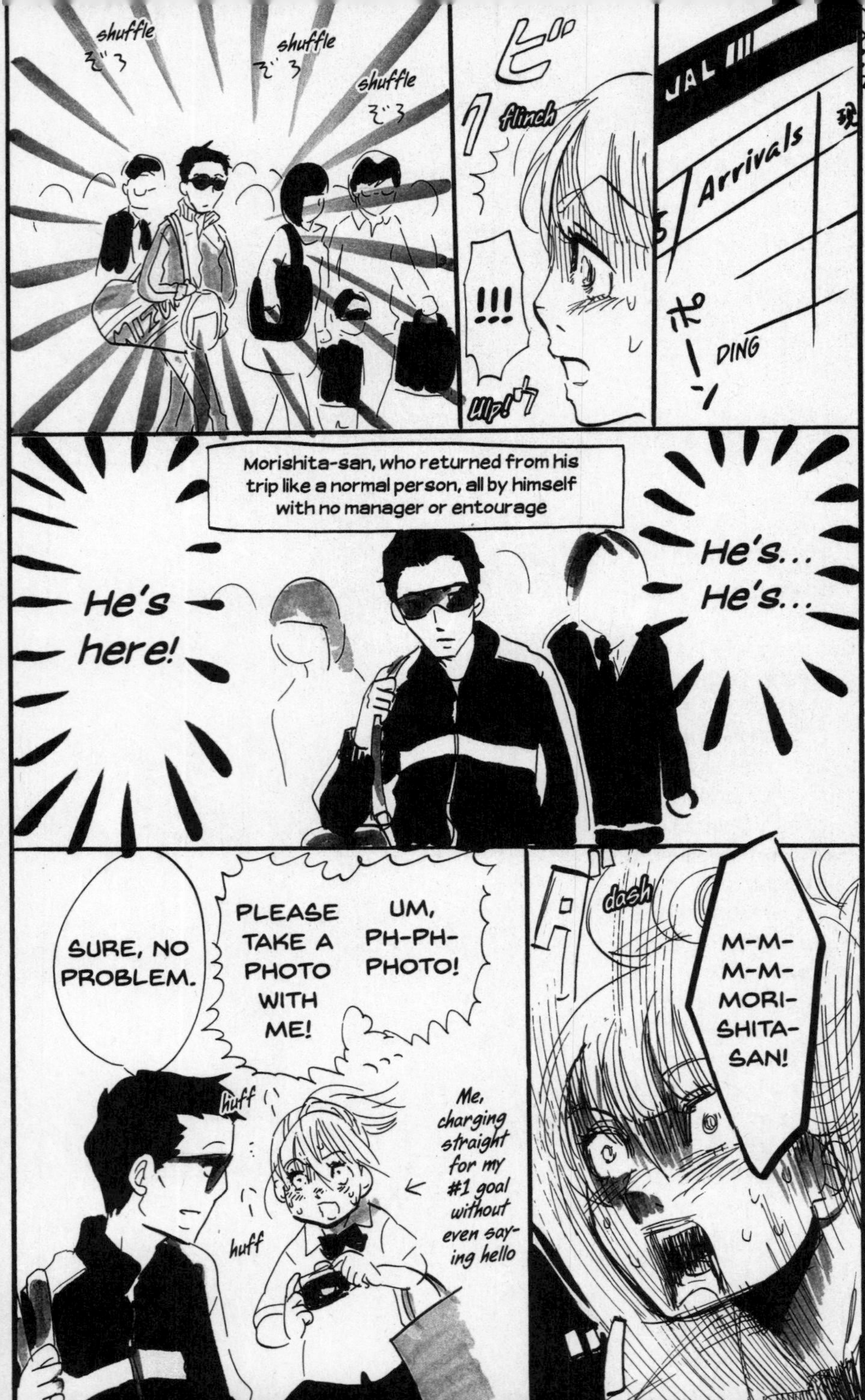

Seen by an assistant!
JAL
Arrivals
DING
flinch
!!!
Ulp!
shuffle
shuffle
shuffle
He's... He's...
Morishita-san, who returned from his trip like a normal person, all by himself with no manager or entourage
He's here!
dash
M-M-M-M-MORI-SHITA-SAN!
UM, PH-PH-PHOTO!
PLEASE TAKE A PHOTO WITH ME!
SURE, NO PROBLEM.
huff
huff
Me, charging straight for my #1 goal without even saying hello

Her editor admonished her and said, "Please end the bonus manga within this Volume! It's just an extra, so don't drag it out so much!" To which Higashimura-sensei retorted, with a completely straight face, "What? I was planning to spend years and years with this story."

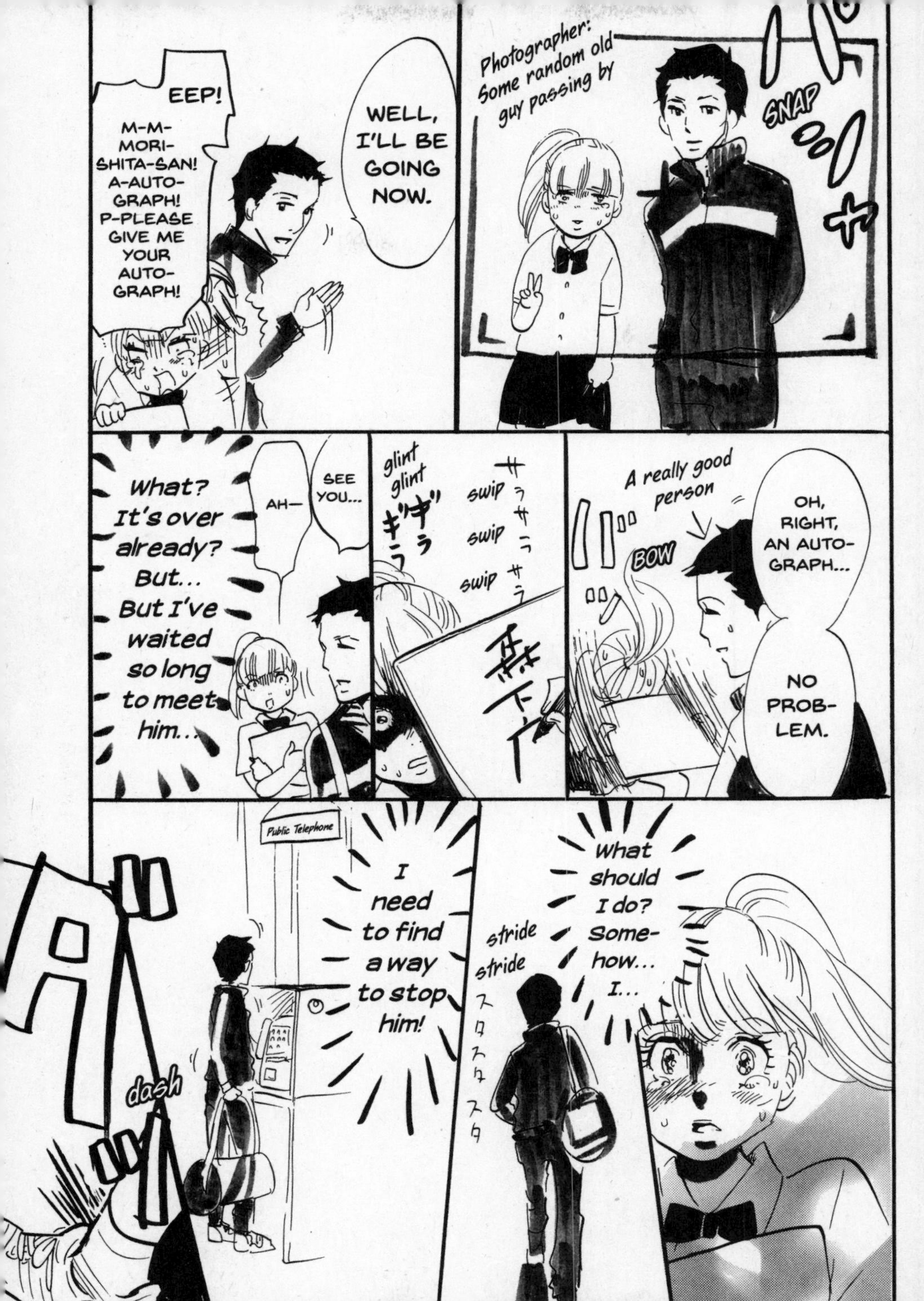
Photographer: Some random old guy passing by
SNAP
WELL, I'LL BE GOING NOW.
EEP!
M-M-MORI-SHITA-SAN! A-AUTO-GRAPH! P-PLEASE GIVE ME YOUR AUTO-GRAPH!
A really good person
OH, RIGHT, AN AUTO-GRAPH...
BOW
NO PROB-LEM.
glint glint
swip swip swip
SEE YOU...
AH—
What? It's over already? But… But I've waited so long to meet him…
What should I do? Some-how… I…
stride stride
I need to find a way to stop him!
Public Telephone
dash

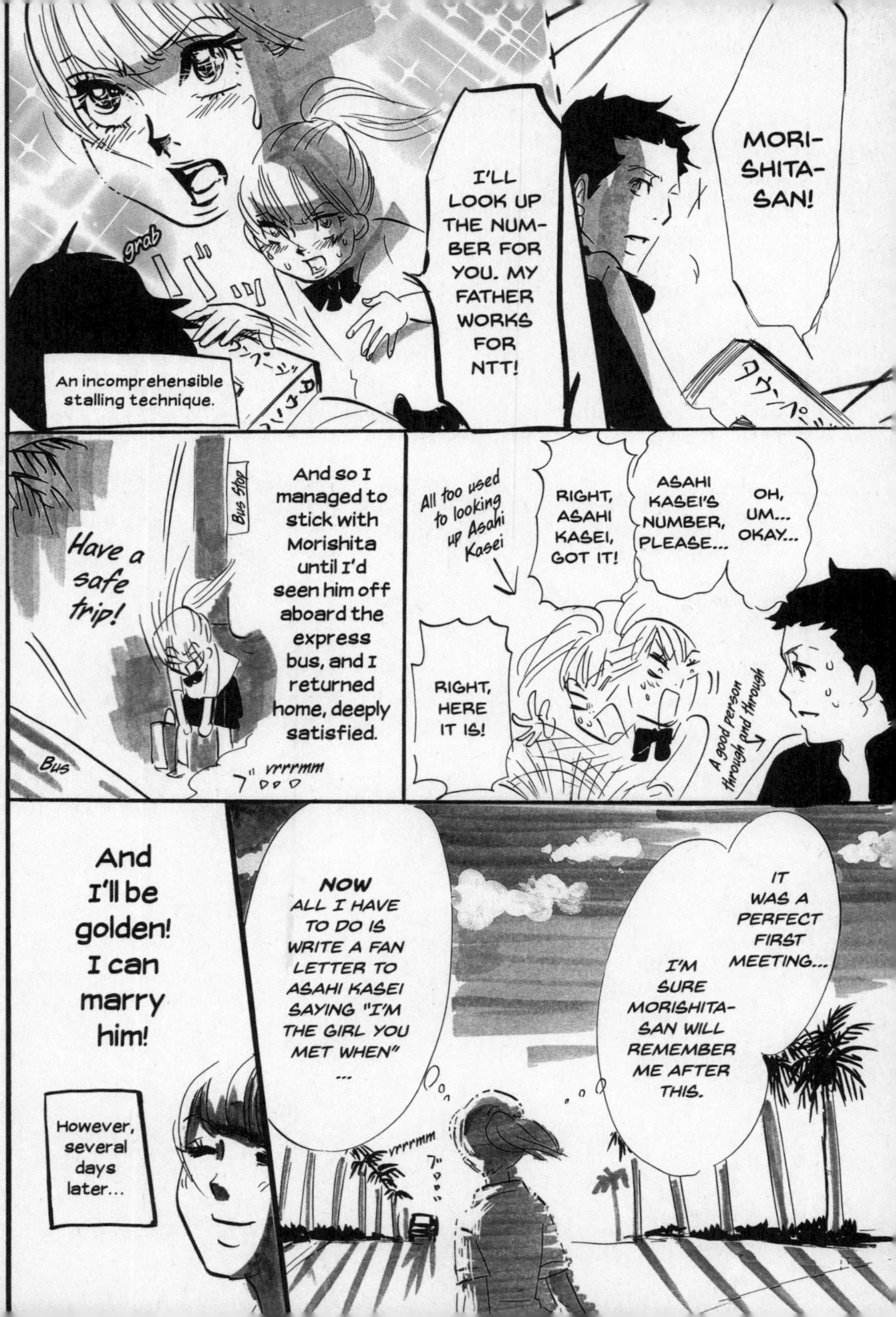
MORI-SHITA-SAN!
I'LL LOOK UP THE NUMBER FOR YOU. MY FATHER WORKS FOR NTT!
grab
An incomprehensible stalling technique.
OH, UM... OKAY...
ASAHI KASEI'S NUMBER, PLEASE...
RIGHT, ASAHI KASEI, GOT IT!
All too used to looking up Asahi Kasei
A good person through and through
RIGHT, HERE IT IS!
And so I managed to stick with Morishita until I'd seen him off aboard the express bus, and I returned home, deeply satisfied.
Bus Stop
Have a safe trip!
Bus
vrrrmm
IT WAS A PERFECT FIRST MEETING...
I'M SURE MORISHITA-SAN WILL REMEMBER ME AFTER THIS.
NOW ALL I HAVE TO DO IS WRITE A FAN LETTER TO ASAHI KASEI SAYING "I'M THE GIRL YOU MET WHEN" ...
vrrrmm
And I'll be golden! I can marry him!
However, several days later...

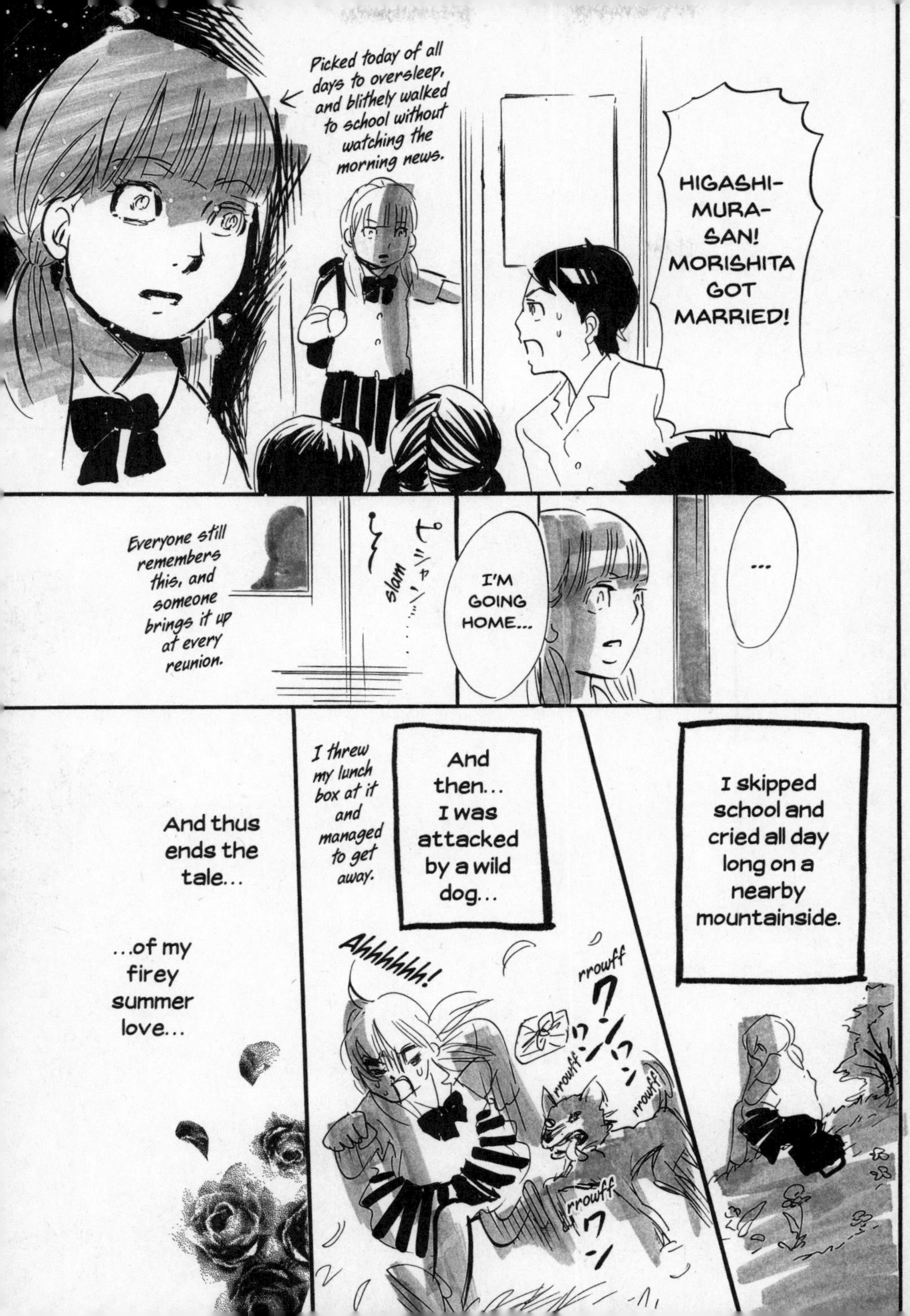
HIGASHI-MURA-SAN! MORISHITA GOT MARRIED!
Picked today of all days to oversleep, and blithely walked to school without watching the morning news.
...
I'M GOING HOME...
slam
Everyone still remembers this, and someone brings it up at every reunion.
I skipped school and cried all day long on a nearby mountainside.
And then... I was attacked by a wild dog...
I threw my lunch box at it and managed to get away.
Ahhhhhh!
rrowff
rrowff
rrowff
rrowff
And thus ends the tale...
...of my firey summer love...

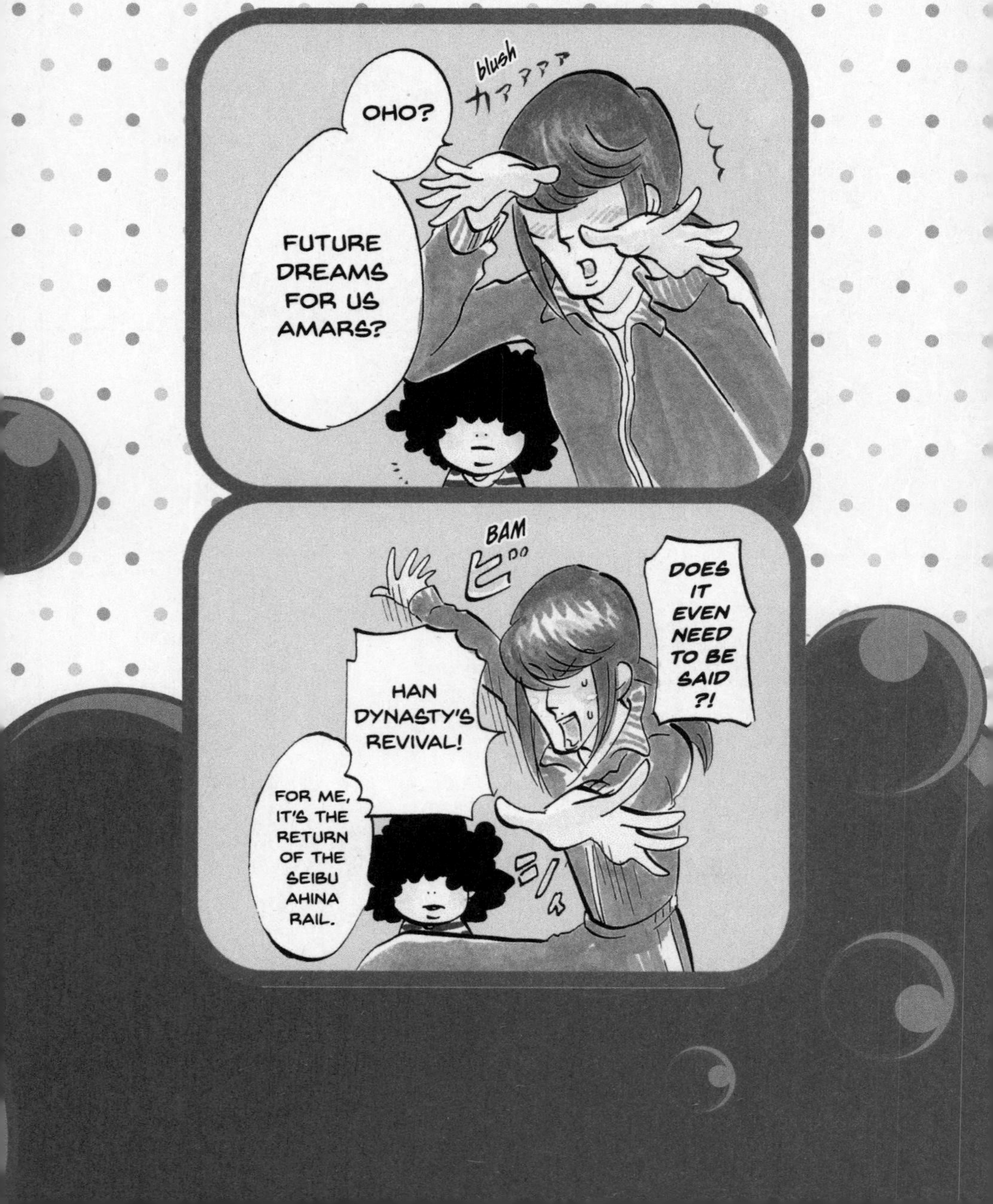
blush
カァァァ
OHO?
FUTURE DREAMS FOR US AMARS?
DOES IT EVEN NEED TO BE SAID ?!
BAM
ビッ
HAN DYNASTY'S REVIVAL!
FOR ME, IT'S THE RETURN OF THE SEIBU AHINA RAIL.

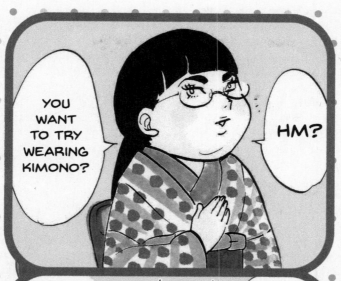

HM?
YOU WANT TO TRY WEARING KIMONO?
AH, YES, I SEE. WELL, BRINGING IN KIMONO TO YOUR EVERYDAY WAR-DROBE IS QUITE EASY. FIRST, YOU JUST NEED A SPE-CIAL UNDERSHIRT, UNDERPANTS, STIFF FABRIC FOR UNDER YOUR OBI, TABI SOCKS, A LEASH BELT, AND MAYBE THREE OR FOUR BRAIDED CORDS, AS WELL AS A NICE COLLAR FOR UNDER YOUR KI-MONO. OH, OH, AND DON'T FOR-GET THE CORE FOR THE COLLAR, TOO.
pant pant
AND THAT'S NOT ALL, YOU KNOW. SINCE THE MOST IMPORTANT PART IS THE SHOES—GETA, ZORI SANDALS, WHICHEVER IS FINE AS LONG AS YOU MATCH IT TO THE TIME, PLACE, AND OCCASION, AS WELL AS YOUR KIMONO. BY THE WAY, THIS TYPE OF KIMONO IS CALLED A MEISEN KIMONO, WHICH, IF YOU DIDN'T ALREADY KNOW, IS PART OF A SILK YARN-DYEING TRADITION. IT WAS QUITE POPULAR IN THE SHOWA ERA AND LET ME TELL YOU WHY...

Translation Notes

Spellbound and Stone Broke, page 6
This name comes from Ryo Takasugi's *Kin'yu Fushoku Retto* novel series, the title of which has been translated various way in English, such as *An Archipelago of Financial Corruption*. The series also inspired several movies, one of which made its way to international film festivals under the title *Jubaku: Spellbound*.

All of you have three-digit balances!, page 7
"Three-digits" could mean anything from 100 yen to 999 yen, which is roughly $1 USD to $10 USD. However, considering that 999 yen equals less than $10 USD at the time of this publication (due to the exchange rate), a three-digit balance is even worse than it sounds!

You'll never join the Katsura that way.
Zakoba will turn you away at the door., page 8
Very accomplished performers of *rakugo*, or comic storytelling, are granted a stage name that gets passed down through generations via formal apprenticeship. The apprentice receives their stage name from their master by taking the last name, and part of the master's first name. Since there are many distinct types and styles of *rakugo*, earning your master's last name reflects not only the school of *rakugo* you learned under, but also the entire "family" you come from, whether it is your master, your colleagues, or your apprentices. "Katsura" is an example of a last name from a famous line of rakugo artists. Not just anyone can take on these stage names—you have to earn them. If you're not good enough, Zakoba will absolutely turn you away at the door. Zakoba's full stage name is Zakoba Katsura II.

Shigeru Mizuki character, page 27
A truly beloved household name. Shigeru Mizuki was a prolific manga author, most famous for *Ge Ge Ge no Kitaro* and other works featuring *yokai*, or ghosts and supernatural creatures from Japanese folklore. His manga style is very distinctive, and Tsukimi is indeed drawn in it occasionally—the top of page 135 is a good example. Mizuki is also known for his manga depicting war and Japanese history. He himself was drafted into the Japanese army during World War II and survived many grave encounters, while also being saved by the kindness of others. This inspired him to create work that reflected compassion and a deep hope for humanity. The *yokai* genre playing a big role in mainstream Japanese media today is in part due to Mizuki's influence.

Tankobon, serial, page 30

You're reading a *tankobon* right now. A *tankobon* is a volume of manga chapters compiled in book format. In Japan, the most common way that manga is published is chapter-by-chapter, in a big anthology that comes out every month, week, or bi-annually, etc. These stories are called "serializations" or "serials" due to their continuous nature. When there are enough of these serialized chapters, the *tankobon* can then be put together from that—the book you're holding contains two *tankobon* published in Japan as Princess Jellyfish volumes three and four. The chapters originally ran in Kodansha's manga magazine called *KISS*. Unfortunately, Mejiro-sensei's past works aren't selling well as *tankobon* at the moment, but she has a new serial running issue-by-issue in a magazine. Let's hope it's a hit!

Mister Donut, page 46

Mister Donut is a popular fast food chain in Japan, best known for their doughnut selection. Their mascot, "Pon De Lion" is a lion with a doughnut mane. This mane is shaped like Mister Donut's famous doughnut called the Pon De Ring, which is made with mochi (glutinous Japanese sweet rice dessert) and is much chewier in texture than a doughnut. On page 70, you can see Hanamori and Sugimocchan meeting at a Mister Donut.

Teru-teru-bozu, page 54

A *teru-teru-bozu* is a doll hung in a window frame or from the eaves as a good-weather charm, to keep the rain away. Its basic form is extremely simple: a round head with a skirt of fabric below that makes it look like a bit like a ghost. These dolls are often hung in groups, and they can be made out of simple tissue paper or plain white cloth. As with all things, crafting enthusiasts make *teru-teru-bozu* far more elaborate and adorable, but Tsukimi makes jellyfish versions.

Bayoeen!, page 72

This is a magical spell that characters Arle and Amitie shout in a series of video games called *Puyo Puyo*, also known as *Puyo Pop* in the English-language releases. Arle's shout is "Cutie!" in English, while Amitie's version is "All Righty!" The spell overwhelms enemies with emotion, temporarily immobilizing them.

Hojicha and yokan, page 102

Hojicha is Japanese green tea that is roasted, turning the leaves brown. Yokan is a traditional Japanese sweet made of jellied azuki beans.

Nippori Fabric Town, page 139
Nippori Fabric Town, also known as Nippori Textile Town, is just what it sounds like: a neighborhood in Tokyo near JR Nippori Station that is devoted exclusively to fabrics, buttons, brocades, sewing equipment, etc.

A wine honoring Guan Yu, page 183
The bottle you're seeing is a real brand of Shaoxing wine. Mayaya likes this brand in particular because the packaging has a picture of Guan Yu on it, and the name of the wine also mentions him. It's called *Kantei*, which is the Japanese reading of one of Guan Yu's alternate names, pronounced "Guan Di" in Chinese.

NTT, page 192
When Higashimura offers to look up a phone number in the phone book for Morishita, she mentions "NTT." She is referring to the Nippon Telegraph and Telephone Corporation (NTT), the largest telecommunications company in Japan. It maintains all telecommunications in Japan.

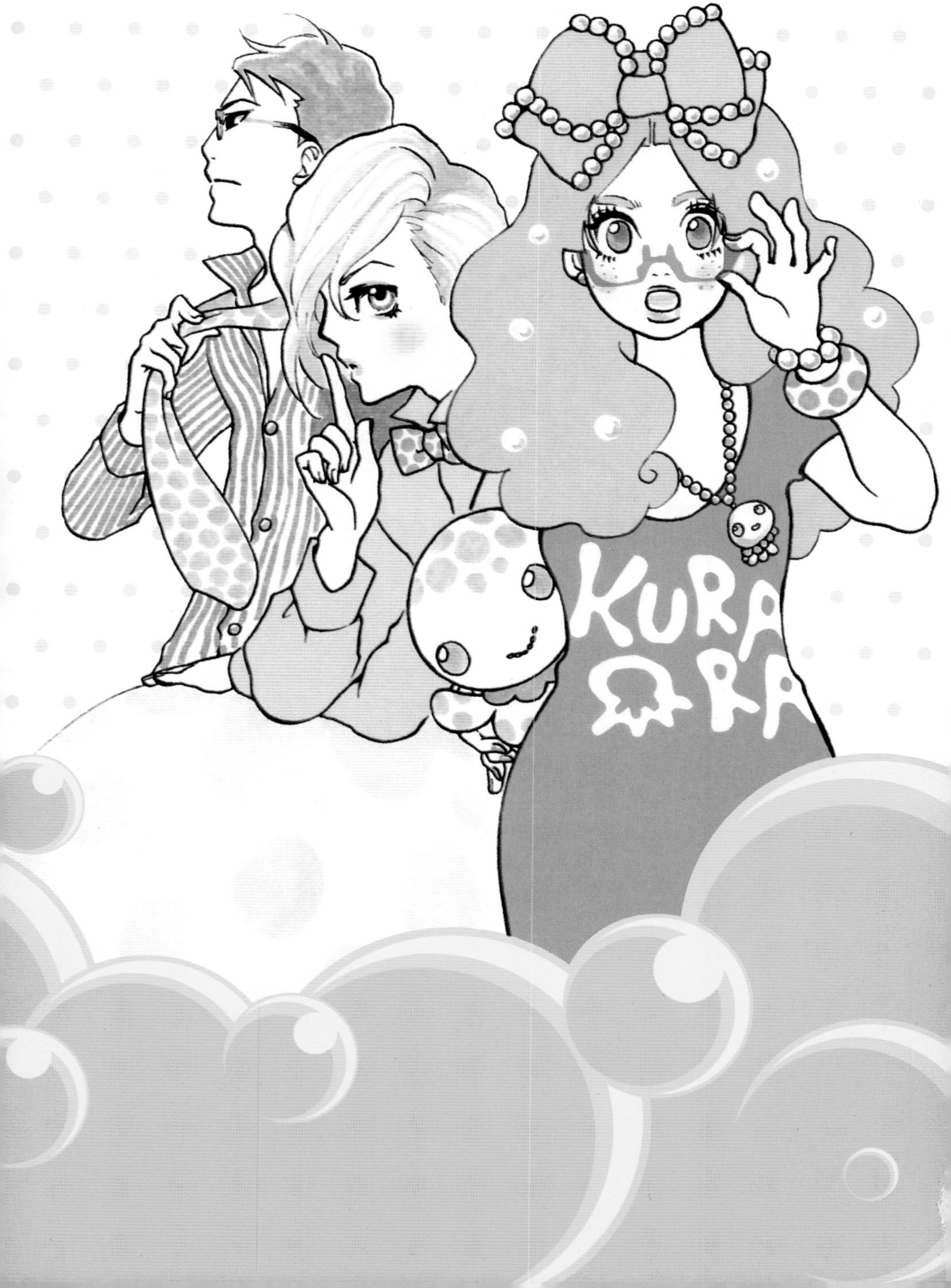
KURA
RA

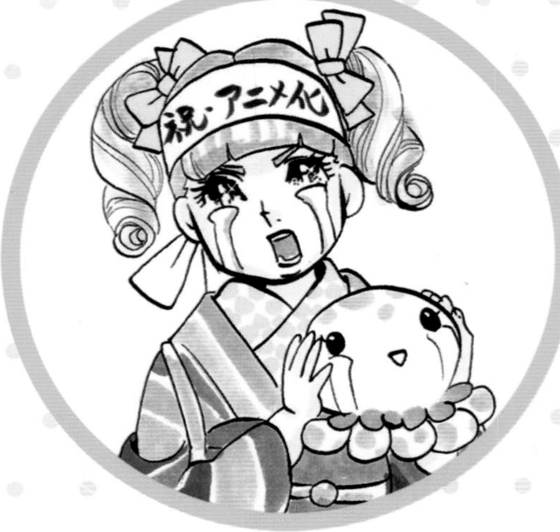
祝・アニメ化

DEAREST READERS!

MAJOR CRISIS! IT'S A RECESSION!
A GREAT DEPRESSION THAT
ONLY OCCURS ONCE IN A
HUNDRED YEARS!
WAIT, WHAT?!
B-BUT YOU'RE STILL SAVING A
NICE CHUNK OF MONEY FOR
THE THINGS THAT YOU LOVE?
HEY, YOU'RE OFFICIALLY
AN AMARS, TOO!
CHEERS!
TO WHATEVER MAKES YOUR EYES
SPARKLE WITH DELIGHT!

-AKIKO HIGASHIMURA

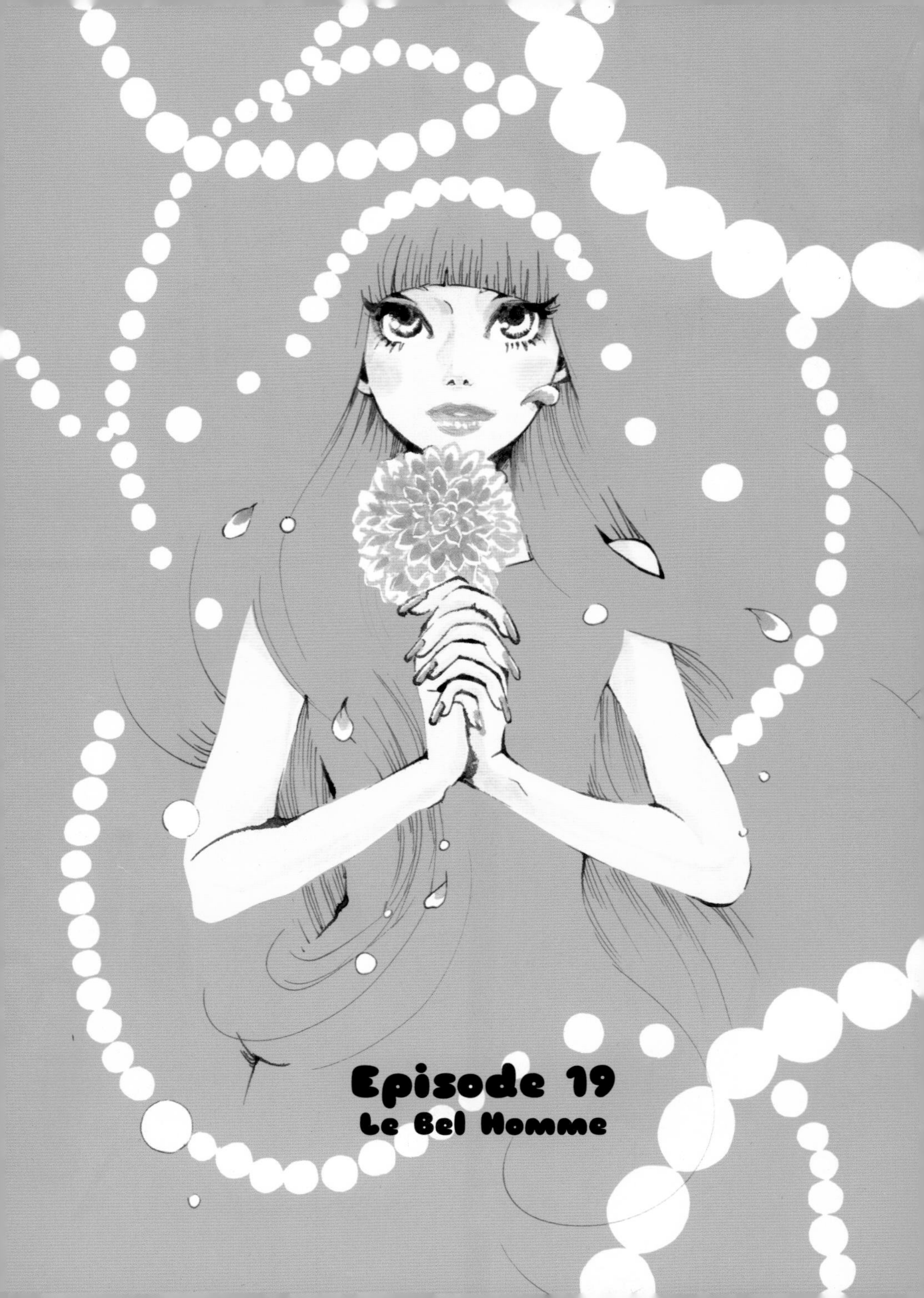
Episode 19
Le Bel Homme

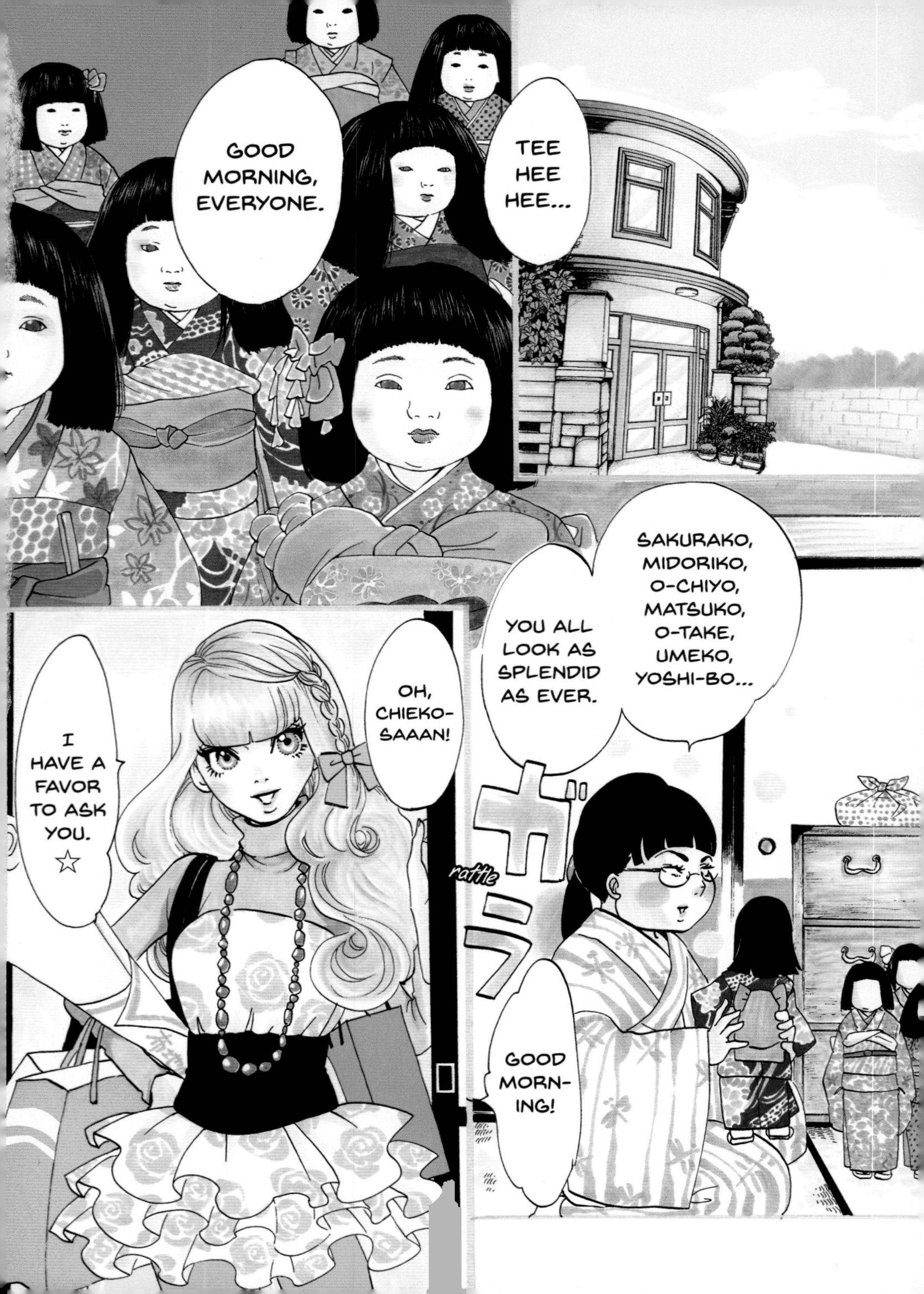
TEE HEE HEE...
GOOD MORNING, EVERYONE.
SAKURAKO, MIDORIKO, O-CHIYO, MATSUKO, O-TAKE, UMEKO, YOSHI-BO...
YOU ALL LOOK AS SPLENDID AS EVER.
ガラ
rattle
GOOD MORN-ING!
OH, CHIEKO-SAAAN!
I HAVE A FAVOR TO ASK YOU. ☆

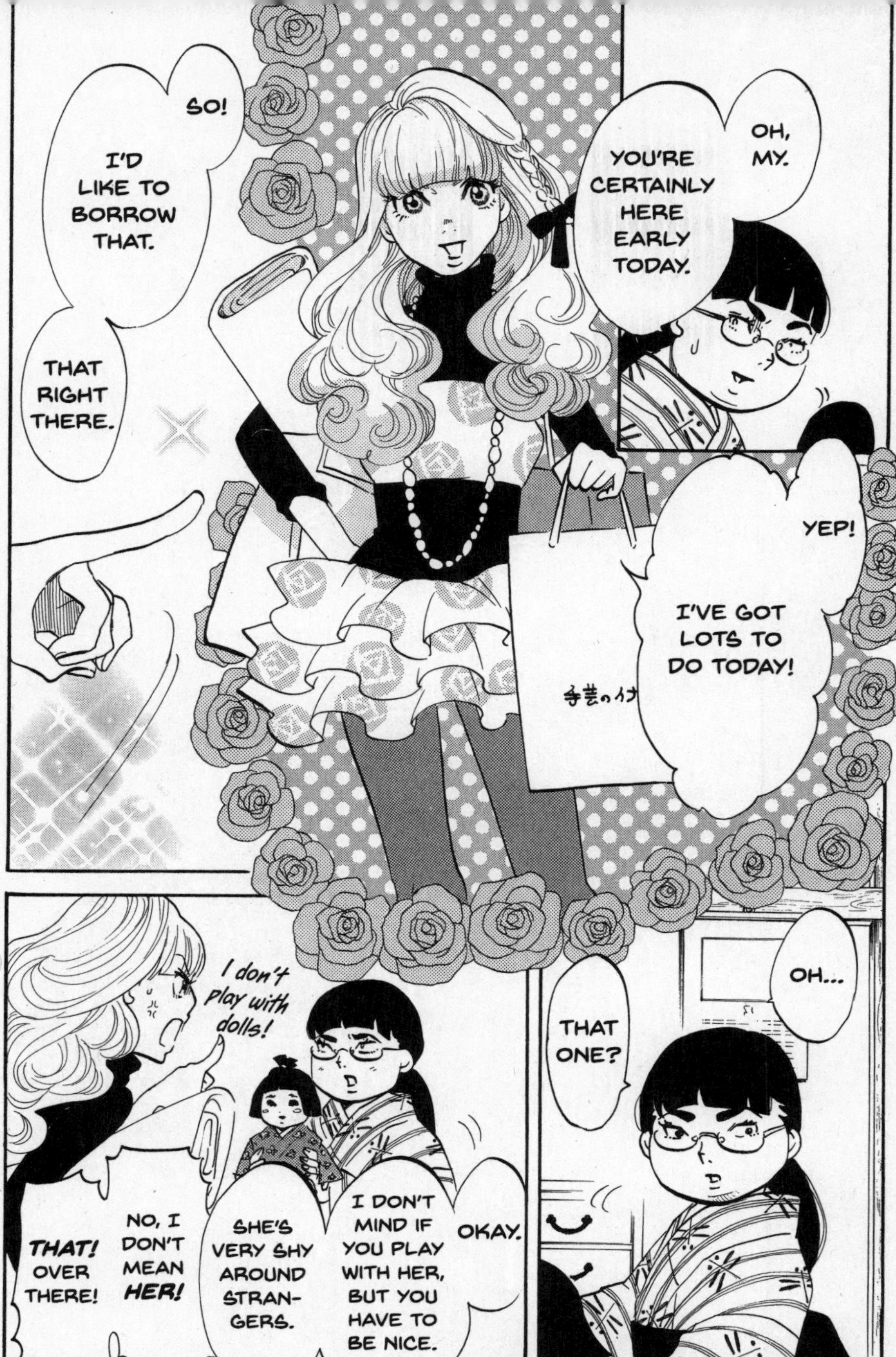
OH, MY.
YOU'RE CERTAINLY HERE EARLY TODAY.
YEP!
I'VE GOT LOTS TO DO TODAY!
SO!
I'D LIKE TO BORROW THAT.
THAT RIGHT THERE.
OH...
THAT ONE?
OKAY.
I DON'T MIND IF YOU PLAY WITH HER, BUT YOU HAVE TO BE NICE.
SHE'S VERY SHY AROUND STRAN-GERS.
I don't play with dolls!
NO, I DON'T MEAN HER!
THAT! OVER THERE!

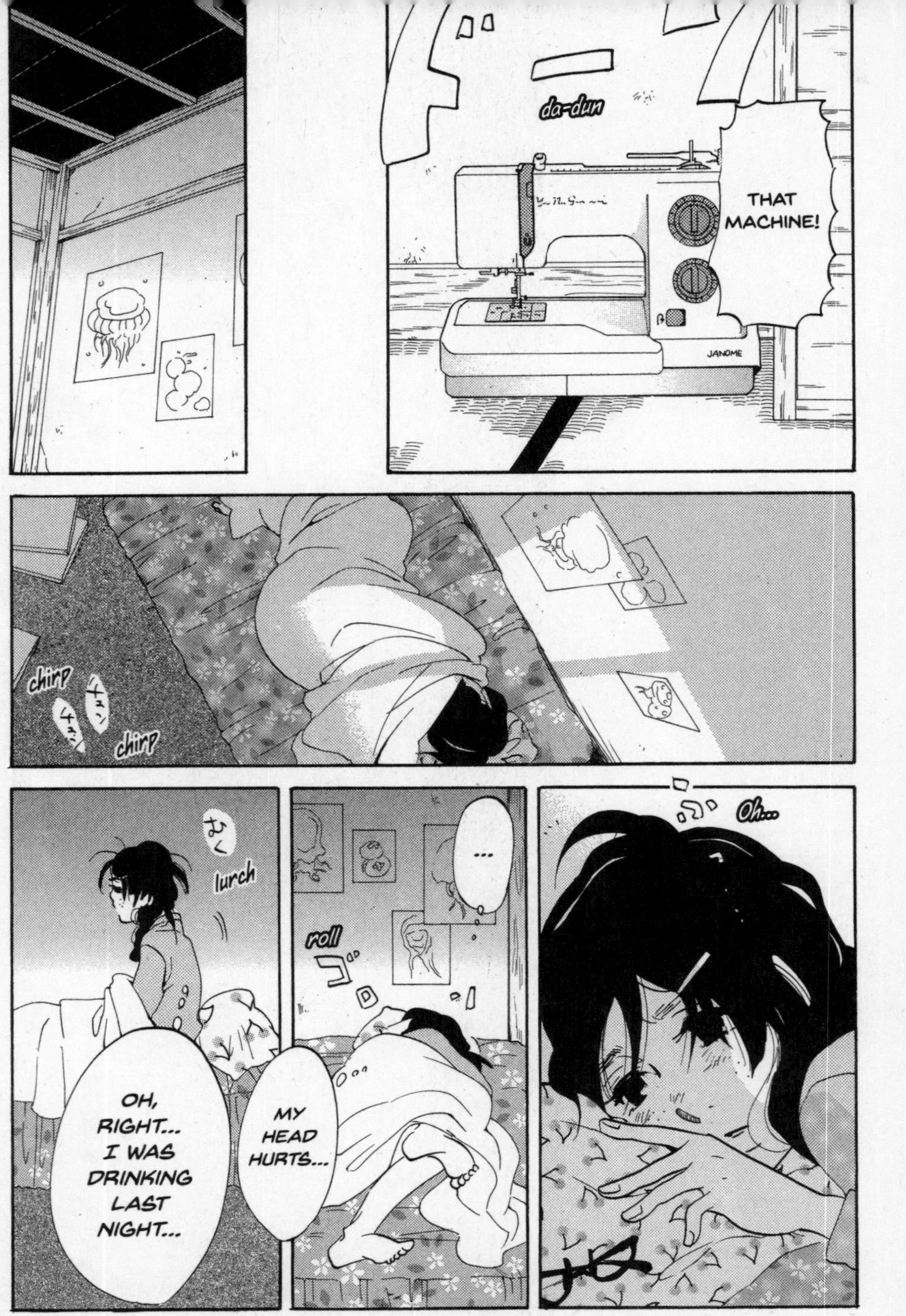

da-dun
THAT MACHINE!
JANOME
chirp
chirp
Oh...
...
roll
MY HEAD HURTS...
むく
lurch
OH, RIGHT... I WAS DRINKING LAST NIGHT...

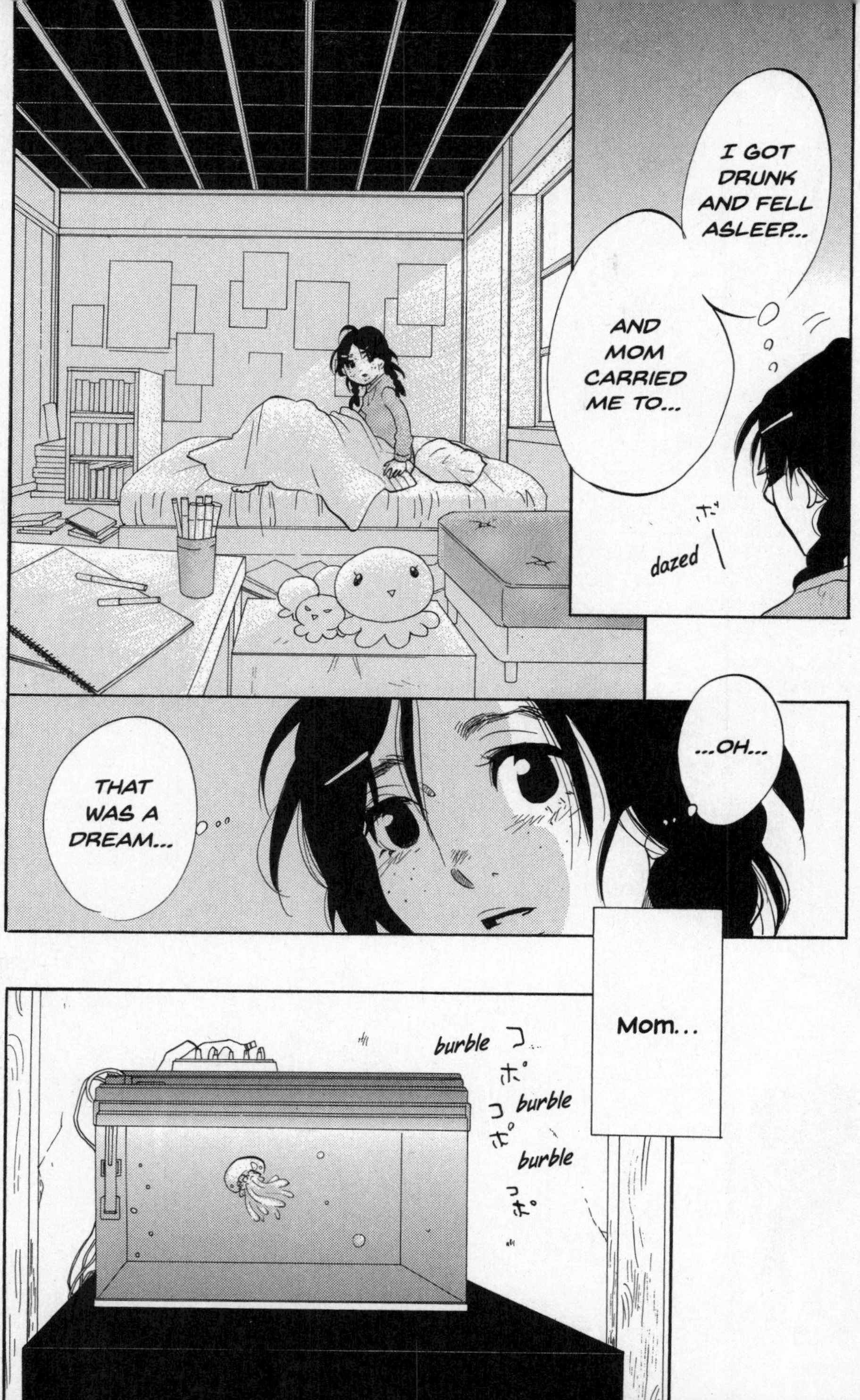

I GOT DRUNK AND FELL ASLEEP..
AND MOM CARRIED ME TO...
dazed
...OH...
THAT WAS A DREAM...
Mom...
burble
burble
burble

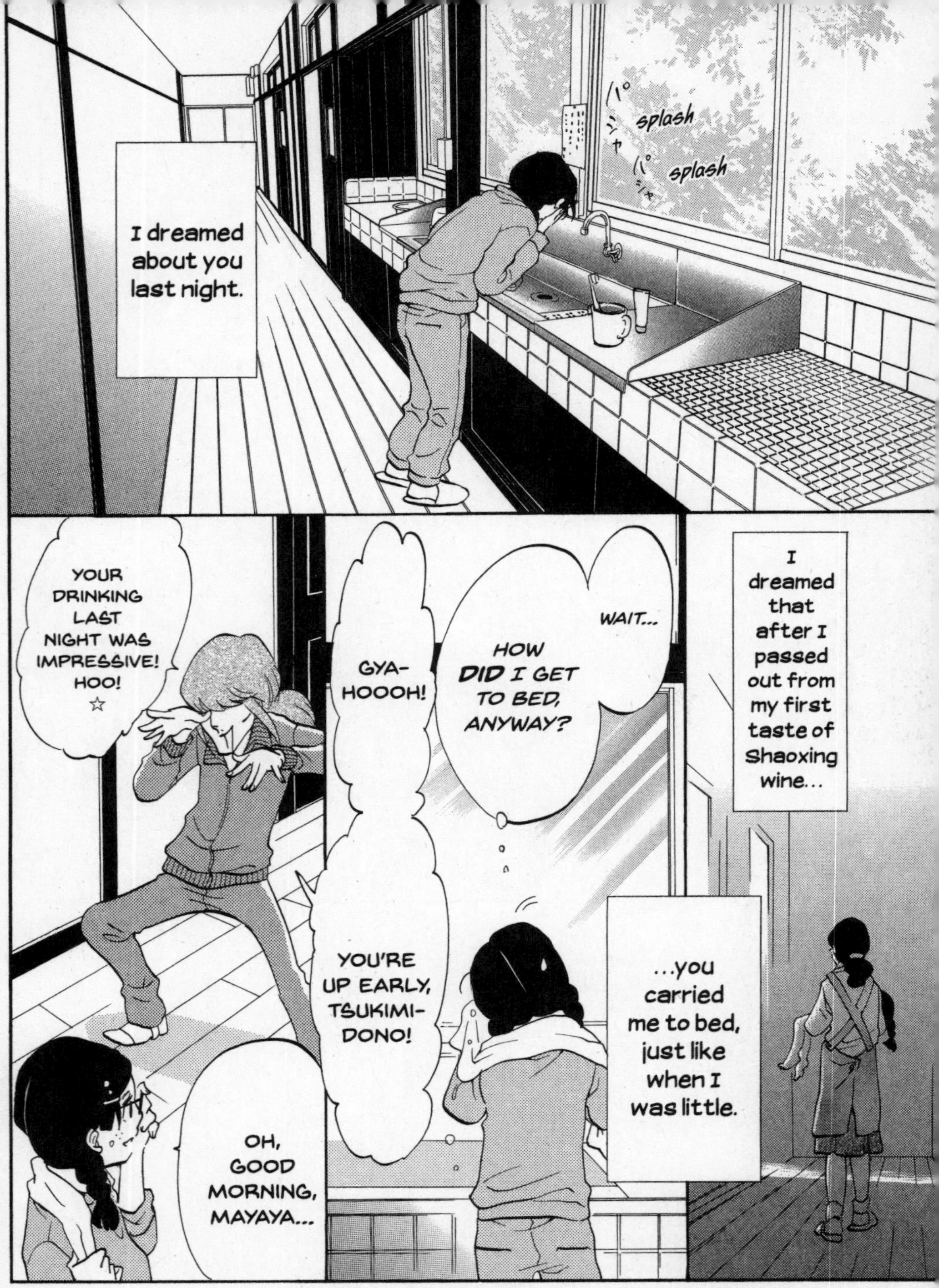
パシャ
splash
パシャ
splash
I dreamed about you last night.
I dreamed that after I passed out from my first taste of Shaoxing wine...
...you carried me to bed, just like when I was little.
WAIT... HOW DID I GET TO BED, ANYWAY?
GYA-HOOOH! YOU'RE UP EARLY, TSUKIMI-DONO!
OH, GOOD MORNING, MAYAYA...
YOUR DRINKING LAST NIGHT WAS IMPRESSIVE! HOO! ☆

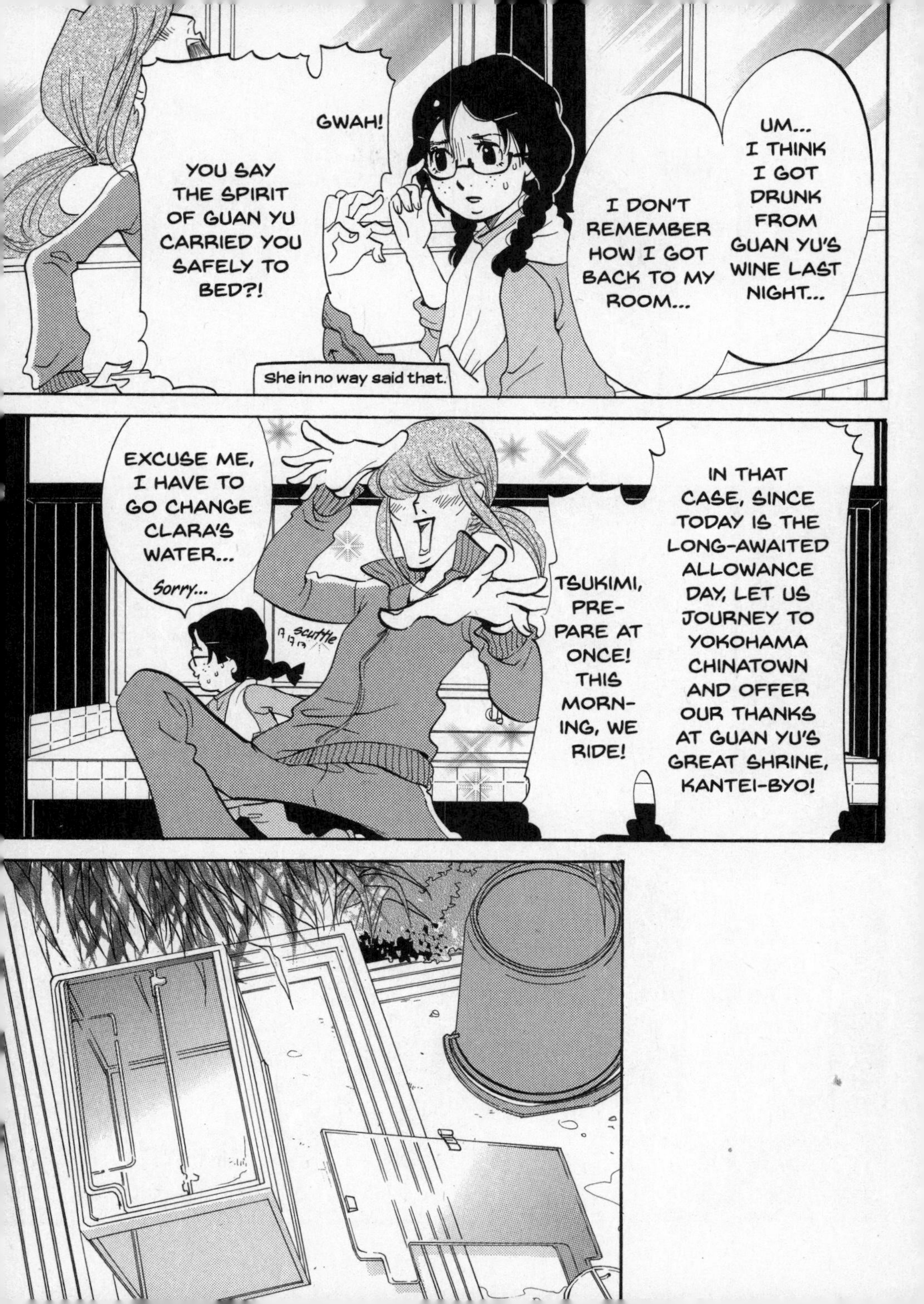
UM... I THINK I GOT DRUNK FROM GUAN YU'S WINE LAST NIGHT...
I DON'T REMEMBER HOW I GOT BACK TO MY ROOM...
GWAH!
YOU SAY THE SPIRIT OF GUAN YU CARRIED YOU SAFELY TO BED?!
She in no way said that.
IN THAT CASE, SINCE TODAY IS THE LONG-AWAITED ALLOWANCE DAY, LET US JOURNEY TO YOKOHAMA CHINATOWN AND OFFER OUR THANKS AT GUAN YU'S GREAT SHRINE, KANTEI-BYO!
TSUKIMI, PRE-PARE AT ONCE! THIS MORN-ING, WE RIDE!
scuttle
EXCUSE ME, I HAVE TO GO CHANGE CLARA'S WATER...
Sorry...

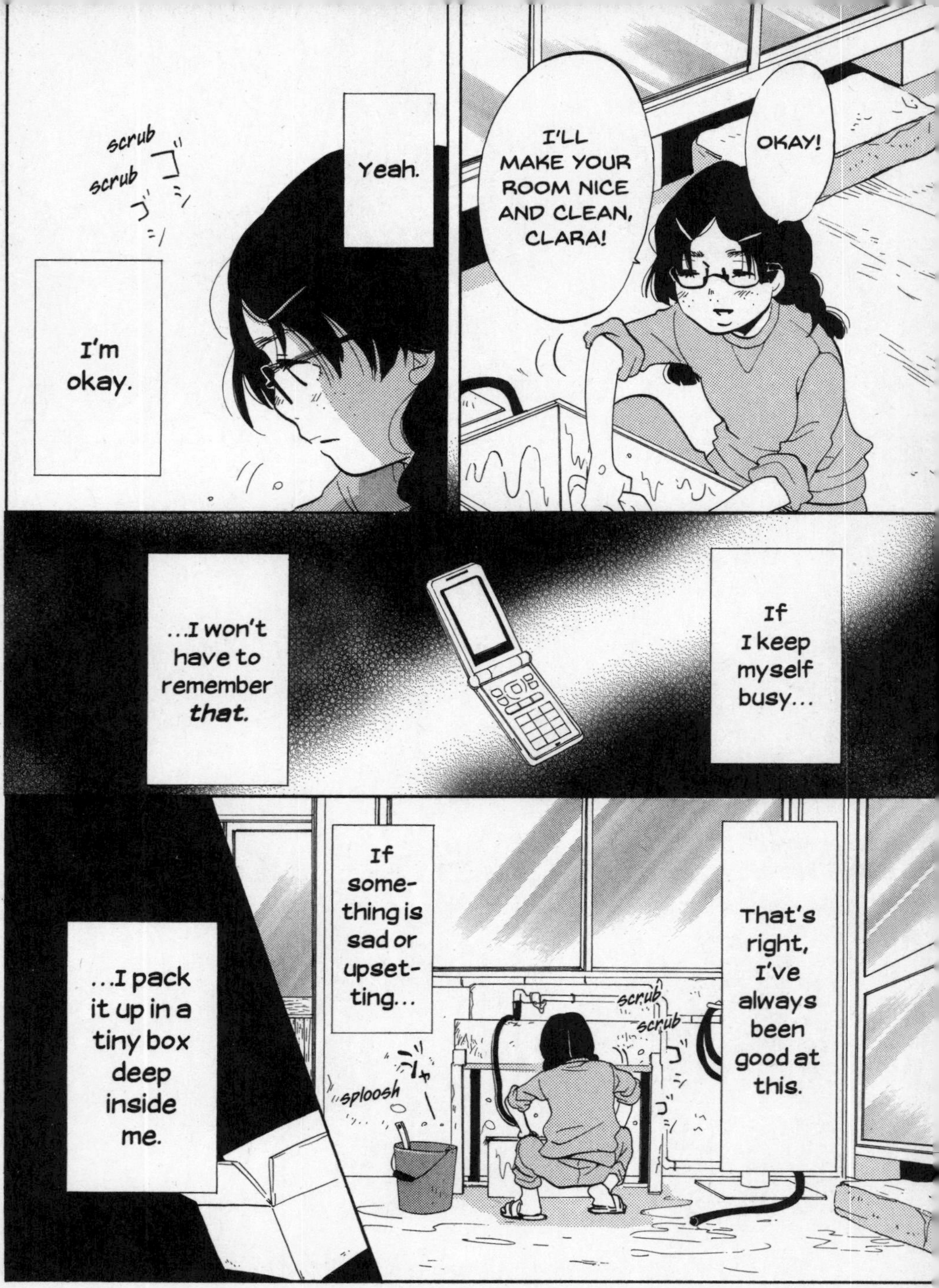
OKAY!
I'LL MAKE YOUR ROOM NICE AND CLEAN, CLARA!
Yeah.
I'm okay.
scrub scrub
If I keep myself busy...
...I won't have to remember *that.*
That's right, I've always been good at this.
scrub scrub
If something is sad or upsetting...
sploosh
...I pack it up in a tiny box deep inside me.

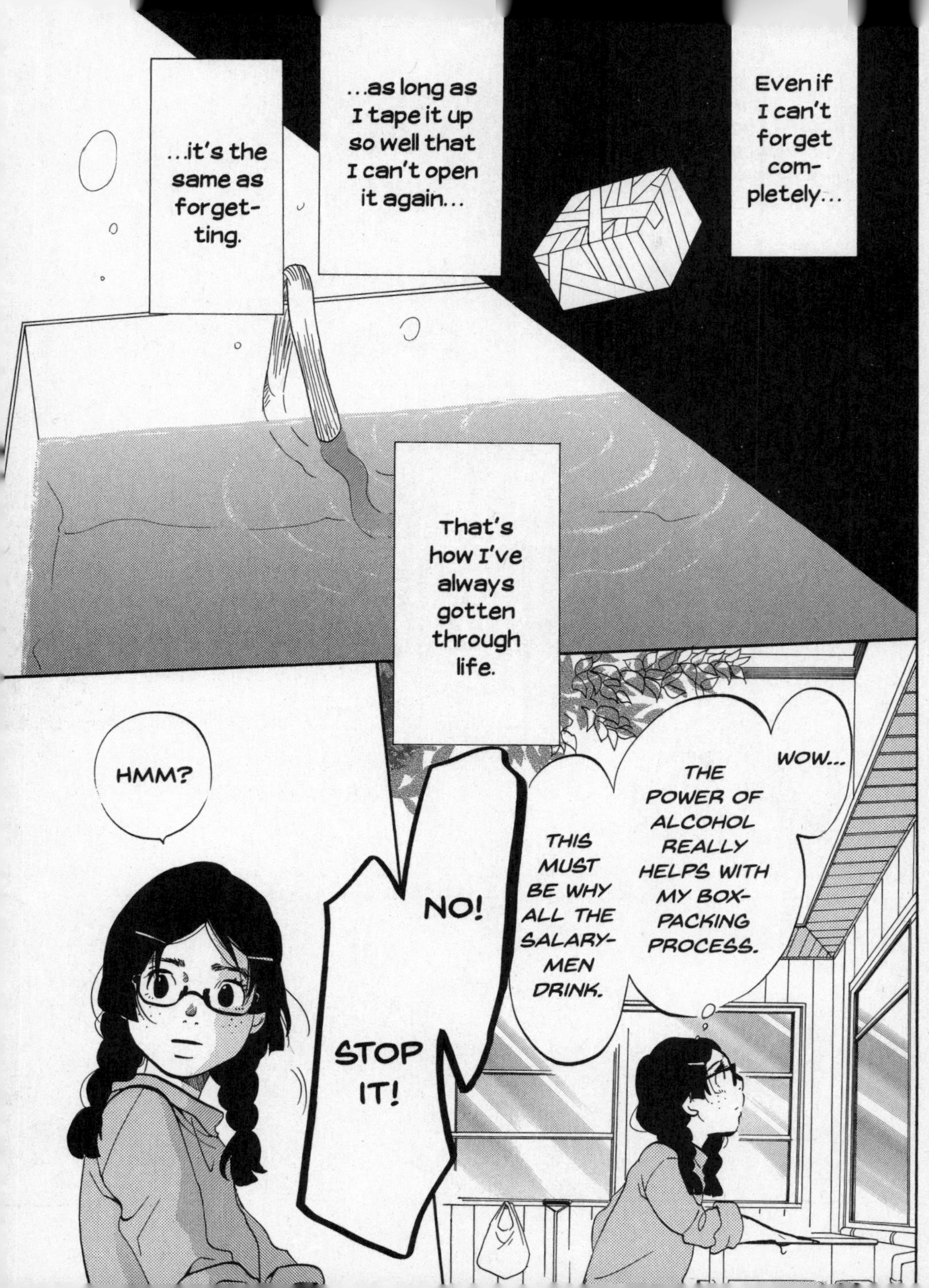
Even if I can't forget completely...
...as long as I tape it up so well that I can't open it again...
...it's the same as forgetting.
That's how I've always gotten through life.
WOW...
THE POWER OF ALCOHOL REALLY HELPS WITH MY BOX-PACKING PROCESS.
THIS MUST BE WHY ALL THE SALARYMEN DRINK.
NO!
STOP IT!
HMM?

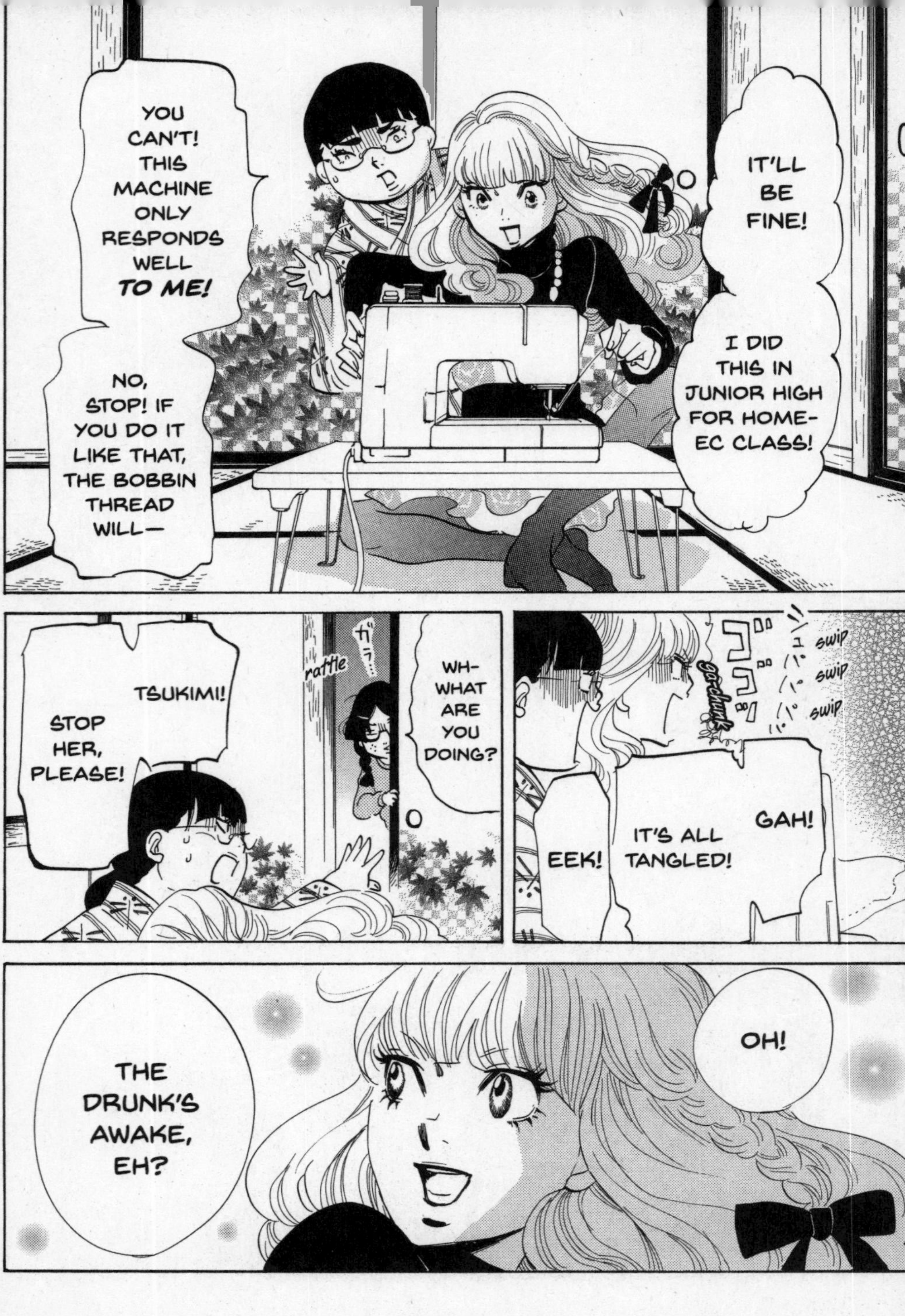
IT'LL BE FINE!
YOU CAN'T! THIS MACHINE ONLY RESPONDS WELL TO ME!
I DID THIS IN JUNIOR HIGH FOR HOME-EC CLASS!
NO, STOP! IF YOU DO IT LIKE THAT, THE BOBBIN THREAD WILL—
swip
swip
swip
ga-chunk
GAH!
IT'S ALL TANGLED!
EEK!
rattle
WH-WHAT ARE YOU DOING?
TSUKIMI!
STOP HER, PLEASE!
OH!
THE DRUNK'S AWAKE, EH?

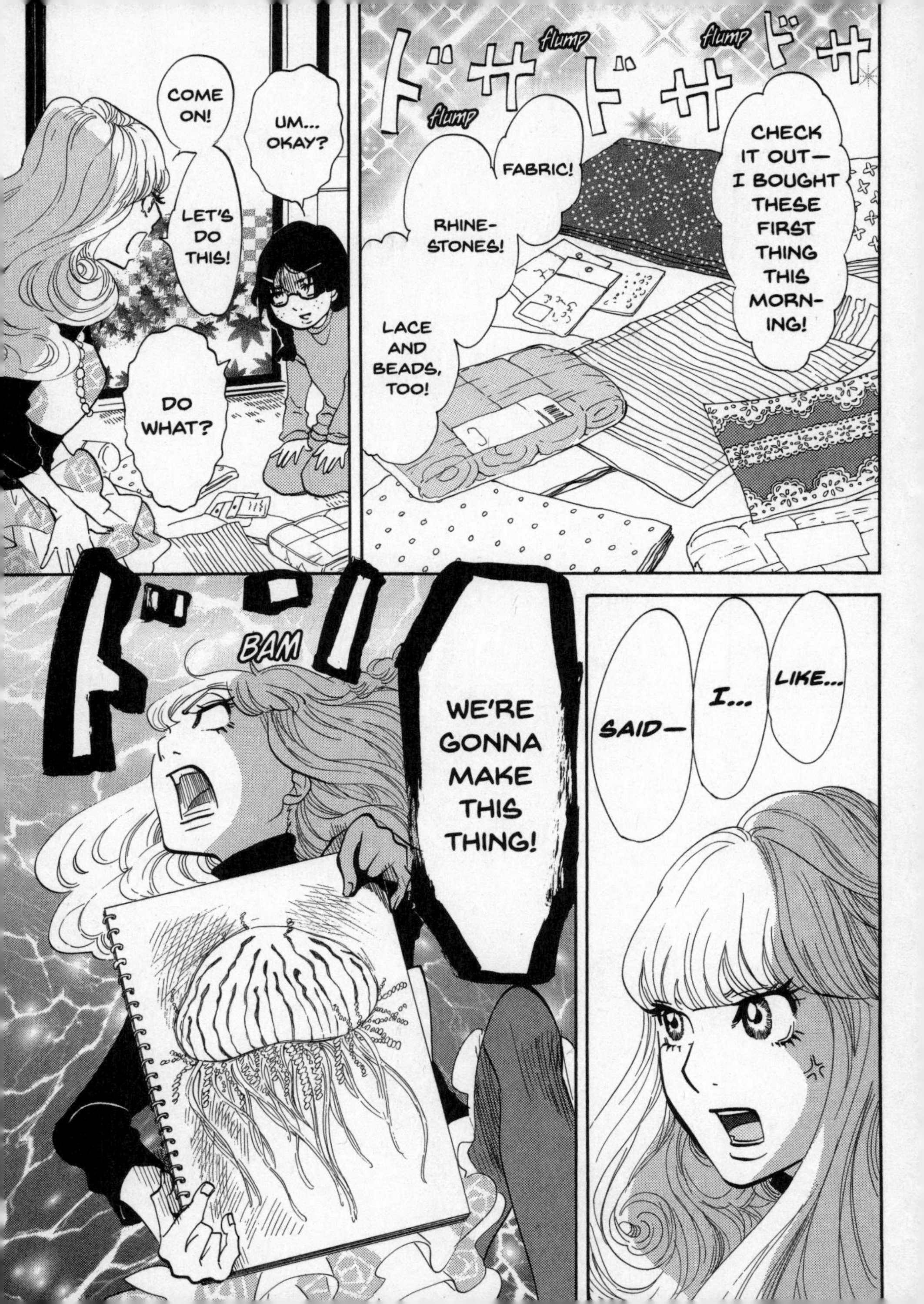
ドサ
flump
ドサ
flump
ドサ
flump
CHECK IT OUT— I BOUGHT THESE FIRST THING THIS MORNING!
FABRIC!
RHINE-STONES!
LACE AND BEADS, TOO!
COME ON!
UM... OKAY?
LET'S DO THIS!
DO WHAT?
LIKE...
I...
SAID—
ドン
BAM
WE'RE GONNA MAKE THIS THING!

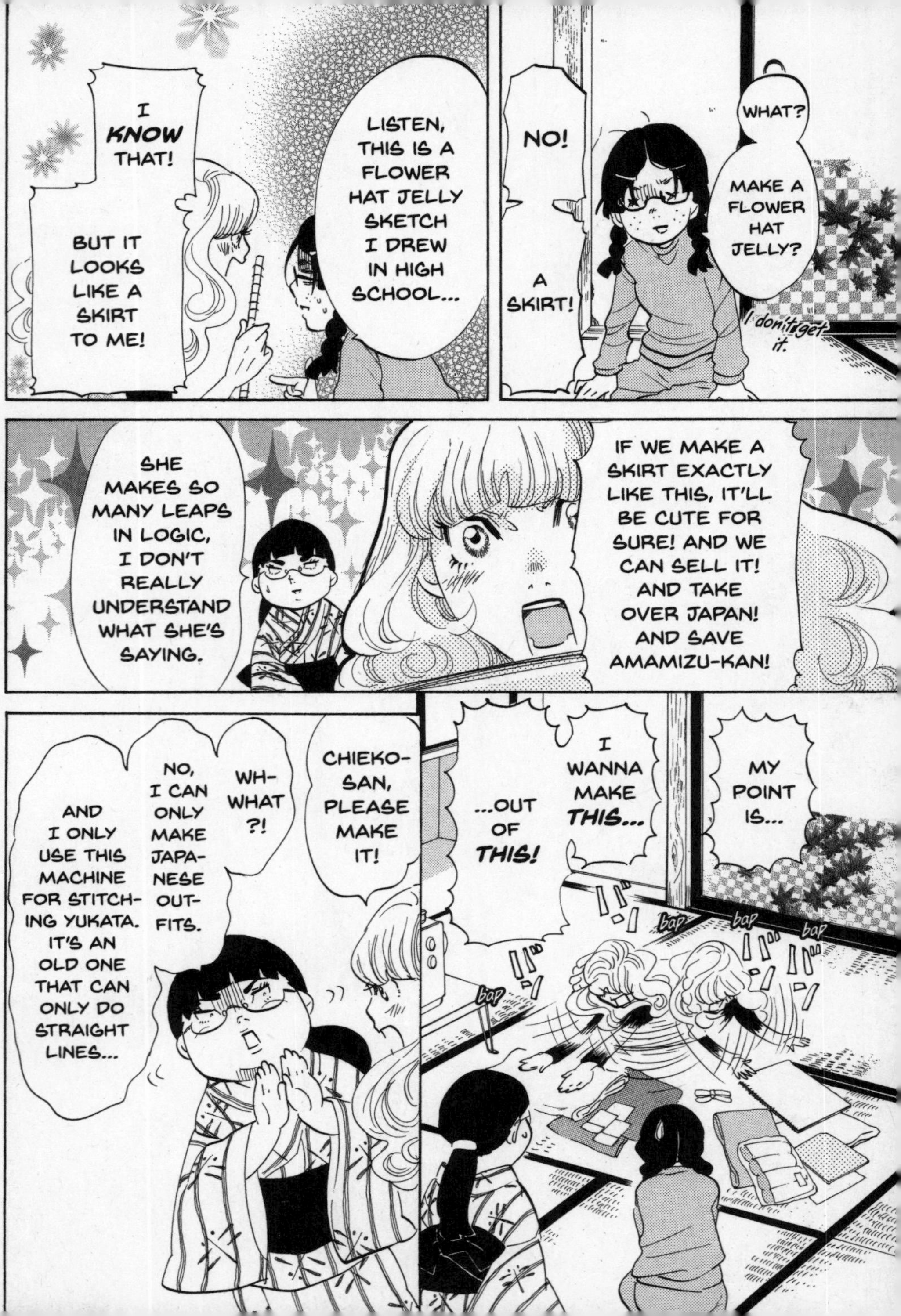
WHAT?
MAKE A FLOWER HAT JELLY?
I don't get it.
NO!
A SKIRT!
LISTEN, THIS IS A FLOWER HAT JELLY SKETCH I DREW IN HIGH SCHOOL...
I KNOW THAT!
BUT IT LOOKS LIKE A SKIRT TO ME!
IF WE MAKE A SKIRT EXACTLY LIKE THIS, IT'LL BE CUTE FOR SURE! AND WE CAN SELL IT! AND TAKE OVER JAPAN! AND SAVE AMAMIZU-KAN!
SHE MAKES SO MANY LEAPS IN LOGIC, I DON'T REALLY UNDERSTAND WHAT SHE'S SAYING.
MY POINT IS...
I WANNA MAKE THIS...
...OUT OF THIS!
bap
bap
bap
bap
CHIEKO-SAN, PLEASE MAKE IT!
WH-WHAT?!
NO, I CAN ONLY MAKE JAPA-NESE OUT-FITS.
AND I ONLY USE THIS MACHINE FOR STITCH-ING YUKATA. IT'S AN OLD ONE THAT CAN ONLY DO STRAIGHT LINES...

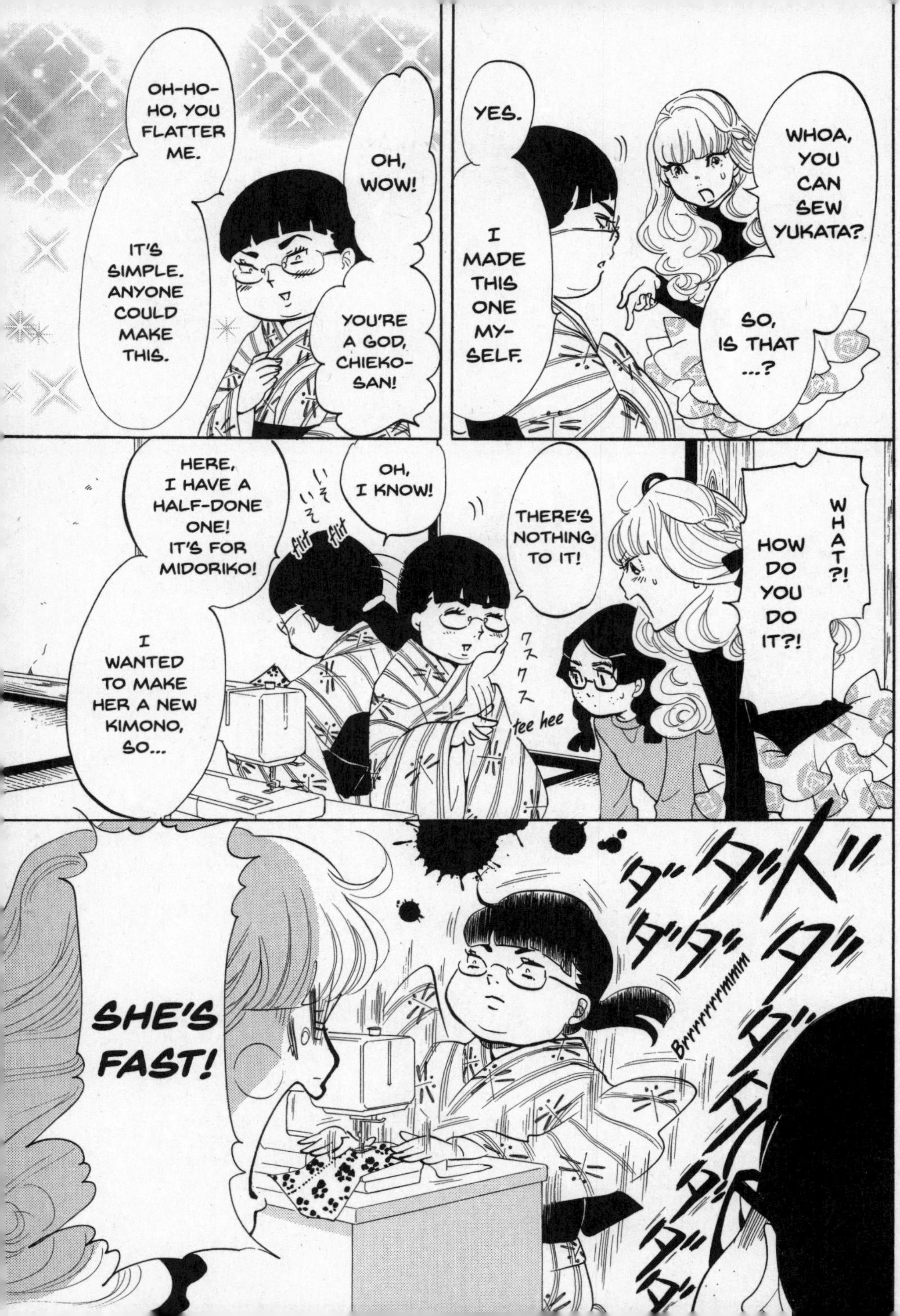
WHOA, YOU CAN SEW YUKATA?
SO, IS THAT ...?
YES.
I MADE THIS ONE MYSELF.
OH, WOW!
YOU'RE A GOD, CHIEKO-SAN!
OH-HO-HO, YOU FLATTER ME.
IT'S SIMPLE. ANYONE COULD MAKE THIS.
WHAT?!
HOW DO YOU DO IT?!
THERE'S NOTHING TO IT!
クスクス
tee hee
OH, I KNOW!
いそいそ
flit flit
HERE, I HAVE A HALF-DONE ONE! IT'S FOR MIDORIKO!
I WANTED TO MAKE HER A NEW KIMONO, SO...
ドドドド
ダダダダダダダ
Brrrrrrrmmm
SHE'S FAST!

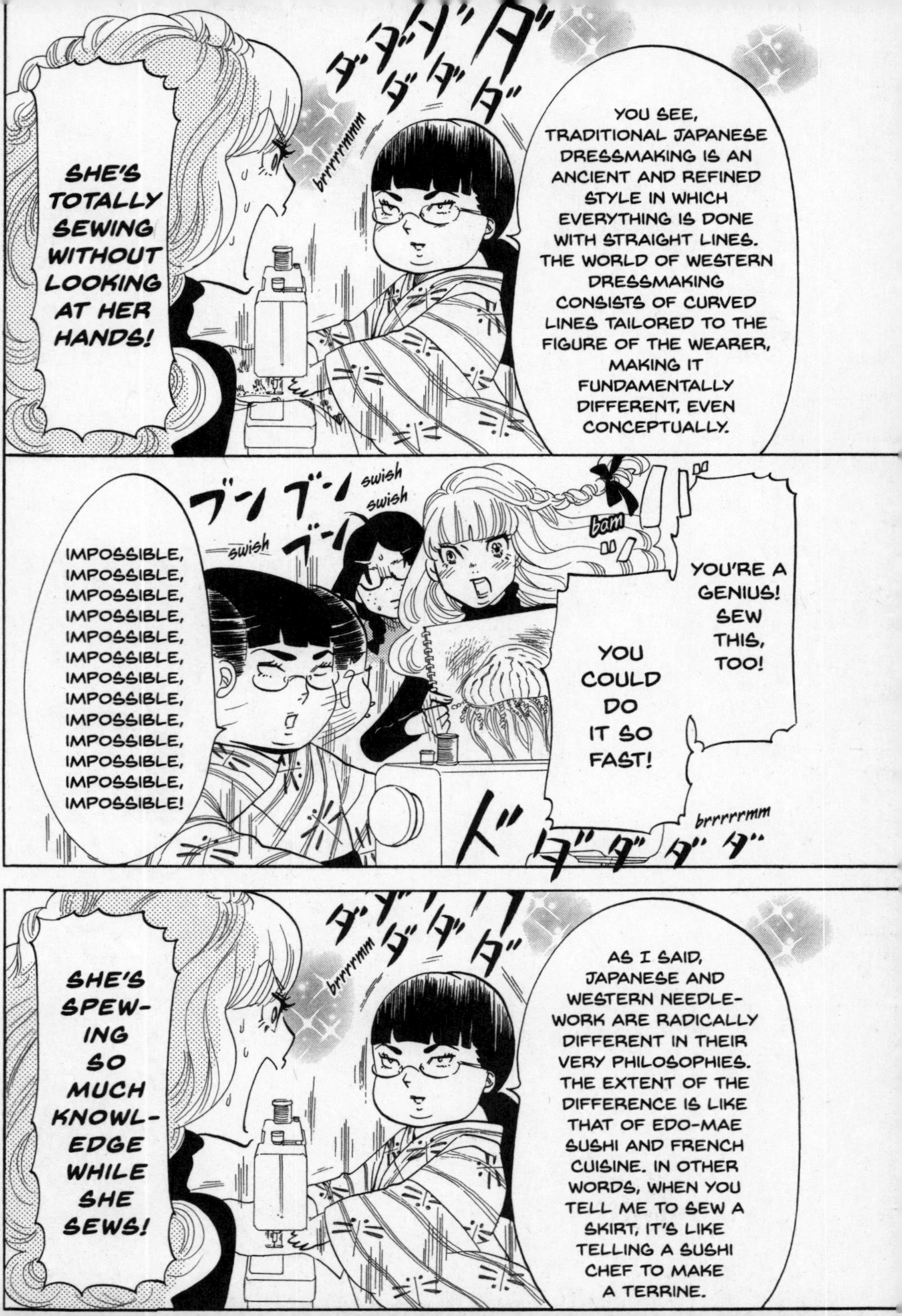
YOU SEE, TRADITIONAL JAPANESE DRESSMAKING IS AN ANCIENT AND REFINED STYLE IN WHICH EVERYTHING IS DONE WITH STRAIGHT LINES. THE WORLD OF WESTERN DRESSMAKING CONSISTS OF CURVED LINES TAILORED TO THE FIGURE OF THE WEARER, MAKING IT FUNDAMENTALLY DIFFERENT, EVEN CONCEPTUALLY.
brrrrrmmm
SHE'S TOTALLY SEWING WITHOUT LOOKING AT HER HANDS!
bam
YOU'RE A GENIUS! SEW THIS, TOO!
YOU COULD DO IT SO FAST!
swish swish
swish
brrrrrmm
IMPOSSIBLE, IMPOSSIBLE, IMPOSSIBLE, IMPOSSIBLE, IMPOSSIBLE, IMPOSSIBLE, IMPOSSIBLE, IMPOSSIBLE, IMPOSSIBLE, IMPOSSIBLE, IMPOSSIBLE, IMPOSSIBLE, IMPOSSIBLE!
AS I SAID, JAPANESE AND WESTERN NEEDLE-WORK ARE RADICALLY DIFFERENT IN THEIR VERY PHILOSOPHIES. THE EXTENT OF THE DIFFERENCE IS LIKE THAT OF EDO-MAE SUSHI AND FRENCH CUISINE. IN OTHER WORDS, WHEN YOU TELL ME TO SEW A SKIRT, IT'S LIKE TELLING A SUSHI CHEF TO MAKE A TERRINE.
brrrrrmm
SHE'S SPEW-ING SO MUCH KNOWL-EDGE WHILE SHE SEWS!

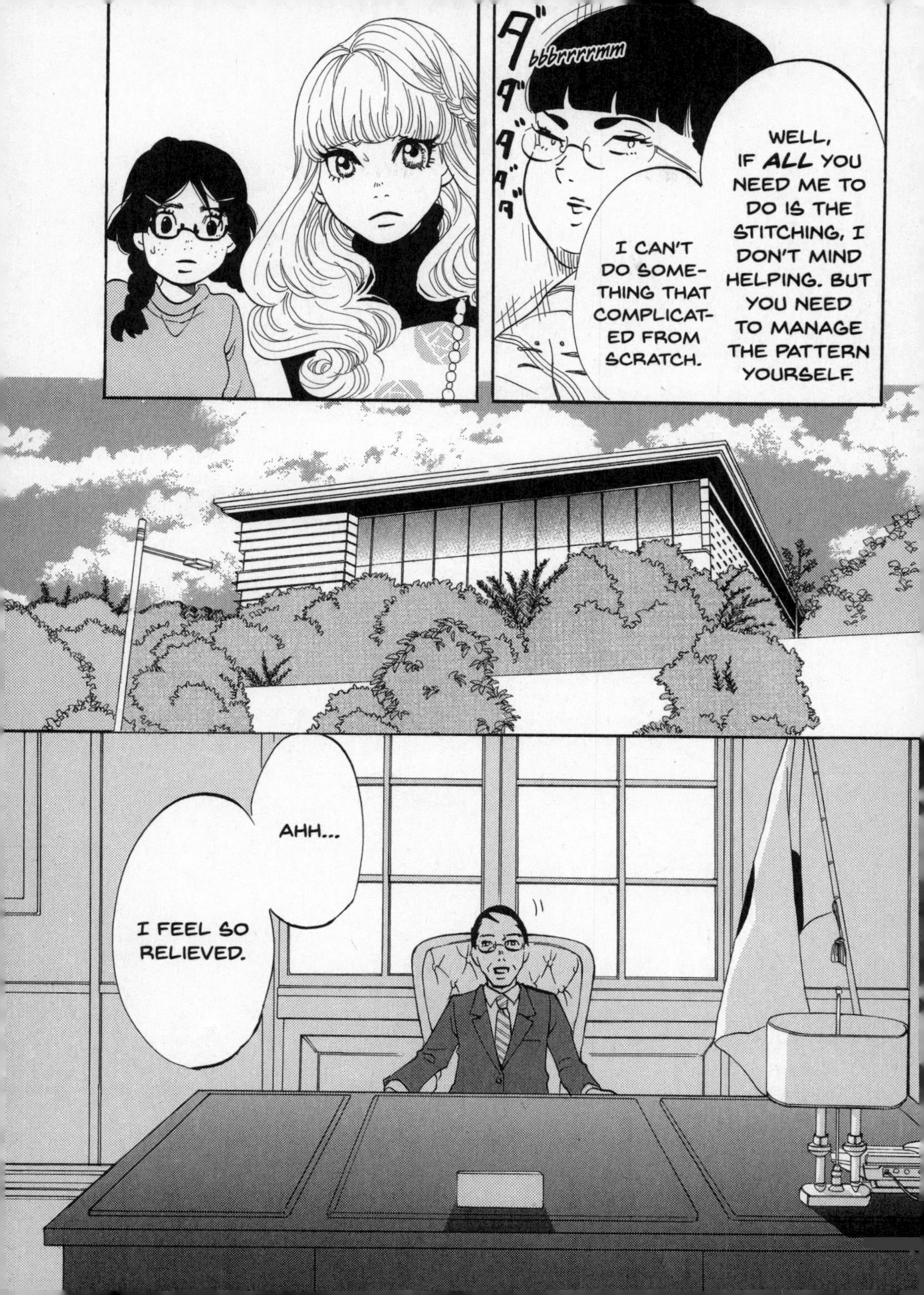
WELL, IF ALL YOU NEED ME TO DO IS THE STITCHING, I DON'T MIND HELPING. BUT YOU NEED TO MANAGE THE PATTERN YOURSELF.
I CAN'T DO SOMETHING THAT COMPLICATED FROM SCRATCH.
ダダダダダ
bbbrrrrrmm
AHH...
I FEEL SO RELIEVED.

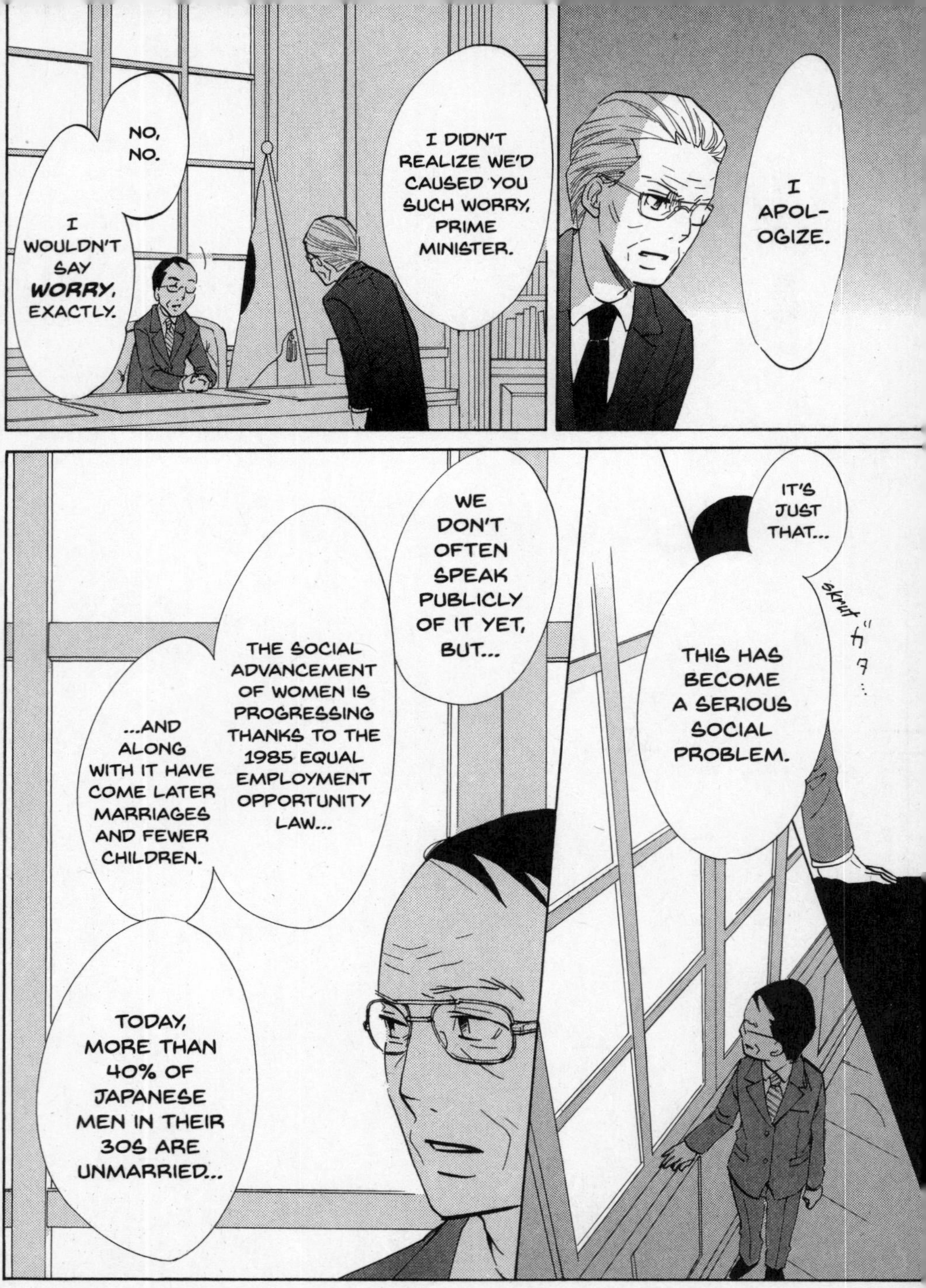
I APOLOGIZE.
I DIDN'T REALIZE WE'D CAUSED YOU SUCH WORRY, PRIME MINISTER.
NO, NO.
I WOULDN'T SAY **WORRY**, EXACTLY.
IT'S JUST THAT...
skrut
THIS HAS BECOME A SERIOUS SOCIAL PROBLEM.
WE DON'T OFTEN SPEAK PUBLICLY OF IT YET, BUT...
THE SOCIAL ADVANCEMENT OF WOMEN IS PROGRESSING THANKS TO THE 1985 EQUAL EMPLOYMENT OPPORTUNITY LAW...
...AND ALONG WITH IT HAVE COME LATER MARRIAGES AND FEWER CHILDREN.
TODAY, MORE THAN 40% OF JAPANESE MEN IN THEIR 30S ARE UNMARRIED...

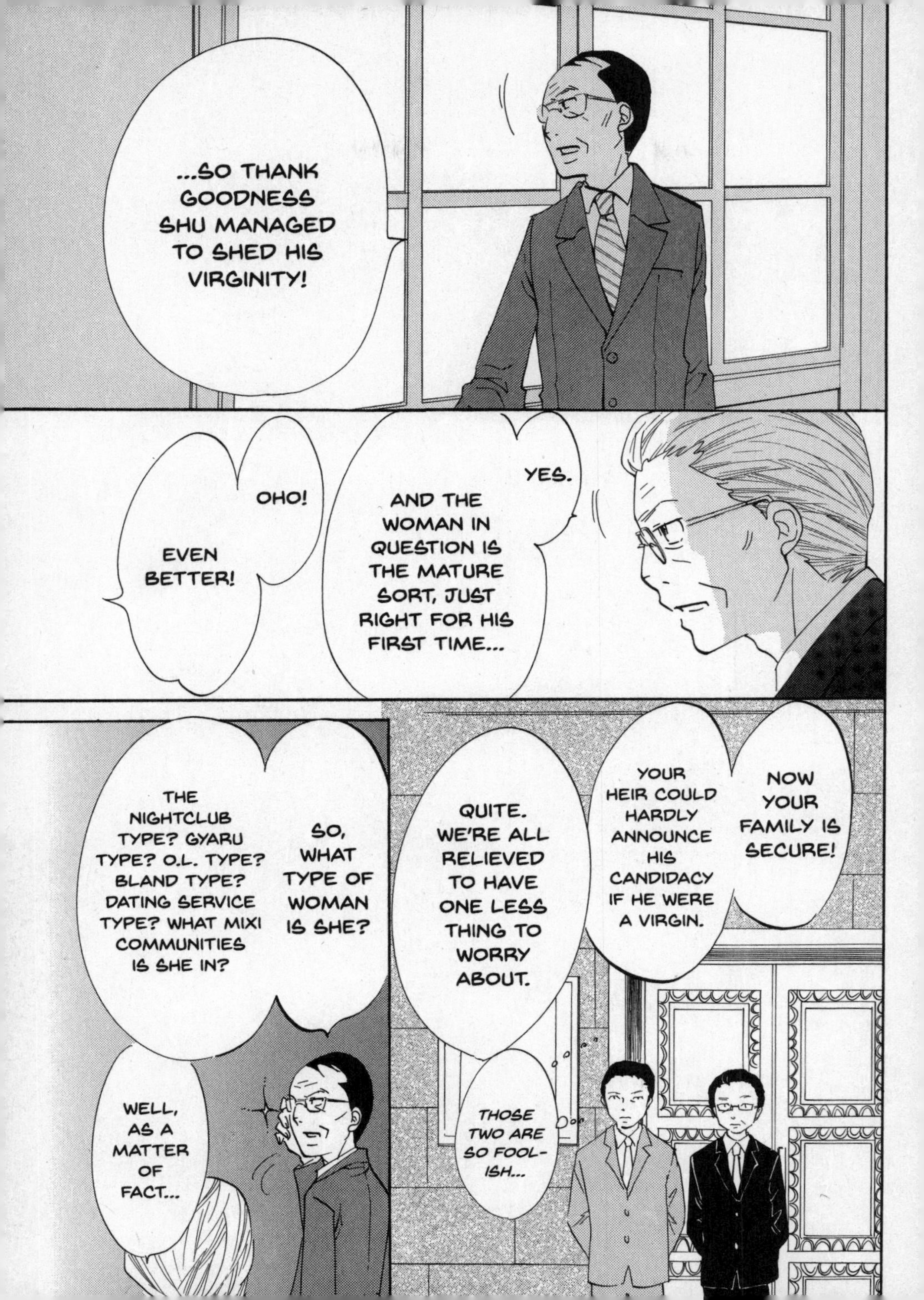
...SO THANK GOODNESS SHU MANAGED TO SHED HIS VIRGINITY!
YES.
AND THE WOMAN IN QUESTION IS THE MATURE SORT, JUST RIGHT FOR HIS FIRST TIME...
OHO!
EVEN BETTER!
NOW YOUR FAMILY IS SECURE!
YOUR HEIR COULD HARDLY ANNOUNCE HIS CANDIDACY IF HE WERE A VIRGIN.
QUITE. WE'RE ALL RELIEVED TO HAVE ONE LESS THING TO WORRY ABOUT.
THOSE TWO ARE SO FOOL-ISH...
SO, WHAT TYPE OF WOMAN IS SHE?
THE NIGHTCLUB TYPE? GYARU TYPE? O.L. TYPE? BLAND TYPE? DATING SERVICE TYPE? WHAT MIXI COMMUNITIES IS SHE IN?
WELL, AS A MATTER OF FACT...

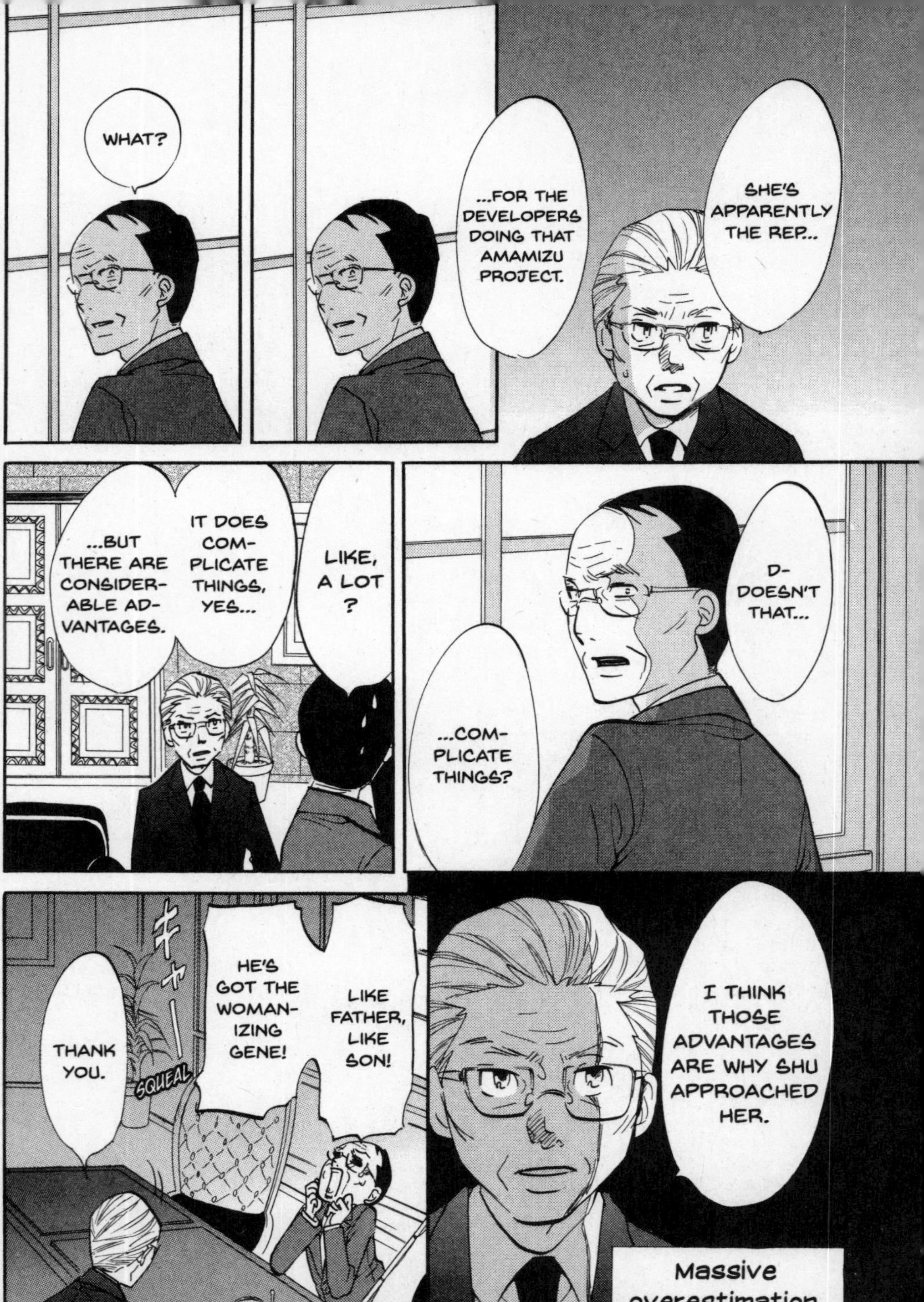
SHE'S APPARENTLY THE REP...
...FOR THE DEVELOPERS DOING THAT AMAMIZU PROJECT.
WHAT?
D-DOESN'T THAT...
...COMPLICATE THINGS?
LIKE, A LOT?
IT DOES COMPLICATE THINGS, YES...
...BUT THERE ARE CONSIDERABLE ADVANTAGES.
I THINK THOSE ADVANTAGES ARE WHY SHU APPROACHED HER.
Massive overestimation
LIKE FATHER, LIKE SON!
HE'S GOT THE WOMANIZING GENE!
SQUEAL
THANK YOU.

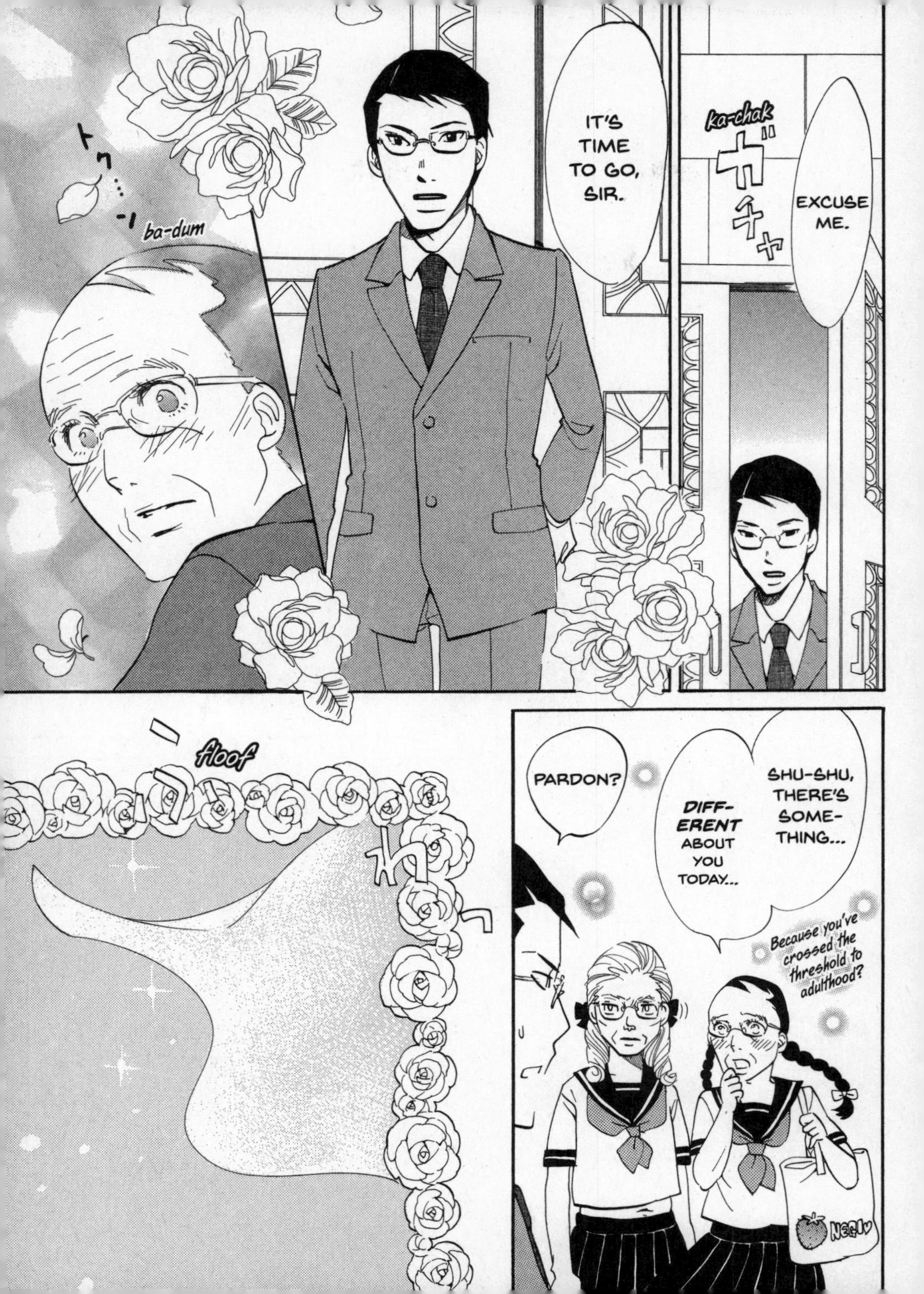
ka-chak
EXCUSE ME.
IT'S TIME TO GO, SIR.
ba-dum
SHU-SHU, THERE'S SOME-THING...
DIFF-ERENT ABOUT YOU TODAY...
PARDON?
Because you've crossed the threshold to adulthood?
floof

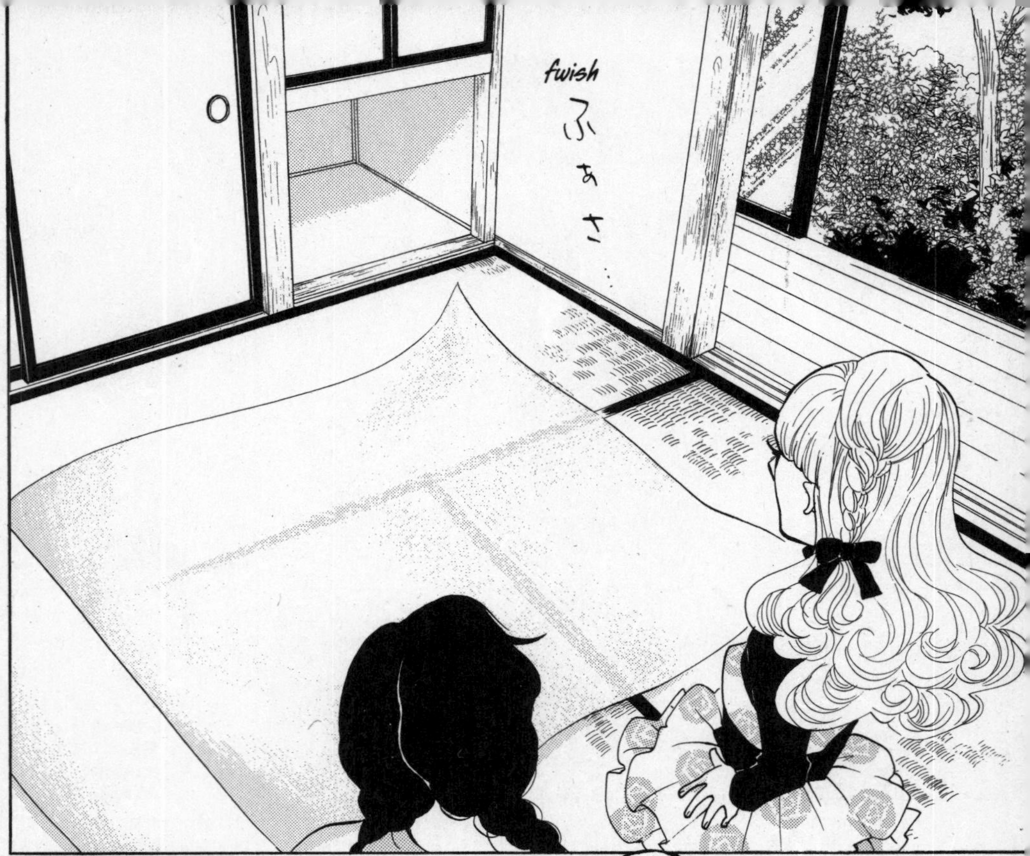
fwish
ふぁさ…

*About $250 USD.

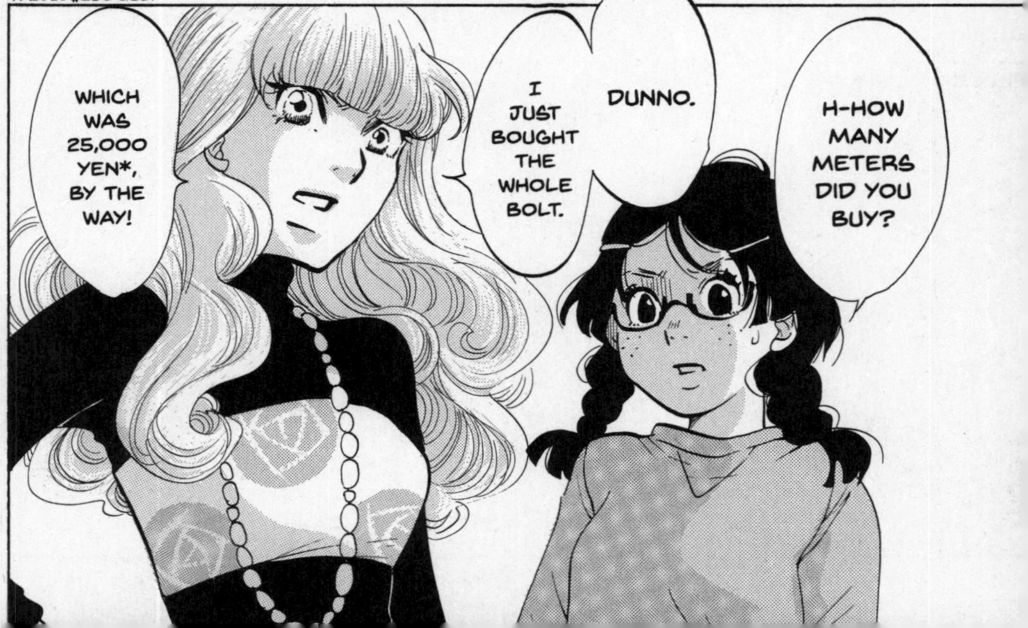
H-HOW MANY METERS DID YOU BUY?
DUNNO.
I JUST BOUGHT THE WHOLE BOLT.
WHICH WAS 25,000 YEN*, BY THE WAY!

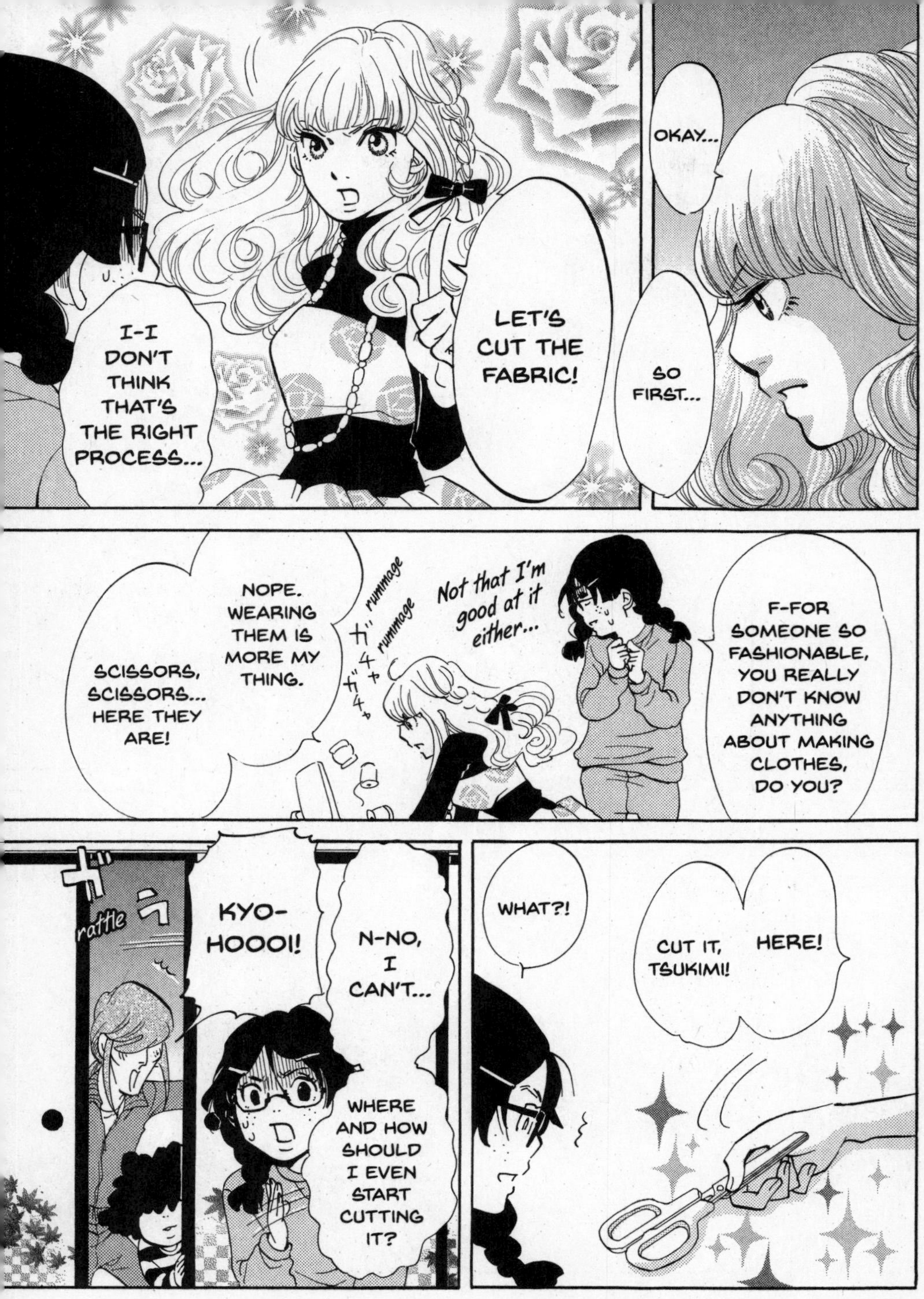
OKAY...
SO FIRST...
LET'S CUT THE FABRIC!
I-I DON'T THINK THAT'S THE RIGHT PROCESS...
F-FOR SOMEONE SO FASHIONABLE, YOU REALLY DON'T KNOW ANYTHING ABOUT MAKING CLOTHES, DO YOU?
Not that I'm good at it either...
rummage rummage
NOPE. WEARING THEM IS MORE MY THING.
SCISSORS, SCISSORS... HERE THEY ARE!
HERE!
CUT IT, TSUKIMI!
WHAT?!
N-NO, I CAN'T...
WHERE AND HOW SHOULD I EVEN START CUTTING IT?
KYO-HOOOI!
rattle

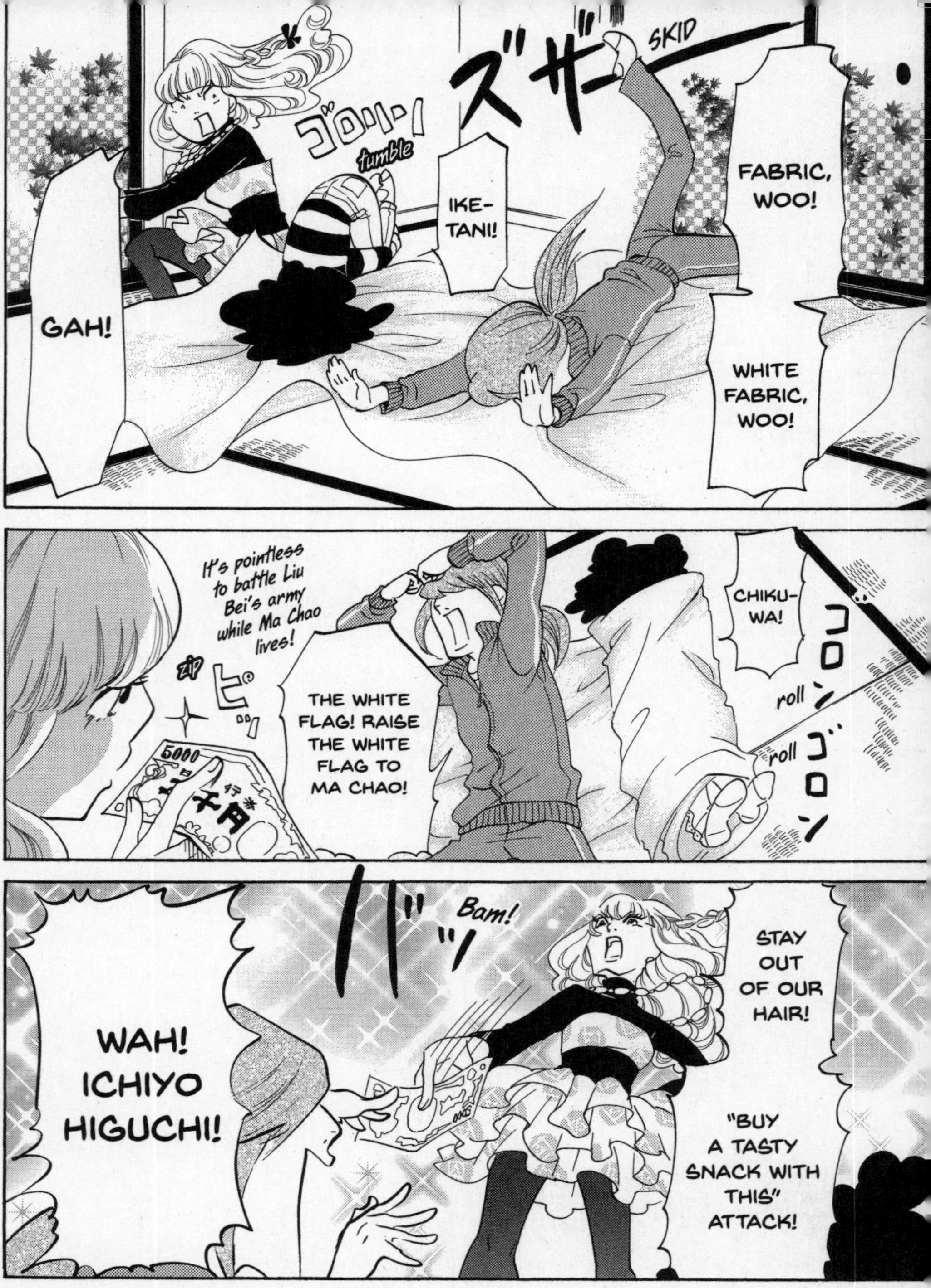
SKID
FABRIC, WOO!
IKE-TANI!
tumble
WHITE FABRIC, WOO!
GAH!
CHIKU-WA!
roll
roll
THE WHITE FLAG! RAISE THE WHITE FLAG TO MA CHAO!
It's pointless to battle Liu Bei's army while Ma Chao lives!
zip
STAY OUT OF OUR HAIR!
Bam!
"BUY A TASTY SNACK WITH THIS" ATTACK!
WAH! ICHIYO HIGUCHI!

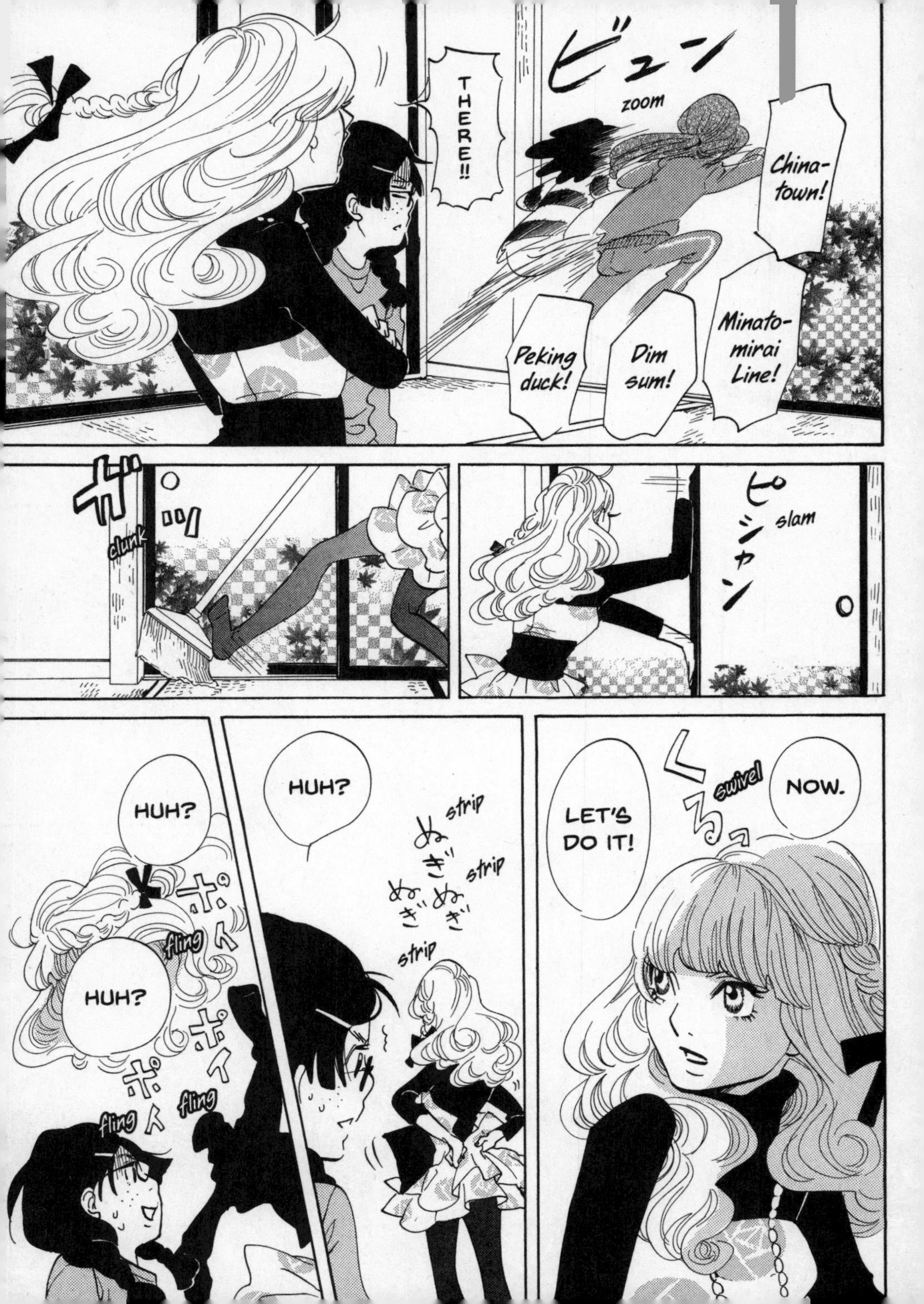
ビュン
zoom
China-town!
Minato-mirai Line!
Dim sum!
Peking duck!
THERE!!
ピシャン
slam
ガッ
clunk
くるっ
swivel
NOW.
LET'S DO IT!
HUH?
ぬぎ
strip
ぬぎ ぬぎ
strip
strip
HUH?
ポイ
fling
HUH?
ポイ
fling
ポイ
fling

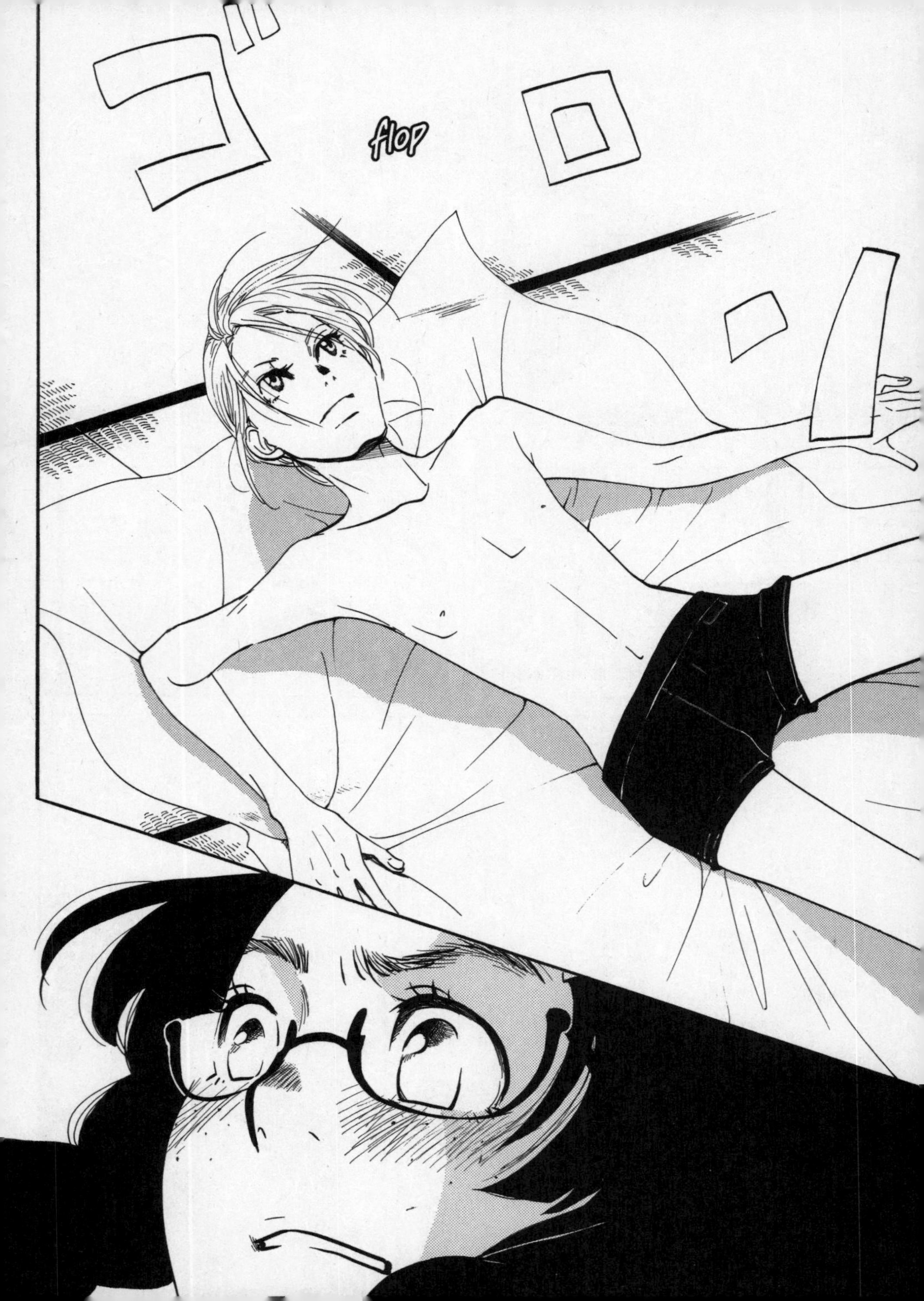
ゴロ
flop

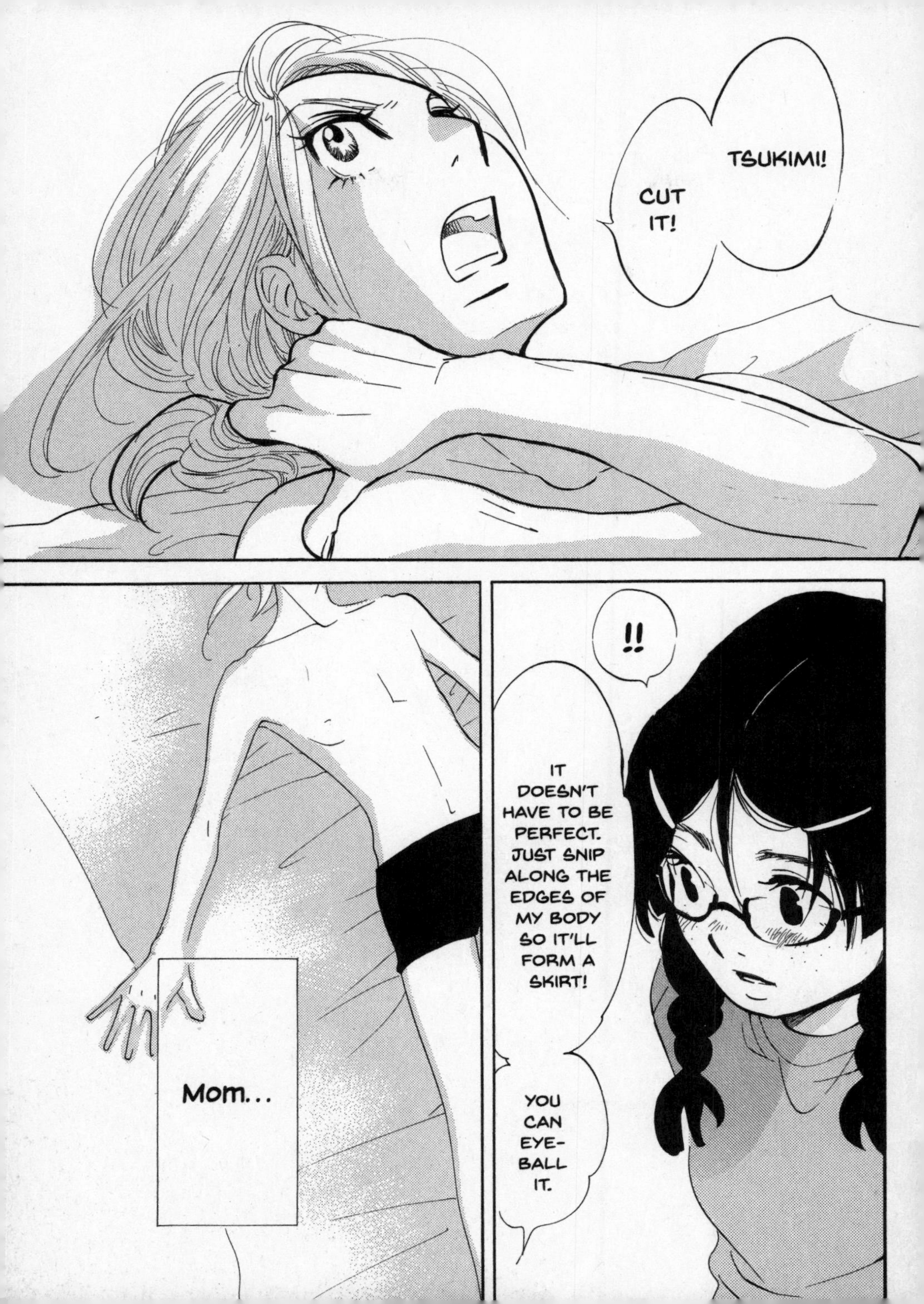
TSUKIMI! CUT IT!
!!
IT DOESN'T HAVE TO BE PERFECT. JUST SNIP ALONG THE EDGES OF MY BODY SO IT'LL FORM A SKIRT!
YOU CAN EYE-BALL IT.
Mom...

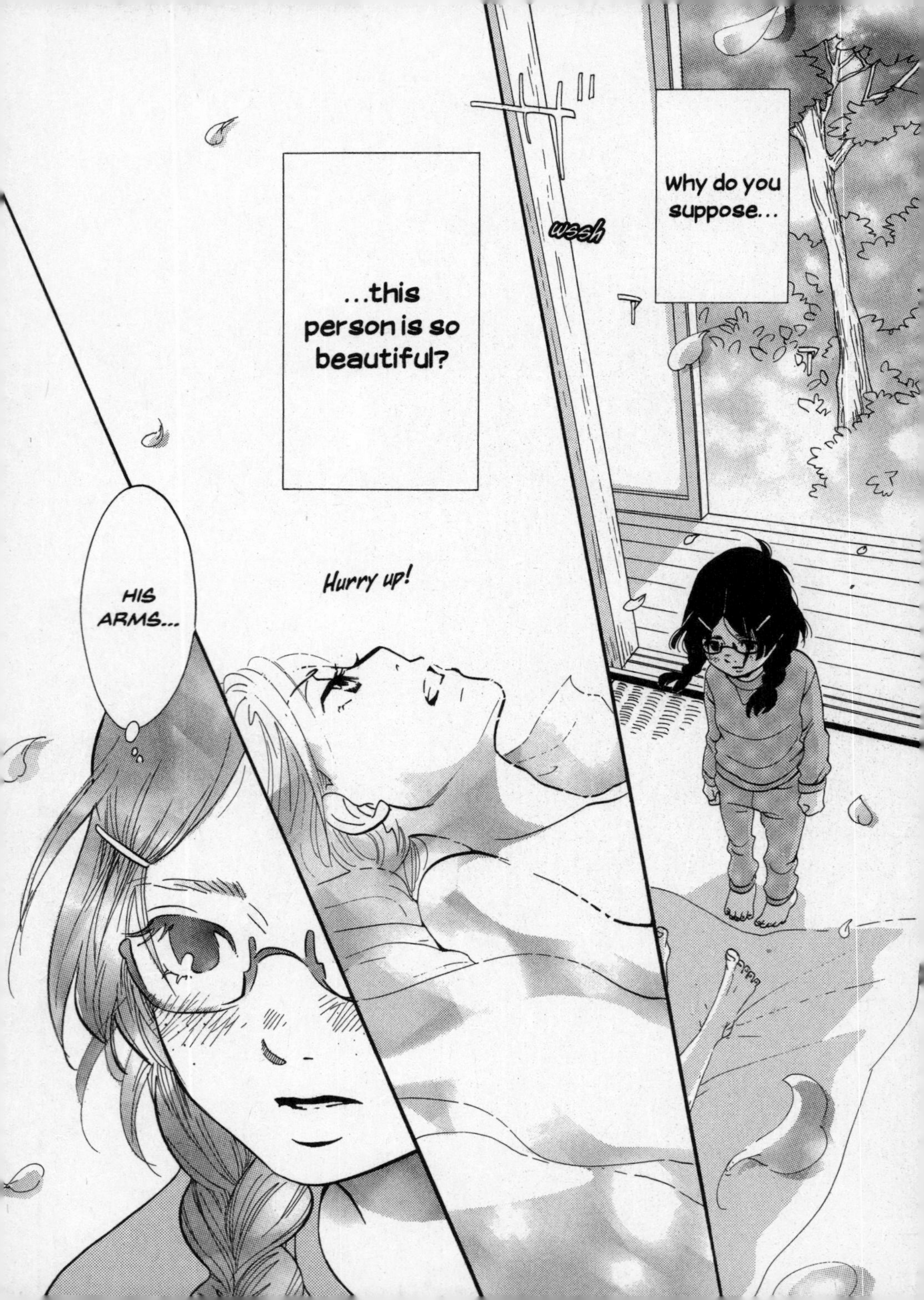
Why do you suppose...
wssh
...this person is so beautiful?
Hurry up!
HIS ARMS...

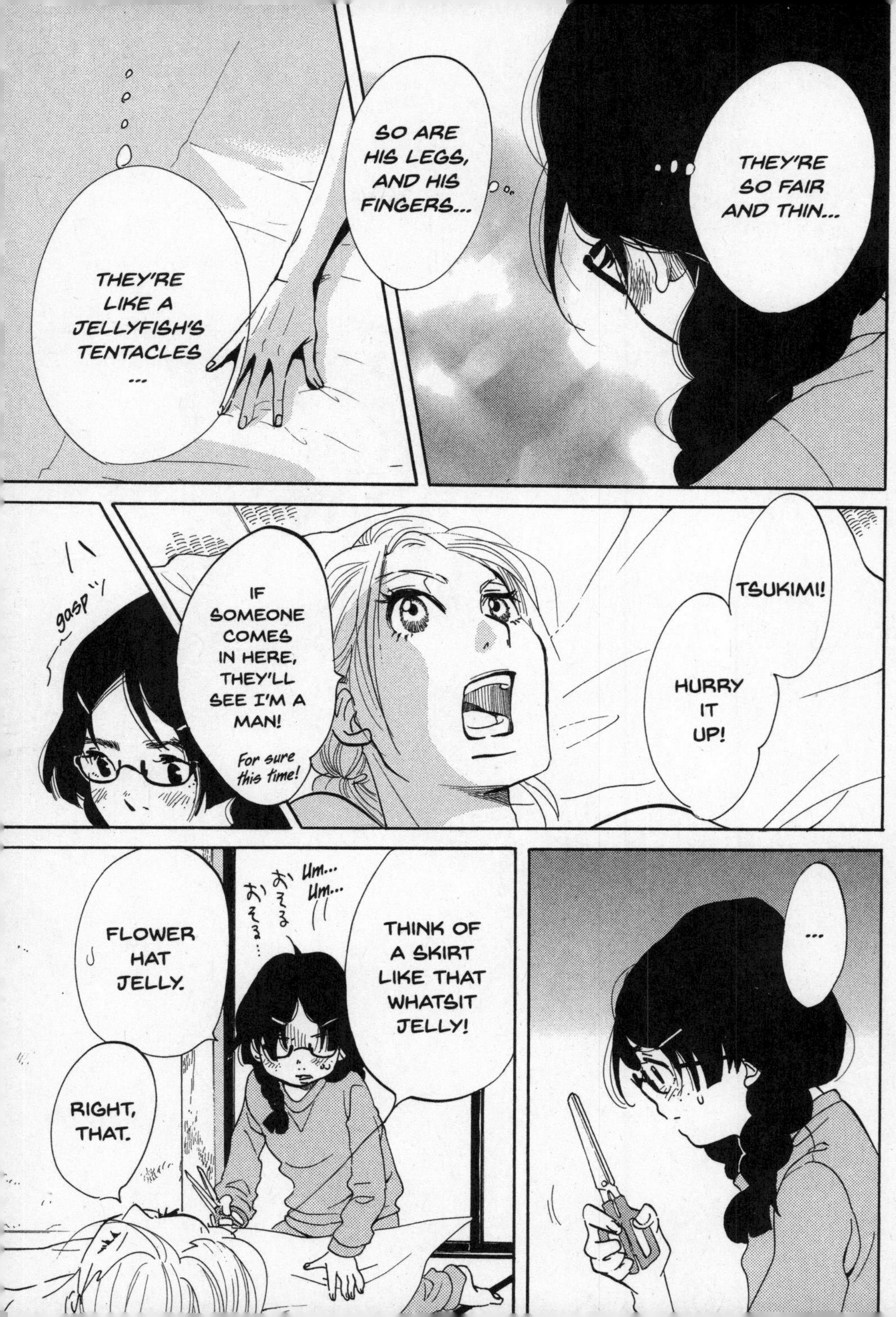
THEY'RE SO FAIR AND THIN...
SO ARE HIS LEGS, AND HIS FINGERS...
THEY'RE LIKE A JELLYFISH'S TENTACLES ...
TSUKIMI!
HURRY IT UP!
IF SOMEONE COMES IN HERE, THEY'LL SEE I'M A MAN!
For sure this time!
gasp
...
THINK OF A SKIRT LIKE THAT WHATSIT JELLY!
Um... Um...
おそるおそる...
FLOWER HAT JELLY.
RIGHT, THAT.

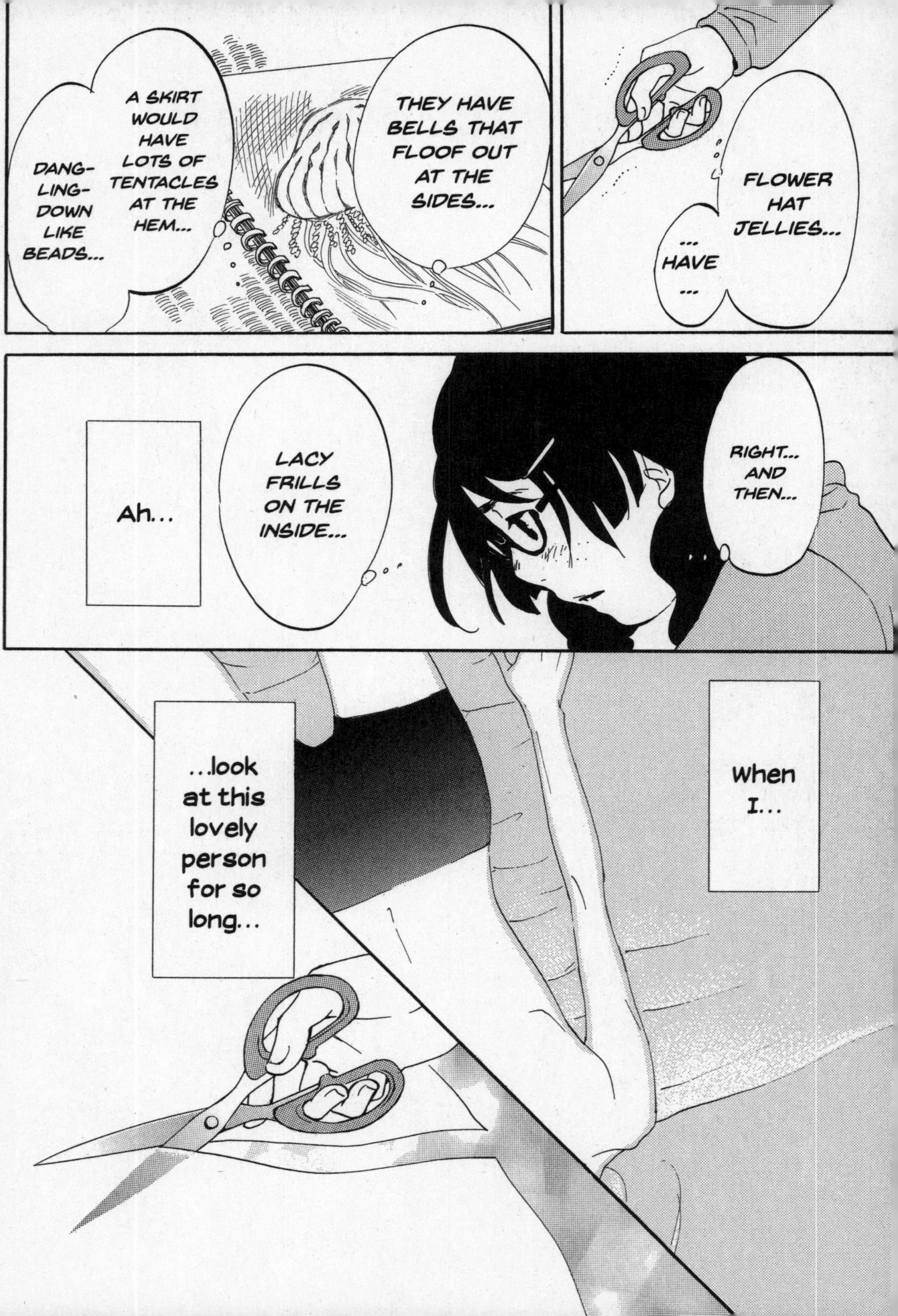
FLOWER HAT JELLIES...
... HAVE ...
THEY HAVE BELLS THAT FLOOF OUT AT THE SIDES...
A SKIRT WOULD HAVE LOTS OF TENTACLES AT THE HEM...
DANG-LING-DOWN LIKE BEADS...
RIGHT... AND THEN...
LACY FRILLS ON THE INSIDE...
Ah...
When I...
...look at this lovely person for so long...

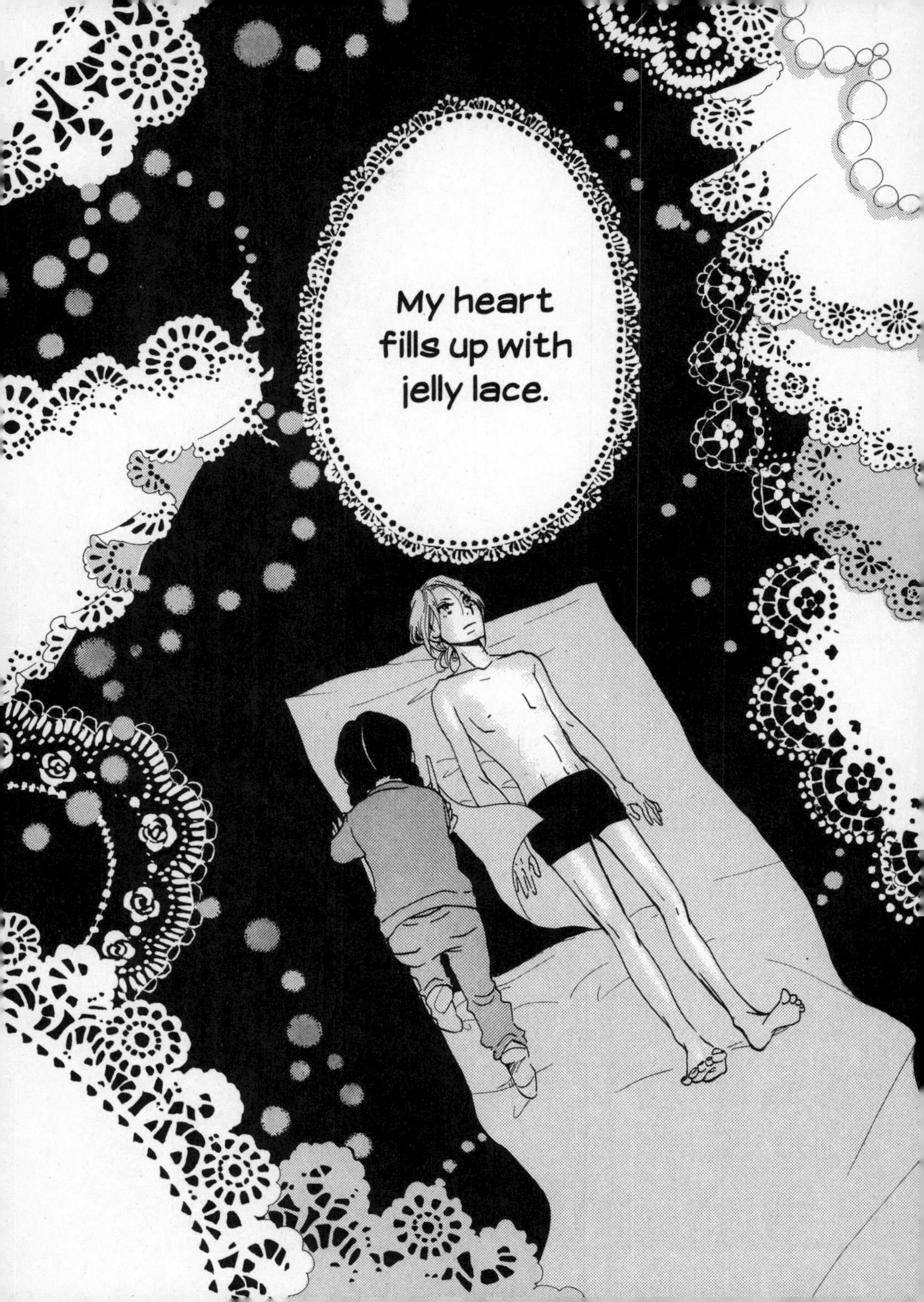
My heart fills up with jelly lace.

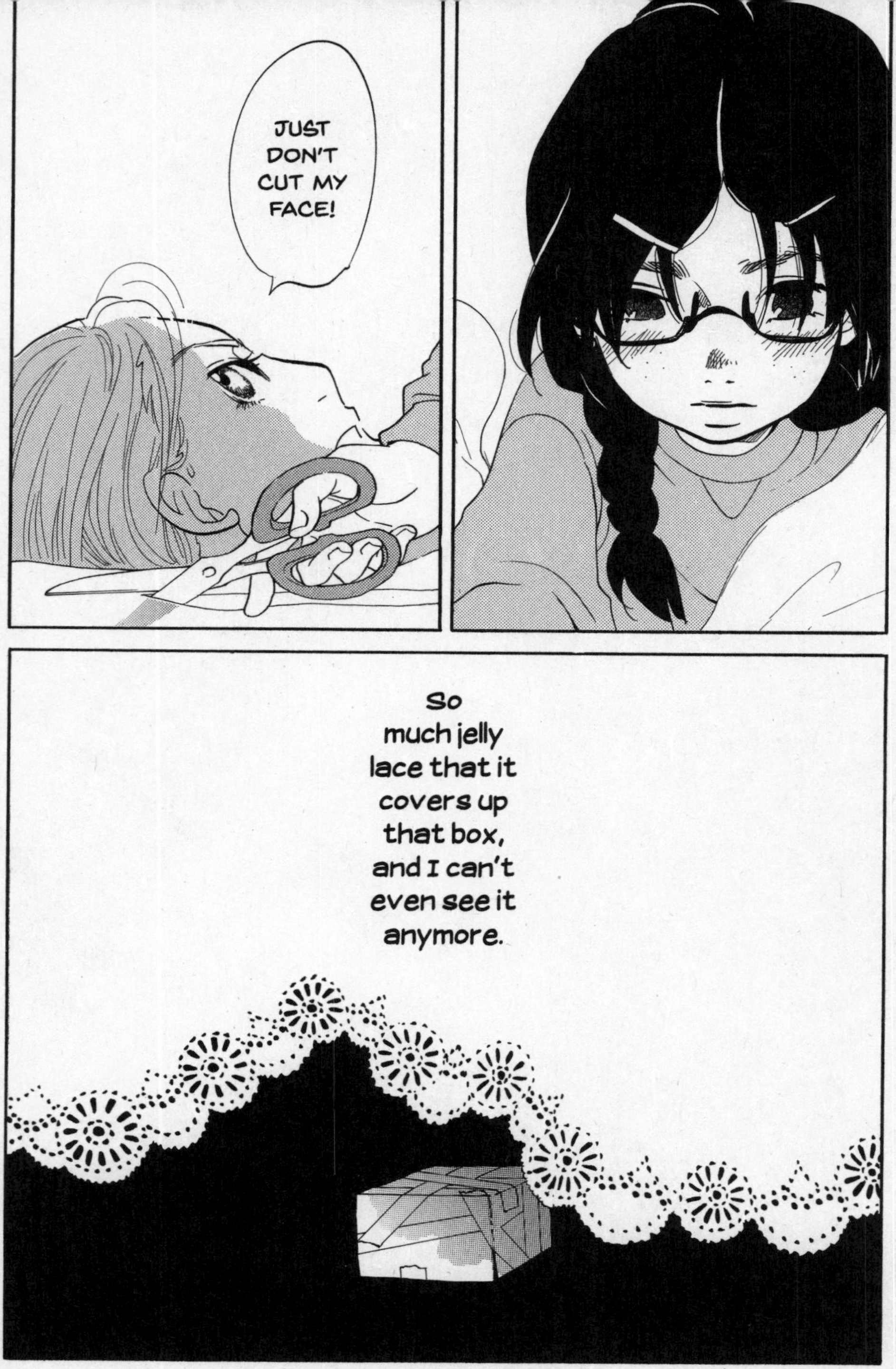
JUST DON'T CUT MY FACE!
So much jelly lace that it covers up that box, and I can't even see it anymore.

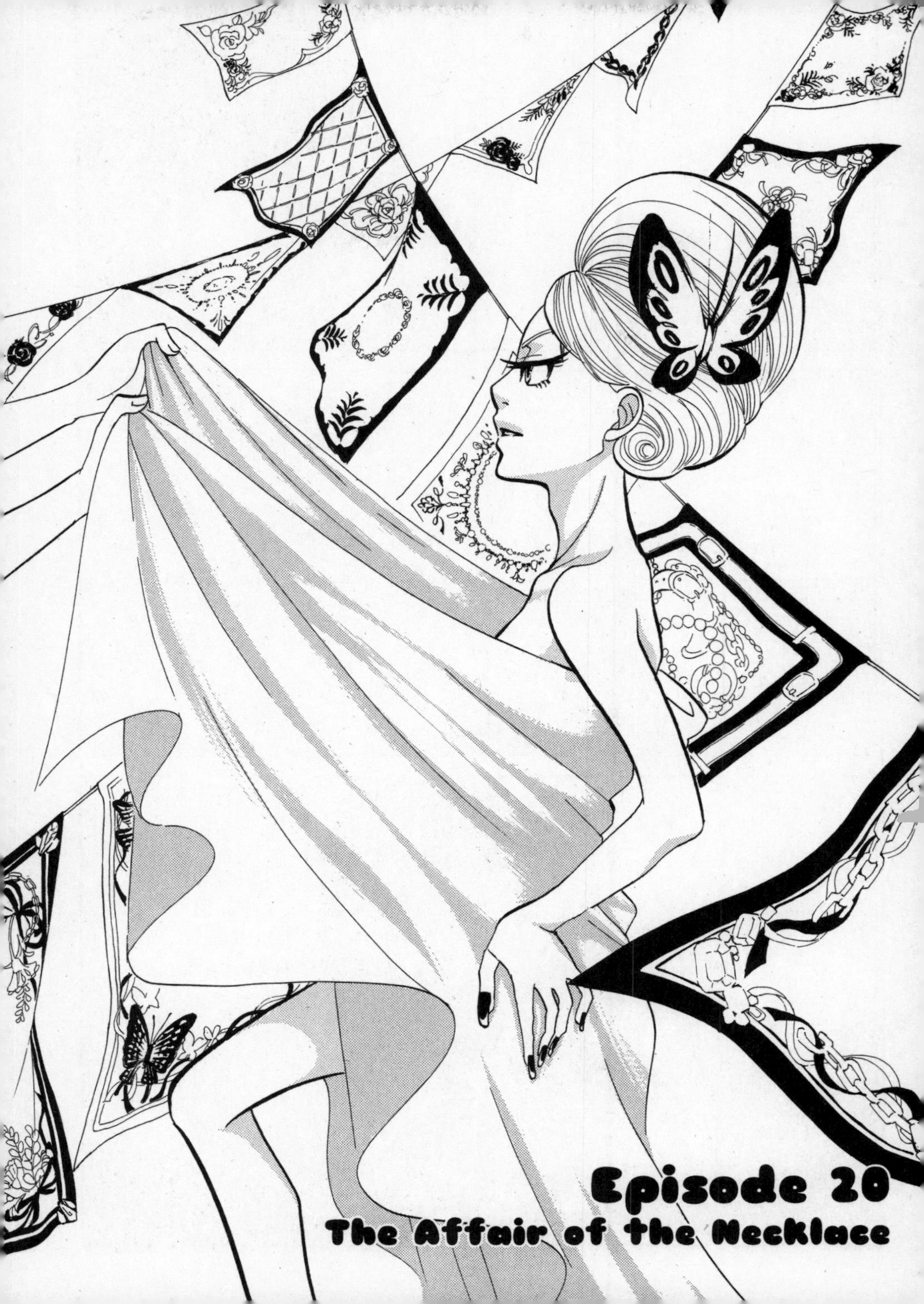
Episode 20
The Affair of the Necklace

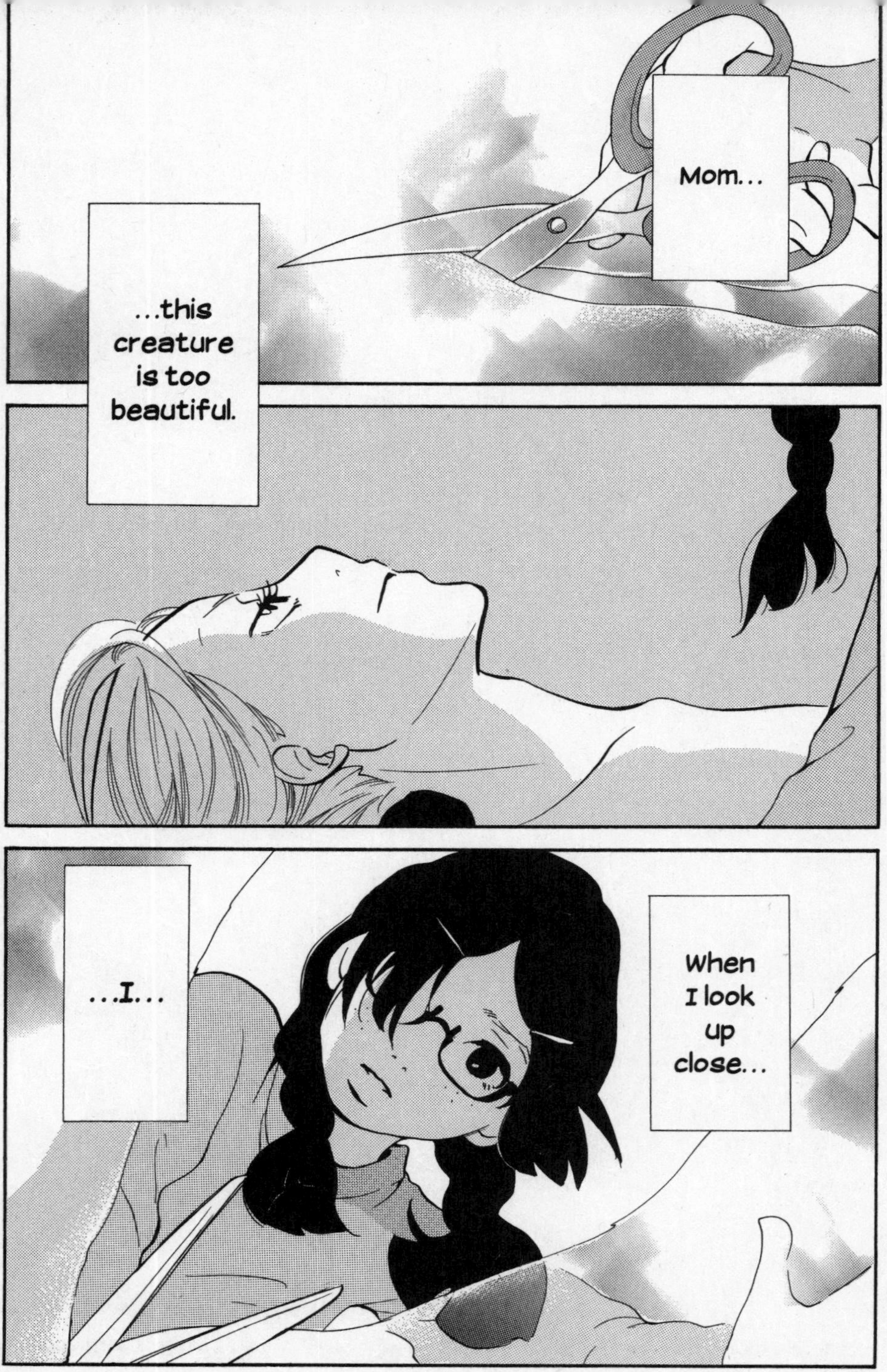
Mom...
...this creature is too beautiful.
When I look up close...
...I...

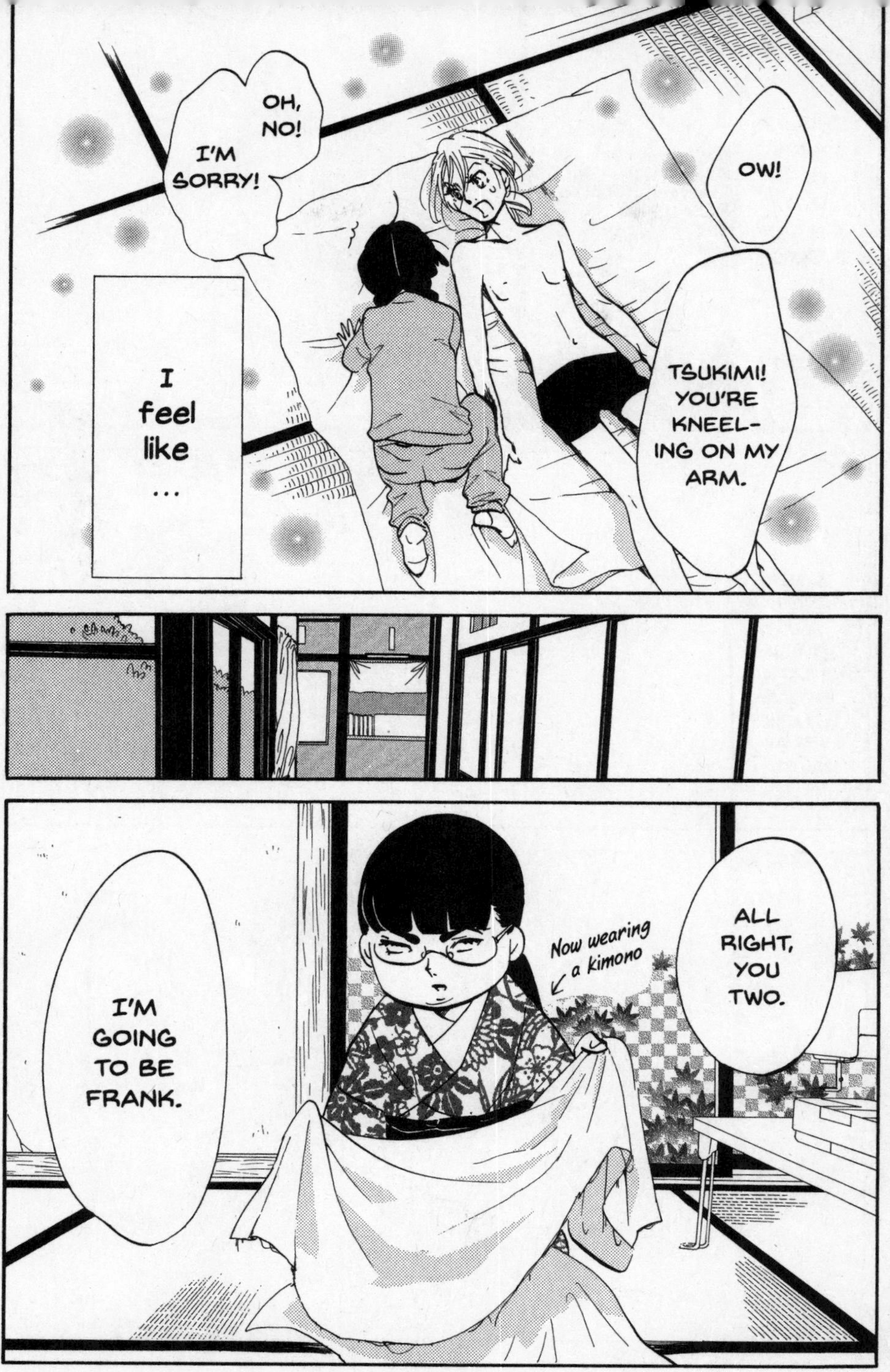
OW!
TSUKIMI! YOU'RE KNEEL-ING ON MY ARM.
OH, NO! I'M SORRY!
I feel like ...
ALL RIGHT, YOU TWO.
Now wearing a kimono
I'M GOING TO BE FRANK.

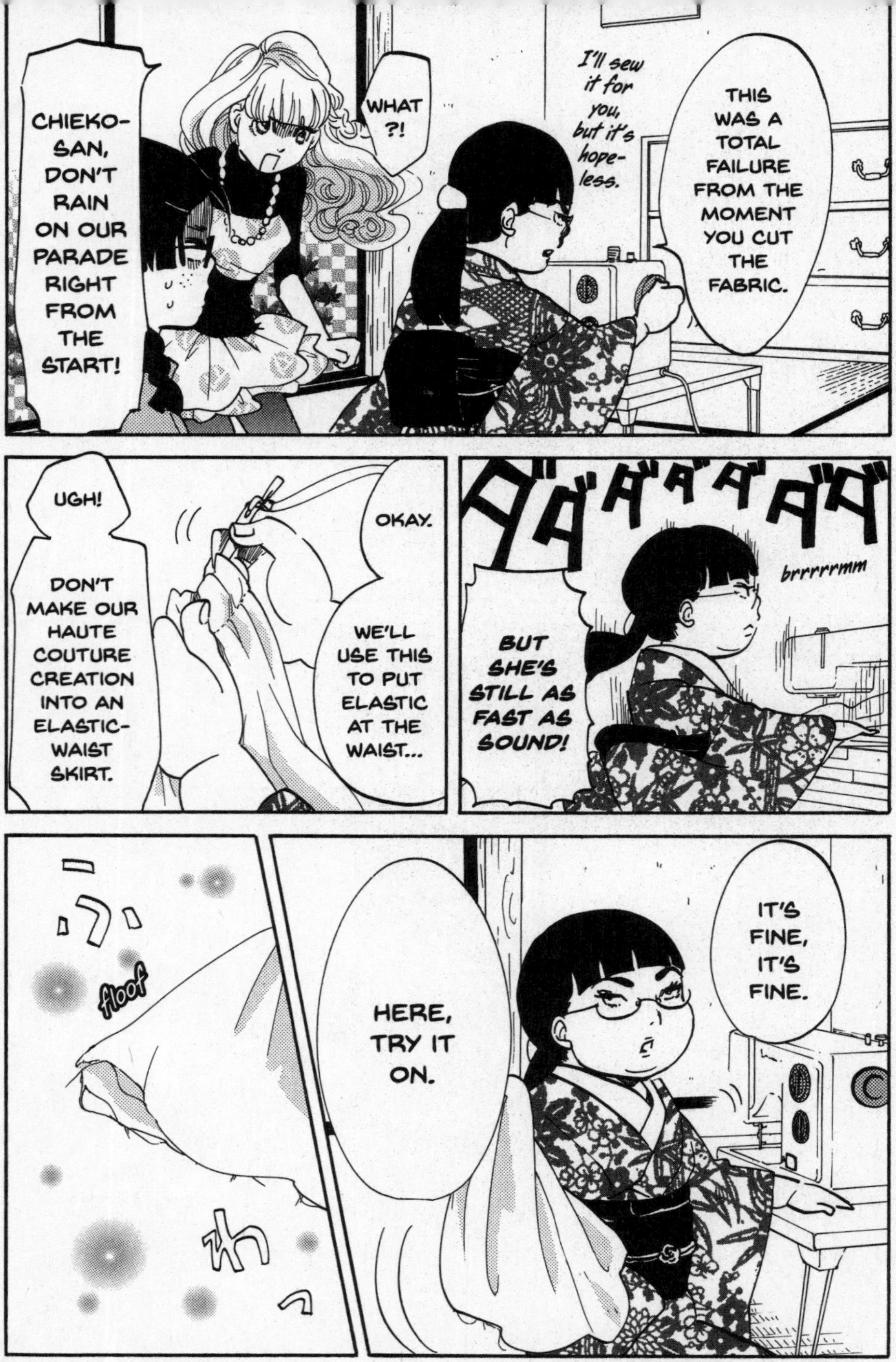
THIS WAS A TOTAL FAILURE FROM THE MOMENT YOU CUT THE FABRIC.
I'll sew it for you, but it's hopeless.
WHAT?!
CHIEKO-SAN, DON'T RAIN ON OUR PARADE RIGHT FROM THE START!
ダダダダダダダ
brrrrrmm
BUT SHE'S STILL AS FAST AS SOUND!
OKAY.
WE'LL USE THIS TO PUT ELASTIC AT THE WAIST...
UGH!
DON'T MAKE OUR HAUTE COUTURE CREATION INTO AN ELASTIC-WAIST SKIRT.
IT'S FINE, IT'S FINE.
HERE, TRY IT ON.
floof

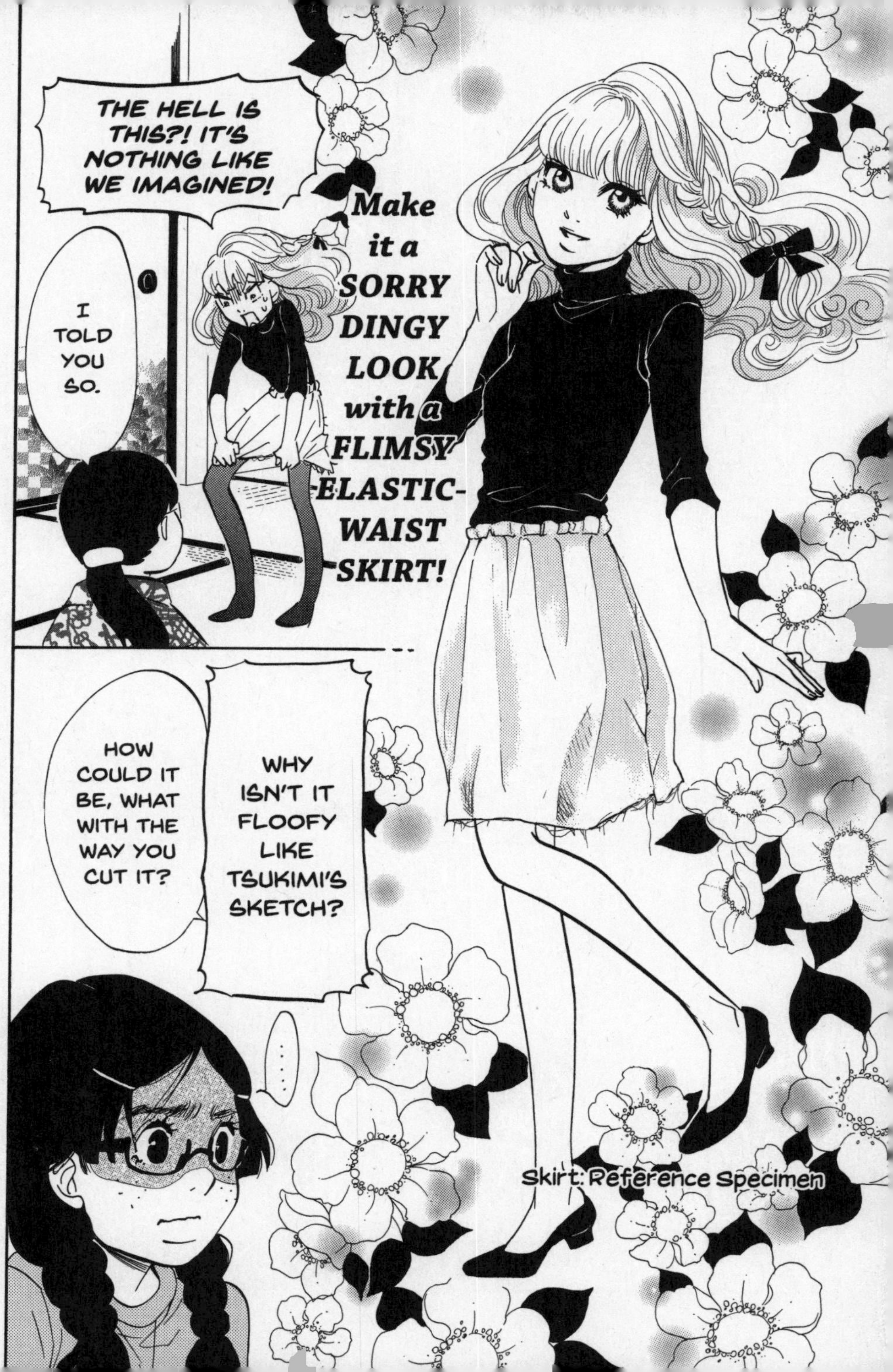
Make it a SORRY DINGY LOOK with a FLIMSY ELASTIC-WAIST SKIRT!
Skirt: Reference Specimen
THE HELL IS THIS?! IT'S NOTHING LIKE WE IMAGINED!
I TOLD YOU SO.
WHY ISN'T IT FLOOFY LIKE TSUKIMI'S SKETCH?
HOW COULD IT BE, WHAT WITH THE WAY YOU CUT IT?
......

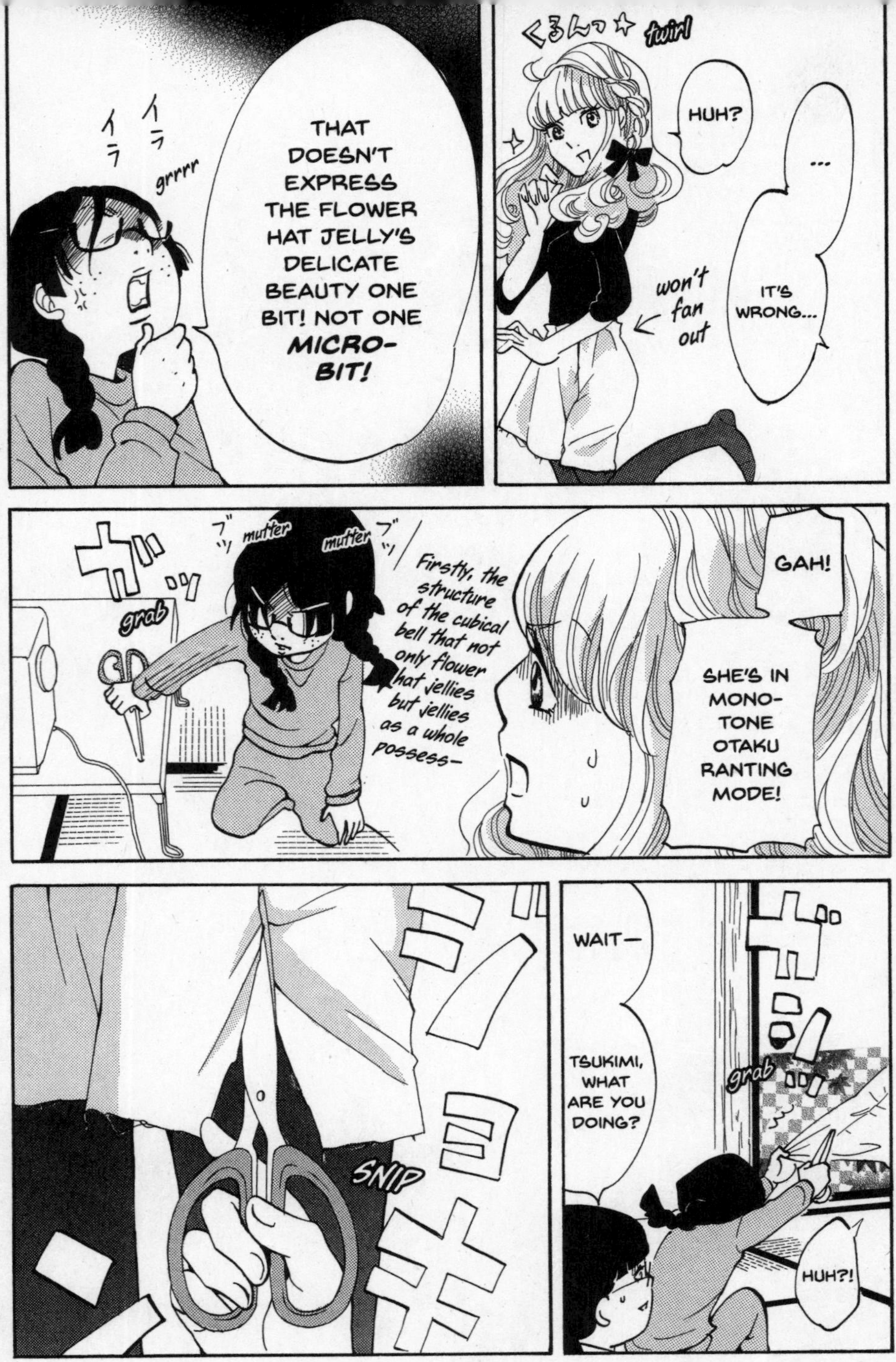
くるんっ☆ twirl
HUH?
...
IT'S WRONG...
won't fan out
イラ イラ
grrrr
THAT DOESN'T EXPRESS THE FLOWER HAT JELLY'S DELICATE BEAUTY ONE BIT! NOT ONE MICRO-BIT!
GAH!
SHE'S IN MONOTONE OTAKU RANTING MODE!
Firstly, the structure of the cubical bell that not only flower hat jellies but jellies as a whole possess—
mutter mutter
grab
WAIT—
TSUKIMI, WHAT ARE YOU DOING?
HUH?!
grab
SNIP

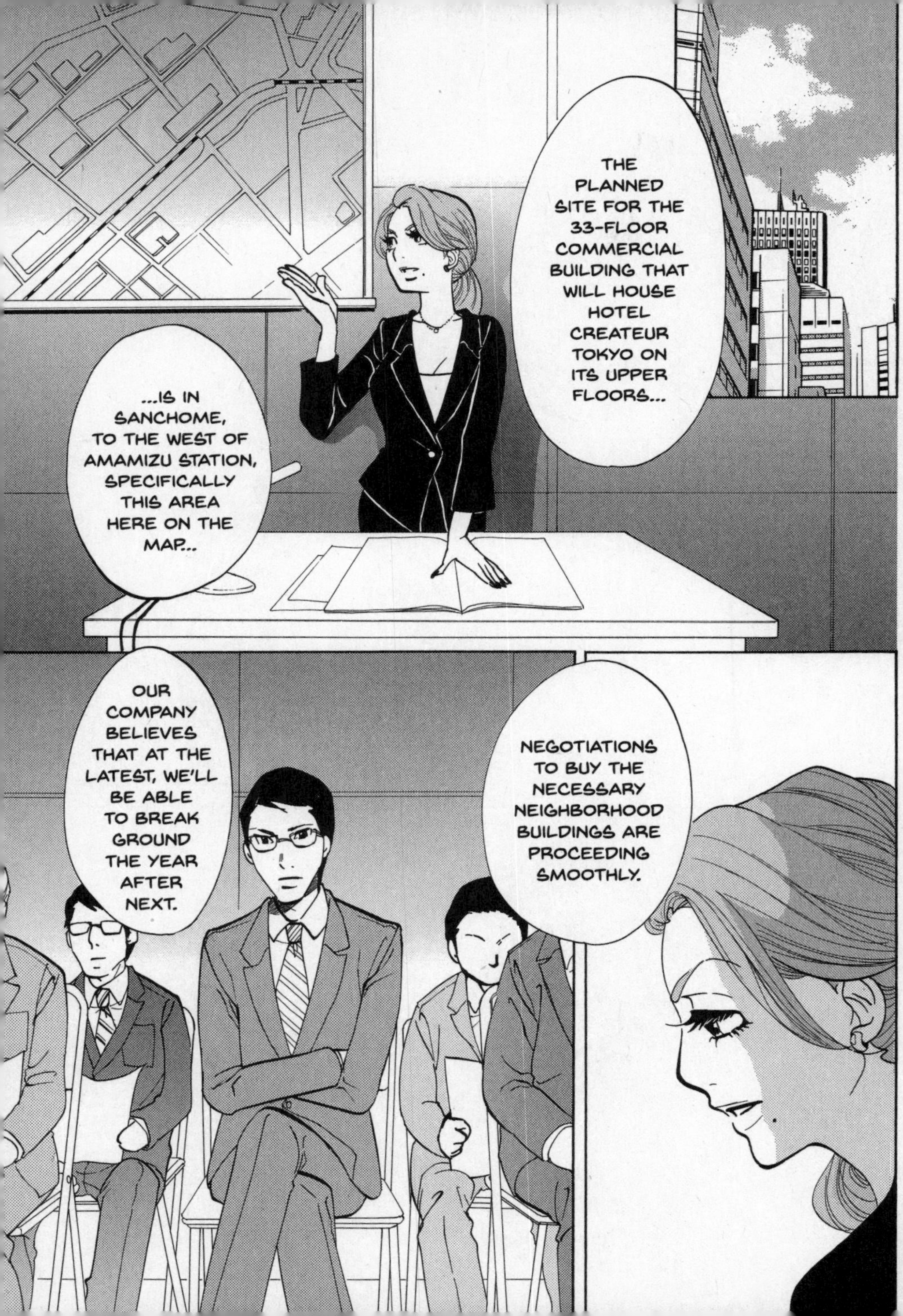
THE PLANNED SITE FOR THE 33-FLOOR COMMERCIAL BUILDING THAT WILL HOUSE HOTEL CREATEUR TOKYO ON ITS UPPER FLOORS...
...IS IN SANCHOME, TO THE WEST OF AMAMIZU STATION, SPECIFICALLY THIS AREA HERE ON THE MAP...
NEGOTIATIONS TO BUY THE NECESSARY NEIGHBORHOOD BUILDINGS ARE PROCEEDING SMOOTHLY.
OUR COMPANY BELIEVES THAT AT THE LATEST, WE'LL BE ABLE TO BREAK GROUND THE YEAR AFTER NEXT.

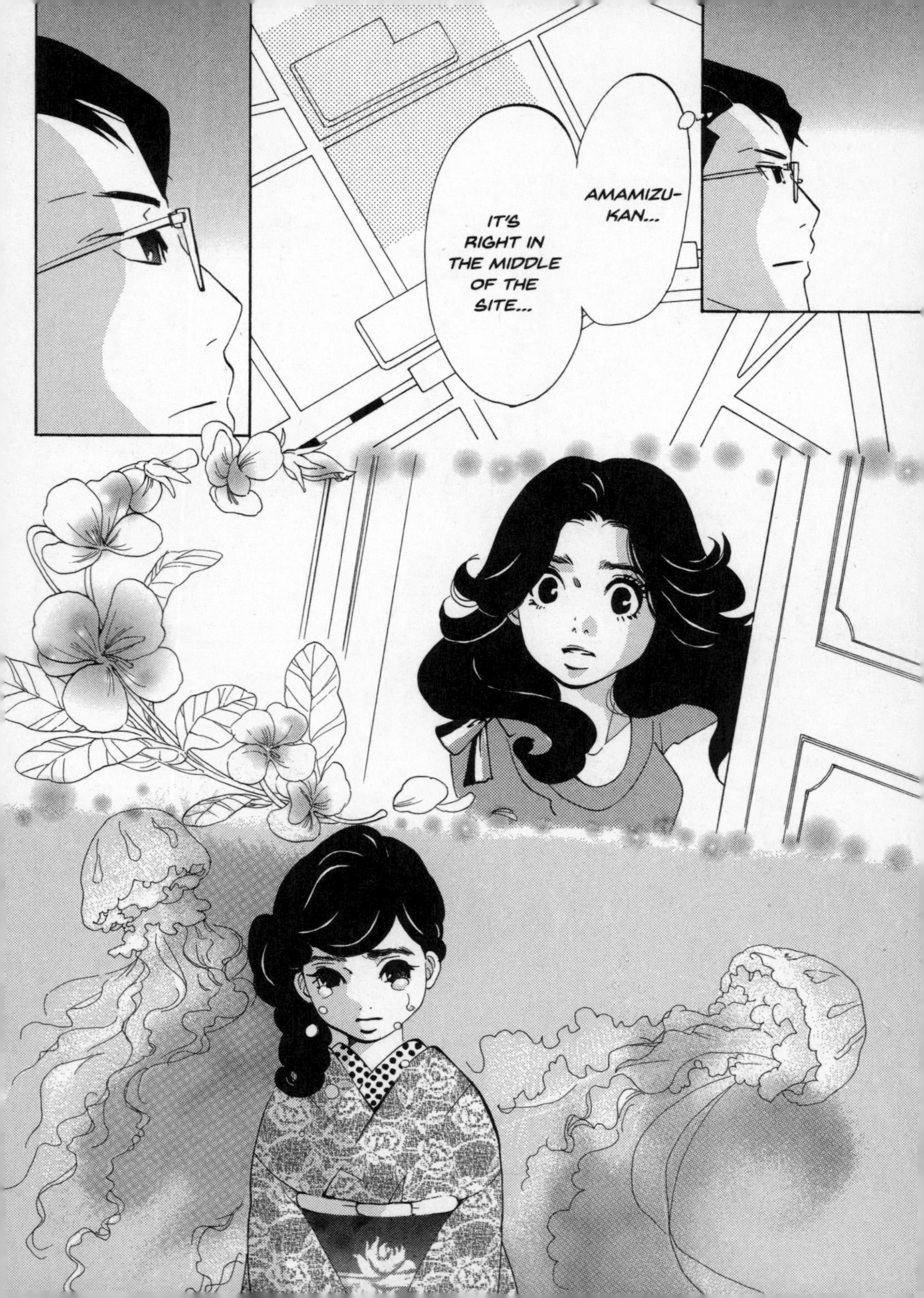
AMAMIZU-KAN...
IT'S RIGHT IN THE MIDDLE OF THE SITE...

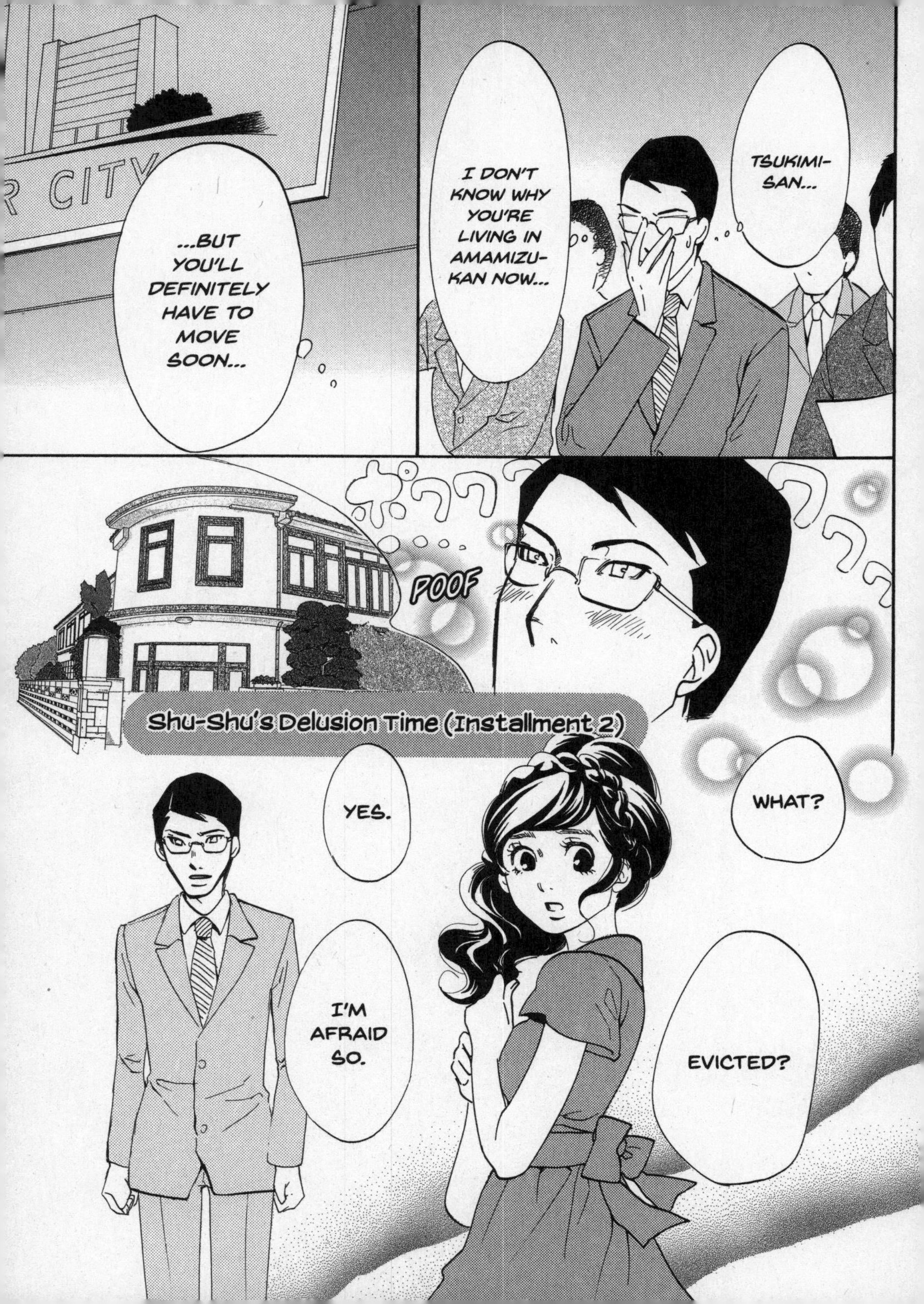
TSUKIMI-SAN...
I DON'T KNOW WHY YOU'RE LIVING IN AMAMIZU-KAN NOW...
...BUT YOU'LL DEFINITELY HAVE TO MOVE SOON...
POOF
Shu-Shu's Delusion Time (Installment 2)
WHAT?
YES.
EVICTED?
I'M AFRAID SO.

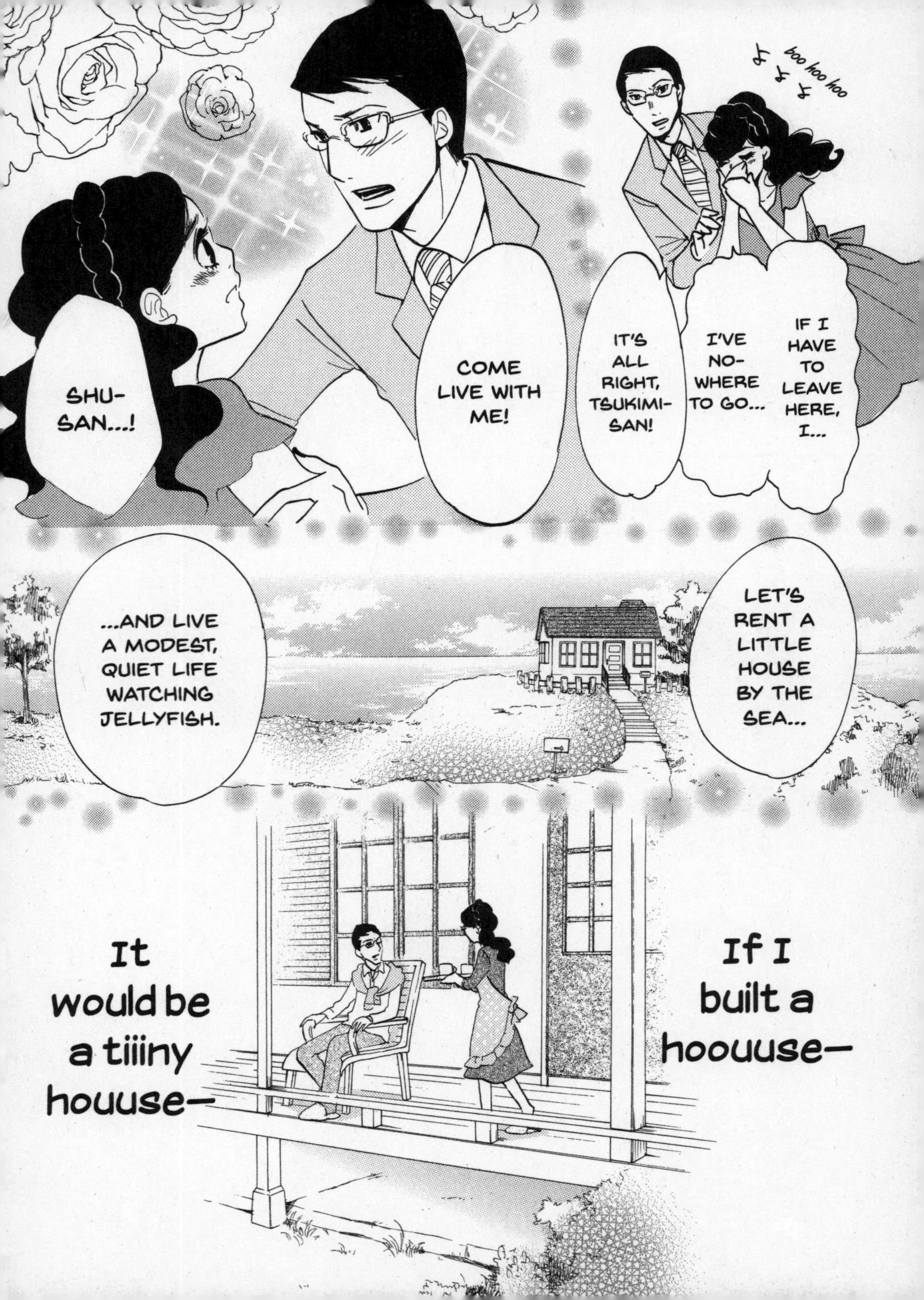
boo hoo hoo
よよよ
IF I HAVE TO LEAVE HERE, I...
I'VE NO-WHERE TO GO...
IT'S ALL RIGHT, TSUKIMI-SAN!
COME LIVE WITH ME!
SHU-SAN...!
LET'S RENT A LITTLE HOUSE BY THE SEA...
...AND LIVE A MODEST, QUIET LIFE WATCHING JELLYFISH.
If I built a hoouuse—
It would be a tiiiny houuse—

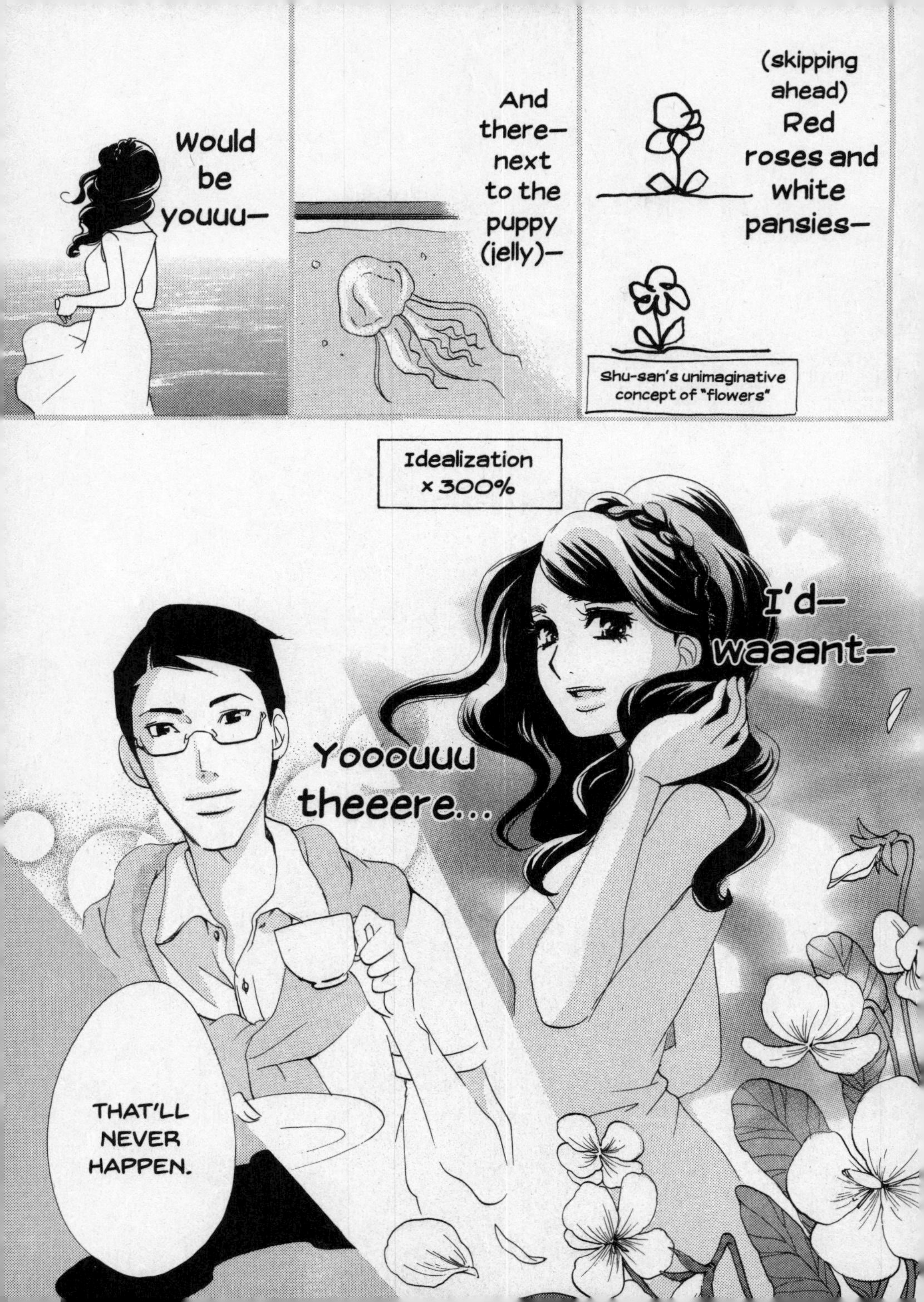
(skipping ahead) Red roses and white pansies—
Shu-san's unimaginative concept of "flowers"
And there— next to the puppy (jelly)—
Would be youuu—
Idealization x 300%
I'd— waaant—
Yooouuu theeere...
THAT'LL NEVER HAPPEN.

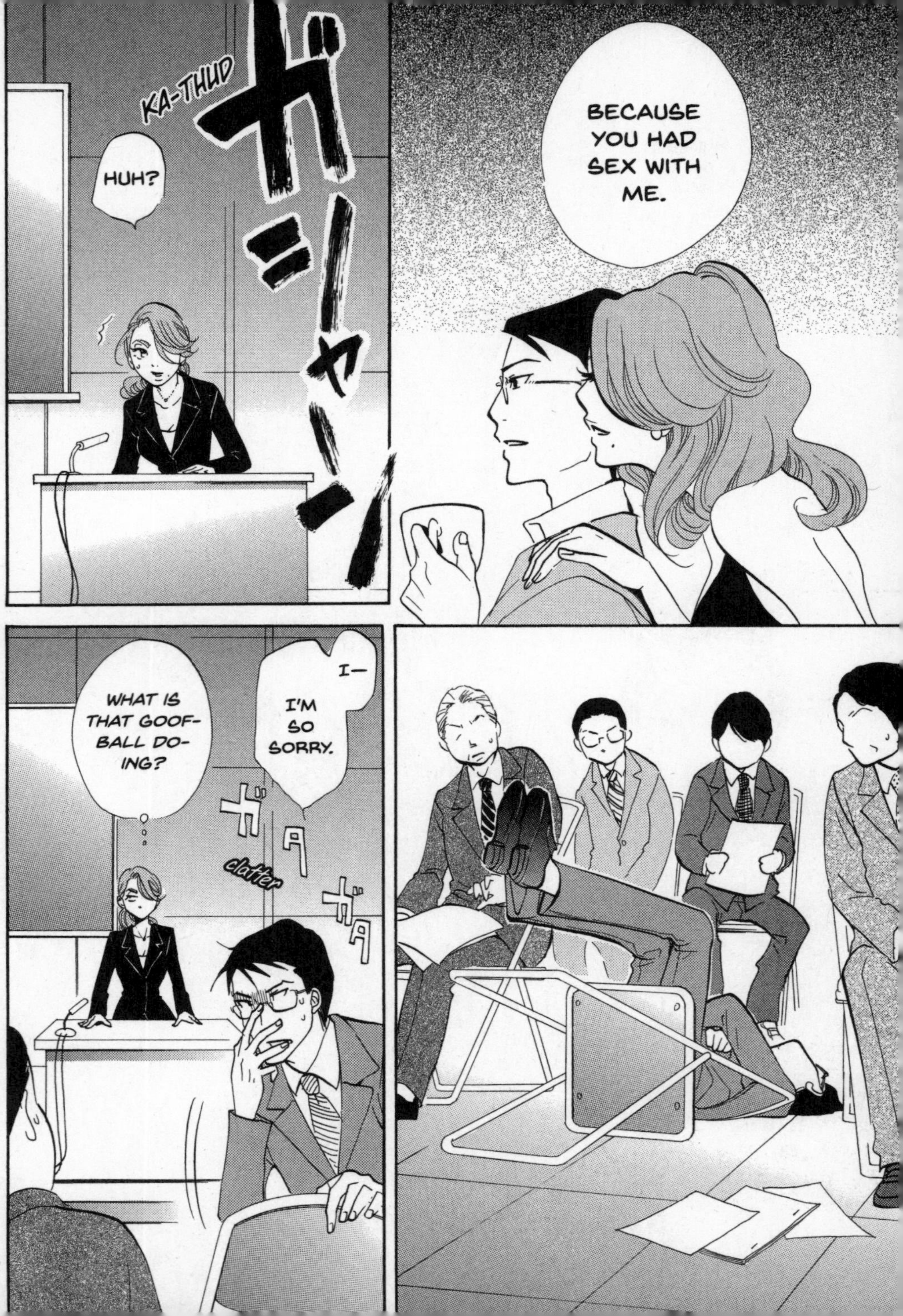
BECAUSE YOU HAD SEX WITH ME.
KA-THUD
HUH?
I—
I'M SO SORRY.
WHAT IS THAT GOOF-BALL DOING?
ガタ
clatter
ガタ

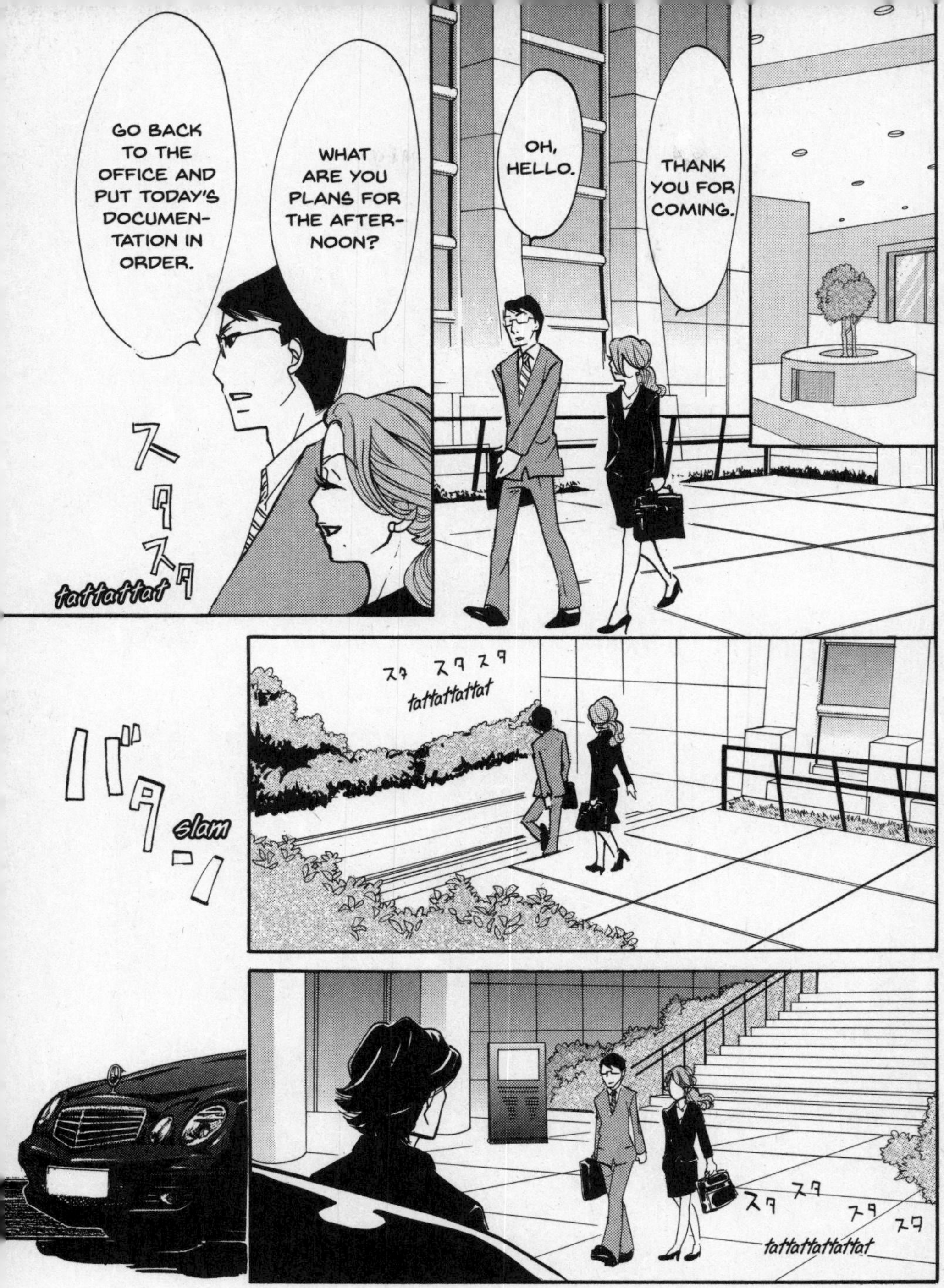
THANK YOU FOR COMING.
OH, HELLO.
WHAT ARE YOU PLANS FOR THE AFTER-NOON?
GO BACK TO THE OFFICE AND PUT TODAY'S DOCUMEN-TATION IN ORDER.
スタスタ
tattattat
スタ スタスタ
tattattattat
バタン
slam
スタ スタ スタ スタ
tattattattattat

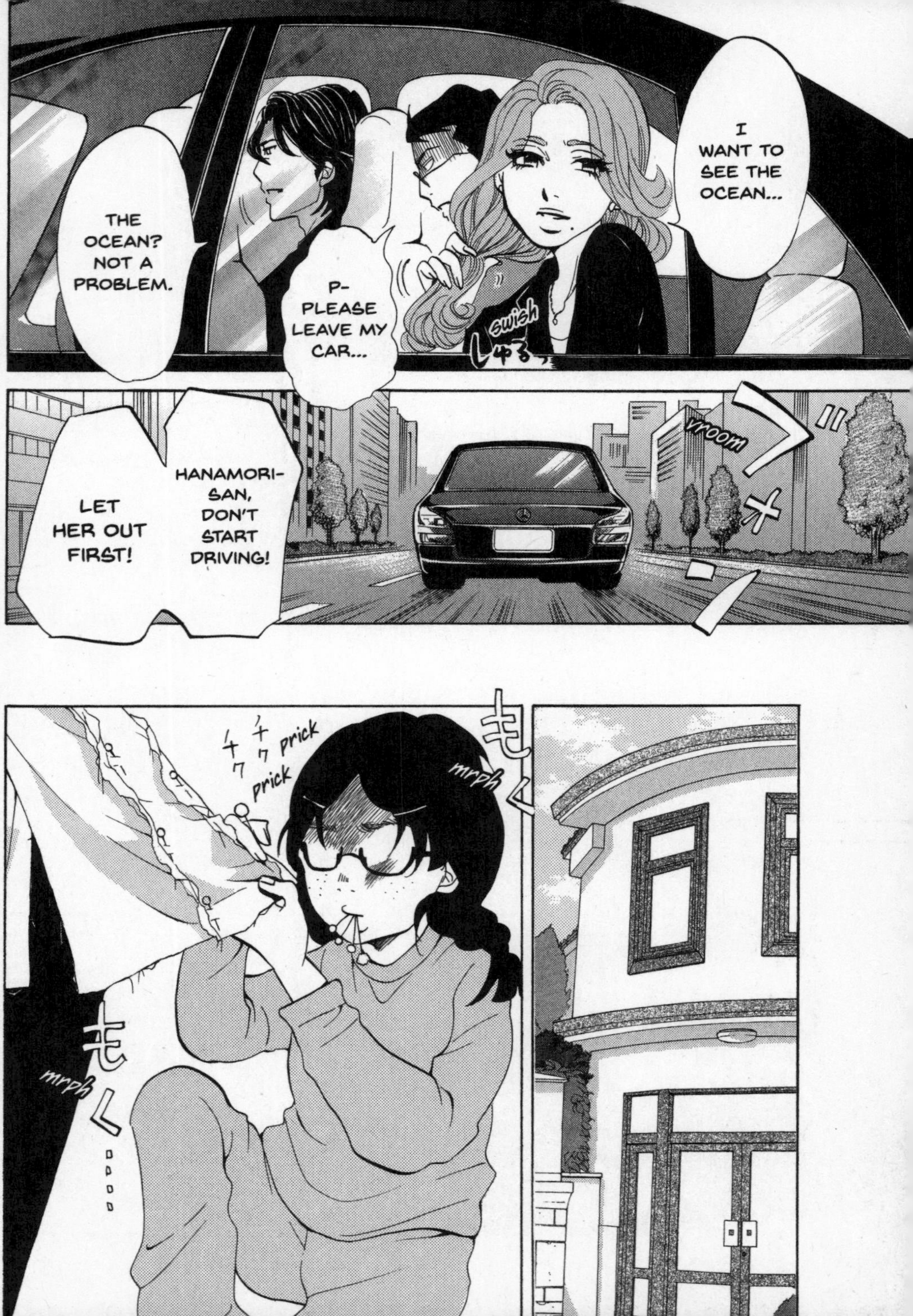
I WANT TO SEE THE OCEAN...
THE OCEAN? NOT A PROBLEM.
P- PLEASE LEAVE MY CAR...
swish
vroom
HANAMORI-SAN, DON'T START DRIVING!
LET HER OUT FIRST!
mrph
prick prick
mrph

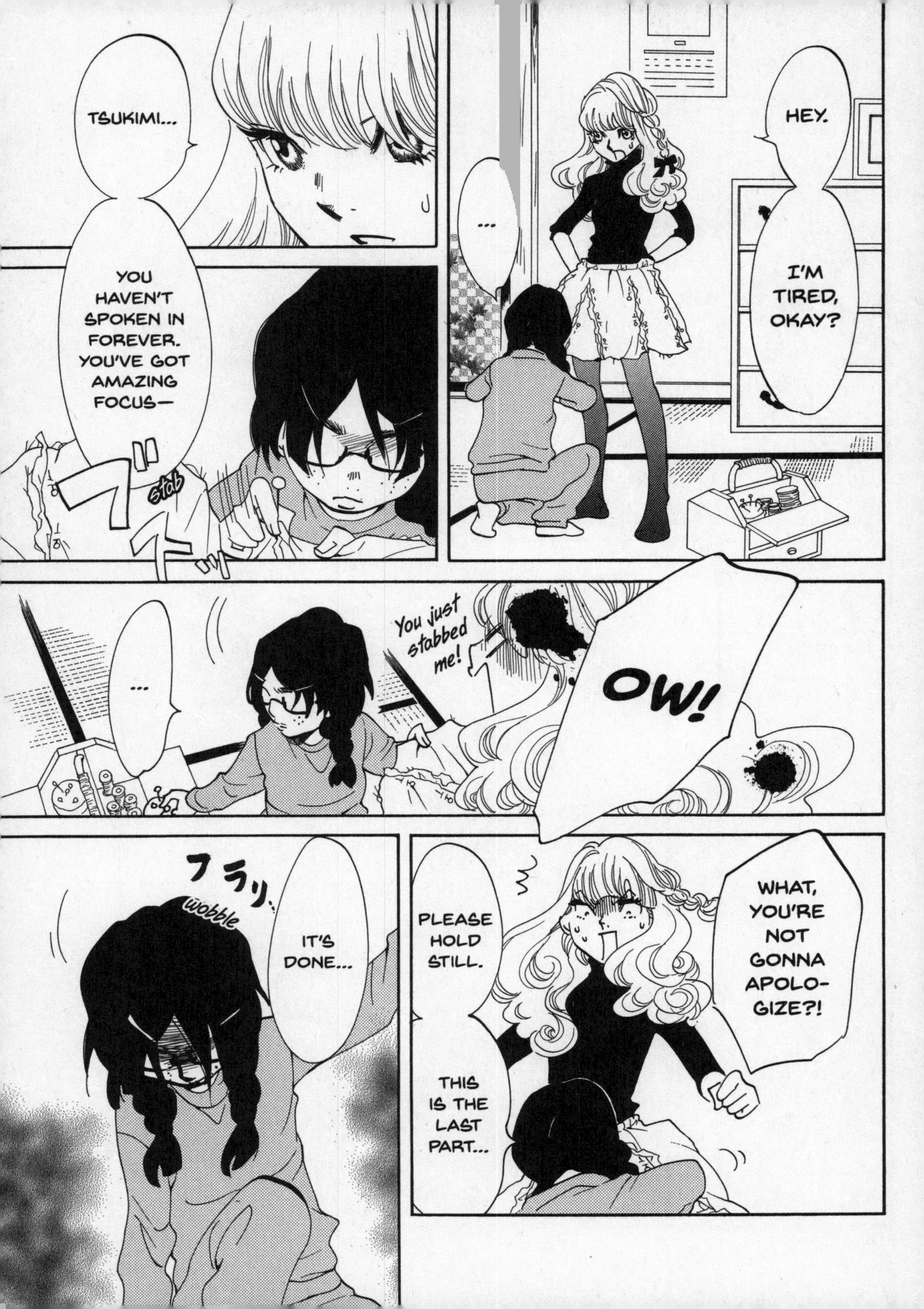
HEY.
I'M TIRED, OKAY?
...
TSUKIMI...
YOU HAVEN'T SPOKEN IN FOREVER. YOU'VE GOT AMAZING FOCUS—
stab
OW!
You just stabbed me!
...
WHAT, YOU'RE NOT GONNA APOLOGIZE?!
PLEASE HOLD STILL.
THIS IS THE LAST PART...
IT'S DONE...
フラリ
wobble

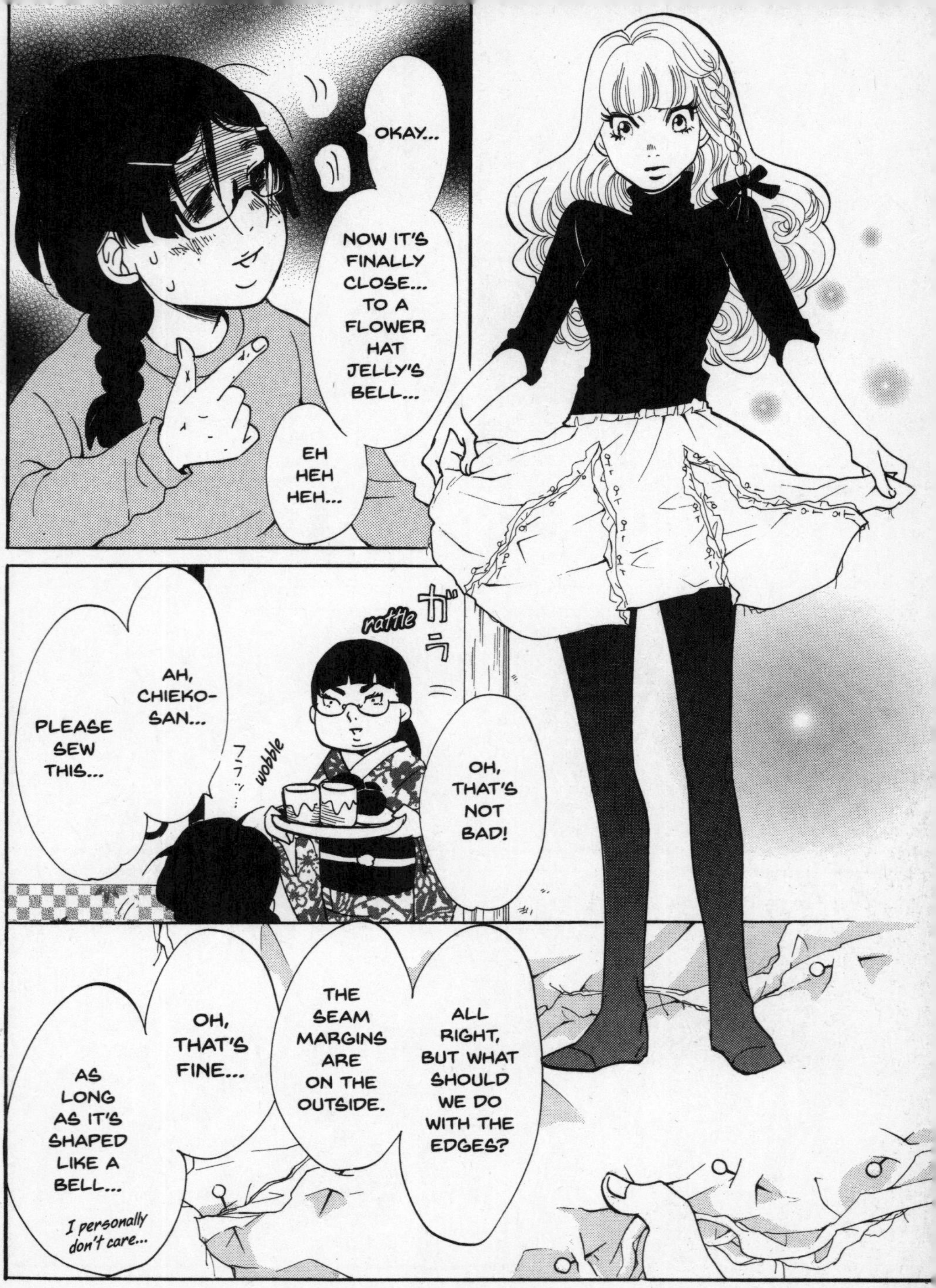
OKAY...
NOW IT'S FINALLY CLOSE... TO A FLOWER HAT JELLY'S BELL...
EH HEH HEH...
ガラ
rattle
OH, THAT'S NOT BAD!
AH, CHIEKO-SAN...
PLEASE SEW THIS...
フラッ…
wobble
ALL RIGHT, BUT WHAT SHOULD WE DO WITH THE EDGES?
THE SEAM MARGINS ARE ON THE OUTSIDE.
OH, THAT'S FINE...
AS LONG AS IT'S SHAPED LIKE A BELL...
I personally don't care...

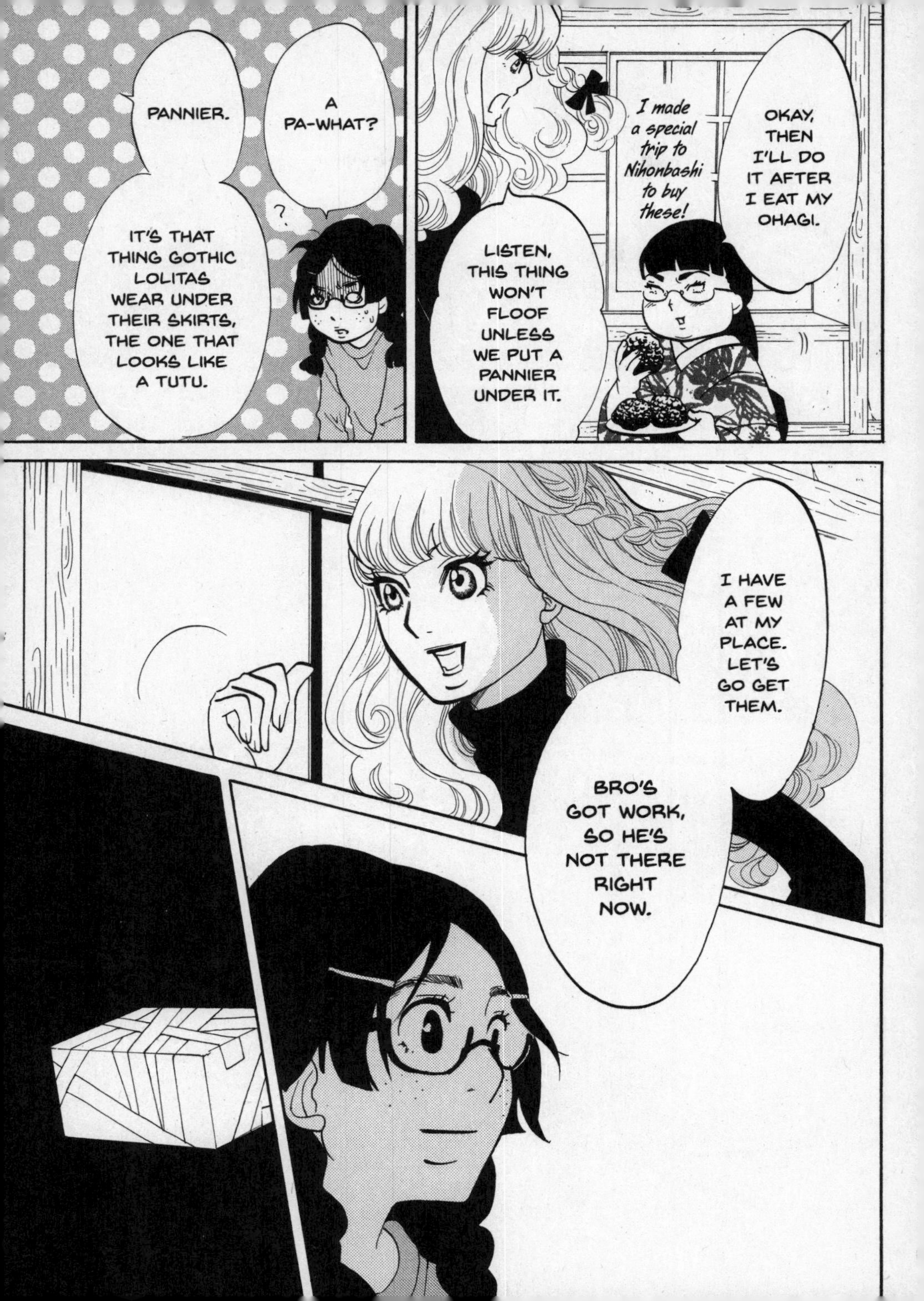
OKAY, THEN I'LL DO IT AFTER I EAT MY OHAGI.
I made a special trip to Nihonbashi to buy these!
LISTEN, THIS THING WON'T FLOOF UNLESS WE PUT A PANNIER UNDER IT.
A PA-WHAT?
?
PANNIER.
IT'S THAT THING GOTHIC LOLITAS WEAR UNDER THEIR SKIRTS, THE ONE THAT LOOKS LIKE A TUTU.
I HAVE A FEW AT MY PLACE. LET'S GO GET THEM.
BRO'S GOT WORK, SO HE'S NOT THERE RIGHT NOW.

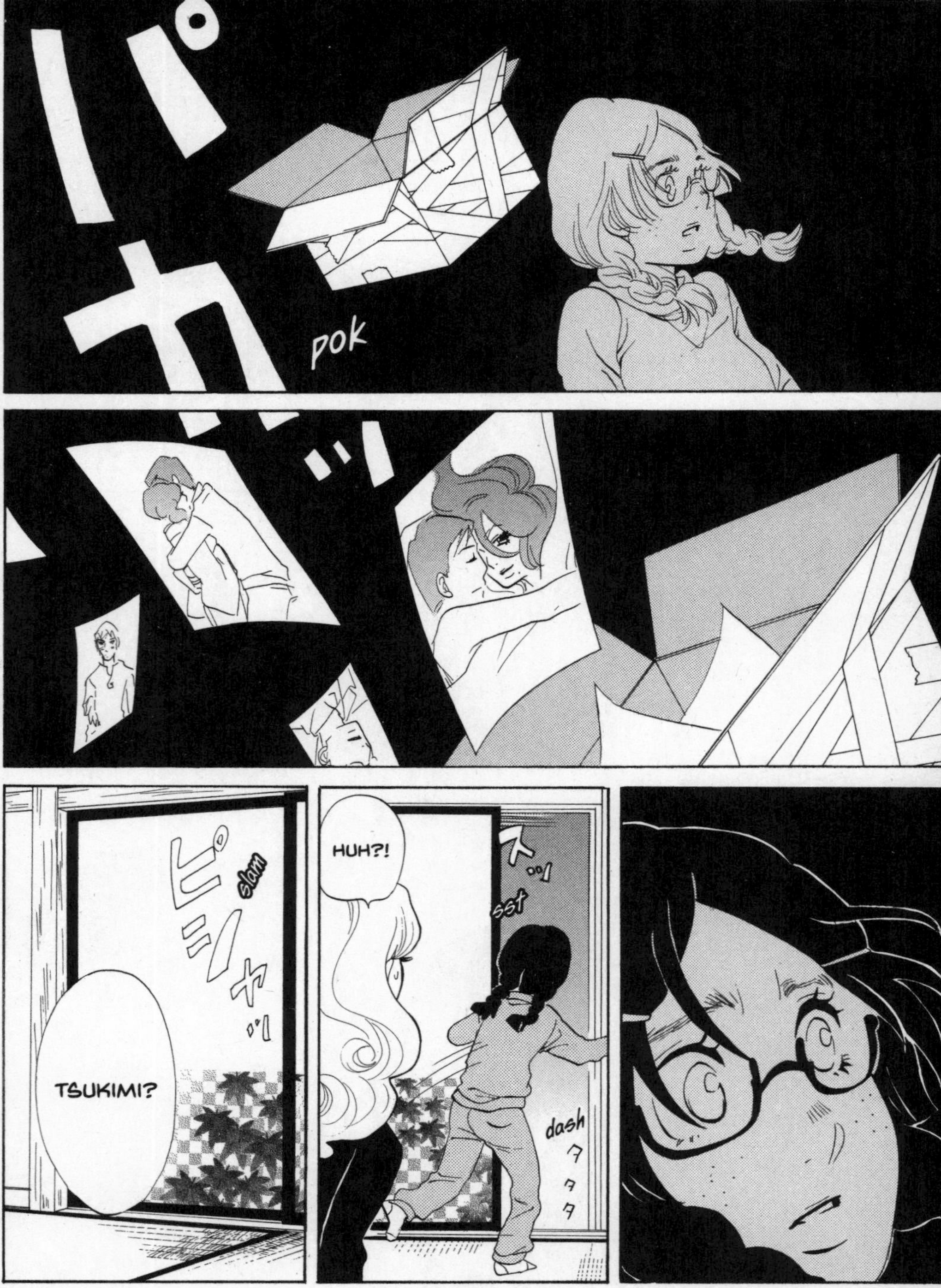
パカッ
pok
HUH?!
スッ
sst
dash
タタタ
ピシャッ
slam
TSUKIMI?

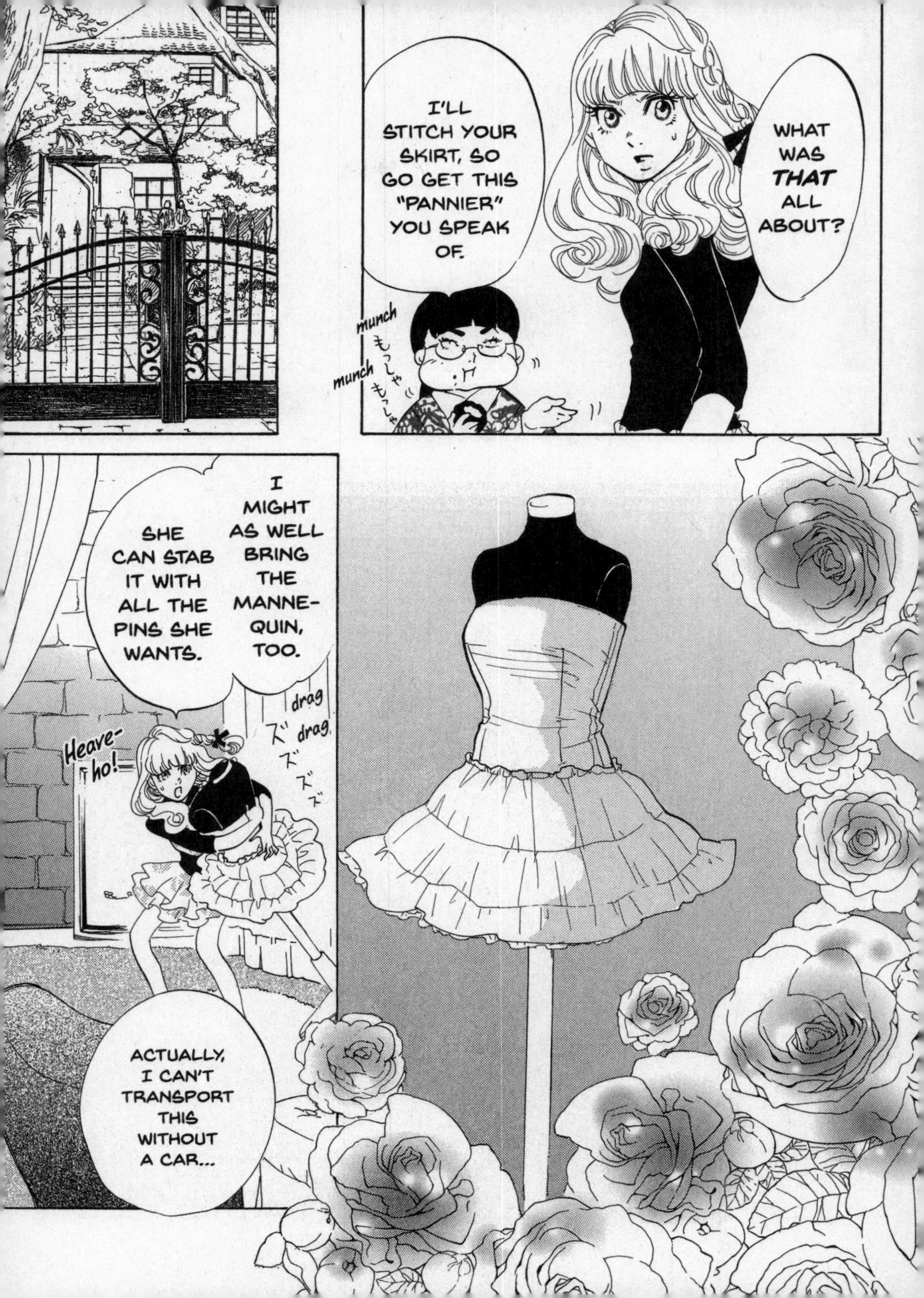
WHAT WAS ***THAT*** ALL ABOUT?
I'LL STITCH YOUR SKIRT, SO GO GET THIS "PANNIER" YOU SPEAK OF.
munch もっしゃ
munch もっしゃ
I MIGHT AS WELL BRING THE MANNEQUIN, TOO.
SHE CAN STAB IT WITH ALL THE PINS SHE WANTS.
drag ズ
drag ズズズ
Heave-ho!
ACTUALLY, I CAN'T TRANSPORT THIS WITHOUT A CAR...

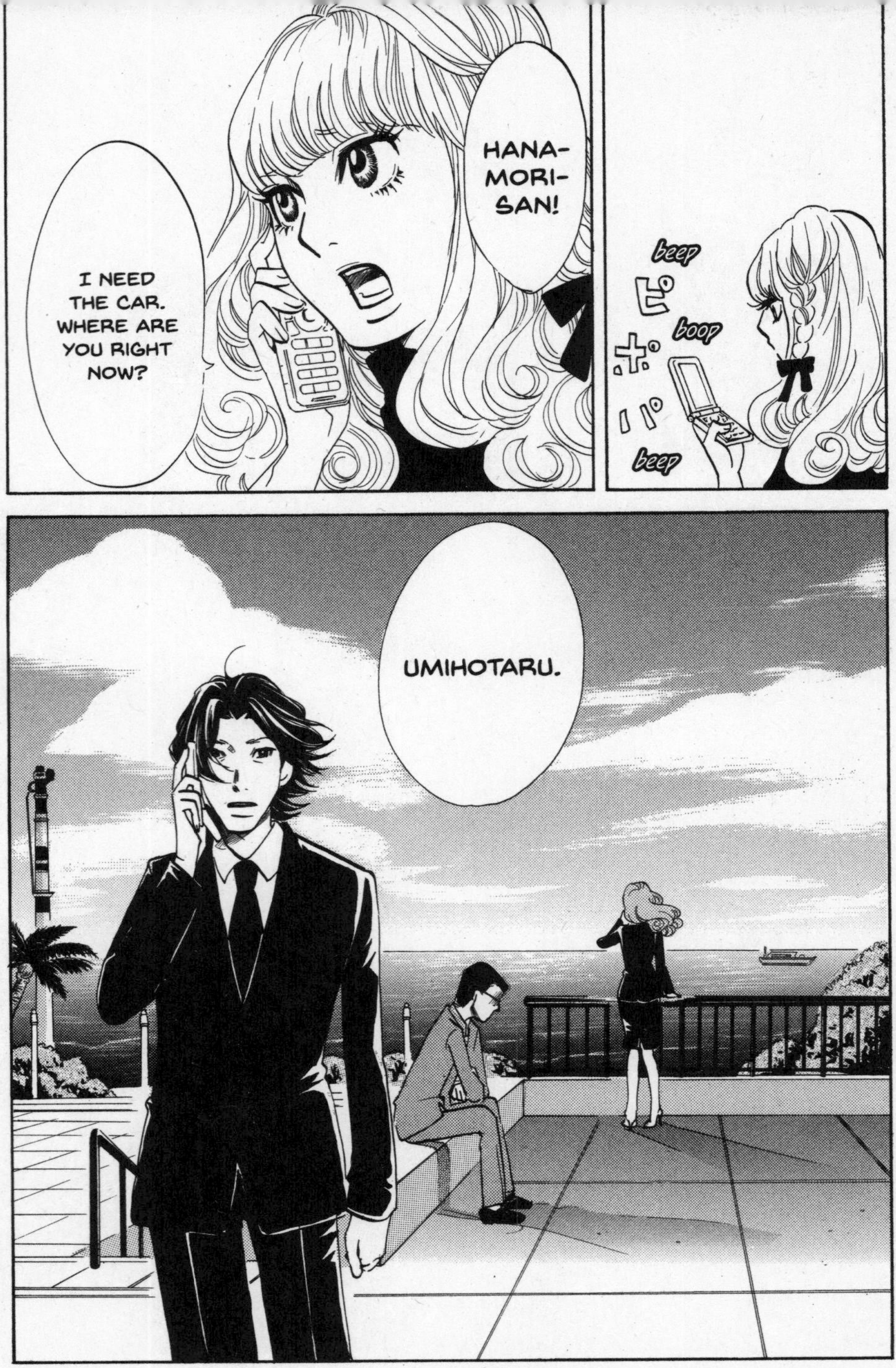
beep
ピ
boop
ポ
パ
beep
HANA-MORI-SAN!
I NEED THE CAR. WHERE ARE YOU RIGHT NOW?
UMIHOTARU.

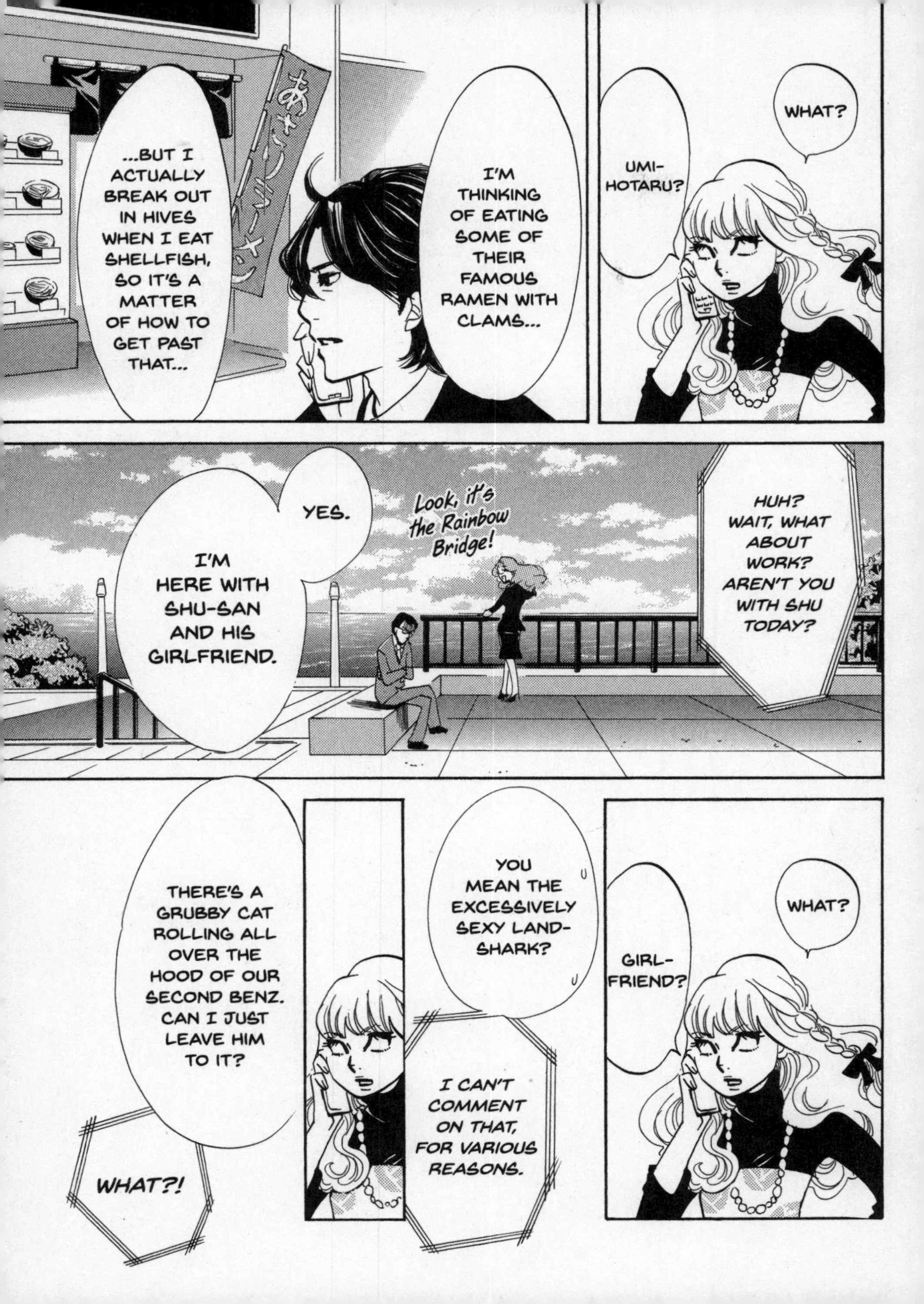
WHAT?
UMI-HOTARU?
I'M THINKING OF EATING SOME OF THEIR FAMOUS RAMEN WITH CLAMS...
...BUT I ACTUALLY BREAK OUT IN HIVES WHEN I EAT SHELLFISH, SO IT'S A MATTER OF HOW TO GET PAST THAT...
HUH? WAIT, WHAT ABOUT WORK? AREN'T YOU WITH SHU TODAY?
Look, it's the Rainbow Bridge!
YES.
I'M HERE WITH SHU-SAN AND HIS GIRLFRIEND.
WHAT?
GIRL-FRIEND?
YOU MEAN THE EXCESSIVELY SEXY LAND-SHARK?
I CAN'T COMMENT ON THAT, FOR VARIOUS REASONS.
THERE'S A GRUBBY CAT ROLLING ALL OVER THE HOOD OF OUR SECOND BENZ. CAN I JUST LEAVE HIM TO IT?
WHAT?!

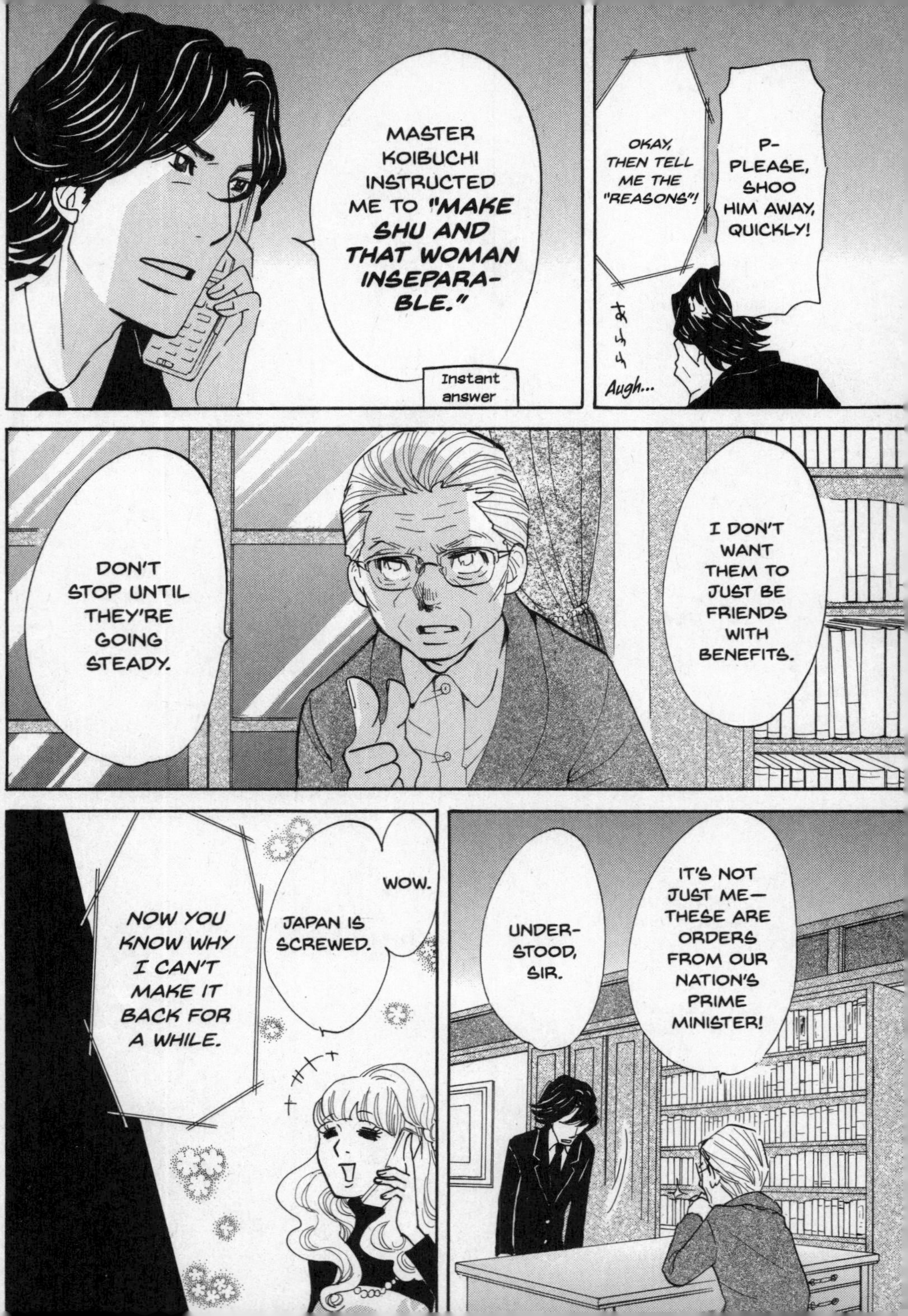
P- PLEASE, SHOO HIM AWAY, QUICKLY!
OKAY, THEN TELL ME THE "REASONS"!
Augh...
MASTER KOIBUCHI INSTRUCTED ME TO "MAKE SHU AND THAT WOMAN INSEPARABLE."
Instant answer
I DON'T WANT THEM TO JUST BE FRIENDS WITH BENEFITS.
DON'T STOP UNTIL THEY'RE GOING STEADY.
IT'S NOT JUST ME— THESE ARE ORDERS FROM OUR NATION'S PRIME MINISTER!
UNDER-STOOD, SIR.
WOW.
JAPAN IS SCREWED.
NOW YOU KNOW WHY I CAN'T MAKE IT BACK FOR A WHILE.

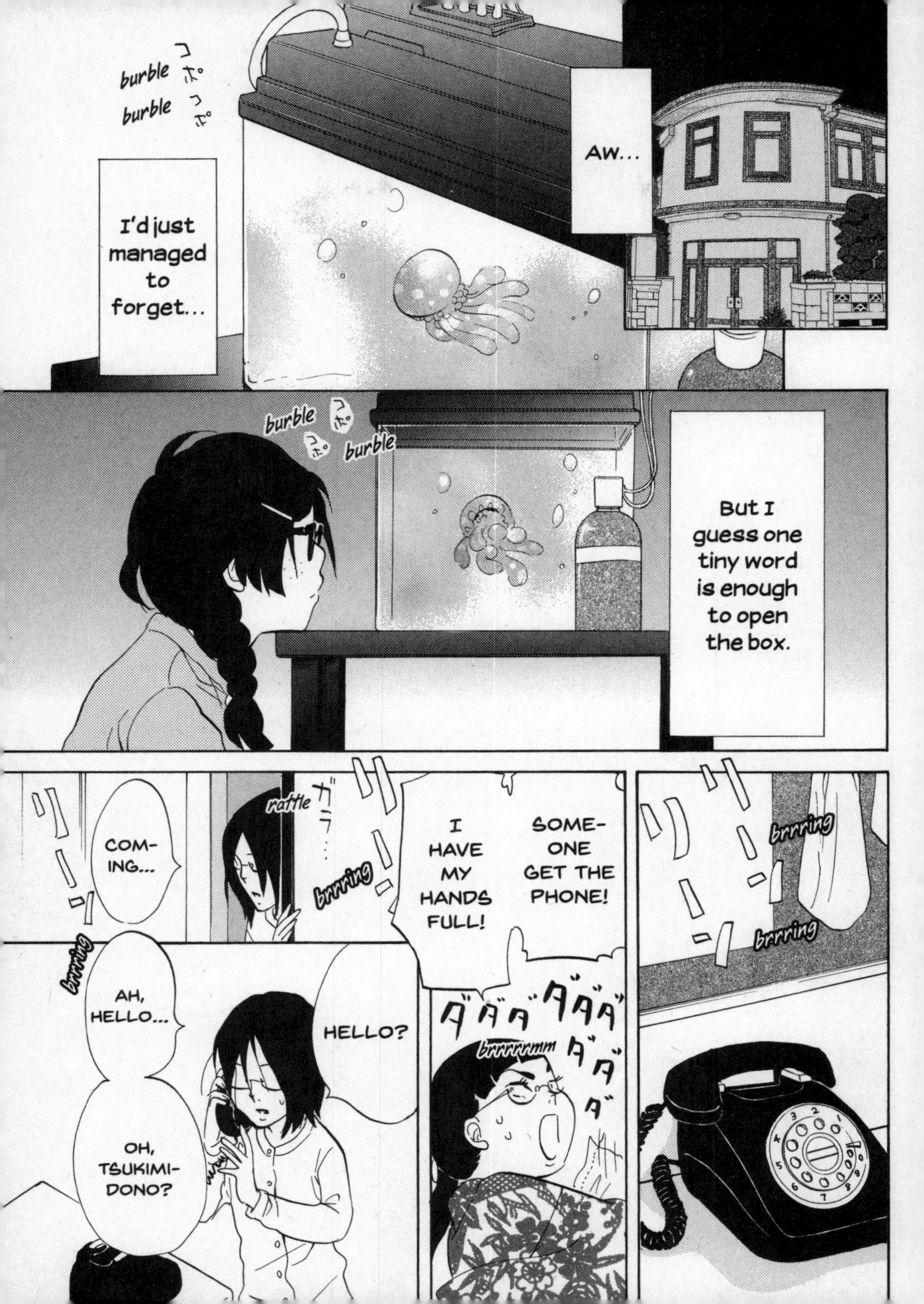
AW...
burble
burble
コポコポ
I'd just managed to forget...
burble
burble
コポコポ
But I guess one tiny word is enough to open the box.
brrring
brrring
SOME-ONE GET THE PHONE!
I HAVE MY HANDS FULL!
rattle
ガラ…
brrring
COM-ING...
brrrrrmm
ダダダダダダダダダ
HELLO?
brrring
AH, HELLO...
OH, TSUKIMI-DONO?

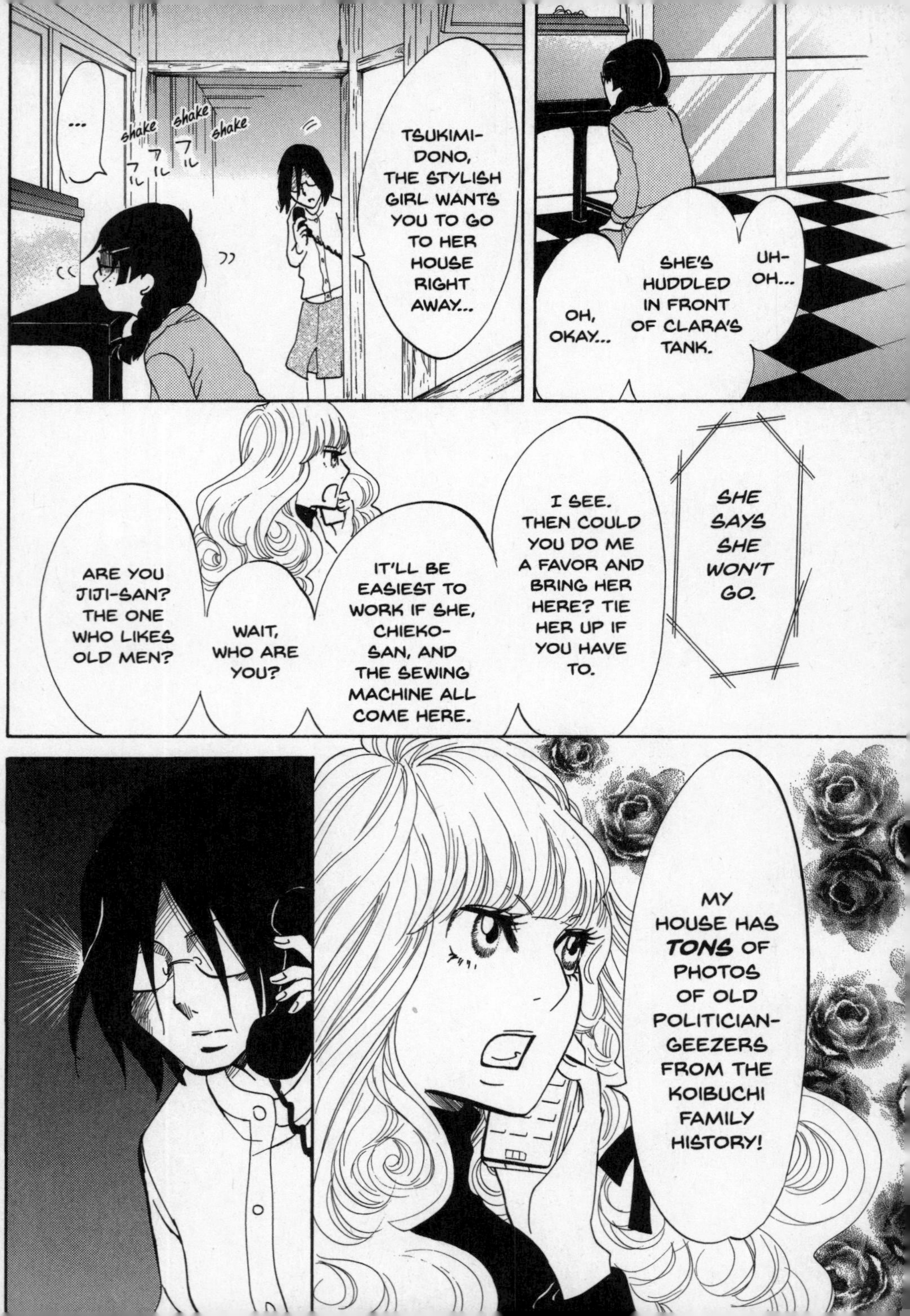
UH-OH...
SHE'S HUDDLED IN FRONT OF CLARA'S TANK.
OH, OKAY...
TSUKIMI-DONO, THE STYLISH GIRL WANTS YOU TO GO TO HER HOUSE RIGHT AWAY...
shake shake shake
フル フル
...
SHE SAYS SHE WON'T GO.
I SEE. THEN COULD YOU DO ME A FAVOR AND BRING HER HERE? TIE HER UP IF YOU HAVE TO.
IT'LL BE EASIEST TO WORK IF SHE, CHIEKO-SAN, AND THE SEWING MACHINE ALL COME HERE.
WAIT, WHO ARE YOU?
ARE YOU JIJI-SAN? THE ONE WHO LIKES OLD MEN?
MY HOUSE HAS **TONS** OF PHOTOS OF OLD POLITICIAN-GEEZERS FROM THE KOIBUCHI FAMILY HISTORY!

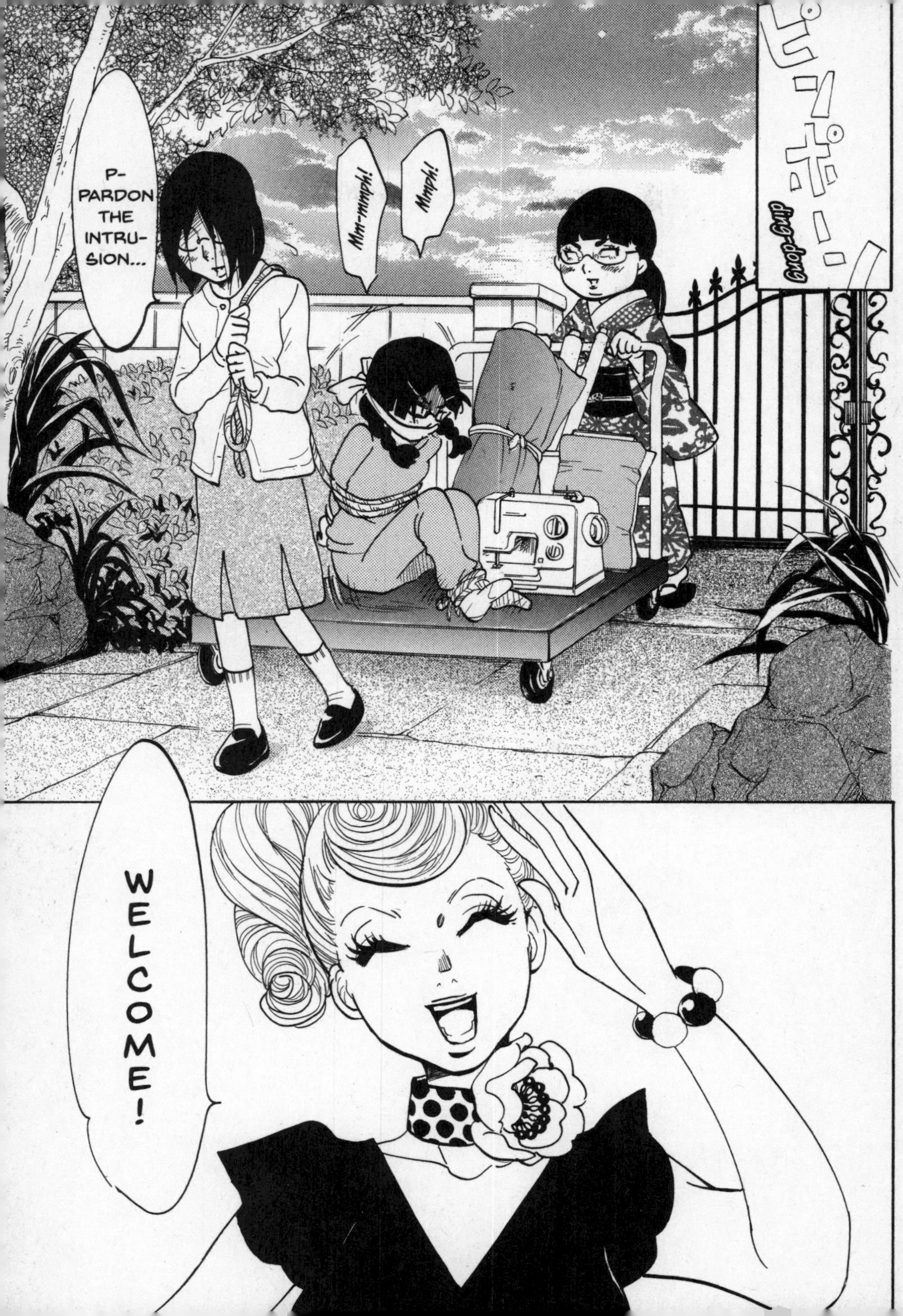
ピンポーン
ding-dong
Mmph!
Mm-mmph!
P-PARDON THE INTRUSION...
WELCOME!

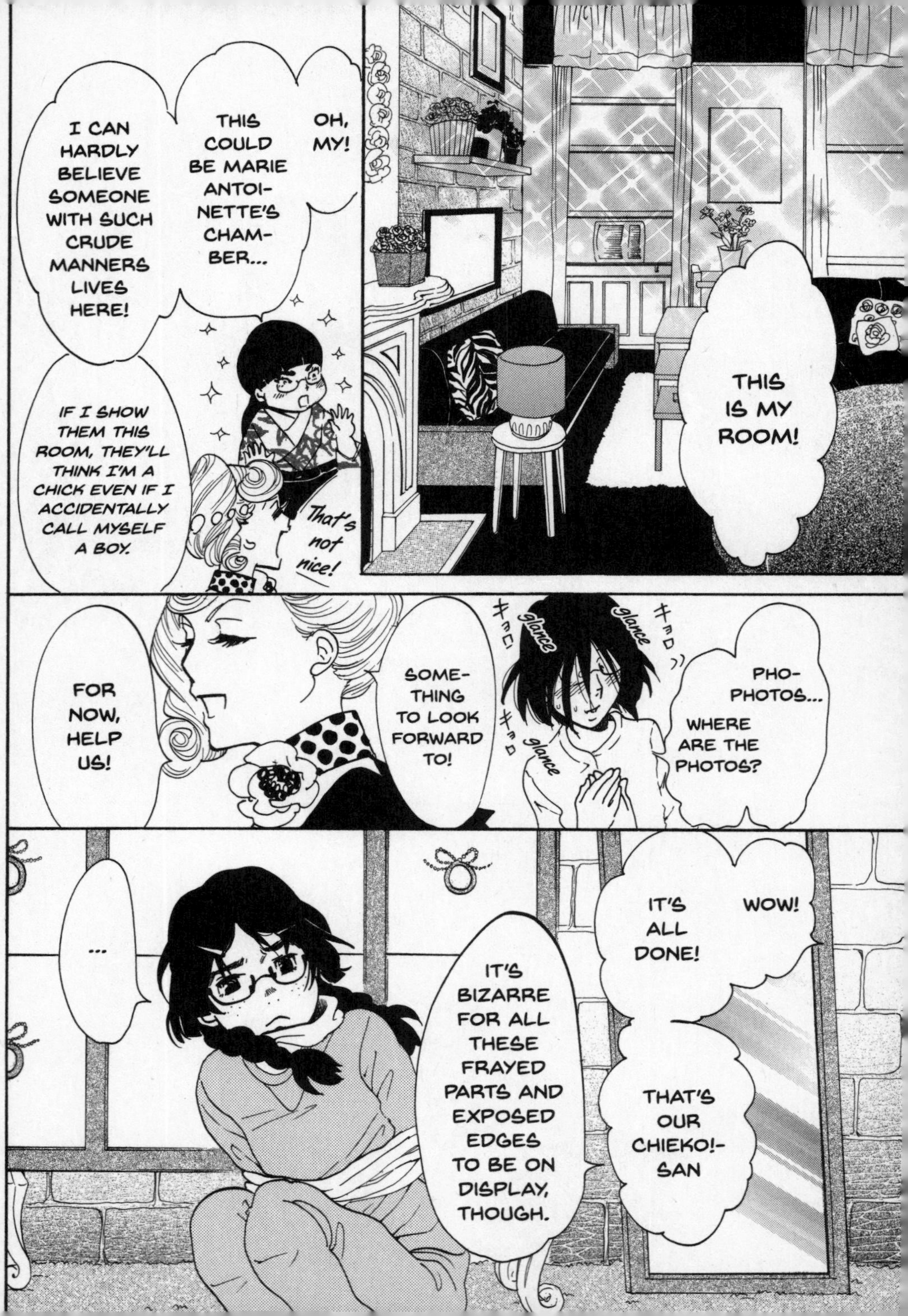
THIS IS MY ROOM!
OH, MY!
THIS COULD BE MARIE ANTOINETTE'S CHAMBER...
I CAN HARDLY BELIEVE SOMEONE WITH SUCH CRUDE MANNERS LIVES HERE!
That's not nice!
IF I SHOW THEM THIS ROOM, THEY'LL THINK I'M A CHICK EVEN IF I ACCIDENTALLY CALL MYSELF A BOY.
PHO-PHOTOS...
WHERE ARE THE PHOTOS?
glance
glance
glance
SOME-THING TO LOOK FORWARD TO!
FOR NOW, HELP US!
WOW!
IT'S ALL DONE!
THAT'S OUR CHIEKO!-SAN
IT'S BIZARRE FOR ALL THESE FRAYED PARTS AND EXPOSED EDGES TO BE ON DISPLAY, THOUGH.
...

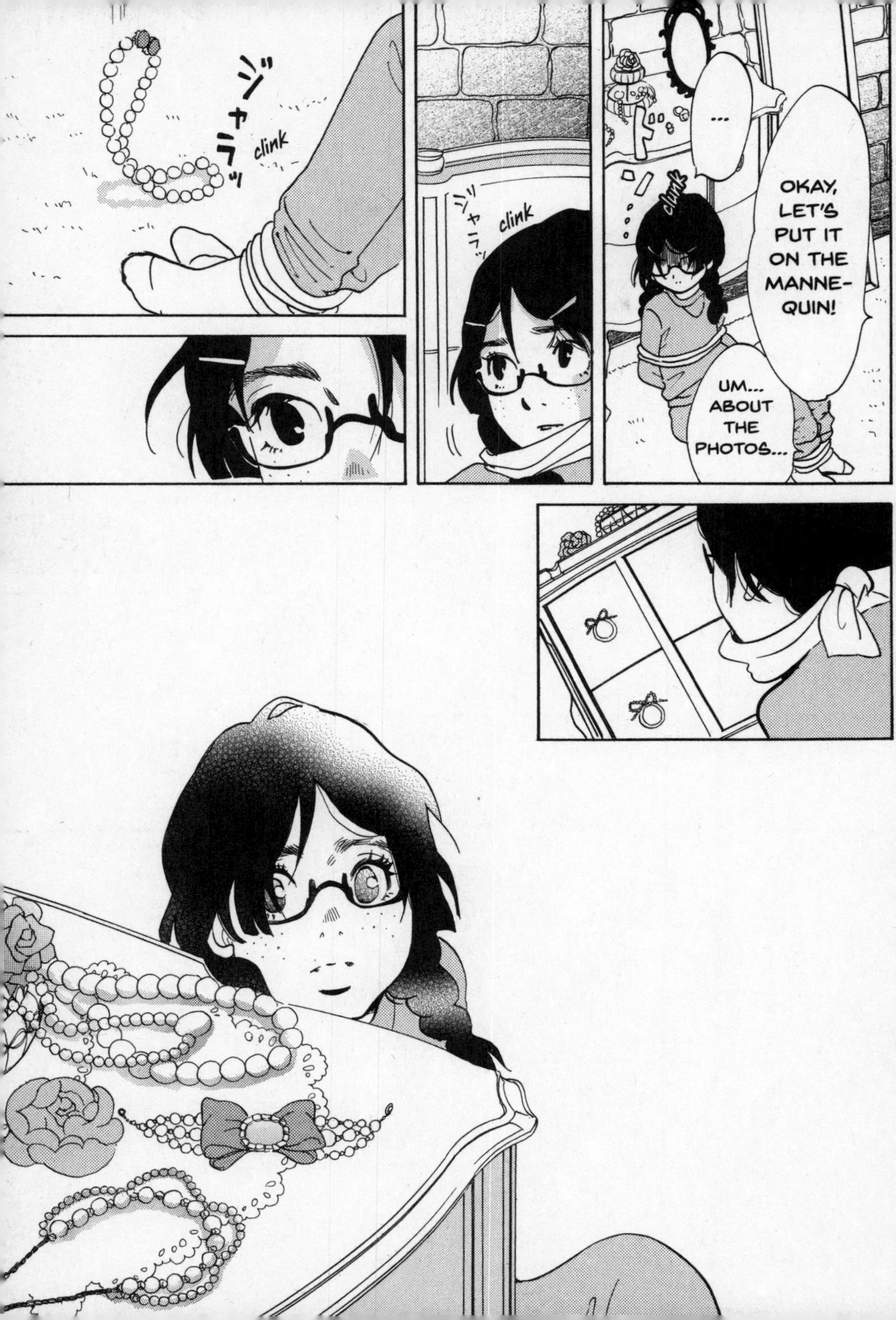
...
OKAY, LET'S PUT IT ON THE MANNE-QUIN!
clink
UM... ABOUT THE PHOTOS...
ジャラッ
clink
ジャラッ
clink

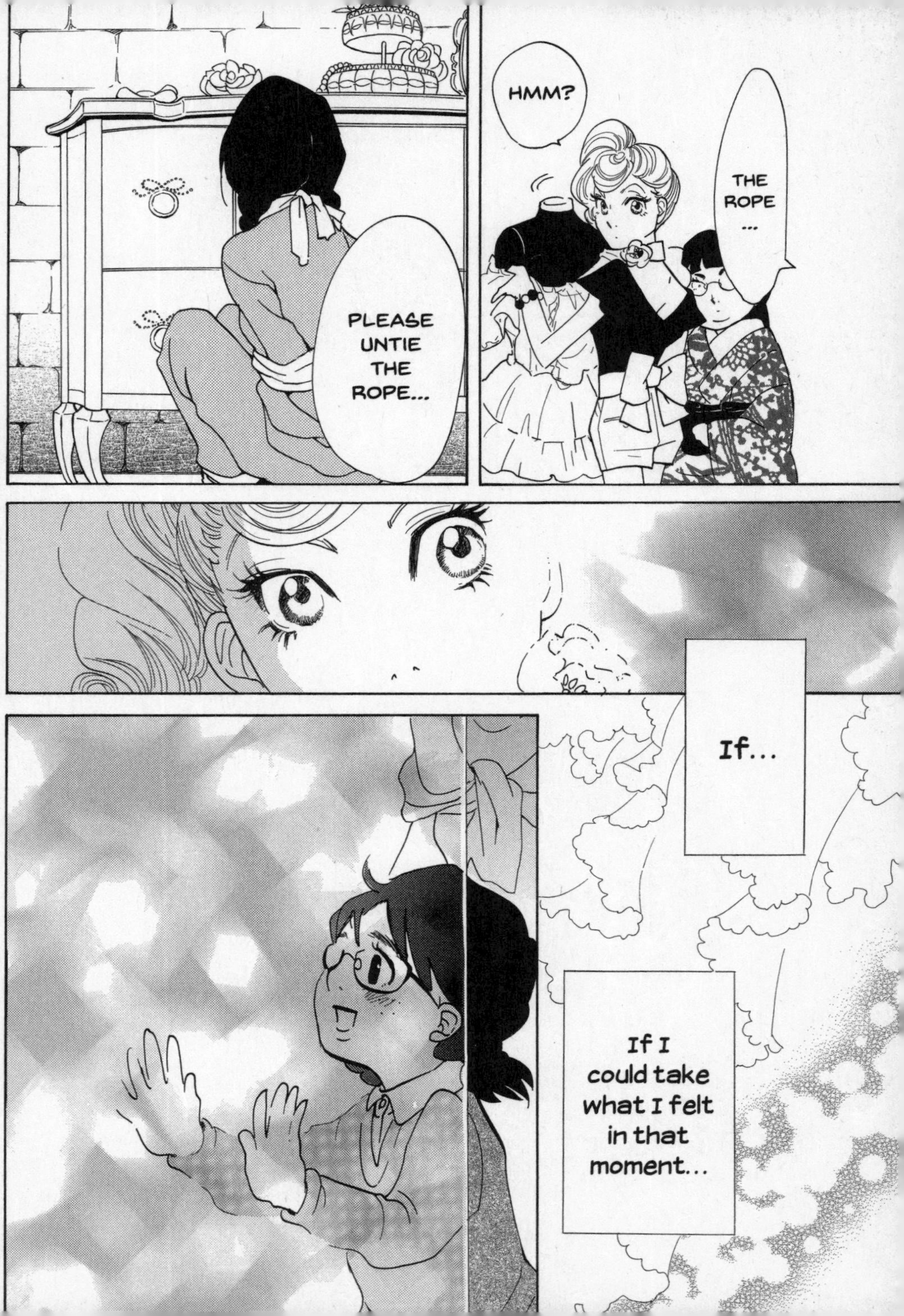
THE ROPE...
HMM?
PLEASE UNTIE THE ROPE...
If...
If I could take what I felt in that moment...

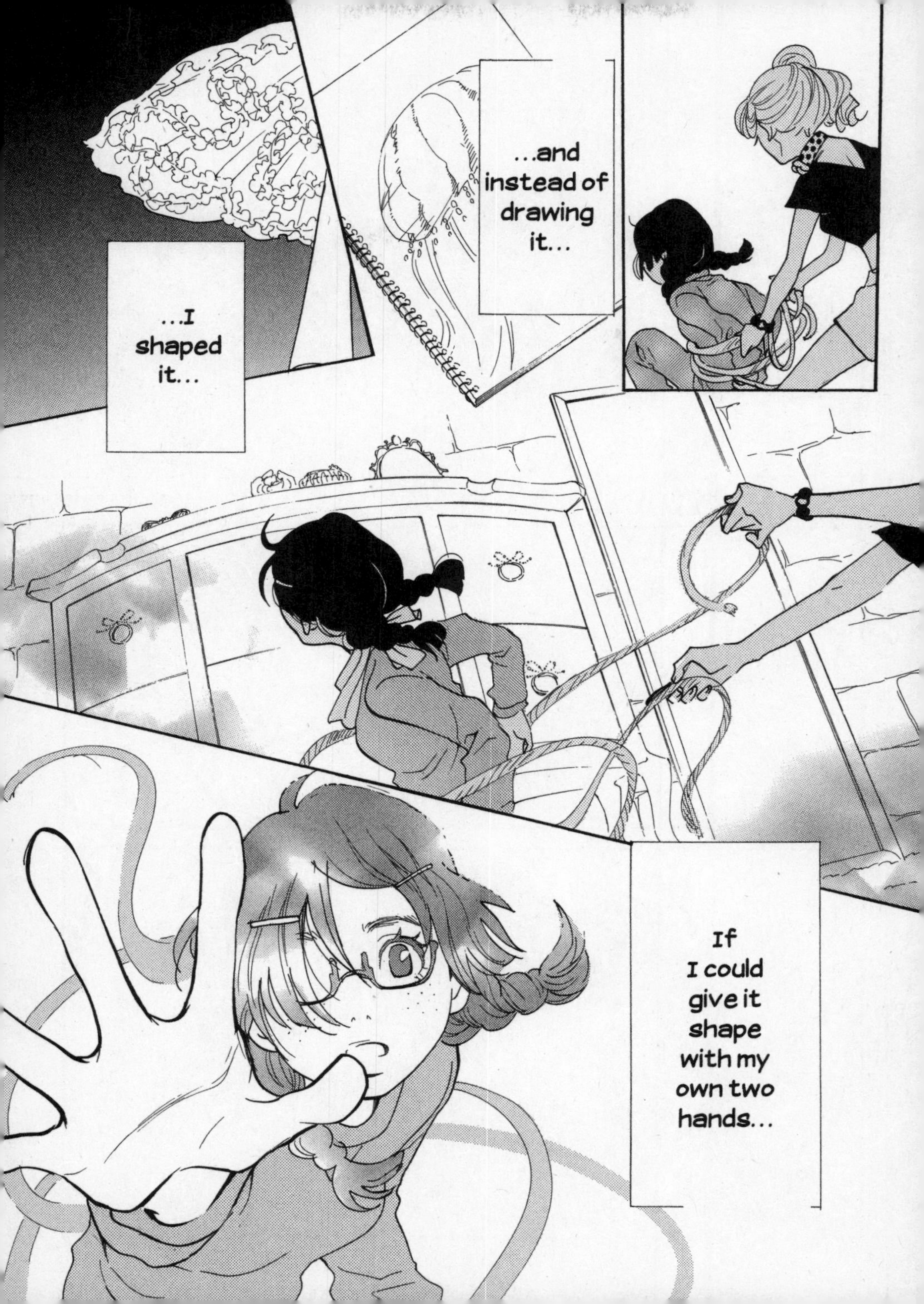
...and instead of drawing it...
...I shaped it...
If I could give it shape with my own two hands...

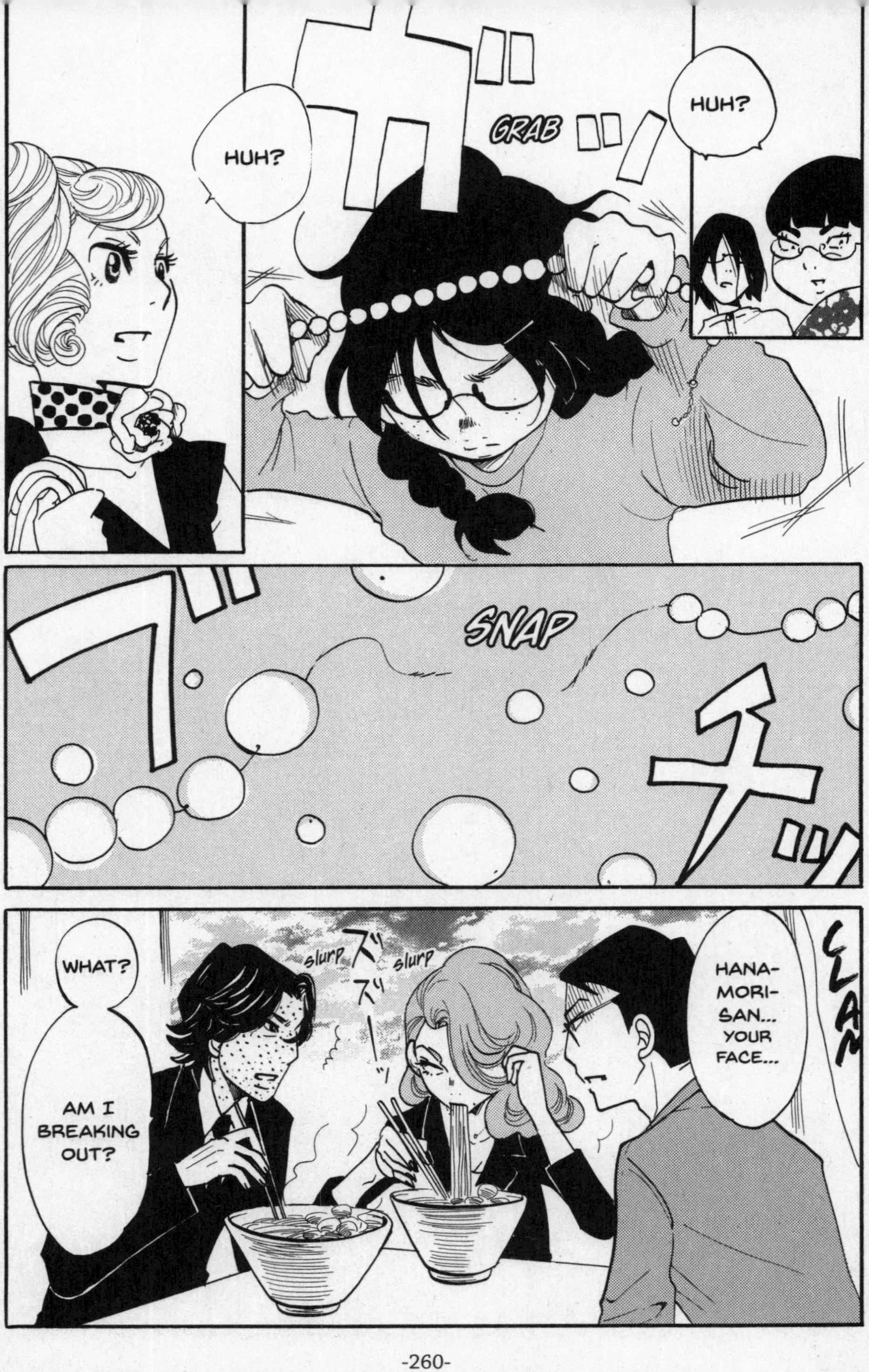
HUH?
GRAB
HUH?
SNAP
SLAM
HANA-MORI-SAN... YOUR FACE...
slurp
slurp
WHAT?
AM I BREAKING OUT?

Episode 21
ER

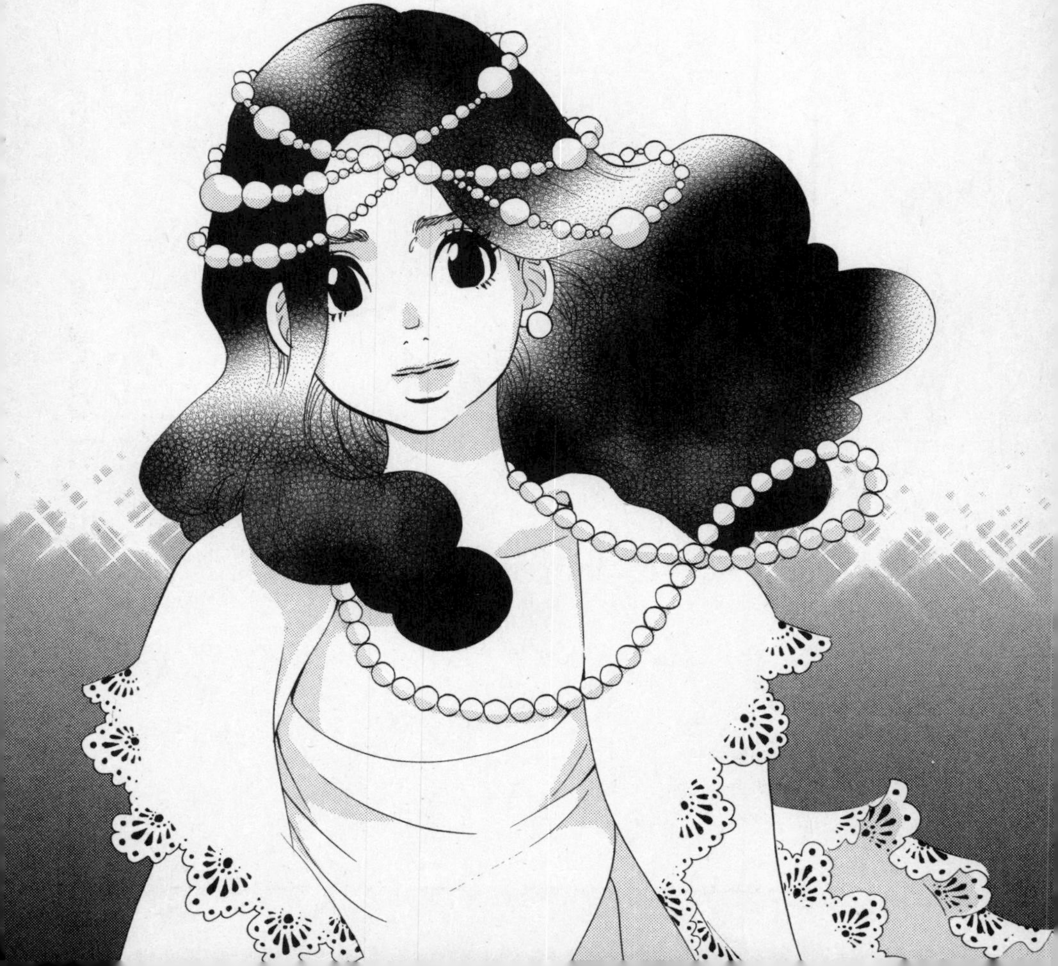

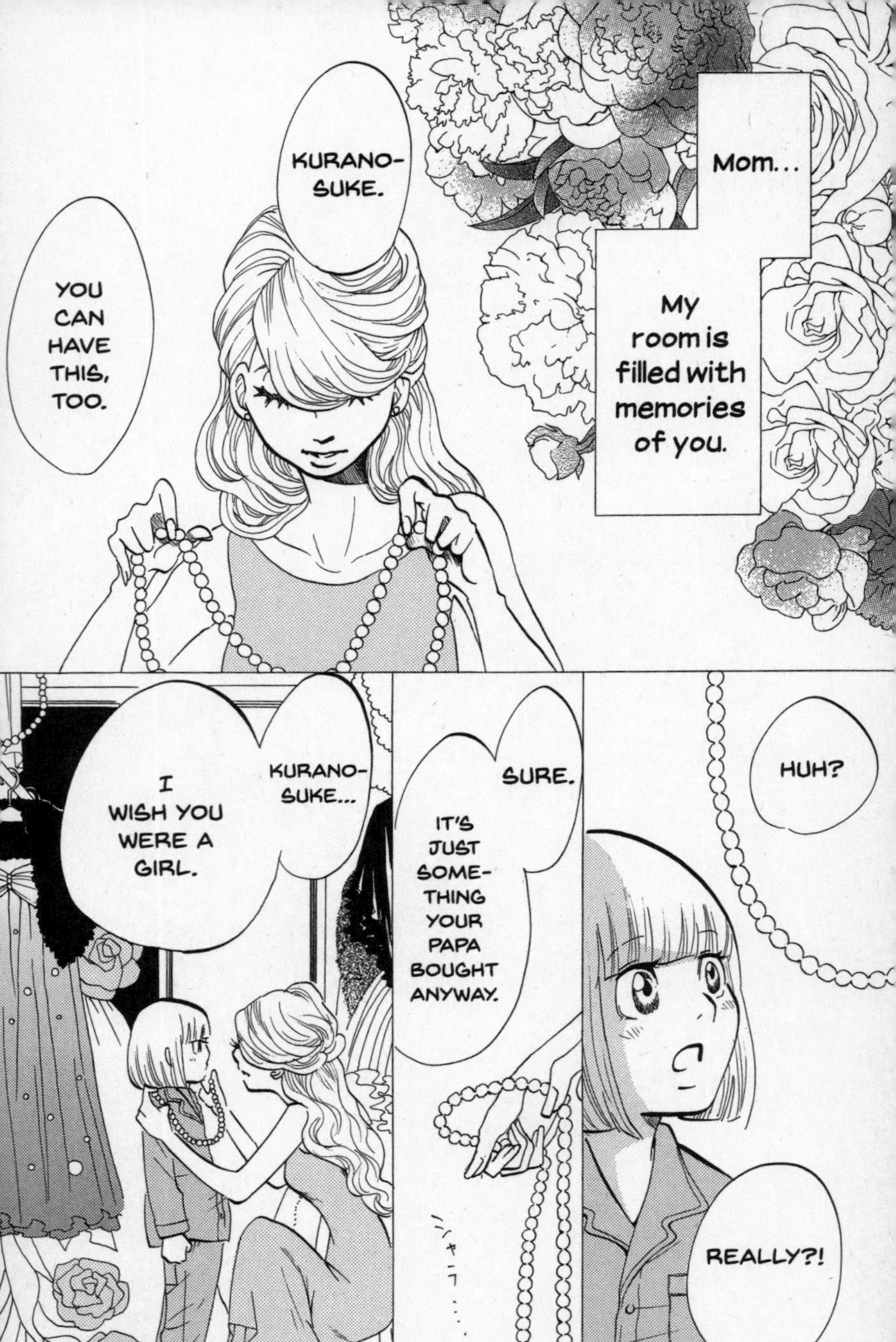
Mom...
My room is filled with memories of you.
KURANO-SUKE.
YOU CAN HAVE THIS, TOO.
HUH?
REALLY?!
SURE.
IT'S JUST SOMETHING YOUR PAPA BOUGHT ANYWAY.
KURANO-SUKE...
I WISH YOU WERE A GIRL.

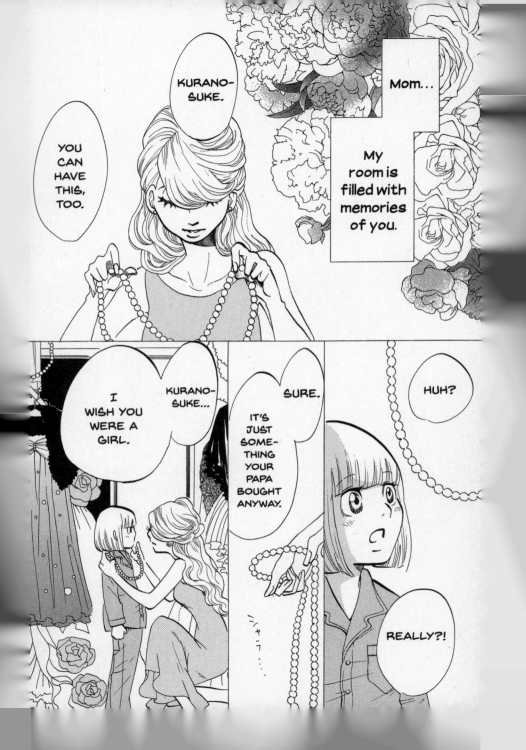

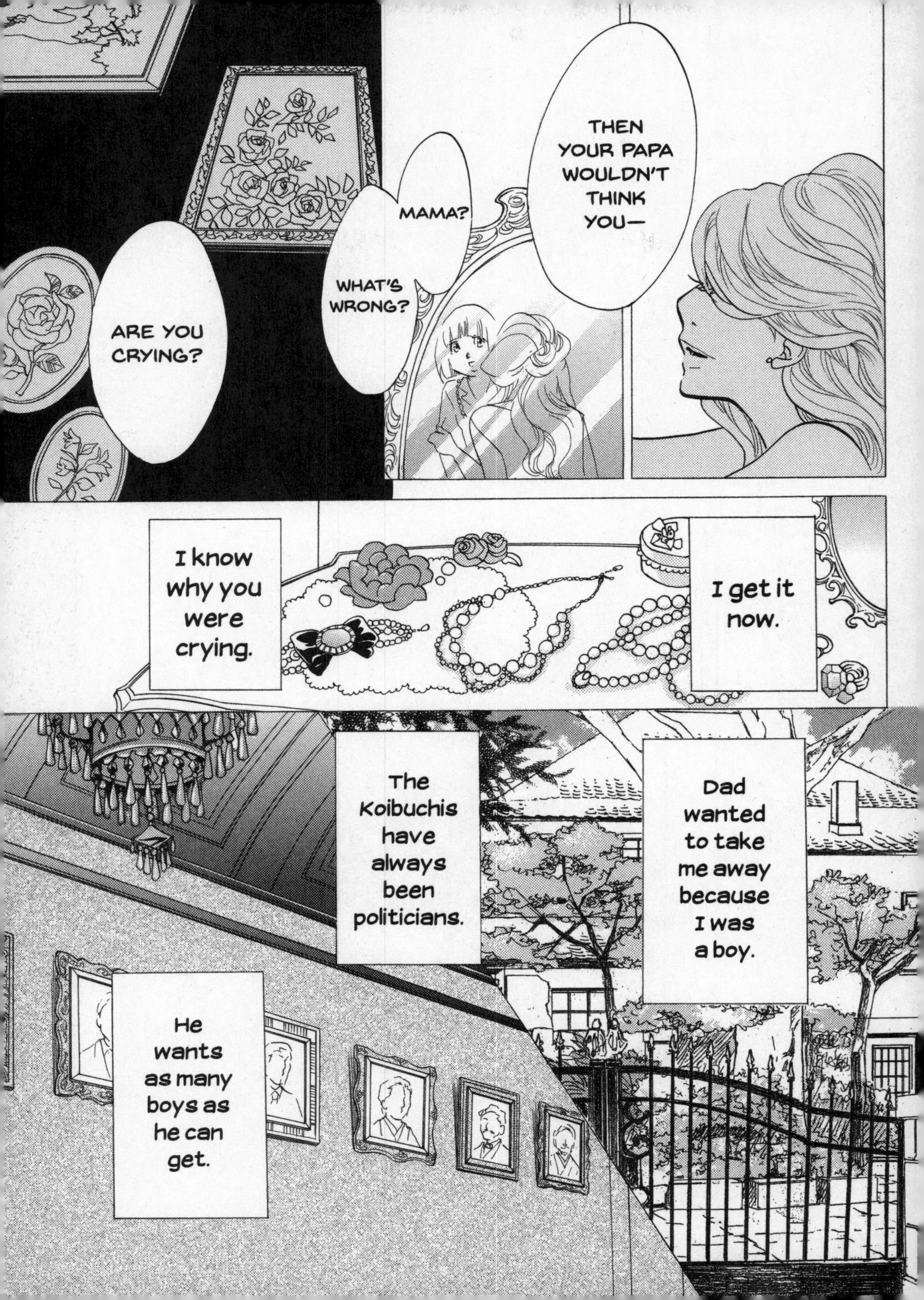
THEN YOUR PAPA WOULDN'T THINK YOU—
MAMA?
WHAT'S WRONG?
ARE YOU CRYING?
I get it now.
I know why you were crying.
Dad wanted to take me away because I was a boy.
The Koibuchis have always been politicians.
He wants as many boys as he can get.

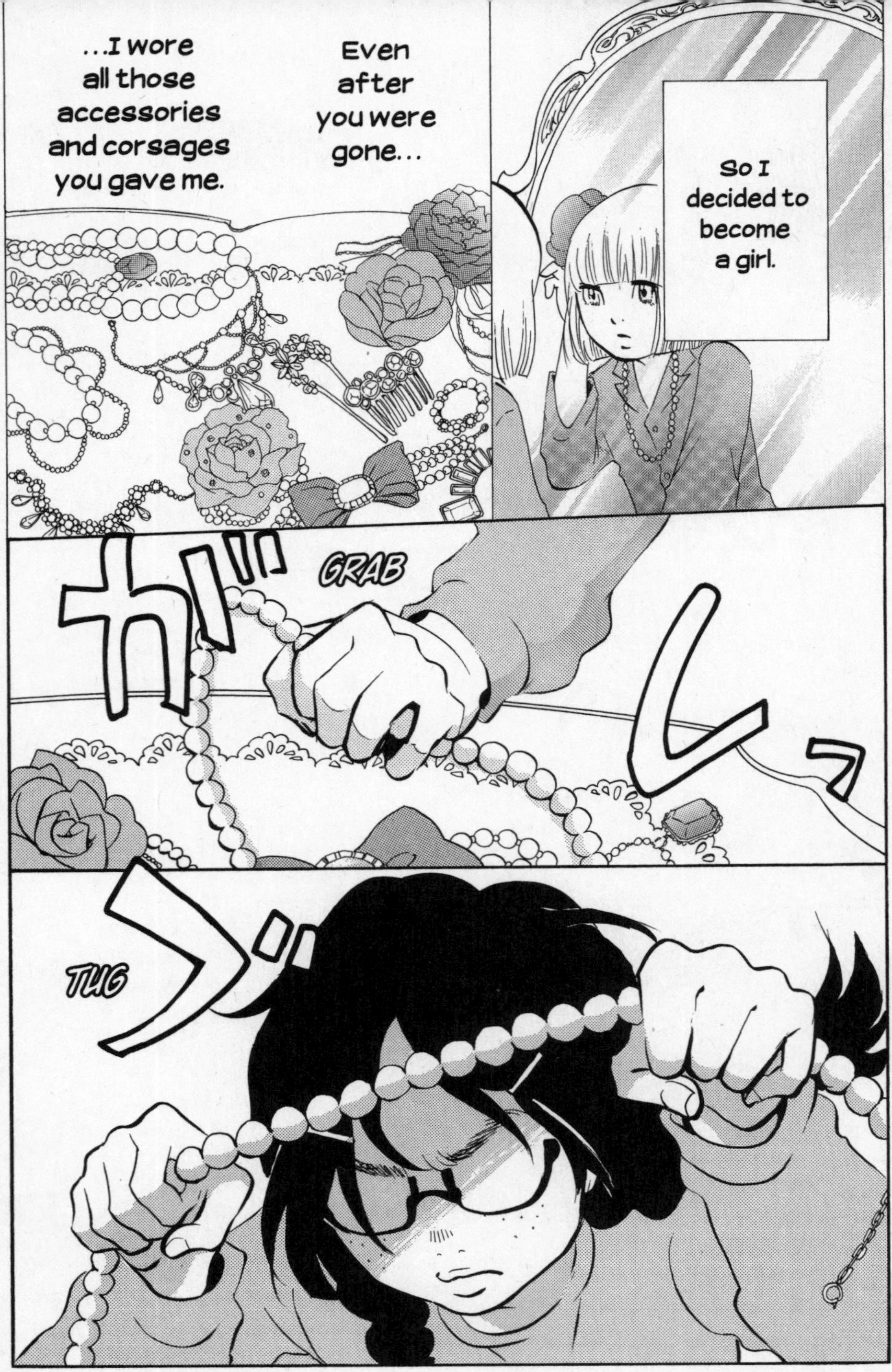
So I decided to become a girl.
Even after you were gone...
...I wore all those accessories and corsages you gave me.
がしっ
GRAB
ぐ
TUG

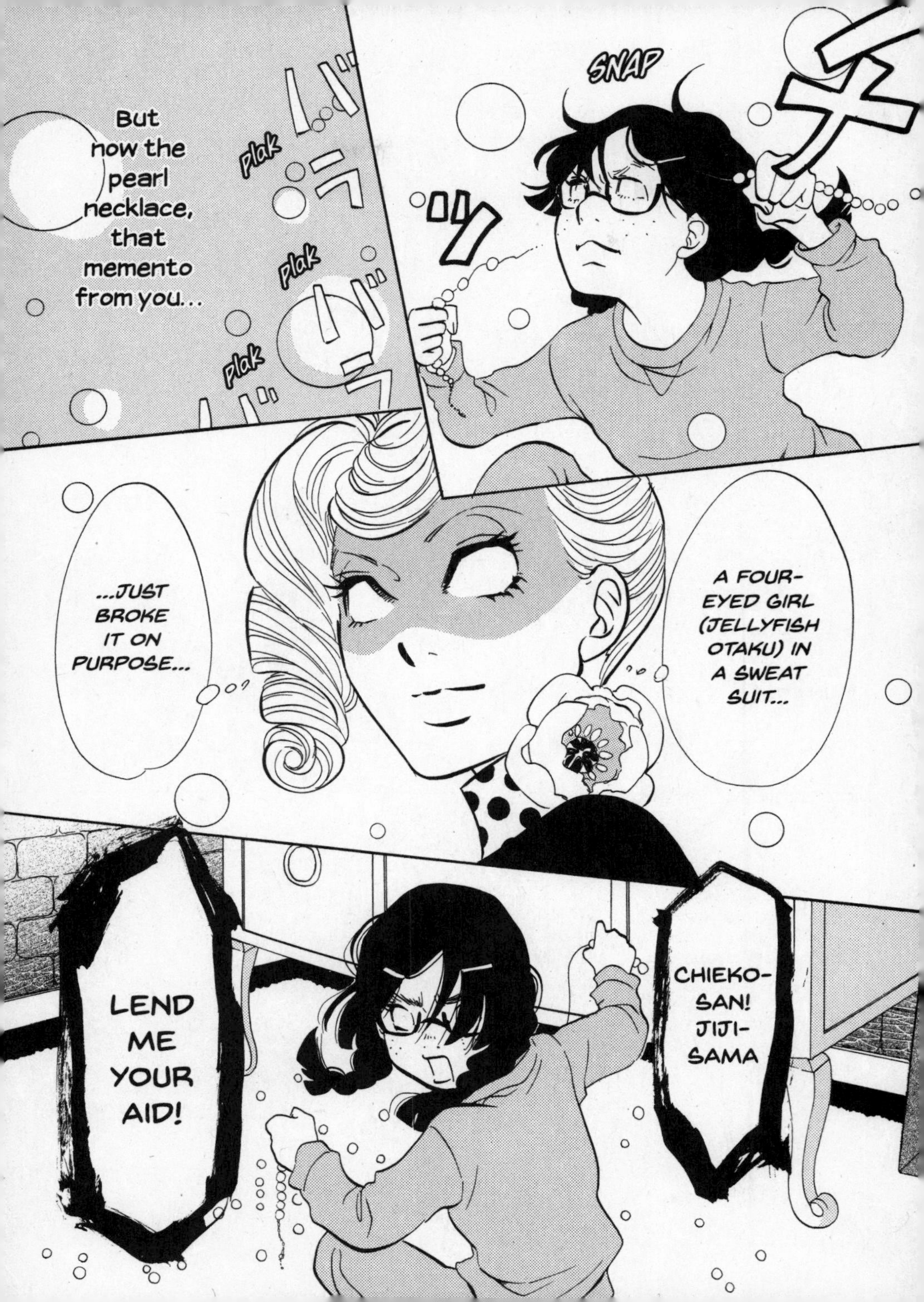
SNAP
But now the pearl necklace, that memento from you...
plak
plak
plak
A FOUR-EYED GIRL (JELLYFISH OTAKU) IN A SWEAT SUIT...
...JUST BROKE IT ON PURPOSE...
CHIEKO-SAN! JIJI-SAMA
LEND ME YOUR AID!

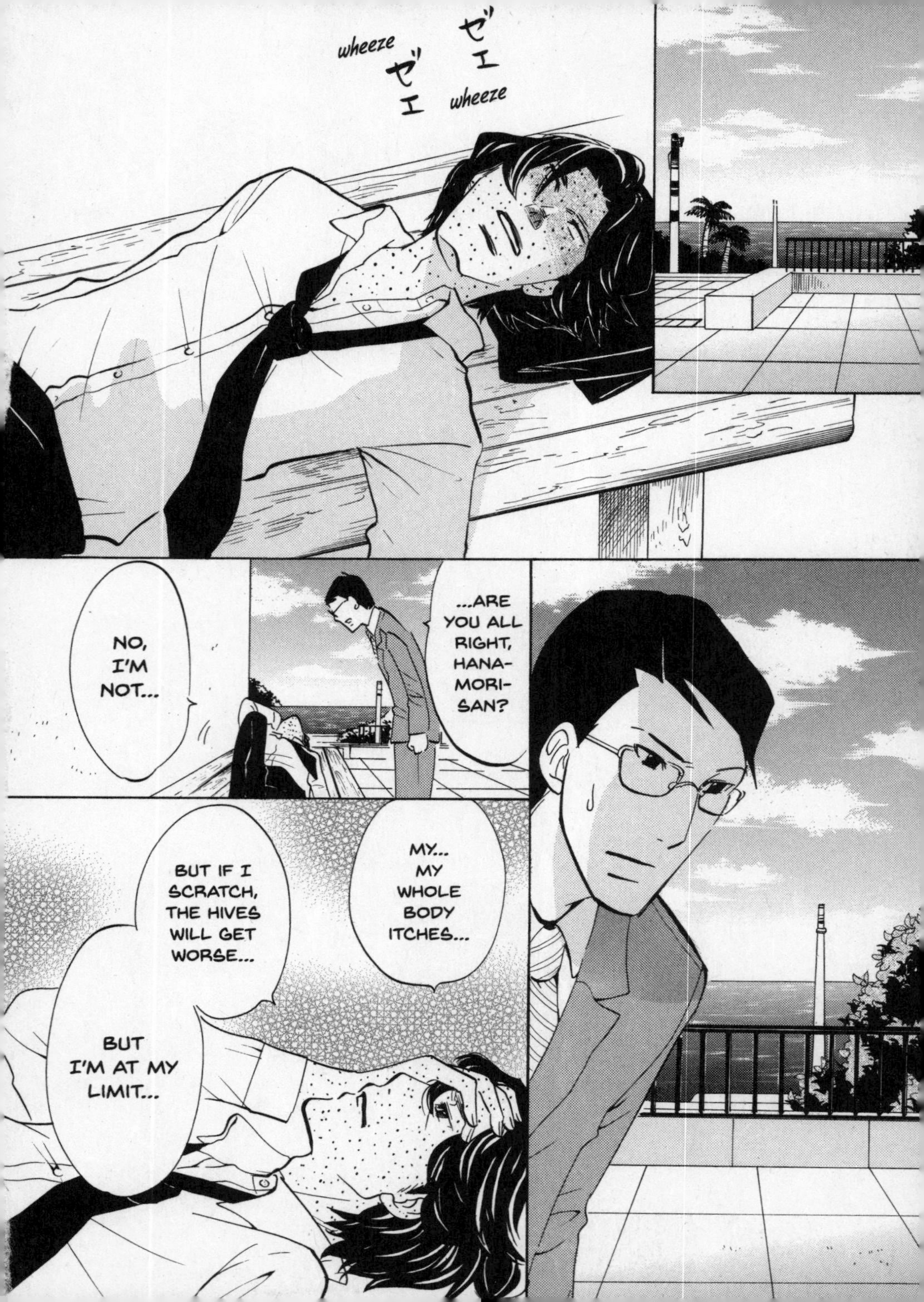
ゼエ wheeze
ゼエ wheeze
...ARE YOU ALL RIGHT, HANA-MORI-SAN?
NO, I'M NOT...
MY... MY WHOLE BODY ITCHES...
BUT IF I SCRATCH, THE HIVES WILL GET WORSE...
BUT I'M AT MY LIMIT...

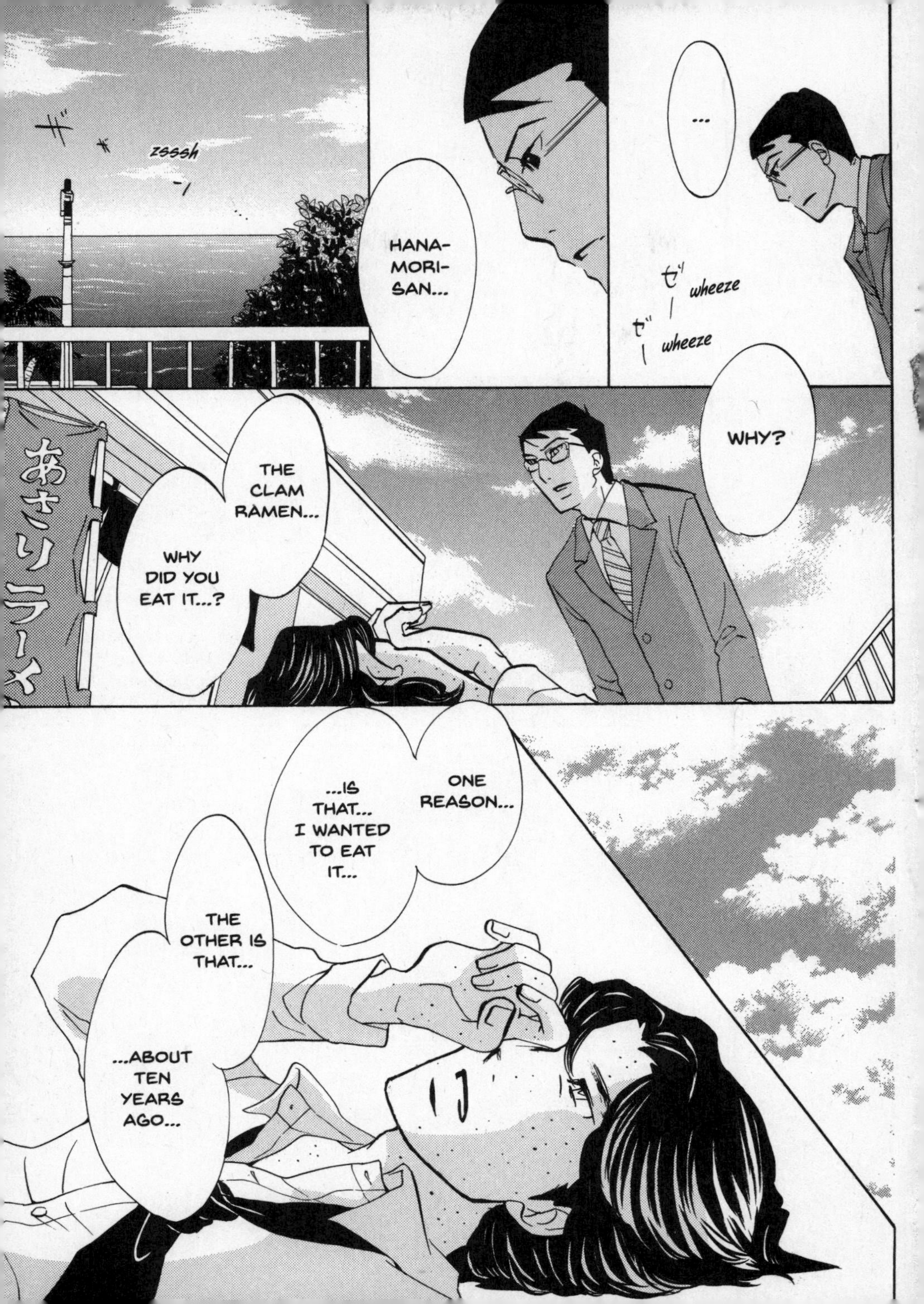
...
wheeze
wheeze
HANA-MORI-SAN...
zsssh
WHY?
THE CLAM RAMEN...
WHY DID YOU EAT IT...?
あさりラー
ONE REASON...
...IS THAT... I WANTED TO EAT IT...
THE OTHER IS THAT...
...ABOUT TEN YEARS AGO...

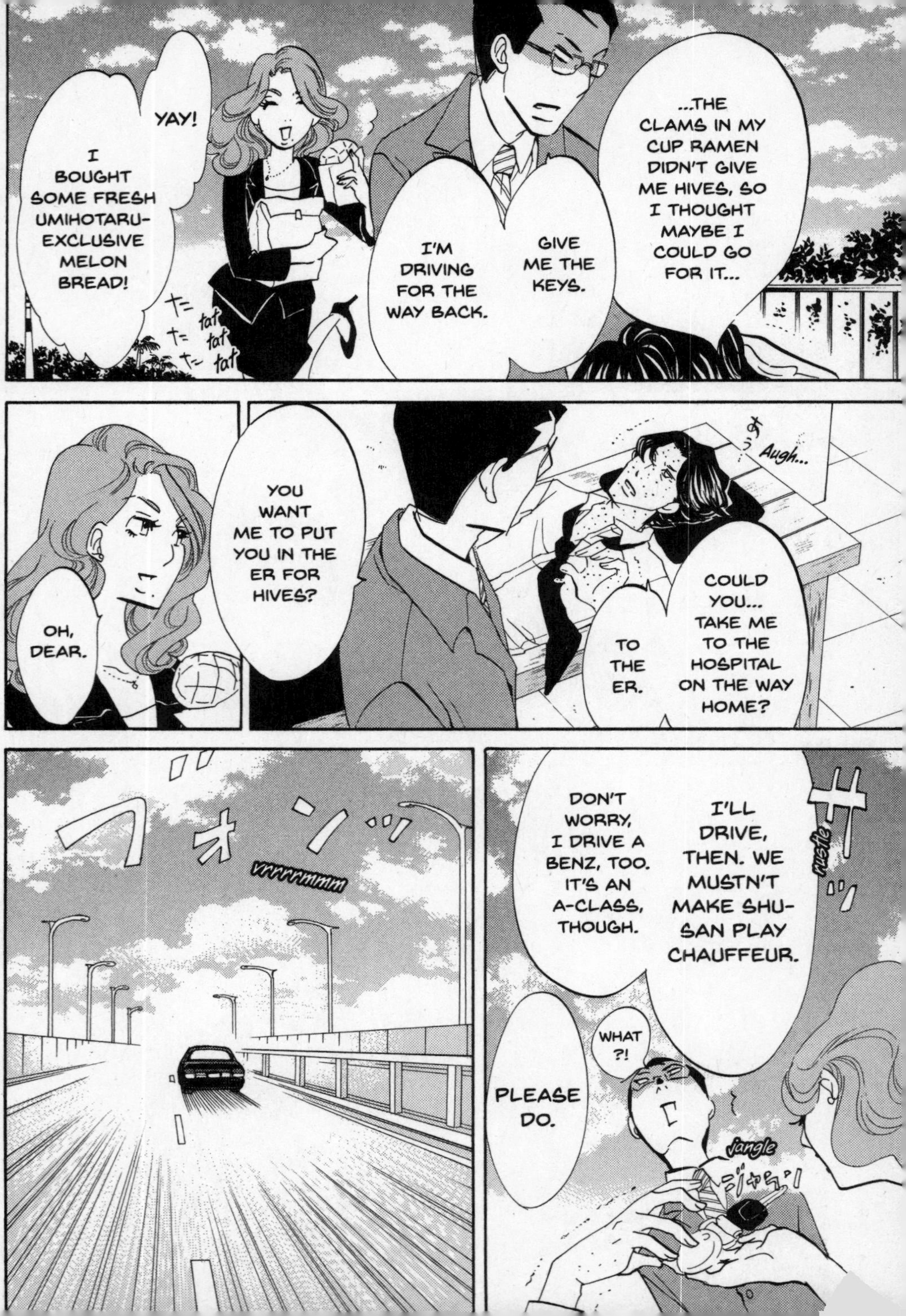
...THE CLAMS IN MY CUP RAMEN DIDN'T GIVE ME HIVES, SO I THOUGHT MAYBE I COULD GO FOR IT...
GIVE ME THE KEYS.
I'M DRIVING FOR THE WAY BACK.
YAY!
I BOUGHT SOME FRESH UMIHOTARU-EXCLUSIVE MELON BREAD!
tat tat tat
Augh...
COULD YOU... TAKE ME TO THE HOSPITAL ON THE WAY HOME?
TO THE ER.
YOU WANT ME TO PUT YOU IN THE ER FOR HIVES?
OH, DEAR.
rustle
I'LL DRIVE, THEN. WE MUSTN'T MAKE SHU-SAN PLAY CHAUFFEUR.
DON'T WORRY, I DRIVE A BENZ, TOO. IT'S AN A-CLASS, THOUGH.
WHAT?!
PLEASE DO.
jangle
vrrrrmmm

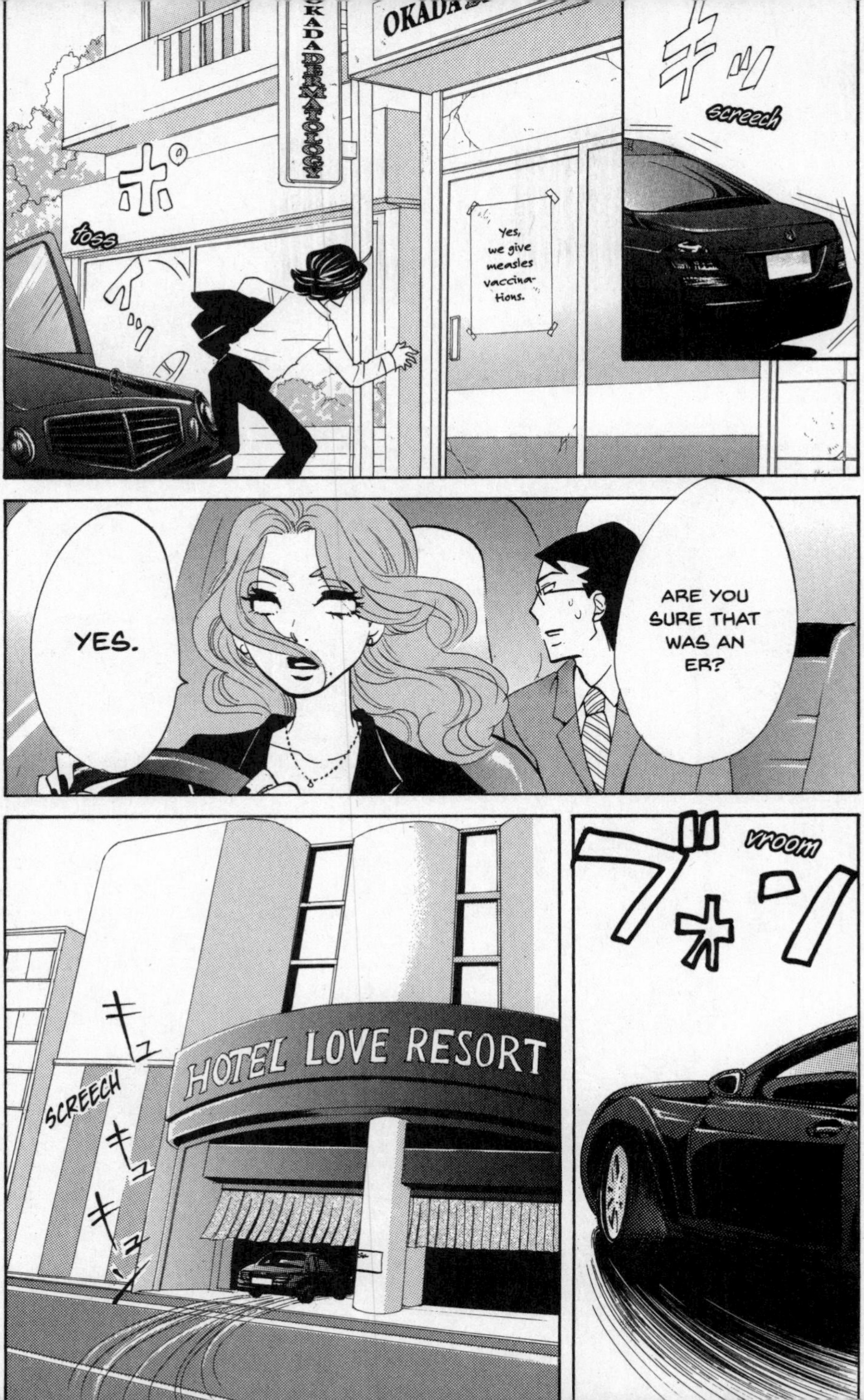
screech
OKADA
OKADA DERMATOLOGY
toss
Yes, we give measles vaccinations.
ARE YOU SURE THAT WAS AN ER?
YES.
vroom
HOTEL LOVE RESORT
SCREECH

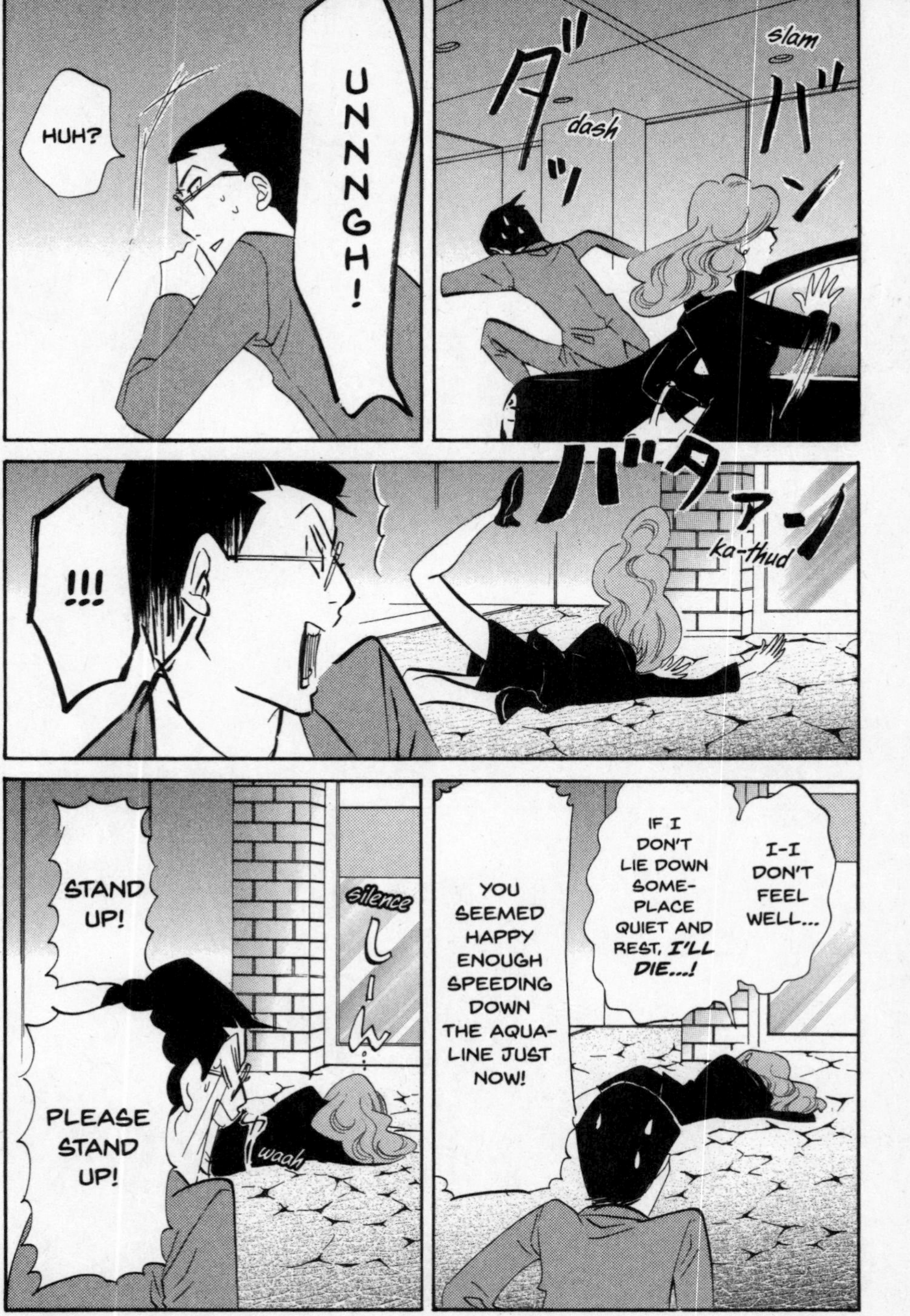
slam
dash
UNNNNGH!
HUH?
ka-thud
!!!
I-I DON'T FEEL WELL...
IF I DON'T LIE DOWN SOME-PLACE QUIET AND REST, *I'LL DIE...!*
YOU SEEMED HAPPY ENOUGH SPEEDING DOWN THE AQUA-LINE JUST NOW!
silence
STAND UP!
PLEASE STAND UP!
waah

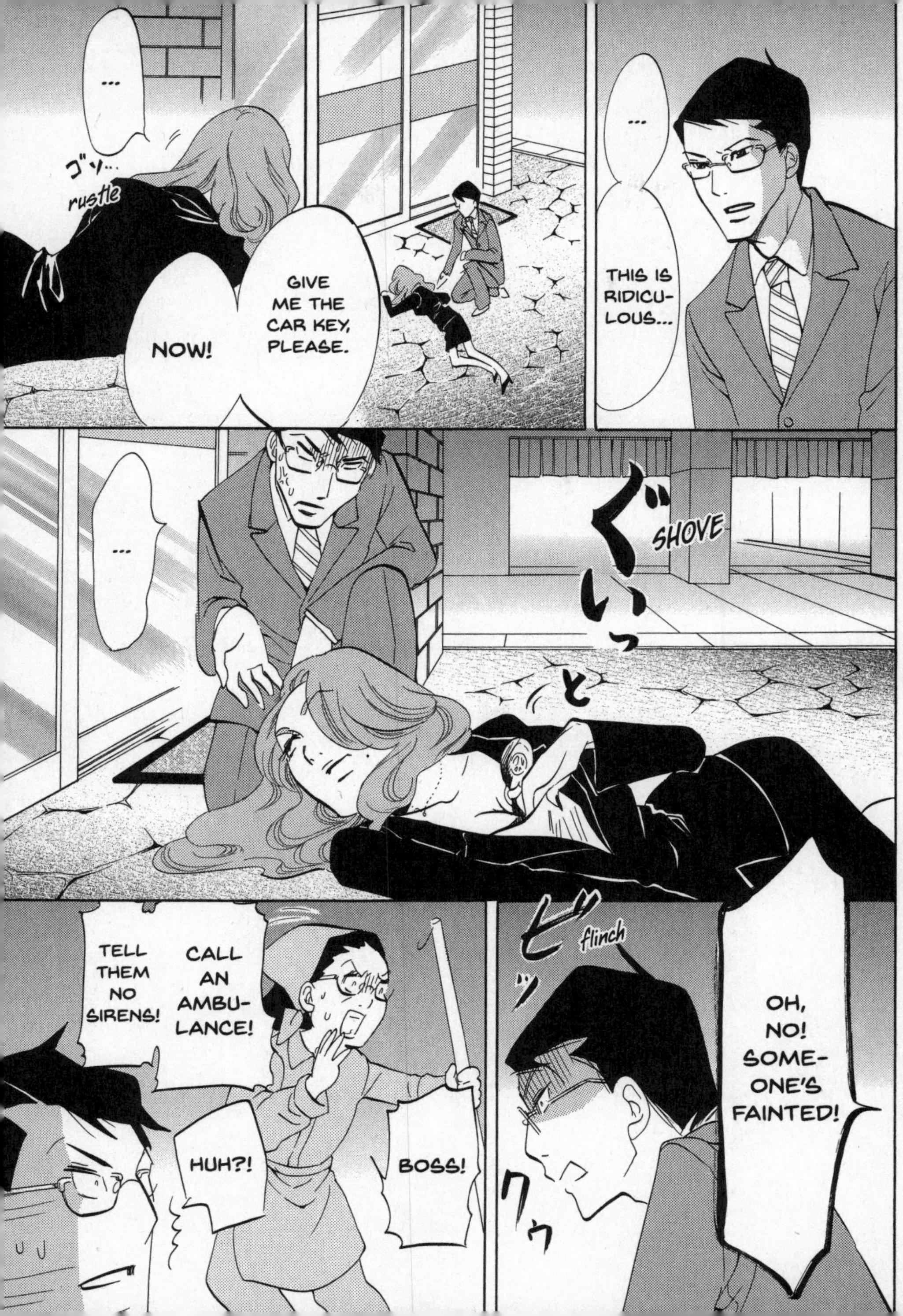
...
THIS IS RIDICULOUS...
...
ゴソ...
rustle
GIVE ME THE CAR KEY, PLEASE.
NOW!
ぐいっ
SHOVE
と
...
ビッ
flinch
OH, NO! SOMEONE'S FAINTED!
クゥ
CALL AN AMBULANCE!
TELL THEM NO SIRENS!
BOSS!
HUH?!

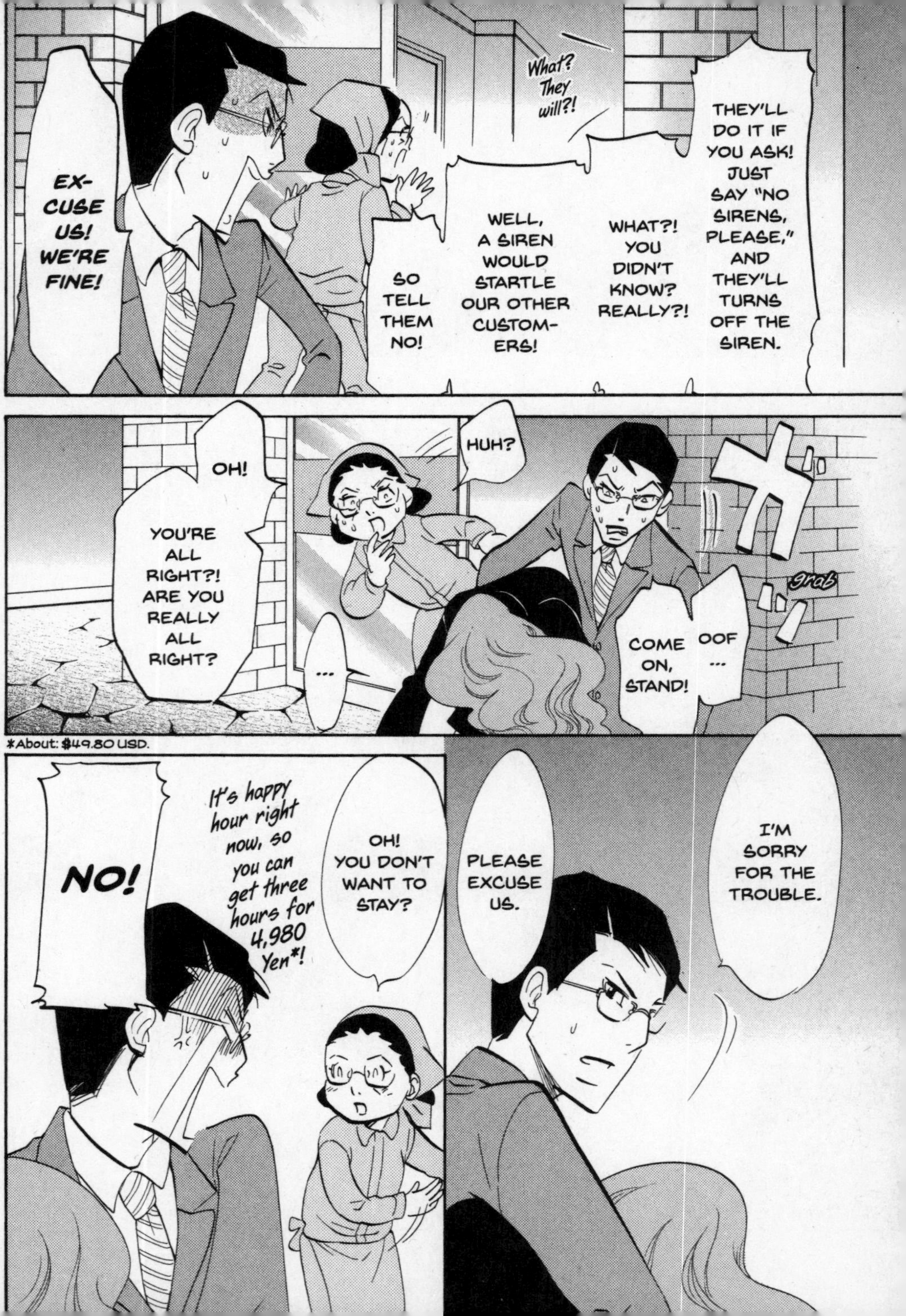
THEY'LL DO IT IF YOU ASK! JUST SAY "NO SIRENS, PLEASE," AND THEY'LL TURNS OFF THE SIREN.
What? They will?!
WHAT?! YOU DIDN'T KNOW? REALLY?!
WELL, A SIREN WOULD STARTLE OUR OTHER CUSTOM-ERS!
SO TELL THEM NO!
EX-CUSE US! WE'RE FINE!
grab
OOF ...
COME ON, STAND!
HUH?
...
OH!
YOU'RE ALL RIGHT?! ARE YOU REALLY ALL RIGHT?
I'M SORRY FOR THE TROUBLE.
PLEASE EXCUSE US.
OH! YOU DON'T WANT TO STAY?
It's happy hour right now, so you can get three hours for 4,980 Yen*!
NO!

*About: $49.80 USD.

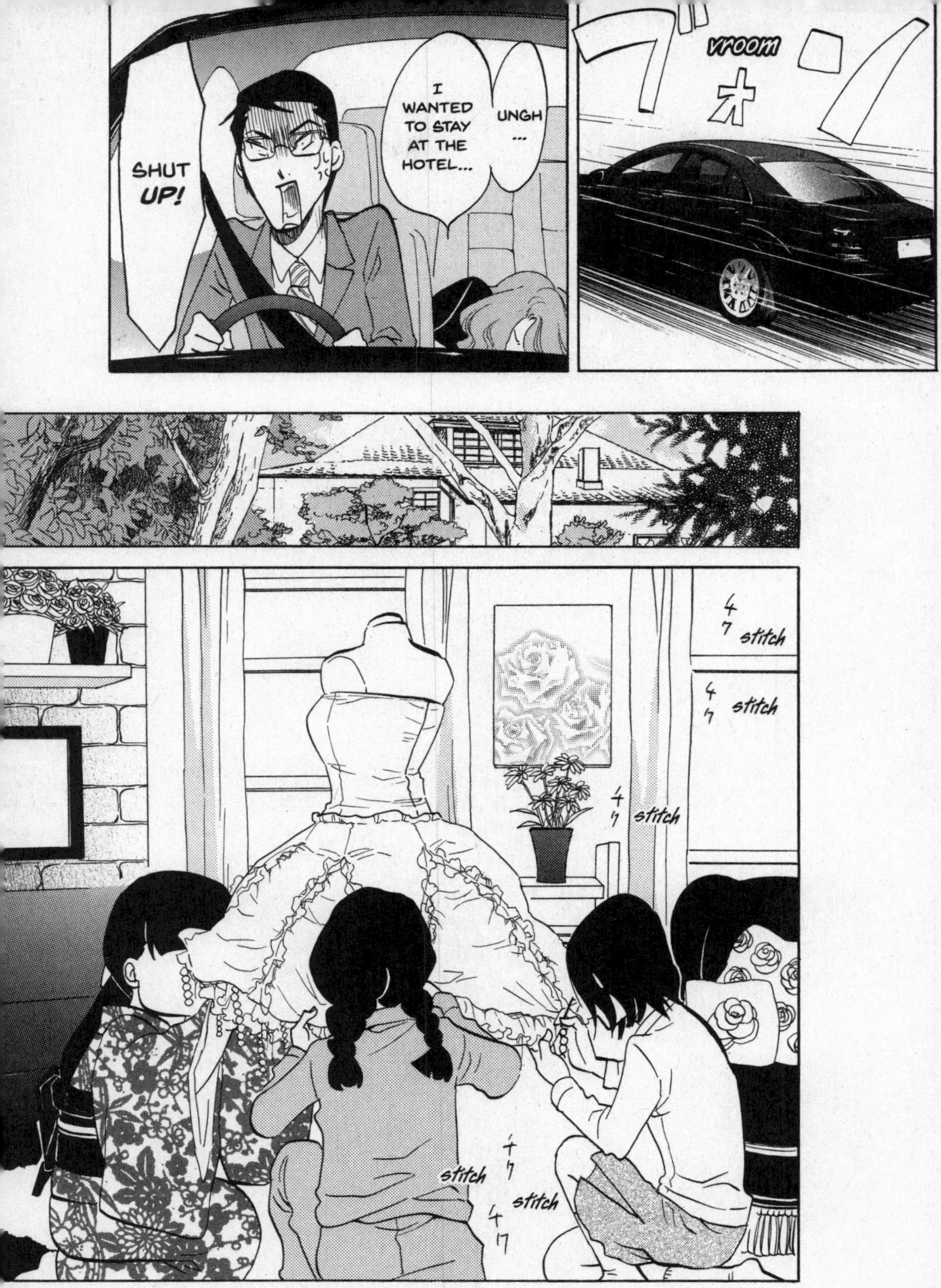
vroom
UNGH ...
I WANTED TO STAY AT THE HOTEL...
SHUT UP!
stitch
stitch
stitch
stitch
stitch

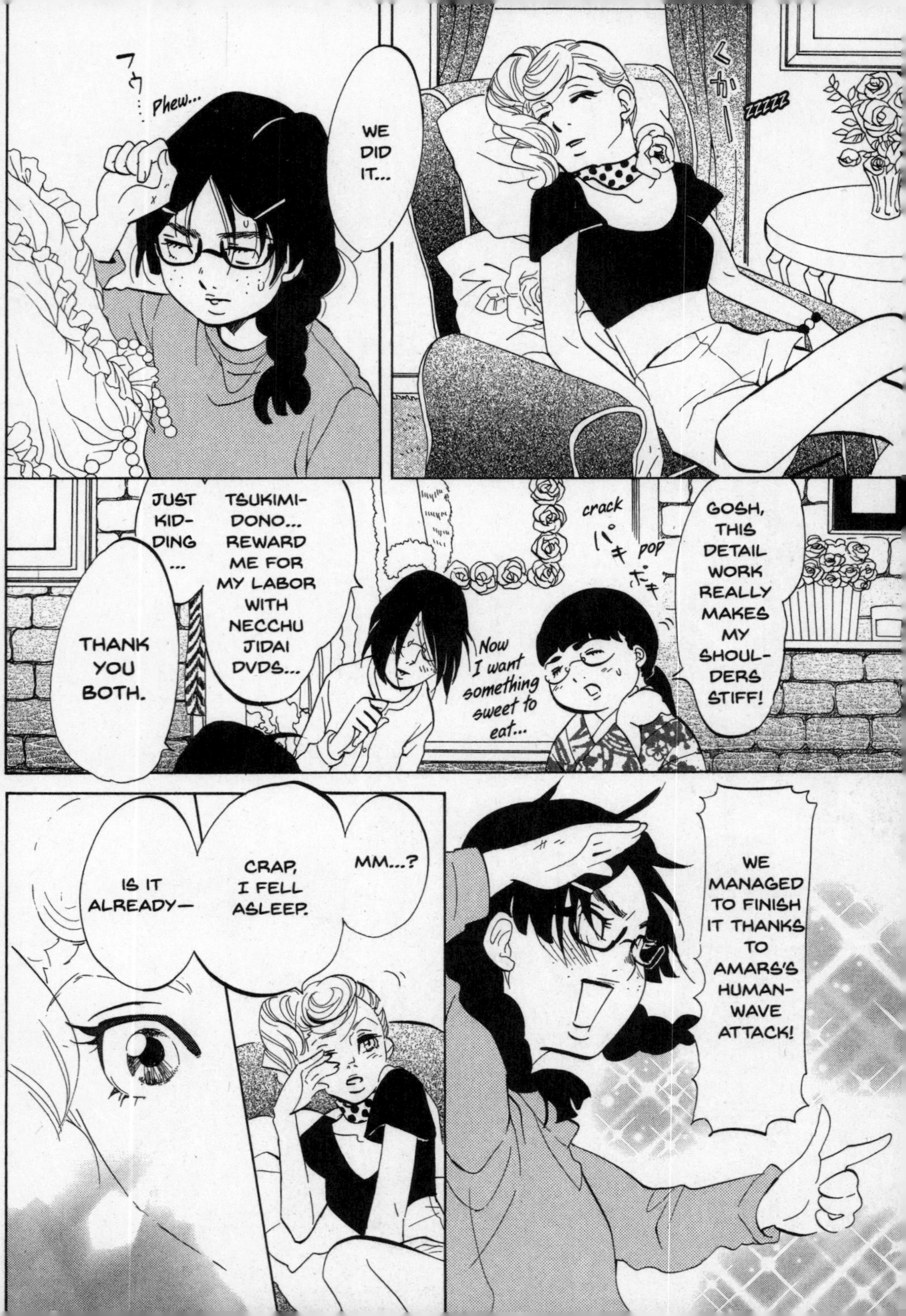
くかー
ZZZZZ
フゥ… Phew...
WE DID IT...
GOSH, THIS DETAIL WORK REALLY MAKES MY SHOULDERS STIFF!
crack パキ
pop ポキ
Now I want something sweet to eat...
TSUKIMI-DONO... REWARD ME FOR MY LABOR WITH NECCHU JIDAI DVDS...
JUST KID-DING...
THANK YOU BOTH.
WE MANAGED TO FINISH IT THANKS TO AMARS'S HUMAN-WAVE ATTACK!
MM...?
CRAP, I FELL ASLEEP.
IS IT ALREADY—

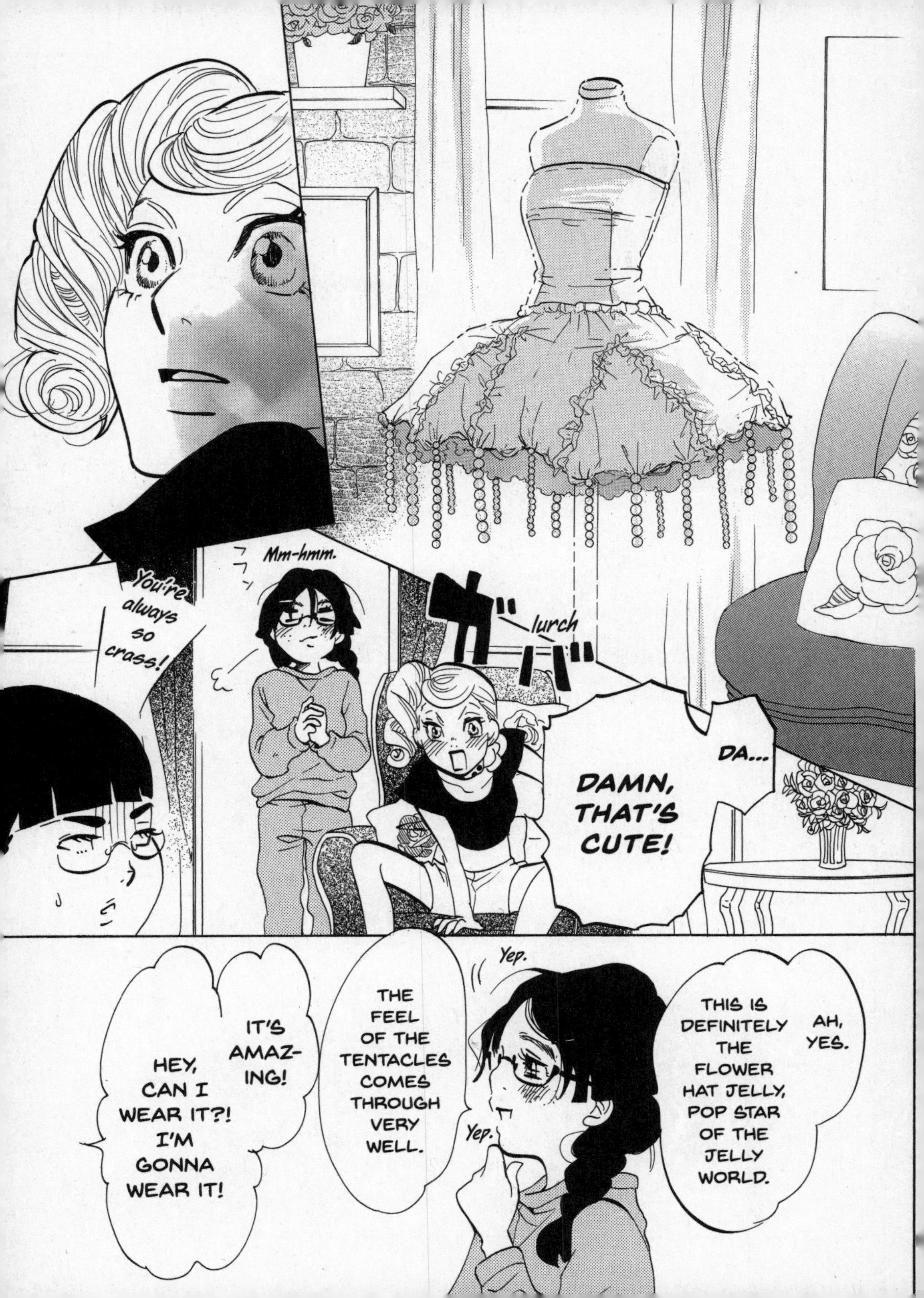
DA...
DAMN, THAT'S CUTE!
lurch
Mm-hmm.
You're always so crass!
AH, YES.
THIS IS DEFINITELY THE FLOWER HAT JELLY, POP STAR OF THE JELLY WORLD.
Yep.
Yep.
THE FEEL OF THE TENTACLES COMES THROUGH VERY WELL.
IT'S AMAZ-ING!
HEY, CAN I WEAR IT?! I'M GONNA WEAR IT!

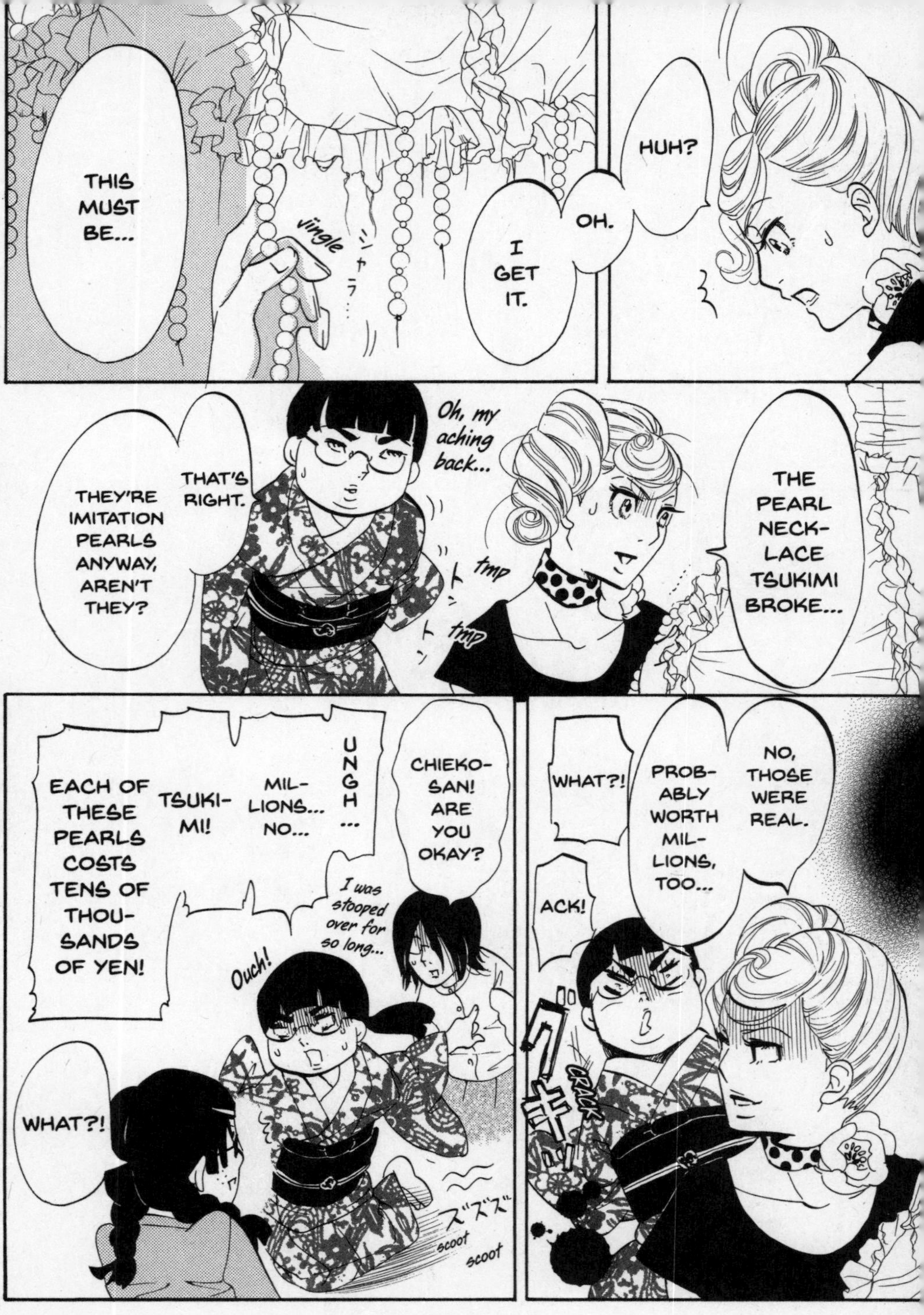
HUH?
OH.
I GET IT.
THIS MUST BE...
jingle
THE PEARL NECKLACE TSUKIMI BROKE...
Oh, my aching back...
tmp
tmp
THAT'S RIGHT.
THEY'RE IMITATION PEARLS ANYWAY, AREN'T THEY?
NO, THOSE WERE REAL.
PROBABLY WORTH MILLIONS, TOO...
WHAT?!
ACK!
CRACK
CHIEKO-SAN! ARE YOU OKAY?
UNGH...
MILLIONS... NO...
TSUKIMI!
EACH OF THESE PEARLS COSTS TENS OF THOUSANDS OF YEN!
I was stooped over for so long...
Ouch!
WHAT?!
scoot scoot

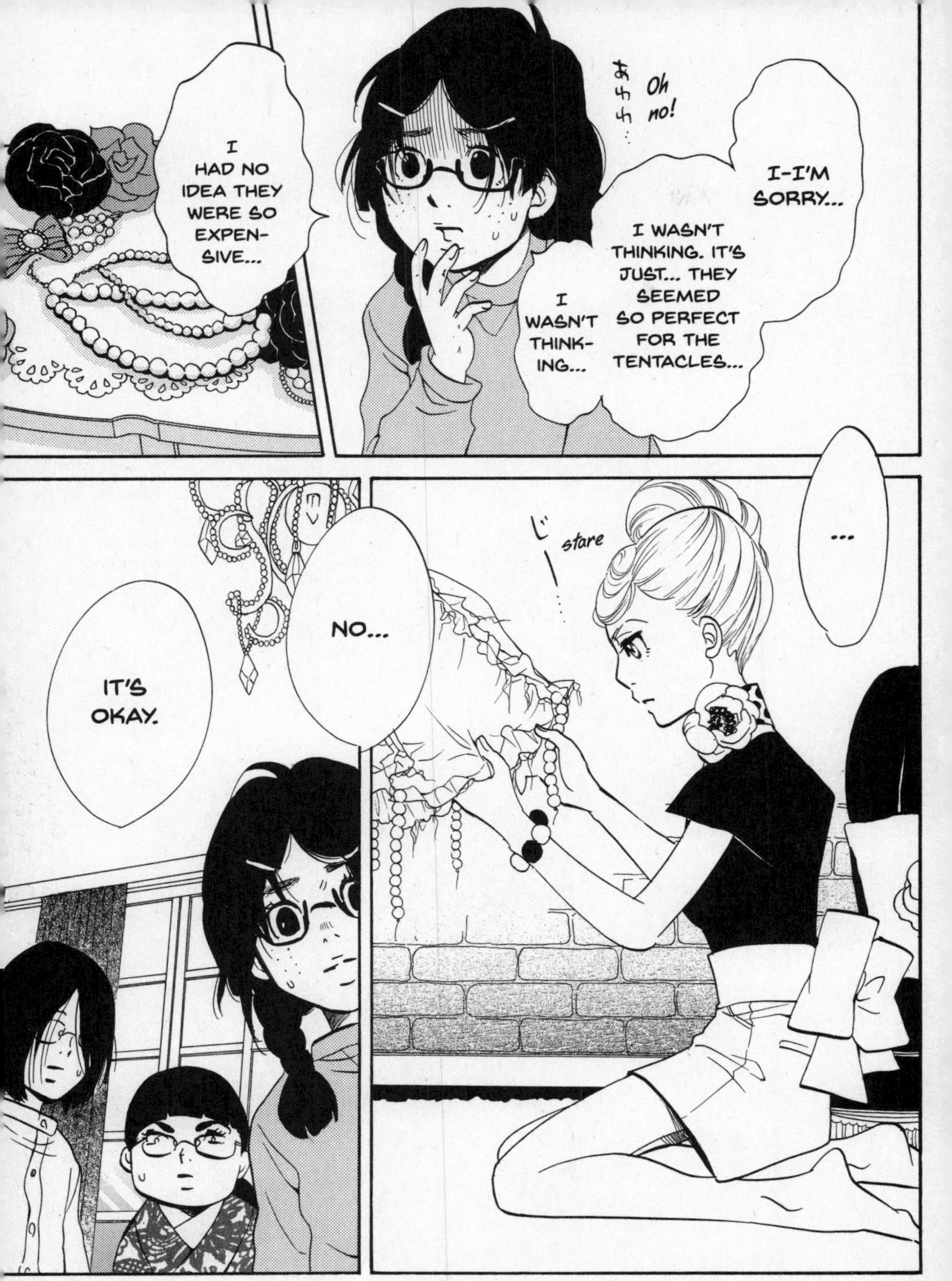
あわわ…
Oh no!
I-I'M SORRY...
I WASN'T THINKING. IT'S JUST... THEY SEEMED SO PERFECT FOR THE TENTACLES...
I WASN'T THINKING...
I HAD NO IDEA THEY WERE SO EXPENSIVE...
じー…
stare
...
NO...
IT'S OKAY.

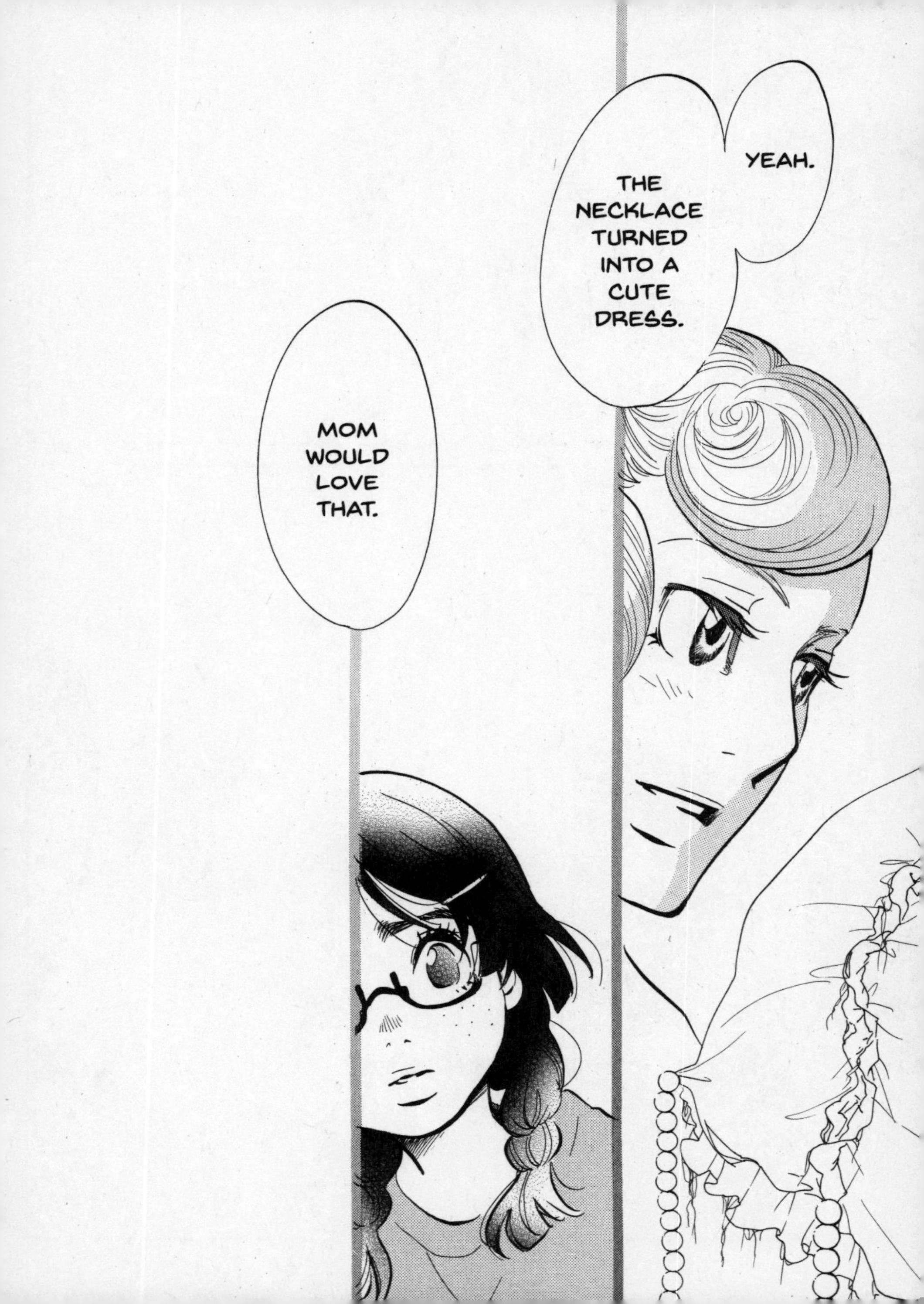
YEAH. THE NECKLACE TURNED INTO A CUTE DRESS.
MOM WOULD LOVE THAT.

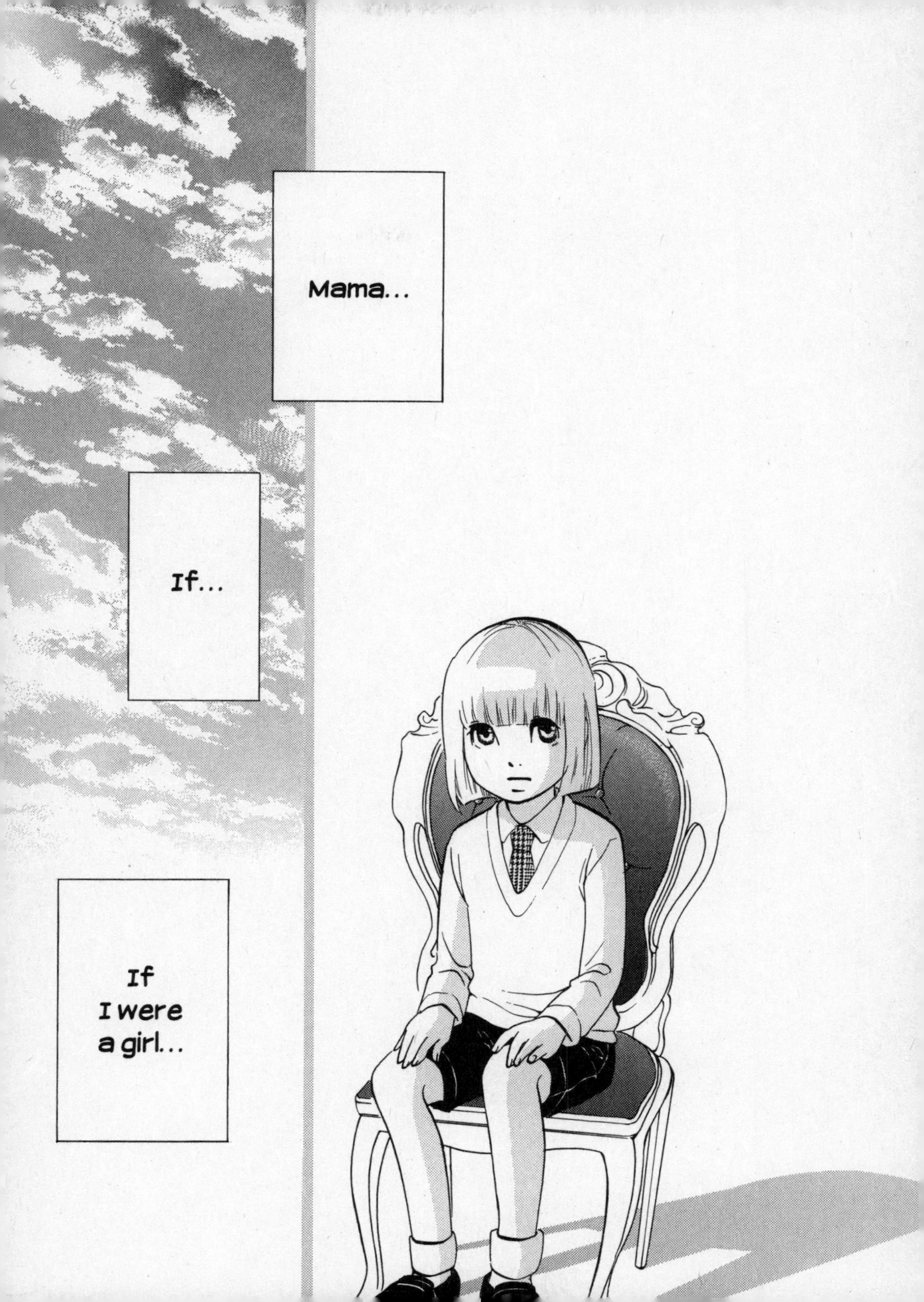
Mama...
If...
If I were a girl...

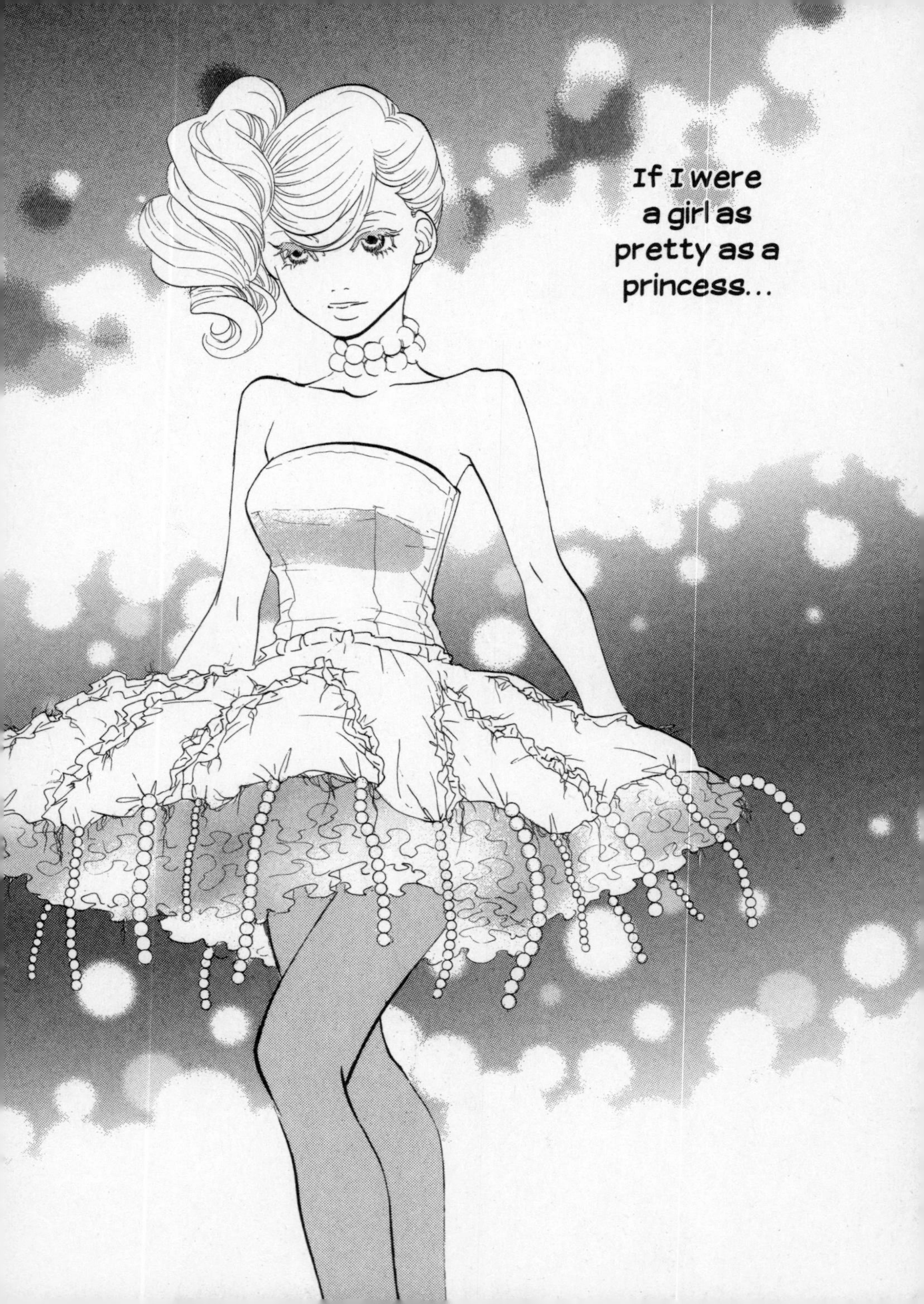
If I were a girl as pretty as a princess...

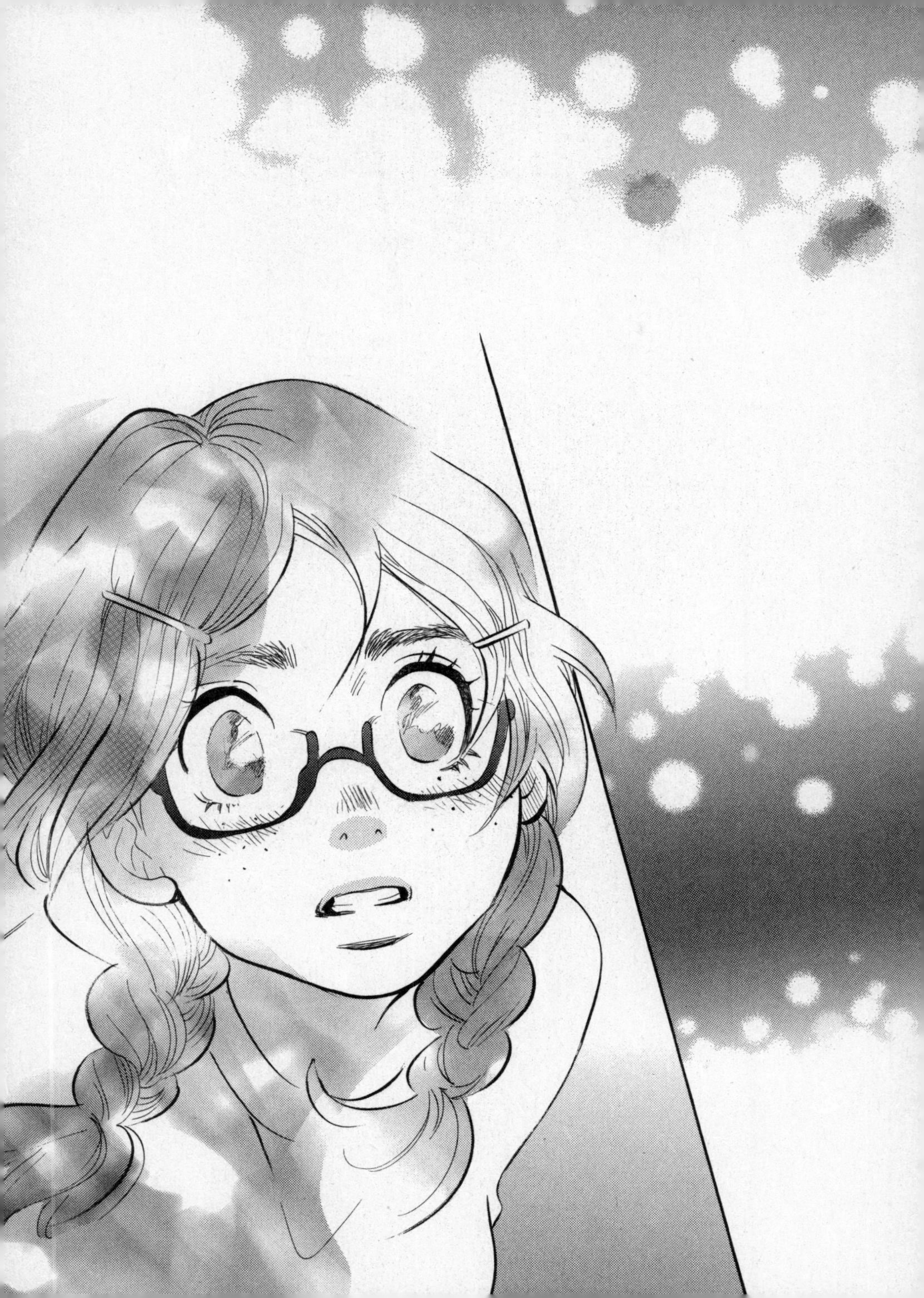

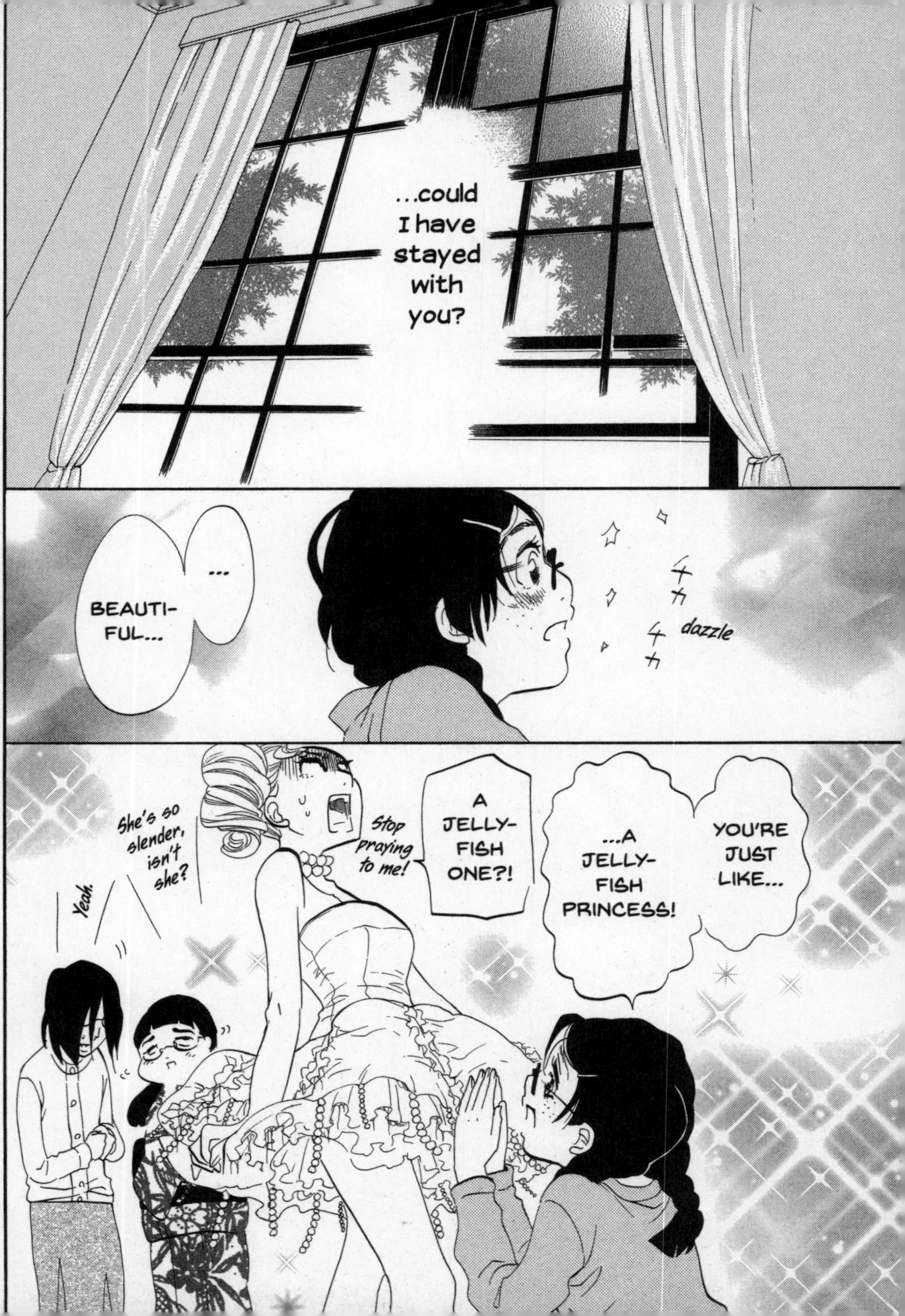
...could I have stayed with you?
... BEAUTIFUL...
dazzle
YOU'RE JUST LIKE...
...A JELLY-FISH PRINCESS!
A JELLY-FISH ONE?!
Stop praying to me!
She's so slender, isn't she?
Yeah.

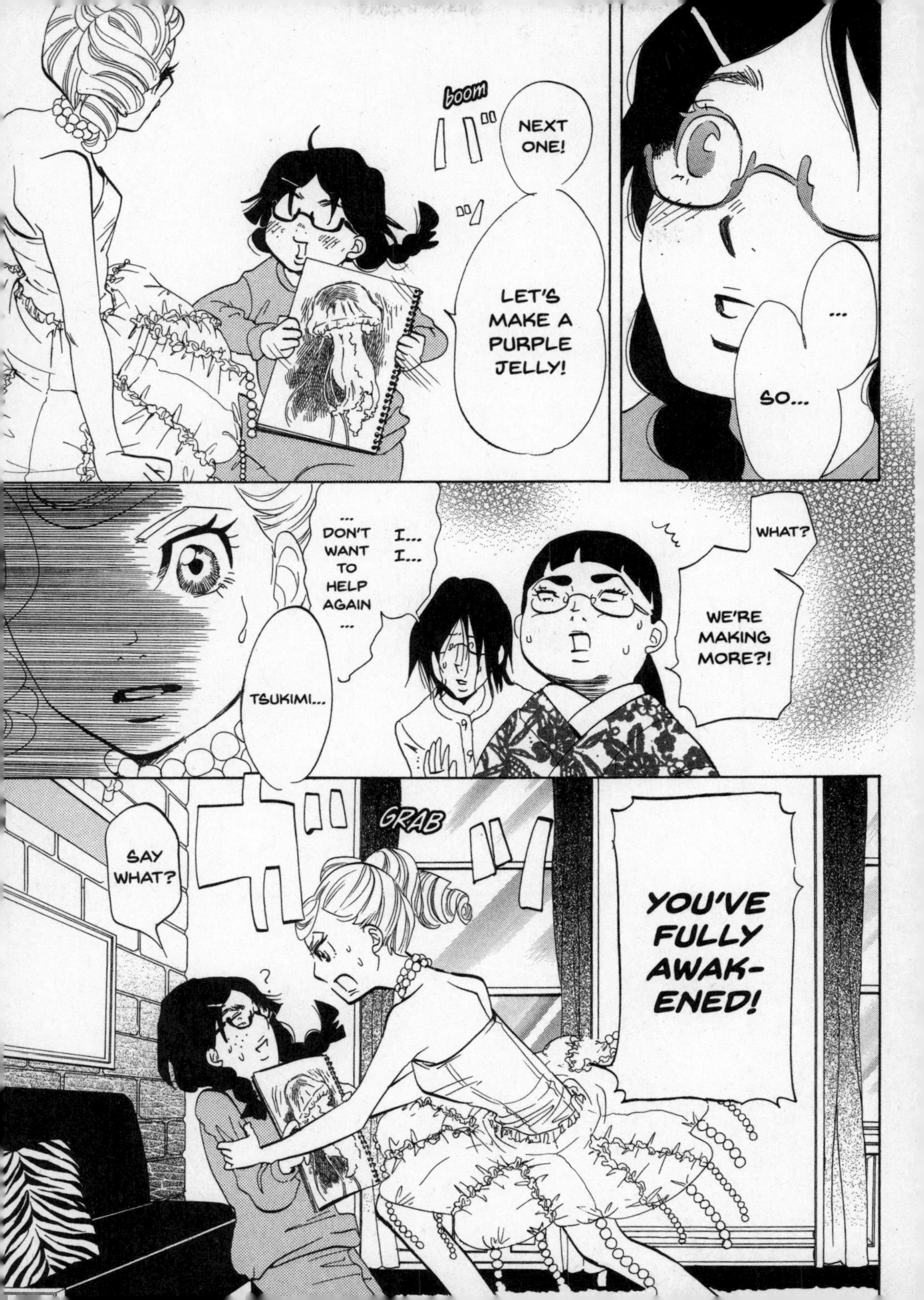
...
SO...
boom
NEXT ONE!
LET'S MAKE A PURPLE JELLY!
WHAT?
WE'RE MAKING MORE?!
I... I...
... DON'T WANT TO HELP AGAIN ...
TSUKIMI...
YOU'VE FULLY AWAK-ENED!
GRAB
SAY WHAT?

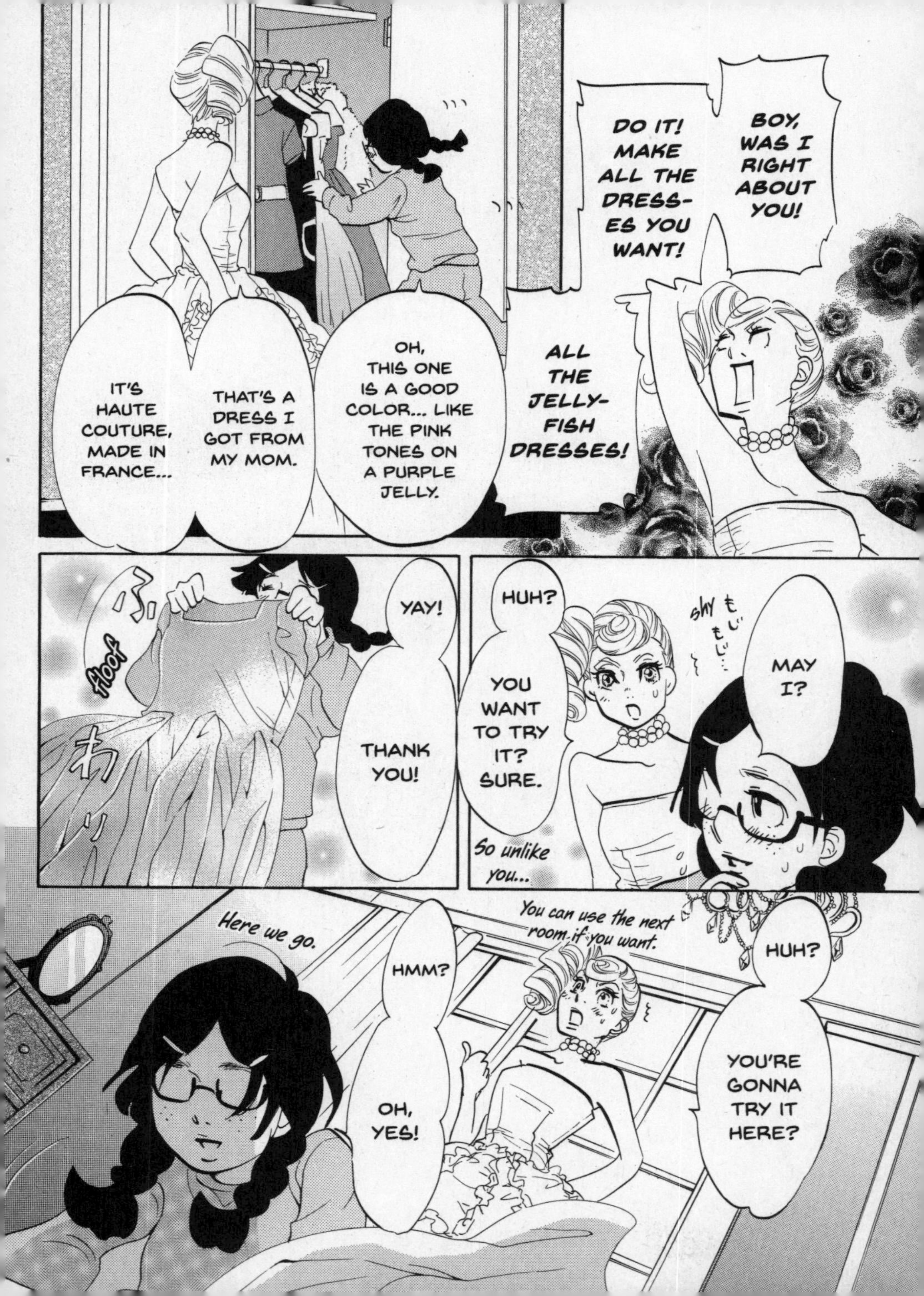
BOY, WAS I RIGHT ABOUT YOU!
DO IT! MAKE ALL THE DRESSES YOU WANT!
ALL THE JELLYFISH DRESSES!
OH, THIS ONE IS A GOOD COLOR... LIKE THE PINK TONES ON A PURPLE JELLY.
THAT'S A DRESS I GOT FROM MY MOM.
IT'S HAUTE COUTURE, MADE IN FRANCE...
shy もじもじ...
MAY I?
HUH?
YOU WANT TO TRY IT? SURE.
So unlike you...
YAY!
THANK YOU!
ふわり
floof
HUH?
YOU'RE GONNA TRY IT HERE?
You can use the next room if you want.
HMM?
OH, YES!
Here we go.

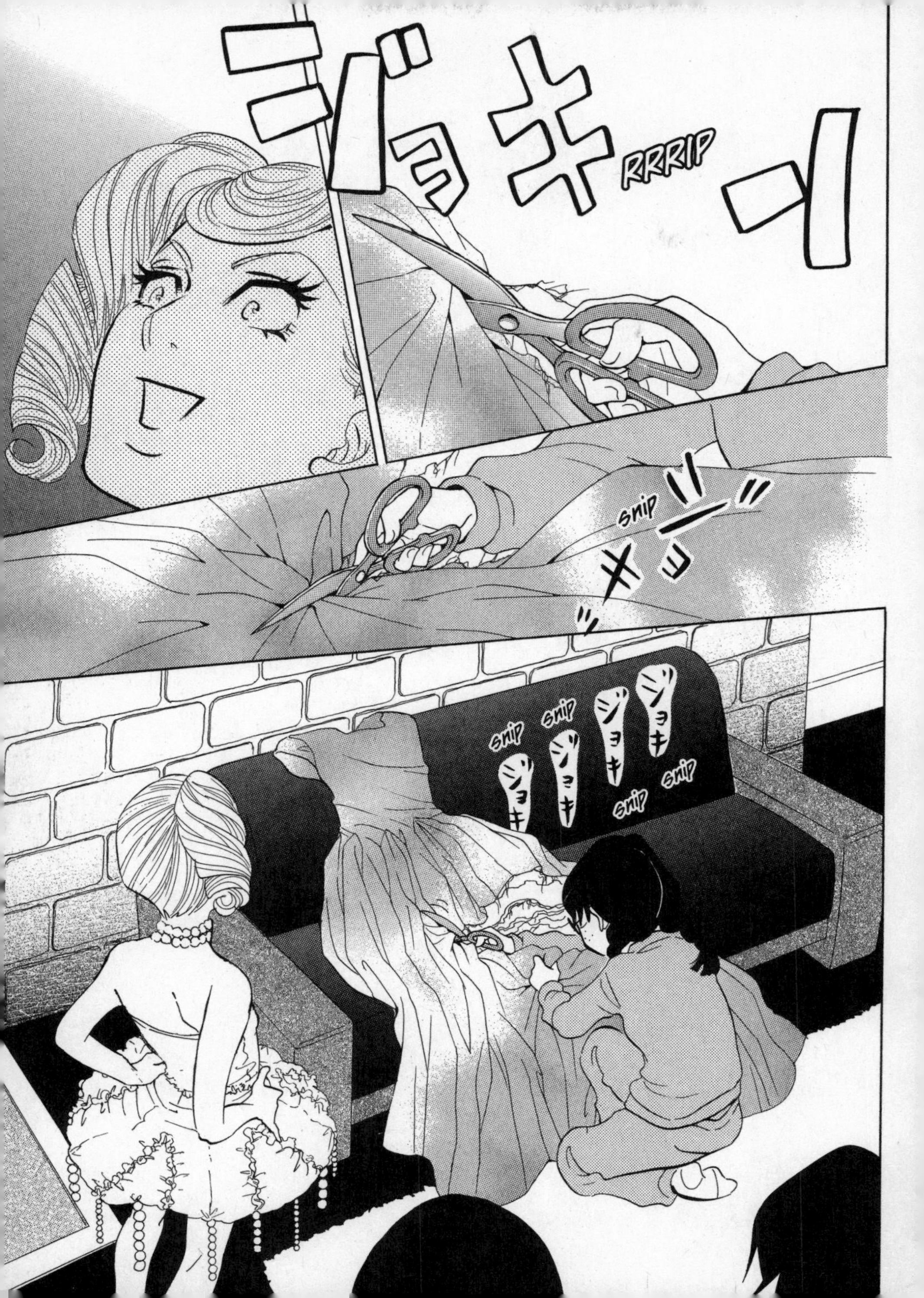
ジョキーッ
RRRIP
ジョキッ
snip
ジョキ
ジョキ
ジョキ
ジョキ
snip
snip
snip
snip
snip

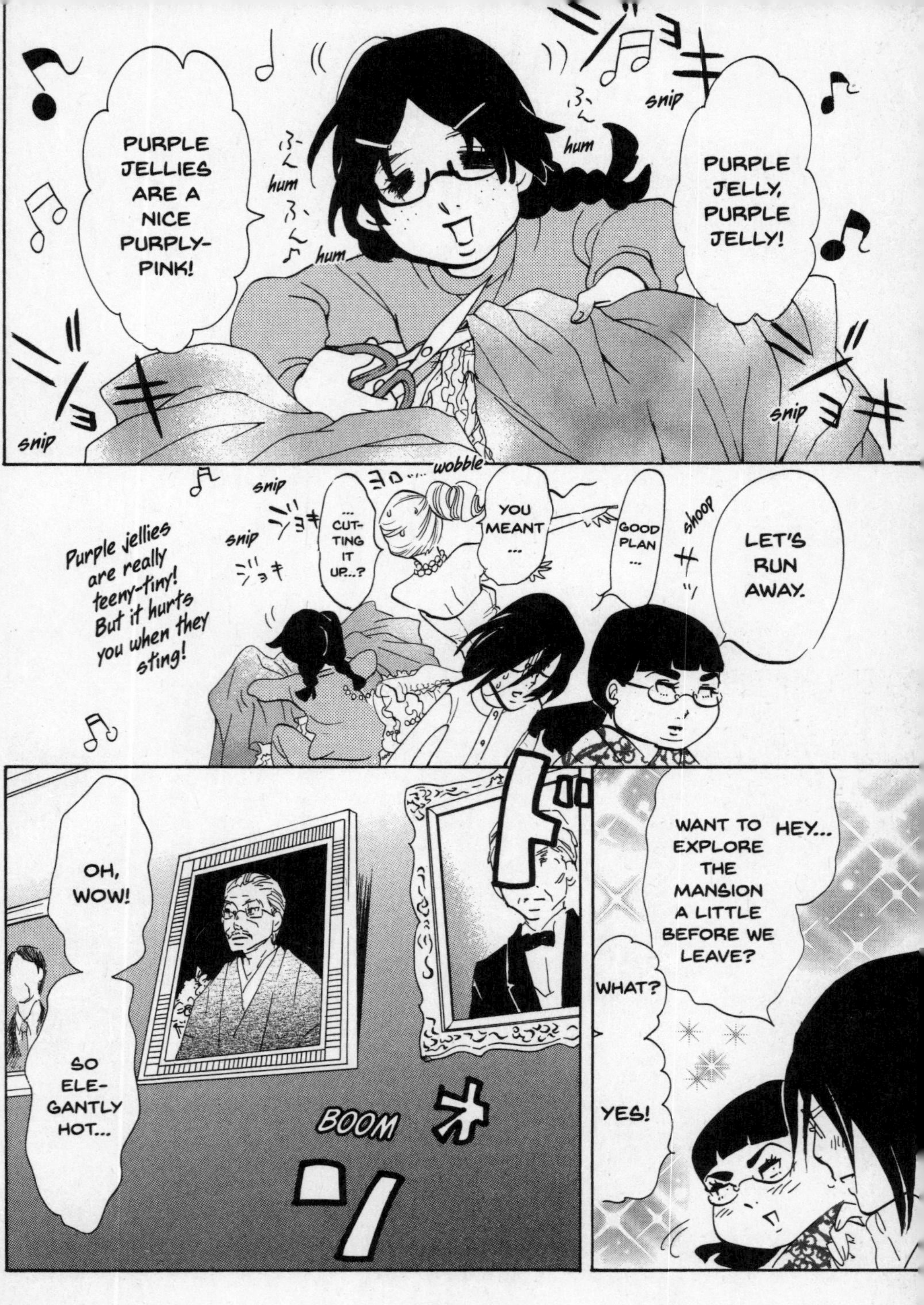
snip
PURPLE JELLY, PURPLE JELLY!
hum
ふん
hum
ふん
ふん
hum
PURPLE JELLIES ARE A NICE PURPLY-PINK!
snip
snip
shoop
LET'S RUN AWAY.
GOOD PLAN...
YOU MEANT...
wobble
ヨロ…
...CUTTING IT UP...?
snip
ジョキ
snip
ジョキ
Purple jellies are really teeny-tiny! But it hurts you when they sting!
HEY...
WANT TO EXPLORE THE MANSION A LITTLE BEFORE WE LEAVE?
WHAT?
YES!
OH, WOW!
SO ELEGANTLY HOT...
BOOM

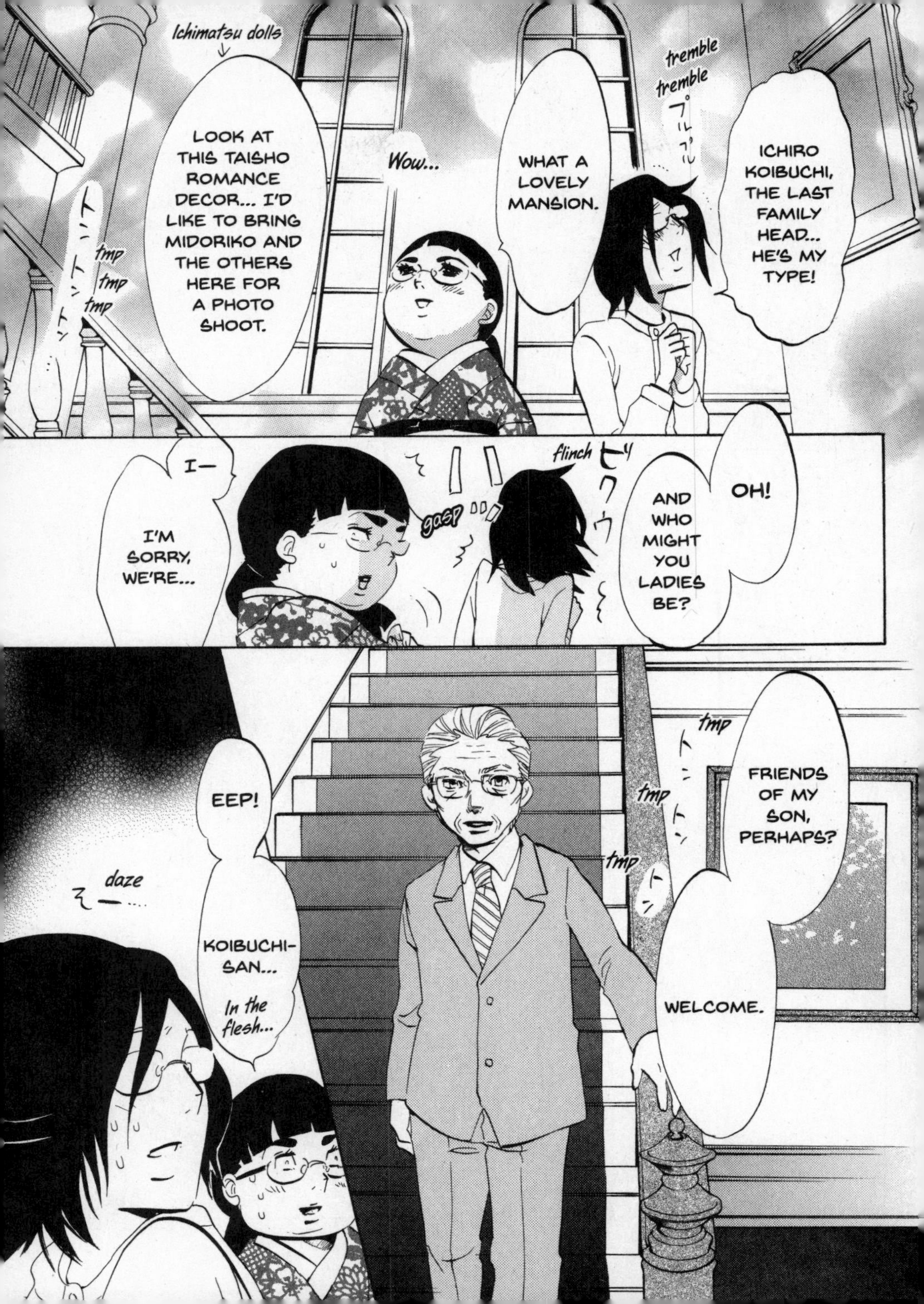
tremble tremble
ICHIRO KOIBUCHI, THE LAST FAMILY HEAD... HE'S MY TYPE!
WHAT A LOVELY MANSION.
Wow...
Ichimatsu dolls
LOOK AT THIS TAISHO ROMANCE DECOR... I'D LIKE TO BRING MIDORIKO AND THE OTHERS HERE FOR A PHOTO SHOOT.
tmp tmp tmp
OH!
AND WHO MIGHT YOU LADIES BE?
flinch
gasp
I—
I'M SORRY, WE'RE...
tmp tmp tmp
FRIENDS OF MY SON, PERHAPS?
WELCOME.
EEP!
KOIBUCHI-SAN...
In the flesh...
daze

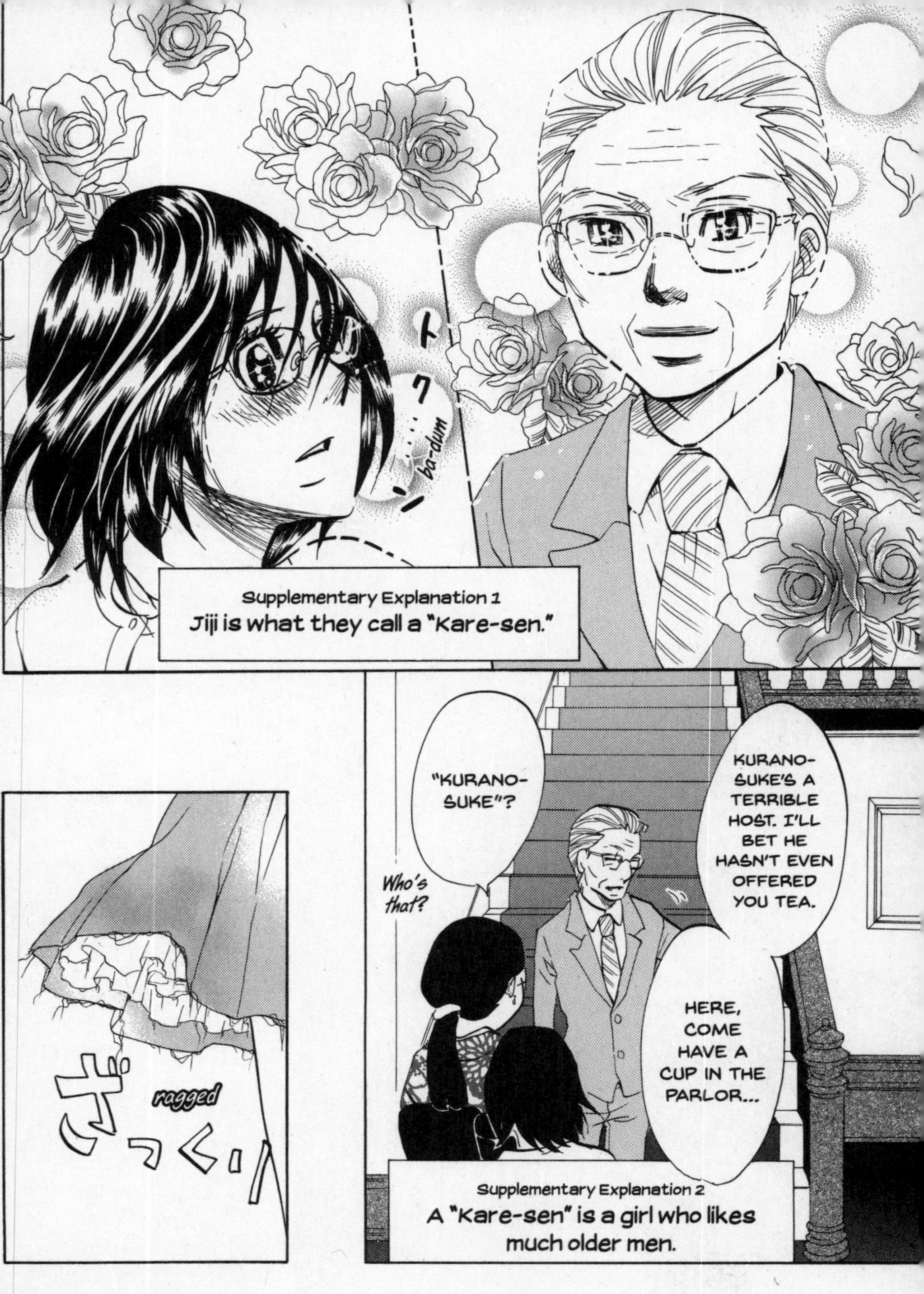
ba-dum
Supplementary Explanation 1
Jiji is what they call a "Kare-sen."
KURANO-SUKE'S A TERRIBLE HOST. I'LL BET HE HASN'T EVEN OFFERED YOU TEA.
HERE, COME HAVE A CUP IN THE PARLOR...
"KURANO-SUKE"?
Who's that?
Supplementary Explanation 2
A "Kare-sen" is a girl who likes much older men.
ragged

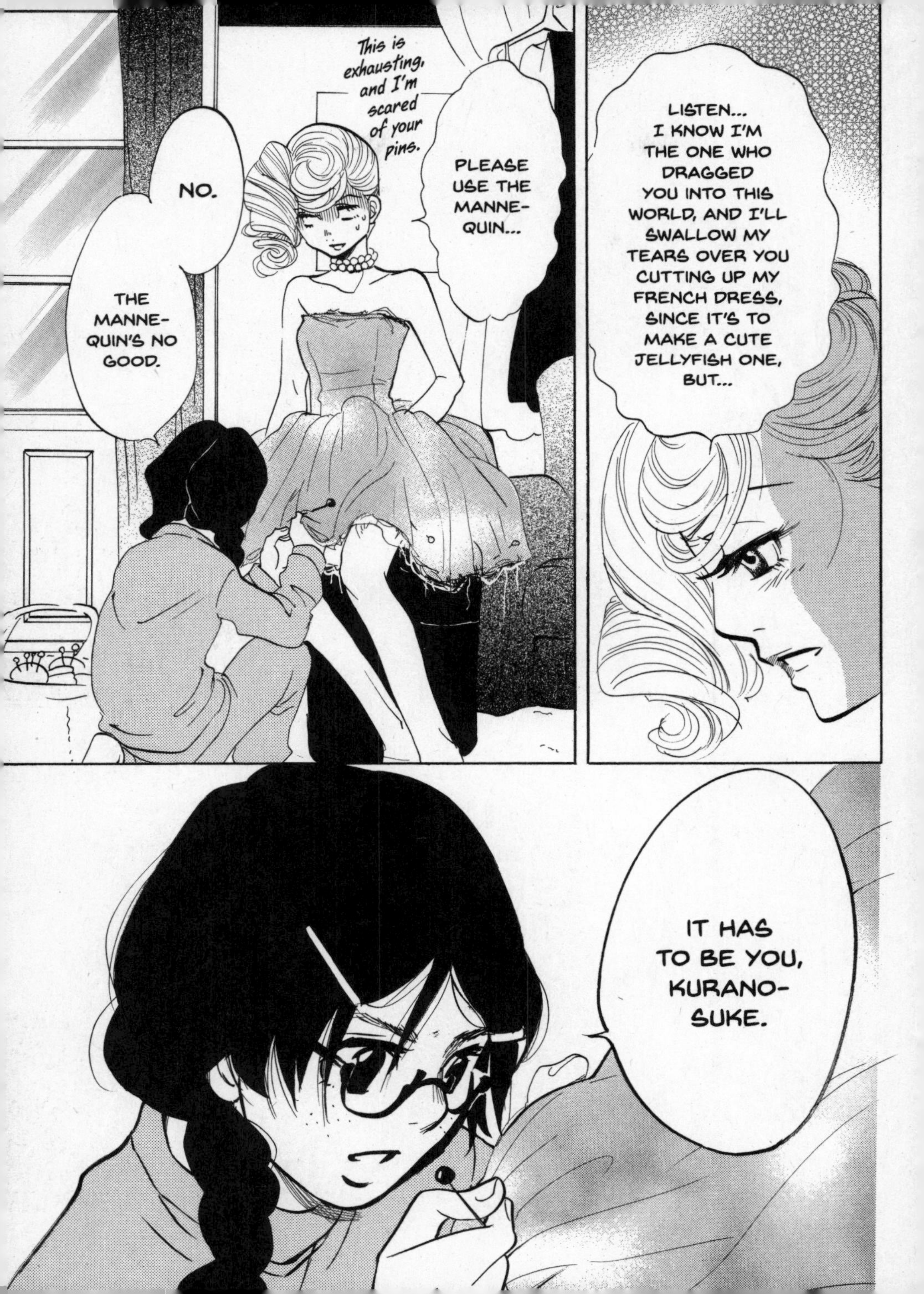
LISTEN... I KNOW I'M THE ONE WHO DRAGGED YOU INTO THIS WORLD, AND I'LL SWALLOW MY TEARS OVER YOU CUTTING UP MY FRENCH DRESS, SINCE IT'S TO MAKE A CUTE JELLYFISH ONE, BUT...
PLEASE USE THE MANNE-QUIN...
This is exhausting, and I'm scared of your pins.
NO.
THE MANNE-QUIN'S NO GOOD.
IT HAS TO BE YOU, KURANO-SUKE.

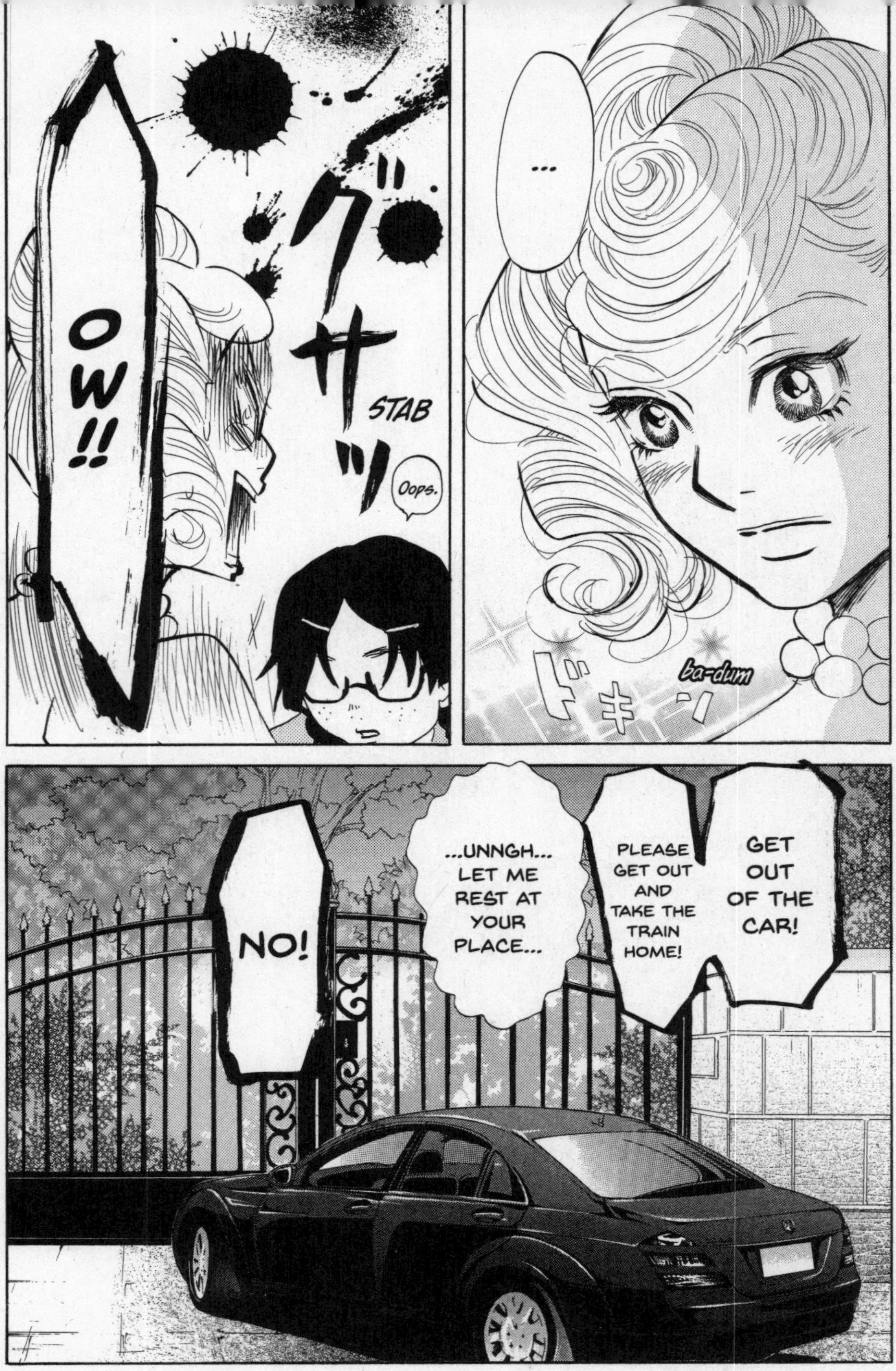
...
ba-dum
STAB
Oops.
OW!!
GET OUT OF THE CAR!
PLEASE GET OUT AND TAKE THE TRAIN HOME!
...UNNGH... LET ME REST AT YOUR PLACE...
NO!

Because you've crossed the threshold to adulthood?

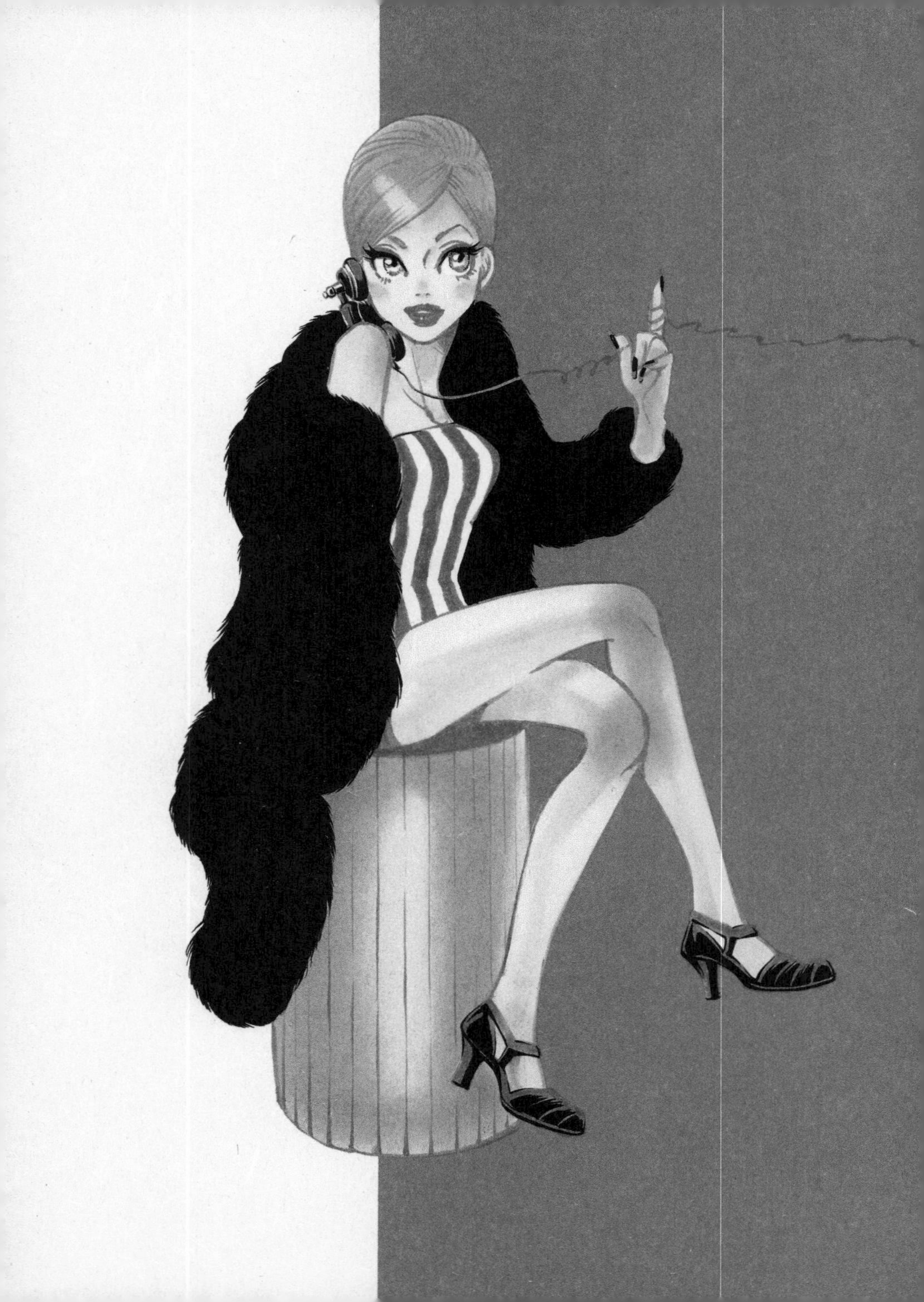

Episode 22
Some Like It Hot?

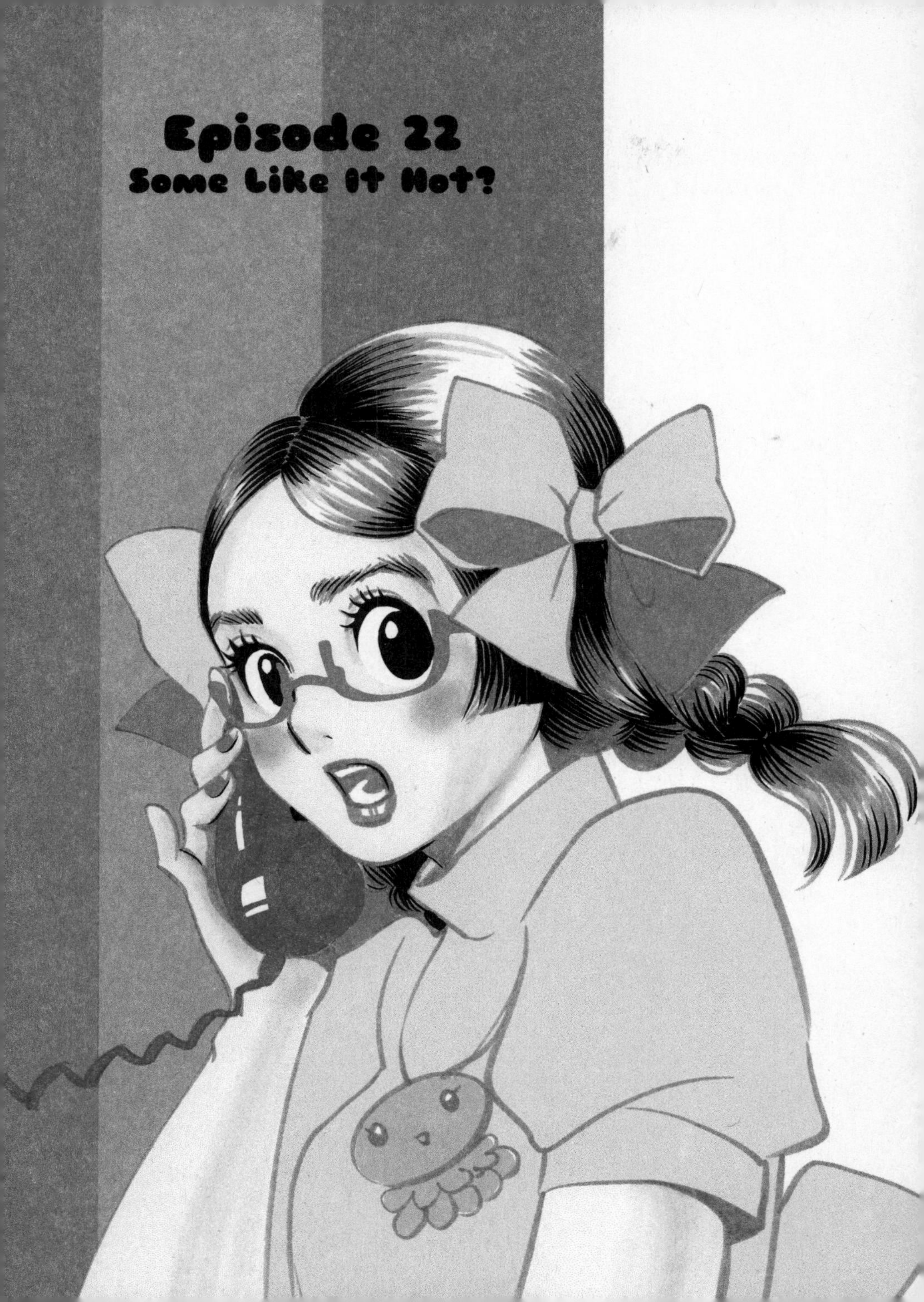

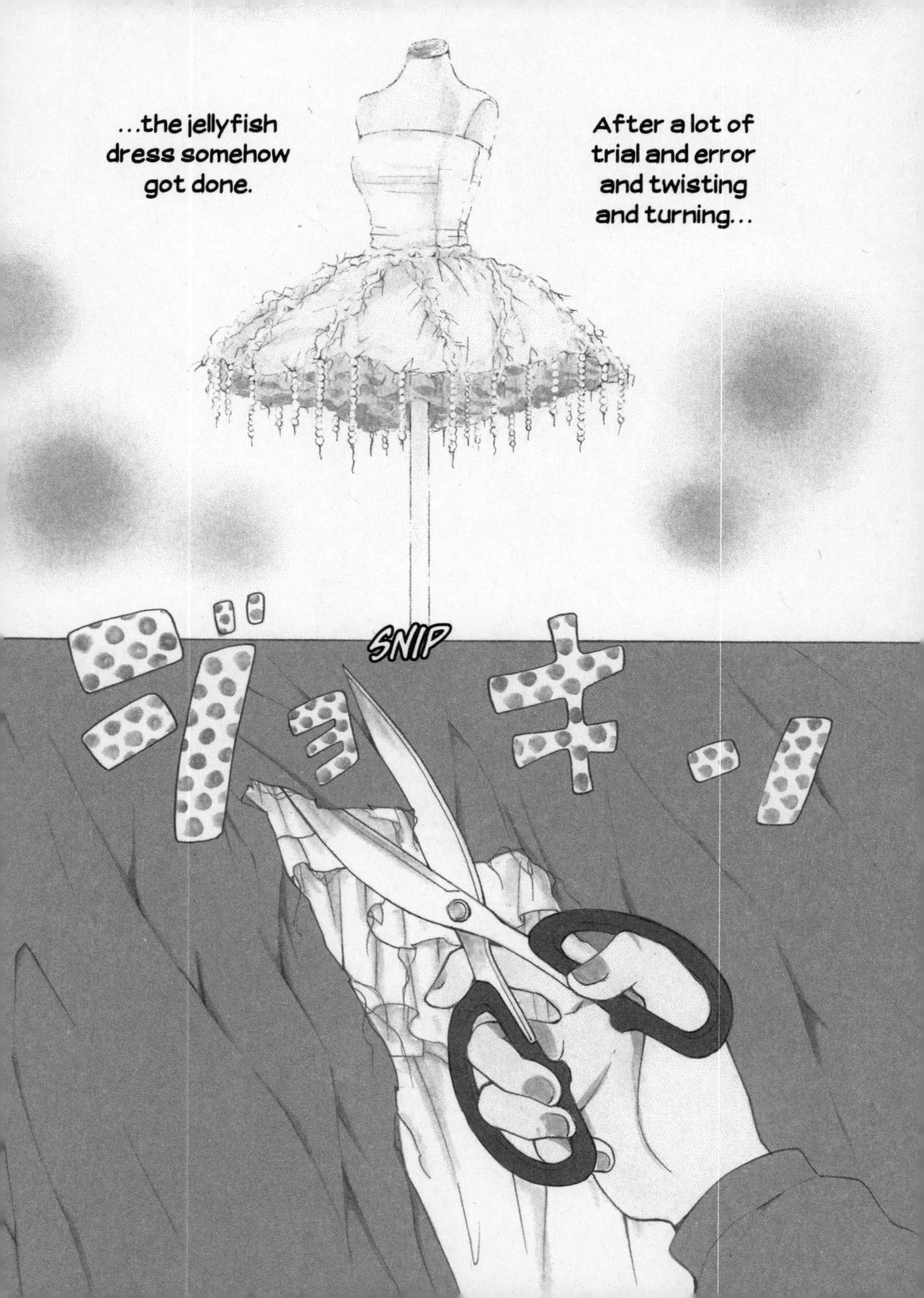
After a lot of trial and error and twisting and turning...
...the jellyfish dress somehow got done.
SNIP
ジョキッ

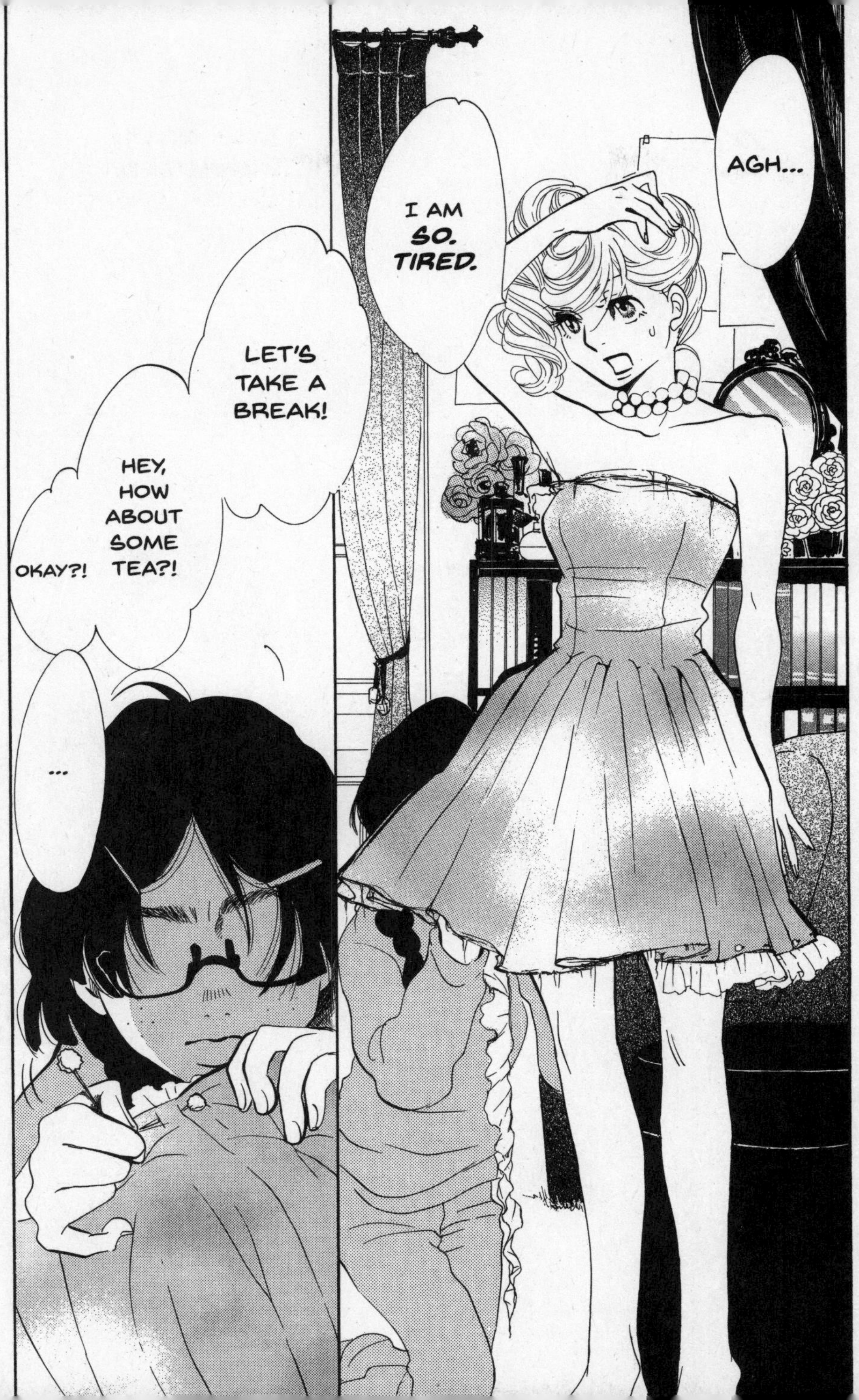
AGH...
I AM SO. TIRED.
LET'S TAKE A BREAK!
HEY, HOW ABOUT SOME TEA?!
OKAY?!
...

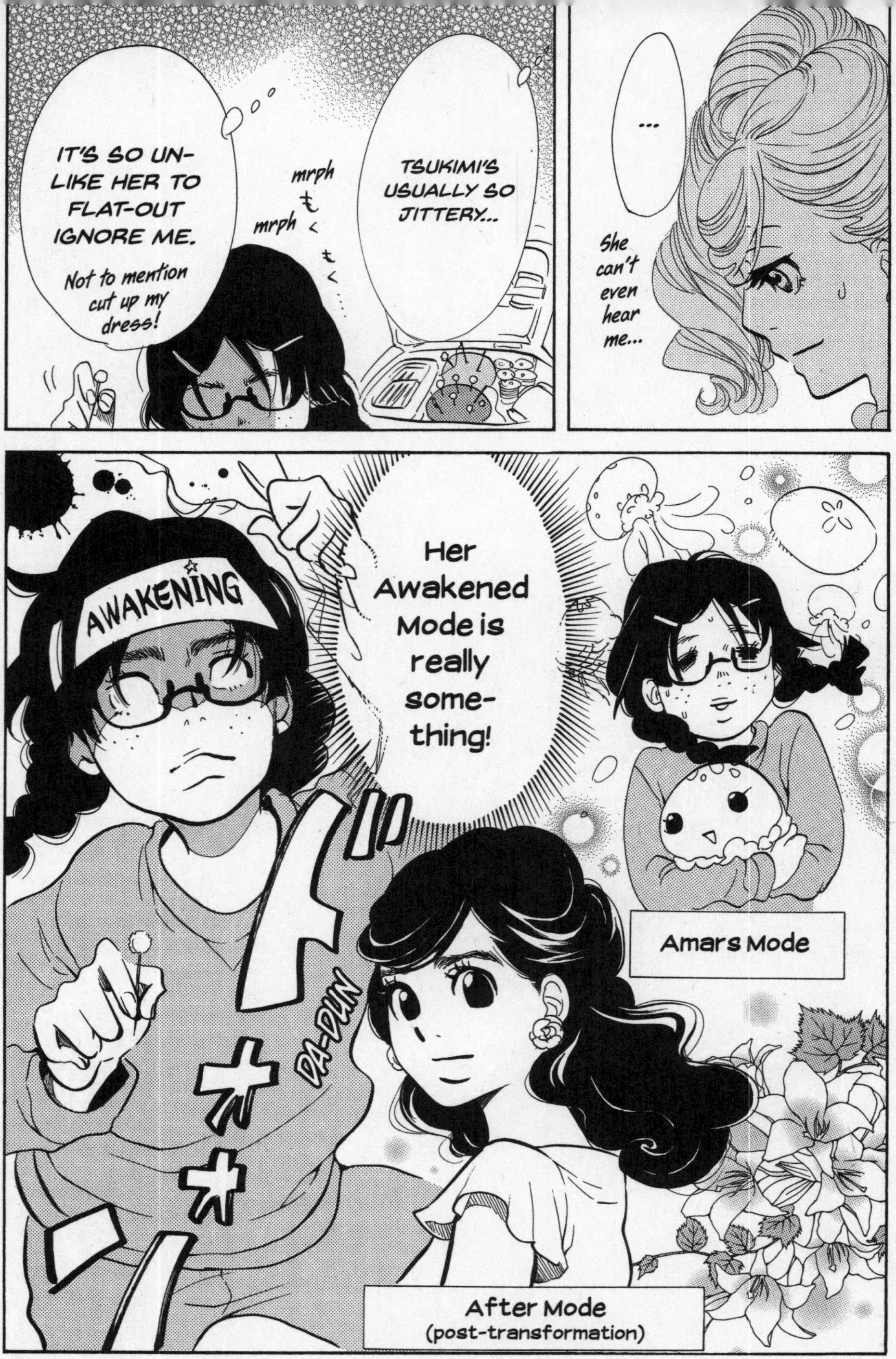
...
She can't even hear me...
TSUKIMI'S USUALLY SO JITTERY...
mrph
mrph
IT'S SO UN-LIKE HER TO FLAT-OUT IGNORE ME.
Not to mention cut up my dress!
Her Awakened Mode is really some-thing!
Amars Mode
AWAKENING
DA-DUN
After Mode
(post-transformation)

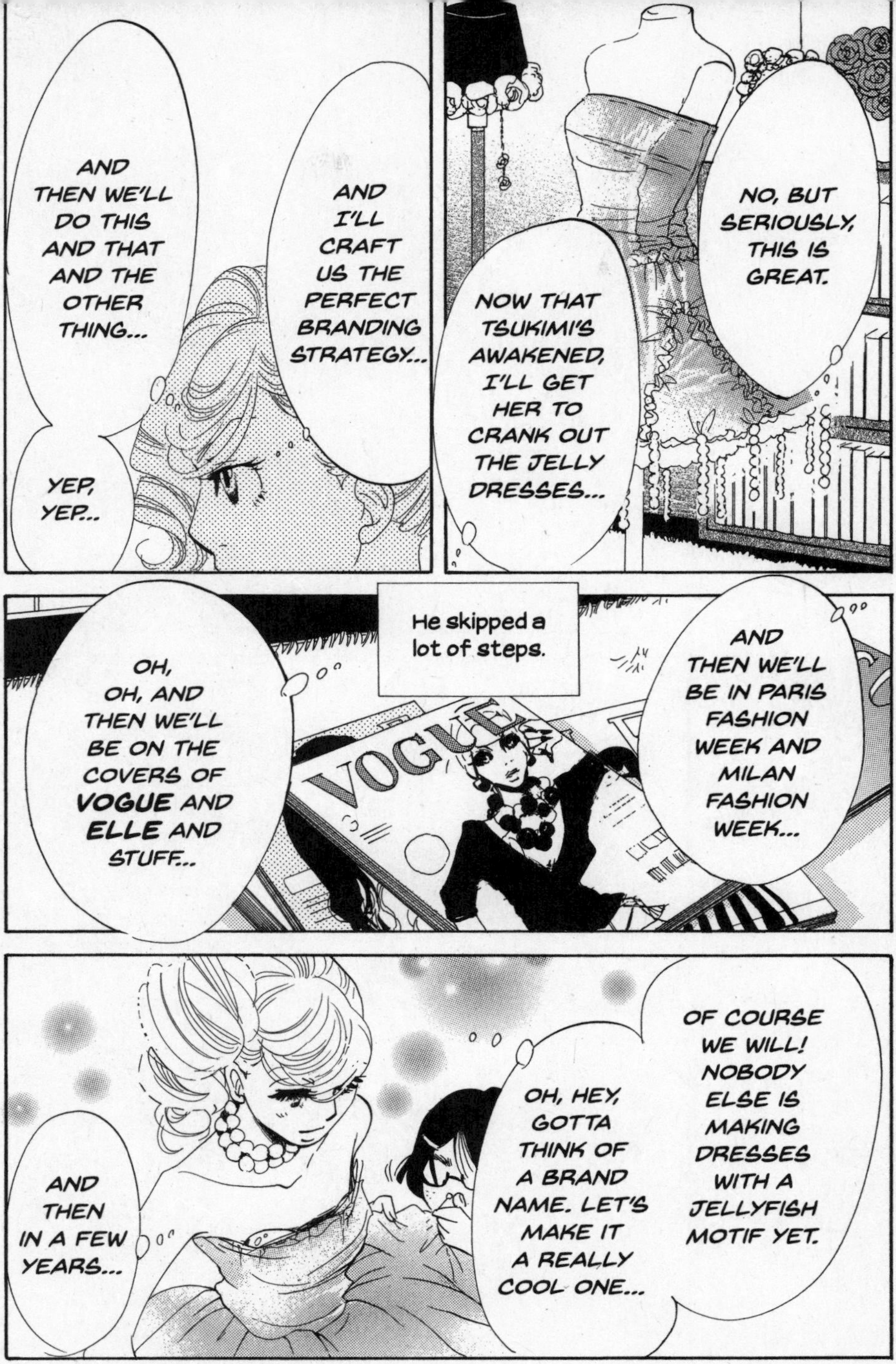
NO, BUT SERIOUSLY, THIS IS GREAT.
NOW THAT TSUKIMI'S AWAKENED, I'LL GET HER TO CRANK OUT THE JELLY DRESSES...
AND I'LL CRAFT US THE PERFECT BRANDING STRATEGY...
AND THEN WE'LL DO THIS AND THAT AND THE OTHER THING...
YEP, YEP...
AND THEN WE'LL BE IN PARIS FASHION WEEK AND MILAN FASHION WEEK...
OH, OH, AND THEN WE'LL BE ON THE COVERS OF VOGUE AND ELLE AND STUFF...
He skipped a lot of steps.
VOGUE
OF COURSE WE WILL! NOBODY ELSE IS MAKING DRESSES WITH A JELLYFISH MOTIF YET.
OH, HEY, GOTTA THINK OF A BRAND NAME. LET'S MAKE IT A REALLY COOL ONE...
AND THEN IN A FEW YEARS...

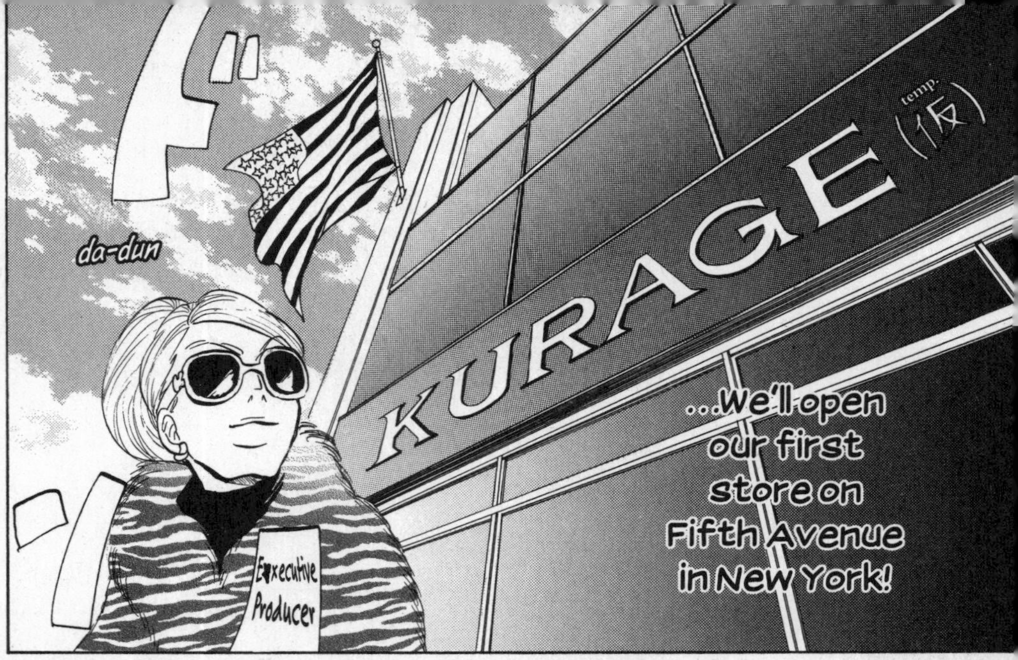
KURAGE
temp.
仮
da-dun
...We'll open our first store on Fifth Avenue in New York!
Executive Producer
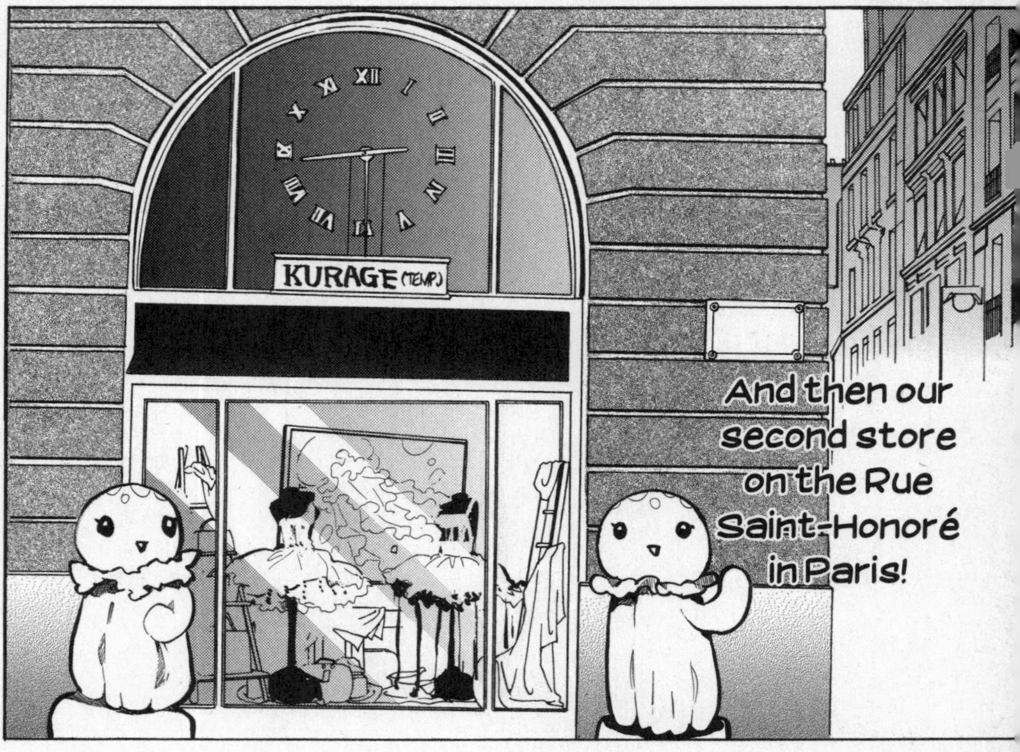
KURAGE (TEMP.)
And then our second store on the Rue Saint-Honoré in Paris!

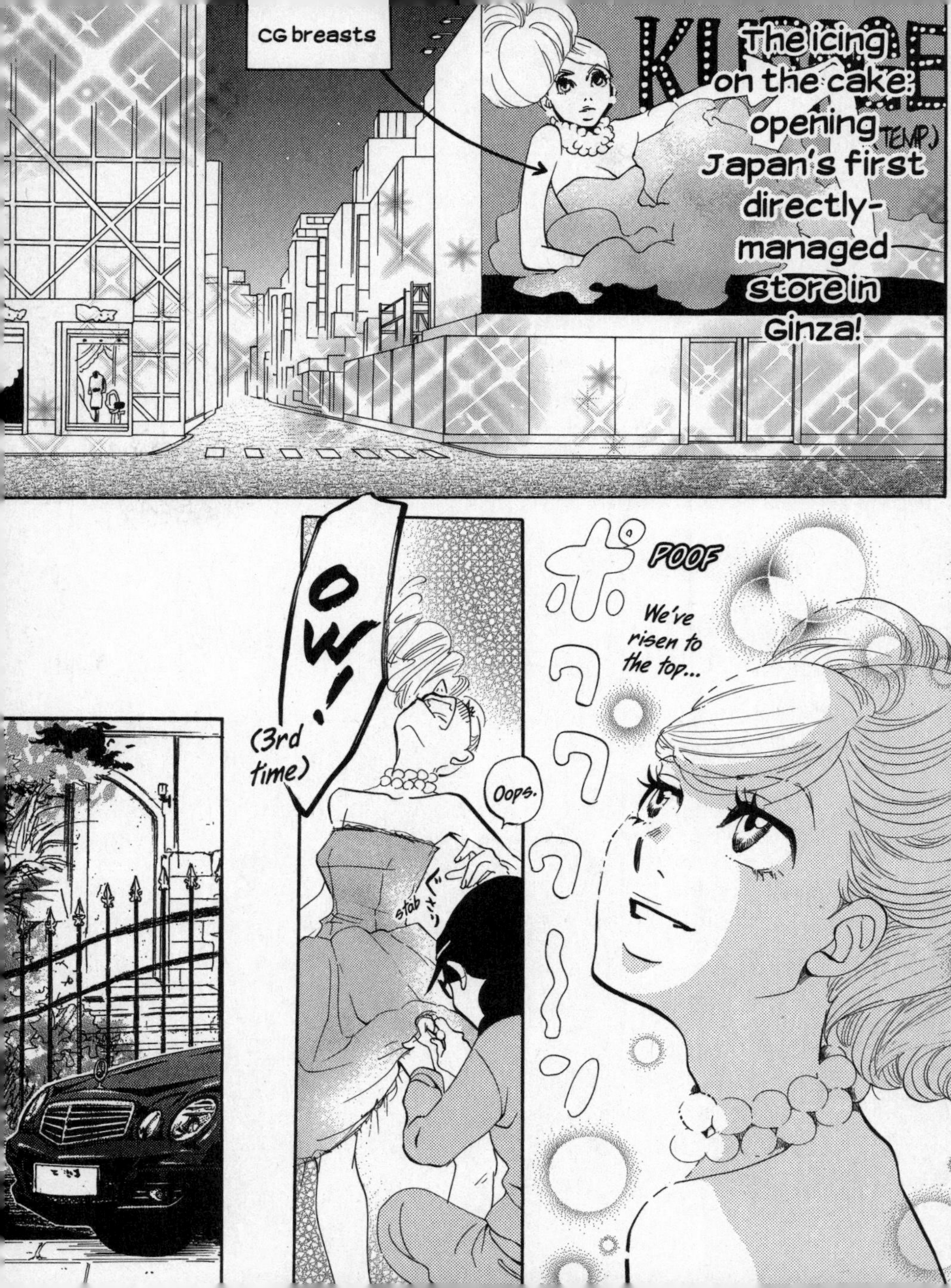
The icing on the cake: opening (TEMP.) Japan's first directly-managed store in Ginza!
CG breasts
POOF
We've risen to the top...
OW!
(3rd time)
Oops.
stab

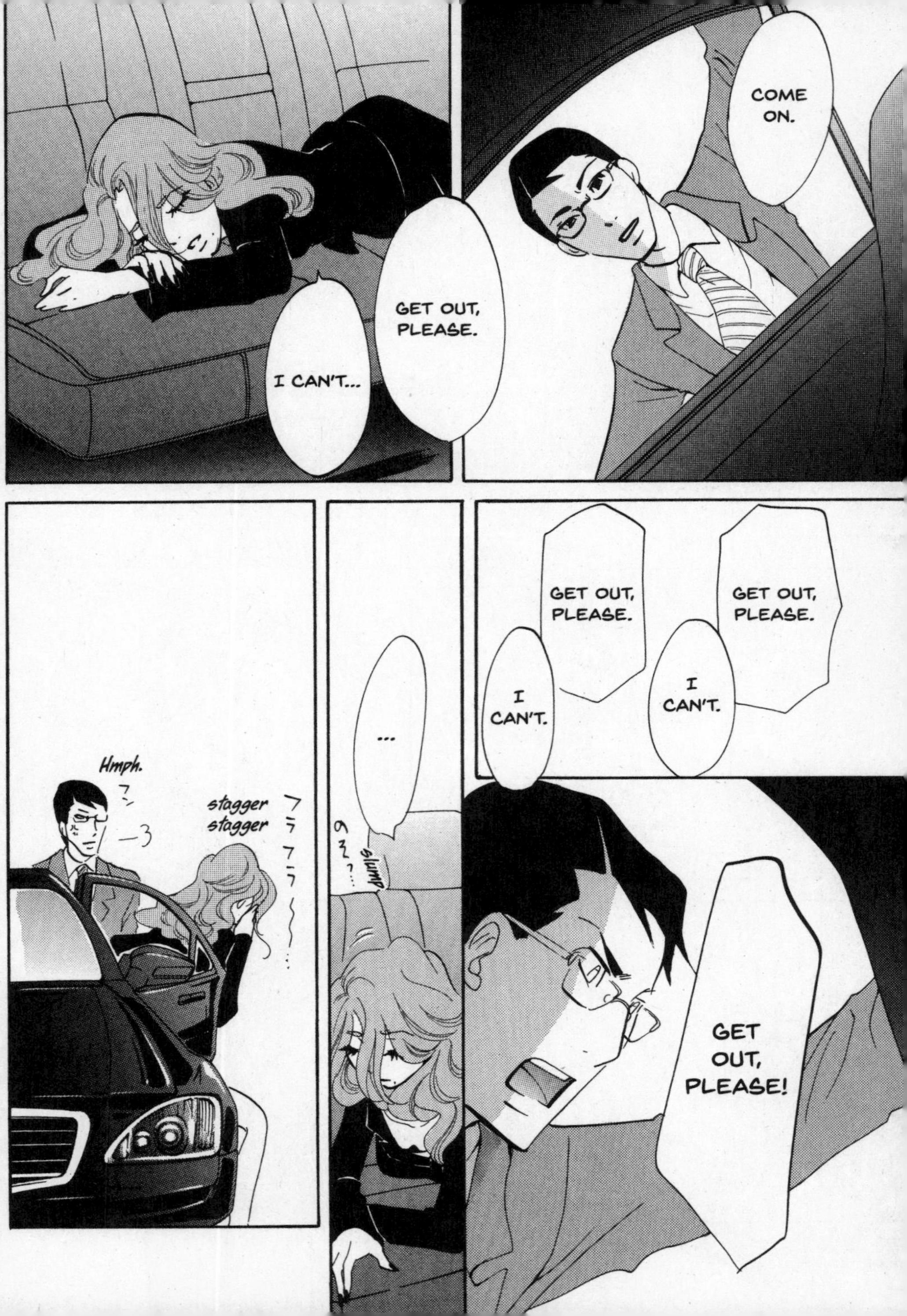

COME ON.
GET OUT, PLEASE.
I CAN'T...
GET OUT, PLEASE.
I CAN'T.
GET OUT, PLEASE.
I CAN'T.
GET OUT, PLEASE!
...
slump
Hmph.
stagger stagger

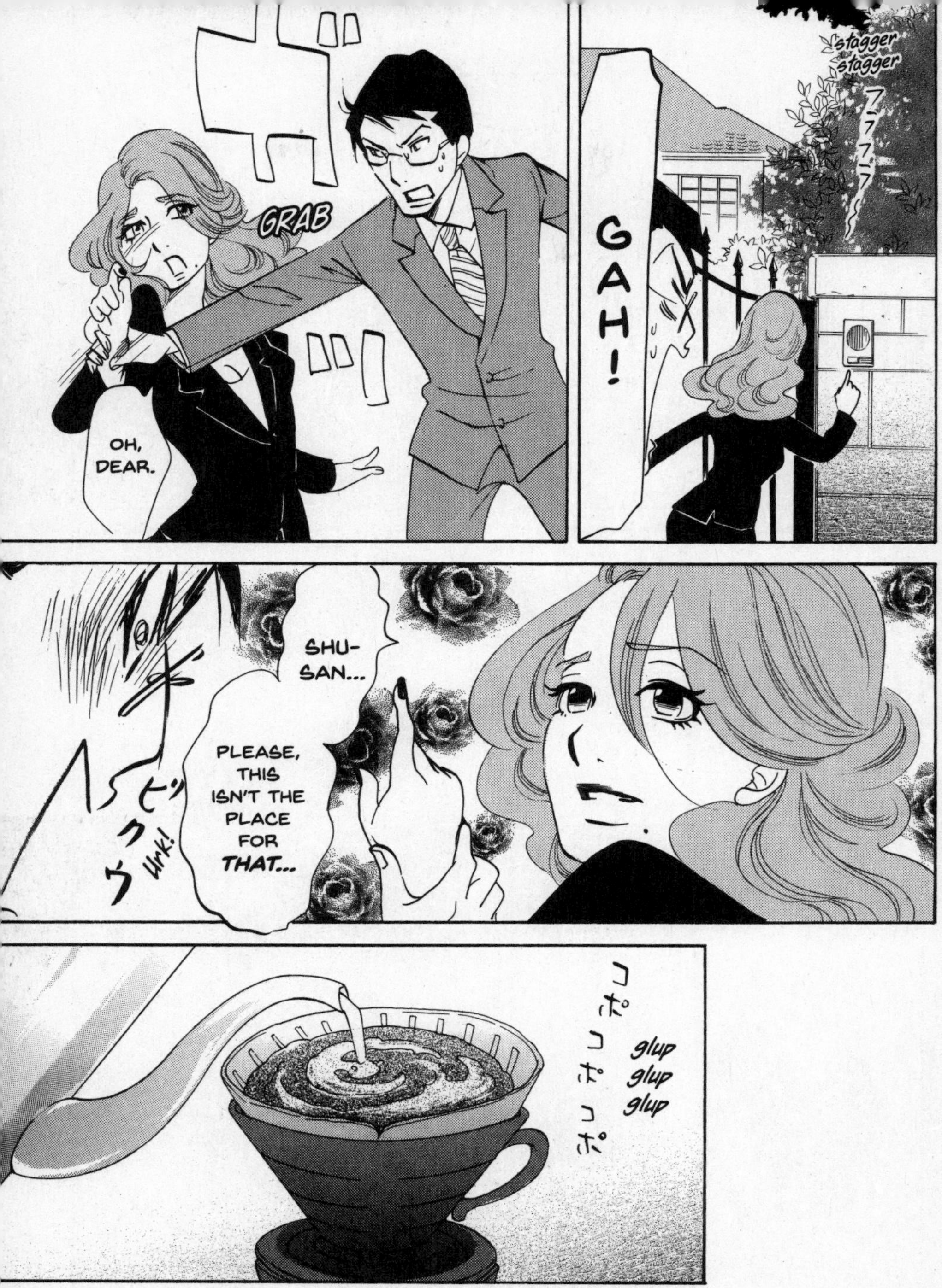
stagger stagger
フラフラ
GAH!
GRAB
OH, DEAR.
SHU-SAN...
PLEASE, THIS ISN'T THE PLACE FOR THAT...
ビクゥ
Urk!
コポコポコポ
glup glup glup

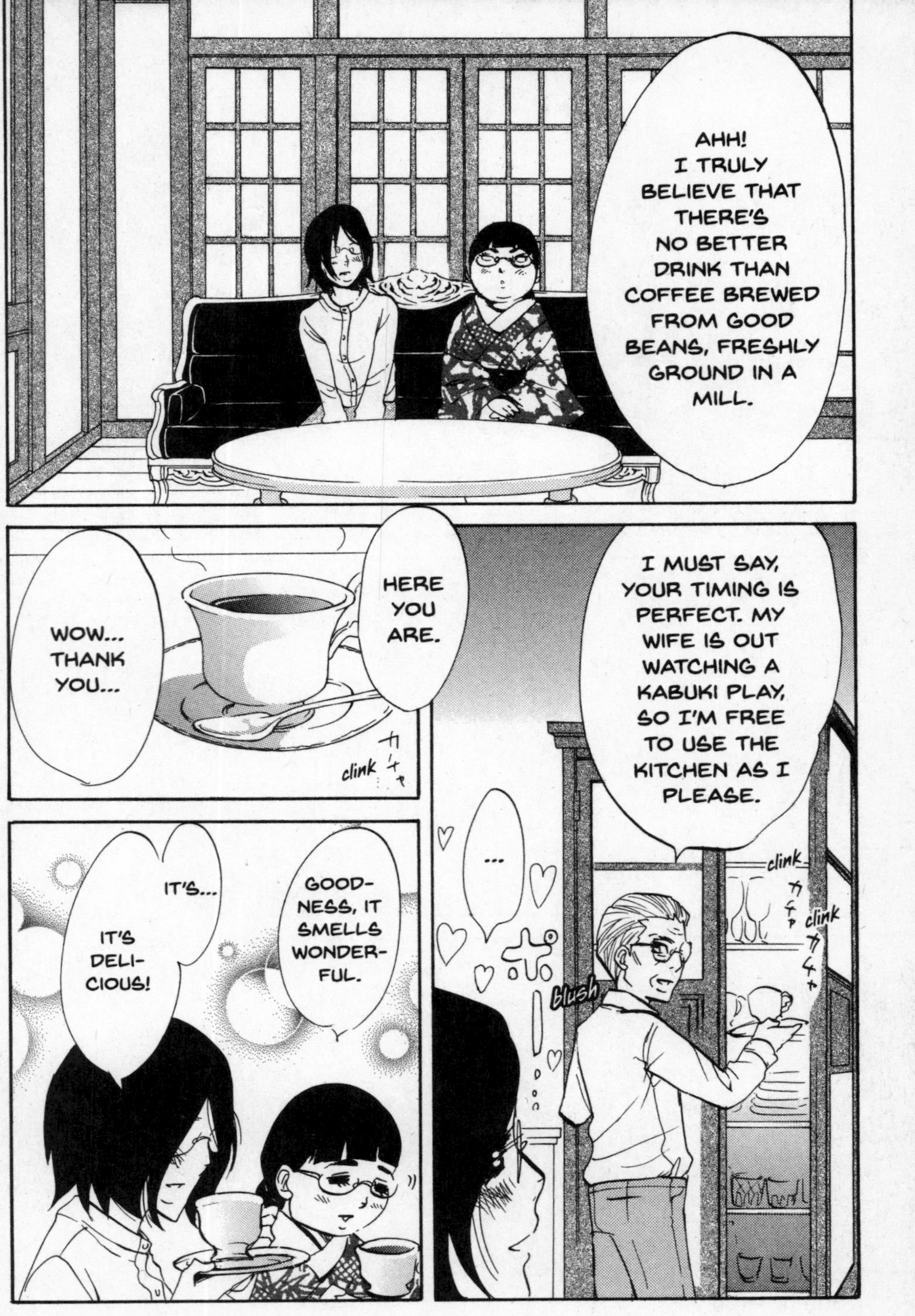
AHH! I TRULY BELIEVE THAT THERE'S NO BETTER DRINK THAN COFFEE BREWED FROM GOOD BEANS, FRESHLY GROUND IN A MILL.
I MUST SAY, YOUR TIMING IS PERFECT. MY WIFE IS OUT WATCHING A KABUKI PLAY, SO I'M FREE TO USE THE KITCHEN AS I PLEASE.
clink
clink
...
blush
HERE YOU ARE.
WOW... THANK YOU...
clink
GOOD-NESS, IT SMELLS WONDER-FUL.
IT'S...
IT'S DELI-CIOUS!

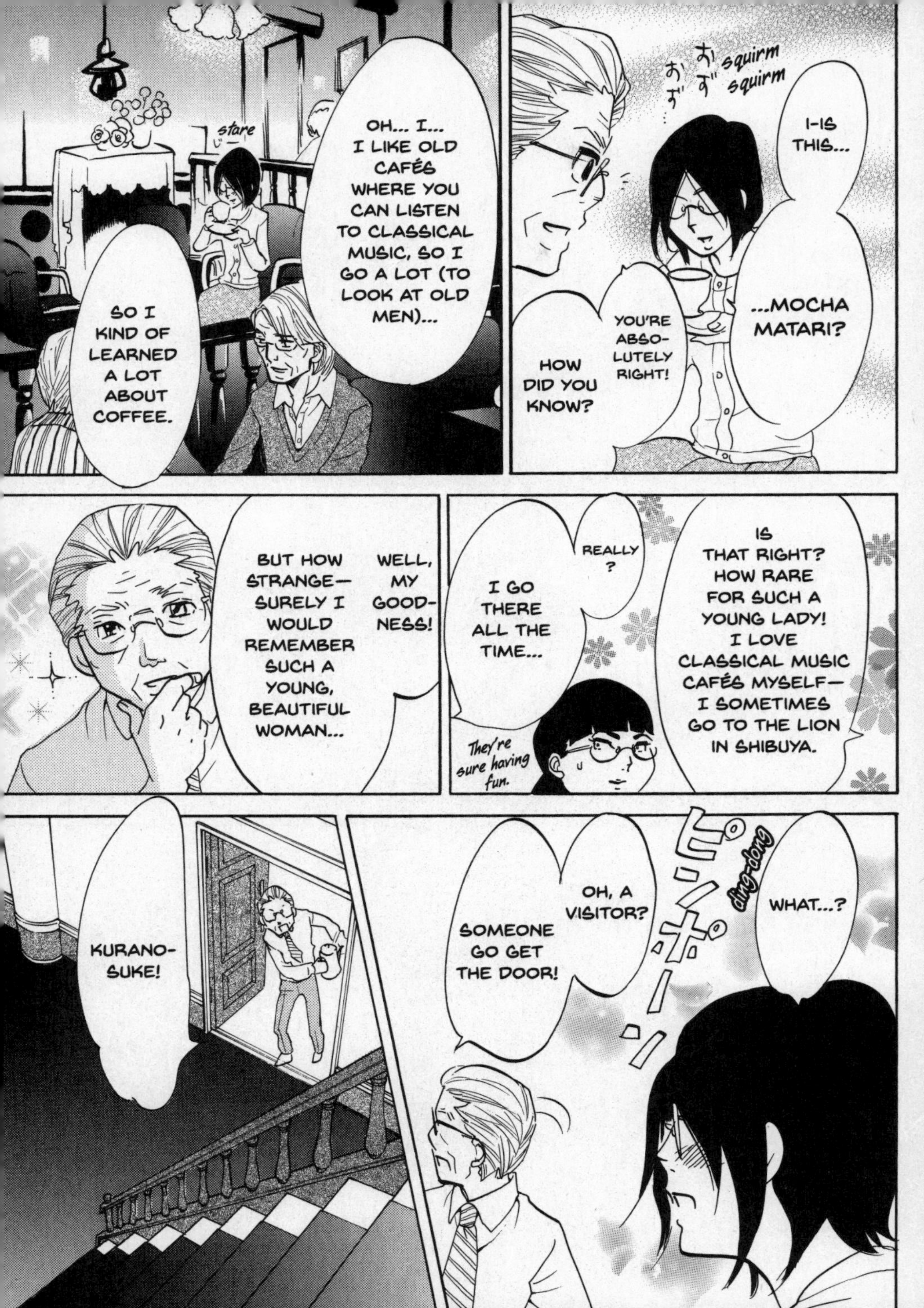
squirm squirm
I-IS THIS...
...MOCHA MATARI?
YOU'RE ABSOLUTELY RIGHT!
HOW DID YOU KNOW?
stare
OH... I... I LIKE OLD CAFÉS WHERE YOU CAN LISTEN TO CLASSICAL MUSIC, SO I GO A LOT (TO LOOK AT OLD MEN)...
SO I KIND OF LEARNED A LOT ABOUT COFFEE.
IS THAT RIGHT? HOW RARE FOR SUCH A YOUNG LADY! I LOVE CLASSICAL MUSIC CAFÉS MYSELF—I SOMETIMES GO TO THE LION IN SHIBUYA.
REALLY?
I GO THERE ALL THE TIME...
They're sure having fun.
WELL, MY GOODNESS!
BUT HOW STRANGE—SURELY I WOULD REMEMBER SUCH A YOUNG, BEAUTIFUL WOMAN...
WHAT...?
ding-dong
OH, A VISITOR?
SOMEONE GO GET THE DOOR!
KURANOSUKE!

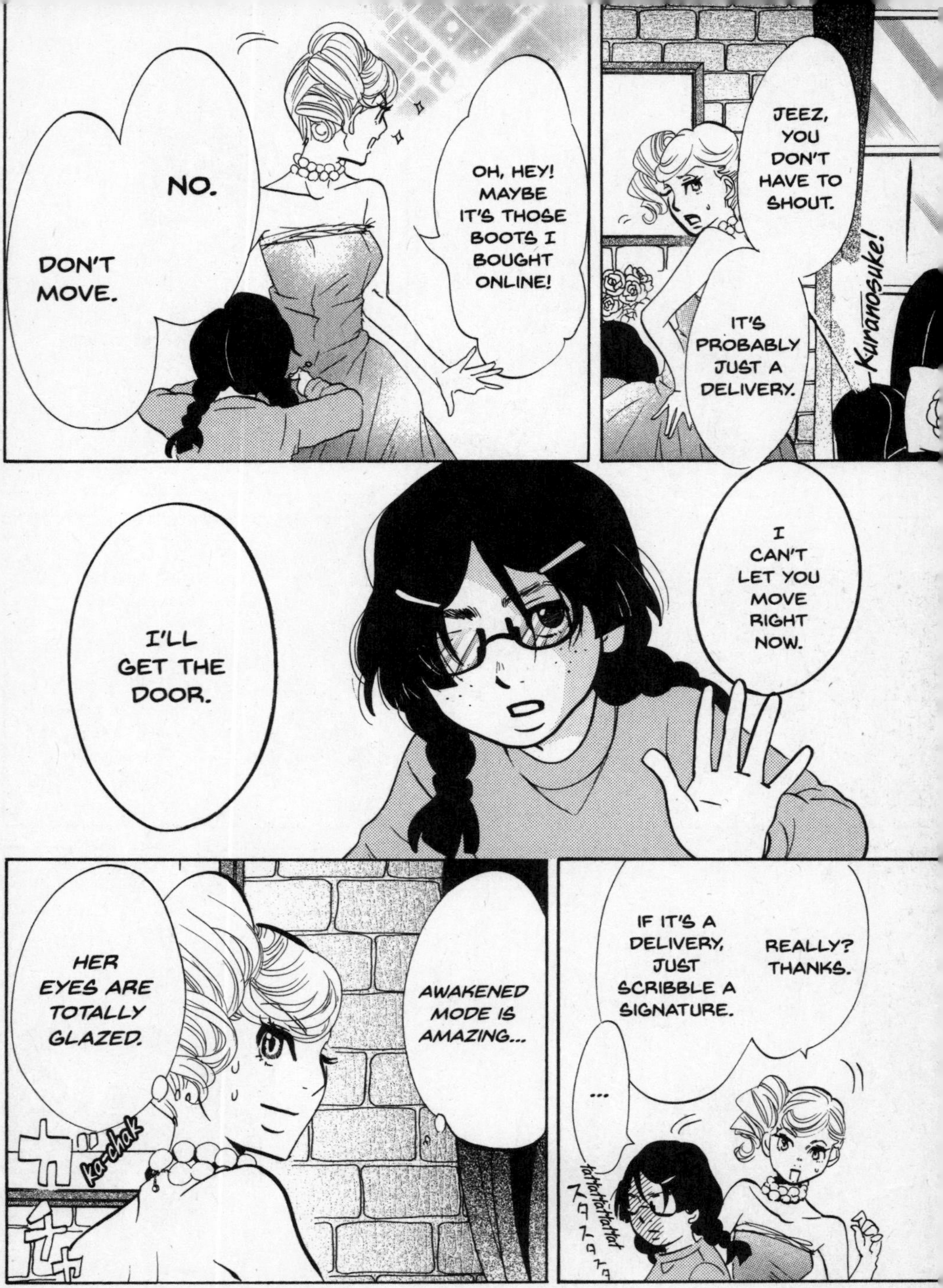
JEEZ, YOU DON'T HAVE TO SHOUT.
Kuranosuke!
IT'S PROBABLY JUST A DELIVERY.
OH, HEY! MAYBE IT'S THOSE BOOTS I BOUGHT ONLINE!
NO.
DON'T MOVE.
I CAN'T LET YOU MOVE RIGHT NOW.
I'LL GET THE DOOR.
REALLY? THANKS.
IF IT'S A DELIVERY, JUST SCRIBBLE A SIGNATURE.
...
tattattattattat
AWAKENED MODE IS AMAZING...
HER EYES ARE TOTALLY GLAZED.
ka-chak

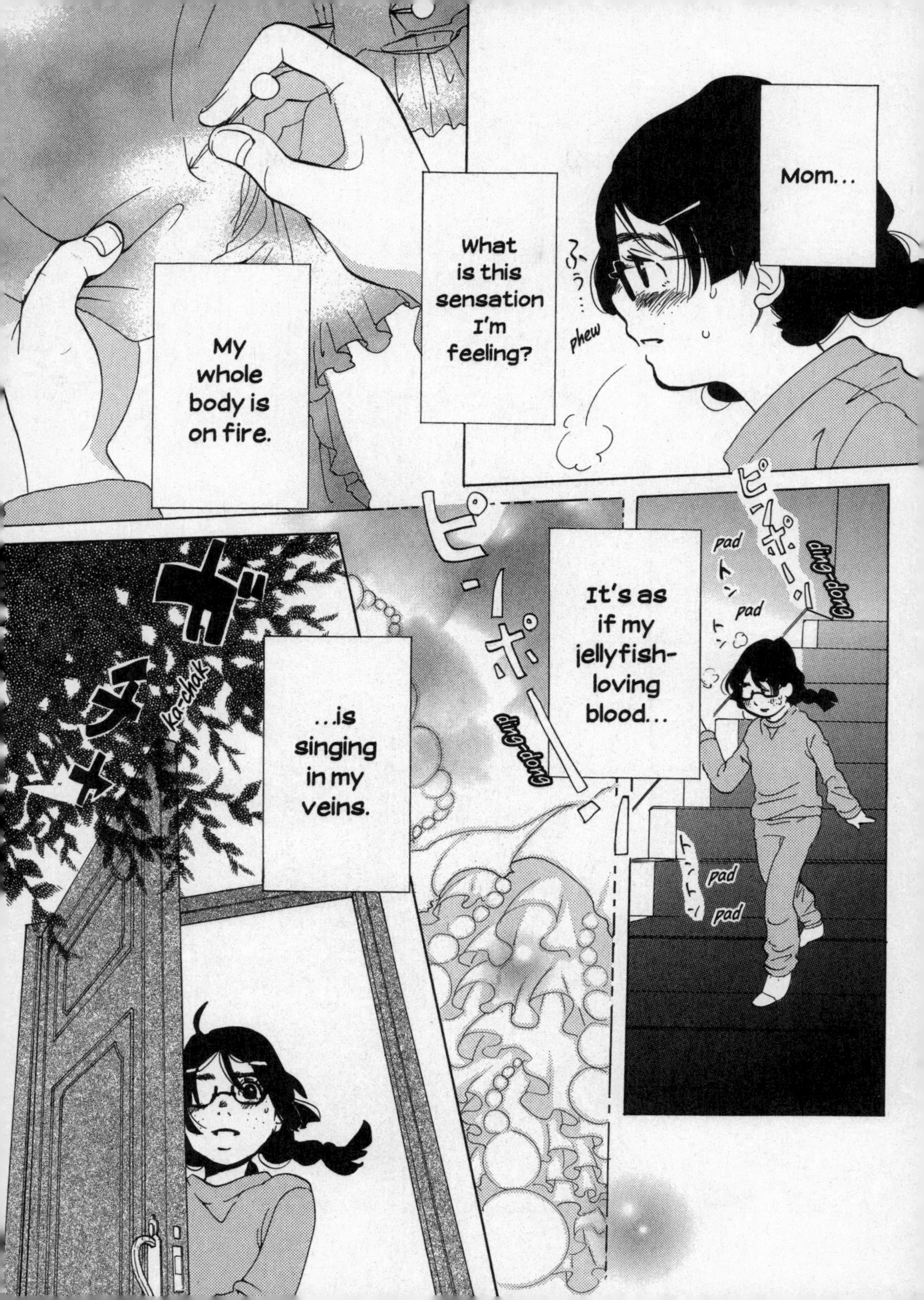
Mom...
ふう…
phew
What is this sensation I'm feeling?
My whole body is on fire.
ピンポーン
ding-dong
トン
pad
トン
pad
It's as if my jellyfish-loving blood...
トントン
pad
pad
ピーンポーン
ding-dong
...is singing in my veins.
ガチャ
ka-chak

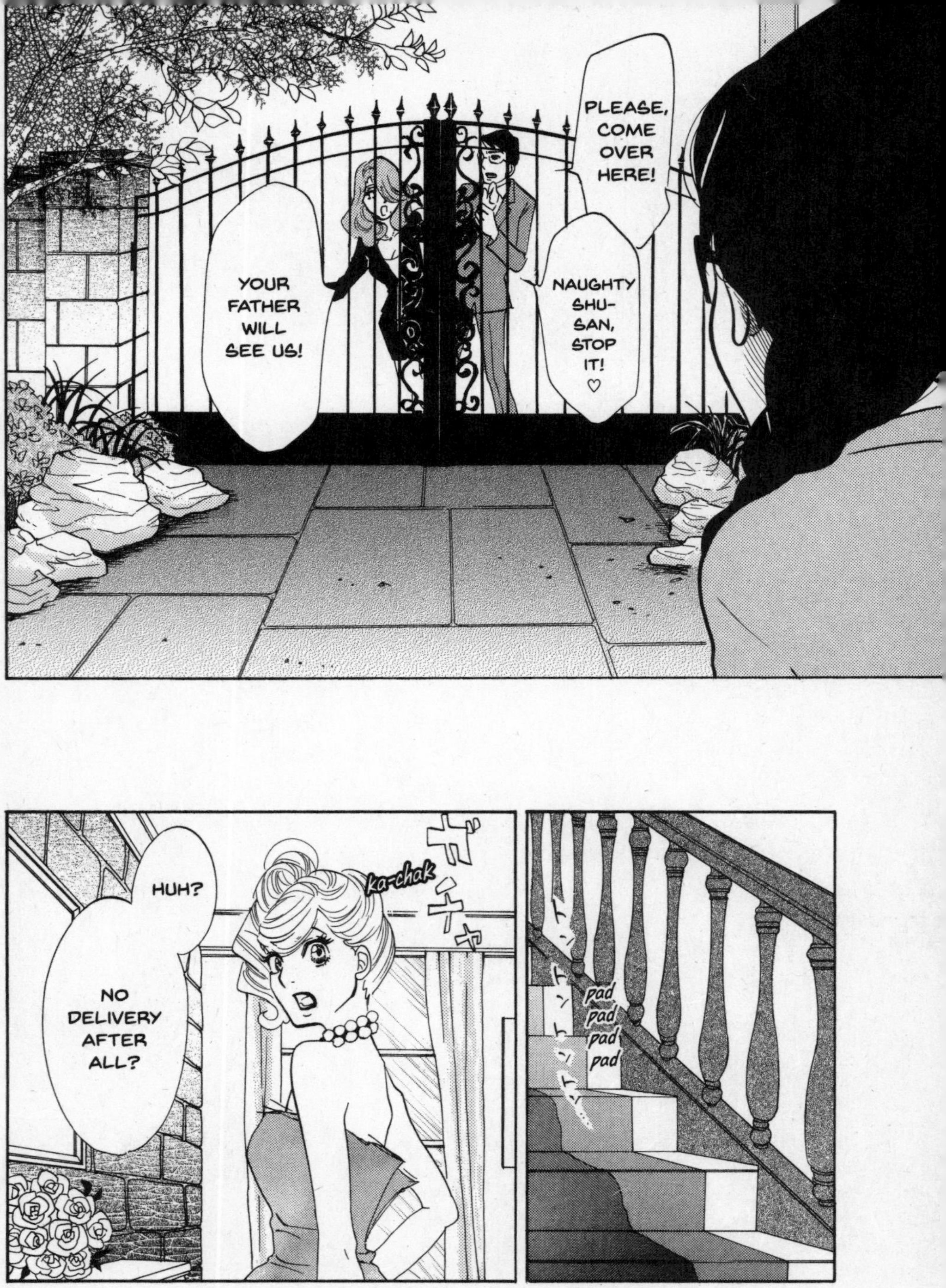
PLEASE, COME OVER HERE!
NAUGHTY SHU-SAN, STOP IT! ♡
YOUR FATHER WILL SEE US!
pad pad pad pad
ka-chak
HUH?
NO DELIVERY AFTER ALL?

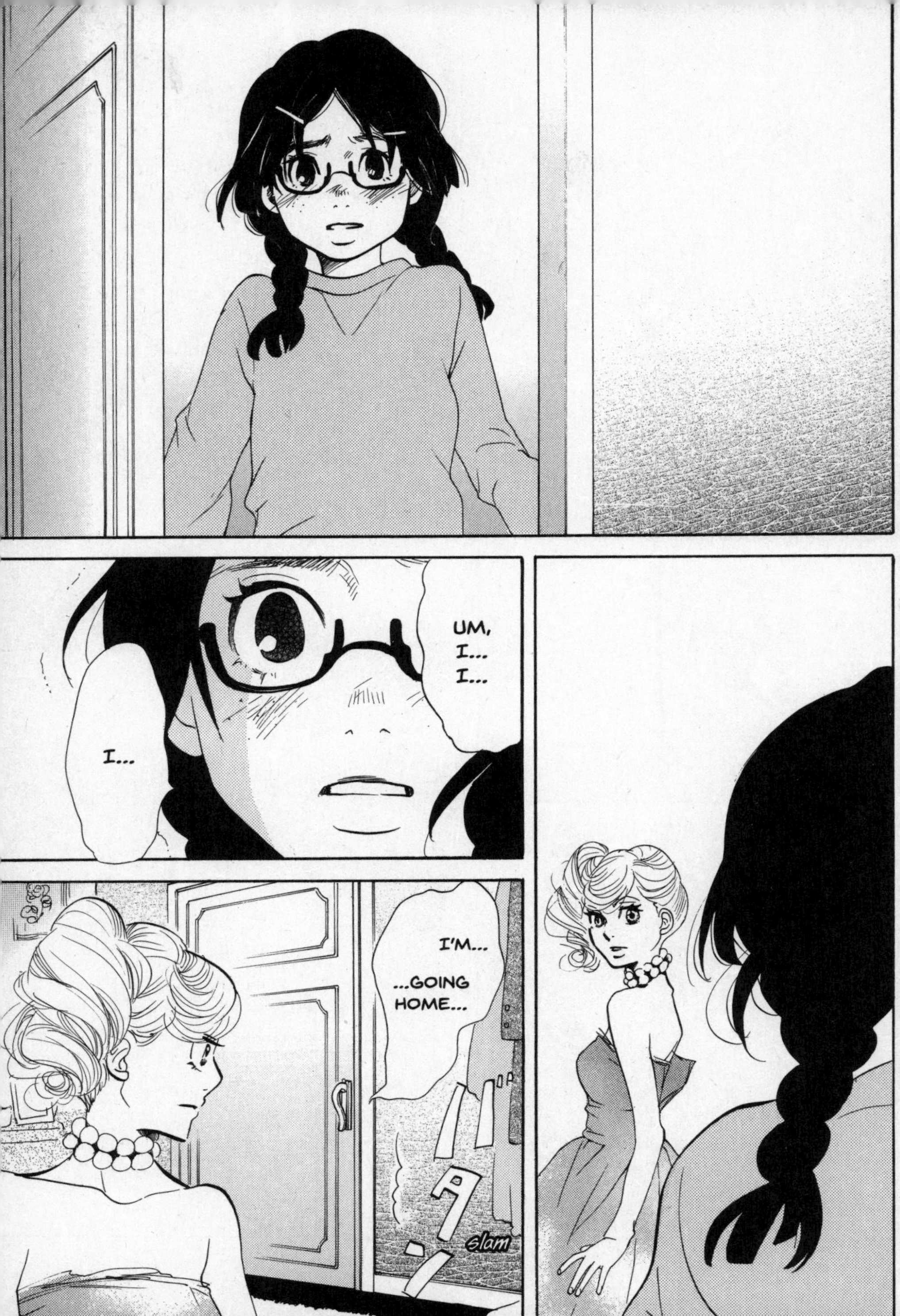
UM, I... I...
I...
I'M...
...GOING HOME...
slam

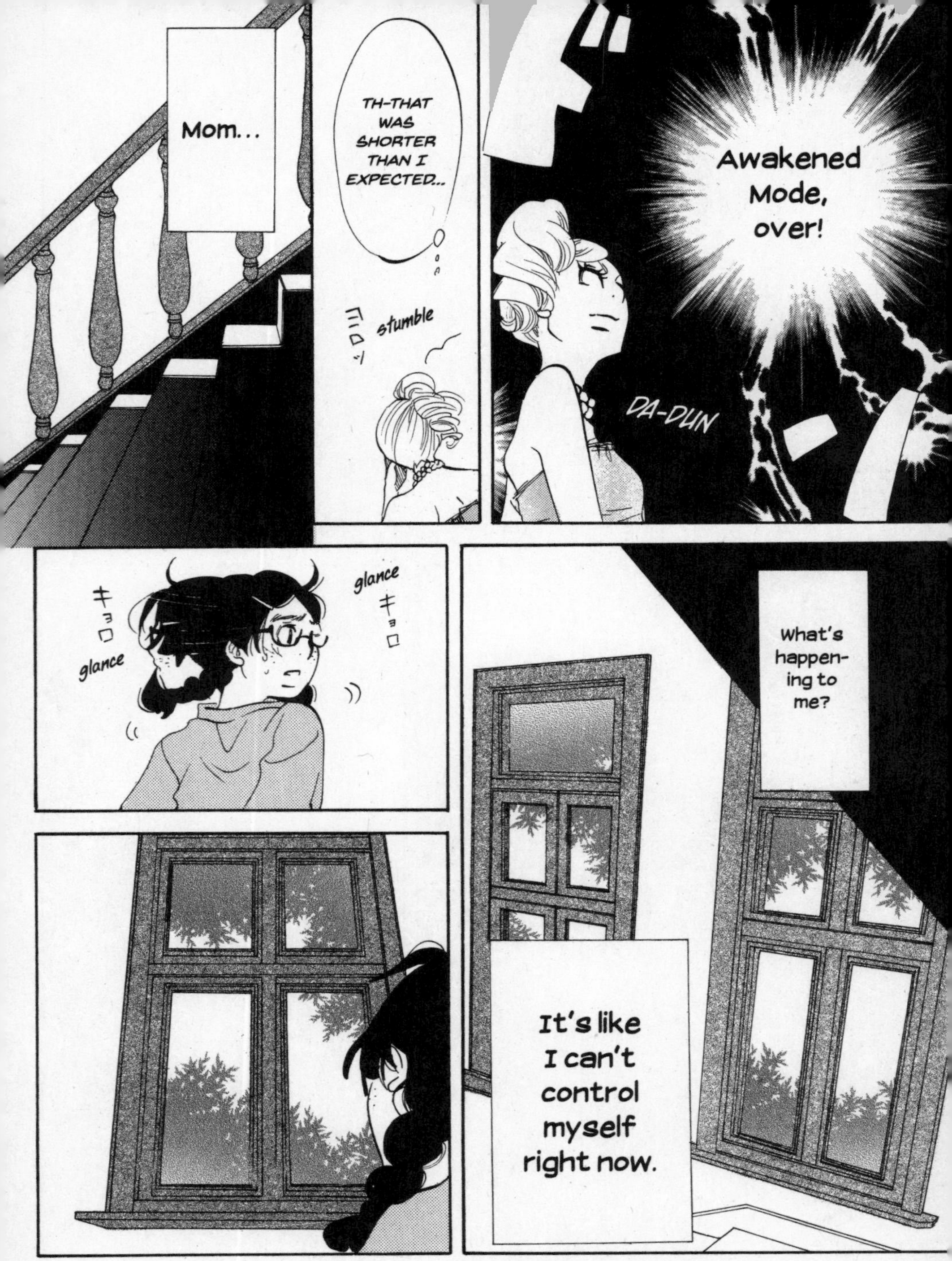
Awakened Mode, over!
DA-DUN
TH-THAT WAS SHORTER THAN I EXPECTED...
ヨロッ
stumble
Mom...
What's happening to me?
It's like I can't control myself right now.
キョロ
glance
キョロ
glance

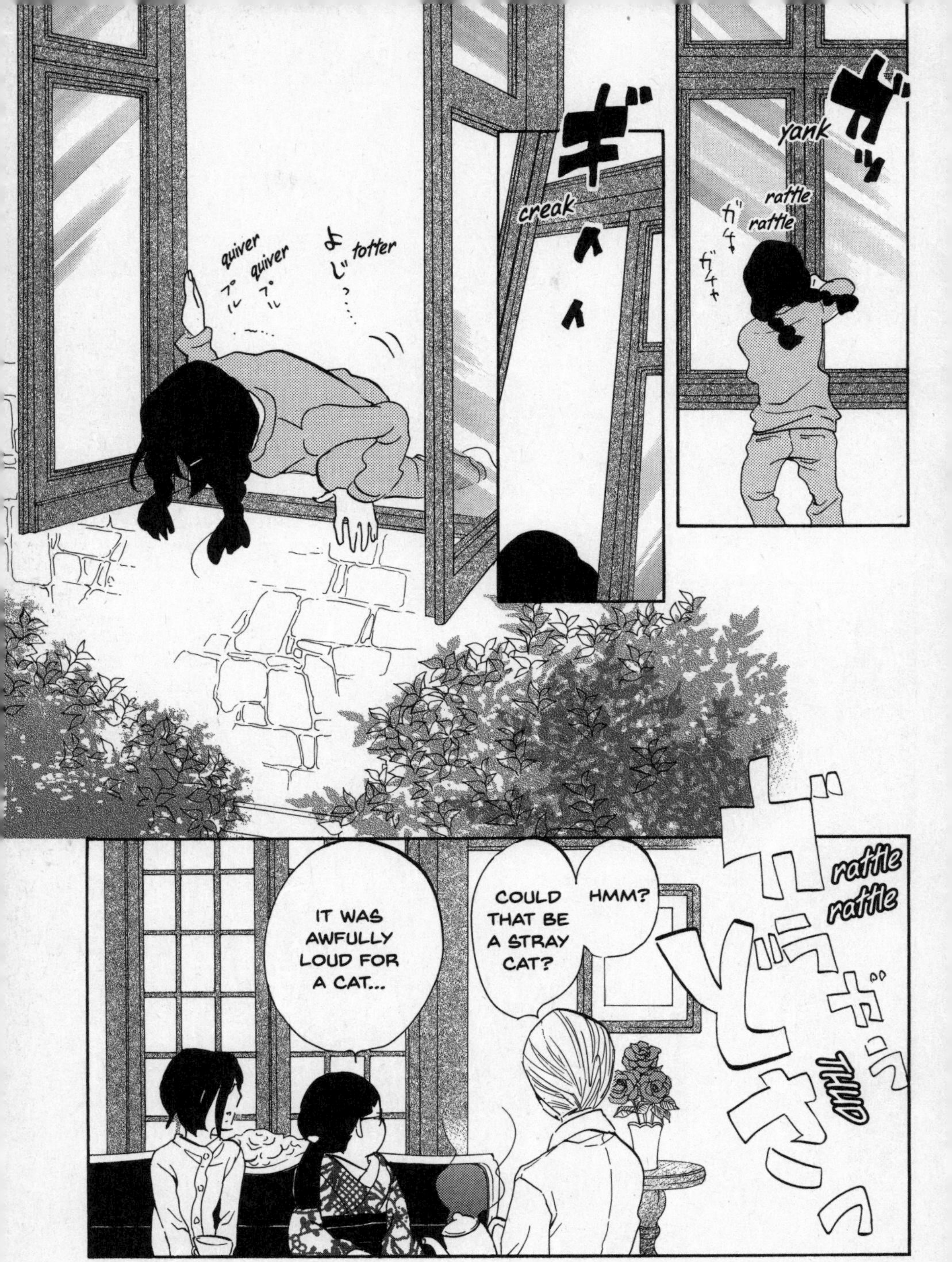
yank
rattle rattle
creak
quiver quiver
totter
rattle rattle
THUD
HMM?
COULD THAT BE A STRAY CAT?
IT WAS AWFULLY LOUD FOR A CAT...

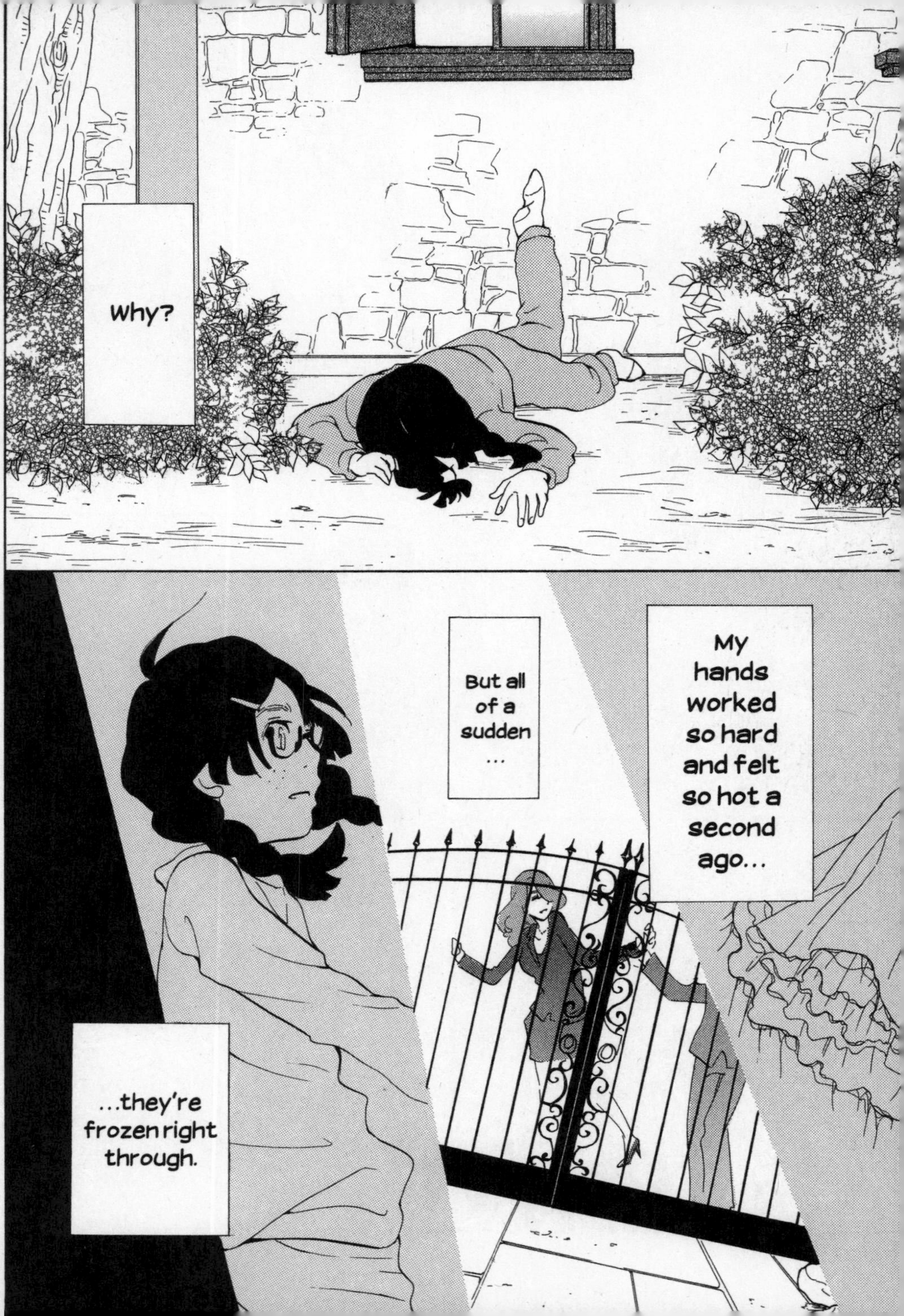
Why?
My hands worked so hard and felt so hot a second ago...
But all of a sudden ...
...they're frozen right through.

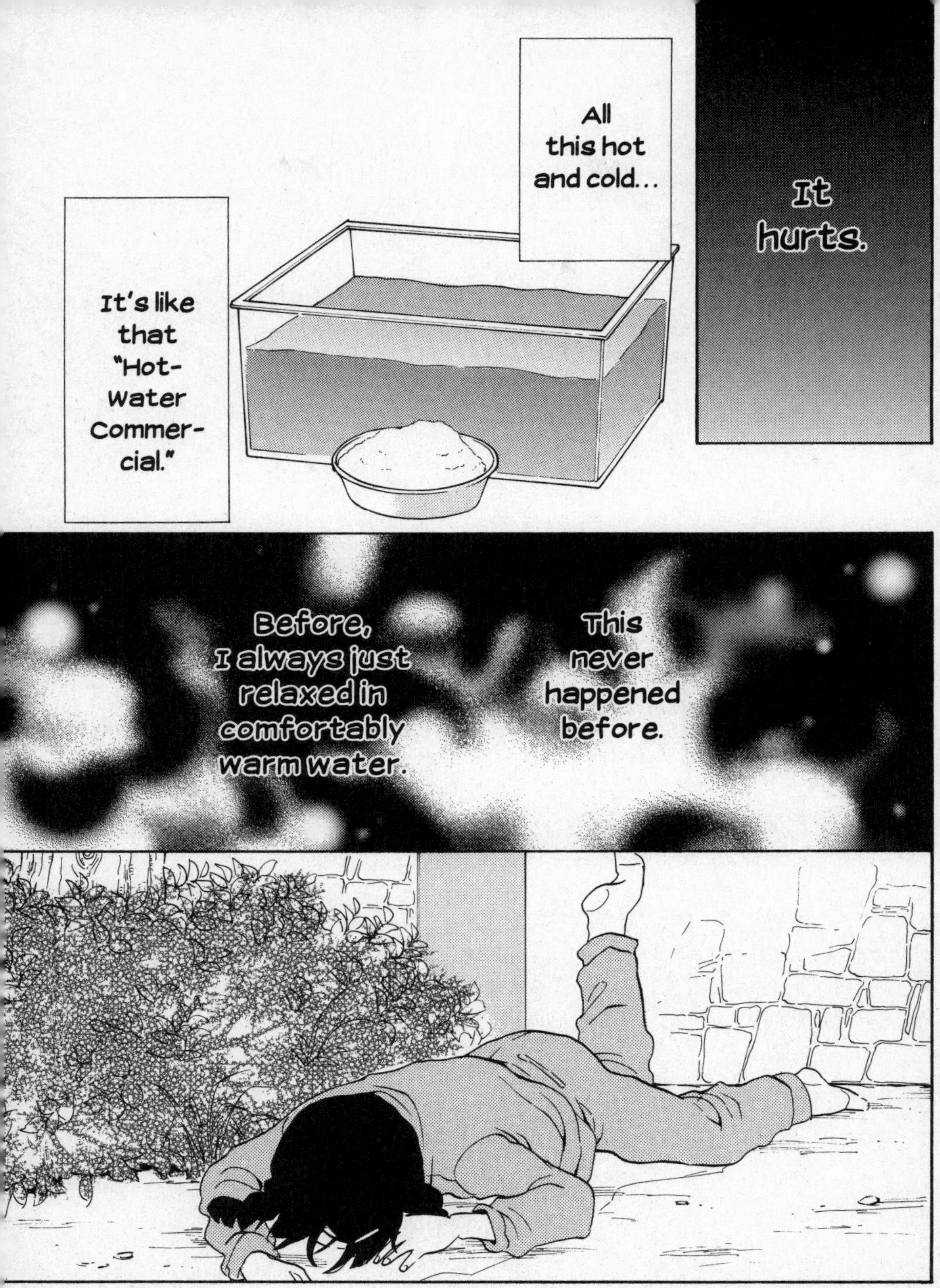
It hurts.
All this hot and cold...
It's like that "Hot-Water Commercial."
This never happened before.
Before, I always just relaxed in comfortably warm water.

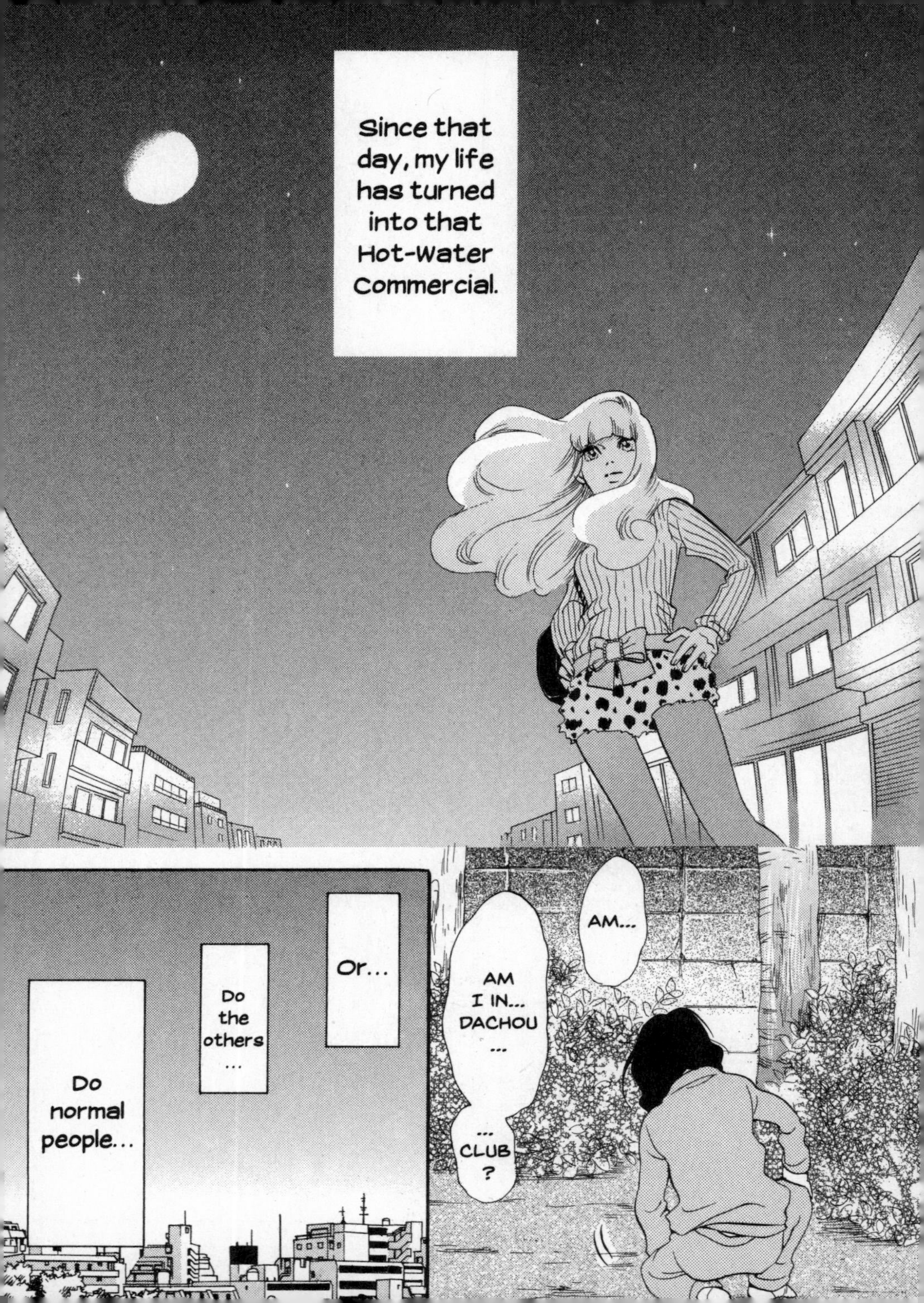
Since that day, my life has turned into that Hot-Water Commercial.
AM...
AM I IN... DACHOU ... ... CLUB ?
Or...
Do the others ...
Do normal people...

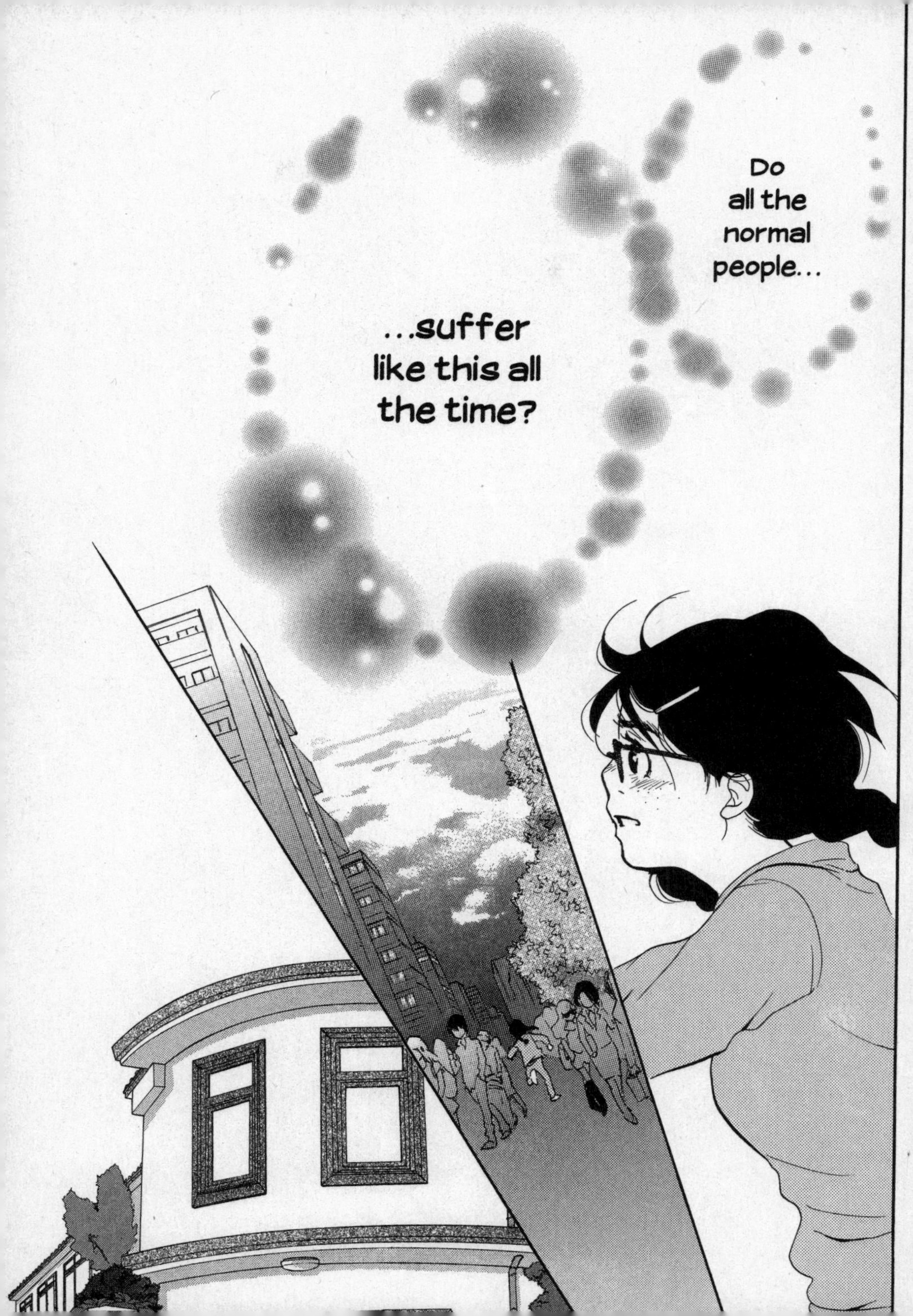
Do all the normal people...
...suffer like this all the time?

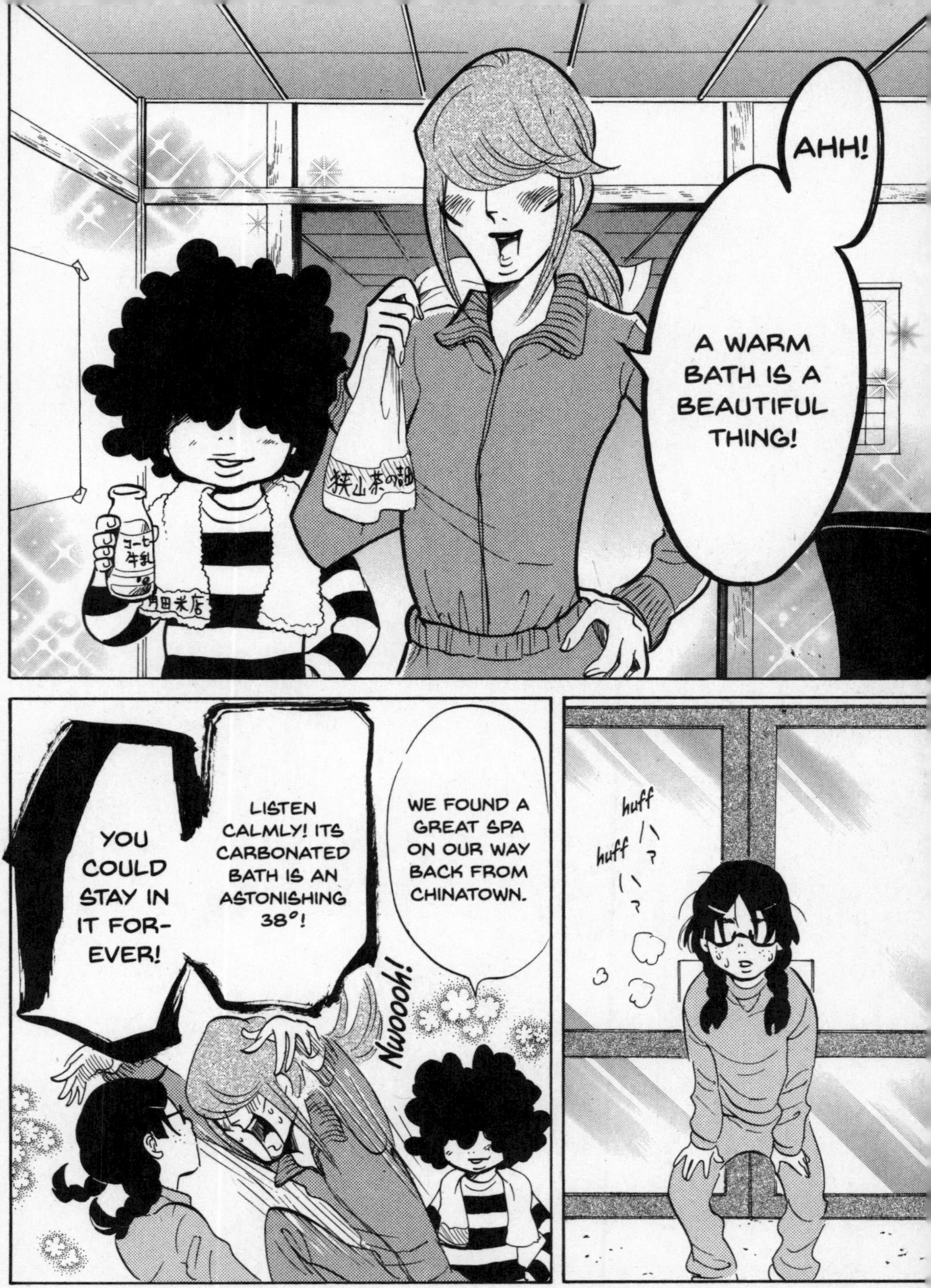
AHH!
A WARM BATH IS A BEAUTIFUL THING!
huff huff
WE FOUND A GREAT SPA ON OUR WAY BACK FROM CHINATOWN.
Nwoooh!
LISTEN CALMLY! ITS CARBONATED BATH IS AN ASTONISHING 38°!
YOU COULD STAY IN IT FOR-EVER!

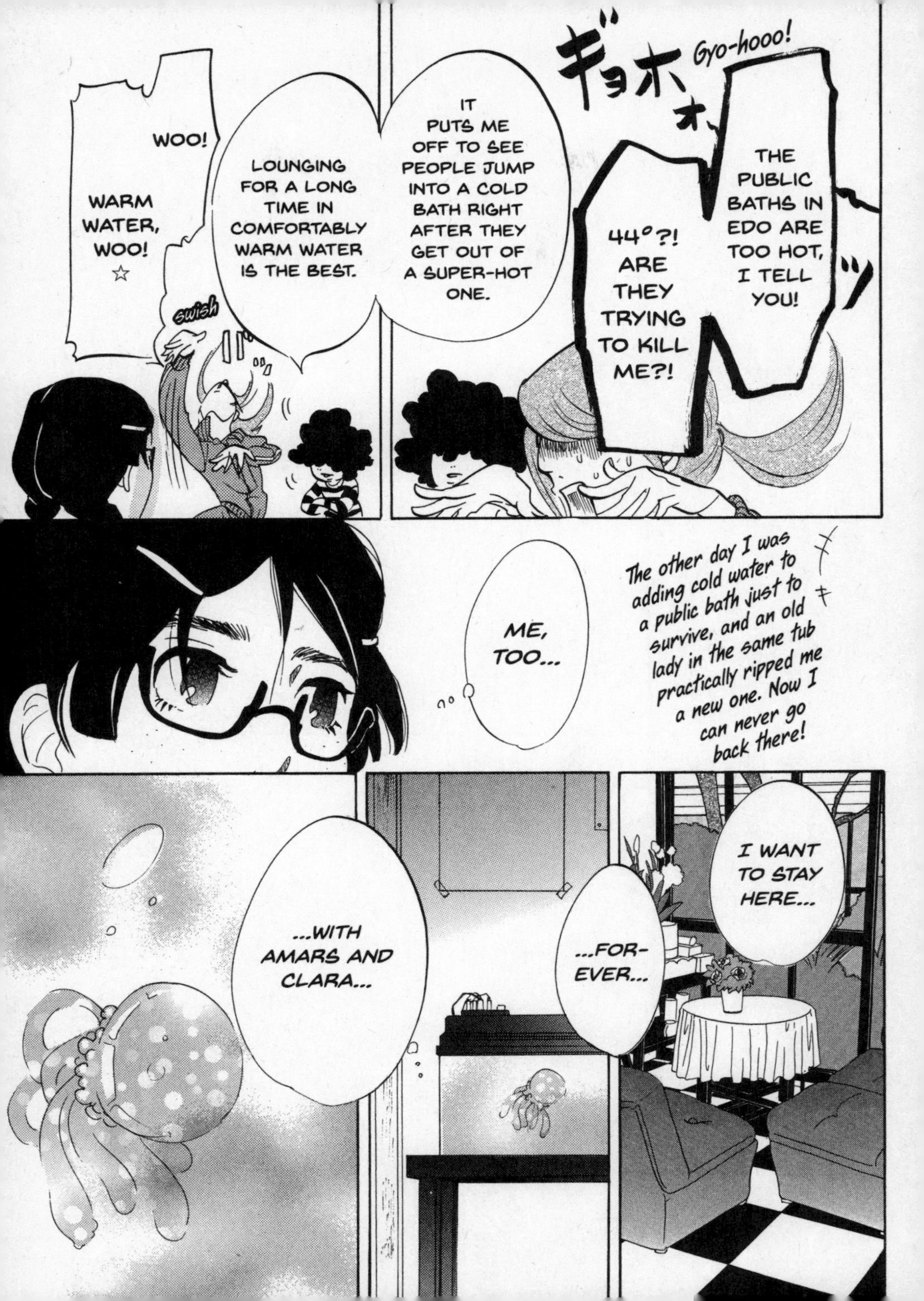
Gyo-hooo!
THE PUBLIC BATHS IN EDO ARE TOO HOT, I TELL YOU!
44°?! ARE THEY TRYING TO KILL ME?!
IT PUTS ME OFF TO SEE PEOPLE JUMP INTO A COLD BATH RIGHT AFTER THEY GET OUT OF A SUPER-HOT ONE.
LOUNGING FOR A LONG TIME IN COMFORTABLY WARM WATER IS THE BEST.
WOO!
WARM WATER, WOO! ☆
swish
The other day I was adding cold water to a public bath just to survive, and an old lady in the same tub practically ripped me a new one. Now I can never go back there!
ME, TOO...
I WANT TO STAY HERE...
...FOR-EVER...
...WITH AMARS AND CLARA...

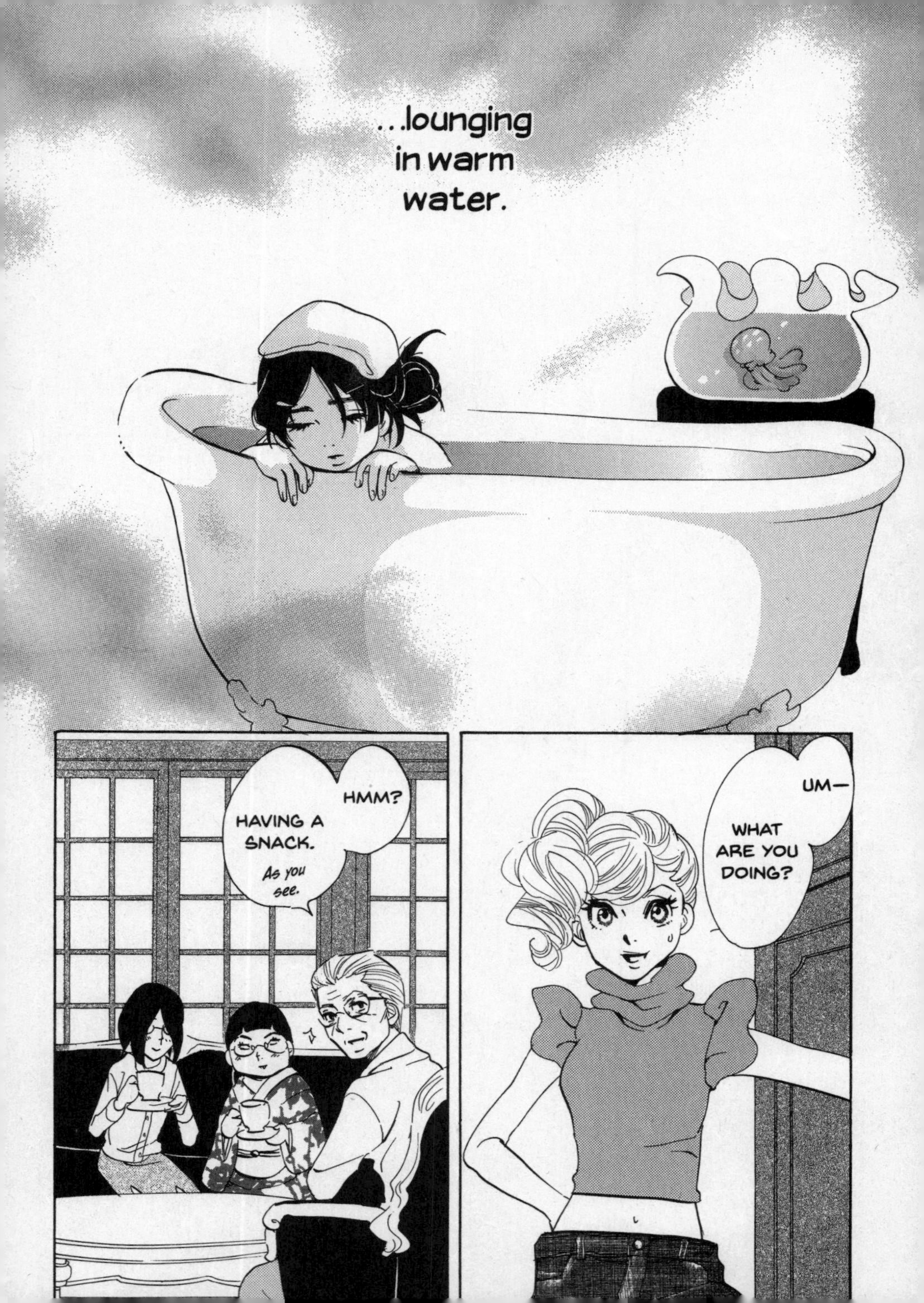
...lounging in warm water.
UM—
WHAT ARE YOU DOING?
HMM?
HAVING A SNACK.
As you see.

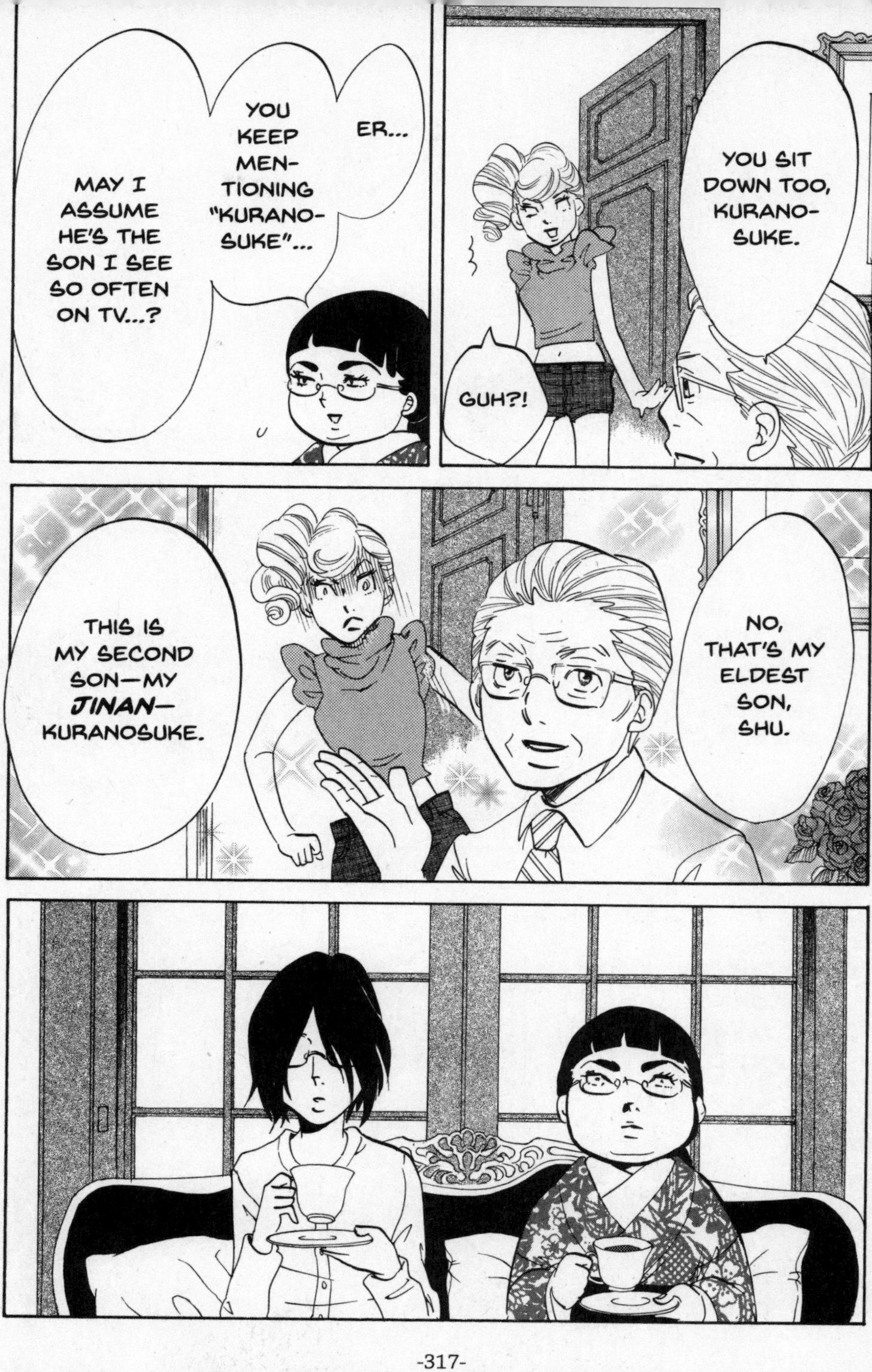
YOU SIT DOWN TOO, KURANOSUKE.
GUH?!
ER...
YOU KEEP MENTIONING "KURANOSUKE"...
MAY I ASSUME HE'S THE SON I SEE SO OFTEN ON TV...?
NO, THAT'S MY ELDEST SON, SHU.
THIS IS MY SECOND SON—MY *JINAN*—KURANOSUKE.

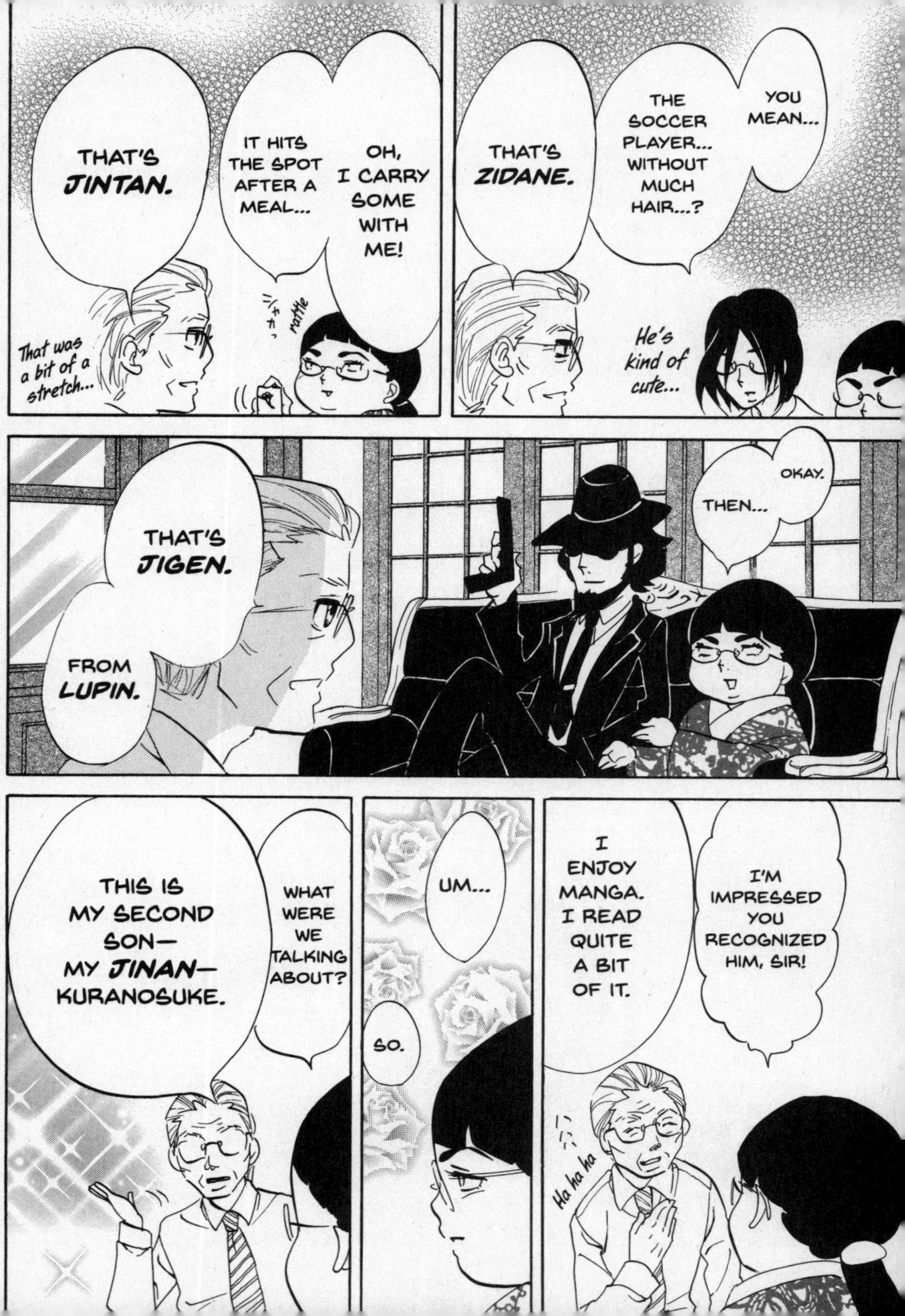
YOU MEAN...
THE SOCCER PLAYER... WITHOUT MUCH HAIR...?
THAT'S ZIDANE.
He's kind of cute...
OH, I CARRY SOME WITH ME!
IT HITS THE SPOT AFTER A MEAL...
rattle
THAT'S JINTAN.
That was a bit of a stretch...
OKAY.
THEN...
THAT'S JIGEN.
FROM LUPIN.
I'M IMPRESSED YOU RECOGNIZED HIM, SIR!
I ENJOY MANGA. I READ QUITE A BIT OF IT.
Ha ha ha
UM...
SO.
WHAT WERE WE TALKING ABOUT?
THIS IS MY SECOND SON— MY JINAN— KURANOSUKE.

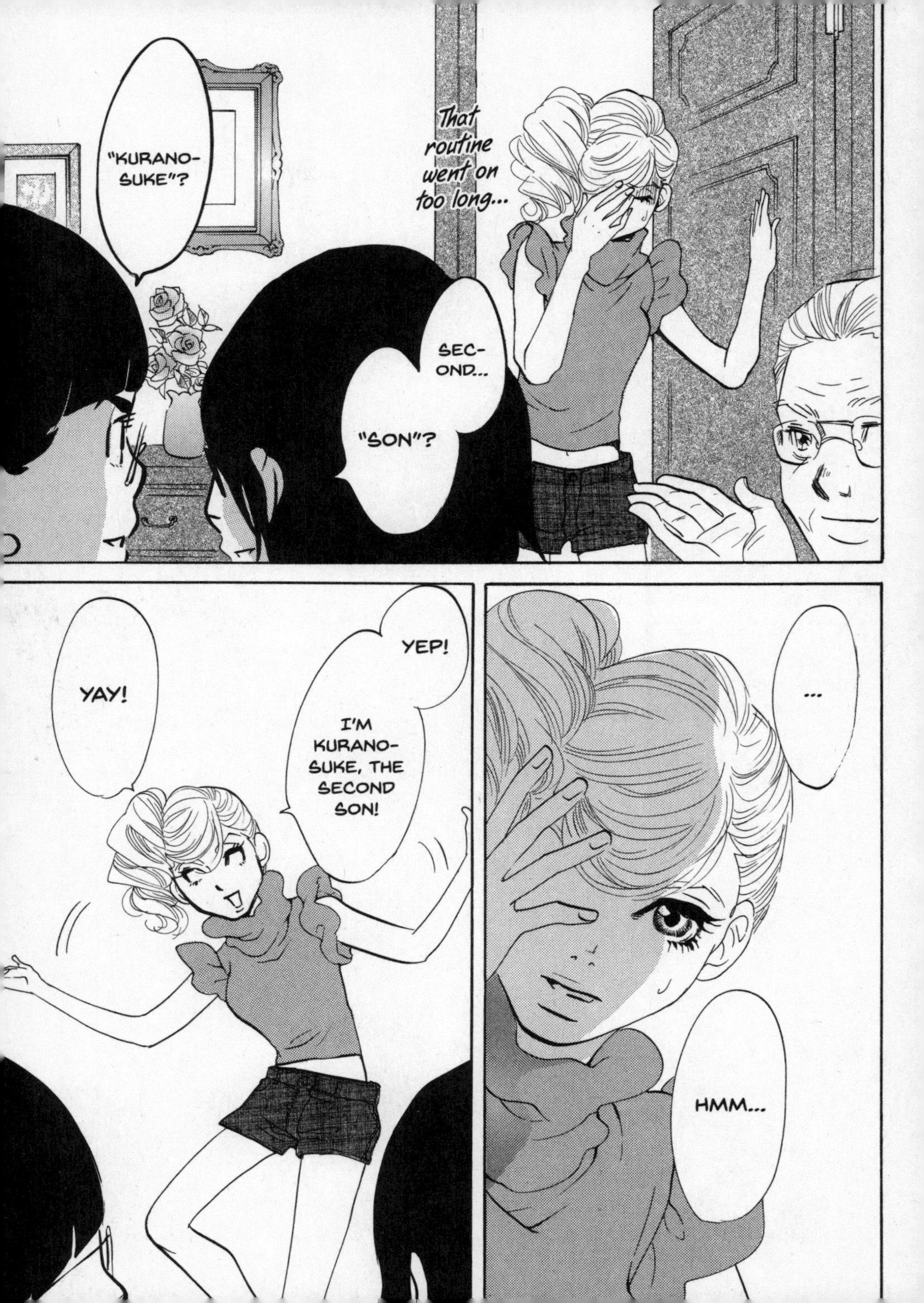
That routine went on too long...
SEC-OND... "SON"?
"KURANO-SUKE"?
...
HMM...
YEP! I'M KURANO-SUKE, THE SECOND SON!
YAY!

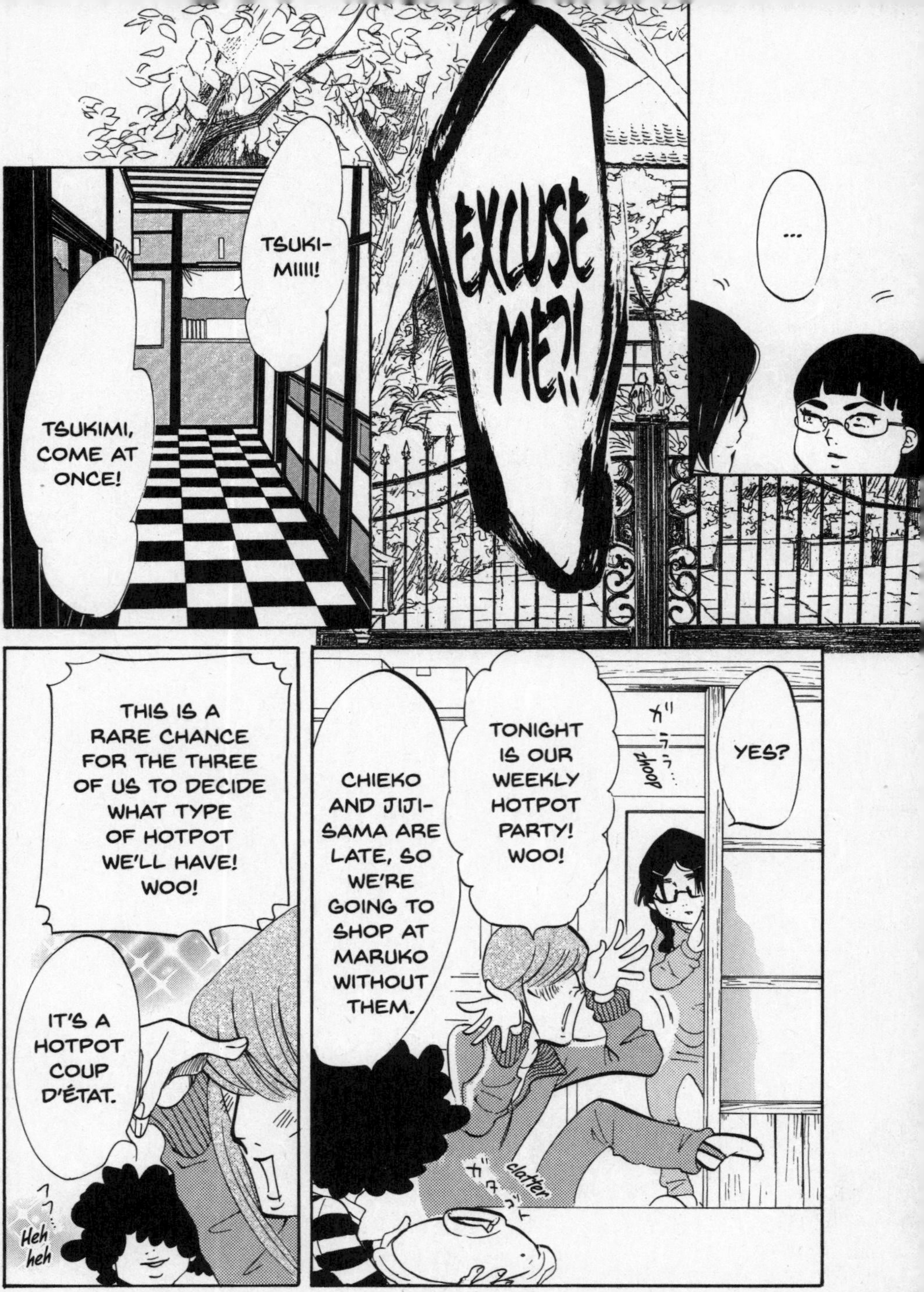
...
EXCUSE ME?!
TSUKI-MIIII!
TSUKIMI, COME AT ONCE!
YES?
zhoop
TONIGHT IS OUR WEEKLY HOTPOT PARTY! WOO!
CHIEKO AND JIJI-SAMA ARE LATE, SO WE'RE GOING TO SHOP AT MARUKO WITHOUT THEM.
clatter
THIS IS A RARE CHANCE FOR THE THREE OF US TO DECIDE WHAT TYPE OF HOTPOT WE'LL HAVE! WOO!
IT'S A HOTPOT COUP D'ÉTAT.
Heh heh

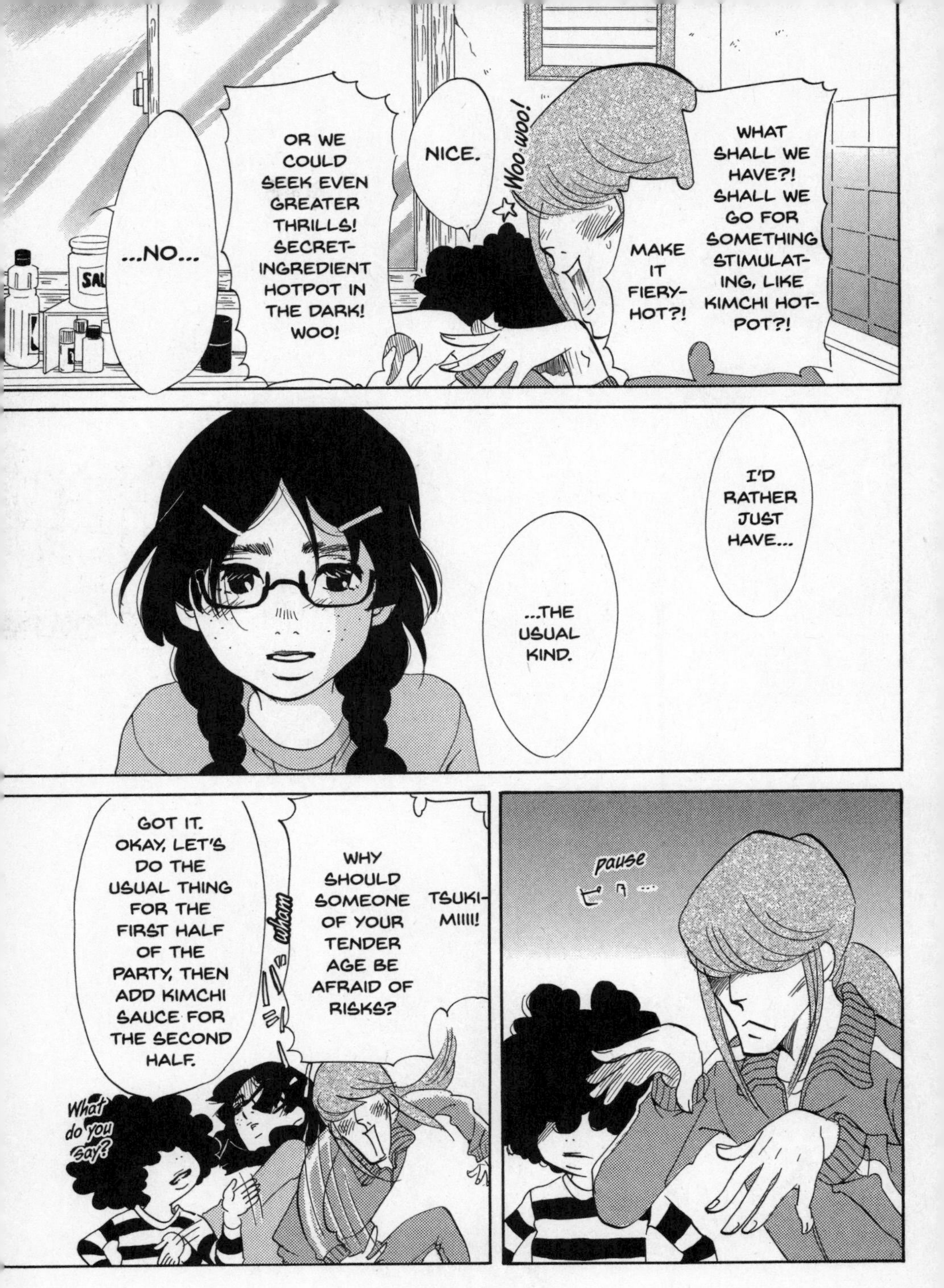
WHAT SHALL WE HAVE?! SHALL WE GO FOR SOMETHING STIMULAT-ING, LIKE KIMCHI HOT-POT?!
MAKE IT FIERY-HOT?!
Woo-woo!
NICE.
OR WE COULD SEEK EVEN GREATER THRILLS! SECRET-INGREDIENT HOTPOT IN THE DARK! WOO!
...NO...
I'D RATHER JUST HAVE...
...THE USUAL KIND.
pause
TSUKI-MIIII!
WHY SHOULD SOMEONE OF YOUR TENDER AGE BE AFRAID OF RISKS?
wham
GOT IT. OKAY, LET'S DO THE USUAL THING FOR THE FIRST HALF OF THE PARTY, THEN ADD KIMCHI SAUCE FOR THE SECOND HALF.
What do you say?

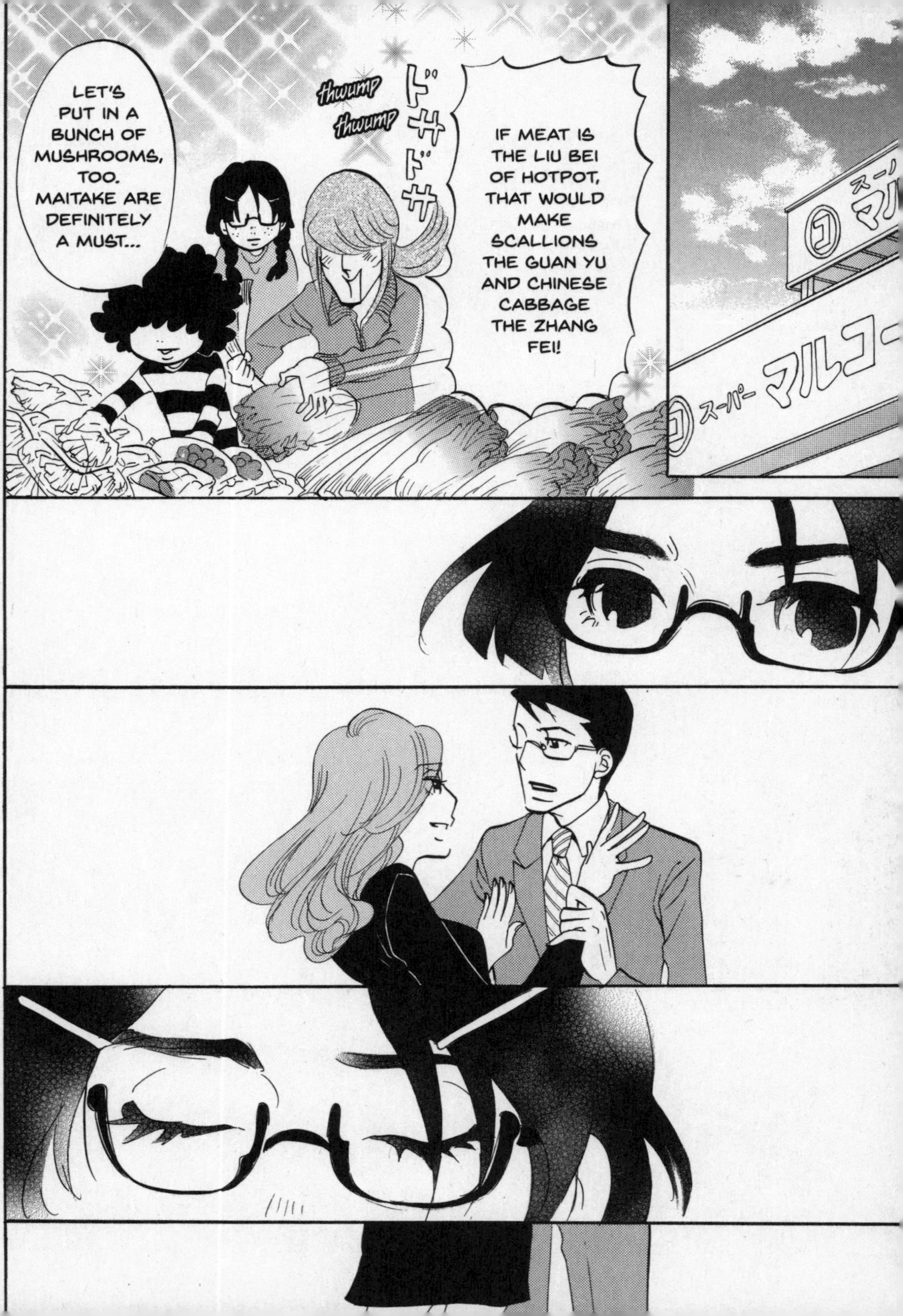

スーパー マルコー
IF MEAT IS THE LIU BEI OF HOTPOT, THAT WOULD MAKE SCALLIONS THE GUAN YU AND CHINESE CABBAGE THE ZHANG FEI!
ドサドサ
thwump thwump
LET'S PUT IN A BUNCH OF MUSHROOMS, TOO. MAITAKE ARE DEFINITELY A MUST...

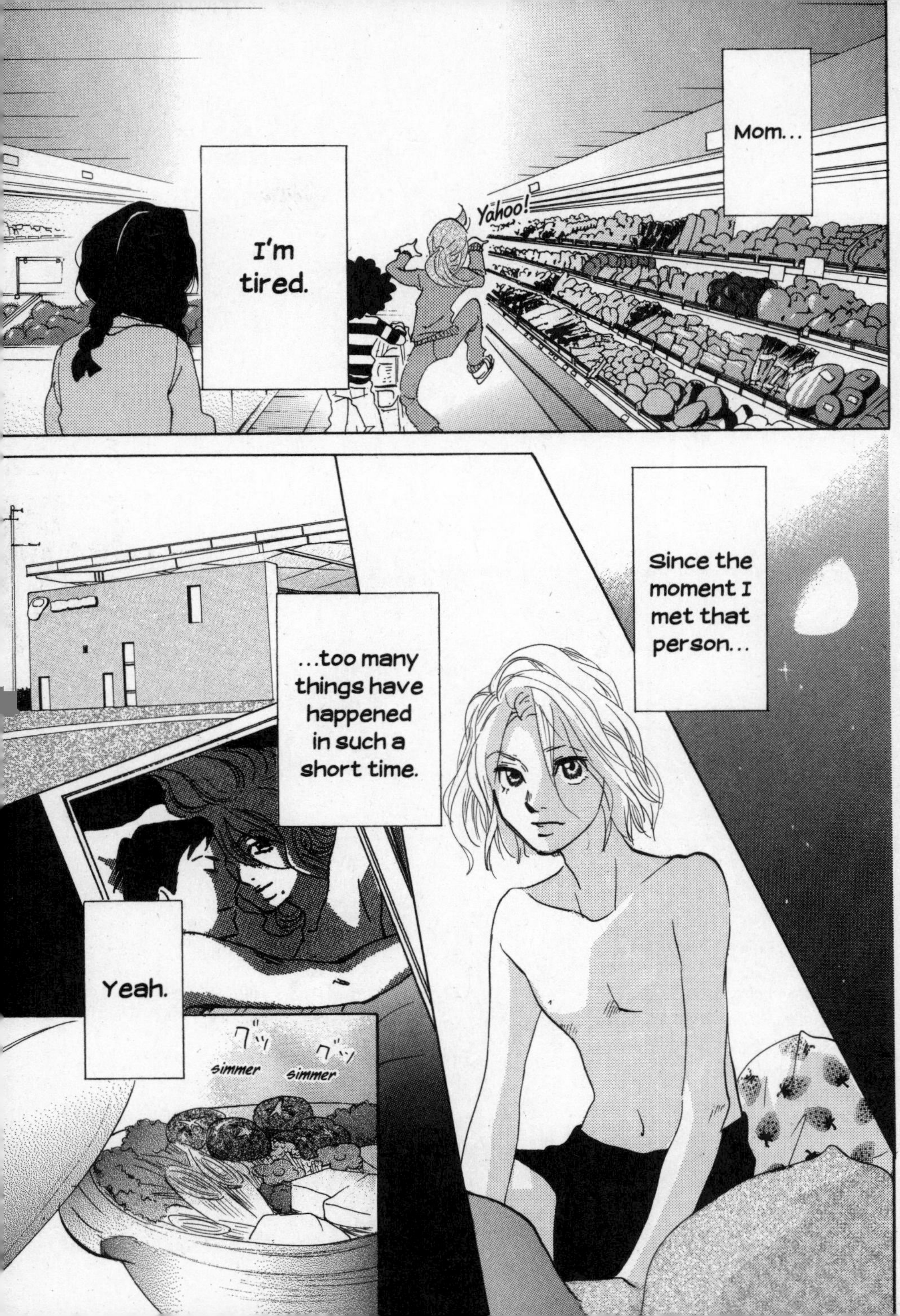
Mom...
Yahoo!
I'm tired.
Since the moment I met that person...
...too many things have happened in such a short time.
Yeah.
グツ simmer
グツ simmer

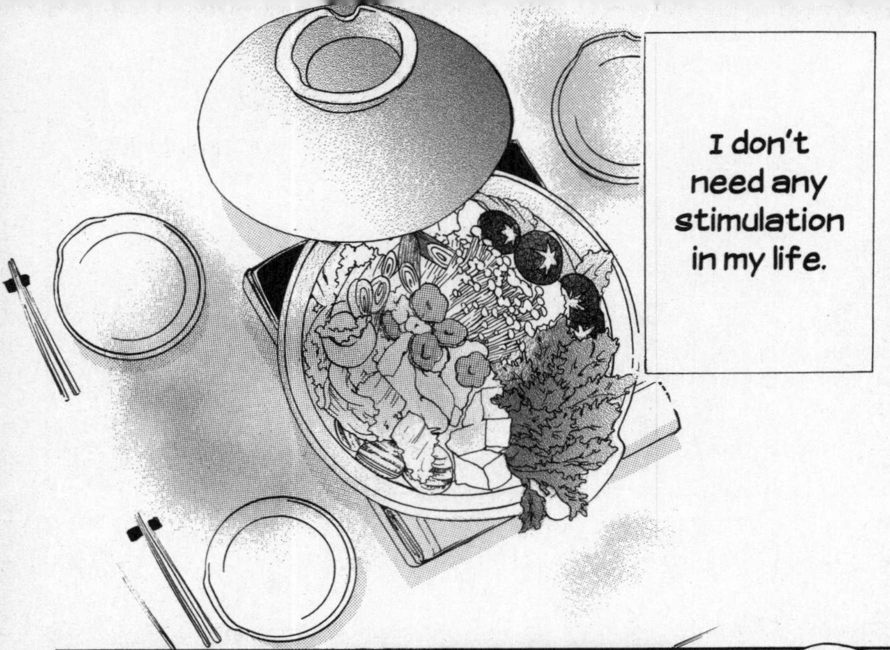
I don't need any stimulation in my life.

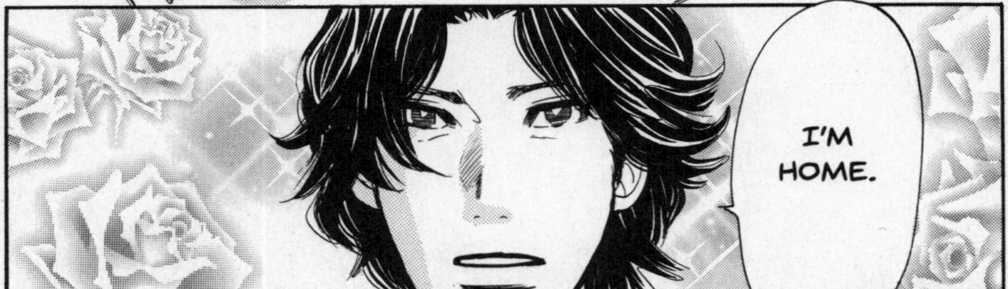
I'M HOME.

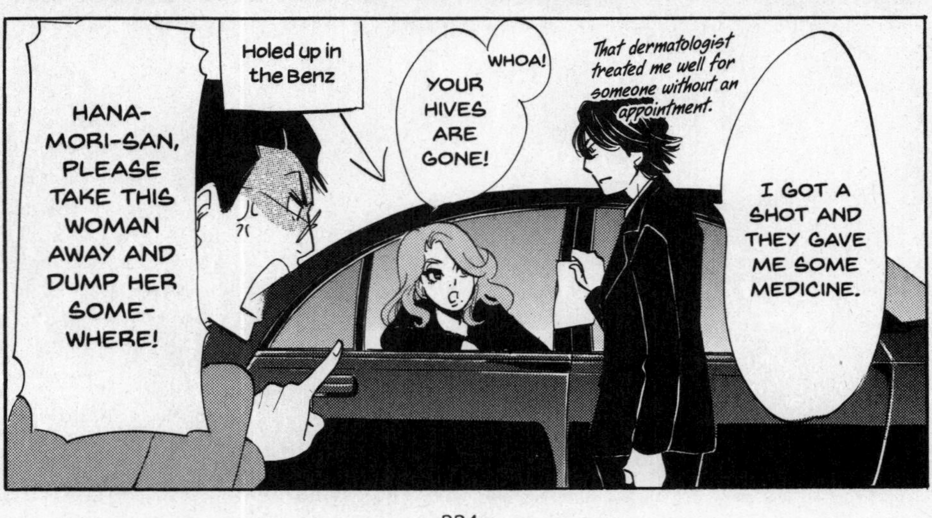
I GOT A SHOT AND THEY GAVE ME SOME MEDICINE.
That dermatologist treated me well for someone without an appointment.
WHOA!
YOUR HIVES ARE GONE!
Holed up in the Benz
HANA-MORI-SAN, PLEASE TAKE THIS WOMAN AWAY AND DUMP HER SOME-WHERE!

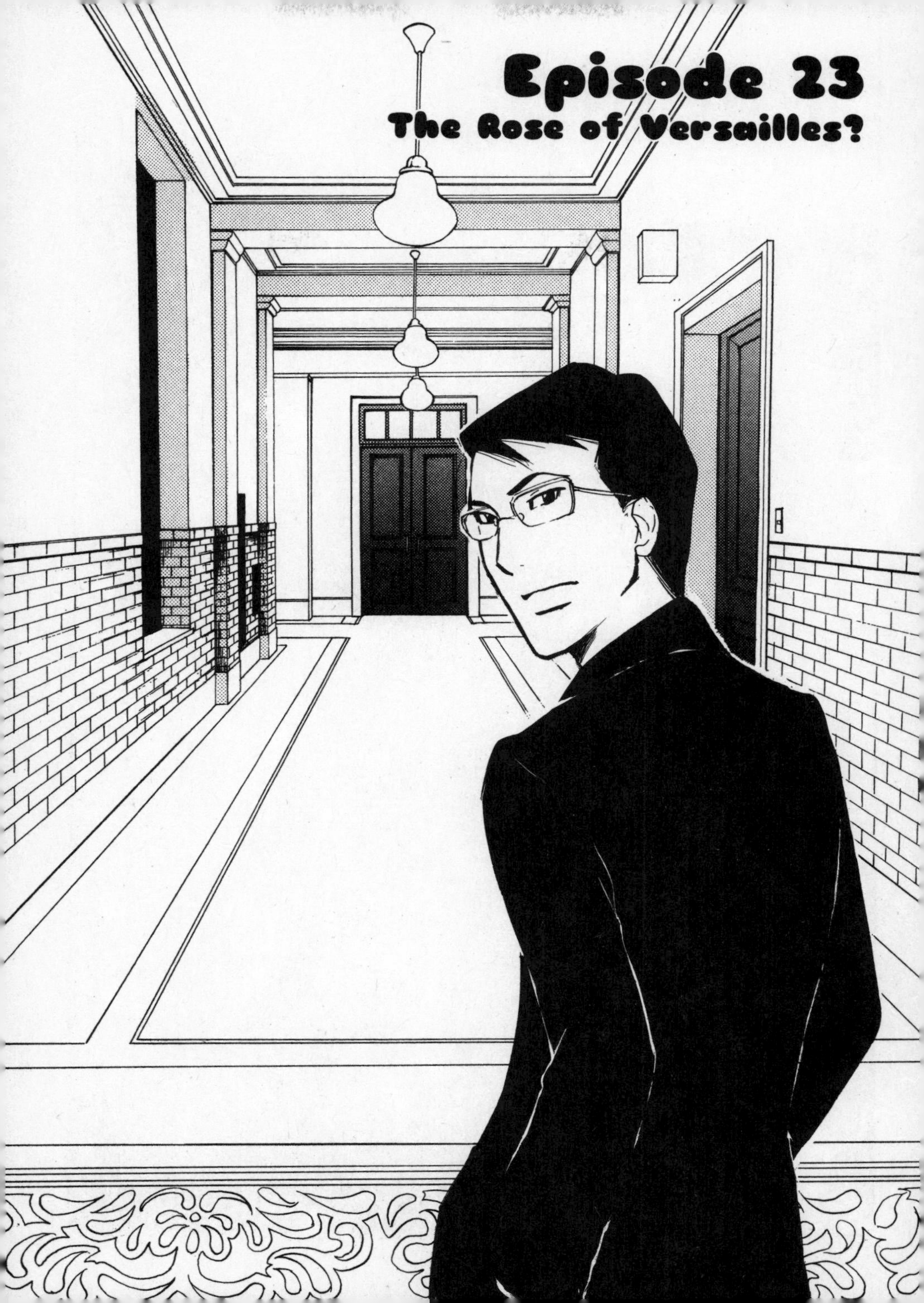
Episode 23
The Rose of Versailles?

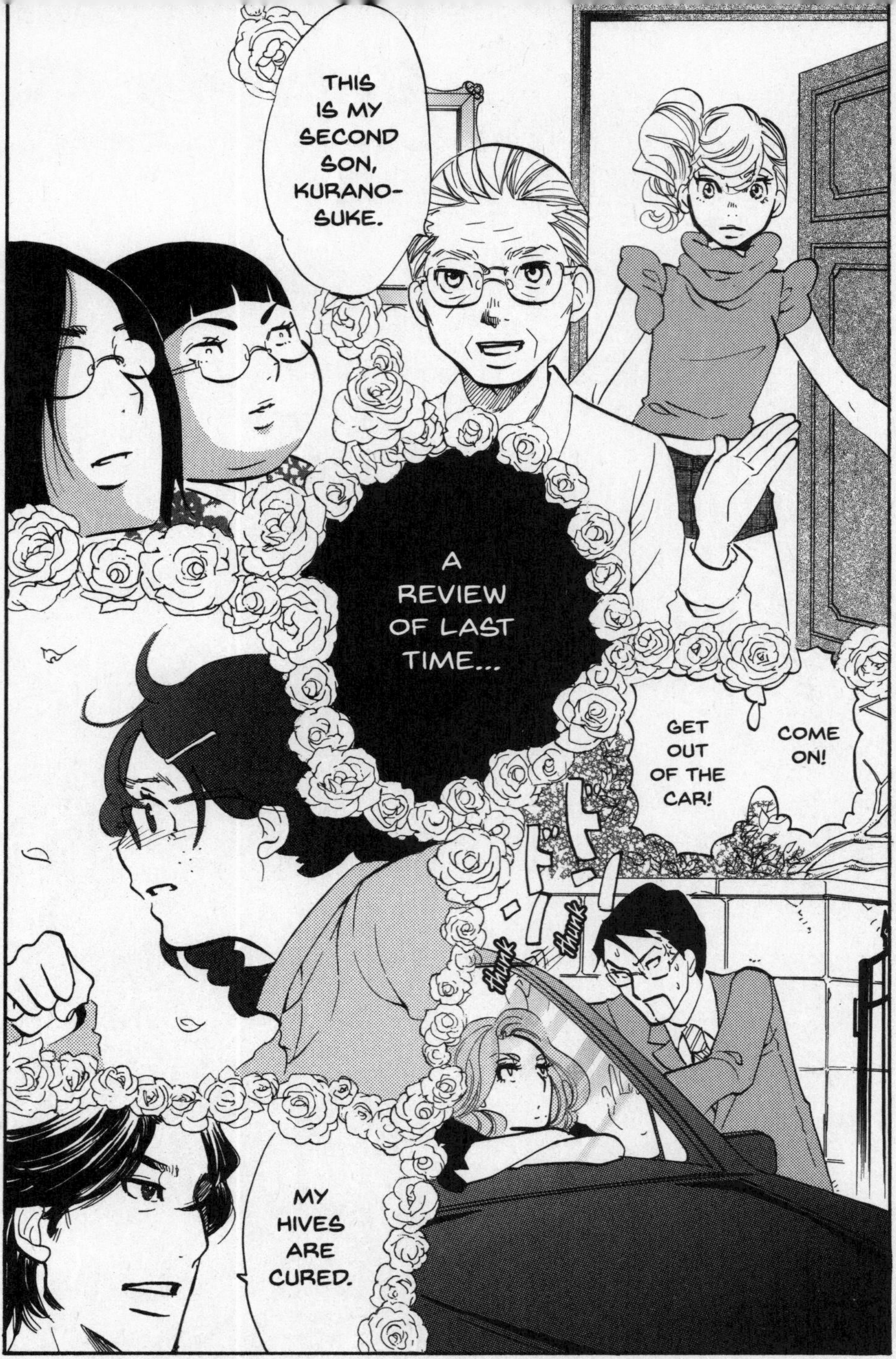
THIS IS MY SECOND SON, KURANOSUKE.
A REVIEW OF LAST TIME...
COME ON!
GET OUT OF THE CAR!
thunk
thunk
thunk
MY HIVES ARE CURED.

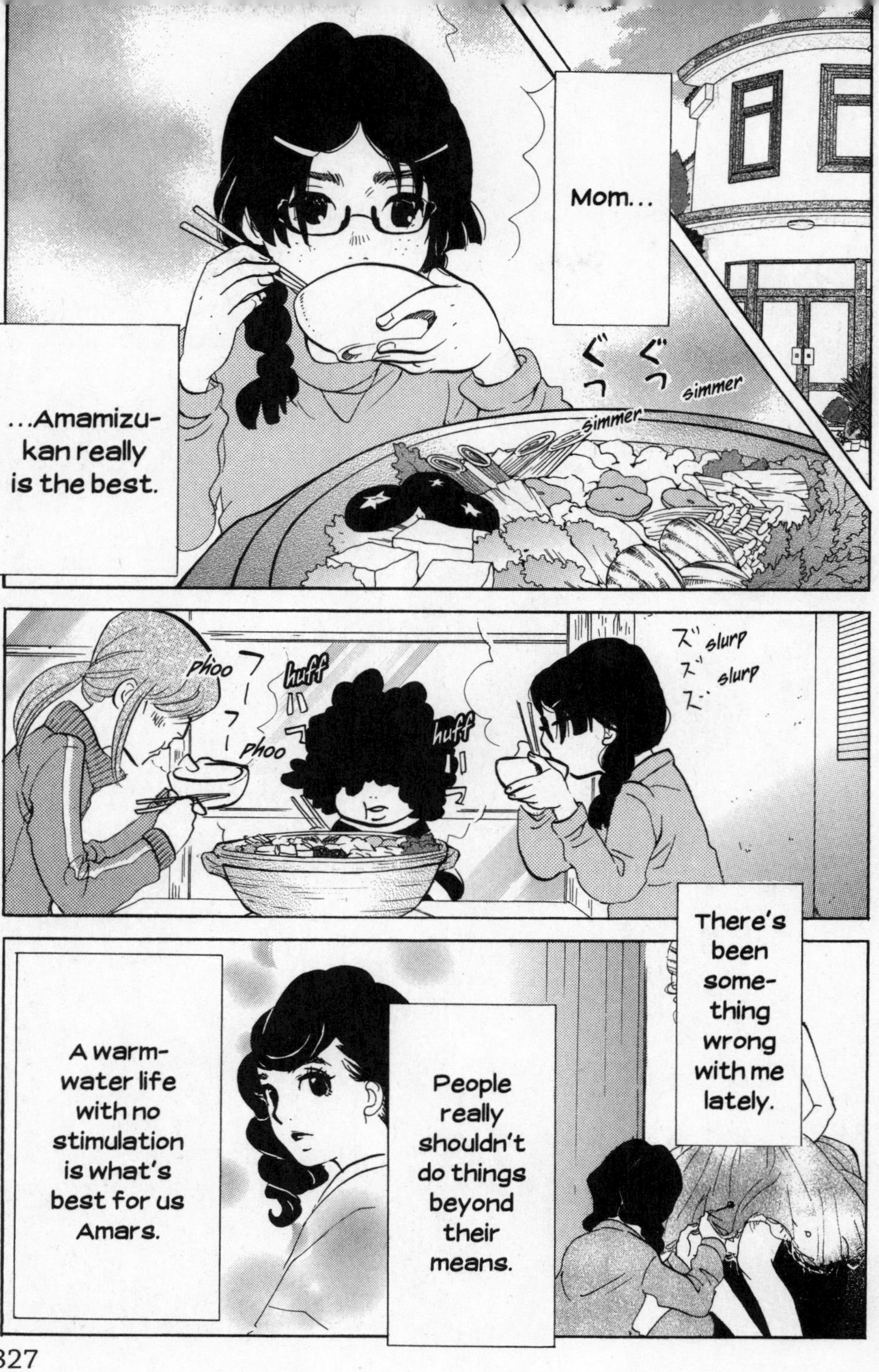
Mom...
ぐつぐつ
simmer
simmer
...Amamizu-kan really is the best.
ズズズ
slurp
slurp
ハフハフ
huff
huff
フーフー
phoo
phoo
There's been some-thing wrong with me lately.
People really shouldn't do things beyond their means.
A warm-water life with no stimulation is what's best for us Amars.

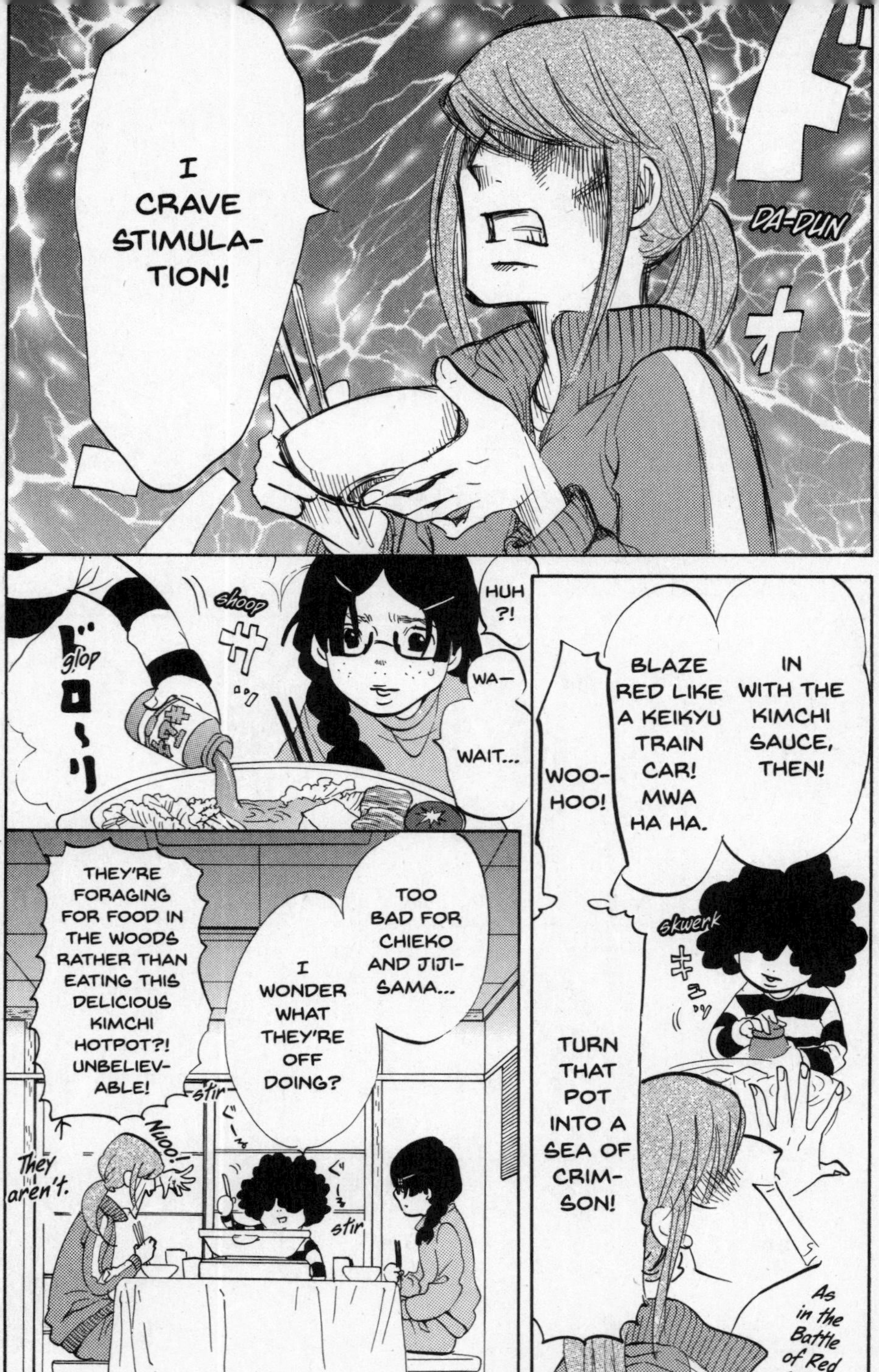
I CRAVE STIMULA-TION!
DA-DUN
IN WITH THE KIMCHI SAUCE, THEN!
BLAZE RED LIKE A KEIKYU TRAIN CAR! MWA HA HA.
WOO-HOO!
skwerk
TURN THAT POT INTO A SEA OF CRIM-SON!
As in the Battle of Red Cliffs!
HUH ?!
WA—
WAIT...
shoop
glop
TOO BAD FOR CHIEKO AND JIJI-SAMA...
I WONDER WHAT THEY'RE OFF DOING?
THEY'RE FORAGING FOR FOOD IN THE WOODS RATHER THAN EATING THIS DELICIOUS KIMCHI HOTPOT?! UNBELIEV-ABLE!
stir
Nuoo!
stir
They aren't.

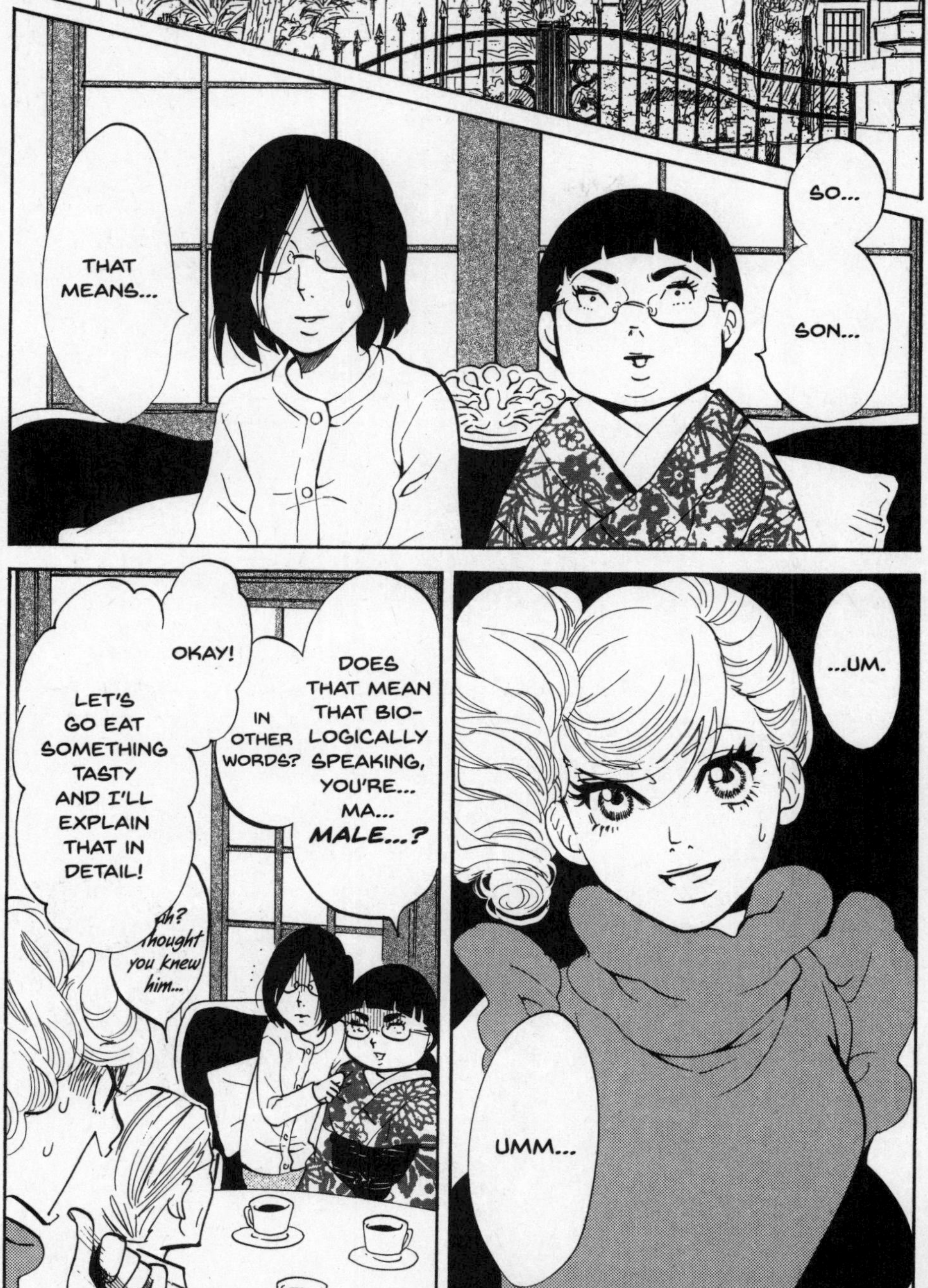
SO... SON...
THAT MEANS...
...UM.
UMM...
DOES THAT MEAN THAT BIO-LOGICALLY SPEAKING, YOU'RE... MA... *MALE...?*
IN OTHER WORDS?
OKAY! LET'S GO EAT SOMETHING TASTY AND I'LL EXPLAIN THAT IN DETAIL!
you knew him...

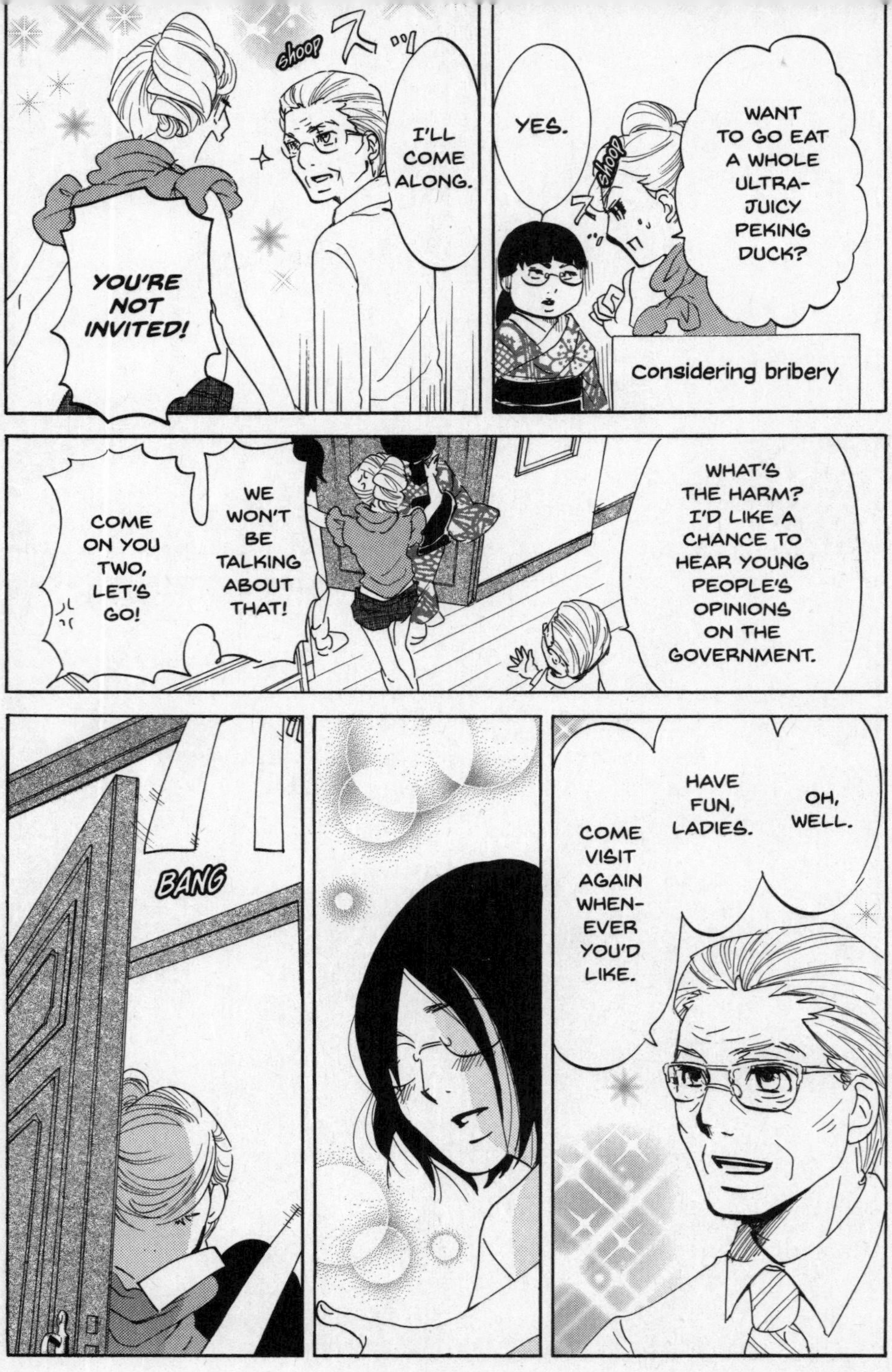
WANT TO GO EAT A WHOLE ULTRA-JUICY PEKING DUCK?
YES.
shoop
Considering bribery
I'LL COME ALONG.
shoop
YOU'RE NOT INVITED!
WHAT'S THE HARM? I'D LIKE A CHANCE TO HEAR YOUNG PEOPLE'S OPINIONS ON THE GOVERNMENT.
WE WON'T BE TALKING ABOUT THAT!
COME ON YOU TWO, LET'S GO!
OH, WELL.
HAVE FUN, LADIES.
COME VISIT AGAIN WHEN-EVER YOU'D LIKE.
BANG

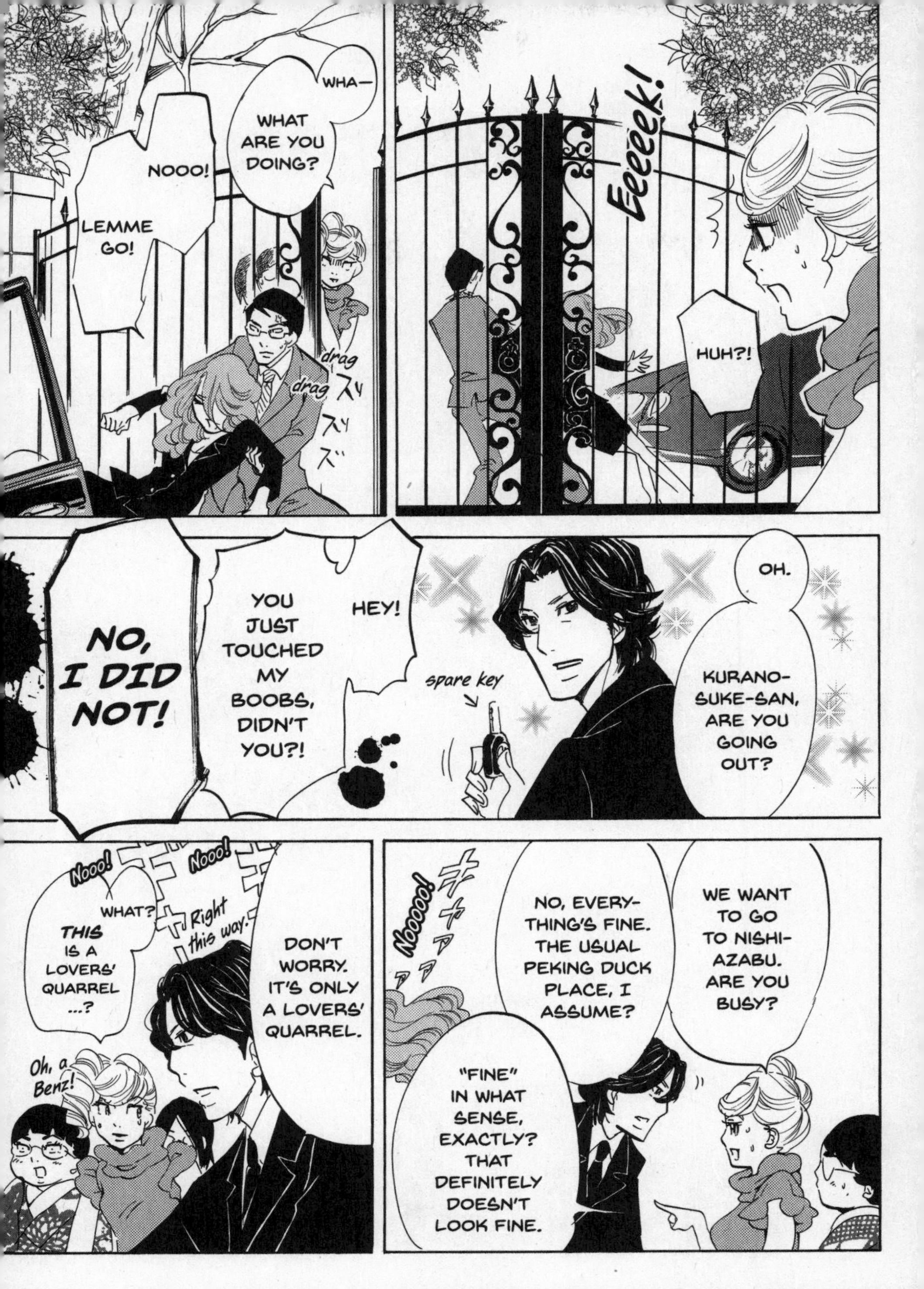
Eeeeek!
HUH?!
WHA—
WHAT ARE YOU DOING?
NOOO!
LEMME GO!
drag
drag
ズリ
ズリ
ズ
OH.
KURANOSUKE-SAN, ARE YOU GOING OUT?
spare key
HEY!
YOU JUST TOUCHED MY BOOBS, DIDN'T YOU?!
NO, I DID NOT!
WE WANT TO GO TO NISHI-AZABU. ARE YOU BUSY?
NO, EVERYTHING'S FINE. THE USUAL PEKING DUCK PLACE, I ASSUME?
Nooooo!
"FINE" IN WHAT SENSE, EXACTLY? THAT DEFINITELY DOESN'T LOOK FINE.
DON'T WORRY. IT'S ONLY A LOVERS' QUARREL.
Right this way.
Nooo!
Nooo!
WHAT?
THIS IS A LOVERS' QUARREL ...?
Oh, a Benz!

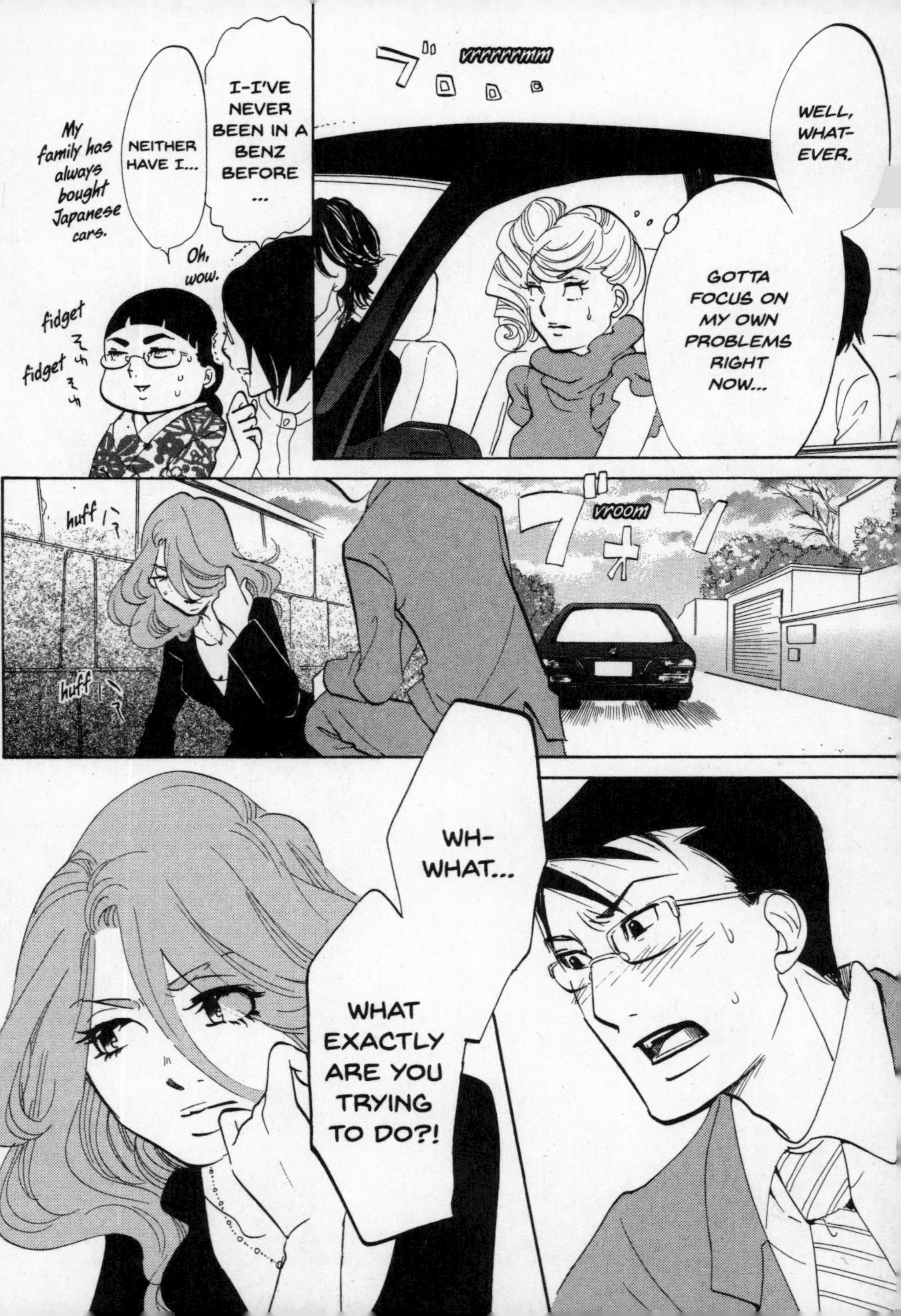
vrrrrrrmm
WELL, WHAT-EVER.
GOTTA FOCUS ON MY OWN PROBLEMS RIGHT NOW...
I-I'VE NEVER BEEN IN A BENZ BEFORE ...
NEITHER HAVE I...
My family has always bought Japanese cars.
Oh, wow.
fidget
fidget
vroom
huff
huff
WH- WHAT...
WHAT EXACTLY ARE YOU TRYING TO DO?!

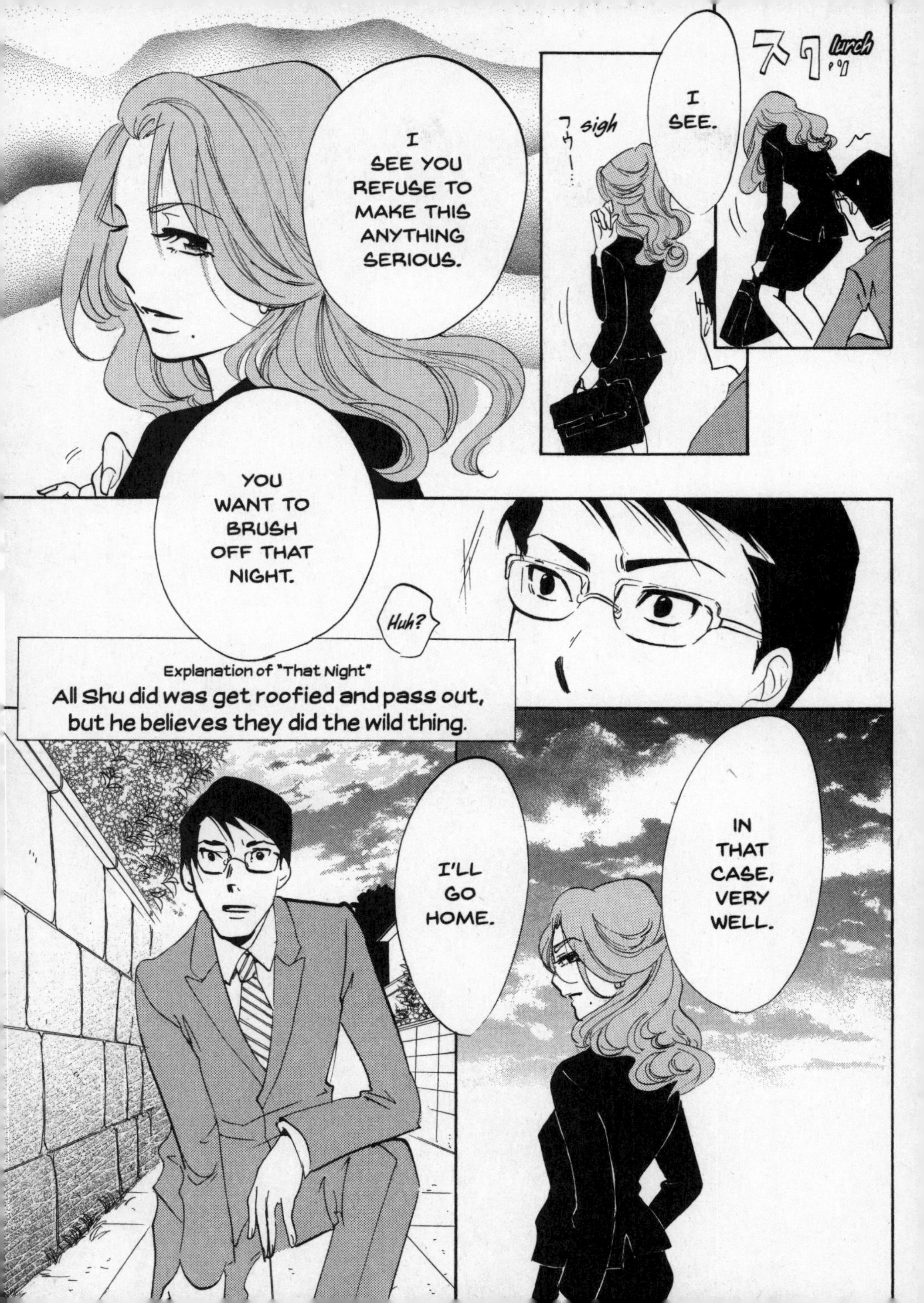
lurch
I SEE.
sigh
I SEE YOU REFUSE TO MAKE THIS ANYTHING SERIOUS.
YOU WANT TO BRUSH OFF THAT NIGHT.
Huh?
Explanation of "That Night"
All Shu did was get roofied and pass out, but he believes they did the wild thing.
IN THAT CASE, VERY WELL.
I'LL GO HOME.

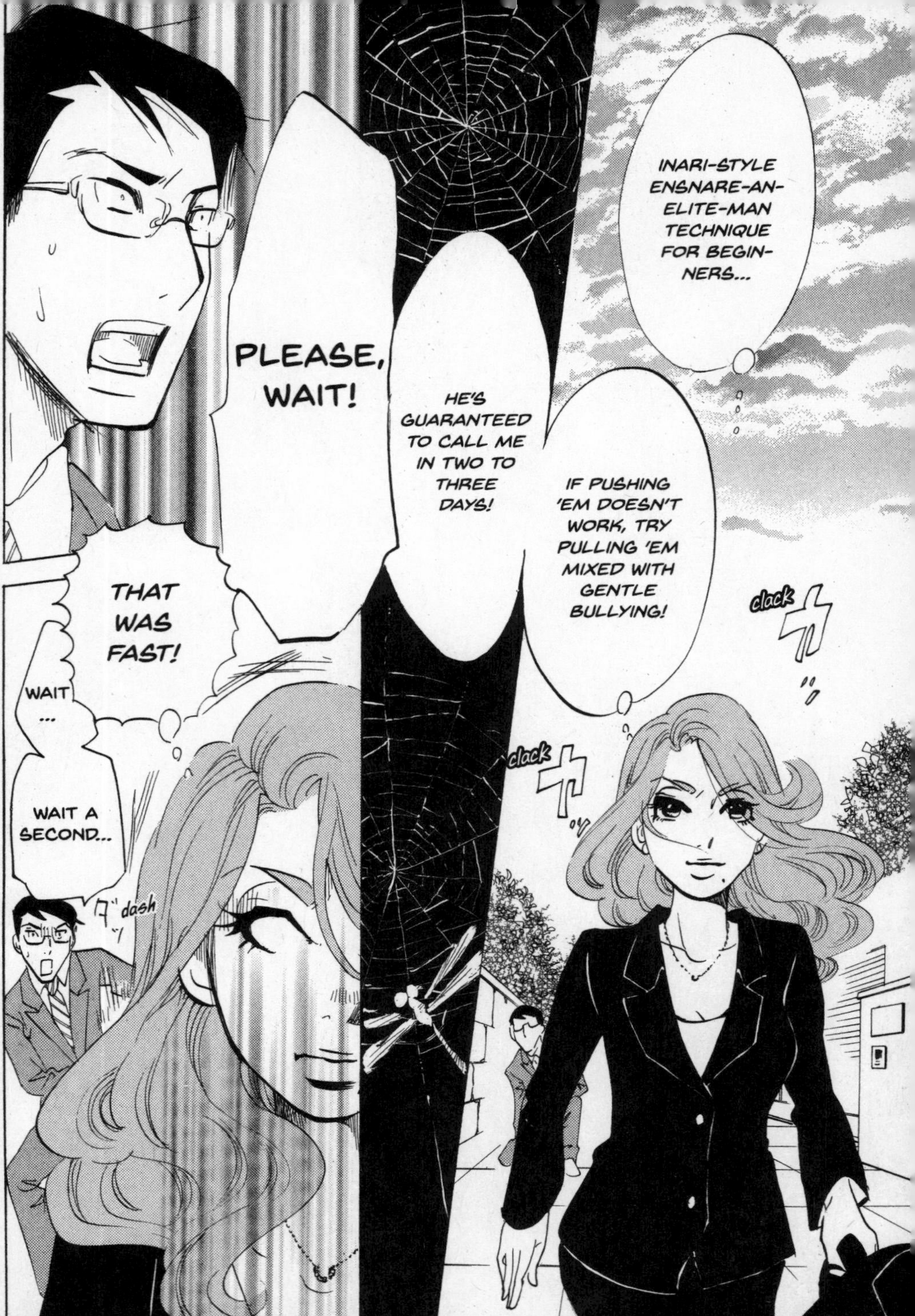
INARI-STYLE ENSNARE-AN-ELITE-MAN TECHNIQUE FOR BEGINNERS...
IF PUSHING 'EM DOESN'T WORK, TRY PULLING 'EM MIXED WITH GENTLE BULLYING!
clack
clack
HE'S GUARANTEED TO CALL ME IN TWO TO THREE DAYS!
PLEASE, WAIT!
THAT WAS FAST!
WAIT...
WAIT A SECOND...
dash

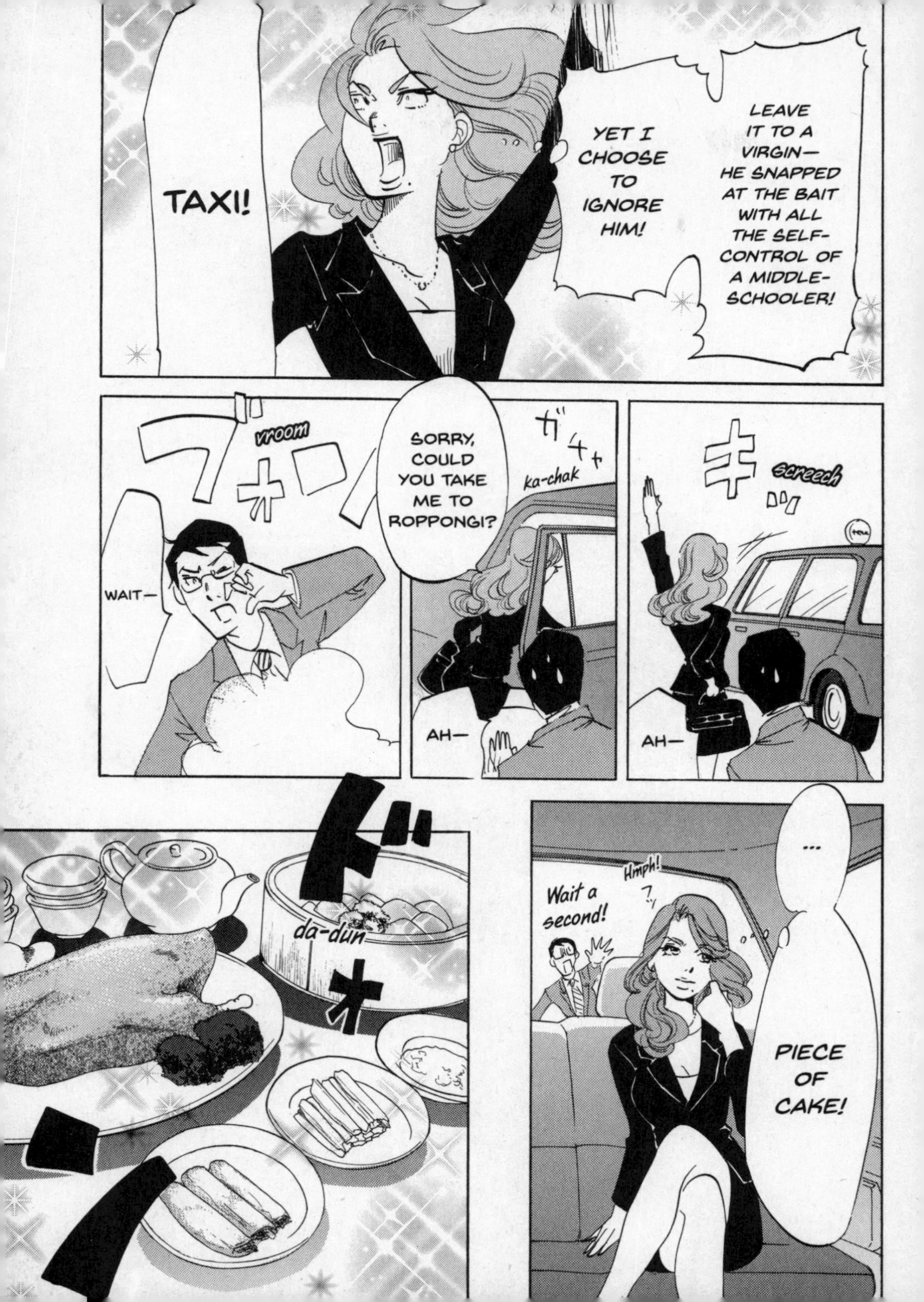
LEAVE IT TO A VIRGIN— HE SNAPPED AT THE BAIT WITH ALL THE SELF-CONTROL OF A MIDDLE-SCHOOLER!
YET I CHOOSE TO IGNORE HIM!
TAXI!
screech
AH—
SORRY, COULD YOU TAKE ME TO ROPPONGI?
ka-chak
AH—
vroom
WAIT—
...
Hmph!
Wait a second!
PIECE OF CAKE!
da-dun

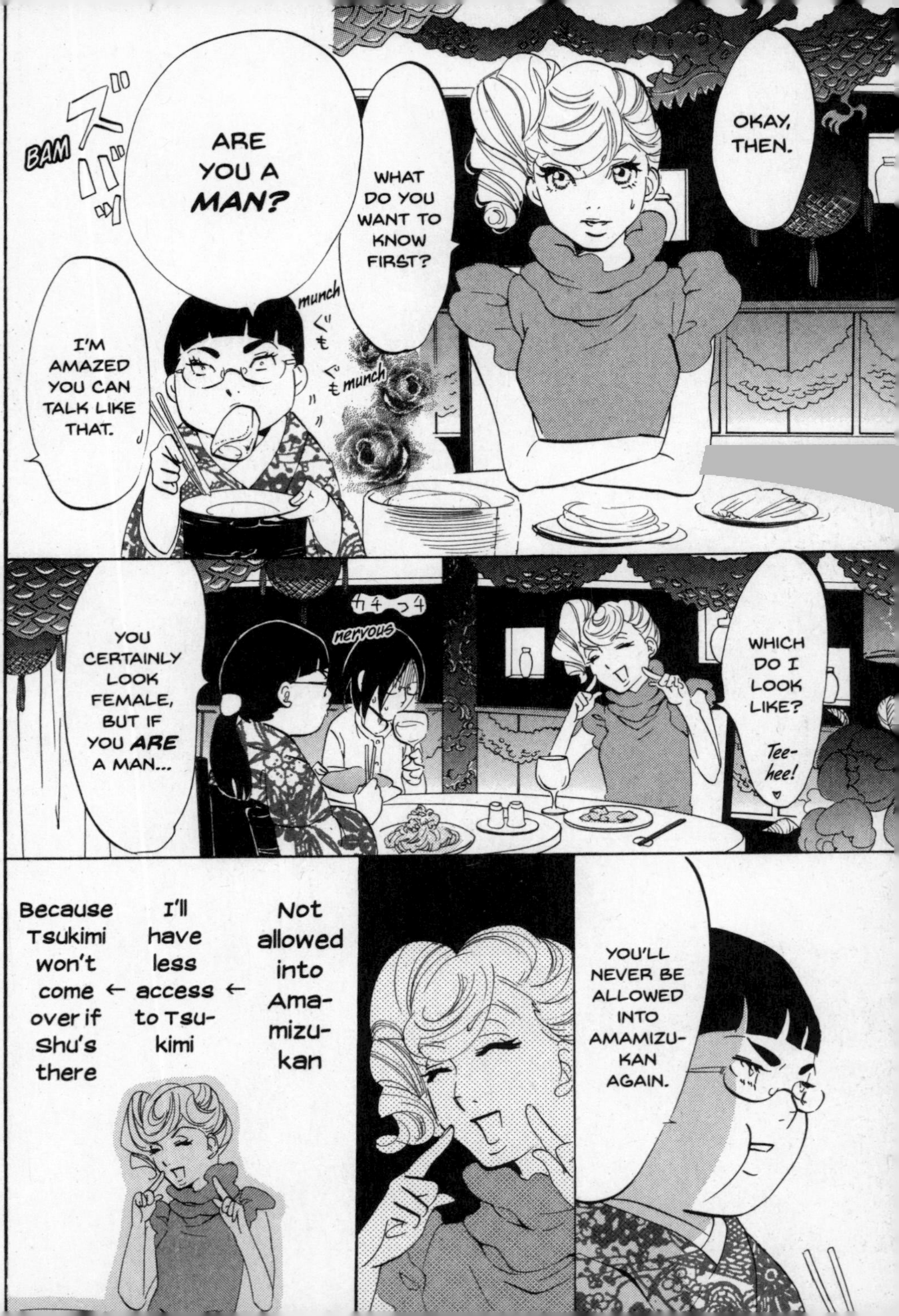
OKAY, THEN.
WHAT DO YOU WANT TO KNOW FIRST?
ARE YOU A MAN?
BAM
munch munch
I'M AMAZED YOU CAN TALK LIKE THAT.
WHICH DO I LOOK LIKE? Tee-hee!
nervous
YOU CERTAINLY LOOK FEMALE, BUT IF YOU ARE A MAN...
YOU'LL NEVER BE ALLOWED INTO AMAMIZUKAN AGAIN.
Not allowed into Amamizukan ← I'll have less access to Tsukimi ← Because Tsukimi won't come over if Shu's there

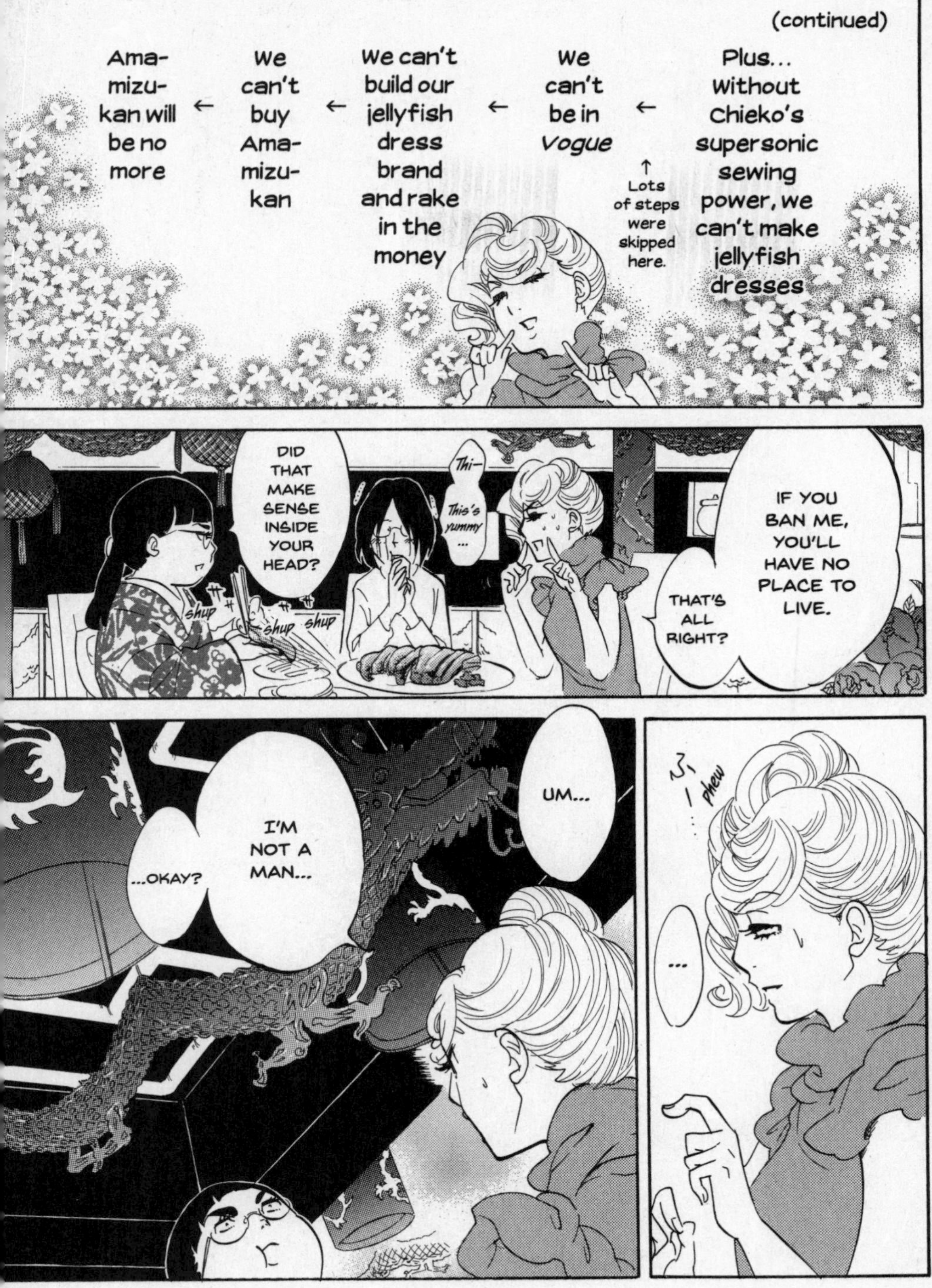
(continued)
Plus... Without Chieko's supersonic sewing power, we can't make jellyfish dresses
← We can't be in *Vogue*
↑ Lots of steps were skipped here.
← We can't build our jellyfish dress brand and rake in the money
← We can't buy Amamizukan
← Amamizukan will be no more
IF YOU BAN ME, YOU'LL HAVE NO PLACE TO LIVE.
THAT'S ALL RIGHT?
Thi-
This's yummy...
DID THAT MAKE SENSE INSIDE YOUR HEAD?
shup shup shup
ふ phew
...
UM...
I'M NOT A MAN...
...OKAY?

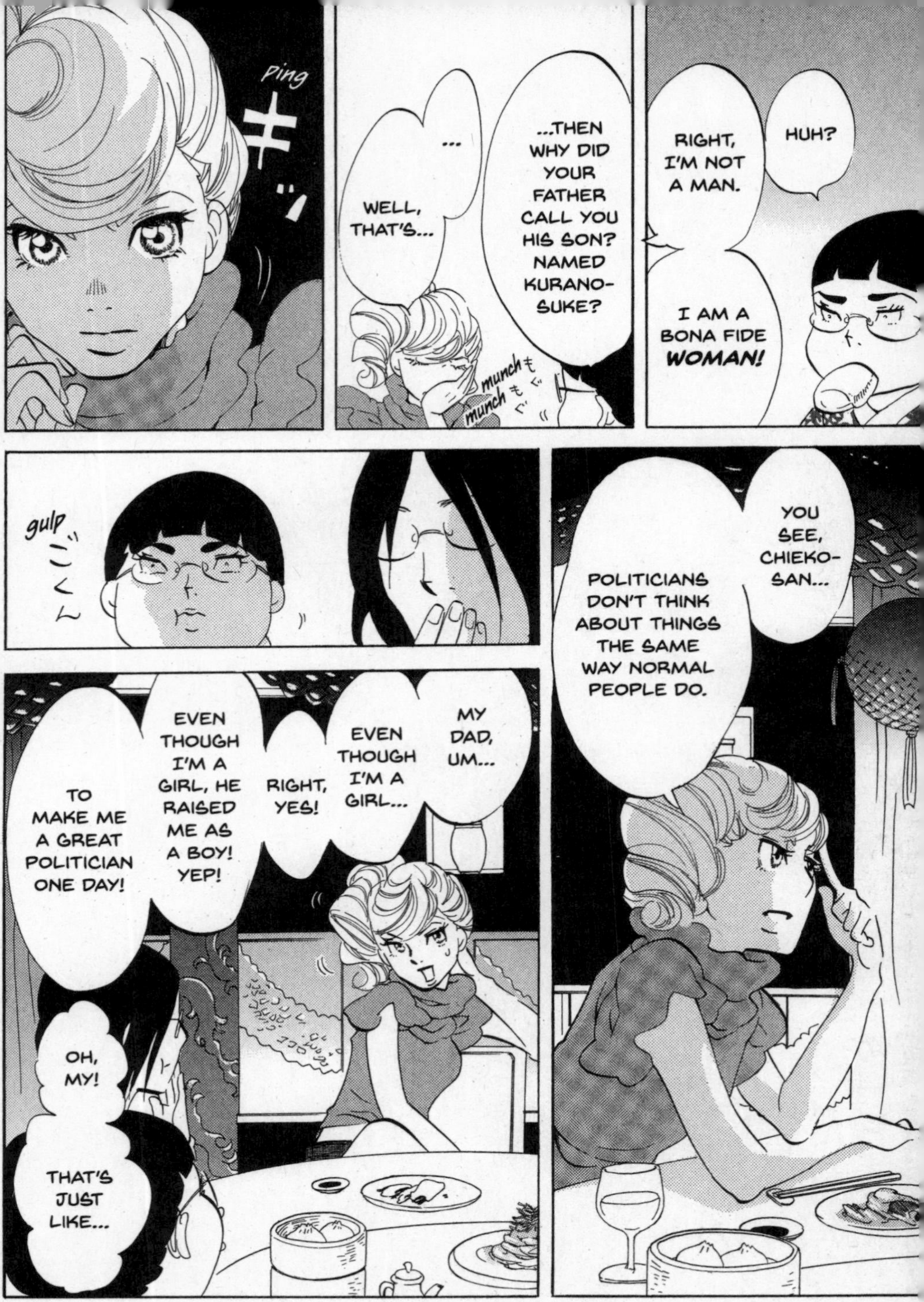
HUH?
RIGHT, I'M NOT A MAN.
I AM A BONA FIDE *WOMAN!*
...THEN WHY DID YOUR FATHER CALL YOU HIS SON? NAMED KURANO-SUKE?
...
WELL, THAT'S...
munch もぐ munch もぐ
ping
キッ
YOU SEE, CHIEKO-SAN...
POLITICIANS DON'T THINK ABOUT THINGS THE SAME WAY NORMAL PEOPLE DO.
gulp
ごくん
MY DAD, UM...
EVEN THOUGH I'M A GIRL...
RIGHT, YES!
EVEN THOUGH I'M A GIRL, HE RAISED ME AS A BOY! YEP!
TO MAKE ME A GREAT POLITICIAN ONE DAY!
OH, MY!
THAT'S JUST LIKE...

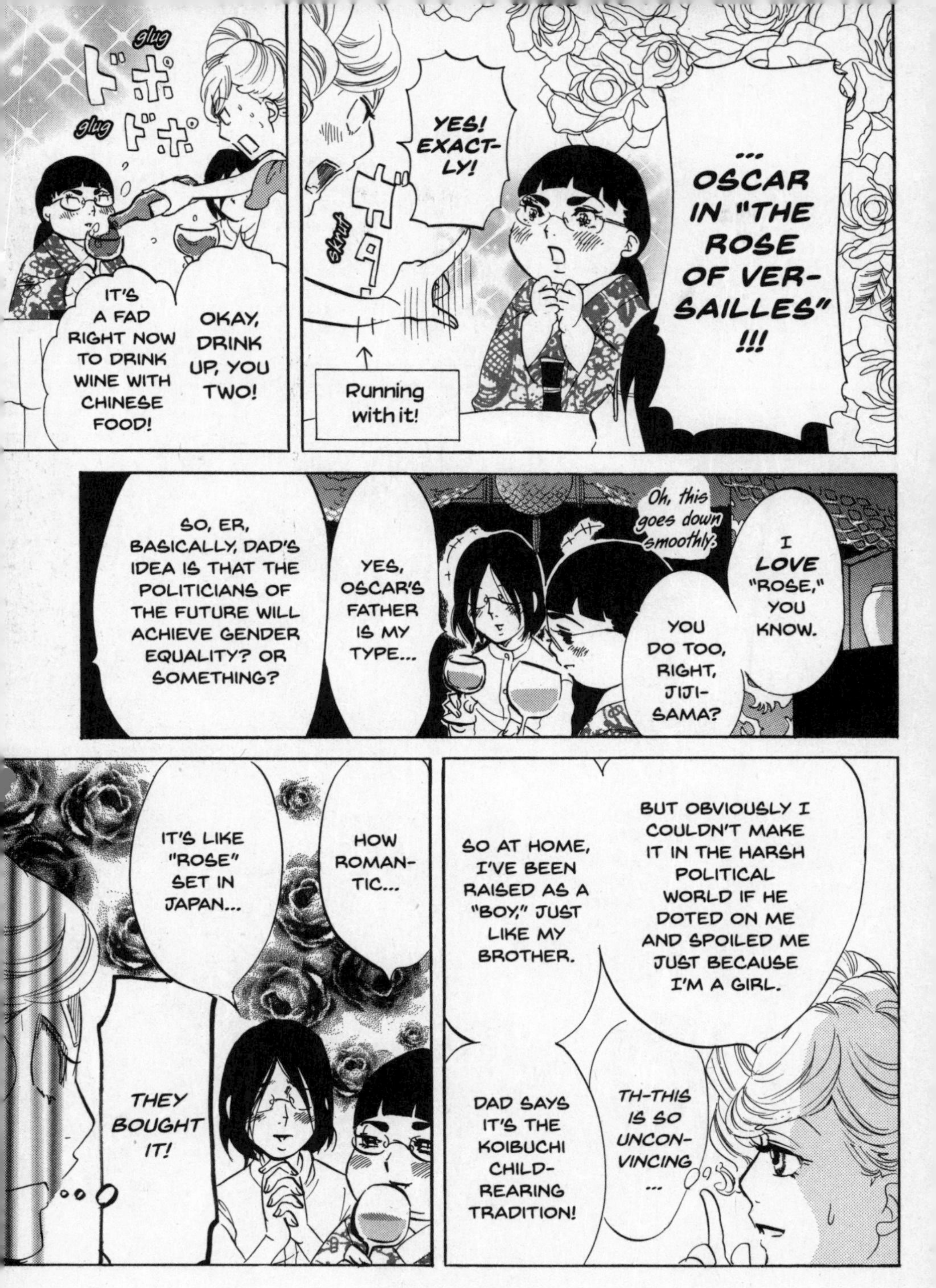
... OSCAR IN "THE ROSE OF VER-SAILLES" !!!
YES! EXACTLY!
skrut
Running with it!
glug
glug
OKAY, DRINK UP, YOU TWO!
IT'S A FAD RIGHT NOW TO DRINK WINE WITH CHINESE FOOD!
Oh, this goes down smoothly.
I LOVE "ROSE," YOU KNOW.
YOU DO TOO, RIGHT, JIJI-SAMA?
YES, OSCAR'S FATHER IS MY TYPE...
SO, ER, BASICALLY, DAD'S IDEA IS THAT THE POLITICIANS OF THE FUTURE WILL ACHIEVE GENDER EQUALITY? OR SOMETHING?
BUT OBVIOUSLY I COULDN'T MAKE IT IN THE HARSH POLITICAL WORLD IF HE DOTED ON ME AND SPOILED ME JUST BECAUSE I'M A GIRL.
SO AT HOME, I'VE BEEN RAISED AS A "BOY," JUST LIKE MY BROTHER.
TH-THIS IS SO UNCONVINCING ...
DAD SAYS IT'S THE KOIBUCHI CHILD-REARING TRADITION!
HOW ROMAN-TIC...
IT'S LIKE "ROSE" SET IN JAPAN...
THEY BOUGHT IT!
...

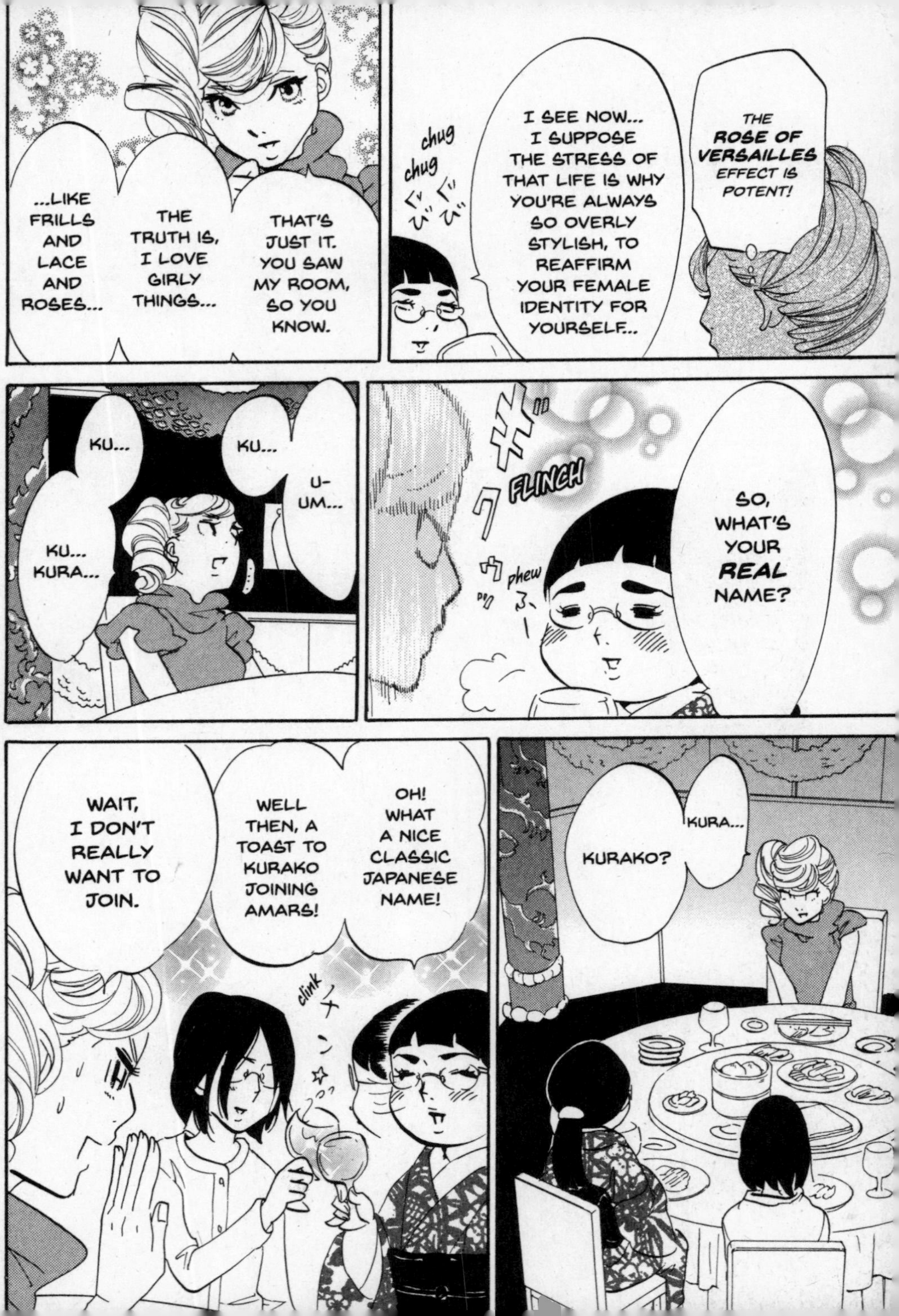
THE ROSE OF VERSAILLES EFFECT IS POTENT!
I SEE NOW... I SUPPOSE THE STRESS OF THAT LIFE IS WHY YOU'RE ALWAYS SO OVERLY STYLISH, TO REAFFIRM YOUR FEMALE IDENTITY FOR YOURSELF...
chug chug
ぐびぐび
THAT'S JUST IT. YOU SAW MY ROOM, SO YOU KNOW.
THE TRUTH IS, I LOVE GIRLY THINGS...
...LIKE FRILLS AND LACE AND ROSES...
SO, WHAT'S YOUR REAL NAME?
ギクッ
FLINCH
phew
ふー
U-UM...
KU...
KU...
KU... KURA...
KURA...
KURAKO?
OH! WHAT A NICE CLASSIC JAPANESE NAME!
WELL THEN, A TOAST TO KURAKO JOINING AMARS!
WAIT, I DON'T REALLY WANT TO JOIN.
clink

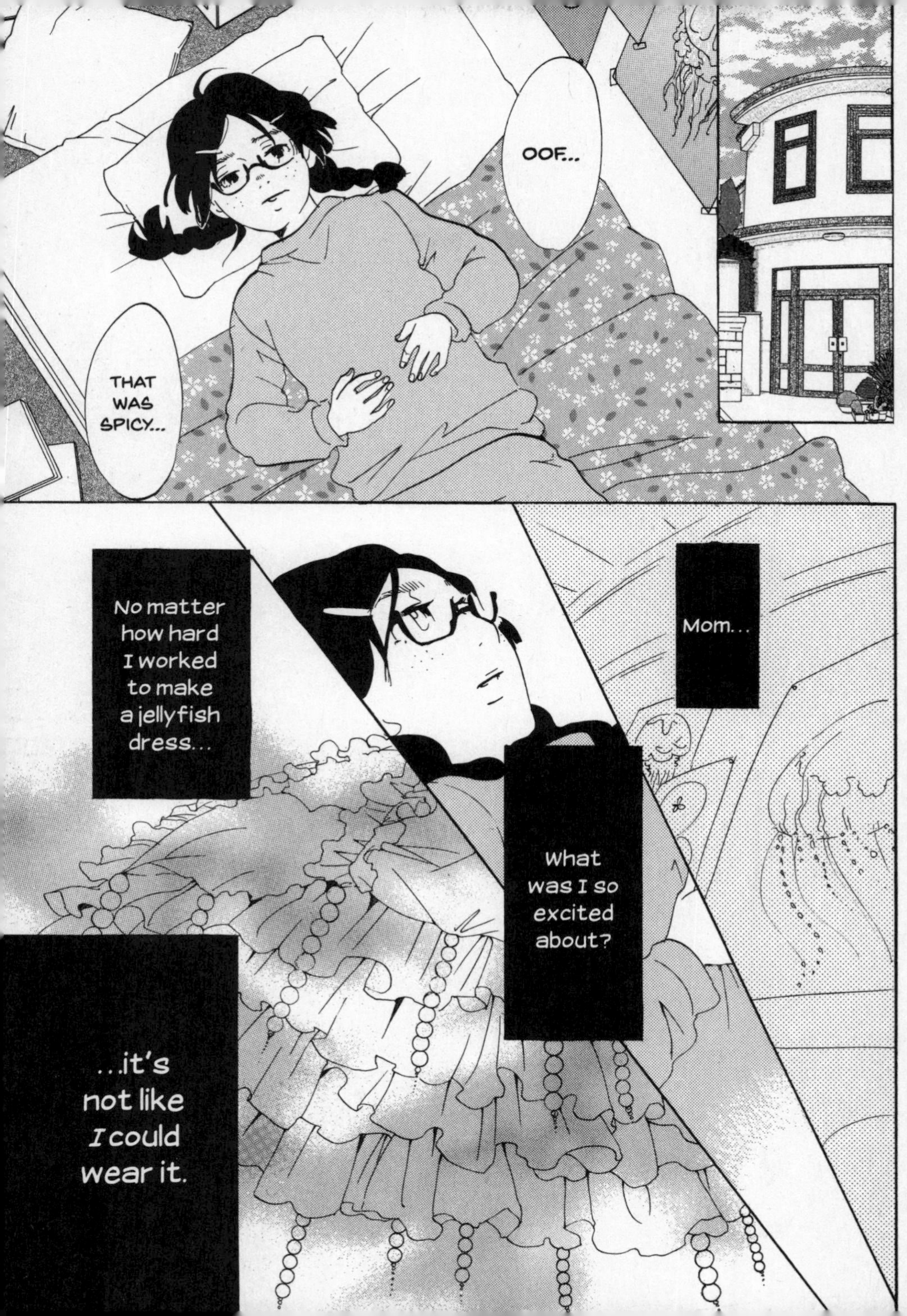
OOF...
THAT WAS SPICY...
Mom...
What was I so excited about?
No matter how hard I worked to make a jellyfish dress...
...it's not like I could wear it.

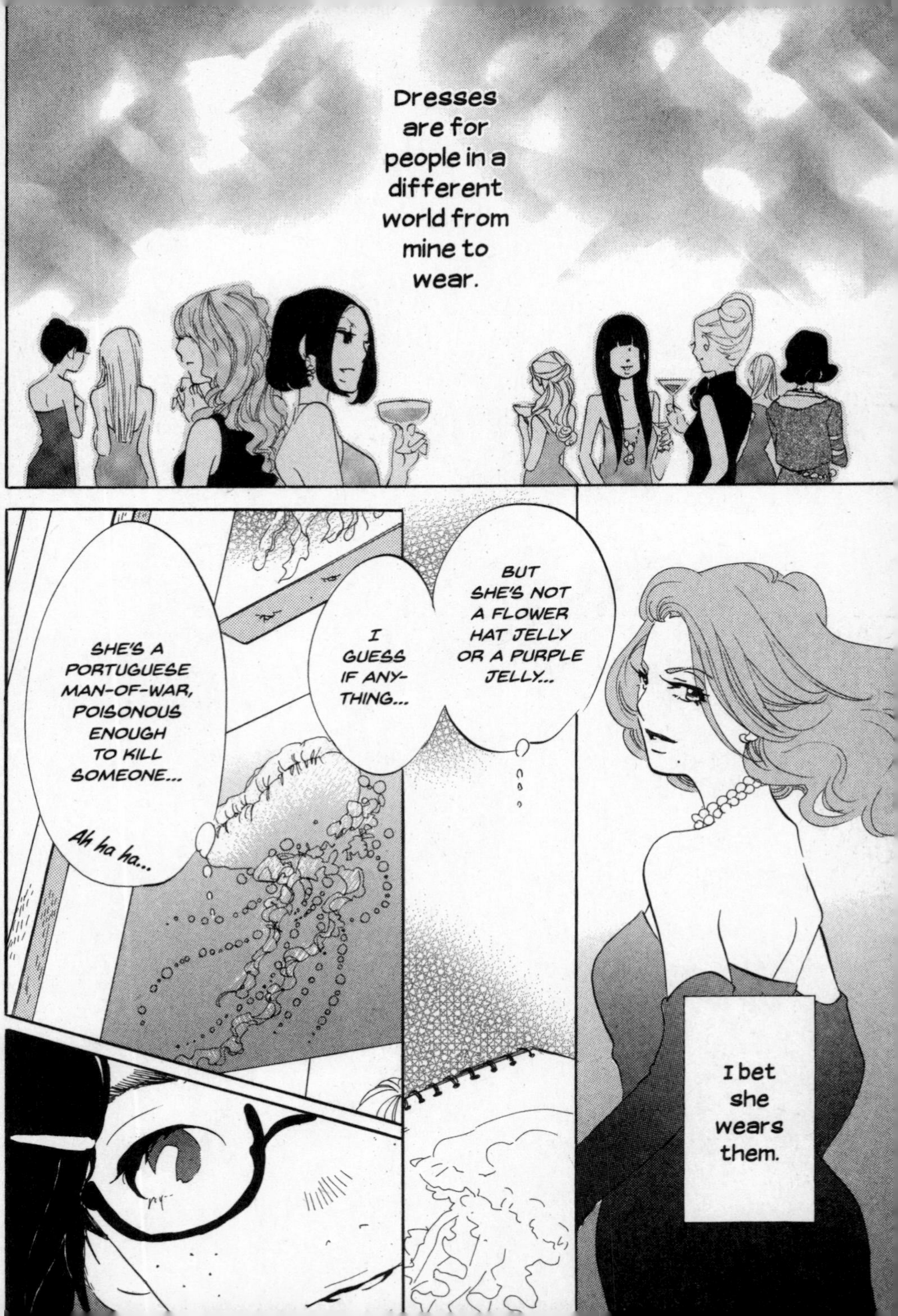
Dresses are for people in a different world from mine to wear.
I bet she wears them.
BUT SHE'S NOT A FLOWER HAT JELLY OR A PURPLE JELLY...
I GUESS IF ANY-THING...
SHE'S A PORTUGUESE MAN-OF-WAR, POISONOUS ENOUGH TO KILL SOMEONE...
Ah ha ha...

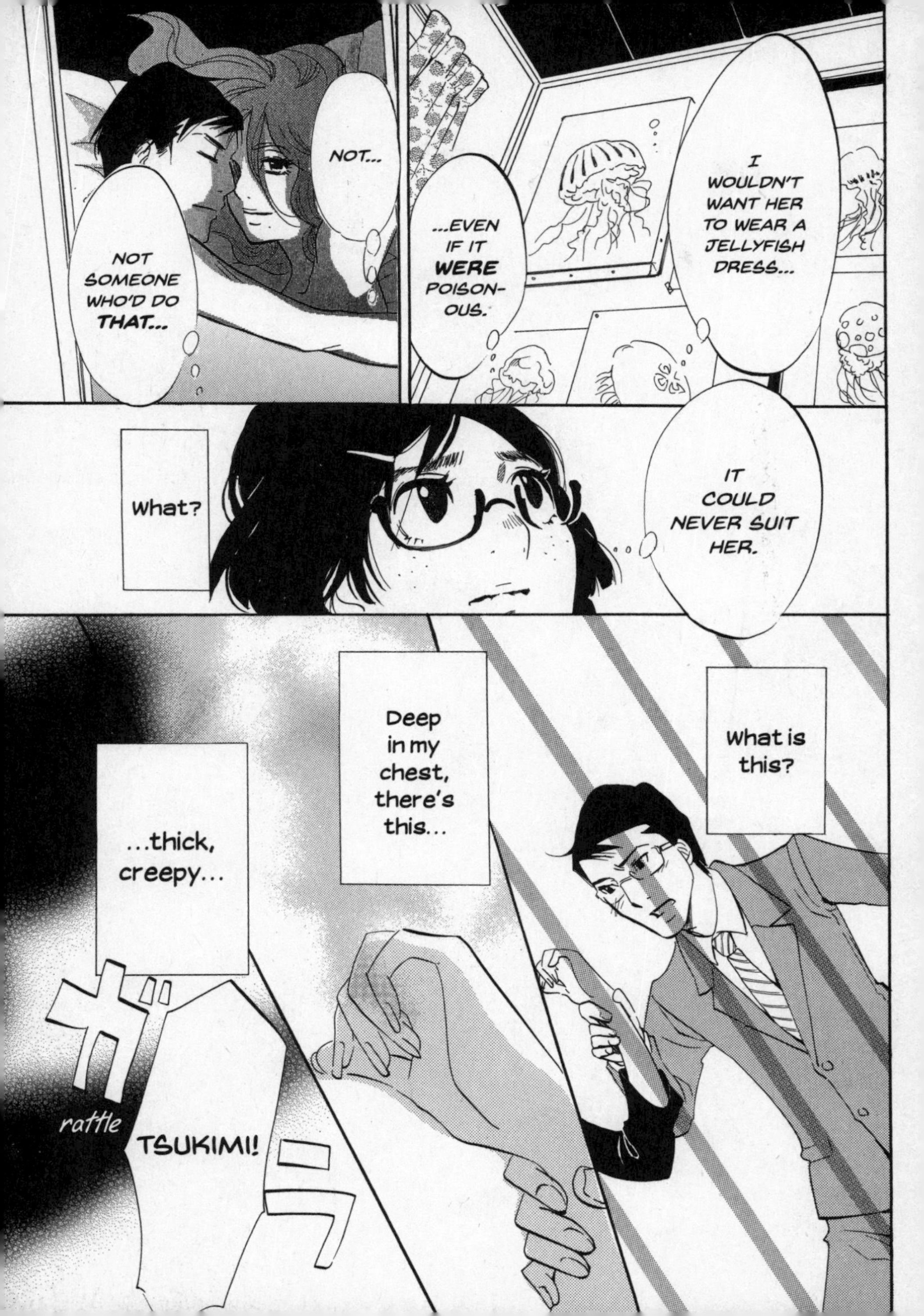
I WOULDN'T WANT HER TO WEAR A JELLYFISH DRESS...
...EVEN IF IT WERE POISONOUS.
NOT...
NOT SOMEONE WHO'D DO THAT...
IT COULD NEVER SUIT HER.
What?
What is this?
Deep in my chest, there's this...
...thick, creepy...
ガラ
rattle
TSUKIMI!

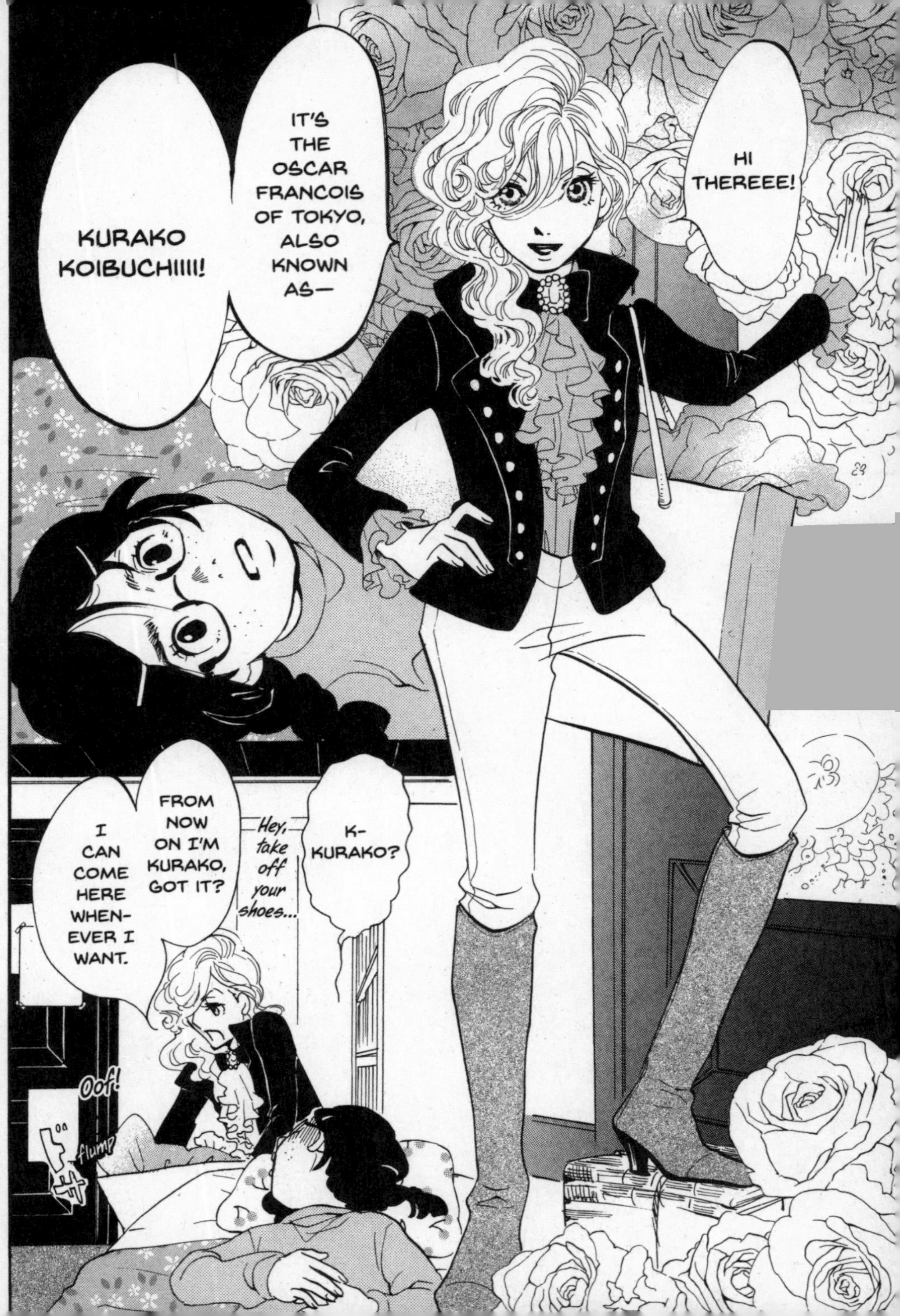
HI THEREEE!
IT'S THE OSCAR FRANCOIS OF TOKYO, ALSO KNOWN AS—
KURAKO KOIBUCHIIIII!
K-KURAKO?
Hey, take off your shoes...
FROM NOW ON I'M KURAKO, GOT IT?
I CAN COME HERE WHEN-EVER I WANT.
Oof!
flump

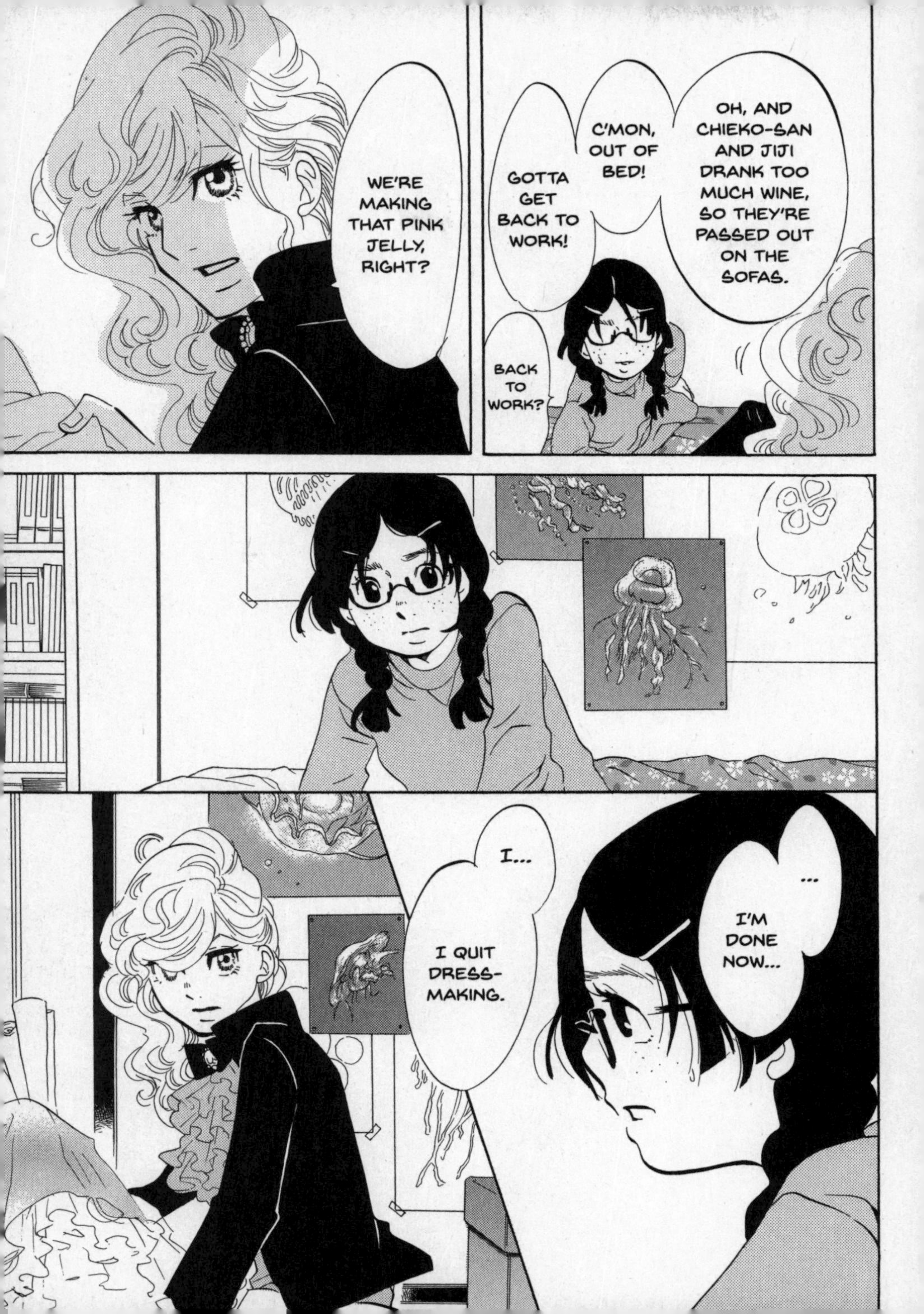
OH, AND CHIEKO-SAN AND JIJI DRANK TOO MUCH WINE, SO THEY'RE PASSED OUT ON THE SOFAS.
C'MON, OUT OF BED!
GOTTA GET BACK TO WORK!
BACK TO WORK?
WE'RE MAKING THAT PINK JELLY, RIGHT?
... I'M DONE NOW...
I...
I QUIT DRESS-MAKING.

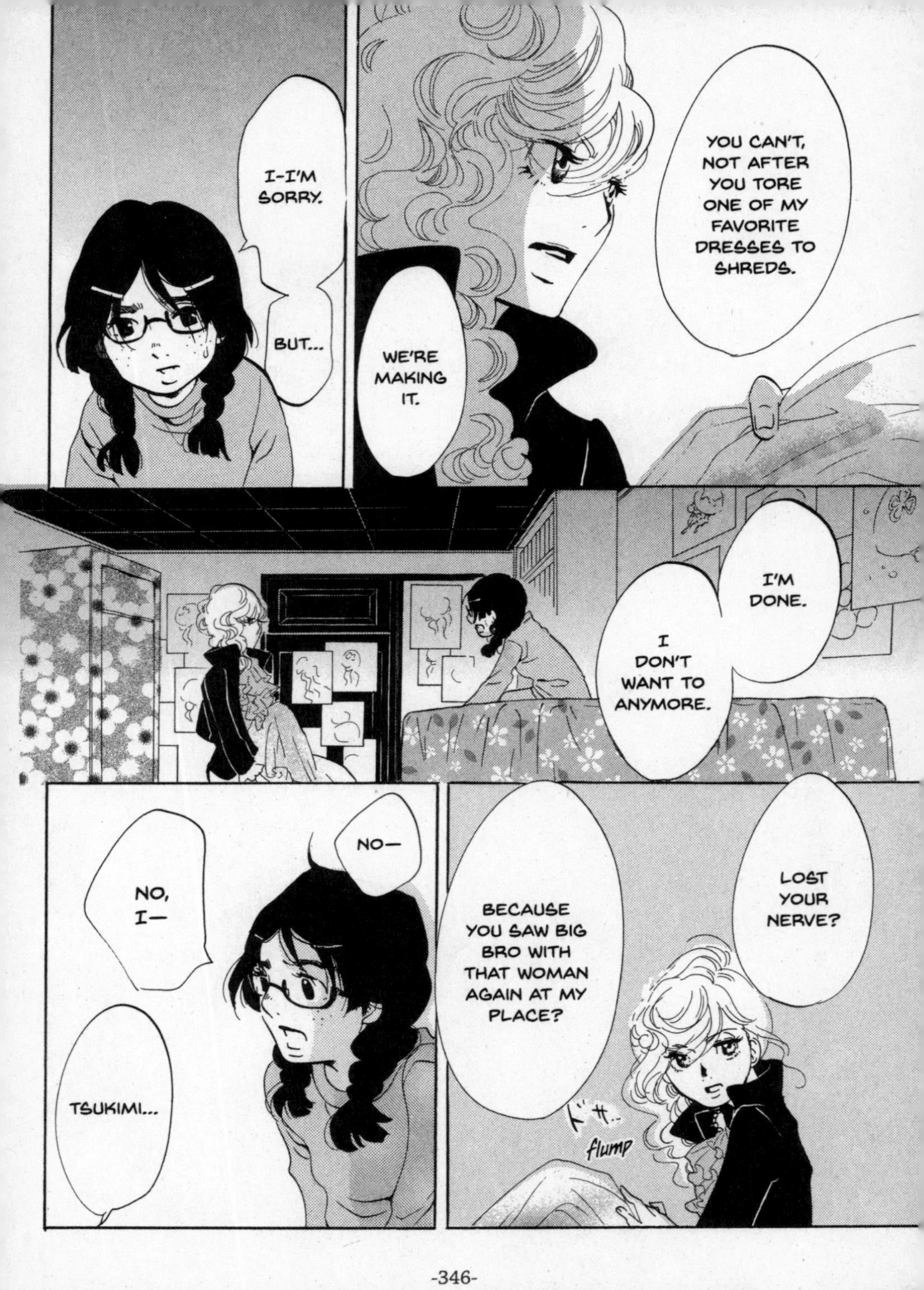
YOU CAN'T, NOT AFTER YOU TORE ONE OF MY FAVORITE DRESSES TO SHREDS.
WE'RE MAKING IT.
I-I'M SORRY.
BUT...
I'M DONE.
I DON'T WANT TO ANYMORE.
LOST YOUR NERVE?
BECAUSE YOU SAW BIG BRO WITH THAT WOMAN AGAIN AT MY PLACE?
flump
NO—
NO, I—
TSUKIMI...

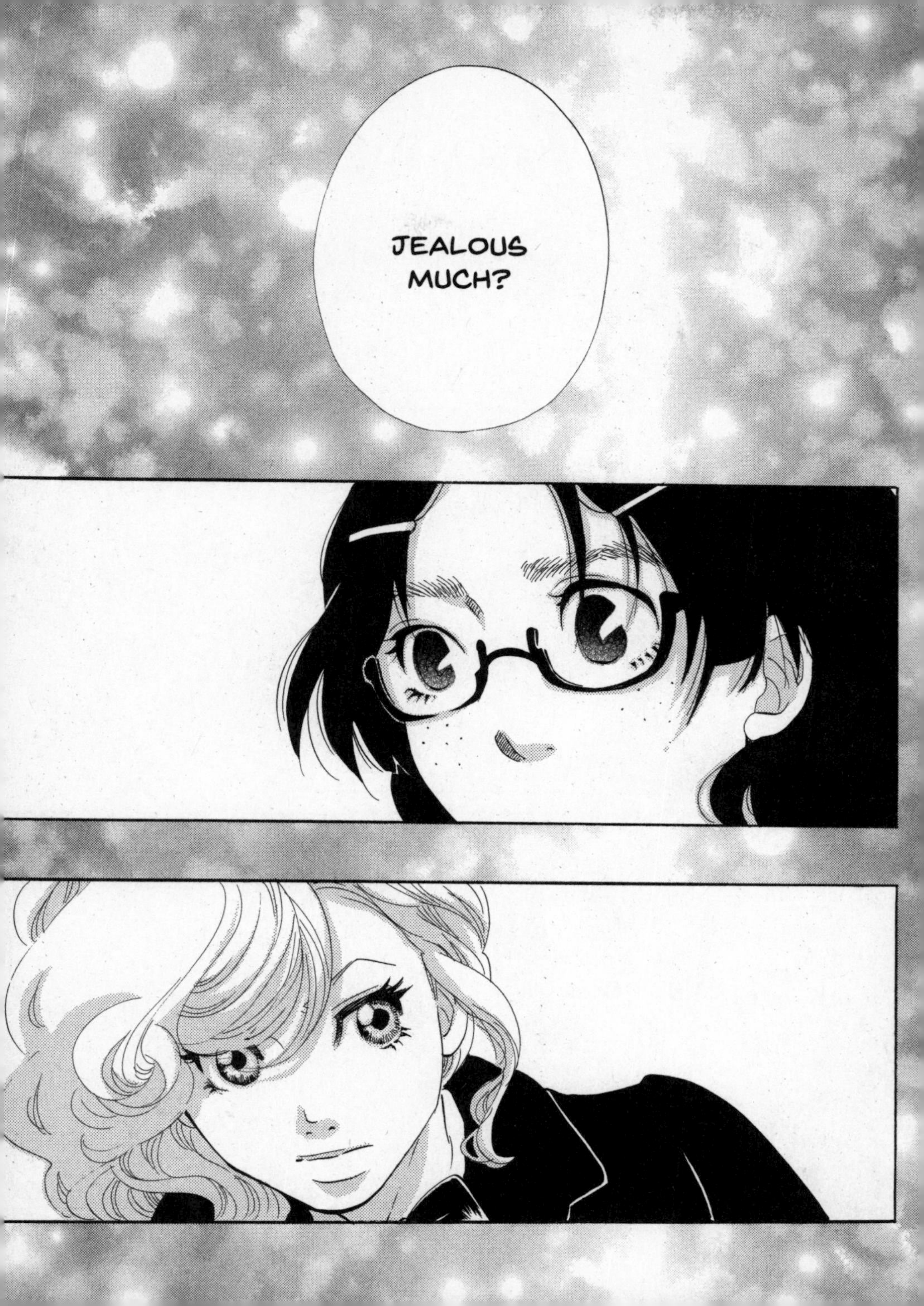
JEALOUS MUCH?

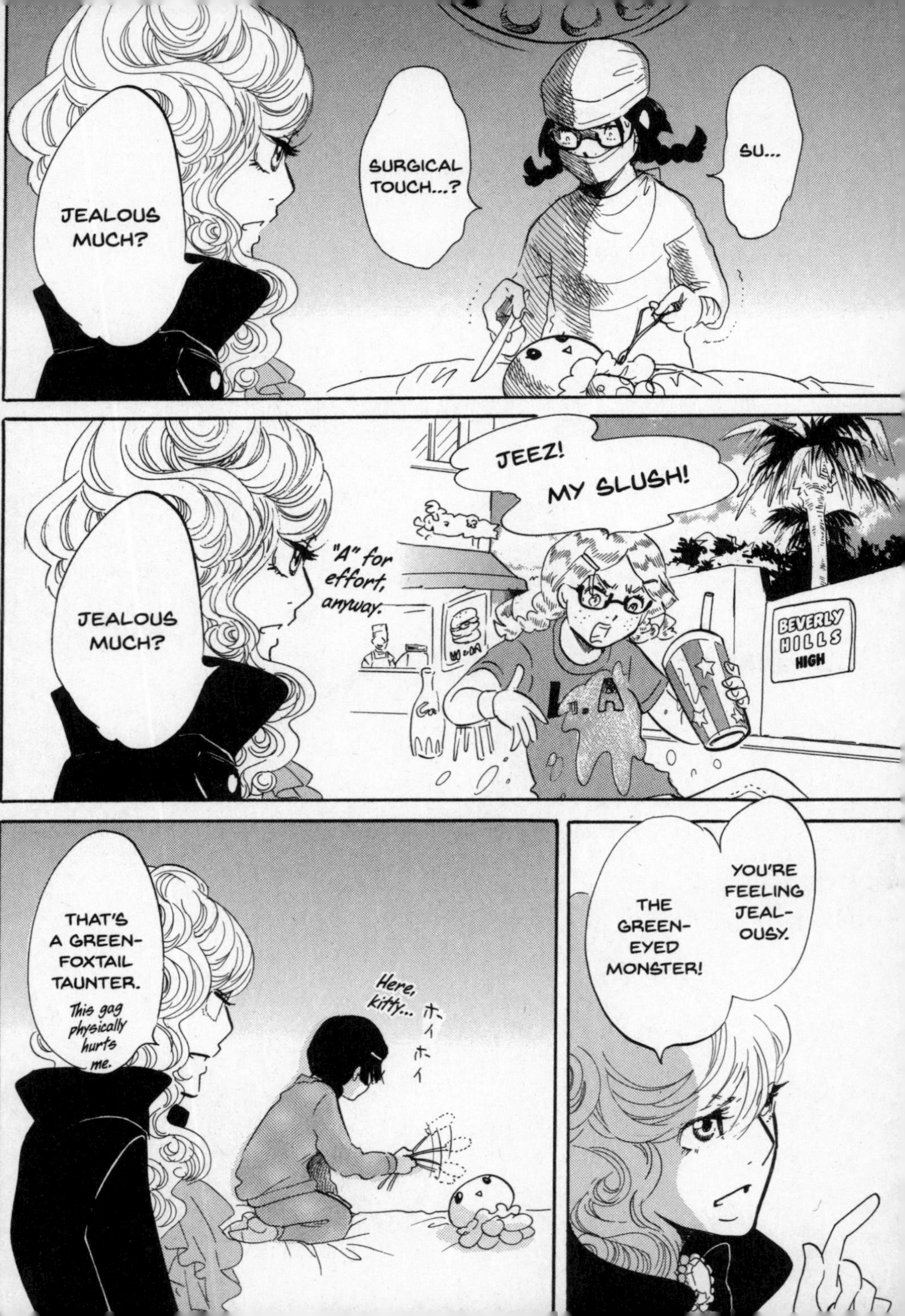
SU...
SURGICAL TOUCH...?
JEALOUS MUCH?
JEEZ! MY SLUSH!
BEVERLY HILLS HIGH
"A" for effort, anyway.
JEALOUS MUCH?
YOU'RE FEELING JEAL-OUSY.
THE GREEN-EYED MONSTER!
THAT'S A GREEN-FOXTAIL TAUNTER.
This gag physically hurts me.
Here, kitty...
ホイホイ

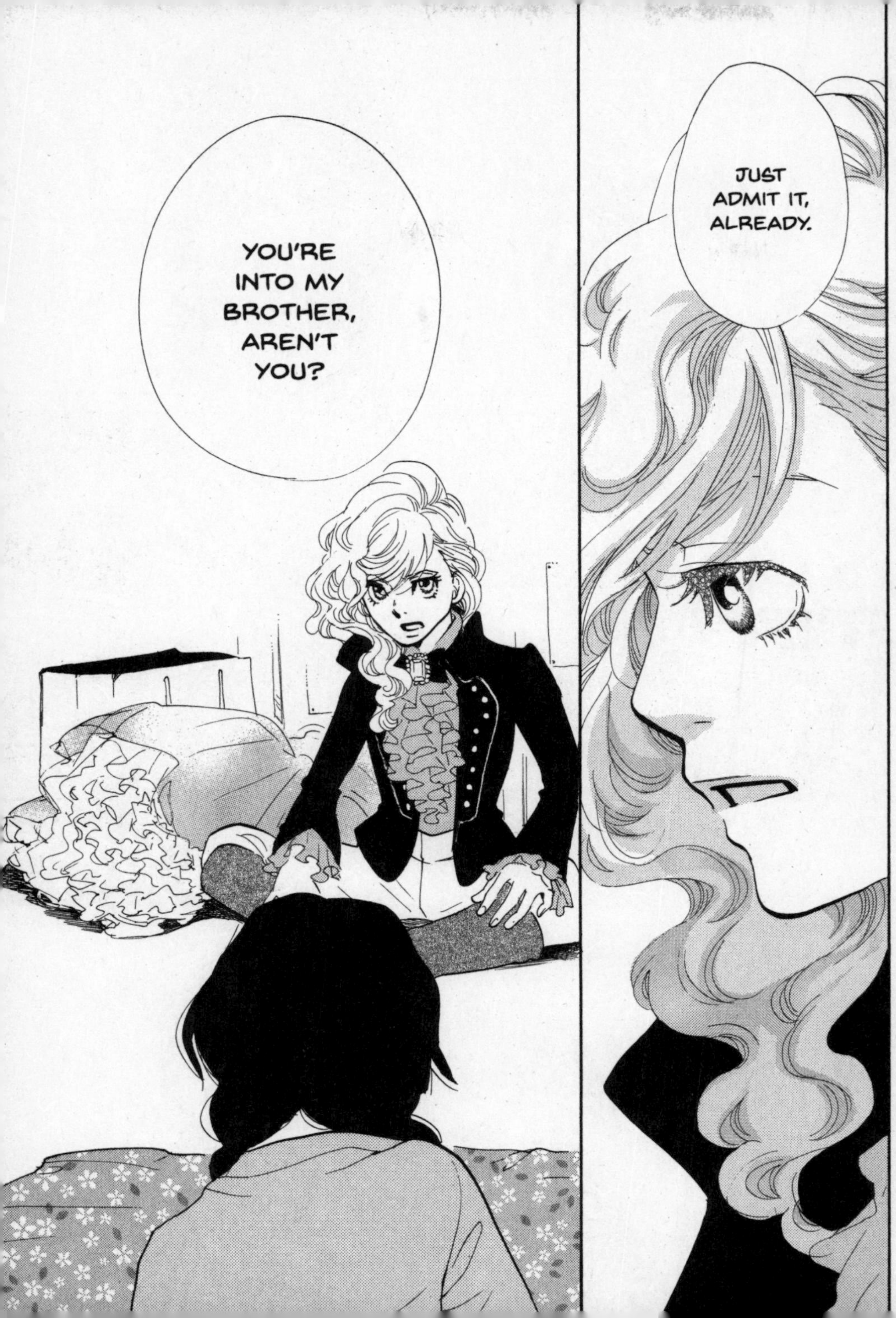
JUST ADMIT IT, ALREADY.
YOU'RE INTO MY BROTHER, AREN'T YOU?

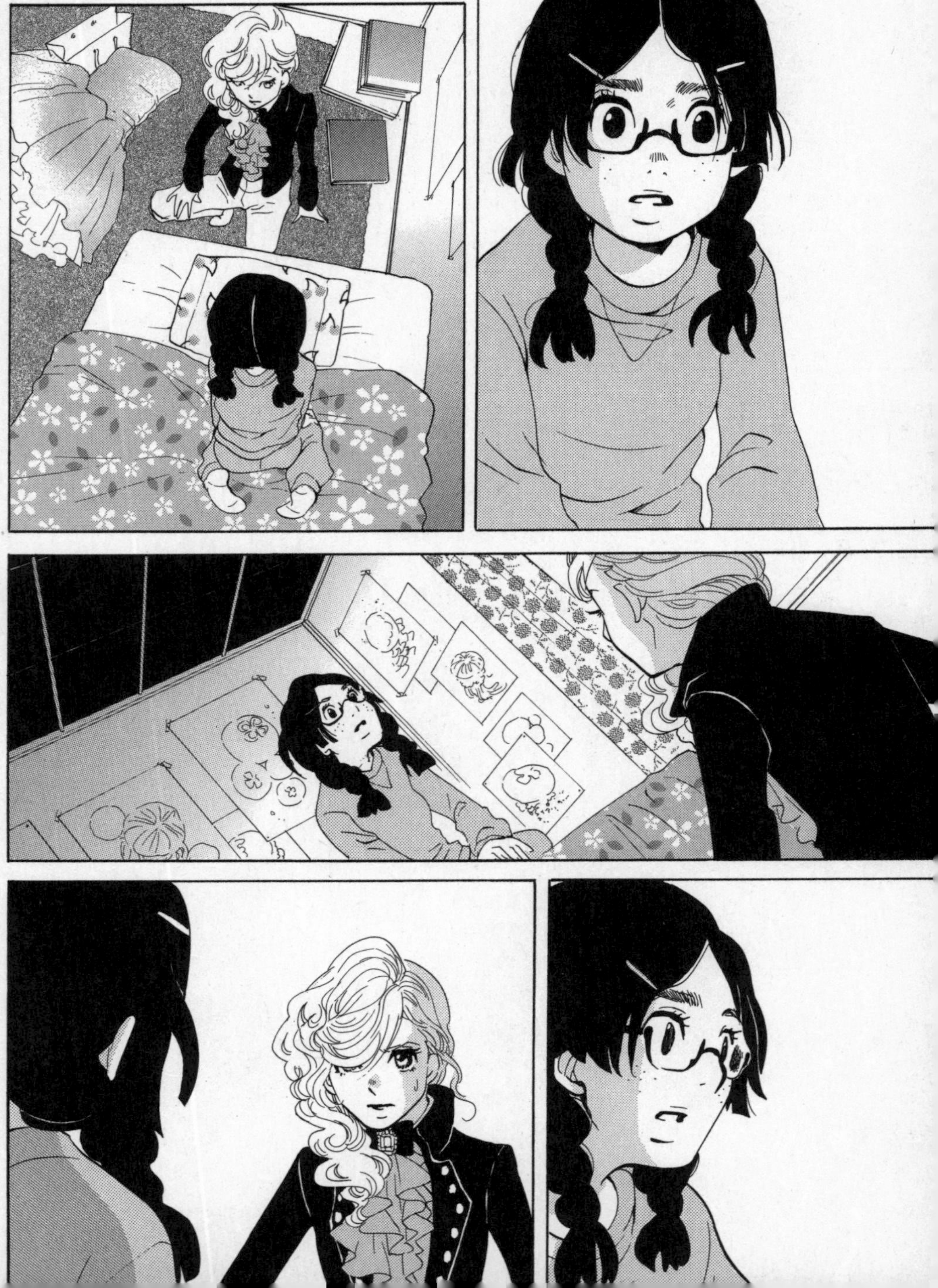

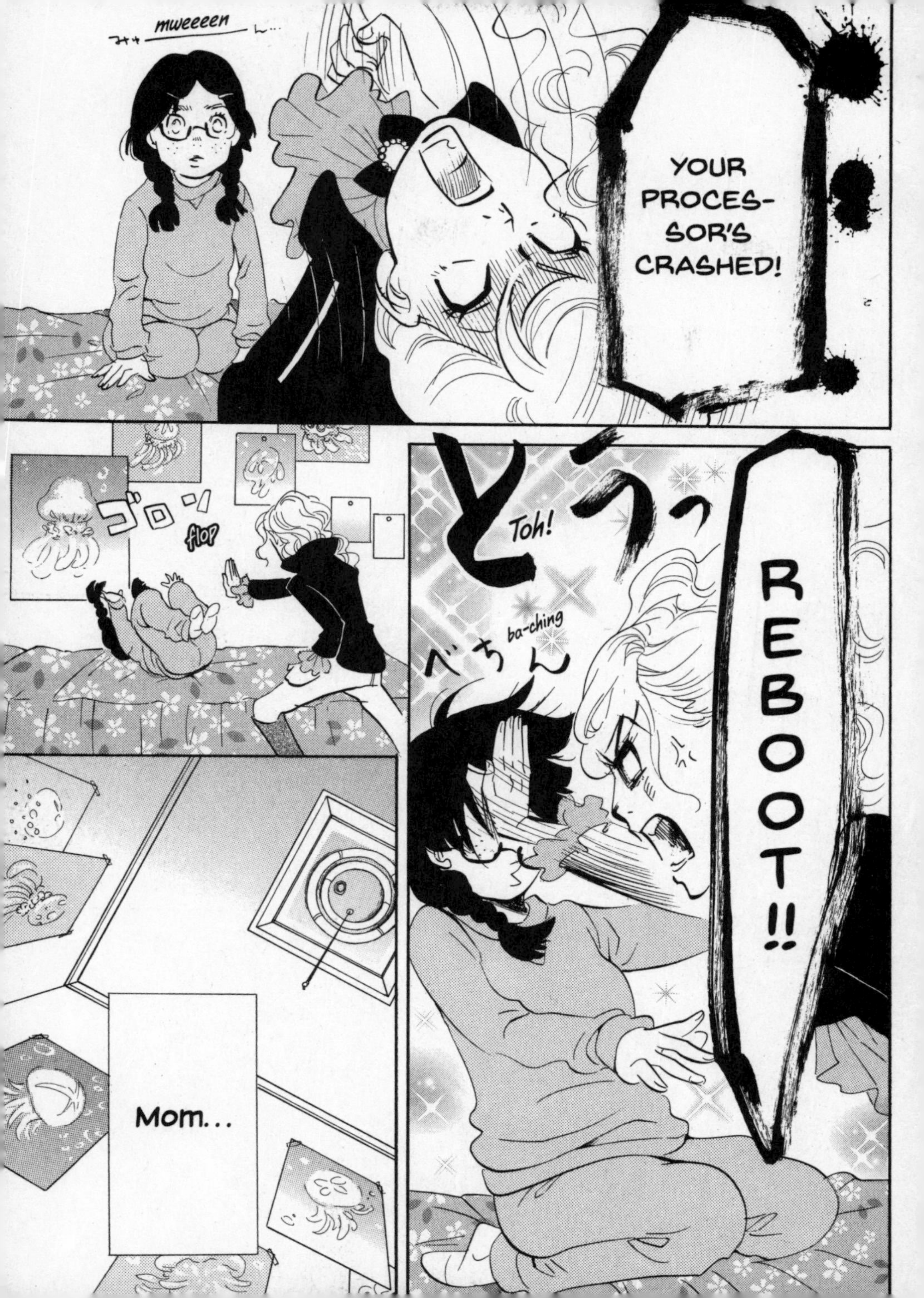
YOUR PROCES-SOR'S CRASHED!
みゃ mweeeen ん…
とうっ
Toh!
REBOOT!!
べちん
ba-ching
ゴロッ
flop
Mom...

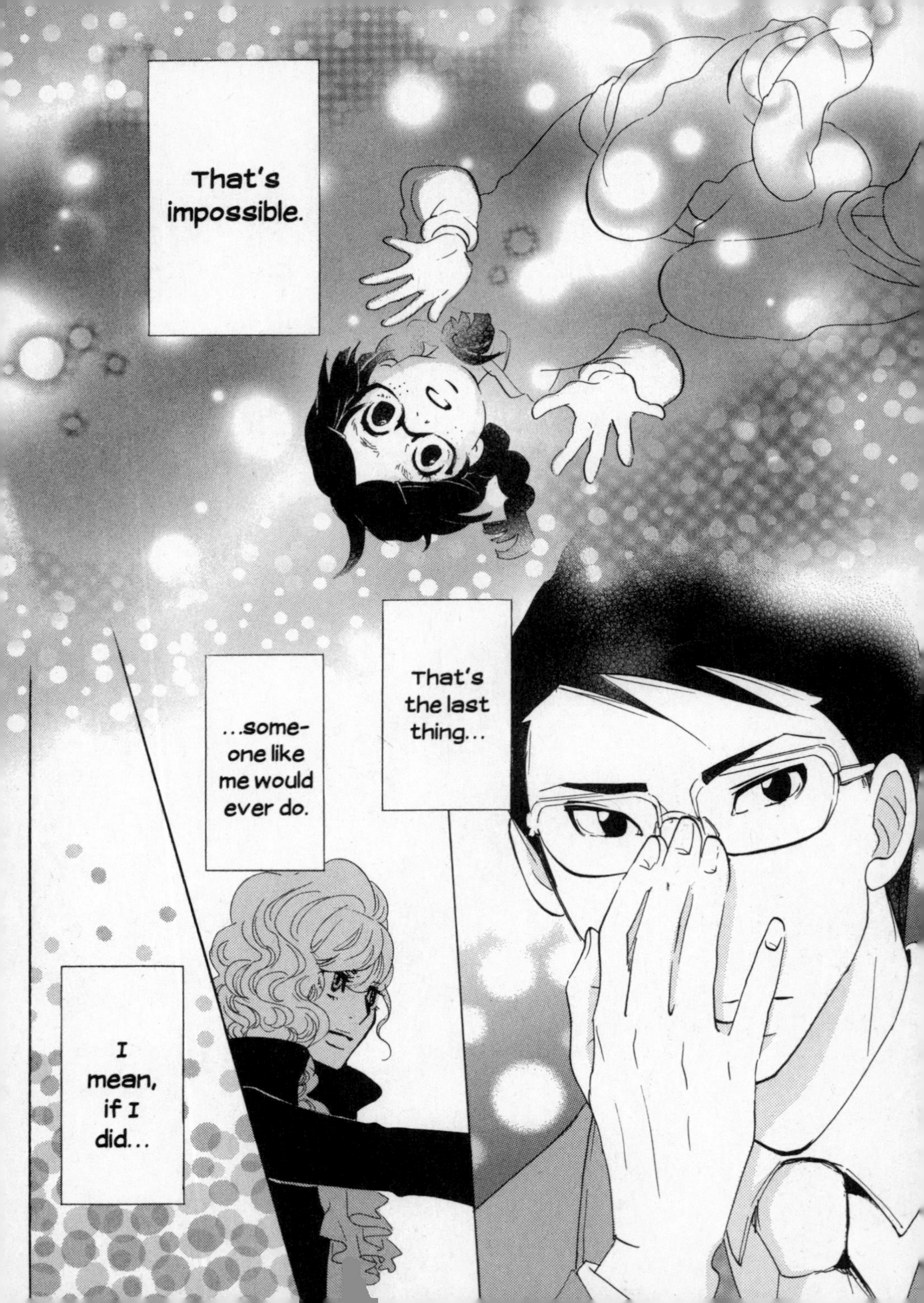
That's impossible.
That's the last thing...
...some-one like me would ever do.
I mean, if I did...

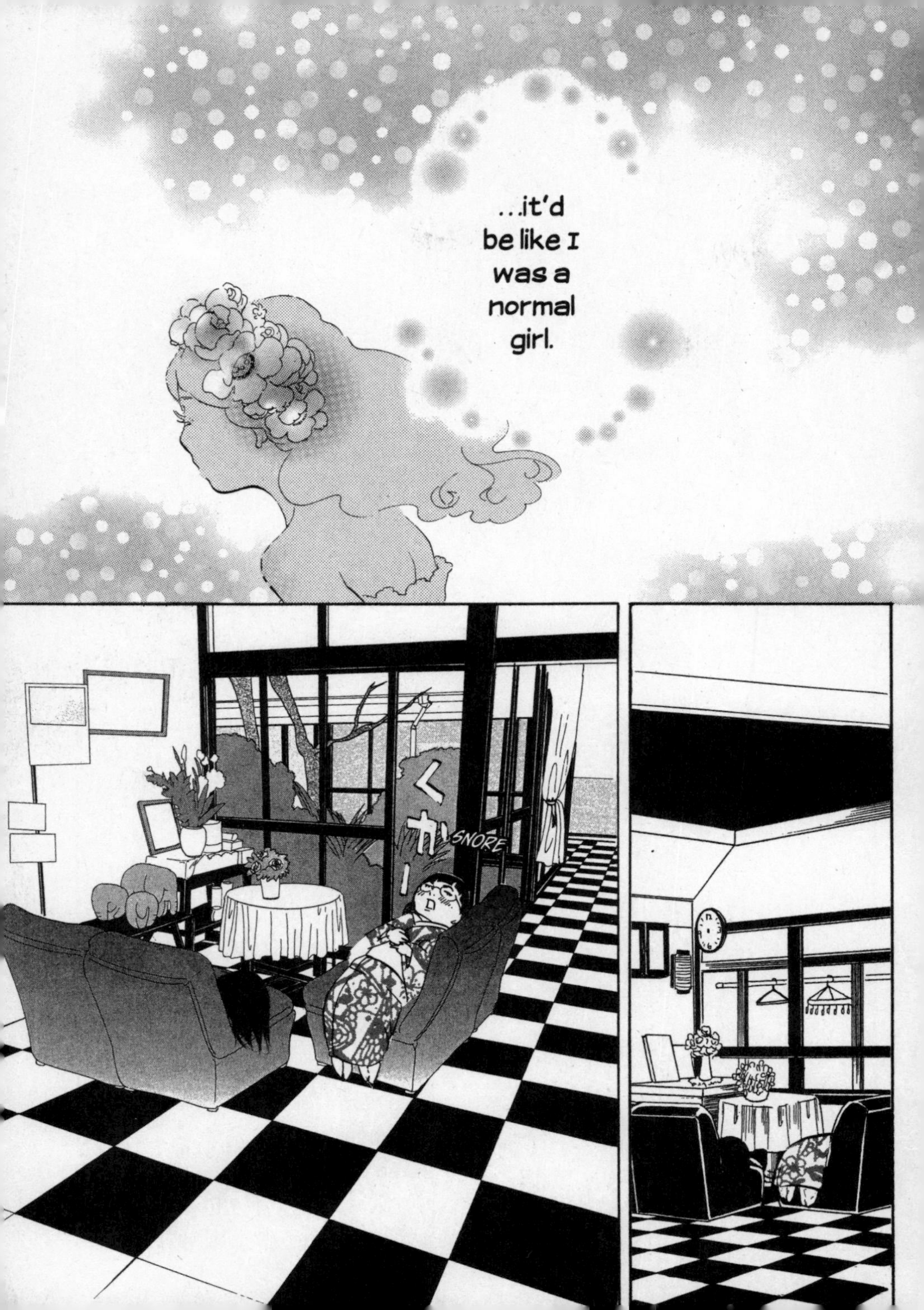
...it'd be like I was a normal girl.
SNORE

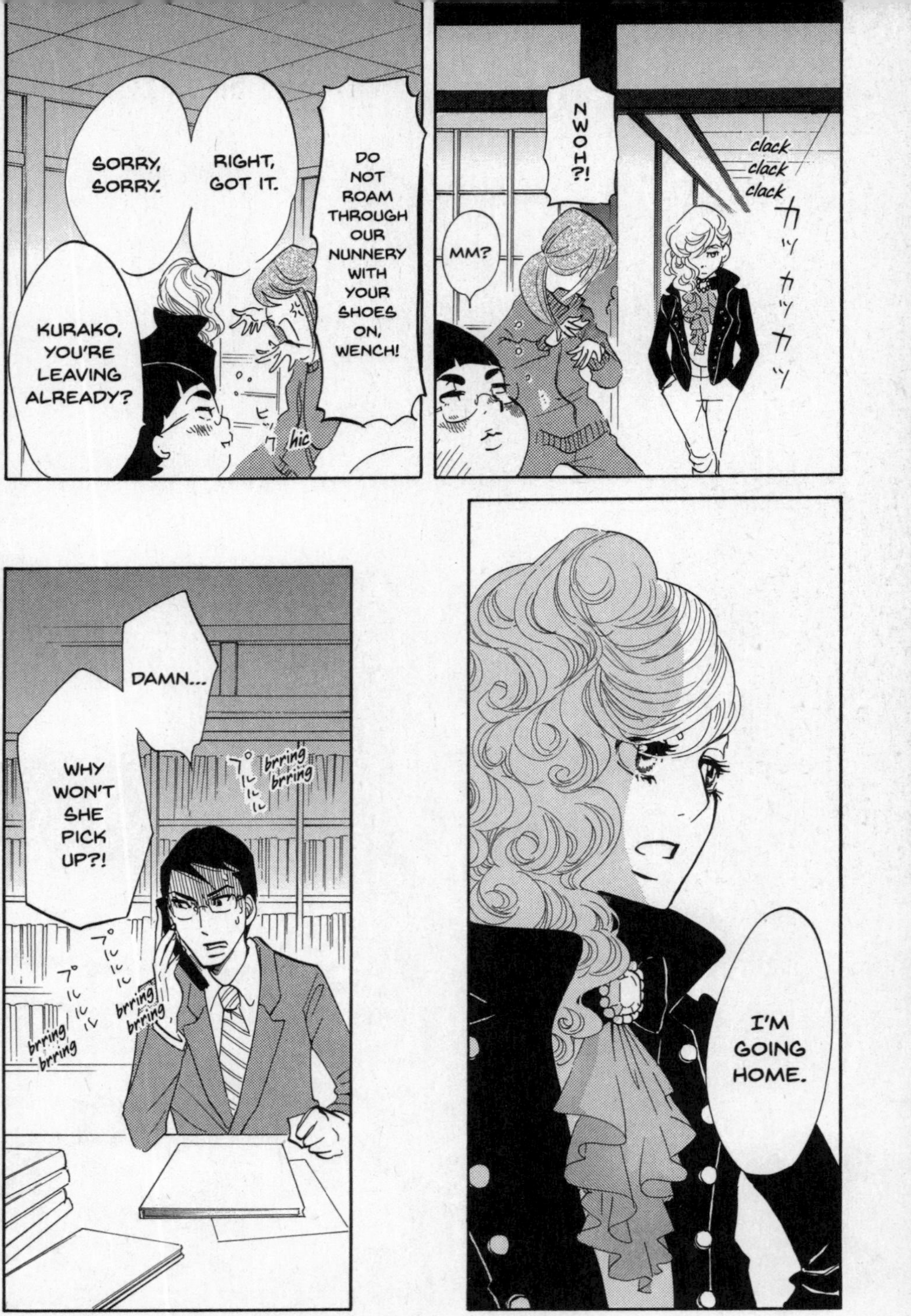
NWOH?!
clack
clack
clack
カッ
カッ
カッ
カッ
MM?
DO NOT ROAM THROUGH OUR NUNNERY WITH YOUR SHOES ON, WENCH!
RIGHT, GOT IT.
SORRY, SORRY.
KURAKO, YOU'RE LEAVING ALREADY?
ヒック
hic
I'M GOING HOME.
DAMN...
WHY WON'T SHE PICK UP?!
プルルル
brring
brring
プルルル
brring
brring
プルルル
brring
brring

Episode 24

Close Encounters of the Third Kind

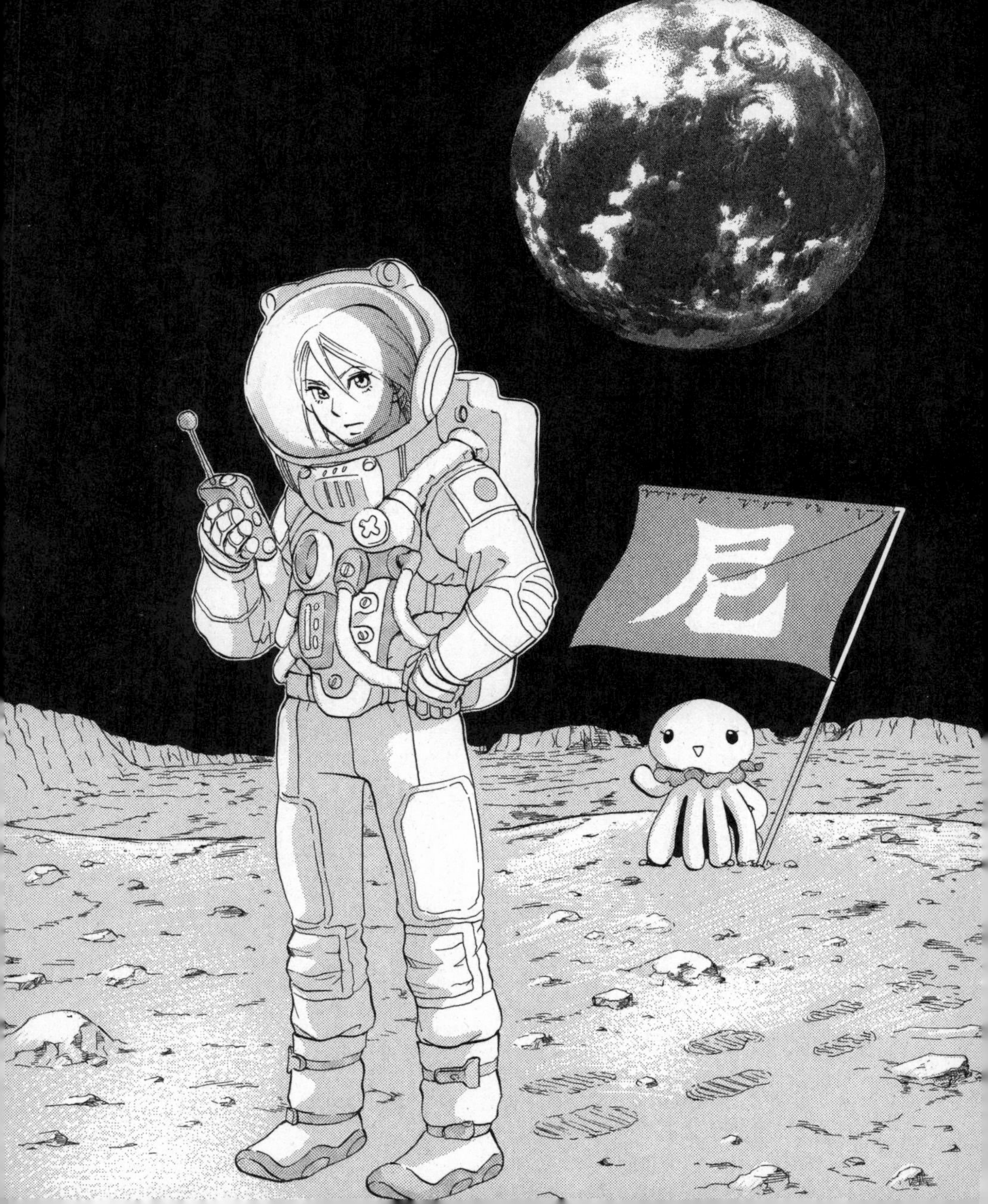
尼

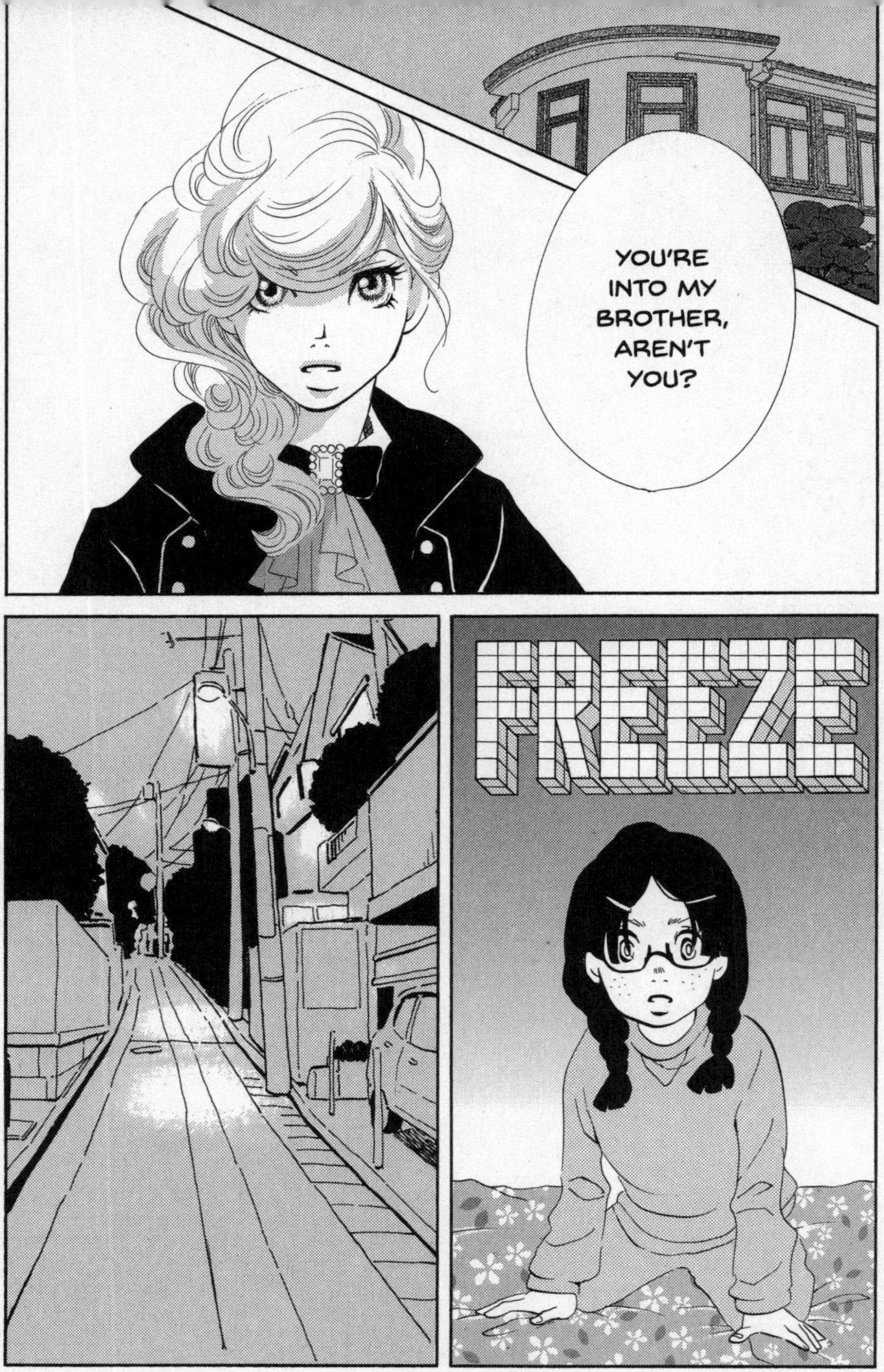
YOU'RE INTO MY BROTHER, AREN'T YOU?
FREEZE

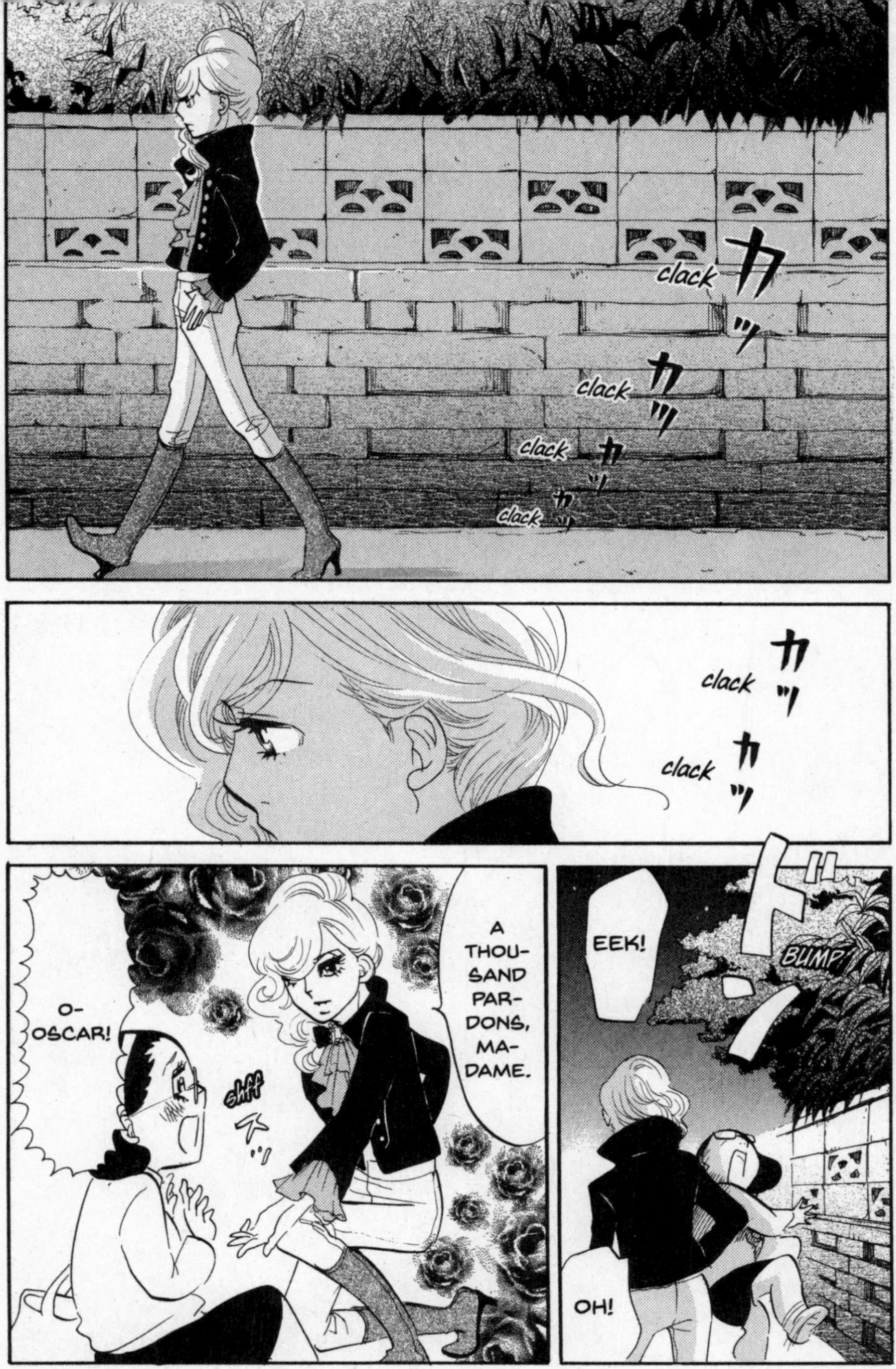
カッ
clack
カッ
clack
カッ
clack
カッ
clack
カッ
clack
カッ
clack
EEK!
BUMP!
OH!
A THOUSAND PARDONS, MADAME.
O-OSCAR!
shff

AW, JEEZ...

...

clack clack clack

grr grr grr

Even though I knew it already, it still pisses me off. But I can't categorize the reason I'm pissed off!

ROMANCE

SYMPATHY

LOVE

FRIENDSHIP

GIVE ME ANYTHING BUT THE UPPER-RIGHT ZONE!

NO, NO, NO!

da-dun

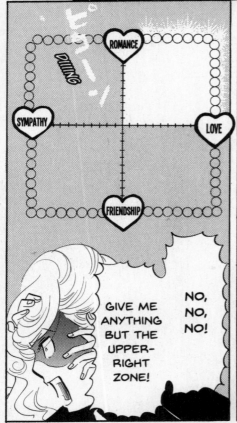

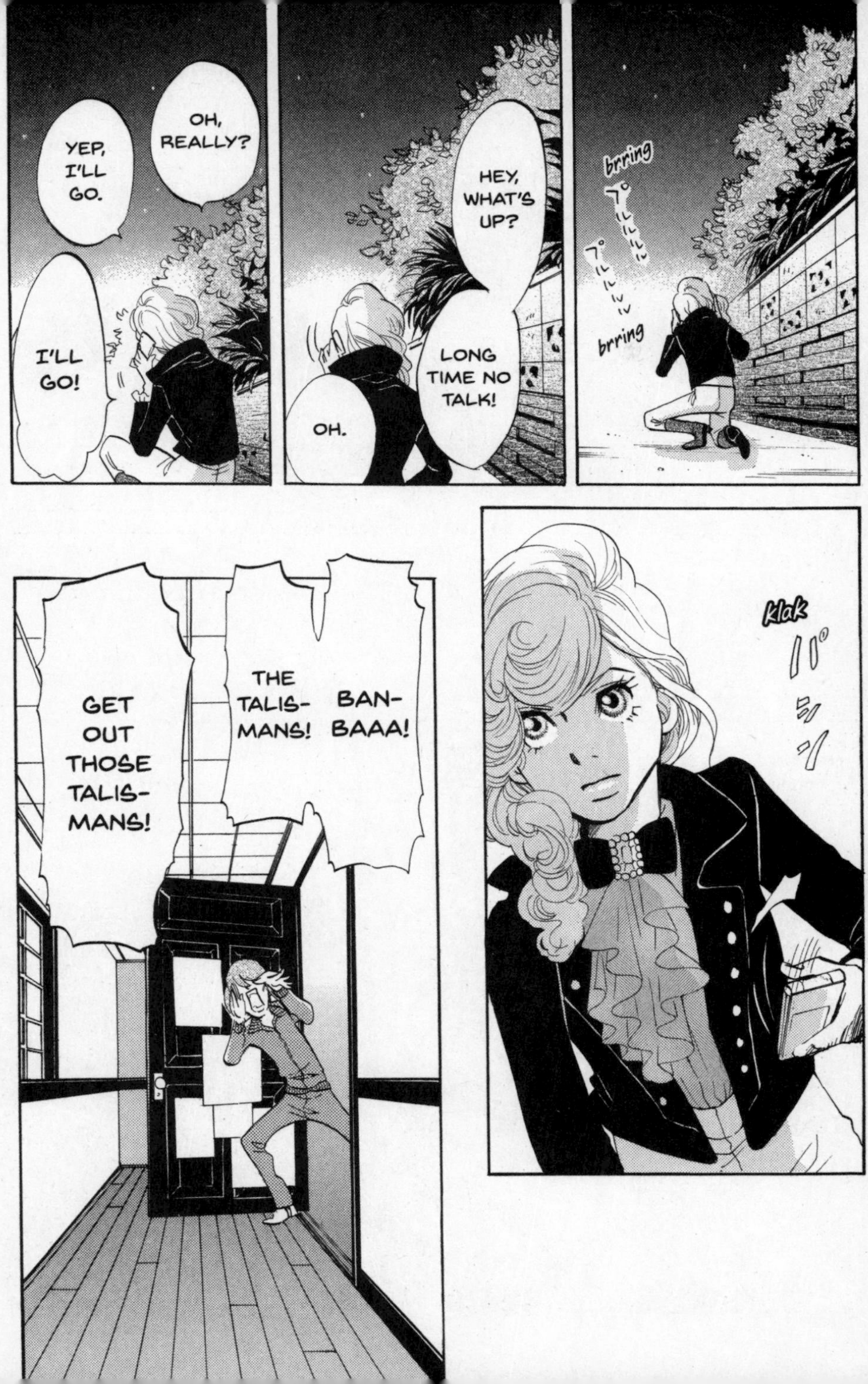
brring
brring
HEY, WHAT'S UP?
LONG TIME NO TALK!
OH.
OH, REALLY?
YEP, I'LL GO.
I'LL GO!
Klak
BAN-BAAA!
THE TALIS-MANS!
GET OUT THOSE TALIS-MANS!

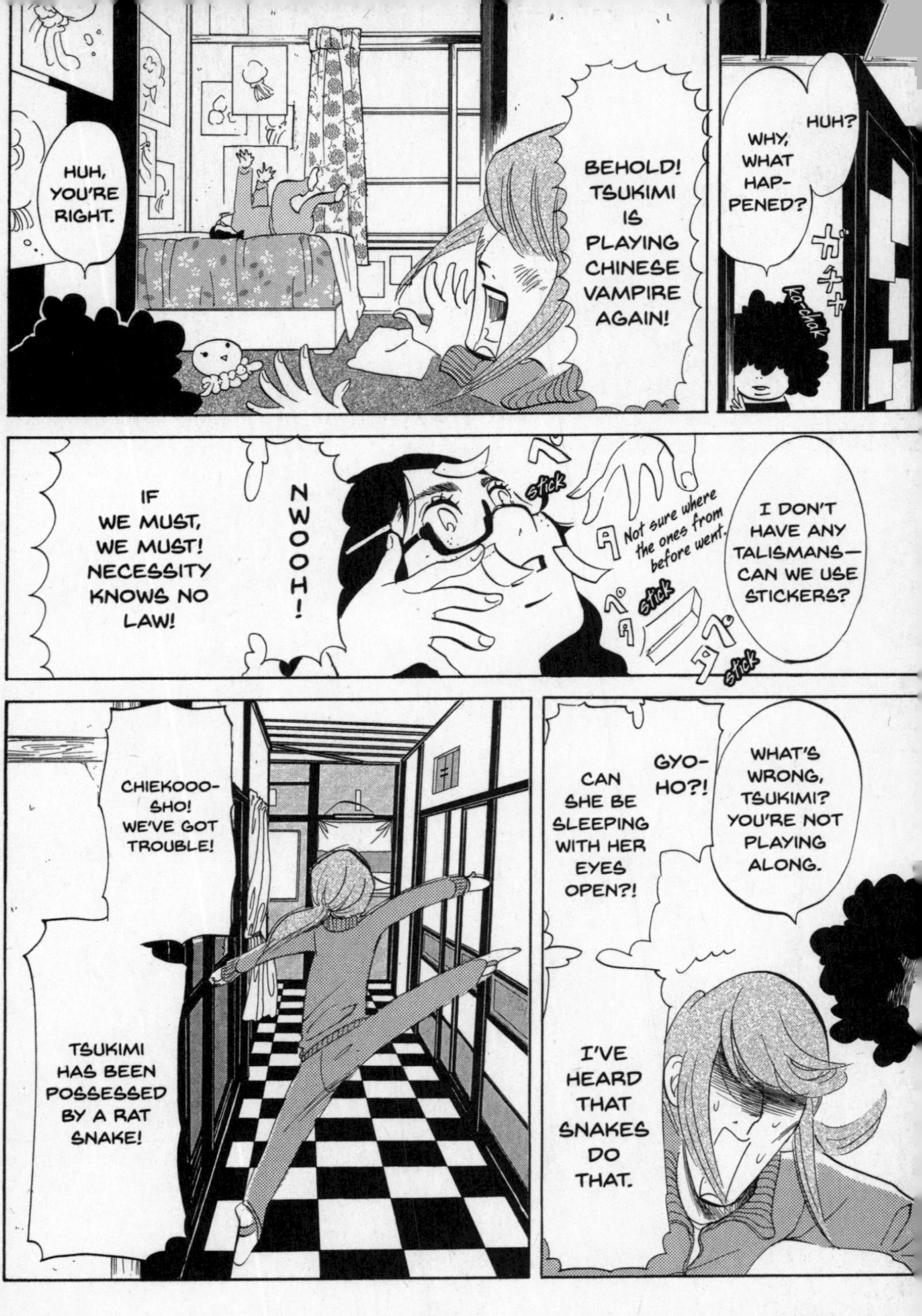
HUH?
WHY, WHAT HAP-PENED?
ka-chak
BEHOLD! TSUKIMI IS PLAYING CHINESE VAMPIRE AGAIN!
HUH, YOU'RE RIGHT.
I DON'T HAVE ANY TALISMANS—CAN WE USE STICKERS?
Not sure where the ones from before went.
stick
stick
stick
NWOOOH!
IF WE MUST, WE MUST! NECESSITY KNOWS NO LAW!
WHAT'S WRONG, TSUKIMI? YOU'RE NOT PLAYING ALONG.
GYO-HO?!
CAN SHE BE SLEEPING WITH HER EYES OPEN?!
I'VE HEARD THAT SNAKES DO THAT.
CHIEKOOOO-SHO! WE'VE GOT TROUBLE!
TSUKIMI HAS BEEN POSSESSED BY A RAT SNAKE!

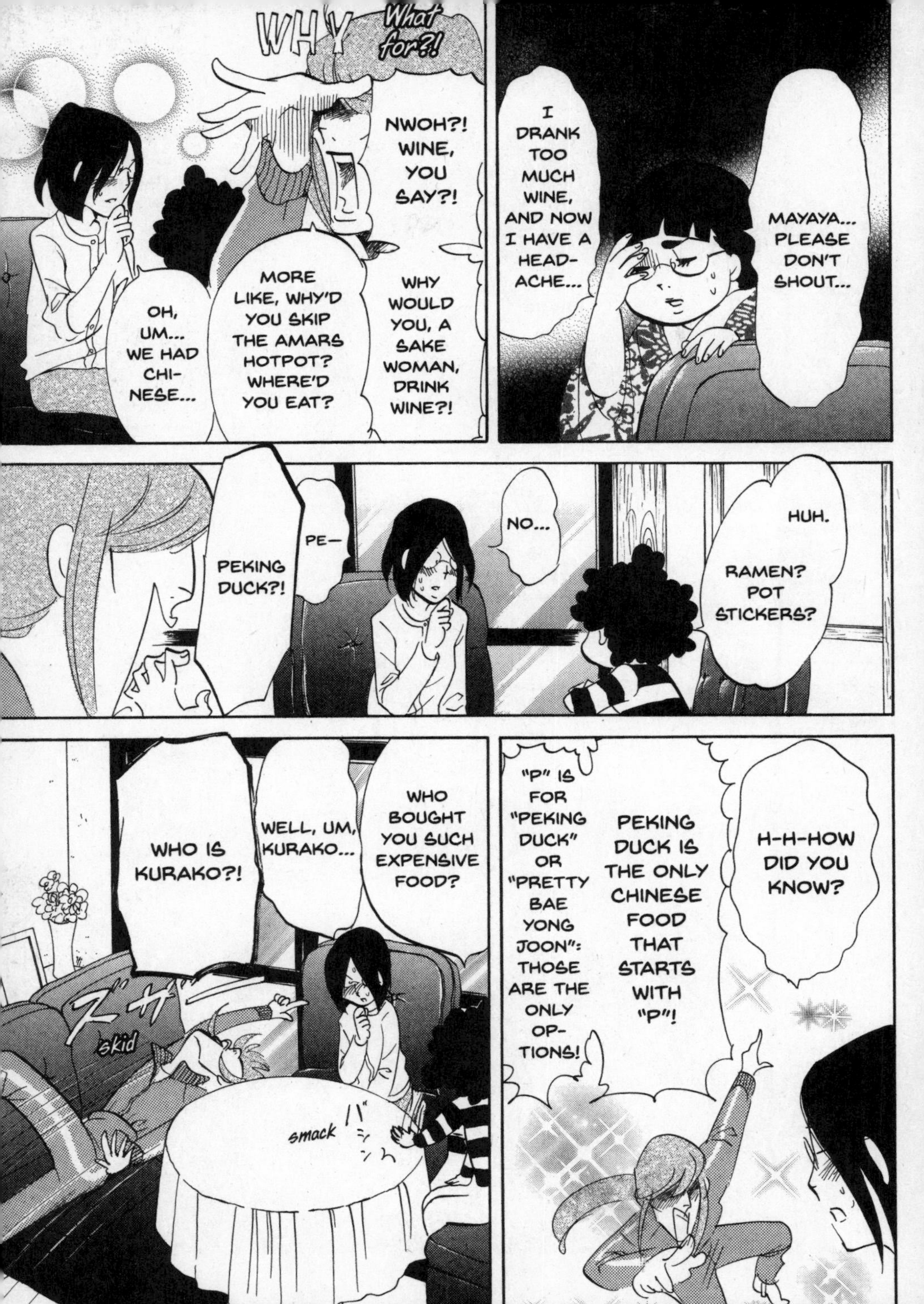
MAYAYA... PLEASE DON'T SHOUT...
I DRANK TOO MUCH WINE, AND NOW I HAVE A HEAD-ACHE...
WHY
What for?!
NWOH?! WINE, YOU SAY?!
WHY WOULD YOU, A SAKE WOMAN, DRINK WINE?!
MORE LIKE, WHY'D YOU SKIP THE AMARS HOTPOT? WHERE'D YOU EAT?
OH, UM... WE HAD CHI-NESE...
HUH.
RAMEN? POT STICKERS?
NO...
PE—
PEKING DUCK?!
H-H-HOW DID YOU KNOW?
PEKING DUCK IS THE ONLY CHINESE FOOD THAT STARTS WITH "P"!
"P" IS FOR "PEKING DUCK" OR "PRETTY BAE YONG JOON": THOSE ARE THE ONLY OP-TIONS!
WHO BOUGHT YOU SUCH EXPENSIVE FOOD?
WELL, UM, KURAKO...
WHO IS KURAKO?!
skid
smack

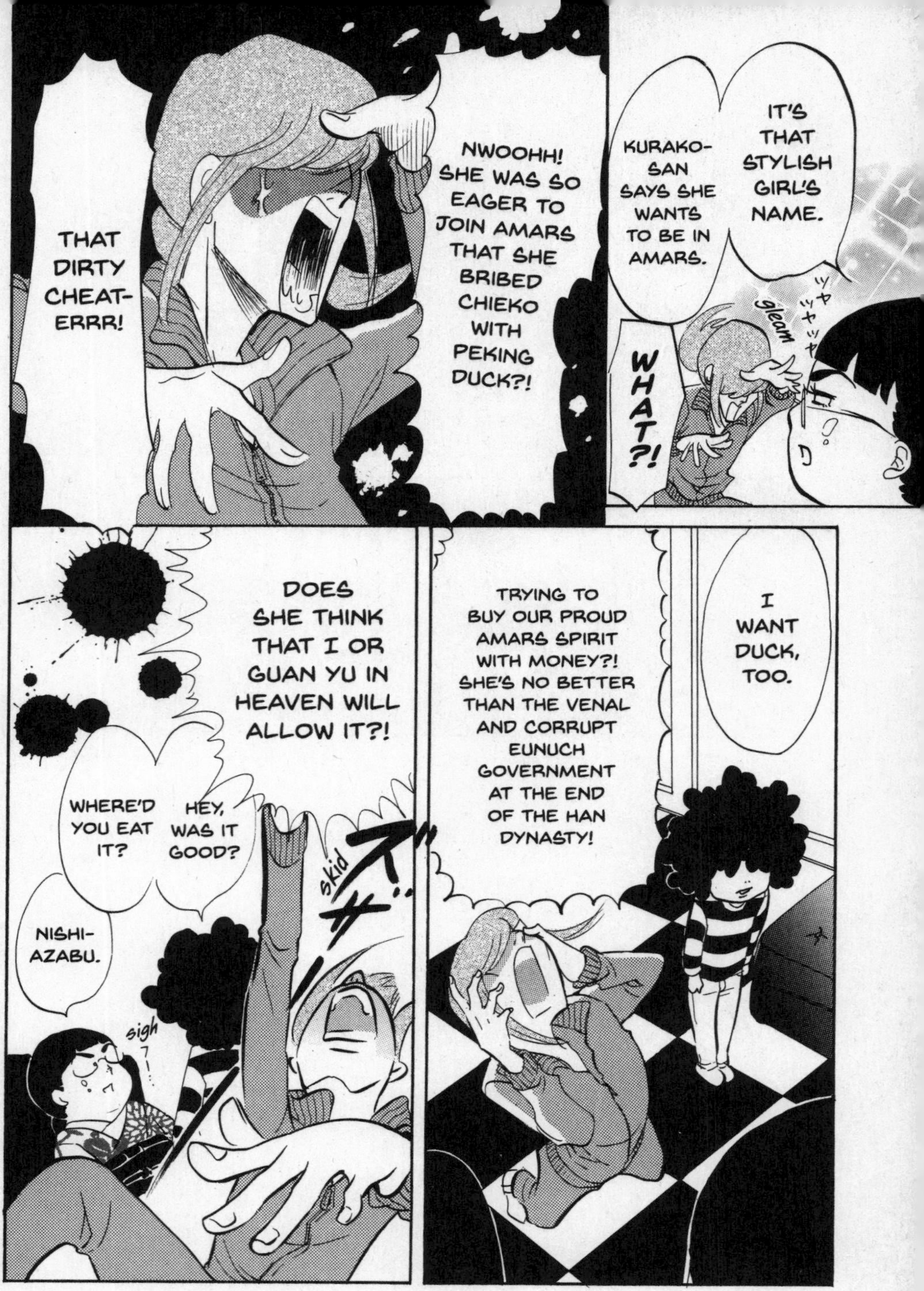
IT'S THAT STYLISH GIRL'S NAME.
KURAKO-SAN SAYS SHE WANTS TO BE IN AMARS.
ツヤツヤツヤ
gleam
WHAT?!
NWOOHH! SHE WAS SO EAGER TO JOIN AMARS THAT SHE BRIBED CHIEKO WITH PEKING DUCK?!
THAT DIRTY CHEAT-ERRR!
I WANT DUCK, TOO.
TRYING TO BUY OUR PROUD AMARS SPIRIT WITH MONEY?! SHE'S NO BETTER THAN THE VENAL AND CORRUPT EUNUCH GOVERNMENT AT THE END OF THE HAN DYNASTY!
DOES SHE THINK THAT I OR GUAN YU IN HEAVEN WILL ALLOW IT?!
skid
HEY, WAS IT GOOD?
WHERE'D YOU EAT IT?
NISHI-AZABU.
sigh

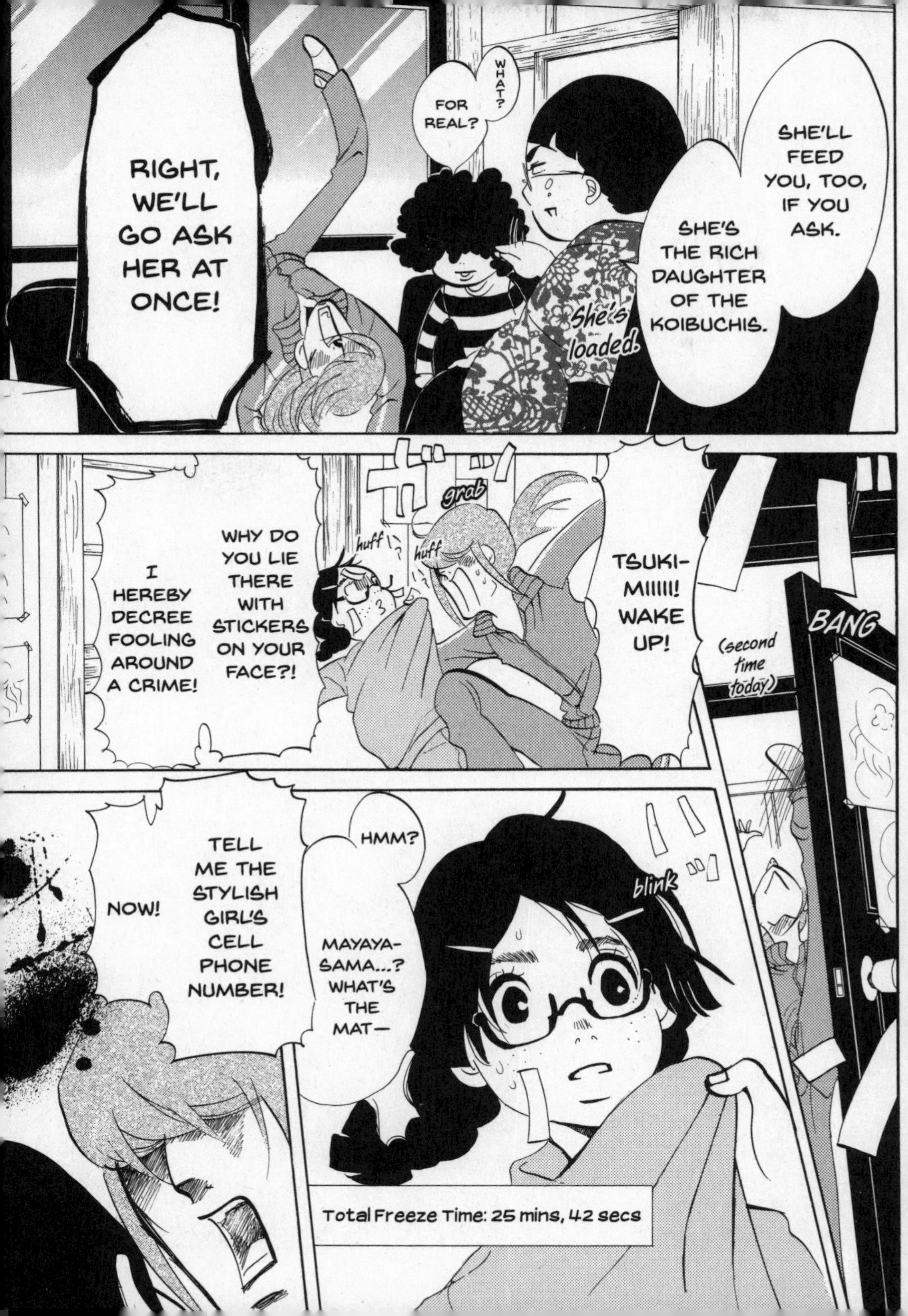
SHE'LL FEED YOU, TOO, IF YOU ASK.
SHE'S THE RICH DAUGHTER OF THE KOIBUCHIS.
She's loaded.
WHAT?
FOR REAL?
RIGHT, WE'LL GO ASK HER AT ONCE!
BANG
(second time today)
TSUKI-MIIIII! WAKE UP!
grab
huff huff
WHY DO YOU LIE THERE WITH STICKERS ON YOUR FACE?!
I HEREBY DECREE FOOLING AROUND A CRIME!
HMM?
blink
MAYAYA-SAMA...? WHAT'S THE MAT—
TELL ME THE STYLISH GIRL'S CELL PHONE NUMBER!
NOW!
Total Freeze Time: 25 mins, 42 secs

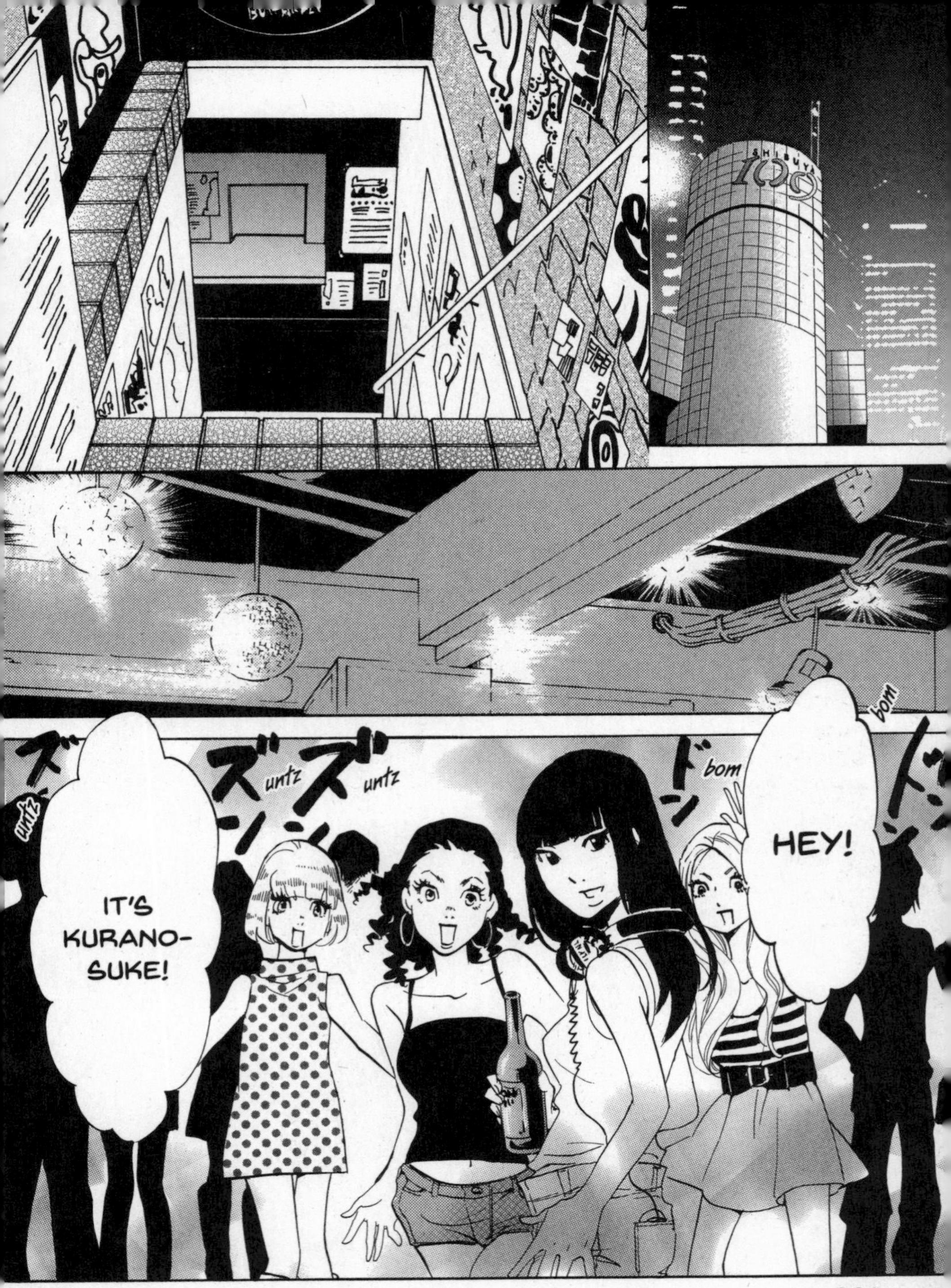
bom
HEY!
bom
untz
untz
untz
IT'S KURANO-SUKE!

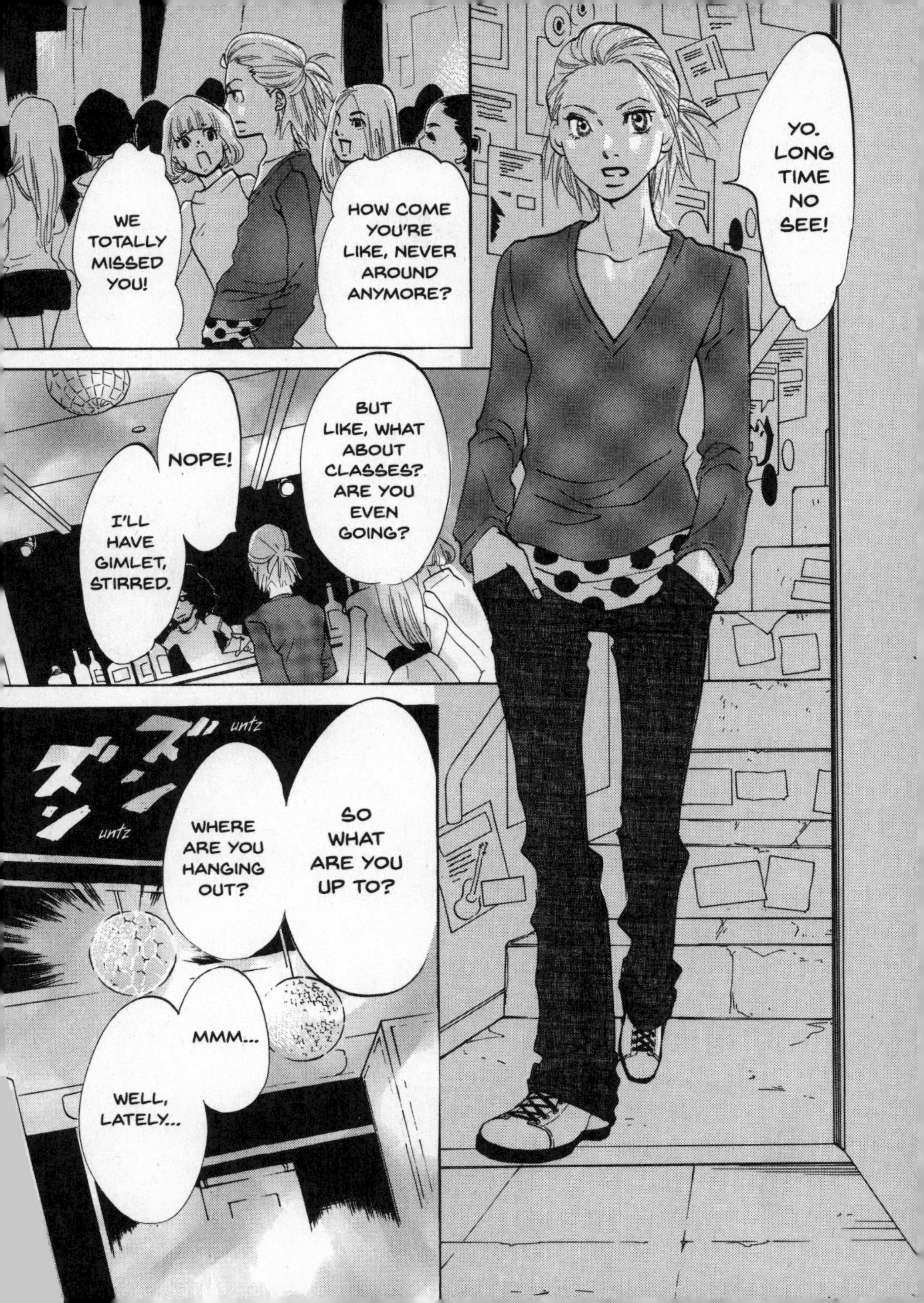
YO. LONG TIME NO SEE!
HOW COME YOU'RE LIKE, NEVER AROUND ANYMORE?
WE TOTALLY MISSED YOU!
BUT LIKE, WHAT ABOUT CLASSES? ARE YOU EVEN GOING?
NOPE!
I'LL HAVE GIMLET, STIRRED.
SO WHAT ARE YOU UP TO?
WHERE ARE YOU HANGING OUT?
untz
untz
MMM...
WELL, LATELY...

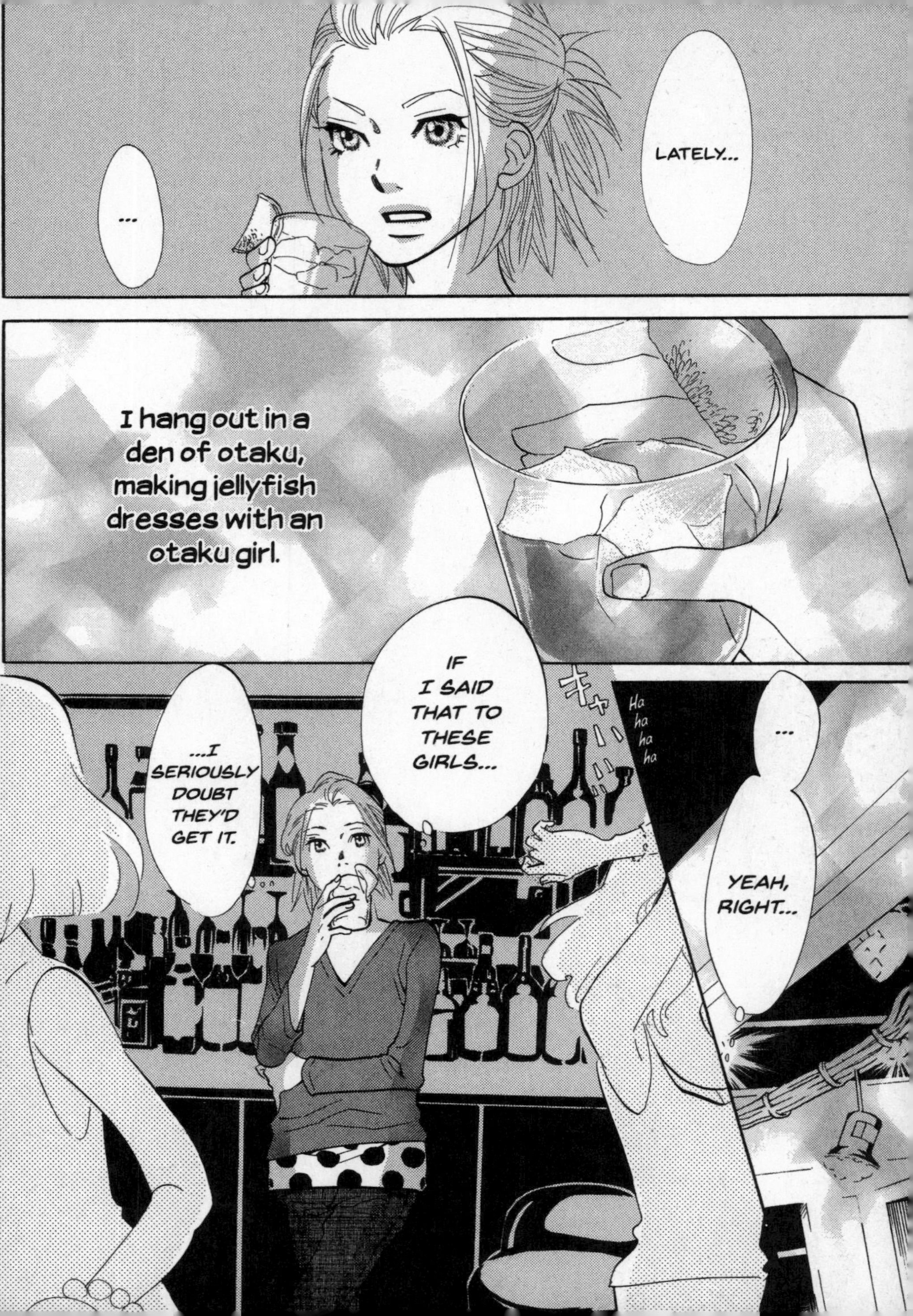
LATELY...
...
I hang out in a den of otaku, making jellyfish dresses with an otaku girl.
...
YEAH, RIGHT...
Ha ha ha ha
IF I SAID THAT TO THESE GIRLS...
...I SERIOUSLY DOUBT THEY'D GET IT.

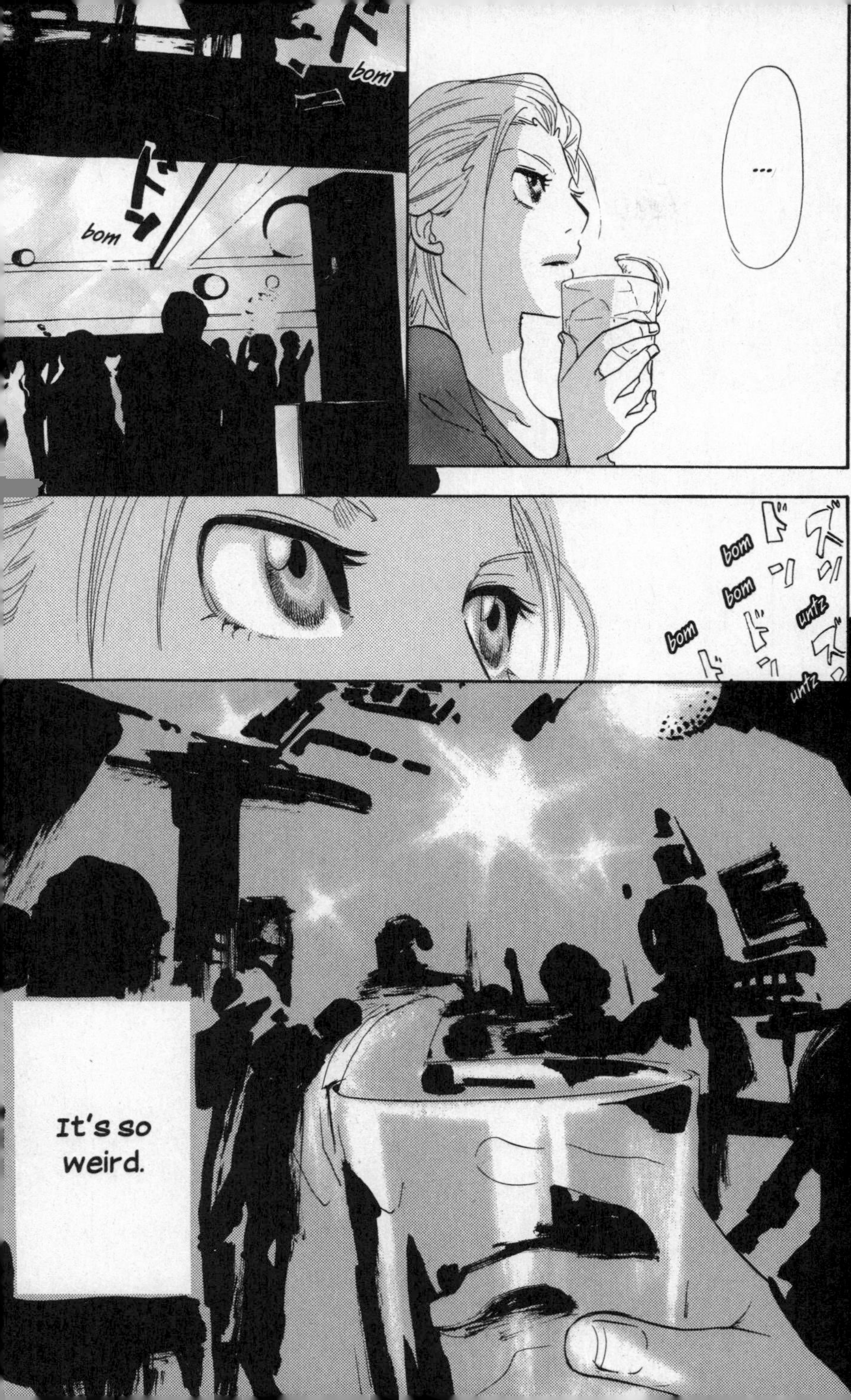
...
ド bom
ドッ bom
bom ドッ
bom ズン
bom ドッ
untz ズン
untz
It's so weird.

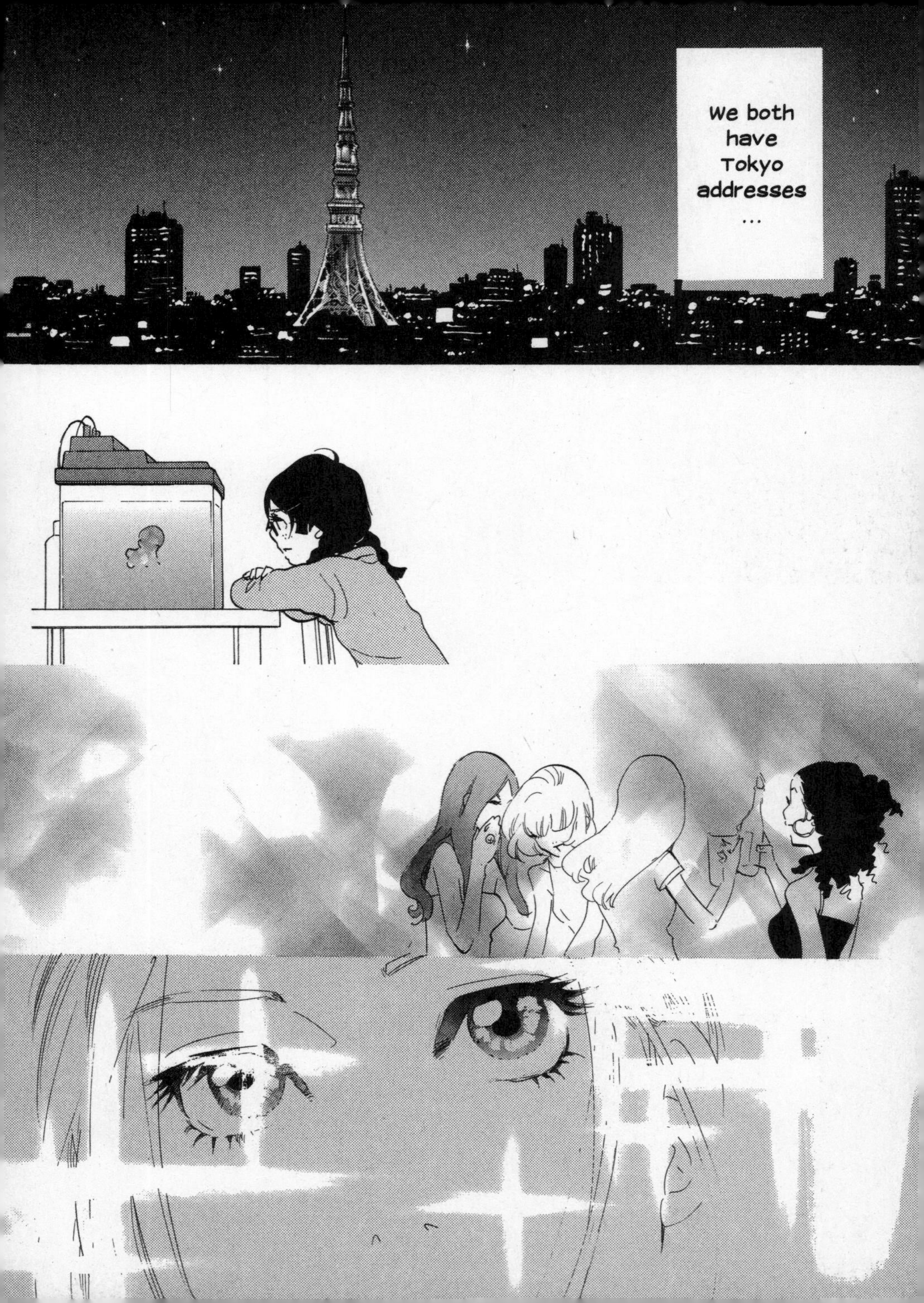
We both have Tokyo addresses
...

...but we live in totally different worlds.
尼
...
ACTUALLY, FORGET OTHER WORLDS...
MORE LIKE... OTHER PLANETS?
Maybe?

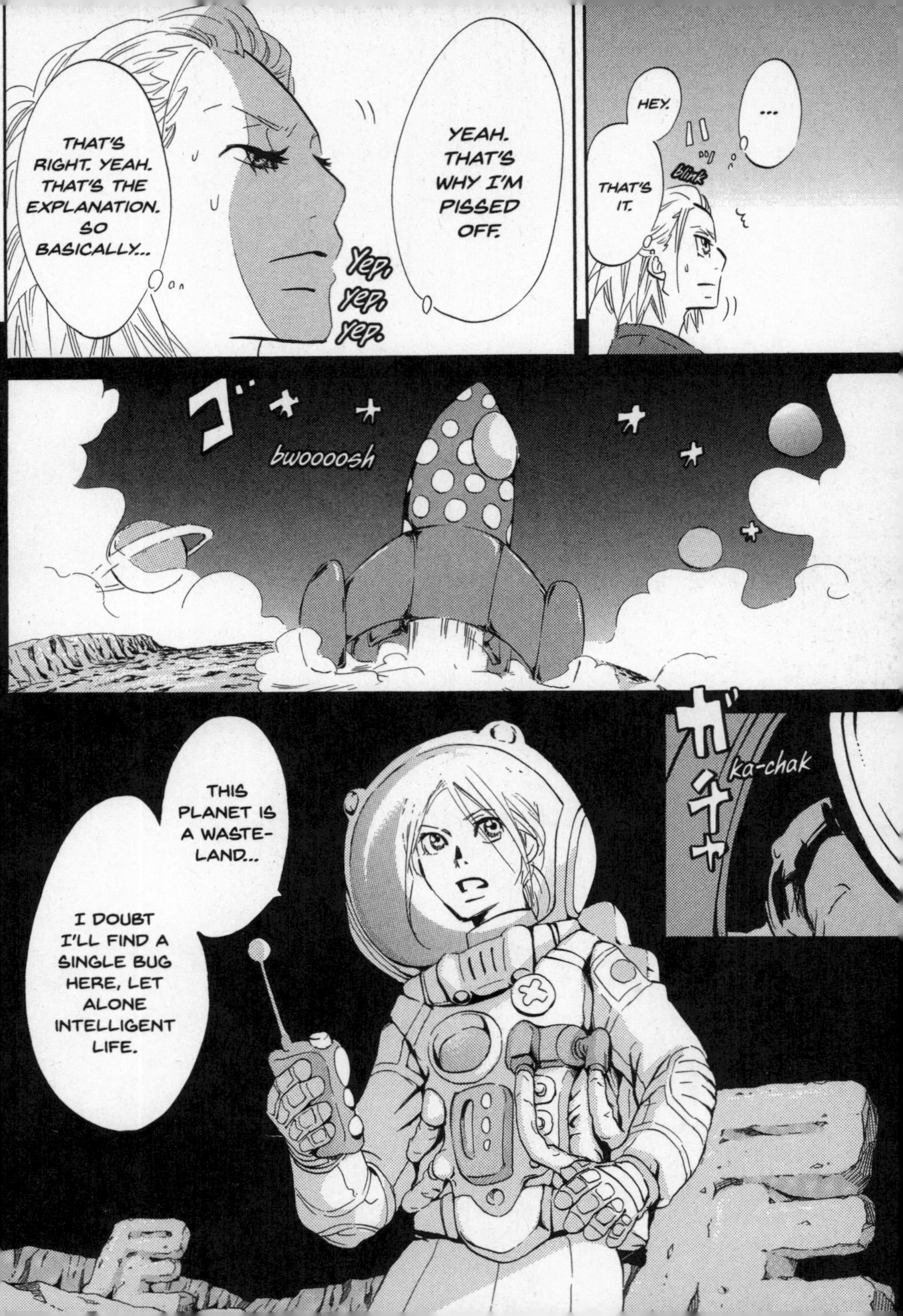
...
HEY.
THAT'S IT.
blink
YEAH. THAT'S WHY I'M PISSED OFF.
Yep, yep, yep.
THAT'S RIGHT. YEAH. THAT'S THE EXPLANATION. SO BASICALLY...
ゴ
bwoooosh
ガチャ
ka-chak
THIS PLANET IS A WASTE-LAND...
I DOUBT I'LL FIND A SINGLE BUG HERE, LET ALONE INTELLIGENT LIFE.

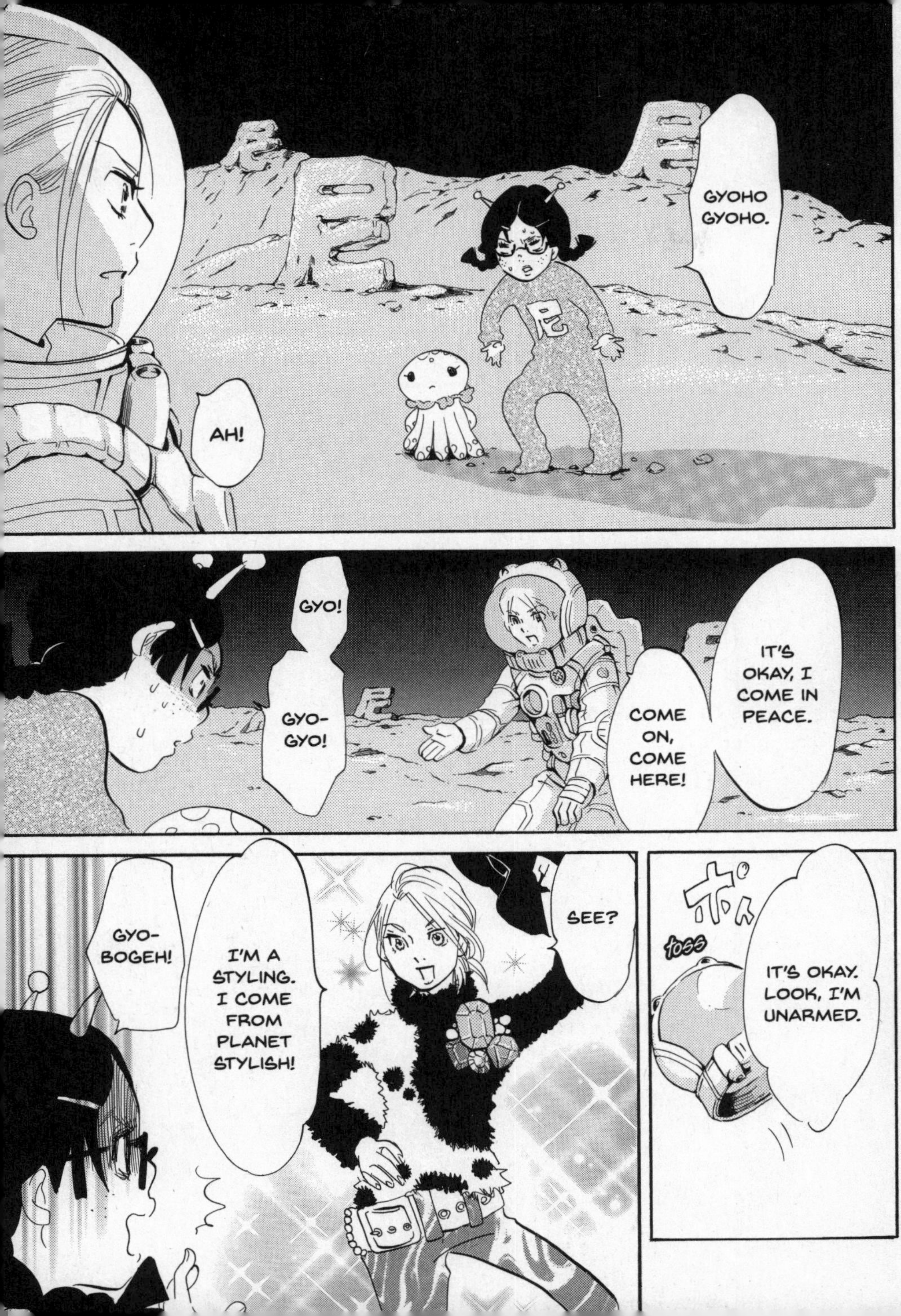
GYOHO GYOHO.
AH!
IT'S OKAY, I COME IN PEACE.
COME ON, COME HERE!
GYO!
GYO-GYO!
toss
IT'S OKAY. LOOK, I'M UNARMED.
SEE?
I'M A STYLING. I COME FROM PLANET STYLISH!
GYO-BOGEH!

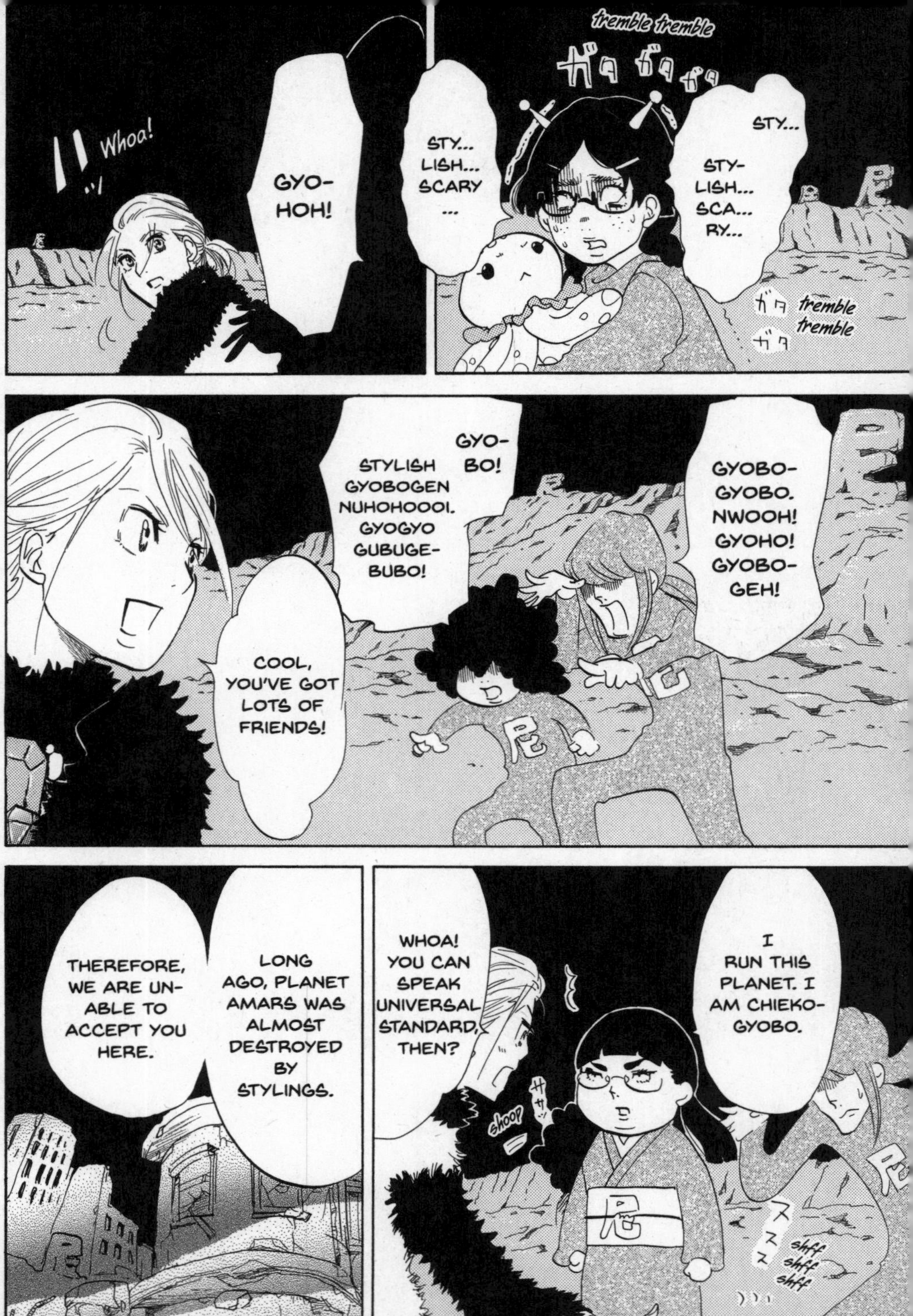
tremble tremble
ガタガタガタ
STY... STY-LISH... SCA... RY...
STY... LISH... SCARY ...
ガタ tremble tremble ガタ
GYO-HOH!
Whoa!
GYOBO-GYOBO. NWOOH! GYOHO! GYOBO-GEH!
GYO-BO!
STYLISH GYOBOGEN NUHOHOOOI. GYOGYO GUBUGE-BUBO!
COOL, YOU'VE GOT LOTS OF FRIENDS!
I RUN THIS PLANET. I AM CHIEKO-GYOBO.
WHOA! YOU CAN SPEAK UNIVERSAL STANDARD, THEN?
shoop
shff shff shff
LONG AGO, PLANET AMARS WAS ALMOST DESTROYED BY STYLINGS.
THEREFORE, WE ARE UN-ABLE TO ACCEPT YOU HERE.

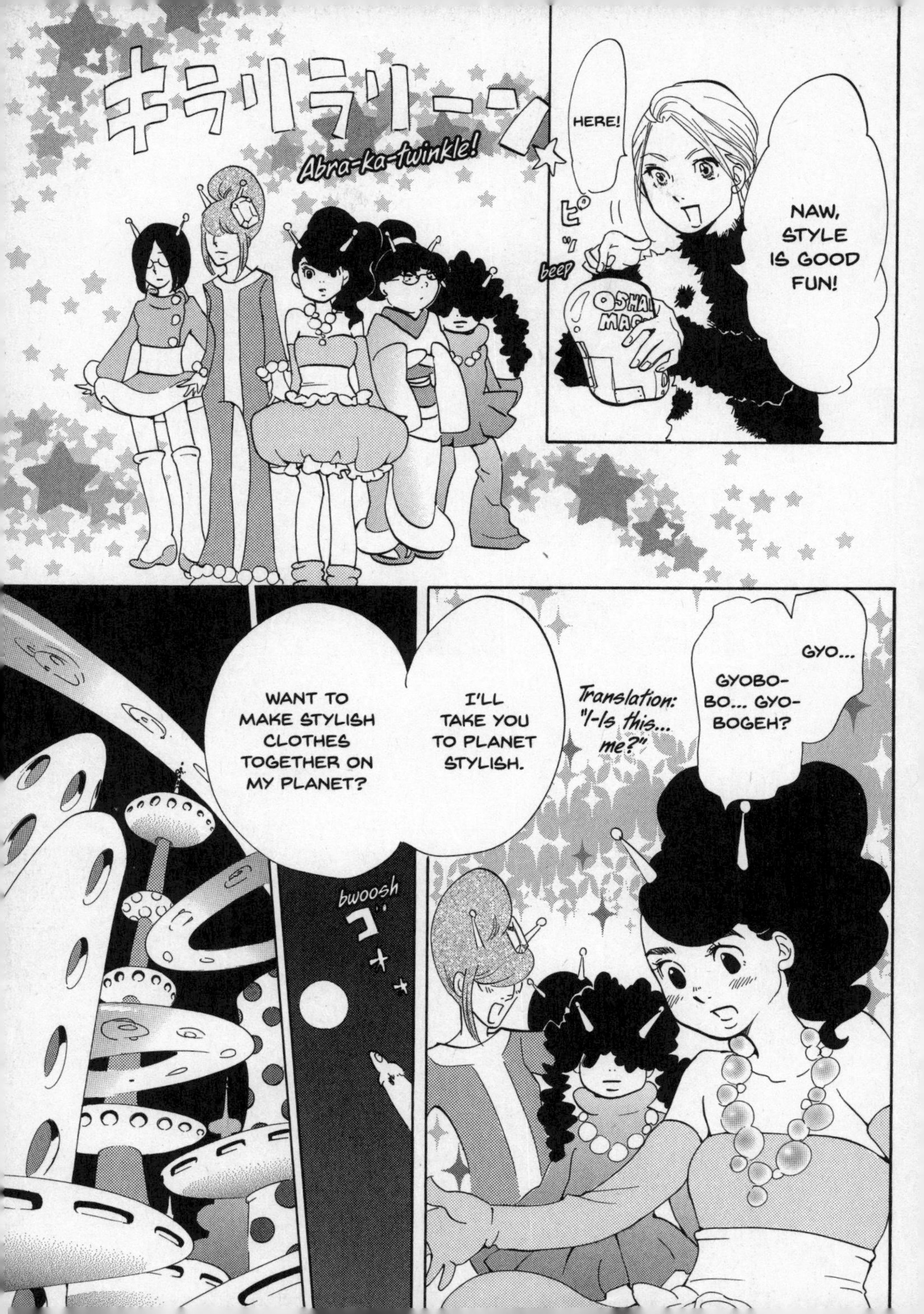
NAW, STYLE IS GOOD FUN!
HERE!
ピッ
beep
キラリラリーン
Abra-ka-twinkle!
GYO...
GYOBOBO... GYO-BOGEH?
Translation: "I-Is this... me?"
I'LL TAKE YOU TO PLANET STYLISH.
WANT TO MAKE STYLISH CLOTHES TOGETHER ON MY PLANET?
bwoosh
ゴォォ

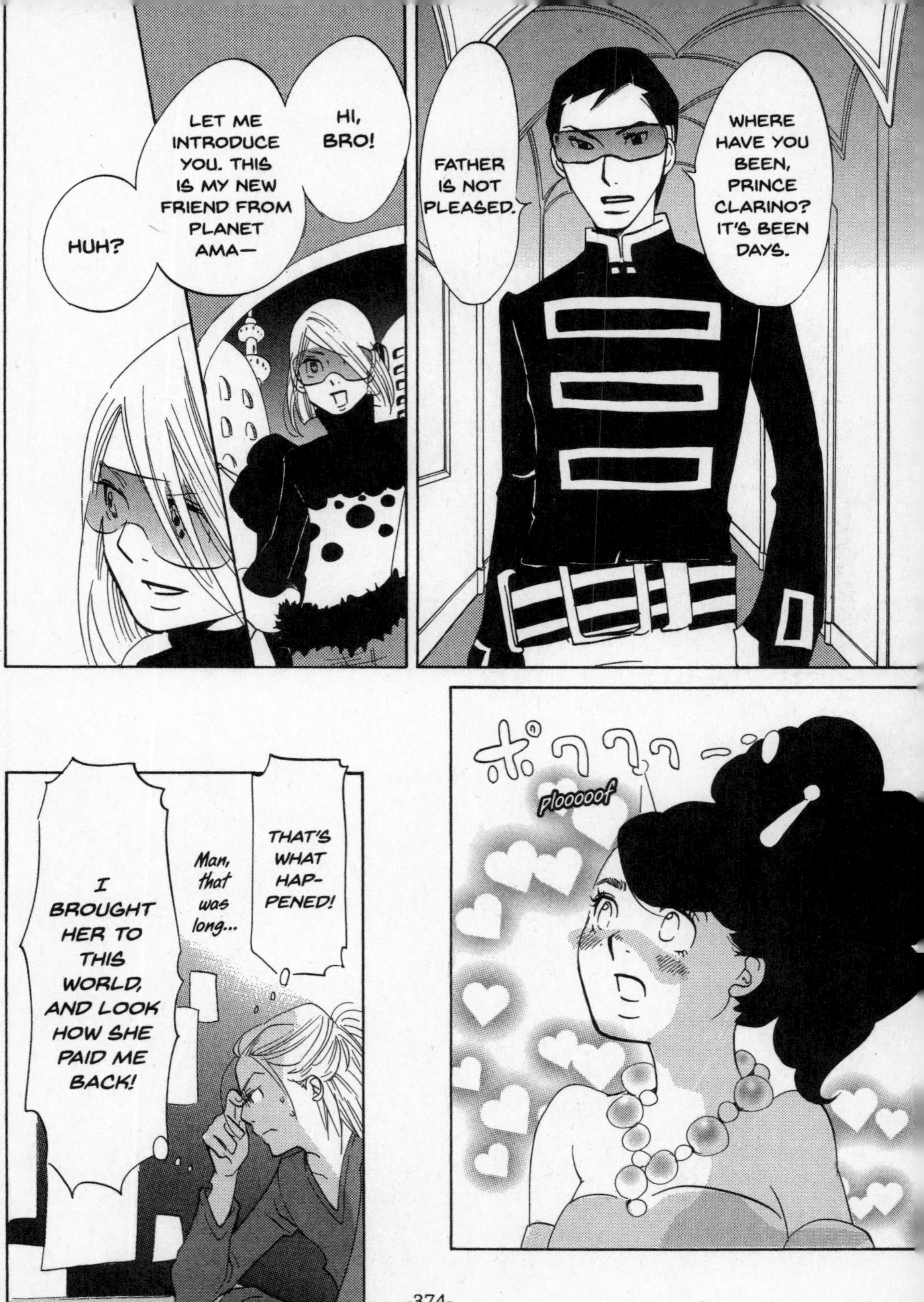
WHERE HAVE YOU BEEN, PRINCE CLARINO? IT'S BEEN DAYS.
FATHER IS NOT PLEASED.
HI, BRO!
LET ME INTRODUCE YOU. THIS IS MY NEW FRIEND FROM PLANET AMA—
HUH?
plooooof
THAT'S WHAT HAP-PENED!
Man, that was long...
I BROUGHT HER TO THIS WORLD, AND LOOK HOW SHE PAID ME BACK!

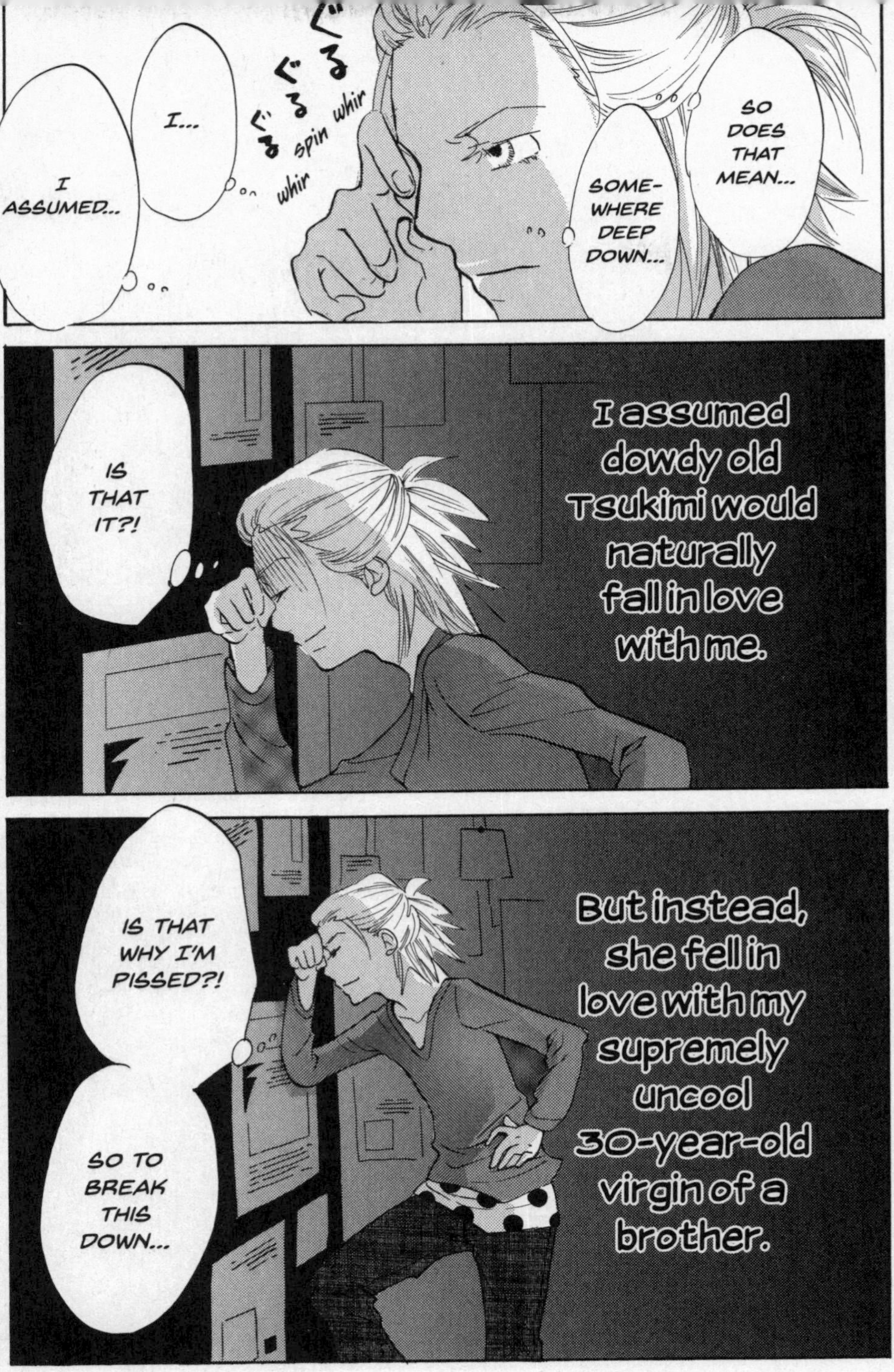
SO DOES THAT MEAN...
SOME-WHERE DEEP DOWN...
ぐるぐるぐる
spin whir whir
I...
I ASSUMED...
I assumed dowdy old Tsukimi would naturally fall in love with me.
IS THAT IT?!
But instead, she fell in love with my supremely uncool 30-year-old virgin of a brother.
IS THAT WHY I'M PISSED?!
SO TO BREAK THIS DOWN...

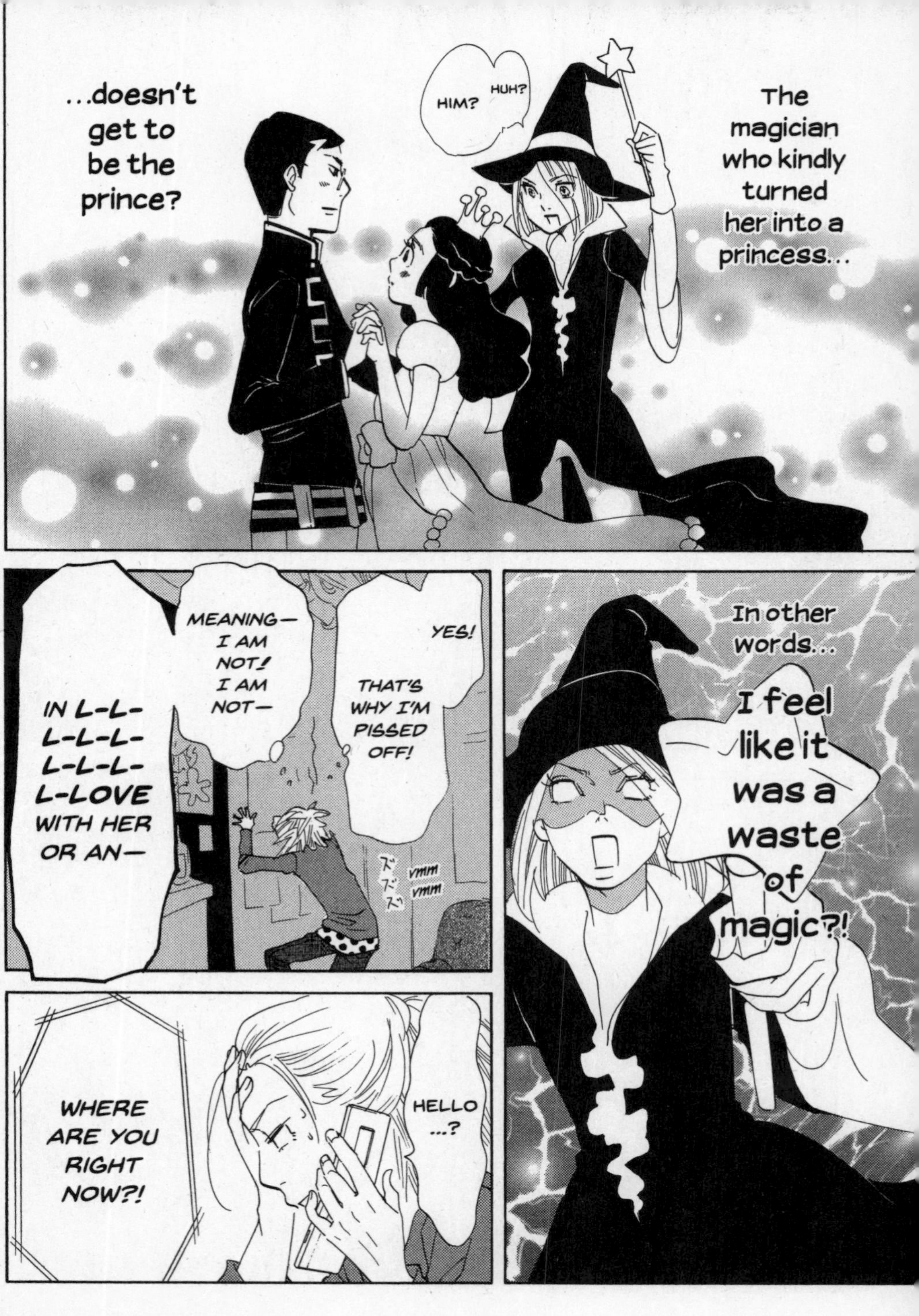
The magician who kindly turned her into a princess...
HUH?
HIM?
...doesn't get to be the prince?
In other words...
I feel like it was a waste of magic?!
YES!
THAT'S WHY I'M PISSED OFF!
MEANING— I AM NOT! I AM NOT—
IN L-L-L-L-L-L-L-L-L-LOVE WITH HER OR AN—
ズズズ
VMM VMM
HELLO ...?
WHERE ARE YOU RIGHT NOW?!

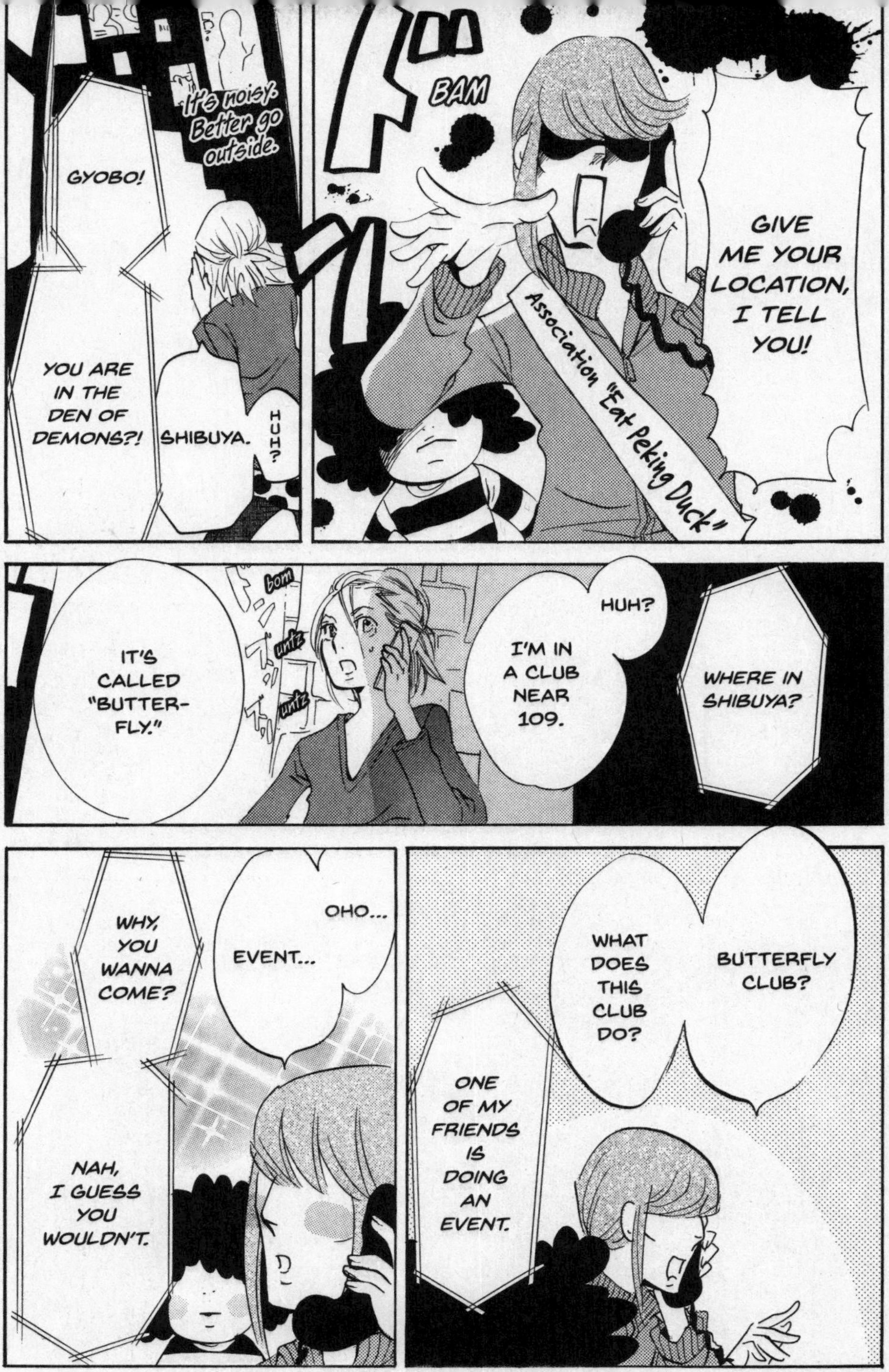
BAM
GIVE ME YOUR LOCATION, I TELL YOU!
Association "Eat Peking Duck"
It's noisy. Better go outside.
HUH?
SHIBUYA.
GYOBO!
YOU ARE IN THE DEN OF DEMONS?!
WHERE IN SHIBUYA?
HUH?
I'M IN A CLUB NEAR 109.
bom
untz
untz
IT'S CALLED "BUTTERFLY."
BUTTERFLY CLUB?
WHAT DOES THIS CLUB DO?
ONE OF MY FRIENDS IS DOING AN EVENT.
OHO...
EVENT...
WHY, YOU WANNA COME?
NAH, I GUESS YOU WOULDN'T.

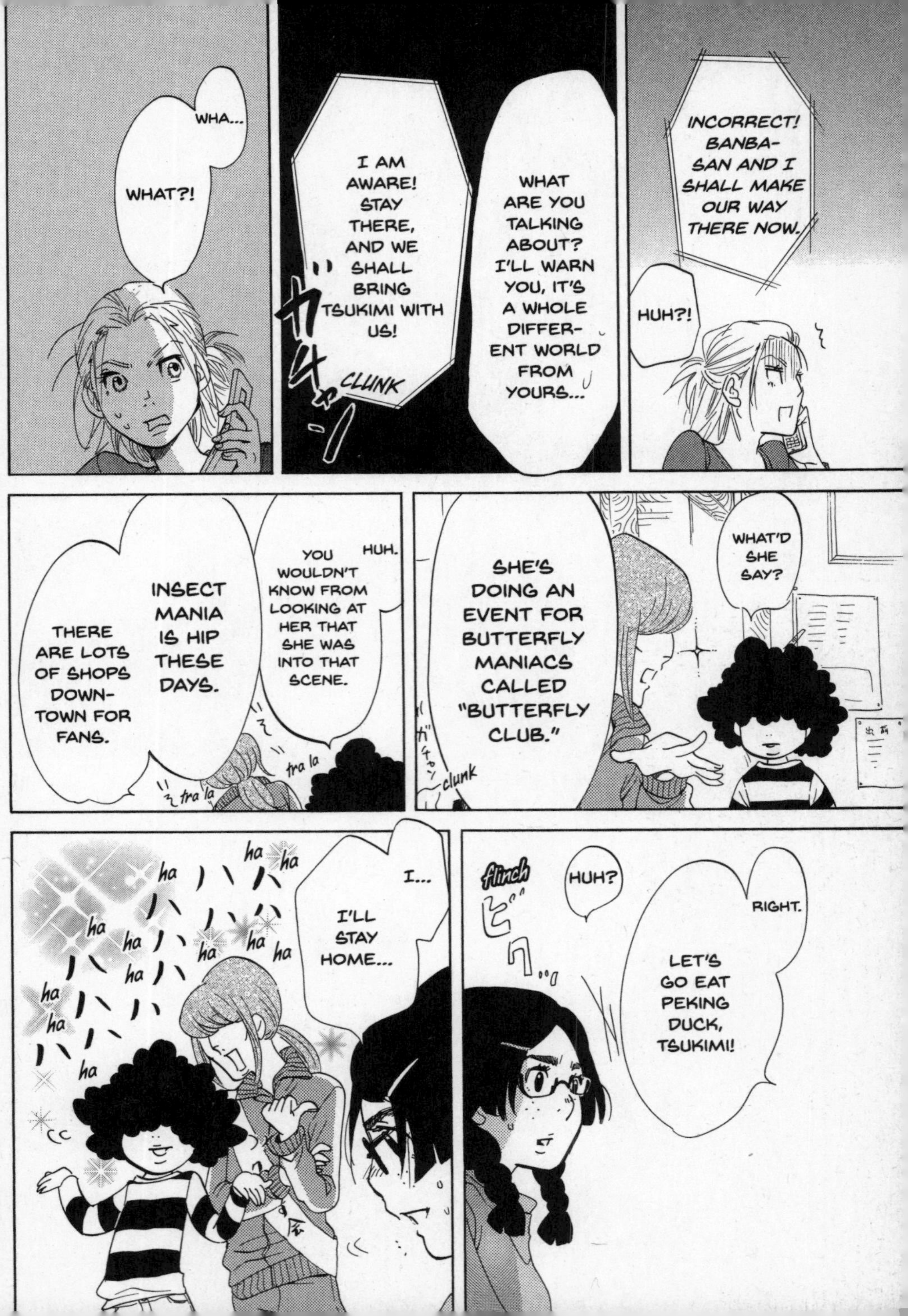
INCORRECT! BANBA-SAN AND I SHALL MAKE OUR WAY THERE NOW.
HUH?!
WHAT ARE YOU TALKING ABOUT? I'LL WARN YOU, IT'S A WHOLE DIFFERENT WORLD FROM YOURS...
I AM AWARE! STAY THERE, AND WE SHALL BRING TSUKIMI WITH US!
CLUNK
WHA...
WHAT?!
WHAT'D SHE SAY?
SHE'S DOING AN EVENT FOR BUTTERFLY MANIACS CALLED "BUTTERFLY CLUB."
clunk
HUH.
YOU WOULDN'T KNOW FROM LOOKING AT HER THAT SHE WAS INTO THAT SCENE.
INSECT MANIA IS HIP THESE DAYS.
THERE ARE LOTS OF SHOPS DOWNTOWN FOR FANS.
tra la
tra la
RIGHT.
LET'S GO EAT PEKING DUCK, TSUKIMI!
HUH?
flinch
I...
I'LL STAY HOME...
ha ha ha ha ha ha ha ha ha ha ha ha

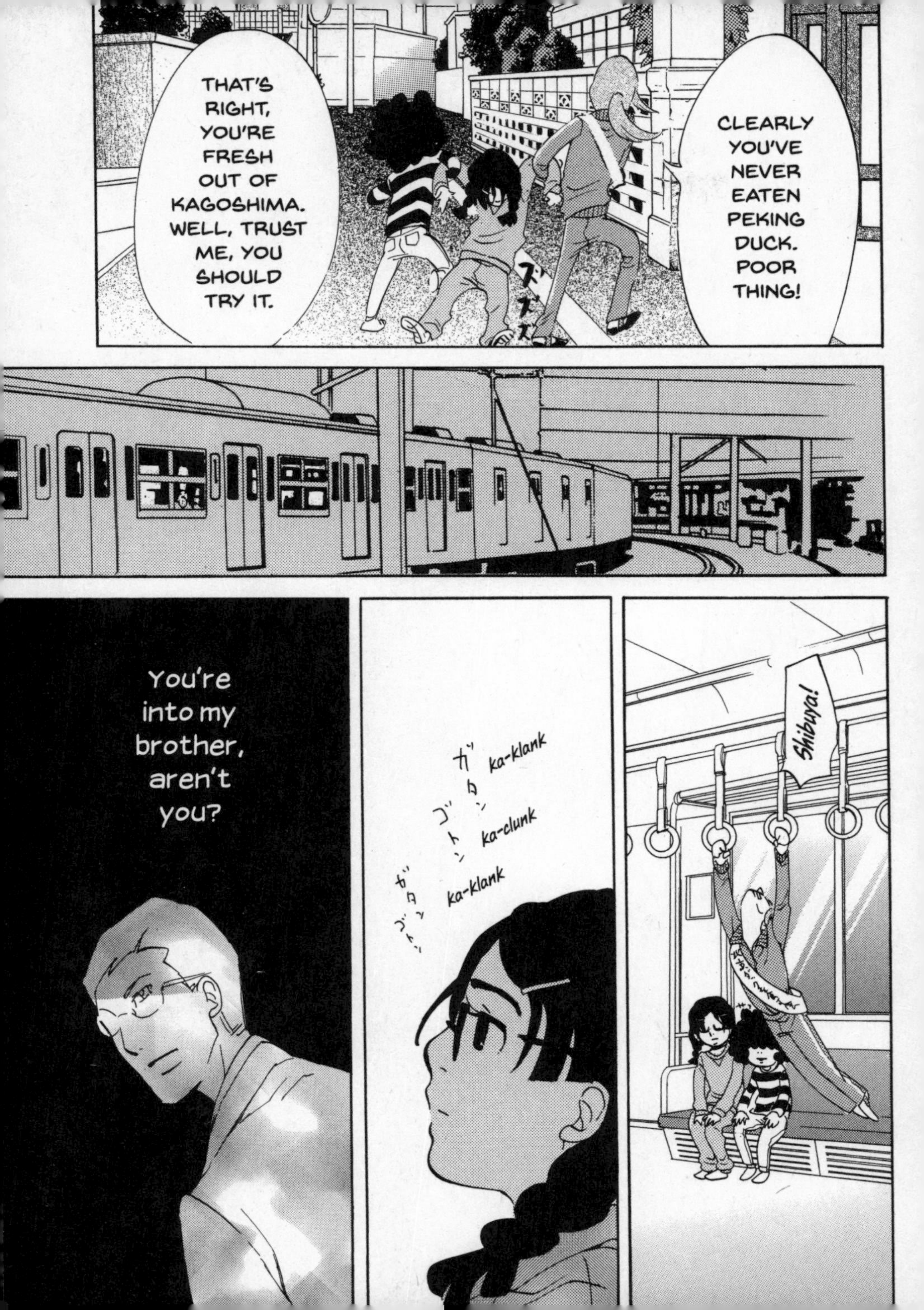
CLEARLY YOU'VE NEVER EATEN PEKING DUCK. POOR THING!
THAT'S RIGHT, YOU'RE FRESH OUT OF KAGOSHIMA. WELL, TRUST ME, YOU SHOULD TRY IT.
Shibuya!
ka-klank
ka-clunk
ka-klank
You're into my brother, aren't you?

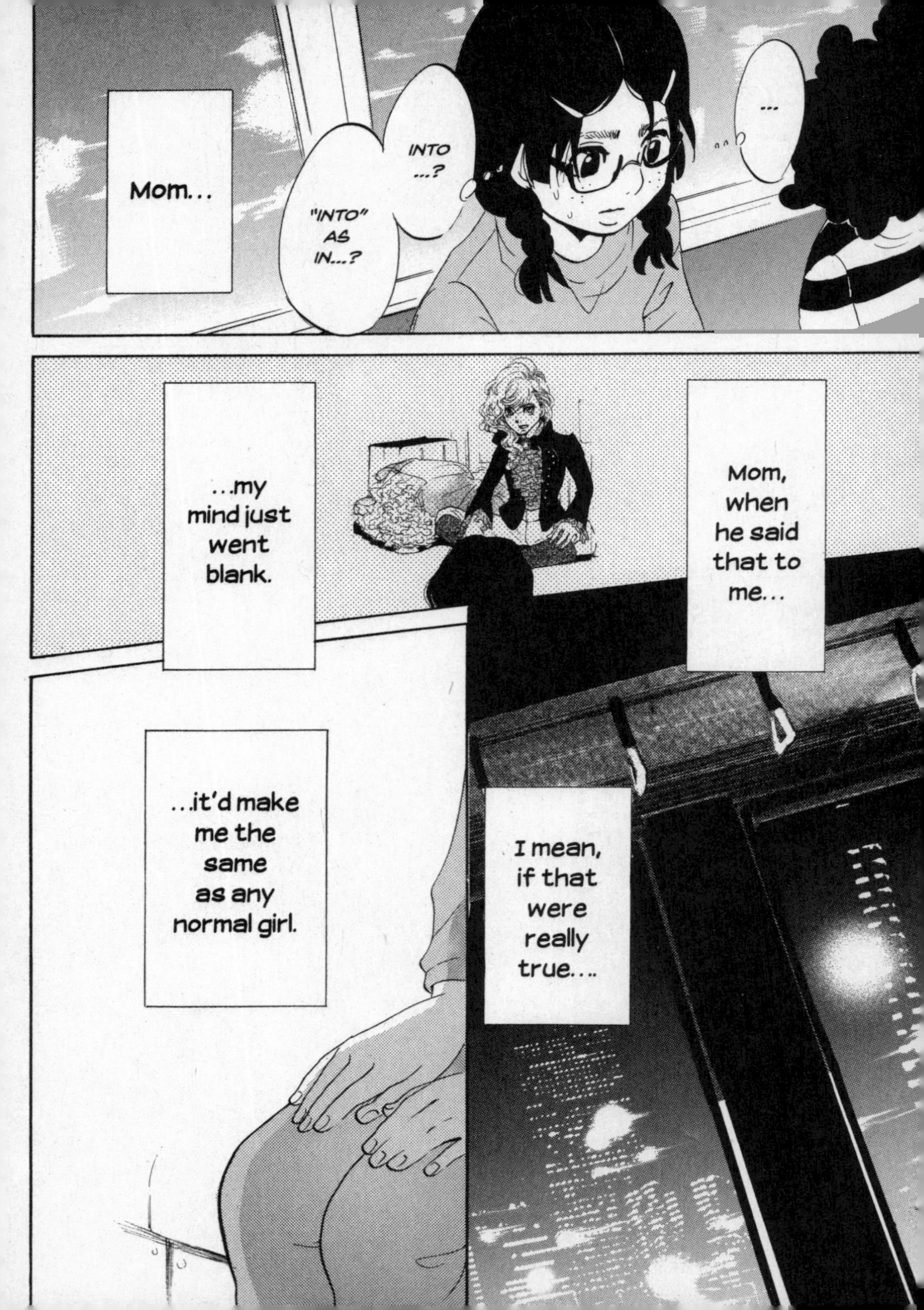
...
INTO ...?
"INTO" AS IN...?
Mom...
Mom, when he said that to me...
...my mind just went blank.
I mean, if that were really true....
...it'd make me the same as any normal girl.

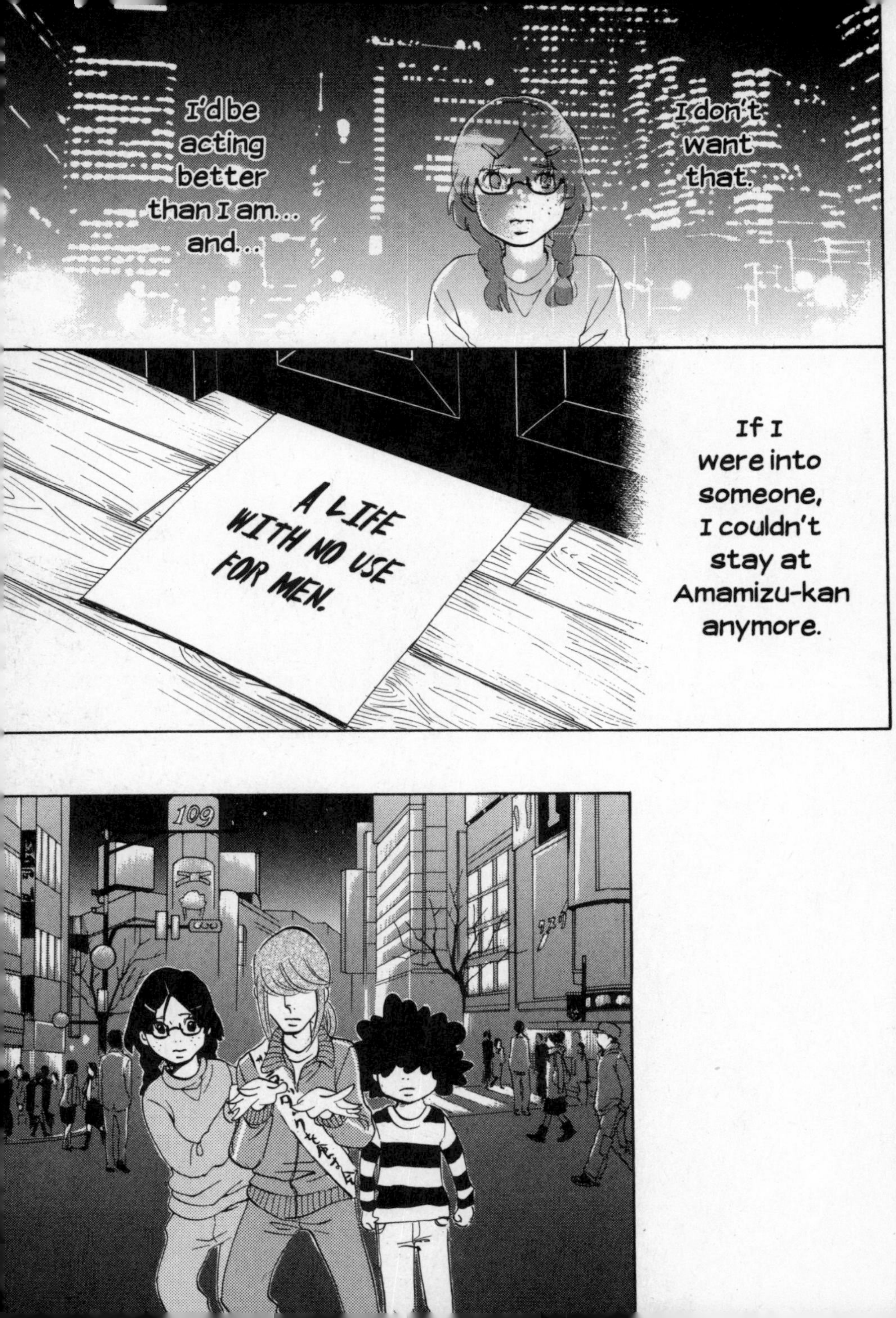
I don't want that.
I'd be acting better than I am... and...
If I were into someone, I couldn't stay at Amamizu-kan anymore.
A LIFE WITH NO USE FOR MEN.
109

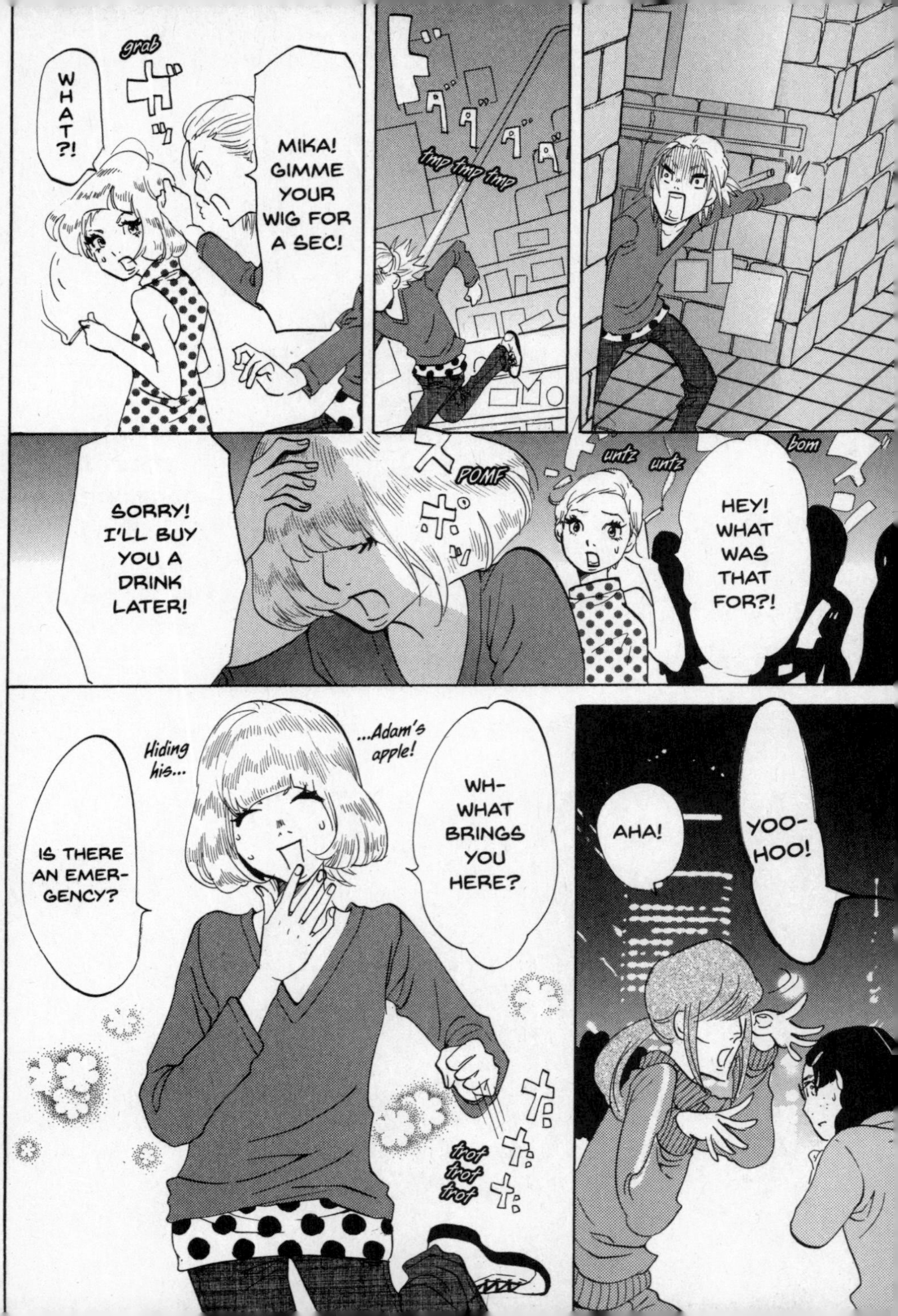
tmp tmp tmp
MIKA! GIMME YOUR WIG FOR A SEC!
grab
WHAT?!
bom
HEY! WHAT WAS THAT FOR?!
untz untz
POMF
SORRY! I'LL BUY YOU A DRINK LATER!
YOO-HOO!
AHA!
...Adam's apple!
WH-WHAT BRINGS YOU HERE?
Hiding his...
IS THERE AN EMERGENCY?
trot trot trot

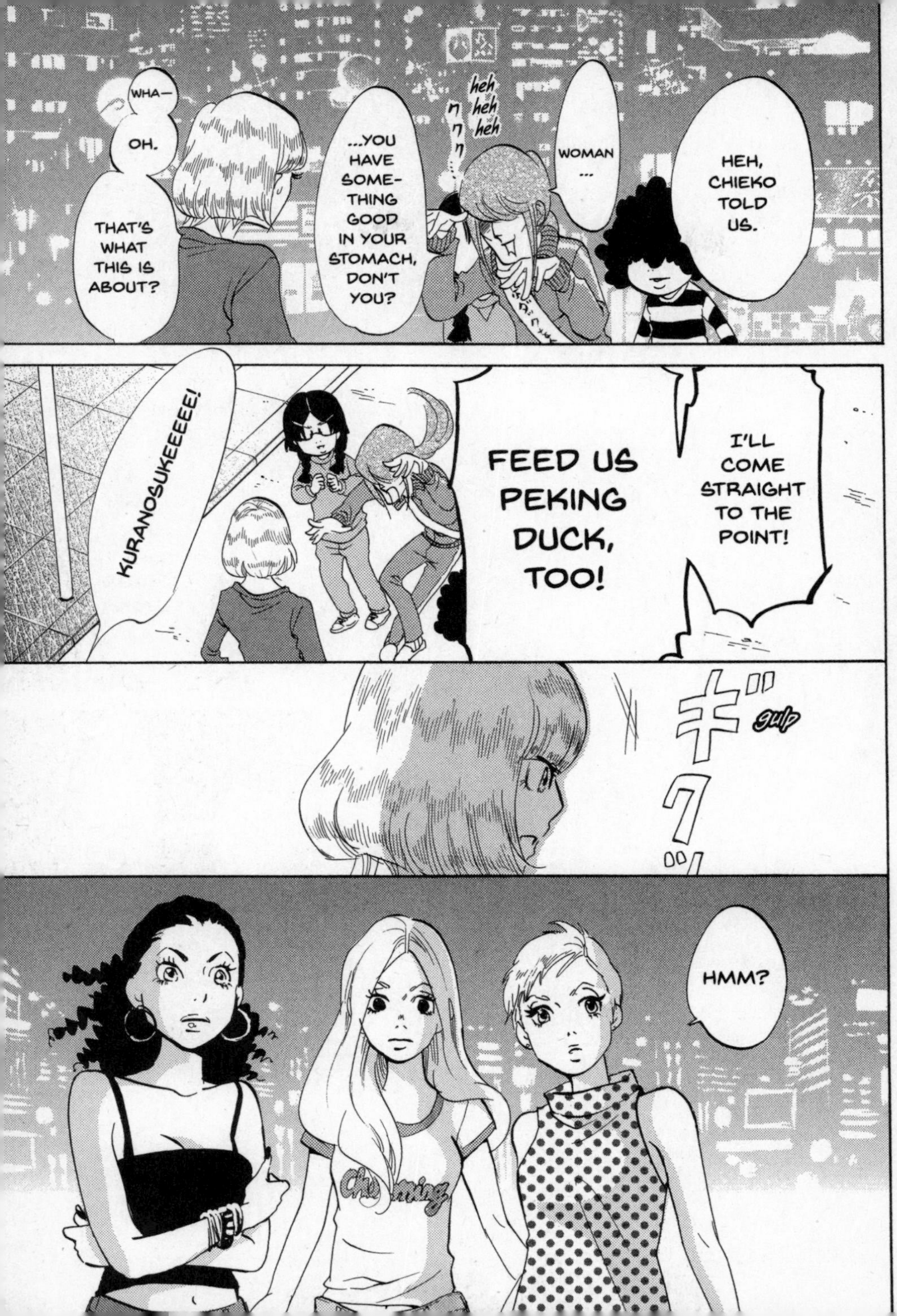
HEH, CHIEKO TOLD US.
WOMAN...
heh heh heh
...YOU HAVE SOME-THING GOOD IN YOUR STOMACH, DON'T YOU?
WHA—
OH.
THAT'S WHAT THIS IS ABOUT?
I'LL COME STRAIGHT TO THE POINT!
FEED US PEKING DUCK, TOO!
KURANOSUKEEEEE!
gulp
HMM?

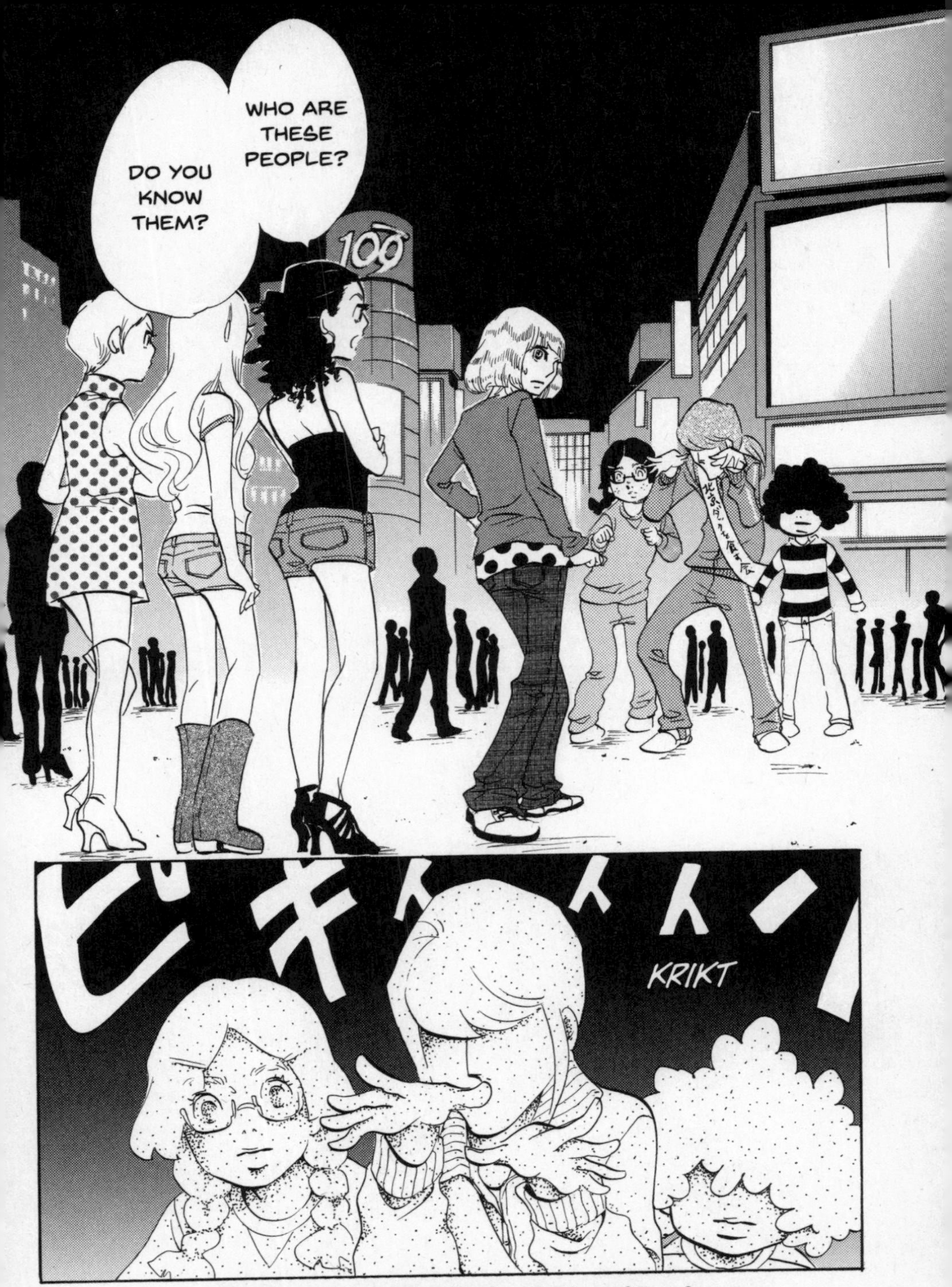
WHO ARE THESE PEOPLE?
DO YOU KNOW THEM?
ピキィィン
KRIKT

Princess Jellyfish Vol. 2/End

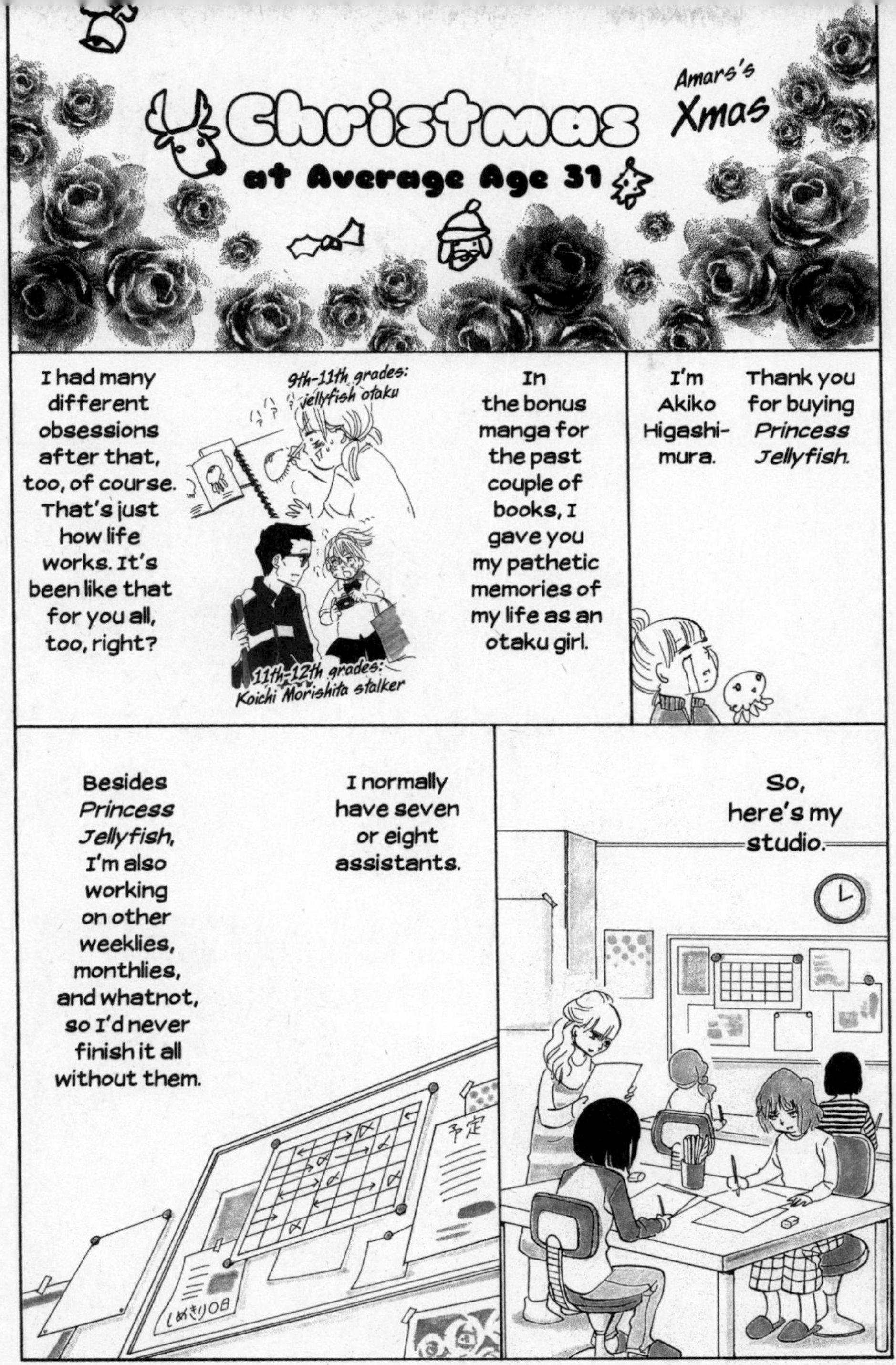
Christmas at Average Age 31
Amars's Xmas
Thank you for buying Princess Jellyfish.
I'm Akiko Higashimura.
In the bonus manga for the past couple of books, I gave you my pathetic memories of my life as an otaku girl.
9th-11th grades: jellyfish otaku
11th-12th grades: Koichi Morishita stalker
I had many different obsessions after that, too, of course. That's just how life works. It's been like that for you all, too, right?
So, here's my studio.
I normally have seven or eight assistants.
Besides Princess Jellyfish, I'm also working on other weeklies, monthlies, and whatnot, so I'd never finish it all without them.
予定
しめきり0日

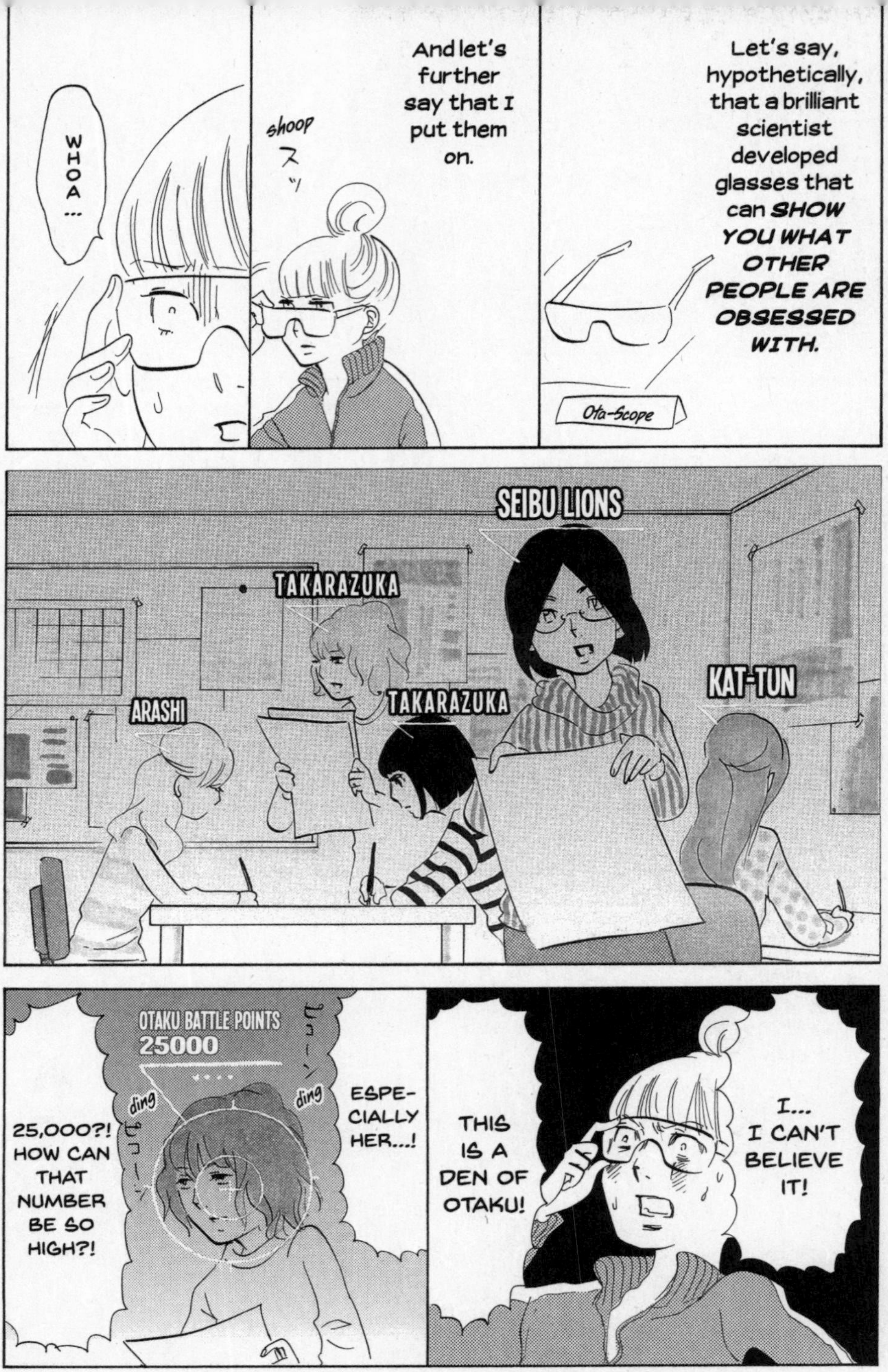
Let's say, hypothetically, that a brilliant scientist developed glasses that can ***SHOW YOU WHAT OTHER PEOPLE ARE OBSESSED WITH.***
Ota-Scope
And let's further say that I put them on.
shoop
スッ
WHOA...
SEIBU LIONS
TAKARAZUKA
KAT-TUN
TAKARAZUKA
ARASHI
I... I CAN'T BELIEVE IT!
THIS IS A DEN OF OTAKU!
ESPE-CIALLY HER...!
OTAKU BATTLE POINTS
25000
ding
ding
25,000?! HOW CAN THAT NUMBER BE SO HIGH?!

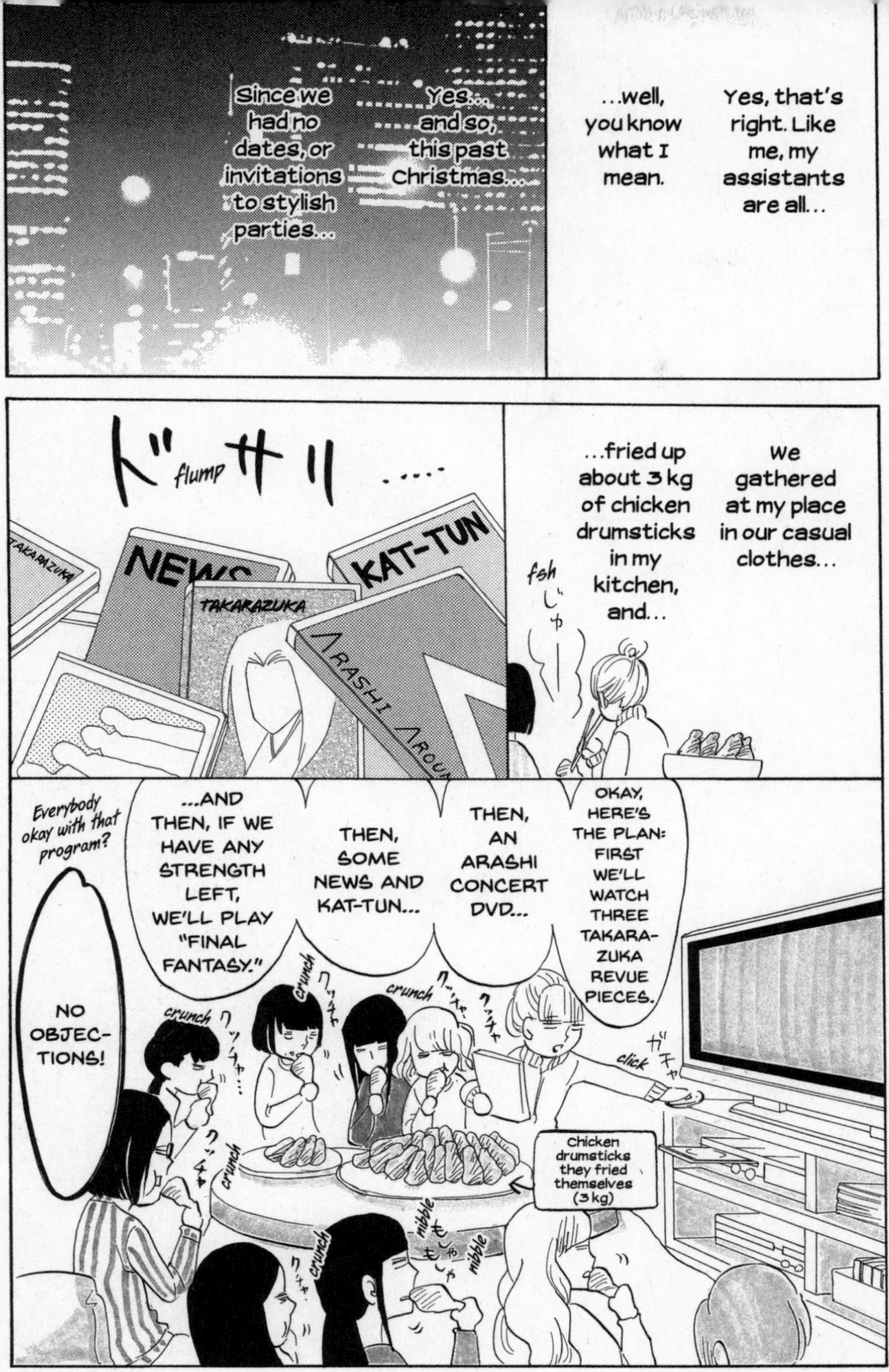
Yes, that's right. Like me, my assistants are all...
...well, you know what I mean.
Yes... and so, this past Christmas...
Since we had no dates, or invitations to stylish parties...
We gathered at my place in our casual clothes...
...fried up about 3 kg of chicken drumsticks in my kitchen, and...
fsh
じゅー
ドサリ flump
....
KAT-TUN
NEWS
TAKARAZUKA
TAKARAZUKA
ARASHI
OKAY, HERE'S THE PLAN: FIRST WE'LL WATCH THREE TAKARAZUKA REVUE PIECES.
THEN, AN ARASHI CONCERT DVD...
THEN, SOME NEWS AND KAT-TUN...
...AND THEN, IF WE HAVE ANY STRENGTH LEFT, WE'LL PLAY "FINAL FANTASY."
Everybody okay with that program?
NO OBJECTIONS!
ガチャ click
crunch
crunch
crunch
crunch
crunch
Chicken drumsticks they fried themselves (3 kg)
nibble
nibble

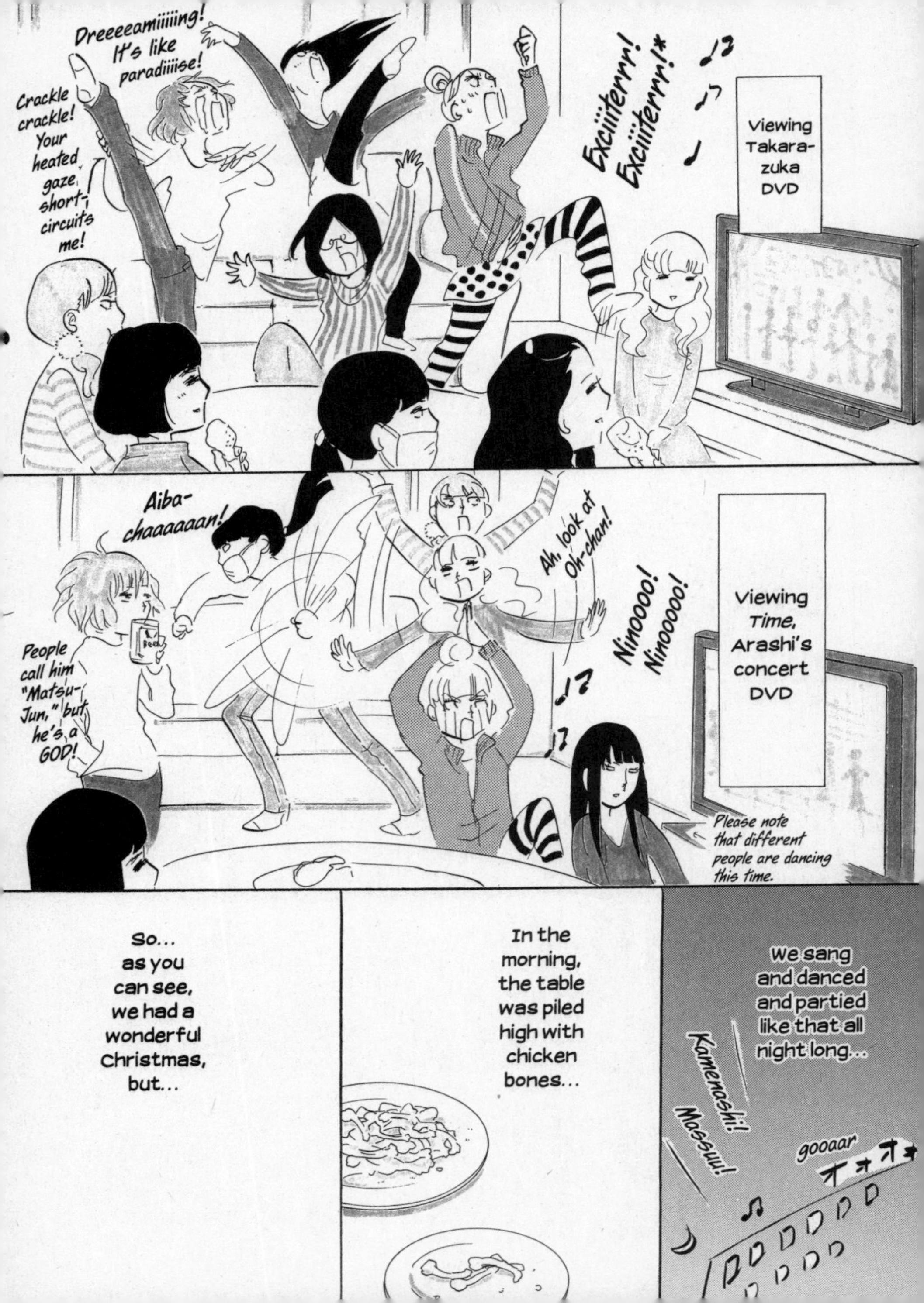

Viewing Takarazuka DVD
Exciiiterrr! Exciiiterrr!*
Dreeeeamiiiiing! It's like paradiiiise!
Crackle crackle! Your heated gaze short-circuits me!
Viewing Time, Arashi's concert DVD
Ninoooo! Ninooooo!
Ah, look at Oh-chan!
Aiba-chaaaaaan!
People call him "Matsu-Jun," but he's a GOD!
Please note that different people are dancing this time.
We sang and danced and partied like that all night long...
Kamenashi!
Massuu!
gooaar
オォオ
In the morning, the table was piled high with chicken bones...
So... as you can see, we had a wonderful Christmas, but...

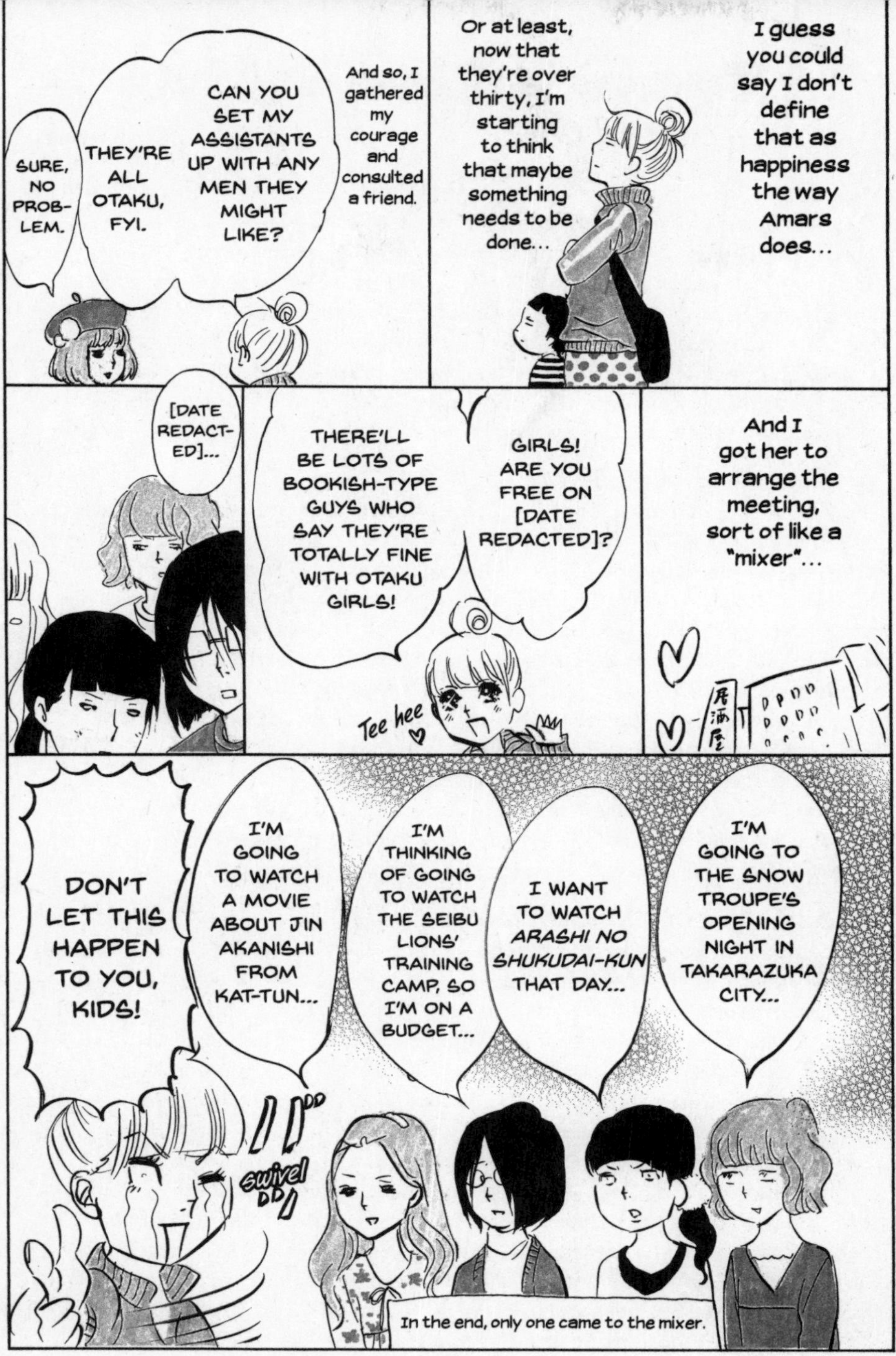
I guess you could say I don't define that as happiness the way Amars does...
Or at least, now that they're over thirty, I'm starting to think that maybe something needs to be done...
And so, I gathered my courage and consulted a friend.
CAN YOU SET MY ASSISTANTS UP WITH ANY MEN THEY MIGHT LIKE?
THEY'RE ALL OTAKU, FYI.
SURE, NO PROB-LEM.
And I got her to arrange the meeting, sort of like a "mixer"...
居酒屋
GIRLS! ARE YOU FREE ON [DATE REDACTED]?
THERE'LL BE LOTS OF BOOKISH-TYPE GUYS WHO SAY THEY'RE TOTALLY FINE WITH OTAKU GIRLS!
Tee hee ♥
[DATE REDACT-ED]...
I'M GOING TO THE SNOW TROUPE'S OPENING NIGHT IN TAKARAZUKA CITY...
I WANT TO WATCH *ARASHI NO SHUKUDAI-KUN* THAT DAY...
I'M THINKING OF GOING TO WATCH THE SEIBU LIONS' TRAINING CAMP, SO I'M ON A BUDGET...
I'M GOING TO WATCH A MOVIE ABOUT JIN AKANISHI FROM KAT-TUN...
DON'T LET THIS HAPPEN TO YOU, KIDS!
swivel
In the end, only one came to the mixer.

Translation Notes

Le Bel Homme, page 201

This isn't a French movie like you might well guess; it's actually a Japanese TV drama called *Utsukushii Hito* that ran in 1999 with the French subtitle *Le Bel Homme*. The show featured a love triangle between a beautiful woman, the abusive husband she's trying to escape, and the widowed plastic surgeon she hires to change her face. The interesting thing about this French alternate title is that it gives the clearer picture of who the title character might really be. *Utsukushii Hito* means "The Beautiful Person," but the gender of that person is unstated. In the French title, on the other hand, the beautiful one is definitively male.

Edo and Edo-mae Sushi, page 214

"Edo" is the old name for the city of Tokyo. While Tokyo is the name used for the city today, the old Edo name still survives in terms that express local flavor or local pride, as well as those which have a long history. (Mayaya will sometimes use Edo instead of Tokyo in strange places, but then, we already knew that Mayaya was stuck in the past.) The owner of Sushi Aoki, a Tokyo sushi restaurant with locations in Ginza and Nishi-Azabu, explains on its website that the term "Edo-mae sushi" (or "Edo-mae-zushi") was coined in the Edo Period to contrast it with the Kansai-style sushi which was then the default. The various sushi of the Kansai cities—Osaka and Kyoto—used more cooked ingredients and more vegetables. Edo-mae's stylistic trademark was to focus on the intrinsic flavor of a single piece of raw seafood. Edo's location along the bay meant access to fresh-caught delights, easy to serve raw. This also meant that when you bought sushi in Edo, you got the seafood that was in season at the time, giving Edo-mae sushi a strongly seasonal character.

Nightclub, Gyaru, O.L., Bland, Dating Service Types, page 217

Here, Prime Minister Negishi references several social "types" or "-kei." *Omizu-kei*, translated here as the Nightclub type, refers to people in *mizu-shobai* type jobs, which refers to the service or entertainment industry and nightlife. Most commonly, *omizu-kei* are hostesses at bars and clubs. *Gyaru*, though initially a borrowed English term "girl," has since become a subculture of Japanese street fashion. *Gyaru* typically bleach and dye their hair lighter and wear a lot of make up. The excessive femininity that gyaru put on is at once an indulgent performance and also a statement that catches one's eyes—they stand out—the male gaze is no match for these young women crafting their *gyaru* look. O.L. stands for "office lady." Not to be confused with the term "career woman" or women who are able to focus on their lifetime careers. On the contrary, O.L.s are women who work as secretaries or clerks, usually right after high school or junior high. O.L.s are expected to support the main staff in a business and bring youthful energy into the office. They have little room for promotion and are expected to leave for marriage before their 30s.

Negishi says *"jimi-kei,"* which translates to "bland." It is comparable to the "Plain Jane" trope–both of which imply a subtle misogynistic nuance of men preferring "average wholesome girls" who won't surprise or trick them, but will "be good for marriage," stability, and support. Dating Service Types, or *deai-kei* refer to people who use dating services, apps, or websites to meet others.

What mixi communities is she in?, page 217
Mixi is a Japanese social networking service. One of its many features is the use of special forums called "communities." The Amars community we see Chieko moderating in Volume 1 is one such mixi community. Though it causes some confusion in English, the company's name is often advertised in lowercase as "mixi."

Iketani, page 222
Yukio Iketani is a gymnast known for his floor exercises. He is an Olympic medalist, winning medals in the 1988 and 1992 Summer Olympics.

Chikuwa, page 222
Chikuwa is fish paste rolled into a tube shape and then cooked, so you can see why it might leap to mind when you roll yourself up in a sheet or blanket (or random bolt of fabric, apparently).

Ichiyo Higuchi!, page 222
Ichiyo Higuchi (1872-1896) is the famous author and poet whose face appears on the 5,000 yen note. She rose to fame during the Meiji period, when Japan was modernizing from its feudal society.

Minatomirai Line, page 223
The subway line connecting Yokohama Station to Yokohama's Chinatown, through a popular district called Minato Mirai 21.

If I built a hoouuse..., page 240
The song playing in the background of Shu's fantasy here is Akiko Kosaka's *Anata* which translates to "You." Although the original lyrics mention a puppy as the family pet, Shu is tethered to reality just enough to realize that he'll need to replace "puppy" with "jelly" in this scenario.

Ohagi, page 247
A traditional Japanese sweet made of sweet rice and sweet red bean paste.

Aqua-Line, page 270
The bridge and tunnel that runs over Tokyo Bay. It connects two prefectures through Kawasaki and Kisarazu.

Reward me for my labor with Necchu Jidai DVDs..., page 274
Necchu Jidai (1970s through 1980s) was a TV drama starring Yutaka Mizutani, whom you may remember from the volume 1 Translation Notes.

All this hot and cold... It's like that "Hot-Water Commercial.", page 311
"Hot-Water Commercial" is a segment on the Beat Takeshi show *Super Jockey*. In it, contestants (generally female) don bathing suits (generally bikinis) and vie to see who can sit in a tank of brutally hot water the longest. This is no innocent hot tub—the experience is explicitly about suffering, and the longer you manage to suffer, the more seconds your company is afforded to do a live advertisement on the show. This panel on page 311 shows the hot water tank, as well as the bucket of ice contestants may choose to rub themselves down with afterward.

Am I in Dachou Club?, page 312
Dachou Club is a comedy trio that also regularly does a hot-water-tank skit. In their case, it's for humorous purposes: they'll do a routine arguing over who should have to try to make it across the tank of hot water, and generally the "loser" will try to climb along the top of it without touching the water, while the other two pledge to give him their full emotional support. As their teammate climbs, he chants, "Don't push me in. Don't push me in. Seriously, don't push me in!" (Spoiler: They push him in.)

Greater thrills! Secret-ingredient hotpot in the dark!, page 321
Yami-nabe, or literally "darkness hotpot," is a hotpot where each person at the table puts in an ingredient they brought...but it's done with the lights off so that nobody can see the ingredients contributed, and then you eat it in the dark so that the meal is a continual surprise for everyone.

Oscar, page 339
It's difficult to overstate the cultural influence of Oscar François de Jarjayes, both upon the genre she inhabits and upon her many fans. This strong-willed, sword-fighting, cross-dressing character from Riyoko Ikeda's 1970s manga *The Rose of Versailles* has become iconic for shojo. Chieko's reaction to the mere idea of Oscar is pretty typical—even stereotypical, perhaps. In the story, which begins slightly before the French Revolution, Oscar's father raises her as a son so that she can follow his career path in the Palace Guards. This gives Oscar a front-row seat for the intrigues of Marie Antoinette and the turbulent politics playing out in France. Along with the revolution taking place in the outer world, Oscar experiences upheaval in her inner world as she questions her allegiances and struggles with the role of gender for someone living out both male and female identities. The original *The Rose of Versailles* manga has been adapted into anime and, famously, Takarazuka Revue musicals.

Prince Clarino, page 374
Kuranosuke's Styling self is appropriately named after a Japanese brand of faux leather products.

Christmas at Average Age 31, page 385
This title is a reference to the award-winning 1994 TV drama *29-sai no Kurisumasu*, which translates to *Christmas at Age 29*. In this story, apparel company employee

Noriko Yabuki's 29th birthday starts with the discovery of a bald spot on her head and only goes downhill from there. In Japan, Christmas is constructed as a holiday that one would spend with their significant other. Furthermore, society used to expect women to be married by 25-years-old, which is why Higashimura mentions that her assistants might benefit from a mixer.

The Assistants' Obsessions (As Seen through the Ota-Scope), page 386
The Seibu Lions are a baseball team; KAT-TUN and Arashi are boy bands (as is NEWS on the next page).

Takarazuka, page 386
The Takarazuka Revue is an all-female cast musical theater in Japan, founded in 1913 by Ichizo Kobayashi as a wholesome tourist attraction for a hot spring resort. It has since become a wildly popular institution with several different theaters across Japan that sell out every seat in the house; the audience is predominantly women as well. They are most well-known for their rendition of *The Rose of Versailles*, and in the US, some may recognize their *Ace Attorney* musical. To be a part of the Takarazuka, young women (aged 14 to 18) must pass a highly selective audition, and once accepted, are designated a role that they must train in for the rest of their time at the prestigious Takarazuka Music School. The *otokoyaku* (male role) are the stars, supported by *musumeyaku* (female role) and the school is very "proper" and strict in the traditional sense. This is because the Takarazuka's success and public image was once hinged on Meiji-era notions of what a "respectable daughter" is. The *otokoyaku* are tall, lithe, husky-voiced, and charming celebrities—a common character trope in shojo manga. The typical make-up and costume for their musicals look exactly like Kuranosuke playing Oscar on page 344. On page 388, the assistants are singing "Exciter," a Takarazuka theme song.

Arashi Name Check, page 388
The assistants are all cheering on their favorite Arashi band members here. "Nino" is a nickname Kazunari Ninomiya; "Oh-chan" is a nickname for Satoshi Ohno; "Aiba-chan" is a nickname for Masaki Aiba, and "Matsu-Jun" is a nickname for Jun Matsumoto. These Arashi members (and more) form a typical Japanese "idol" franchise, meaning that in addition to their musical activities, they're also television personalities. They are known for their TV variety show, *Arashi no Shukudai-kun* (2006-2010) which is mentioned on the very next page.

Kamenashi, Massuu, page 388
Kazuya Kamenashi is a member of KAT-TUN. "Massu" or "Massuu" is a nickname for Takahisa Masuda, a member of NEWS.

Princess Jellyfish volume 2 is a work of fiction. Names, characters, places, and incidents are the products of the author's imagination or are used fictitiously. Any resemblance to actual events, locales, or persons, living or dead, is entirely coincidental.

A Kodansha Comics Trade Paperback Original.

Published in the United States by Kodansha Comics,
an imprint of Kodansha USA Publishing, LLC, New York.

Publication rights for this English edition arranged through Kodansha Ltd., Tokyo.

First published in Japan in 2009 and 2010 by Kodansha Ltd., Tokyo,
as *Kuragehime* volumes 3 & 4.

ISBN 978-1-63236-229-2

Printed in the United States of America.

www.kodanshacomics.com

9 8 7 6 5 4 3 2 1

Translation: Sarah Alys Lindholm
Lettering: Carl Vanstiphout
Additional Layout: Belynda Ungurath
Editing: Haruko Hashimoto
Kodansha Comics Edition Cover Design: Phil Balsman